P9-DTK-834

The ARRL
Operating
Manual

For Radio Amateurs

Eleventh Edition

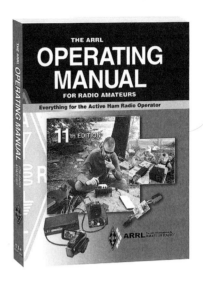

Front cover: In the main photo, Stuart Thomas, KB1HQS, enjoys operating portable with battery powered gear from scenic locations. [Stuart Thomas, KB1HQS, photo] In the inset photo, Ellie Rose Tucker makes a contact at the Escondido (California) Amateur Radio Society Field Day site while Bud Hennessy, AE6BH, assists. [Matthew Tucker, N6EAJ, photo] Lower left: A DVB-T digital amateur television transmitter system, including a Hi-Des modulator, 70 cm linear amplifier, and high-definition camcorder. [Jim Andrews, KH6HTV] Lower right: A voltage reducer for using 16.8 V Lithium-ion polymer (LiPo) battery packs with 13.8 V amateur gear. [Phil Salas, AD5X, photo]

Back cover: Ashley Rattmann, K6NAA, operating the Rookie Roundup contest at the N6TV station. [Bob Wilson, N6TV, photo]

Editor
Mark J. Wilson, K1RO

Editorial Assistant
Maty Weinberg, KB1EIB

Cover Design
Sue Fagan, KB1OKW
Bob Inderbitzen, NQ1R

Production
Jodi Morin, KA1JPA
Michelle Bloom, WB1ENT
David F. Pingree, N1NAS

ARRL The national association for **AMATEUR RADIO**®

Contents

Preface

About the ARRL

ARRL Membership Benefits

The Amateur's Code

1   Basic Station and Operating Techniques

1.1 Assembling a Station

1.2 Basic Operating Procedures

1.3 HF Digital Communications

1.4 VHF/UHF FM, Repeaters, Digital Voice and Data

1.5 VHF/UHF Beyond FM and Repeaters

1.6 Amateur Satellites

1.7 Image Communications

1.8 Portable and Mobile Operation

2   Radio Clubs and Public Service

2.1 Group Activities for the Radio Amateur

2.2 Preparing the Next Generation

2.3 ARRL Field Day

2.4 Public Service Operating

3   On-Air Activities and Radiosport

3.1 Awards — Measuring Operating Achievements

3.2 DXing — Contacting Those Faraway Places

3.3 Confirming the Contact — QSLing

3.4 Contesting — Competitive Wireless

4   Resources for the Active Ham

A collection of useful information to support on-air operating activities.

Preface

Talking to friends. Serving your community. Chasing DX. Adding a new band. Trying a new mode. Working a contest. Having fun with radio. Does any of this sound appealing? If so, you've come to the right place.

Amateur Radio offers a stunning variety of on-air operating activities to try. Once you have your license in hand and have mastered the basics, what else can you try? The 11th edition of the *ARRL Operating Manual* is here to show you some of the many different activities in the world of Amateur Radio. Each section jumps into several different aspects of ham radio, but all of the chapters describe things you can do with your gear. In some cases you may need to pick up another radio, antenna or accessory, but in many cases you already have the hardware needed to get started.

This 11th edition has been prepared and revised by experienced hams who are active on the air. They have "been there, done that" and are happy to share what they have learned so that you can get involved too.

Your station isn't a museum display. It's there to be used and is just waiting for a chance to reach out and contact someone. So what are you waiting for? Get on the air, stretch your comfort zone a bit and see what Amateur Radio has to offer.

About the ARRL

The seed for Amateur Radio was planted in the 1890s, when Guglielmo Marconi began his experiments in wireless telegraphy. Soon he was joined by dozens, then hundreds, of others who were enthusiastic about sending and receiving messages through the air — some with a commercial interest, but others solely out of a love for this new communications medium. The United States government began licensing Amateur Radio operators in 1912.

By 1914, there were thousands of Amateur Radio operators — hams — in the United States. Hiram Percy Maxim, a leading Hartford, Connecticut inventor and industrialist, saw the need for an organization to unify this fledgling group of radio experimenters. In May 1914 he founded the American Radio Relay League (ARRL) to meet that need.

ARRL is the national association for Amateur Radio in the US. Today, with approximately 167,000 members, ARRL numbers within its ranks the vast majority of active radio amateurs in the nation and has a proud history of achievement as the standard-bearer in amateur affairs. ARRL's underpinnings as Amateur Radio's witness, partner, and forum are defined by five pillars: Public Service, Advocacy, Education, Technology, and Membership. ARRL is also International Secretariat for the International Amateur Radio Union, which is made up of similar societies in 150 countries around the world.

ARRL's Mission Statement: To advance the art, science, and enjoyment of Amateur Radio.
ARRL's Vision Statement: As the national association for Amateur Radio in the United States, ARRL:

- Supports the awareness and growth of Amateur Radio worldwide;
- Advocates for meaningful access to radio spectrum;
- Strives for every member to get involved, get active, and get on the air;
- Encourages radio experimentation and, through its members, advances radio technology and education; and
- Organizes and trains volunteers to serve their communities by providing public service and emergency communications.

At ARRL headquarters in the Hartford, Connecticut suburb of Newington, the staff helps serve the needs of members. ARRL publishes the monthly journal *QST* and an interactive digital version of *QST*, as well as newsletters and many publications covering all aspects of Amateur Radio. Its headquarters station, W1AW, transmits bulletins of interest to radio amateurs and Morse code practice sessions. ARRL also coordinates an extensive field organization, which includes volunteers who provide technical information and other support services for radio amateurs as well as communications for public service activities. In addition, ARRL represents US radio amateurs to the Federal Communications Commission and other government agencies in the US and abroad.

Membership in ARRL means much more than receiving *QST* each month. In addition to the services already described, ARRL offers membership services on a personal level, such as the Technical Information Service, where members can get answers — by phone, e-mail, or the ARRL website — to all their technical and operating questions.

A bona fide interest in Amateur Radio is the only essential qualification of membership; an Amateur Radio license is not a prerequisite, although full voting membership is granted only to licensed radio amateurs in the US. Full ARRL membership gives you a voice in how the affairs of the organization are governed. ARRL policy is set by a Board of Directors (one from each of 15 Divisions). Each year, one-third of the ARRL Board of Directors stands for election by the full members they represent. The day-to-day operation of ARRL HQ is managed by a Chief Executive Officer and his/her staff.

Join ARRL Today! No matter what aspect of Amateur Radio attracts you, ARRL membership is relevant and important. There would be no Amateur Radio as we know it today were it not for ARRL. We would be happy to welcome you as a member! Join online at **www.arrl.org/join**. For more information about ARRL and answers to any questions you may have about Amateur Radio, write or call:

ARRL — The national association for Amateur Radio®
225 Main Street
Newington CT 06111-1494
Tel: 860-594-0200
FAX: 860-594-0259
e-mail: **hq@arrl.org**
www.arrl.org

Prospective new radio amateurs call (toll-free):
800-32-NEW HAM (800-326-3942)
You can also contact ARRL via e-mail at **newham@arrl.org**
or check out the ARRL website at **www.arrl.org**

ARRL Membership Benefits

QST Monthly Magazine

QST covers new trends and the latest technology, fiction, humor, news, club activities, rules and regulations, special events, and much more. Here is some of what you will find every month:

- Informative product reviews of the newest radios and accessories
- A monthly conventions and hamfest calendar
- A public service column that keeps you up to date on the public service efforts hams are providing around the country and shows you how you can join in this satisfying aspect of our hobby
- Eclectic Technology, a monthly column that covers emerging Amateur Radio and commercial technology
- A broad spectrum of articles in every issue ranging from challenging topics to straightforward, easy-to-understand projects

ARRL members also get preferred subscription rates for QEX, the ARRL Forum for Communications Experimenters.

Members-Only Web Services

- **QST Digital Edition**
  All ARRL members can access the online digital edition of QST. Enjoy enhanced content, convenient access and a more interactive experience. Apps for Apple and Android devices are also available.
- **QST Archive and Periodicals Search**
  Browse ARRL's extensive online QST archive. A searchable index for QEX and NCJ is also available.
- **Free E-Newsletters**
  Subscribe to a variety of ARRL e-newsletters and e-mail announcements: ham radio news, radio clubs, public service, contesting and more!
- **Product Review Archive**
  Search for, and download, QST Product Reviews published from 1980 to present.
- **E-Mail Forwarding Service**
  E-mail sent to your arrl.net address will be forwarded to any e-mail account you specify.

Technical Information Service (TIS)

Get answers on a variety of technical and operating topics through ARRL's Technical Information Service. Our experts can help you overcome hurdles and answer all your questions.

Member Benefit Programs and Discounts

- **Ham Radio Equipment Insurance Plan**
  Insurance is available to protect you from loss or damage to your station, antennas and mobile equipment by lightning, theft, accident, fire, flood, tornado, and other national disasters.
- **Liberty Mutual® Auto and Home Insurance**
  ARRL members may qualify for special group discounts on home and auto insurance.
- **The ARRL Visa Signature® Card**
  Show your ham radio pride with the ARRL Visa credit card. You earn great rewards and every purchase supports ARRL programs and services.

Outgoing QSL Service

Let us be your mail carrier and handle your overseas QSLing chores. The savings you accumulate through this service alone can pay your membership dues many times over.

Continuing Education/Publications

Find classes to help you prepare to pass your license exam or upgrade your license, learn more about Amateur Radio activities, or train for emergency communications or public service. ARRL also offers hundreds of books, CDs and videos on the technical, operating, and licensing facets of Amateur Radio.

Regulatory Information Branch

Reach out to our Regulatory Information Branch for information on FCC and regulatory questions; problems with antenna, tower and zoning restrictions; and reciprocal licensing procedures.

ARRL as an Advocate

ARRL supports legislation in Washington, D.C. that preserves and protects access to existing Amateur Radio frequencies as a natural resource for the enjoyment of all hams. Members contribute to the efforts to preserve our privileges.

ARRL The national association for **AMATEUR RADIO®**

The Amateur's Code

The Radio Amateur is:

CONSIDERATE...never knowingly operates in such a way as to lessen the pleasure of others.

LOYAL...offers loyalty, encouragement and support to other amateurs, local clubs, and the American Radio Relay League, through which Amateur Radio in the United States is represented nationally and internationally.

PROGRESSIVE...with knowledge abreast of science, a well-built and efficient station and operation above reproach.

FRIENDLY...slow and patient operating when requested; friendly advice and counsel to the beginner; kindly assistance, cooperation and consideration for the interests of others. These are the hallmarks of the amateur spirit.

BALANCED...radio is an avocation, never interfering with duties owed to family, job, school or community.

PATRIOTIC...station and skill always ready for service to country and community.

—The original Amateur's Code was written by Paul M. Segal, W9EEA, in 1928.

Contents

1.1 Assembling a Station
1.1.1 In the Shack — Your Equipment
1.1.2 Station Setup at Home
1.1.3 Antennas
1.1.4 Resources for Assembling a Station

1.2 Basic Operating Procedures
1.2.1 The Bands
1.2.2 Operating — What, Where and How
1.2.3 Recordkeeping
1.2.4 Resources for SSB and CW Operating

1.3 HF Digital Communications
1.3.1 HF Transceivers for Digital Operating
1.3.2 Computers and Software
1.3.3 Digital Modes
1.3.4 WSPR
1.3.5 HF Digital Resources

1.4 VHF/UHF FM, Repeaters, Digital Voice and Data
1.4.1 How Do You Use Repeaters?
1.4.2 Band Plans
1.4.3 Public Service
1.4.4 About Those Tones
1.4.5 Linking and Crossband Repeaters
1.4.6 Internet Linking
1.4.7 Digital Voice (DV) — The New Horizon
1.4.8 VHF/UHF Digital Data Modes
1.4.9 VHF/UHF FM and Digital Resources

1.5 VHF/UHF beyond FM and Repeaters
1.5.1 Overview
1.5.2 Propagation
1.5.3 How Do I Operate on VHF/UHF?
1.5.4 EME: Earth-Moon-Earth
1.5.5 Hilltopping and Portable Operation
1.5.6 Contests
1.5.7 VHF/UHF Resources

1.6 Amateur Satellites
1.6.1 Satellite Orbits and Tracking
1.6.2 Satellite Tracking Software
1.6.3 Satellite Operating
1.6.4 Satellite Resources

1.7 Image Communications
1.7.1 Amateur Television (ATV) Overview
1.7.2 The ATV Station
1.7.3 Licensing, Limits, Repeaters, Identifying
1.7.4 UHF to Microwaves
1.7.5 ATV Applications and Activities
1.7.6 Slow-Scan Television (SSTV)
1.7.7 Image Communication Resources

1.8 Portable and Mobile Operation
1.8.1 Portable Operating
1.8.2 Mobile Stations
1.8.3 Portable and Mobile Resources

Section 1

Basic Station and Operating Techniques

The material in this section is adapted and updated from previous editions of the ARRL Operating Manual. H. Ward Silver, NØAX, originally wrote the introduction, Assembling a Station, Basic Operating Procedures, and Mobile Operating sections. Steve Ford, WB8IMY, originally wrote the HF Digital Communications and Amateur Satellite sections. The information on WSPR is condensed from a QST article by Joe Taylor, K1JT, and Bruce Walker, W1BW. The VHF/UHF FM, Repeaters, Digital Voice and Data section is originally from Gary Pearce, KN4AQ, and the VHF/UHF Beyond FM and Repeaters section is from Michael Owen, W9IP. The Amateur Television (ATV) section is adapted from material written by Art Towslee, WA8RMC, and Tom O'Hara, W6ORG, while the Slow Scan Television (SSTV) section is based on material written by Dave Jones, KB4YZ. Stuart Thomas, KB1HQS, wrote the section on Portable Operating which is new to this edition.

Amateur Radio is all about operating — all the technology and procedures in the world are no substitute for hams getting on the air and making contact. That's what this book is about — how hams send their signals and why. Hams have found dozens of ways to have fun and engage in useful activities on the air. You'll find many of those described here — both to provide guidance in participating and for your general interest in unfamiliar forms of Amateur Radio.

You may have taken an interest in ham radio because of a specific need or activity — public service, emergency communications, interest in electronics or even radio controlled models! Right away, you'll find yourself immersed in Amateur Radio, learning the ropes of your preferred activity. As you operate and become more skilled, a curious thing will happen. You'll discover that there is considerable magic behind the front panel of your radio, out there between the antennas, and in the minds of your compatriot hams! Your Amateur Radio license is the gateway to exploring as much of that magic as you wish.

In addition to operating from home, hams enjoy operating from their vehicles or taking portable stations to interesting or unusual locations. Stuart Thomas, KB1HQS, combines ham radio with his love of hiking in the outdoors and discusses portable operation later in this book. [Stuart Thomas, KB1HQS, photo]

Bud, N7CW, and several friends set up their station on a boat and operated near San Clemente Island off the coast of southern California. [Courtesy Jim Price, K6ZH]

it's an opportunity to serve your community and make your neighborhood a better place to live.

With all the communications technology available in the modern world, is there still a useful role for Amateur Radio? Certainly, there is! Part of the magic of everyday Amateur Radio arises from the "who's out there?" nature of all those hams sharing the bands. Whether you communicate with a regular circle of friends or spend your time tuning the bands in search of a new call sign, an unexpected surprise may be no farther away than your next CQ ("calling any station"). When disaster strikes and normal communications are knocked out for a time, hams step in and harness that magic for the public's benefit.

This *ARRL Operating Manual* covers the most popular activities in ham radio. No matter if you're completely new to Amateur Radio or an experienced ham looking for information on a new way to communicate, this book can help you decide what to operate, where to operate and how to operate. Think of your participation in Amateur Radio as a never-ending journey — there's always something new to explore, always something new to do!

The Wide Variety of Ham Activities

Hams are involved in all sorts of fun, challenging and fulfilling activities. That means not just from home, but on the move — in a car, or on a bike or hiking in the mountains. You might be on the sea or in the air — even in Earth orbit, where spacefaring hams have enjoyed using their radios from

Many hams start out with a simple hand-held VHF/UHF FM transceiver. Such a radio can be used as the basis of a mobile or home station as well.

aboard the International Space Station.

So what sorts of things do hams do?

NEAR, FAR, WHEREVER YOU ARE

Some enjoy communicating locally or training for public service and disaster communications using small, inexpensive, low-powered VHF/UHF radios that operate on fixed channels using FM voice. Repeaters extend their limited range by amplifying and retransmitting their signals. Depending on where the repeater is located, you can talk with other hams 50 or even 100 miles away. Distances up to 30 miles are common.

Others are enchanted with using the ionosphere to bounce high frequency (HF) signals to and from faraway places thousands of miles away. The object of their quest is

Amateur Radio provides opportunities to learn about and experiment with technology. It's also a way to learn electronic communication skills. It's a means to overcome the limitations of physical handicaps and enter an open arena of communications. It's fun and a great way to make friends. It's an opportunity to participate in public service activities. And

Matt, KF0Q, operates his station with simple wire antennas. [Courtesy Matt Burt, KF0Q]

A recent ARRL CW DX Contest included a very "laid-back" QRP entry by Jim, HI/W8WTS, who used a battery-powered KX3 transceiver and a wire run up into the sun umbrella for many of his QSOs. [Courtesy Jim Galm, W8WTS]

distant stations (DX). They try to contact as many distinct political and geographic areas as they can. The quest is complete when the contact is confirmed with a *QSL* card — a colorful and interesting postcard confirming contact with another station — in the mail or via an online contact confirmation service such as the ARRL's Logbook of The World.

Hybrids of VHF/UHF repeaters and the Internet have been developed by hams to extend the range of communications of those low-power radios to HF distances. Voice over Internet Protocol (VoIP) systems combine radio and digitized voice to connect portable and mobile hams around the world.

DX (ham shorthand for long distance) holds a special fascination for many hams. It can be correctly defined in different ways. To most amateurs, DX is the lure of seeing how far away you can establish a QSO — the greater the distance, the better. DX is a personal achievement, bettering some previous "best distance worked," involving a set of self-imposed rules.

DXers often aim for one of the DX-oriented awards such as ARRL's DX Century Club. DXing can be a full-time goal for some hams and a just-for-fun challenge for others. Regardless of whether you turn into a serious DXer or just have a little fun searching for entities you have yet to work, DXing is one of the most fascinating aspects of Amateur Radio.

Some enjoy the thrill and adventure of travel to and operating from the "other side of the pileup" from distant and exotic places. Hams often operate on a vacation trip to a warm island in the Caribbean to escape the freezing winter weather, or on a business trip to Europe or Asia. Others take special trips called *DXpeditions* to the ends of the Earth — Antarctica, desert islands and mountain kingdoms. There they make contacts at high rates for a few days as DXers around the world try to get their call signs "in the log." DXing is covered in much more detail in Section 3 of this book.

Amateur satellites in low Earth orbit can be accessed with a small handheld antenna and an FM transceiver. Here, Jim, AA0CW, makes some contacts from his home in Ridgeway, Colorado. [Courtesy Jim Adams, AA0CW]

OUT OF THIS WORLD!

Hams are not limited to communication on the Earth. Many enjoy talking with astronauts and cosmonauts in orbit. Hams have been communicating with astronauts since Owen Garriott, W5LFL, took his 2 meter handheld radio to orbit on Space Shuttle mission STS-9 in 1983. Today, nearly all residents of the International Space Station (ISS) are hams and regularly make contact with hams on the ground. The ISS ham radio station even has its own call sign, NA1SS.

Hams also communicate with each other through satellites that hams themselves have designed and built. One such amateur organization is AMSAT, the Radio Amateur Satellite Corporation. It is fully funded by amateurs and builds professional quality "birds." Some hams even bounce their signals to each other off the Moon. Others reflect their transmissions off of the active aurora or a short-lived meteor trail. Hams have been pioneers in many modes of communication, paving the way for many different commercial uses.

COMPETITIONS

The thrill of competition calls some hams to enter on-the-air contests for a weekend of intense activity. It's a way to test station capability and operator skills. For the busy ham, it's a great way to cram a lot of contacts into a short period of time. For others, a contest involves operating away from home — perhaps with friends at a "super station" or on the road as a mobile or rover.

Contesting is to Amateur Radio what the Olympic Games are to worldwide amateur athletic competition: a showcase to display talent and learned skills, as well as a stimulus for further achievement through competition. Increased operating skills and greater station effectiveness may be the end result of Ama-

Astronaut Reid Wiseman, KF5LKT, operated Field Day from station NA1SS aboard the International Space Station. He also took part in several contacts with schools as part of the Amateur Radio on the International Space Station (ARISS) program. [NASA photo]

Marty, KC1CWF, enjoys operating in contests as part of a team at the K6ND station. There's no better way to get your feet wet than to connect with a group of experienced operators. [Will Angenent, K6ND, photo]

The North Carolina Mountain State Fair included an Amateur Radio tent organized and staffed by several area radio clubs. Most of the antenna farm is visible in the background. [Karl Bowman, W4CHX, photo]

Keith, K7KAR, enjoys operating radioteletype (RTTY) from his station in Montana. [Keith Regli, K7KAR, photo]

teur Radio contesting, but the most common experience is *fun*.

Competition takes many forms. Hams who love to collect awards compete against themselves. Are they able to make contact with all the states? All the counties? All the prefectures of Japan or the provinces of Spain? Awards and certificates for various operating accomplishments are offered by the ARRL, other national amateur societies, private clubs, and contest groups. Many of the awards are very handsome paper certificates or intricately designed plaques very much in demand by awards chasers.

Some hams take to foot or vehicle with direction-finding equipment to see who's the best at finding a hidden transmitter. Their competitions may be local or international, such as the Amateur Radio Direction-Finding contests.

Contests and awards are covered in more detail in Section 3 of this book.

WORKING COOPERATIVELY

Those involved in *public service*, including *disaster communications* (also called emergency communications or "emcomm"), have to work together cooperatively to get the job done. Over many years of training and practice, hams have developed on-the-air procedures and organizations to communicate efficiently and effectively. By studying them and practicing with your local groups, you will become a valued member of an important volunteer service. Public service communications make Amateur Radio a valuable public resource, one that has been recognized by Congress and a whole host of federal, state and local agencies that serve the public.

Traffic handling involves passing messages to others over the amateur bands. Messages can be informal or follow a set format. Hams handle *third-party traffic* (messages for nonhams) in both routine situations and in times of disaster. Public service communications are covered in more detail in Section 2 of this book.

Nets are regular gatherings of hams who share a mutual interest and who use the net (short for "network") to further that interest. Their most common purpose is to pass traffic or participate in one of the many other ham activities, from awards chasing and DXing to just plain old talking among longtime friends. In an emergency or following a disaster, however, the net transforms into a powerful on-the-air coordination and information-sharing machine!

County and state hunting nets are very popular since they provide a frequency to work that last state for the ARRL WAS (Worked All States) award or a rare county. Service nets are used by mobile and marine stations to request assistance, pass messages, or let their status be known.

There are nets dedicated to beginner or slow-speed CW operation. These can help a newcomer sharpen operating skills. To find the frequencies and meeting times of nets in your area, use the online net search facility via the ARRL Net Directory page on the ARRL website.

"RAG CHEWING"

"Chewing the rag" refers to getting on the air and spending minutes (or hours!) in interesting conversation on virtually any and every topic imaginable. Without a doubt, the most popular operating activity is rag chewing. The rag chew may be something as simple as a brief chat on a 2 meter or 440 MHz FM repeater as you drive across town. It also may be a group of friends who have been meeting on 15 meter SSB every Saturday afternoon for 20 years. The essential element is the same — hams talking to each other on any subject that interests them.

DIGITAL MODES

As computers have become popular — almost essential — in the ham shack, the number of digital modes available to hams has expanded quickly. The first computer-based modes was RTTY (Baudot radiotele-

David, AJ5W and Harry, KC5TRB, prepare a balloon for launch with an Automatic Position Reporting System (APRS) tracker as part of the payload, a science experiment to measure ozone levels. (Scotty Mays, KE5DTZ photo]

type), still in use today. The Automatic Packet Reporting System (APRS®), an offshoot of packet radio, is a popular application.

PSK31 is a digital mode that has become very popular on the HF bands. It is a narrow-band, real-time digital mode that exploits the ubiquitous sound card. The software is even available free of charge over the web.

First conceived as a way for sailing hams to exchange messages while at sea, the Winlink amateur email system has become a staple of public service and message handling. The Winlink system operates on both HF (via the PACTOR family of protocols) and VHF/UHF frequencies (via packet radio), using Amateur Radio to collect and deliver email.

Other popular digital modes include PSK63 and JT65. The development and improvement of digital modes is one of the most active areas of experimentation by amateurs. We'll discuss digital modes in detail later in this section.

1.1 Assembling a Station

Technician licensees have full privileges on the VHF and UHF amateur bands and limited privileges on some of the HF bands. Getting on the air may be as simple as finding a new (or used) VHF handheld radio, charging the batteries and then talking with new ham friends through a local FM repeater. This is exactly how many hams begin their amateur operation — reliable, fun communication with a small group of friends in their own and nearby communities. Technicians can also can talk through the amateur satellites or to space shuttle astronauts. With some additional equipment and some easy-to-find software, they can explore the VHF digital modes such as APRS. In addition, they can use SSB voice or CW (Morse code) to contact other stations on the VHF and UHF bands. These modes require transceivers and antennas that are different from those used for FM.

Technician licensees have the same privi-

Bob, WA1Z, operated from this nicely laid out station of Ed, VP9GE, in Bermuda. [Kurt Pauer, W6PH, photo]

leges on the HF bands as Novice licensees. That means they can use CW on portions of the 80, 40, and 15 meters bands. On 10 meters, they can try CW, SSB, RTTY and other digital modes!

It's hard to resist the lure of the HF bands, where many of today's most experienced hams got their start. You'll hear hams on the repeater or at your radio club talking enthusiastically about their adventures on those lower-frequency bands. Someone may regale you with tales of how they have made friends many thousands of miles away, across oceans and continents. To earn the right to transmit on *all* the HF bands, you'll need to pass the General license exam. At the summit is the Amateur Extra license, which allows access to every part of every ham band. The General license provides you with the opportunity to try every bit of ham radio there is — you'll never regret making the effort to upgrade!

1.1.1 In the Shack — Your Equipment

The first step in selecting your station should be to make up a list to answer a few questions. Will you be operating HF or only VHF? How much room do you have — in other words, how big can your "shack" or operating position be? Do you have room outside for long antennas, such as HF dipoles, or high antennas such as HF verticals and VHF/UHF arrays? How much do you plan to spend, including transceiver, accessories, furniture, coax feed line and wire?

Some of these questions may not apply to your situation, and you may need to answer other questions not discussed here. The result of making your personal list, however, is to give you an idea of what you want, as well as your limitations.

The next step is to do some research. Take your time deciding what gear to get. Many sources of information on ham gear are available to you.

1) *Hands-on experience.* Try to use many different pieces of gear before you decide. This applies to VHF/UHF as well as HF gear. Ask a nearby ham friend or one or more of your fellow radio club members if you can use their station. Try your club's station. Note what you like and what features you don't care for in each of the stations you tried.

2) *Radio club members.* Ask members of your local radio club about their personal preferences in gear and antennas. Be prepared for a great volume of input. Every amateur

has an opinion on the best equipment and antennas. Years of experimentation usually go into finding just the right station equipment to meet a particular amateur's needs. Listen and take note of each ham's choices and reasons for selecting a particular kind of gear. There's a lot of experience, time, effort, and money behind each of those choices.

3) *Advertisements.* QST is chock-full of ads for all the newest up-to-date equipment.

Manufacturers' websites often have comparison charts and instruction manuals you can download for free. If there is a dealer close to you, pay a visit and let them demonstrate some of the gear to you.

4) *Product Reviews.* QST also carries detailed Product Reviews that include reliable measurements made in the ARRL Laboratory. These definitive reviews describe the features of the equipment being evaluated.

Hamfests and conventions are excellent places to see the latest equipment and look for used gear. Although the Dayton Hamvention® shown here is the biggest and best known in the US, there are frequent events sponsored by local radio clubs. Check the Convention and Hamfest Calendar in *QST* for one near you. [Steve Ford, WB8IMY, photo]

Steve, WGØAT, enjoys hiking and portable operating with this simple CW transceiver and paddle that fit in the palm of his hand. [Courtesy Steve Galchutt, WGØAT]

5) *Websites and Internet interest groups.* A number of websites are devoted to equipment reviews and discussion. They range from general-interest sites that let members review all kinds of ham gear, to discussion groups or sites devoted to one manufacturer or even a specific model. Try using your favorite Internet search engine to look for information on models that interest you.

Several possible sources of new and used equipment are:

1) *Local amateurs.* Nearby hams may be willing to part with spare gear at a reasonable price. If you are new to the hobby and you buy a rig from a local club member, you may be able to talk him or her into helping you with the rig's installation and operation. Local clubs are the safest source of used equipment.

2) *Hamfests/flea markets.* Many radio clubs run small conventions called hamfests. Usually one of the big attractions of these events is a flea market where hams buy and sell used radios, antennas, and accessories. Much used gear, usually in passable shape, can be found at reasonable prices. Local distributors and manufacturers of new ham gear and materials sometimes show up at these events, as well.

3) *Local ham radio or electronics dealers.* If you are lucky enough to live near a ham radio dealer or an electronics distributor that handles a line or two of ham gear, so much the better. The dealer can usually answer any questions you may have, will usually have a demonstration unit and will be pleased to assist you in purchasing your new gear. They may also have used gear taken on trade or consignment.

4) *Internet.* You'll find ham gear on popular auction sites such as eBay, as well as the "classified ad" sections of ham websites such as eHam.net, QRZ.com, and QTH.com.

If you are experienced with tools and basic electronic construction, you may even consider building some simple gear from a kit or from an article in a magazine or book.

How Much Power?

On HF, most hams run 100 to 150 W, the power level of typical transceivers. There are times when it is necessary to run the full legal power limit of 1500 W output to establish and

Jordan, NL7Z, arranged his station so that his computer is in front of him, his transceiver is off to the side, and accessories are on a shelf above. His microphone is mounted on a boom to keep his hands free to operate the transceiver and computer. [Courtesy Jordan Johns, NL7Z]

maintain solid communications or to compete effectively in a DX contest on certain bands. Most often, the 100 W level is more than enough to provide excellent contacts.

Some hams find the low initial cost of low power (QRP) HF equipment very attractive, especially since some are available in kit form. Beginning operators who are still developing the skills of making contacts often find QRP frustrating, however. By all means, try QRP any time, but it's recommended that you first get some experience at the 100 W level so that you know what to expect on the HF bands.

On VHF the situation is slightly different. Unless you are trying to work several hundred miles in an opening or operate a weak-signal mode, 5 to 10 W is enough power when coupled with a good antenna for excellent local communications. Handheld transceivers typically run 5 W, while mobile transceivers typically run about 50 W.

VHF/UHF Gear

If you're interested mainly in voice and maybe APRS or packet radio communication with local amateurs, all you need is a VHF/UHF FM transceiver. Portable, mobile, and home (fixed) FM transceivers and antennas can be used to create a station that suits your needs from wherever you operate.

1) *Handheld transceivers.* Handheld transceivers put out from under a watt to 5 W or more. If the handheld you're considering is capable of high-power operation, you'll want to be able to switch to low power when possible to conserve the battery. Most handhelds offer a HIGH/LOW power switch. If you use your handheld rig while inside the car, you'll probably be disappointed with the performance of the attached flexible "rubber duck" antenna. A mobile antenna outside the metal shell of the car will work much better.

2) *Mobile transceivers* have power outputs ranging from 10 to 50 W or more and are used with *mag-mount* or permanently attached mobile antennas mounted on the vehicle. In populated areas with many repeaters, 10 W is probably enough.

3) *Fixed-station transceivers.* A mobile rig connected to a power supply or 12-V automotive battery makes a good fixed station radio. It also can be disconnected and moved into the car for mobile operation. Powering the rig from a battery has the added advantage of allowing operation when the local power lines go down in a storm. A growing number of *all-band* fixed-station radios operate on the HF bands, as well as VHF and UHF. If you plan on operating HF from home, these would be a good choice. Home stations on VHF/UHF should always use external antennas if more than a few watts of power will be used.

4) *VHF packet radio.* Most VHF packet

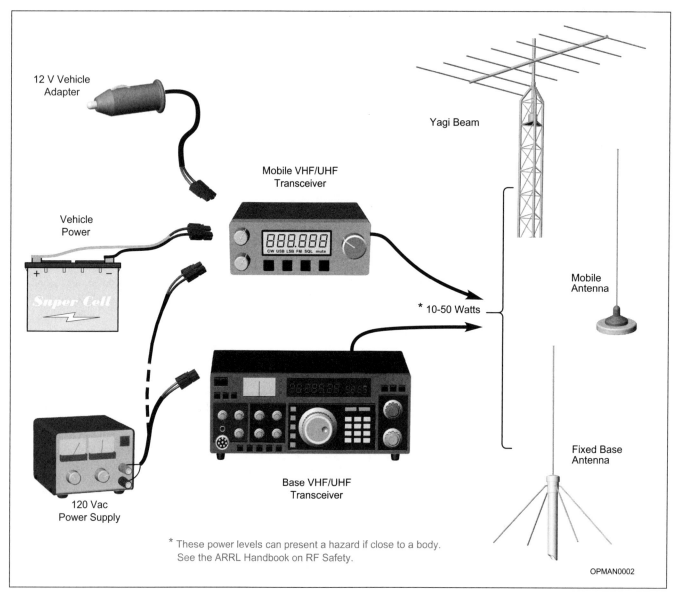

Starting with the radio — a handheld transceiver or mobile rig — forms the basis for a VHF/UHF station at home, on the road, or carried in your hand. Combine the basic radios with accessories and antennas to create the station that suits your needs.

radio operation, including APRS, takes place on the 2 meter and 440 MHz bands. A mobile transceiver makes a good packet-radio station rig, too. You'll need a computer or terminal, plus a terminal node controller (TNC).

Remember that higher power levels can create an RF safety hazard. At the higher power levels of mobile and base transceivers, use external antennas and place mobile antennas away from the passenger compartment. For the higher-powered handheld transceivers, use a detachable speaker-mike and belt clip to keep the antenna away from your eyes and head. This important topic is discussed in the Safety chapter of *The ARRL Handbook*.

HF Equipment

It is a bit more challenging to put together

an HF station than a VHF station. HF equipment generally covers more bands and modes and has greater requirements for frequency stability than an FM-only radio. Thus, HF gear is generally more expensive, and the antennas at HF are bigger.

There are so many different possible HF station configurations that it may be hard to choose the very best station to start out with. Most hams face other constraints — such as having a limited budget to spend for ham gear, or having restrictions on the size and location of antennas. Some hams have a difficult time installing any sort of antenna outdoors and they must resort to indoor or perhaps easily hidden "stealth" wire antennas.

HF transceivers (a transmitter plus a receiver) have been common since the late 1960s. Like all older gear, older transceiv-

ers are likely to have maintenance problems. Transceivers manufactured after about 1980 featured fully solid-state designs. Tuning mechanisms had fewer mechanical parts to wear, and all-band operation became common.

Equipment manufactured in the past 10 years is the most desirable. These radios are fully solid-state, microprocessor-controlled, and have data and control interfaces for digital modes and station accessories. Later models also incorporate *digital signal processing* (DSP) features that provide advanced filtering and noise reduction. The improved performance and reliability are well worth the relatively small premium in price over older equipment now approaching collectible status.

Accessories

In addition to the transceiver, consider a few useful accessories to help you set up, test, and operate your equipment.

SWR INDICATOR OR POWER METER

This device is handy for testing an antenna and feed line when the antenna is first erected, and later to make sure the antenna is still in good shape. If an antenna tuner is used with a multiband antenna system, such as a 135-foot dipole or a G5RV antenna, an SWR (standing-wave ratio) indicator is essential for ensuring the tuner is adjusted for a reasonable SWR. All modern HF transceivers include an SWR indicator. If you plan to operate both VHF and HF you will probably have to buy one for HF and a second for VHF/UHF.

ANTENNA TUNER

Although many transceivers include an internal antenna tuner, there are a number of reasons to have a separate tuner. They generally tune a wider range of impedances, are available with higher power handling ability, can be dedicated to specific antennas, and so forth. There are many antenna tuners available on the market. More expensive models handle higher power and/or use microprocessor circuits for automatic adjustment.

KEYS, KEYERS, AND PADDLES

If you're interested in CW, you will need some means of sending code. You should

Used with an electronic CW keyer, a keyer paddle send a string of dits when one lever is pressed, and a string of dahs (dashes) when the other lever is pressed. Keyers are built into many current transceivers, and others (often with more sophisticated features) are separate accessories.

start with a straight key until you feel you have the proper rhythm. The next step is to buy an electronic keyer and paddles, or use your computer to send code. Most modern transceivers have keyers built in, so all you need is a paddle. Paddles may be standard or *iambic* — able to send alternating dots and dashes. The iambic type requires less hand motion but takes a bit longer to master. Code-transmitting programs are available for most computers.

COMPUTERS

Computers have become a very valuable part of the ham shack. It is common to use a computer to send and receive Morse code, digital modes, or slow-scan TV. The same computer can be used for logging and record keeping, as well as connecting to the Internet. Many radios and accessories have computer control interfaces via USB or RS-232.

Most ham computers are *Windows*-compatible, although the *Linux* and Macintosh communities are well-represented. If you plan on using your computer to control amateur equipment, you may need at least one COM (serial) port or a USB-to-serial converter.

When considering a computer for the shack, remember that a computer uses various oscillators inside that can generate annoying spurious signals in your receiver. These signals may interfere with on-air signals you are trying to hear. Some computers can be very sensitive to the presence of radio-frequency energy (RF), such as that generated by your nearby transceiver. For help with this topic see *The ARRL RFI Book*, which contains an entire chapter on solving computer problems in the shack.

TEST METER

An inexpensive digital multimeter capable of measuring voltage, current, and resistance is very helpful around the shack. High accuracy is not needed for most projects. An inexpensive unit will pay for itself the first time you need to check the integrity of a coax connector you've just installed.

1.1.2 Station Setup at Home

How you set up a home station is determined by how much space you have, and how much equipment you have to squeeze into it. The table should be about 30 inches high and 30 inches deep. An old desk makes a good operating table. Stacking radios on top of one another prevents ventilation and may cause them to overheat. Build shelves for your equipment — office supply and home improvement stores often have inexpensive desktop shelves that work well for radios. It's also easier to change cables and move equipment around when you use shelves. Make sure you can get behind the gear to plug or unplug cables.

Assuming you use a computer, its monitor should be centered in front of your keyboard at a comfortable viewing height. Avoid neck and eye strain — don't place the monitor too far above or to the sides of the keyboard. Place

This fine station belongs to Randy, KØEU. Note the use of shelves to keep everything within easy reach. [Randy Martin, KØEU, photo]

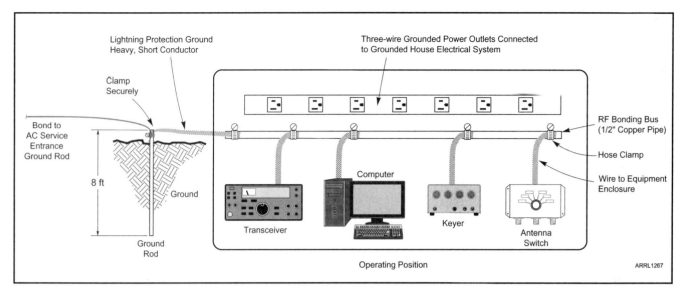

An RF bonding bus connects all of the equipment enclosures together to keep them at the same RF voltage. If the bus is connected to a lightning protection ground, use a heavy conductor, fastened securely. All ground rods must be bonded together and to the residence's ac service entry ground rod. The RF bonding bus should also be connected to the ac safety ground.

the radios to one side of the keyboard. Check that you can see the frequency display and reach the operating controls of your radios easily. Continuously reaching across a computer keyboard to tune or operate a radio will cause strain on your back, shoulder and arms.

To prevent fatigue when operating on CW, place your key or paddle far enough from the edge of the table so your entire arm is supported. If you're not using a headset with a boom microphone, the microphone can be mounted on a stand placed on the table or on an extension that reaches in from the back or side.

The best way to test the arrangement of your station is to sit in the operating chair and operate. Don't be afraid to rearrange your equipment if the layout turns out to be uncomfortable. This is also a good reason not to make your first layout too permanent! Adjust the height and angle of all equipment until it's easy to see and use. If some knobs are too low, try placing spacers or blocks under the

front feet of the rig. Too high? Try placing the spacers under the rear legs.

AC and RF Grounding

Be sure to have an ac safety ground at your station and connected to all equipment. It's a good idea to not even plug in equipment until its case is grounded. Electrical codes require all recent construction to have grounded (three-wire) ac outlets.

Place a grounding strap or *bus* at the back of the equipment and ground all equipment to it with short leads. Then connect the ground bus to an earth ground (ground rod) as directly as possible using copper strap, heavy wire, or strips of flashing copper. Connect the ground bus to your ac safety ground. An RF bonding bus connects all of the equipment enclosures together to keep them at the same RF voltage. If the bus is connected to a lightning protection ground, use a heavy conductor, fastened securely. All ground rods must be bonded

together and to the residence's ac service entry ground rod. The RF bonding bus should also be connected to the ac safety ground. The path from the ground bus to the earth should be as short and direct as possible.

If you live on a higher floor and a direct connection to an earth ground is not available, use an RF bonding bus and be sure all equipment is connected to it. This keeps all equipment at the same RF potential, giving RF current no reason to flow between the various pieces and cause problems.

Safety should be a prime consideration. Make sure that other people in the house know how to cut off power to your station. Consider running your shack through a *GFCI* (ground fault circuit interrupt) outlet. Unfortunately not all ham gear, especially older units, will operate with these devices. By detecting unbalanced line currents and shutting off the voltage when unbalance occurs, however, they could save your life!

1.1.3 Antennas

Antennas are important. The best (and biggest) transmitter in the world will not do any good if the signal is not radiated into the air. A good rule of thumb to follow is "always erect as much antenna as possible." The better your antennas, the better your radiated signal will be and the better you'll hear other stations. A good antenna system can make up for inadequacies or shortcomings in station equipment.

Antenna Safety

Whatever antennas you select, install them safely. Don't endanger your life or someone else's for your hobby!
 • Keep the antenna and its support well clear of any power lines, including the ac power service to your home.
 • Make sure if the antenna or its support falls, it can't contact power lines.
 • Install the antenna where it can't be easily contacted by people.
 There are thorough discussions of antenna safety in *The ARRL Handbook* and *The ARRL Antenna Book*.

If you are thinking of a tower, talk to a few local hams before starting construction (or applying for a building permit). Local rules and ordinances may have a large impact on your plans. Many homes are also subject to *restrictive covenants* or other restrictions on external antennas. Be sure you know what you're allowed to do before digging a hole for a tower base, and get whatever building permits are required!

First VHF/UHF Antennas

One of the nice things about VHF and UHF operation is that the simplest antennas, if mounted high enough and clear of surrounding objects, will often do an excellent job. Ground planes, J-poles and simple beams can either be purchased at a reasonable cost or constructed in a home workshop.

A simple ground-plane antenna can be mounted by taping the feed line and bottom connector to a pole so that the antenna extends above the top of the pole. It can also be suspended by a length of fishing line or synthetic twine by lengthening the vertical element and bending the extra length into a loop. One end of the line is fastened to the loop and the other end is supported by a tree branch or rafter.

A Simple HF Antenna

The most popular — and a very effective — first HF antenna is the half-wavelength dipole. It consists of a half wavelength of wire divided in the center by an insulator. The insulator is where a feed line from your station is connected to each half of the wire. The dipole is very easy to erect and has a low SWR (standing wave ratio). SWR is the measure of how well an antenna is tuned to the desired frequency and of the match between its feed point impedance and the feed line's characteristic impedance.

A dipole can be fed with 50 Ω coaxial cable and used on one band. A single-band dipole fed with low-loss feed line, such as window or open-wire line, can also be used on other bands. In fact with an antenna tuner, a balun, and a random-length center-fed dipole you can actually operate on any HF band.

The antenna should be as high and as far away from surrounding trees and structures as possible. Never put an antenna near power lines! A dipole requires one support at each of its ends (perhaps trees, poles or even house or garage eaves), so survey your potential antenna site with this in mind. If you find space is so limited that you can't put up a straight-line dipole, don't give up! The dipole can also be held up by a single support in the middle with the ends secured closer to the ground — this is called an *inverted V*.

You can also slope or bend the dipole and it will still make plenty of contacts. You can put up an antenna under almost any circumstances, but you may need to use your imagination. Antennas want to work!

Dipole Antenna Parts

If this is the first time you have tried to put up a dipole by yourself the following parts list will give you some guidance.

1) *Antenna wire.* #12 or #14 hard-drawn Copperweld (copper-clad steel) is preferred, so the antenna won't stretch. Stranded or solid copper wire will also work but if used for a long antenna, the wire will probably have to be trimmed once it's been under tension for a while. Wire of this gauge is strong enough to support itself as well as the weight of the feed line connected at its center. Always buy plenty of wire. It never goes to waste!

2) *Insulators.* You need one center and two end antenna insulators for a simple dipole.

3) *Clamp.* Large enough to fit over two diameters of your coaxial cable to provide mechanical support.

4) *Coaxial Cable or "Coax."* Feed line made of a center conductor surrounded by an insulating dielectric. This in turn is surrounded by a braid called the shield and an outer insulating jacket. Use good quality RG-58, RG-8X, RG-8, RG-213, or an equivalent.

A good alternative to coax is balanced open-wire or window line. Open-wire line is constructed using two parallel pieces of wire connected and spaced with plastic rods. Window line has a plastic jacket similar to TV 300-Ω wire with pieces of the center plastic removed to form "windows," lightening the line and reducing its losses. If you are sure you want to build a single-band dipole, stay with coax feed line, otherwise consider the tuner, balun, and open-wire configuration.

5) *Connector.* Connects coaxial feed line to your rig. The standard connector on HF equipment is the SO-239 or "UHF" connector. You'll need a matching PL-259 connector for the coax. If your radio needs a different type of connector, check your radio's instruction manual for installation information. You also need connectors for the coax lines between your antenna tuner, SWR meter and your rig.

6) *Electrical tape and coax sealant.* This is needed to waterproof the connection between the coax feed line and the antenna. Otherwise water can get into the coax, eventually ruining the feed line.

7) *Supporting rope or cord.* You need enough to tie the ends of the antenna to a supporting structure and also reach the ground when the antenna is lowered. That's about twice the height of the support plus the distance from the support to the end of the antenna. Use UV-resistant cord or rope to avoid degradation from exposure.

8) *SWR meter or antenna analyzer.* If your radio doesn't have an SWR meter built-in, you'll need to purchase a separate unit. The SWR meter is required for antenna adjustment and then for antenna tuner adjustment when operating. SWR meters are readily available and inexpensive, making them easier to buy than to build. An antenna analyzer is a self-contained device that connects

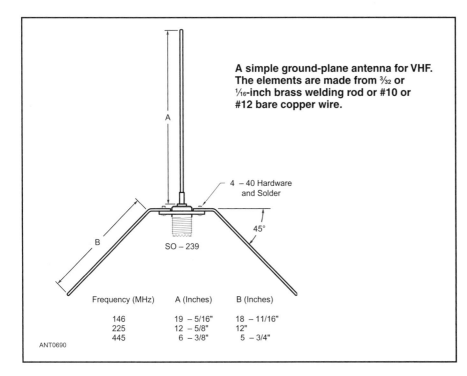

A simple ground-plane antenna for VHF. The elements are made from ³⁄₃₂ or ¹⁄₁₆-inch brass welding rod or #10 or #12 bare copper wire.

A
4 – 40 Hardware and Solder
45°
B
SO – 239
ANT0690

Frequency (MHz)	A (Inches)	B (Inches)
146	19 – 5/16"	18 – 11/16"
225	12 – 5/8"	12"
445	6 – 3/8"	5 – 3/4"

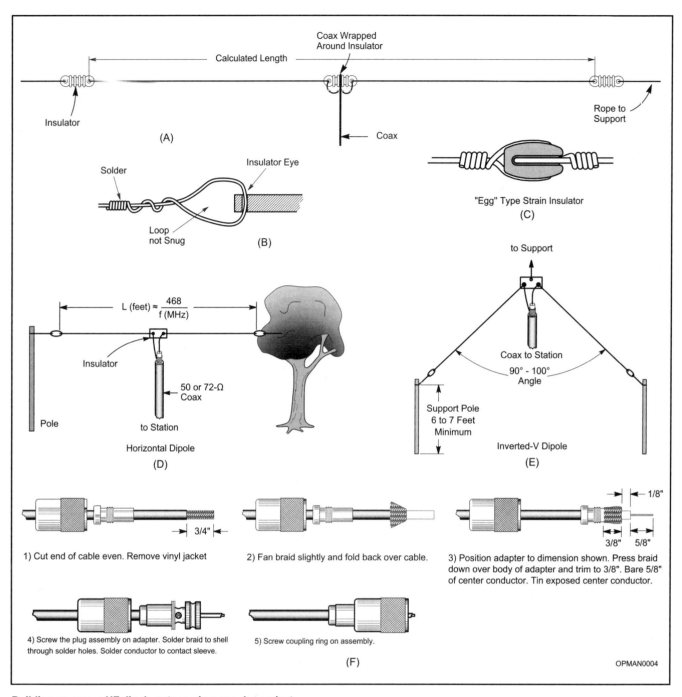

Building your own HF dipole antenna is a popular project.

to the antenna feed line and transmits a very low power signal to display the antenna SWR over a range of frequencies.

Putting It Together

Assembly is quite simple. Your dipole consists of two lengths of wire, each approximately ¼ wavelength long at your chosen (or lowest) operating frequency. These two

Table 1.1
Antenna Lengths in Feet

	½ wavelength	¼ wavelength
80 m	126' 6"	63' 3"
40 m	65' 8"	32' 10"
15 m	22' 2"	11' 11"
10 m	16' 7"	8' 3"

Remember to add about 1 foot to each end of the dipole for tuning adjustment.

wires are connected in the center, at an insulator, to the feed line. In our antenna the feed line, which brings the signals to and from your radio, is coaxial cable. Calculate the length of the half-wave dipole by using this simple formula: antenna length in feet = 468/frequency in MHz

(The information in **Table 1.1** has approximate lengths already calculated.) Now measure the antenna wire, keeping it as straight as possible. To the length in the table, add an additional 8 inches on each end of the wire (that's 16 inches per antenna half) to allow for the mechanical loop through the insulator.

Carefully assemble your antenna, paying special attention to waterproofing the coax connections at the center insulator. Don't solder the antenna ends until later, when tuning is completed. Just twist them for now. Route the coax to your station, leaving a drip loop wherever the cable goes through a wall or window. Cut the coax to a length that will leave some excess for strain relief so your rig won't be pulled around during strong winds! Install the connectors according to the diagrams. If you use an external SWR meter, connect it between the end of the antenna feed line and the transmitter.

Raise the antenna into place and test it! Turn on your radio and reduce power to 10 W output or less. Follow the instructions in the radio's instruction manual to measure SWR at several frequencies across the band for which the dipole was designed. Be sure to listen first and find a clear frequency so you don't unintentionally interfere with other hams using the band.

If the minimum SWR occurs at or near the desired operating frequency and the SWR is lower than 2:1 or so, your antenna is correctly tuned. Lower it, solder the ends of the antenna that are twisted around the insulators and

hoist it back into place. Go operate!

If the *resonant frequency* at the minimum SWR is too low, the antenna is too long and it will need to be shortened. Lower it and remove six inches from each side of the dipole, then test SWR again. Keep notes! Assuming the resonant frequency increased when the antenna was shortened, keep shortening and testing until the resonant frequency is approximately correct. If the resonant frequency was too high, you can splice the antenna and add some length on each end. As the last step, when you are sure the length of the dipole is correct, solder the wire wrapped around the end insulators. When you complete the antenna, take a final set of SWR readings and keep them in a notebook for future reference, should you need to troubleshoot the antenna or feed line.

If you plan on building a number of antennas, a better way to tune the antenna that does not involve transmitting an unmodulated signal is to use an antenna *noise bridge* or an *antenna analyzer*. These instruments use extremely low power signals to measure SWR and are much more portable than a transmitter and SWR meter.

When all systems are go, get on the air and operate. As you settle into that first QSO with your new antenna, enjoy those feelings of pride, accomplishment and fun that will naturally follow. After all, that's what Amateur Radio is all about!

Problems and Cures

Many hams act as though the world will end if they put up an antenna and measure an SWR greater than 1.5:1. For most purposes an SWR of up to 3:1 is perfectly acceptable at HF with good quality feed lines 100 feet or less in length, provided your transceiver will work with an SWR that high (some radios reduce power as SWR increases over 2:1).

A high SWR that does not change when you change the antenna length by a foot or more (HF only) probably means something more serious is wrong with your simple, one-band dipole. Check to see if your coax is open or shorted. Make sure your antenna isn't touching anything and that all your connections are sound.

On bands such as 80 meters, the antenna likely won't have a low SWR over the whole band. In this case, tune the antenna for the highest frequency part of the band on which you wish to operate (the shortest antenna length). When you want to use the lower part of the band, lower the antenna and temporarily attach short lengths of wire at the end insulators, using heavy alligator clips or split-nut wire clamps.

We'll cover mobile and portable stations later in this section.

1.1.4 Resources for Assembling a Station

ARRL website: **www.arrl.org/your-first-antenna**
ARRL website: **www.arrl.org/what-rig-should-i-buy**
ARRL Product Reviews: **www.arrl.org/product-review**
   You can also find more technical information in *The ARRL*

Handbook and *The ARRL Antenna Book*, as well as *Your First Amateur Radio HF Station, Simple and Fun Antennas for Hams, Basic Antennas*, and a number of other antenna-related titles, all available from your favorite ham radio dealer or the ARRL website.

1.2 Basic Operating Procedures

Actual on-the-air operating experience is the best teacher. In this section, we will try to give you enough of the basics to be able to make (and enjoy!) your first QSO. Learn by doing and by listening to others. Don't be afraid to ask questions of someone who might be able to help. After all, we're in this hobby together, and assistance is only as far away as the closest ham.

Since there are established ways of doing things in the Amateur Radio Service because of rules or good practice, you'll learn most effectively by just plain, old-fashioned listening. All you need is a receiver and your ears. Tune around the amateur frequency bands, and just listen, listen, listen. Listen to as many QSOs as you can. Learn how the operators conduct themselves, see what works for other operators and what doesn't, and incorporate those good operating practices into your own operating habits. You'll be surprised how much operator savvy you can pick up just by listening.

When you're ready, fire up the rig to make your first QSO. Go for it! Nothing can compare

with actual on-the-air experience. Remember, everyone on the air today had to make their first QSO at some time or other. They had the same tentativeness you might have now, but they made it just fine. So will you.

It's the nature of the ham to be friendly,

Your First Contact

Are your palms sweaty, hands shaking and is there a queasy herd of butterflies (wearing spikes, perhaps) performing maneuvers in your stomach? Chances are you're facing your first Amateur Radio QSO. If so, take heart! Although some may deny it, the vast majority of hams felt the same way before firing up the rig for their first contact.

Although nervousness is natural, there are some preparations that can make things go a little more smoothly. Practicing QSOs face-to-face with a friend, or perhaps with a member of the local Amateur Radio club, is a good way to ease the jitters.

Some find it useful to write down in advance information you will use during the QSO. You might even go so far as to write a script for what you expect. After a couple of contacts, however, you'll find that you need little prompting.

The ideal security blanket to have with you as you make your first few QSOs is your Elmer or another experienced ham. You'll find that after your initial nervousness wears off you will do just fine by yourself. And you will have honored a ham friend by allowing him or her the privilege of sharing your first on-the-air contacts.

especially toward other members of this wonderful fraternity we all joined when we passed that examination. Trust the operator at the other end of your first QSO to understand your feelings and be as helpful as possible. After all, he or she was once in your situation!

1.2.1 The Bands

Operating on the VHF/UHF bands is relatively straightforward for most modes of operation commonly employed there. Operating on the HF bands is a quite a bit more variable, because the propagation depends on a number of factors that are quite literally in outer space. The main influence on the Earth's ionosphere is the Sun, but the magnetic field of the Earth gets into the act very much as well in determining how HF signals are propagated from one place to another.

The sidebar "Picking a Band" gives you a generalized idea of what to expect on both the HF and the VHF/UHF bands. Never forget, however, that part of the excitement and mystery of the HF bands lies in their unpredictability from day-to-day, or even from hour-to-hour. As this edition is being written, as we head for the solar cycle minimum, the higher HF bands (15, 12, and 10 meters) are quiet much of the time. When sunspots start appearing once again, those bands will fill with signals from around the world!

Table 1.2 shows the Considerate Operator's Frequency Guide for HF. Try these frequencies first when looking for activity on a quiet band. North American VHF and above calling frequencies are discussed in

Picking a Band

By Jim Kearman, KR1S

160 and 80 Meters

Eighty meters, and its phone neighbor, 75 meters, are favorites for ragchewing. I frequently check out the upper frequencies of the CW subband. There I find both newcomers as well as old-timers trying to work the rust out of their fists. Around 3570 kHz you'll find the digital modes, including RTTY, PSK31 and JT65. The QRP frequency is 3560 kHz. If you hear a weak signal calling CQ near 3560, crank down your power and give a call. If you live in the eastern half of North America, listen for W1AW on 3581.5 (CW), 3597.5 (digital) or 3990 kHz (SSB). If you can copy W1AW, you can probably work the East Coast, even with low power. AM operation is generally found between 3870 and 3890 kHz.

Ionospheric absorption is greatest during the day, thus local contacts are common. At night, contacts over 200 miles away are more frequent, even with a poor antenna. Summer lightning storms make for noisy conditions in the

summer, while winter is much quieter. In the winter, especially during low sunspot years, DX contacts are common. You may also be troubled by electrical noise here. A horizontally polarized antenna, especially one as far from buildings as possible, will pick up less electrical noise.

Topband, as 160 meters is often called, is similar to 80 meters. QSOs here tend to be a bit more relaxed with less QRM. DX is frequent at the bottom of the band. Don't let the length of a half-wave dipole for 160 keep you off the band; a "long wire" can give you surprisingly good results if a good ground system is available. One favorite trick is to connect together the center conductor and shield of the coax feed line of a 40- or 80-meter dipole and load the resulting antenna as a "T," working it against the station ground.

60 Meters

Unlike other HF amateur bands, 60 meters is *channelized*. This means that you have to operate on specific frequencies. Amateurs have secondary

VHF/UHF Beyond FM and Repeaters later in this section.

Propagation Beacons

By providing a steady signal on certain frequencies, HF beacons provide a valuable means of checking current propagation conditions — how well signals are traveling at the time you want to transmit.

The Northern California DX Foundation, in cooperation with the International Amateur Radio Union (IARU), has established a widespread, multi-band beacon network. This network operates on 14.100, 18.110, 21.150, 24.930 and 28.200 MHz. These beacons transmit at a sequence of power levels from 100 W down to 0.1 W in a repeating sequence. A full description with the most up-to-date status is on the NCDXF website (**www.ncdxf.org/beacon.htm**).

access to this band. They cannot cause interference to and must accept interference from the Primary Government users. Amateurs can transmit CW and PSK31 on the following channel-center frequencies: 5332.0, 5348.0, 5358.5, 5373.0 and 5405.0 kHz. Amateurs can also transmit upper sideband (USB) voice and PACTOR III on the following suppressed carrier frequencies (the frequencies typically shown on transceiver displays): 5330.5, 5346.5, 5357.0, 5371.5 and 5403.5 kHz.

Amateurs may transmit with an effective radiated power (ERP) of 100 W or less, relative to a half-wave dipole. If you're using a commercial directional antenna, FCC Rules require you to keep a copy of the manufacturer's gain specifications in your station records. If you built the directional antenna yourself, you must calculate the gain and keep the results in your station records.

When using a directional antenna, you must take your antenna gain into account when setting your RF output power. For example, if your antenna offers 3 dB gain, your maximum legal output power on 60 meters should be no more than 50 W (50 W plus 3 dB gain equals 100 W ERP).

Despite the limitations, it has intriguing potential. The propagation on 60 meters combines the best of 80 and 40 meters.

40 and 30 Meters

If I could have a receiver that covered only one band, it would be 40. Running 10 W from my East Coast apartment (indoor antenna) I can work European hams, ragchew up and down the coast, and check into Saturday morning nets. Yes, 40 is a little crowded. Look at the bright side: You won't be lonely. I think it's possible to work someone on 40 any time of the day or night.

In the US, Advanced and Extra licensees have voice privileges starting at 7125 kHz and the General band starts at 7175 kHz. Most other countries have SSB privileges down to 7050 kHz so don't be surprised if you hear voice stations below the US phone band. At night you may hear foreign broadcast stations above 7200 kHz. During the day, they won't bother you much. Forty is a good band for daytime mobile SSB operation, too. You'll find plenty of activity, and propagation conditions tend

to be stable enough to allow you to ragchew as you roll along.

CW QRPers hang around and above 7030 kHz. Digital operators work around 7070 to 7125 kHz. Hams operating AM are typically around 7290 kHz.

The 30 meter band has propagation similar to 40 meters. Skip distances tend to be a little longer on 30 meters, and it's not so crowded. At present, stations in the US are limited to 200 W output on this band. DX stations seem to like the low end of the band, from 10100 to 10115 kHz. Ragchewers often congregate above 10115. We share 30 meters with other services, so be sure you don't interfere with them. SSB isn't allowed on 30, but you can use CW and the digital modes.

20 Meters

As much as I like 40 and 30 meters, I have many fond memories of 20 meters as well. When I upgraded my license to General, I made a beeline to 20 meters. To this day, I can't stay away for long. On 20 meters, you can work the world with a dipole or vertical and 100 W. A 20 meter dipole is only 33 feet long, and that doesn't have to be in a straight line. Many hams consider 20 meters the workhorse DX band. At the peak of the solar cycle, it's open 24 hours a day. Even at the bottom of a solar cycle, 20 meters may be usable in a particular direction for a few hours a day.

There's plenty of room on the band. CW ragchewers hang out from 14025 to 14070 kHz, where you start hearing digital stations. The international QRP frequency is 14060 kHz. The sideband part of the band is sometimes pretty busy and then it may be difficult to make a contact with low power or a modest antenna. Look above 14250 for ragchewers. Impromptu discussion groups that sometimes spring up on 20 SSB make for interesting listening, even if you don't participate. If you like photographs, look around 14230 kHz for slow-scan TV. You'll need some extra equipment (as discussed later in this section) to see the pictures.

17, 15 and 12 Meters

Except during years of high solar activity, you'll do most of your operating during daylight hours. Propagation is usually better during the winter months. Seventeen and 12 meters aren't as

crowded as 15 meters. Fifteen, though, is not nearly as crowded as 20. On 15, the QRP calling frequency is 21060 kHz. Don't forget that CW can be found all the way up to 21200 kHz. No special frequencies are used for QRP operation on 17 and 12. SSB operation is much easier on 17 and 12 because of lower activity. Low activity doesn't mean no activity — when those bands are open, you'll find plenty of stations to work. You only need one at a time, after all. Digital operation is found from 21070 to 21110 kHz, and around 18100 and 24920 kHz.

Practical indoor, outdoor, mobile or portable antennas for these bands are simple to build and install.

10 Meters

The 10 meter band stretches from 28000 to 29700 kHz. During years of high solar activity, 10 to 25 W transceivers will fetch plenty of contacts. When the Sun is quiet, there are still occasional openings of thousands of miles. Ten meters also benefits from sporadic-E propagation. You'll find most sporadic-E openings in the summer, but they can happen anytime. Sporadic-E openings happen suddenly and end just as quickly. You may not be able to ragchew very long, but you'll be amazed at how many stations you can work.

SSB activity is heaviest in the Novice/Technician subband from 28300 to 28500 kHz. The lower end of the band (tune up from the bottom edge) is a good place to look for CW activity, as is the QRP calling frequency at 28060 kHz. You can operate 1200 baud packet radio on 10 meters, whereas we're limited to 300 baud on the lower bands. Digital operation takes place from 28070 to 28120 kHz.

Higher in the band, above 29000 kHz, you'll find amateur FM stations and repeaters, and the amateur satellite subband. AM operation is also popular between 29000 and 29200 kHz.

Operating on 50 MHz and Above

The VHF/UHF/microwave bands offer advantages to the low-power operator. The biggest plus is the relatively smaller antennas used. A good-sized 2 meter beam will easily fit in a closet when not in use. Portable and mobile operation on these bands is also easy and fun. These bands are discussed in detail later in this section.

US Amateur Radio Bands

Effective Date March 5, 2012

ARRL — The national association for AMATEUR RADIO®

US AMATEUR POWER LIMITS

FCC 97.313 An amateur station must use the minimum transmitter power necessary to carry out the desired communications. (b) No station may transmit with a transmitter power exceeding 1.5 kW PEP.

KEY

Note:
CW operation is permitted throughout all amateur bands.
MCW is authorized above 50.1 MHz, except for 144.0-144.1 and 219-220 MHz.
Test transmissions are authorized above 51 MHz, except for 219-220 MHz.

E = Amateur Extra
A = Advanced
G = General
T = Technician
N = Novice

= RTTY and data
= phone and image
= CW only
= SSB phone
= USB phone, CW, RTTY, and data.
= Fixed digital message forwarding systems only

160 Meters (1.8 MHz)

Avoid interference to radiolocation operations from ~.900 to 2.000 MHz

1.800 — 1.900 — 2.000 MHz   E,A,G

80 Meters (3.5 MHz)

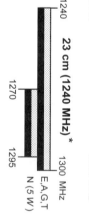

3.500 3.600 3.700 4.000 MHz
3.525 3.600 — 3.800
E / A / G / N,T (200 W)

60 Meters (5.3 MHz)

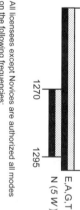

5330.5 5346.5 5357.0 5371.5 5403.5 kHz
⎯ 2.8 kHz ⎯
E,A,G (100 W)

General, Advanced, and Amateur Extra licensees may operate on these five channels on a secondary basis with a maximum effective radiated power (ERP) of 100 W PEP relative to a half-wave dipole. Permitted operating modes include upper sideband voice (USB), CW, RTTY, PSK31 and other digital modes such as PACTOR III as defined by the FCC Report and Order of November 18, 2011. USB is limited to 2.8 kHz centered on 5332, 5348, 5358.5, 5373 and 5405 kHz. CW and digital emissions must be centered 1.5 kHz above the channel frequencies indicated above. Only one signal at a time is permitted on any channel.

40 Meters (7 MHz)

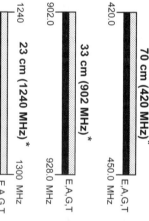

7.00C 7.125 7.175
7.C25 7.125
7.300 MHz
E / A / G / N,T (200 W)

Phone and Image modes are permitted between 7.075 and 7.100 MHz for FCC licensed stations in ITU Regions 1 and 3 and by FCC licensed stations in ITU Region 2 West of 130 degrees West longitude or South of 20 degrees North latitude. See Sections 97.305(c) and 97.307(f)(11). Novice and Technician licensees outside ITU Region 2 may use CW only between 7.025 and 7.075 MHz and between 7.100 ar d 7.125 MHz. 7.200 to 7.300 MHz is not available outside ITU Region 2. See Section 97.301(e). These exemptions do not apply to stations in the continental US.

30 Meters (10.1 MHz)

Avoid interference to fixed services outside the US.

200 Watts PEP

10.100 — 10.150 MHz   E,A,G

20 Meters (14 MHz)

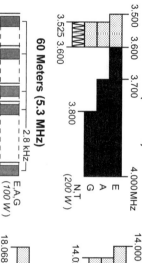

14.000 14.150 14.350 MHz
14.025 14.150 14.225
14.175
E / A / G / N,T (200 W)

17 Meters (18 MHz)

18.068 18.110 18.168 MHz   E,A,G

15 Meters (21 MHz)

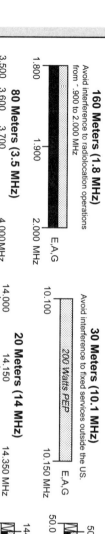

21.000 21.200 21.450 MHz
21.025 21.200
21.225 21.275
E / A / G / N,T (200 W)

12 Meters (24 MHz)

24.890 24.930 24.990 MHz   E,A,G

10 Meters (28 MHz)

28.000 28.300 29.700 MHz
28.000 28.300
28.500
E,A,G / N,T (200 W)

6 Meters (50 MHz)

50.0 50.1 — 54.0 MHz   E,A,G,T

2 Meters (144 MHz)

144.0 144.1 — 148.0 MHz   E,A,G,T

1.25 Meters (222 MHz)

219.0 220.0 — 222.0 — 225.0 MHz
E,A,G,T / N (25 W)

70 cm (420 MHz) *

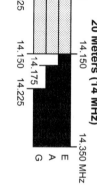

420.0 — 450.0 MHz   E,A,G,T

33 cm (902 MHz) *

902.0 — 928.0 MHz   E,A,G,T

23 cm (1240 MHz) *

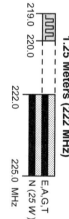

1240 — 1270 — 1295 — 1300 MHz
E,A,G,T / N (5 W)

*Geographical and power restrictions may apply to all bands above 420 MHz. See *The ARRL Operating Manual* for information about your area.

*No pulse emissions

All licensees except Novices are authorized all modes on the following frequencies:

2300-2310 MHz
2390-2450 MHz
3300-3500 MHz
5650-5925 MHz

10.0-10.5 GHz *
24.0-24.25 GHz
47.0-47.2 GHz
76.0-81.0 GHz

122.25-123.0 GHz
134-141 GHz
241-250 GHz
All above 275 GHz

See *ARRLWeb* at www.arrl.org for detailed band plans.

ARRL — We're At Your Service

ARRL Headquarters:
860-594-0200 (Fax 860-594-0259)
email: hq@arrl.org

Publication Orders:
www.arrl.org/shop
Toll-Free 1-888-277-5289 (860-594-0355)
email: orders@arrl.org

Membership/Circulation Desk:
www.arrl.org/membership
Toll-Free 1-888-277-5289 (860-594-0338)
email: membership@arrl.org

Getting Started in Amateur Radio:
Toll-Free 1-800-326-3942 (860-594-0355)
email: newham@arrl.org

Exams: 860-594-0300 email: vec@arrl.org

Copyright © ARRL, 2012   rev. 6/3/2016

Frequency Allocation Chart for US amateurs.

Table 1.2
The Considerate Operator's Frequency Guide
The following frequencies are generally recognized for certain modes or activities (all frequencies are in MHz) during normal conditions. These are not regulations and occasionally a high level of activity, such as during a period of emergency response, DXpedition or contest, may result in stations operating outside these frequency ranges.

Nothing in the rules recognizes a net's, group's or any individual's special privilege to any specific frequency. Section 97.101(b) of the Rules states that "Each station licensee and each control operator must cooperate in selecting transmitting channels and in making the most effective use of the amateur service frequencies. No frequency will be assigned for the exclusive use of any station." No one "owns" a frequency.

It's good practice — and plain old common sense — for any operator, regardless of mode, to check to see if the frequency is in use prior to engaging operation. If you are there first, other operators should make an effort to protect you from interference to the extent possible, given that 100% interference-free operation is an unrealistic expectation in today's congested bands.

Frequencies	Modes/Activities	Frequencies	Modes/Activities
1.800-2.000	CW	18.100-18.105	RTTY/Data
1.800-1.810	Digital Modes	18.105-18.110	Automatically controlled data stations
1.810	CW QRP calling frequency	18.110	IBP/NCDXF beacons
1.843-2.000	SSB, SSTV and other wideband modes	18.162.5	Digital Voice
1.910	SSB QRP	21.060	QRP CW calling frequency
1.995-2.000	Experimental	21.070-21.110	RTTY/Data
1.999-2.000	Beacons	21.090-21.100	Automatically controlled data stations
		21.150	IBP/NCDXF beacons
3.500-3.510	CW DX window	21.340	SSTV
3.560	QRP CW calling frequency	21.385	QRP SSB calling frequency
3.570-3.600	RTTY/Data		
3.585-3.600	Automatically controlled data stations	24.920-24.925	RTTY/Data
3.590	RTTY/Data DX	24.925-24.930	Automatically controlled data stations
3.790-3.800	DX window	24.930	IBP/NCDXF beacons
3.845	SSTV		
3.885	AM calling frequency	28.060	QRP CW calling frequency
3.985	QRP SSB calling frequency	28.070-28.120	RTTY/Data
		28.120-28.189	Automatically controlled data stations
7.030	QRP CW calling frequency	28.190-28.225	Beacons
7.040	RTTY/Data DX	28.200	IBP/NCDXF beacons
7.070-7.125	RTTY/Data	28.385	QRP SSB calling frequency
7.100-7.105	Automatically controlled data stations	28.680	SSTV
7.171	SSTV	29.000-29.200	AM
7.173	D-SSTV	29.300-29.510	Satellite downlinks
7.285	QRP SSB calling frequency	29.520-29.580	Repeater inputs
7.290	AM calling frequency	29.600	FM simplex
		29.620-29.680	Repeater outputs
10.130-10.140	RTTY/Data		
10.140-10.150	Automatically controlled data stations		
14.060	QRP CW calling frequency		
14.070-14.095	RTTY/Data		
14.095-14.0995	Automatically controlled data stations		
14.100	IBP/NCDXF beacons		
14.1005-14.112	Automatically controlled data stations		
14.230	SSTV		
14.233	D-SSTV		
14.236	Digital Voice		
14.285	QRP SSB calling frequency		
14.286	AM calling frequency		

ARRL band plans for frequencies above 28.300 MHz are shown in *The ARRL Repeater Directory* and on **www.arrl.org**.

1.2.2 Operating — What, Where and How

You have read a little about the basics of ham radio and have some ideas about selecting a rig and station equipment and erecting a decent antenna system. Now it's time to learn a little more about how to go about playing the ham radio game.

To communicate effectively with other hams, we all need to use accepted operating procedures. Next we'll briefly describe the major modes of ham radio communication and a few of the procedures and conventions that hams use on the air. Later we will discuss the operating procedures for specialized modes of communication in greater detail. But first we are going to look at operating HF voice and CW (Morse code).

Phone Operating Procedures

These phone or voice operating procedures apply to operation on the HF bands as well as SSB on VHF/UHF. Procedures used on repeaters are different since the operation there is channelized — that is, anyone listening to the repeater will hear you as soon as you begin to transmit. Therefore there is no need to call CQ. Each repeater may use a slightly different procedure. There is a discussion of repeater operations later in this section.

Learning procedures is straightforward: Listen to what others are doing, and incorporate their good habits into your own operating style. Use common sense in your day-to-day phone QSOs, too:

1) Listen before transmitting. Ask if the frequency is in use before making a call on any particular frequency.

2) Give your call sign as needed, using the

Table 1.3
The Phonetic Alphabet

When operating phone, a standard alphabet is often used to ensure understanding of call letters and other spelled-out information. Thus Ward, NØAX, would announce his call as November Zero Alfa X-Ray if he felt the station on the other end could misunderstand his call. Phonetics are not used routinely when operating VHF-FM.

A — Alfa (**AL** FAH)
B — Bravo (**BRAH** VOH)
C — Charlie (**CHAR** LEE)
D — Delta (**DELL** TAH)
E — Echo (**ECK** OH)
F — Foxtrot (**FOX** TROT)
G — Golf (GOLF)
H — Hotel (HOH **TELL**)
I — India (**IN** DEE AH)
J — Juliet (**JEW** LEE ETT)
K — Kilo (**KEY** LOH)
L — Lima (**LEE** MA)
M — Mike (MIKE)
N — November (NO **VEM** BERR)
O — Oscar (**OSS** CAR)
P — Papa (PAH **PAH**)
Q — Quebec (KEY **BECK**)
R — Romeo (**ROW** ME OH)
S — Sierra (SEE **AIR** AH)
T — Tango (**TANG** OH)
U — Uniform (**YOU** NEE FORM)
V — Victor (**VIK** TORE)
W — Whiskey (**WISS** KEY)
X — X-Ray (**EX** RAY)
Y — Yankee (**YANG** KEY)
Z — Zulu (**ZOO** LOU)

The boldfaced syllables are emphasized.

Table 1.4
The RST System

The RST reporting system is used on both CW and voice; leave out the "tone" report on voice.

Readability
1 — Unreadable
2 — Barely readable, occasional words distinguishable
3 — Readable with considerable difficulty
4 — Readable with practically no difficulty
5 — Perfectly readable

Signal Strength
1 — Faint signals, barely perceptible
2 — Very weak signals
3 — Weak signals
4 — Fair signals
5 — Fairly good signals
6 — Good signals
7 — Moderately strong signals
8 — Strong signals
9 — Extremely strong signals

Tone
1 — Sixty-cycle ac or less, very rough and broad
2 — Very rough ac, very harsh and broad
3 — Rough ac tone, rectified but not filtered
4 — Rough note, some trace of filtering
5 — Filtered rectified ac but strongly ripple-modulated
6 — Filtered tone, definite trace of ripple modulation
7 — Near pure tone, trace of ripple modulation
8 — Near perfect tone, slight trace of ripple modulation
9 — Perfect tone, no trace of ripple or modulation of any kind

On CW, if the signal has chirp, add the letter C. Similarly for a key click, add K.

---

approved ITU (International Telecommunication Union) phonetics. These phonetics are given in **Table 1.3**.

3) Make sure your signal is clean and your audio undistorted. Do not turn your microphone gain up too high. If you have a speech processor, use it only when you are sure it is properly adjusted. Don't take the chance of transmitting spurious (out of band) signals.

4) Only occupy the frequency as long as you need it. This gives as many operators as possible a chance to use the frequency spectrum.

5) Give honest signal reports. **Table 1.4** lists what the various RST reports mean.

Whatever band, mode or type of operating you choose, there are three fundamental things to remember. The first is that courtesy costs very little and is often amply rewarded by bringing out the best in others. The second is that the aim of each radio contact should be 100% effective communication. The good operator is never satisfied with anything less. The third is that "private" conversations with another station are actually *public*. Keep in mind that many amateurs are uncomfortable discussing so-called controversial subjects such as sex, religion, or politics over the air.

Also, never unnecessarily give any information on the air that might be of assistance to the criminally inclined, such as when you are going to be out of town!

Using the proper procedure is very important. Voice operators say what they want to have understood, while CW operators have to spell it out or abbreviate. Correct phone operation is more challenging than it first may appear, even though it does not require the use of code or special abbreviations. Remember that the other operator can't see you. Understanding you depends solely on your voice coming over the airwaves. It's easy to acquire bad habits of speech, so be prepared to put in a bit of effort to speak clearly and not too quickly. This is particularly important when talking to a DX station that speaks a different language.

Avoid using CW abbreviations and Q signals on phone, although QRZ (for "who is calling?") has become accepted. Otherwise, plain language should be used. Keep jargon to a minimum. Some hams use "we" instead of "I," "handle" instead of "name," and "roger" instead of "that's correct." These expressions are not necessary and do not contribute to better operating. No doubt you will hear many more.

Initiating a Contact

There are three ways to initiate a voice contact: call CQ (a general call to any station),

answer a CQ, or call at the end of the other person's contact. If activity on a band seems low and you have a reasonable signal, a CQ call may be worthwhile.

Before calling CQ, it is important to find a frequency that appears unoccupied by any other station. This may not be easy, particularly in crowded band conditions. Listen carefully — perhaps a weak DX station is on frequency.

Always listen before transmitting. Make sure the frequency isn't being used *before* you call. If, after a reasonable time, the frequency seems clear, ask if the frequency is in use, followed by your call: "Is the frequency in use? This is N1OJS." If as far as you can determine no one responds, you are ready to make your call.

CQ calls should be kept short. Long calls are unnecessary. If no one answers, you can always call again. Think of each CQ as an advertisement for your station. A caller tuning across your signal should hear a friendly voice, clean audio, and plenty of time between your CQs for them to respond.

If you do transmit a long call, a potential contact may become impatient and tune elsewhere. You may also interfere with stations that were already on the frequency but whom you didn't hear in the initial check. If two or three calls produce no answer, there may be interference on the frequency. It's also possible that the band isn't open.

An example of a short CQ call would be: "CQ CQ Calling CQ. This is N1OJS, November-One-Oscar-Juliet-Sierra, November-One-Oscar-Juliet-Sierra, calling CQ and standing by."

When replying to a CQ, give both call signs clearly — yours and the CQing station. Use the standard phonetics to make sure the other station gets your call correctly. Phonetics are necessary when calling in a DX pileup and initially in most HF contacts but not usually used when calling into an FM repeater.

When you are calling a specific station, it is good practice to keep calls short and to say the call sign of the station called only once followed by your call repeated twice. VOX (voice operated switch) operation is helpful. If properly adjusted, it enables you to listen between phrases so that you know what is happening on the frequency. "N1OJS, this is W2GD, Whiskey-Two-Golf-Delta, Over."

Once contact has been established, it is no longer necessary to use the phonetic alphabet or sign the other station's call. According to FCC regulations, you need only sign your call every 10 minutes, or at the conclusion of the contact. (The exception is handling international third-party traffic; you must sign both calls in this instance.) A normal two-way conversation can thus be enjoyed, without the need for continual identification. The words "Over" or "Go Ahead" may be used at the end of a transmission to show you are ready for a reply from the other station.

Signal reports on phone are two-digit numbers using the RS portion of the RST system (no tone report is required). The maximum signal report would be "59"; that is, readability 5, strength 9. On FM repeaters, RS reports are not appropriate. When a signal has fully captured the repeater, this is called "full quieting."

CW Operating

Using Morse code is a common bond among many HF operators who take pride in their code proficiency. It takes practice to master the art of sending good code on a hand key, bug (semi-automatic key) or electronic keyer. It takes practice to get that smooth rhythm, practice to get that smooth spacing between words and characters, and practice to learn the sound of whole words and phrases, rather than just individual letters.

CW (standing for *continuous wave*) is an effective mode of communication. CW transceivers are simpler than their phone counterparts, and a CW signal can usually get through very heavy QRM (interference) much more effectively than a phone signal.

To reduce transmission time and increase efficiency when using Morse code, hams use shortcuts and abbreviations such as UR for your, or PSE for please during a CW QSO.

Tom, K7TPD, is shown here operating 40 meter CW on an outing with the Radio Society of Tucson K7RST.

Many were developed within the ham fraternity, while some are borrowed from old-time telegraph operators. *Q signals* are among the most useful of these abbreviations. A few of the most popular Q signals are shown in **Table 1.5**. You don't have to memorize all the Q-signals, just keep a copy handy to your operating table.

After using some of the Q signals and abbreviations a few times you will quickly learn the most common ones without needing any reference. With time, you'll find that as your CW proficiency rises, you will be able to communicate almost as quickly on CW as you can on the voice modes.

Your CW sending and receiving speed will rise very quickly with on-the-air practice. For your first few QSOs, carefully choose to answer the calls from stations sending at a speed you can copy (perhaps another first timer on the band?). Courtesy on the ham bands dictates that an operator will slow his or her code speed to accommodate another operator. Don't be afraid to call someone who is sending just a bit faster than you can

copy comfortably. That operator will generally slow down to meet your CW speed. If necessary, ask the other operator to "PSE QRS" to slow down a little. Helping each other is the name of the game in ham radio.

Correct CW Procedures

The best way to establish a contact, especially at first, is to listen until you hear someone calling CQ. CQ means, "I wish to contact any amateur station." Avoid the common operating pitfall of calling CQ endlessly; it clutters up the airwaves and keeps others from calling you. The typical CQ would sound like this: CQ CQ CQ DE KB3VVE KB3VVE KB3VVE repeated once or twice and followed by K. The letter K is a prosign inviting any station to go ahead. If there is no answer, pause for 10 seconds or so and repeat the call.

If you hear a CQ, wait until the ham finishes transmitting (by ending with the letter K), then call: KB3VVE DE W6LEN W6LEN AR. (AR is equivalent to *over*). In answer to your call, the called station will begin the reply by

Table 1.5
Q Signals
These Q signals are the ones used most often on the air. (Q abbreviations take the form of questions only when they are sent followed by a question mark.)

QRL	Are you busy? I am busy (or I am busy with ___).Please do not interfere.
QRM	Is my transmission being interfered with? Your transmission is being interfered with.
QRN	Are you troubled by static? I am troubled by static.)
QRO	Shall I increase power? Increase power.
QRP	Shall I decrease power? Decrease power.
QRS	Shall I send more slowly? Send more slowly (___ WPM).
QRT	Shall I stop sending? Stop sending.
QRZ	Who is calling me? You are being called by _____.
QSL	Can you acknowledge receipt (of a message or transmission)? I am acknowledging receipt.
QSO	Can you communicate with direct or by relay? I can communicate with ___ direct (or relay through).
QTH	What is your location? My location is ___ .

sending W6LEN DE KB3VVE R. That R (*roger*) means that he has received your call correctly. Suppose KB3VVE heard someone calling her, but didn't quite catch the call because of interference (QRM) or static (QRN). Then she might come back with QRZ? DE KB3VVE K (Who is calling me?).

The QSO

During the contact, it is necessary to identify your station only once every 10 minutes and at the end of the communication. Keep the contact on a friendly and cordial level, remembering that the conversation is not private and many others, including nonamateurs, may be listening. It may be helpful at the beginning to have a fully written-out script typical of the first couple of exchanges in front of you. A typical first transmission might sound like this: W6LEN DE KB3VVE R TNX CALL. UR 599 599 QTH PENNSYLVANIA NAME EMILY HW? W6LEN DE KB3VVE KN. This is the basic exchange that begins most QSOs. Once these basics are exchanged the conversation can turn in almost any direction. Many people talk about their jobs, other hobbies, families, travel experiences, and so on.

Both on CW and phone, it is possible to be informal, friendly and conversational; this is what makes the Amateur Radio QSO enjoyable. During a CW contact, when you want the other station to take a turn, the recommended signal is KN (*go ahead, only*), meaning that you want *only* the contacted station to come back to you. If you don't mind someone else breaking in to join the contact, just K (*go ahead*) is sufficient.

Ending the QSO

When you decide to end the contact or the other ham expresses the desire to end it, don't keep talking. Briefly express your thanks for the contact: TNX QSO or TNX CHAT — and then sign off: 73 KB3VVE DE W6LEN SK. If you are leaving the air, add CL (*closing*) to the end, right after your call sign.

Conducting the Contact

Aside from signal strength, name, and location, it is customary to exchange power level and antenna. This information helps both stations assess conditions. Keep in mind that many hams will not know the charac-

teristics of your equipment. Therefore, you may be better off just saying that your rig runs 100 W output and the antenna is a dipole. Once these routine details are out of the way, you can proceed to discuss virtually anything appropriate and interesting.

DX Contacts

DX can be worked on any HF band as well as occasionally on 6 meters. Keep in mind that while many overseas amateurs have an exceptional command of English, they may not be familiar with many of our colloquialisms. Because of the language differences, some DX stations are more comfortable with the barebones type contact and you should be sensitive to their preferences. In unsettled propagation conditions, it may be necessary to keep the whole contact short. The good operator takes these factors into account when expanding on a basic contact.

Also understand that during a band opening on 10 meters or on VHF, you should keep contacts brief so as many stations as possible can work the DX coming through during what may be a brief opportunity. Brevity is also expected when contacting a DXpedition operating from some exotic location for just a few days.

Additional Recommendations

Listen with care. It is very natural to answer the loudest station that calls, but sometimes you will have to dig deep into the noise and interference to hear the other station.

Use VOX or push-to-talk (PTT). If you use VOX, don't defeat its purpose by saying "aaah" to keep the relay closed. If you use PTT, let go of the mike button every so often to make sure you are not "doubling" (talking at the same time as the other station). Don't filibuster.

Talk at a constant level. Try to maintain the same distance between your mouth and the microphone. Keep the mike gain down to eliminate background noise. Follow the manufacturer's instructions for use of the microphone. Some require close talking, while some need to be turned at an angle to the speaker's mouth.

Speech processing and adjustable transmit audio equalization (often built into contemporary transceivers) is a mixed blessing. It can help you cut through the interference and static, but if improperly adjusted, the audio quality suffers. Make some on-air tests with another station to adjust the controls for the best sounding signal.

UTC Explained

Keeping track of time can be pretty confusing when you are talking to other hams around the world. Europe, for example, is anywhere from 4 to 11 hours ahead of North America. There are literally *dozens* of time zones around the world! Mass confusion would occur if everyone used their own local time without some single common reference time.

To solve the issue of standardizing clocks, the time at Greenwich, England on the Prime Meridian of longitude has been universally recognized as the standard time in all international affairs, including ham radio. This is Coordinated Universal Time (abbreviated UTC). (For many years it was called Greenwich Mean Time or GMT, and is sometimes called Zulu time.) Using UTC when communicating with other hams means that wherever you are, you and the station you contact will be able to reference a common date and time.

Twenty-four-hour time also avoids the equally confusing question about AM and PM. If you hear someone say that a contact was made at 0400 hours UTC (or 0400Z), you will know immediately that this was 4 hours past midnight, UTC, since the new day always starts just after midnight. Likewise, a contact made at 1500 hours UTC was 15 hours past midnight, or 3 PM (15 − 12 = 3) UTC. Each day starts at midnight, 0000 hours. Noon is 1200 hours, and the afternoon hours merely go on from there.

UTC	EDT/AST	CDT/EST	MDT/CST	PDT/MST	PST
0000*	2000	1900	1800	1700	1600
0100	2100	2000	1900	1800	1700
0200	2200	2100	2000	1900	1800
0300	2300	2200	2100	2000	1900
0400	0000*	2300	2200	2100	2000
0500	0100	0000*	2300	2200	2100
0600	0200	0100	0000*	2300	2200
0700	0300	0200	0100	0000*	2300
0800	0400	0300	0200	0100	0000*
0900	0500	0400	0300	0200	0100
1000	0600	0500	0400	0300	0200
1100	0700	0600	0500	0400	0300
1200	0800	0700	0600	0500	0400
1300	0900	0800	0700	0600	0500
1400	1000	0900	0800	0700	0600
1500	1100	1000	0900	0800	0700
1600	1200	1100	1000	0900	0800
1700	1300	1200	1100	1000	0900
1800	1400	1300	1200	1100	1000
1900	1500	1400	1300	1200	1100
2000	1600	1500	1400	1300	1200
2100	1700	1600	1500	1400	1300
2200	1800	1700	1600	1500	1400
2300	1900	1800	1700	1600	1500
2400	2000	1900	1800	1700	1600

*0000 and 2400 are interchangeable. 2400 is associated with the date of the day ending, 0000 with the day just starting.

MFJ-12/24 HOUR DUAL LCD CLOCK
MODEL MFJ-108B

Clocks with a digital readout that show time in a 24-hour format are quite popular as a station accessory. Some show both local time and UTC simultaneously.

1.2.3 Recordkeeping

Although the FCC does not require that amateur stations document their operations except for certain specialized occurrences, you can still benefit by keeping an accurate log. The FCC requires that you record the type of antenna and gain of any antenna other than a dipole that you use on the 60 meter band. This can be recorded in your log or kept on file separately. The FCC will also assume that you were the control operator for all contacts made from your station unless your log (or some other record) indicates otherwise.

Your Station Log

A well-kept log will help you preserve your fondest ham radio memories for years. It will also serve as a bookkeeping system should you embark upon a quest for ham radio awards, or decide to expand your collection of QSL cards.

Many amateurs have decided to computerize their log keeping because of its flexibility and additional features. There are many excellent computer programs for Amateur Radio logging, including specialized programs for contests and other types of operation. For a selection of programs, check the ads in *QST* or try AC6V's website.

Whether paper or electronic, a log entry should include:

1) The call sign of the station worked.
2) The date and time of the QSO. Always use UTC (Universal Coordinated Time, sometimes also called GMT or Zulu time) when entering the date and time. Use UTC whenever you need a time or date in your ham activities. The use of UTC helps all hams avoid confusion through conversion to local time. See the sidebar "UTC Explained" for details.
3) The frequency or frequency band on which the QSO took place.
4) The emission mode used to communicate (SSB, FM, CW, PSK and so on).
5) Signal reports sent and received.
6) Any miscellaneous data, such as the other operator's name or QTH that you care to record.

QSLing

The QSL card is the final courtesy of a QSO. It confirms specific details about your two-way contact with another ham. Whether you want the other station's QSL as a memento of an enjoyable QSO or for an operating award, it's wise to have your own QSL

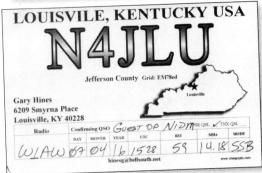

QSL cards are a longstanding ham radio tradition. They're often personalized with artwork and information about station equipment, antennas, or other interests.

cards and know how to fill them out. That way, when you send your card to the other station, it will result in the desired outcome (a confirming card sent back to you). And you'll be ready to respond if the other operator wants a QSL from you.

Paperless confirmation of contacts using computer systems is very popular. The ARRL's Logbook of The World system, for example, currently stores more than 750 mil-lion contacts as of mid-2016! Other popular online logbooks include QRZ.com, ClubLog and eQSL.cc.

To use electronic logbook and QSLing systems, you'll need to store your log on your computer. The logging program then creates lists of your contacts and sends them to the QSLing system where they can be cross-referenced against other submitted contacts. The various QSLing systems all have their own security processes and not all of them are accepted by the many award sponsors, including the ARRL. Check to be sure your electronic contact confirmations will be accepted!

Now Go Make Some Contacts

That finishes our quick tour of operating procedures. Now we'll get into details of some specific modes and activities.

1.2.4 Resources for SSB and CW Operating

ARRL Net Directory: **www.arrl.org/arrl-net-directory-search**
ARRL Logbook of The World:
   www.arrl.org/logbook-of-the-world
Colorful frequency chart:
   www.arrl.org/graphical-frequency-allocations
FCC Rules and Regulations:
   www.arrl.org/part-97-amateur-radio

Logging software:
   www.ac6v.com/logging.htm
NCDXF/IARU Beacons: **www.ncdxf.org/beacon/**
   You may also be interested in *Morse Code Operating for Amateur Radio*, *Propagation and Radio Science*, *The ARRL Logbook*, and the ARRL *Minilog*, all available from your favorite ham radio dealer or the ARRL website.

1.3 HF Digital Communications

With the ubiquity of the personal computer, digital communication has become increasingly popular on HF. This has been particularly true for amateurs who are forced to operate in restricted situations using such things as hidden antennas and low output power. They've discovered that a few watts with a digital mode can still take them considerable distances, even around the world. This section will show how to get started with today's popular digital modes.

The modern HF digital station centers around a computer and sound card running appropriate software. Here Jeff, WK6I, operates RTTY contests using multiple radios and large screens. [Tom Taormina, K5RC, photo]

1.3.1 HF Transceivers for Digital Operating

You don't need to run out and purchase a special radio with sophisticated features. All you need is an SSB voice transceiver. If your radio dates from about 1990 to the present day, you'll likely be in fine shape. These rigs are stable and most include all the features you'll need for HF digital. The singular exception involves some of the inexpensive SSB transceivers designed for low-power (QRP) operating. These rigs aren't usually intended for digital applications, so their stability may be questionable. They may also not offer connections to external devices through jacks known as *ports*.

Robert Wood, W5AJ, operated an ARRL RTTY Roundup contest from Aruba with the call sign P4ØP.

Transceiver Accessory Ports

Modern radios get along surprisingly well with computers and other external devices. In fact, most modern HF transceivers are designed with external devices in mind. They offer a variety of ports depending on the model in question.

Nearly every HF rig manufactured within the past decade includes an "accessory" port of some kind. Typically these are multipin jacks (as many as 13 pins) that provide connections for audio into and out of the radio, as well as a pin that causes the radio to switch from receive to transmit whenever the pin is grounded. This is often called the *PTT* or *push to talk* line. Some manufacturers also call it the *Send* line.

These accessory ports are ideal for con-

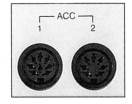

Today's transceivers usually include a multi-pin accessory jack for connecting audio into and out of the radio and for transmit-receive switching. This jack could be labeled ACC or DATA or DIGITAL or a similar name. Check your transceiver manual for detailed information about using this jack.

necting the kinds of interface devices we use to operate HF digital. In addition to the PTT function, accessory ports provide receive audio output at *fixed* levels that never change no matter where the VOLUME knob is set. This is a highly convenient feature that you'll appreciate when operating late at night after everyone has gone to bed. You can turn the VOLUME knob to zero and still have all the receive audio you need!

Transceiver USB Ports

The newest generation transceivers often include a USB port that works for both radio control and digital mode operating. Transmit and receive audio, and transmit/receive keying, are all handled smoothly over a single cable between the radio and your computer — no hardware interfaces required. You only need to keep in mind that the transceiver presents itself as a "sound device" (USB Audio CODEC), which you'll have to select in your software setup.

For transmit/receive keying, the transceiver appears as a virtual serial COM port, and you may have to install a special driver on your computer. For example, recent Kenwood and Icom transceivers use the Silicon Labs CP210x USB to UART Bridge, which assigns each connected radio a COM port number. To find it, access Device Manager in *Windows* and open the list of ports. Find the correct one and configure your software to use that COM port number for rig keying.

What? No Radio Ports?

What if your SSB transceiver doesn't have an accessory or USB port? No problem. You can use the microphone jack as your connection for transmit/receive switching as well as the audio input. For the audio output, you can use the external speaker or headphone jack. This isn't an ideal situation, but it works.

1.3.2 Computers and Software

Most HF digital software does not require powerful computers. Any ordinary off-the-shelf consumer-grade laptop or desktop computer will do the job. If you're thinking about a small netbook, be careful to check the specifications. Some netbooks don't include audio ports, but audio ports are highly important unless your transceiver can operate digital modes via a USB connection as described above.

In terms of operating systems, the vast majority of HF digital software is written for Microsoft *Windows*. There is HF digital software available for *MacOS* as well, although not as much variety. *Linux* users will find a number of HF digital applications, too.

The computer should have as much memory as possible, not just to run the ham applications smoothly, but the operating system as well. Either a built-in wireless (Wi-Fi) modem or an Ethernet port is important if you want to connect your station to the Internet from time to time. You may also need a CD-ROM drive for loading new software that is only available on CD (a less common need today, but don't sell yourself short).

The Rise of the Tablets

More and more applications are being developed for tablets and smartphones. They can send and receive e-mail, display TV shows and movies, browse the Internet, act as e-book readers, become game platforms and do a great deal more. For hundreds of millions of people throughout the world, they are ideal go-anywhere computers. Apple's popular iTunes store offers a staggering variety of applications, known as *apps*, for just about every purpose imaginable. Android tablets are plentiful as well and can also be used with a wide variety of apps designed for those devices. Some developers have released apps for HF digital, primarily for the Apple iPad.

The Importance of Sound

With few exceptions, every computer you are likely to purchase today will include a either a dedicated sound card or a sound chipset. This feature is absolutely critical for HF digital operation because most of the modes you'll enjoy depend on sound devices to act as radio *modems* — *mod*ulators/*dem*odulators.

The audio from your radio enters your computer via the sound device where it is converted (demodulated) to digital data for processing by your software. The results are words or images on your computer monitor. When you want to transmit, this same sound device takes the data from your software, such as the words you are typing, and converts it to shifting audio tones according to whatever mode you are using. This conversion is a form of modulation. The tones are then applied to your radio for transmission.

The simplest built-in sound devices are those found in laptops and tablets. They provide two ports to the outside world: microphone (audio input) and headphone (audio output). These are perfectly adequate for HF digital work. Desktop computers often have a similar arrangement, although the output port is usually labeled *speaker*. A line-level input may also be included for stronger audio signals. In all cases these ports come in the form of ⅛-inch stereo jacks.

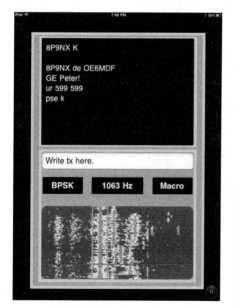

Multimode by Luca Facchinetti, IW2NDH, receiving PSK31 on an Apple iPad.

Fldigi for *Windows* operating PSK31.

Some desktops computers offer sound cards that plug into the motherboard. These devices are more elaborate. Some sound cards can offer as many as 12 external connections.

Software

In the beginning, HF digital programs were designed for one specific mode, such as *DigiPan* for PSK31 (**www.digipan.net**) or *MMTTY* for RTTY (**hamsoft.ca/pages/mmtty.php**). While mode-specific software still exists, the trend has been strongly in favor of multimode software that can operate many different HF digital modes.

Among the most popular *Windows* multimode applications are *MixW* (**mixw.net**), *MultiPSK* (**f6cte.free.fr/index_anglais.htm**), and *Fldigi* (**www.w1hkj.com/Fldigi.html**). *Macintosh* users may select *Cocoamodem* (**www.w7ay.net/site/Applications/cocoaModem/**) or *Multimode* (**www.blackcatsystems.com/software/multimode.html**). *Fldigi* is also available for *Linux*.

The Interface

The simplest interface has only one job to do: to allow the computer to toggle the radio between transmit and receive. It achieves this by using a signal from the computer to switch on a transistor to key the transceiver's *PTT* (push to talk) line and switch to transmit. When the signal from the computer disappears, the transceiver returns to the receive mode.

If an interface can be so straightforward, couldn't you just build your own? Yes, you could. Many amateurs enjoy HF digital with simple homemade interfaces like the one shown here. In addition to the switching circuit, they connect shielded audio cables between the computer and the radio to carry the transmit and receive audio signals.

There are good reasons to roll your own interface, the cost savings being chief among them. On the other hand, if you purchase an interface off the shelf you'll be able to benefit from enhanced design features, depending on how much you want to pay. The short list of useful features includes:

Independent audio level controls. These are knobs on the front panel of the interface that allow you to quickly raise or lower the transmit or receive audio levels instead of doing it in software.

CW keying. Full-featured interfaces handle more than just HF digital. They can also use keying signals from the computer to send Morse code with a separate connection to the transceiver's CW key jack. This allows you to send CW from your keyboard rather than by hand.

FSK keying. If you want to operate RTTY with the FSK function of your transceiver, assuming your rig offers such a function, the FSK keying feature translates keying signals from your computer into the MARK/SPACE data pulses necessary for FSK RTTY.

Microphone input. If you are making HF digital connections to your radio through the microphone jack rather than the rear panel accessory port, you'll need to unplug the interface cable whenever you want to use your microphone for a voice conversation. To make operating more convenient, some interfaces allow you to keep your microphone plugged into the interface at all times, switching between your microphone or computer as necessary.

Transceiver control. Deluxe interfaces include the extra circuitry needed to allow full computer control of your transceiver. Sometimes referred to as *CAT* (computer aided transceiver), this is a separate function that passes all the available controls from your radio to your computer. (If your transceiver has the ability to connect directly to your computer through an RS-232 serial connection, USB cable or Ethernet port, you don't need the CAT feature.) An interface with CAT functionality brings everything together in one affordable box.

Built-in sound device. Several interface designs include a built-in sound device. This is particularly handy in that it liberates the sound device in your computer for other functions. You can enjoy music on your computer, for example, without having to worry that you are meddling with the sound levels you've set up for HF digital operating. In addition, an interface with a built-in sound device greatly reduces the number of cables connecting the computer and radio. The audio signals, as well as transmit/receive keying functions, are all carried over a single USB cable; there are no connections to your computer's sound ports.

Pre-made cables. Most commercial interface manufacturers either include cables specifically wired for your radio free of charge, or offer them at an additional cost. This significantly reduces the hassle of wiring your HF digital station.

When an Interface Isn't an Interface — PACTOR

PACTOR is unique because it is capable of 100% error free communication at global distances on the HF bands. This makes PACTOR

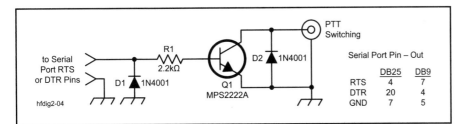

The simplest way to key a radio using a computer is through a single-transistor circuit like this. The input connects to the serial cable coming from the computer (or from the USB/serial adapter). Either the RTS or DTR pins can be used, depending on what your software requires. The pin numbers for 25- and 9-pin plugs are shown.

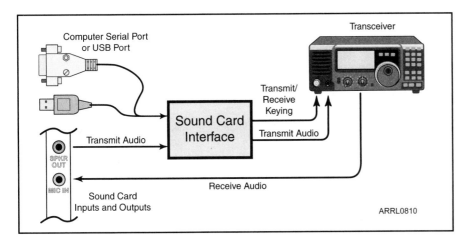

The sound card interface installs between your computer and your HF transceiver. Its primary function is to allow your computer to switch your radio between transmit and receive, but many models perform additional functions such as providing audio isolation.

the hands-down favorite when messages must get through error free. That's why PACTOR is the most widely used digital mode among those who participate on the HF side of the Winlink network. We'll discuss Winlink later.

PACTOR works its magic by sending data in small chunks or *frames*. The receiving station analyzes the data and keeps whatever has arrived without errors. It transmits a short burst back to the originating station and tells it to repeat the frame. With luck, the next retransmission of the frame will arrive with most of the data intact, or with at least enough intact data that the receiving station can mix and match between the "new" and "old" frames to come up with a complete 100% error-free frame.

All of this back-and-forth transmitting makes a characteristic *chirp-chirp-chirp* sound on the air. It also requires a fast-switching transceiver and a lot of computational horsepower. To this date no one has written a computer program that is capable of doing PACTOR with sound devices. The PACTOR timing parameters are too strict and computer operating system timing tends to be too loose.

So, the manufacturers have packaged dedicated microprocessor circuitry into a stand-alone box. This box, often called a *controller*, has the speed and efficiency to meet the requirements for PACTOR. It can do other modes as well such as PSK31 and RTTY. Unlike a desktop or laptop computer, a controller doesn't labor under the burden of an operating system and it isn't required to fulfill a broad range of simultaneous tasks.

If you want PACTOR capability, you must purchase a controller. On the Winlink e-mail network you may be able to get away with

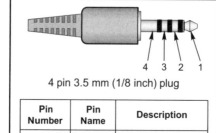

4 pin 3.5 mm (1/8 inch) plug

Pin Number	Pin Name	Description
1	Tip	Left Audio Out
2	Ring	Right Audio Out
3	Ring	Common/Ground
4	Sleeve	Audio In

QS1008-Eclec01

A diagram of the iPad headphone/ microphone plug.

an older PACTOR I controller that you'll find selling for a few hundred dollars, but to step up to modern PACTOR II you will most definitely need one of the units manufactured by SCS Corporation (**www.scs-ptc.com**). In addition to PACTOR II, these controllers will do PSK31, RTTY, CW, slow scan TV, packet radio and more.

Tablet Connections

With the use of tablet computers becoming more widespread, we're seeing an increasing number of amateurs putting these devices to work in their stations. The main problem with using an iPad for HF digital is making the connections to the transceiver and key-

ing the transceiver between transmit and receive. iPads can connect to the outside world through the docking port or the microphone/ headphone jack. If you purchase an Apple Camera Connection Kit and plug it into the docking port, you will suddenly have a USB connection to the iPad.

Unfortunately, this does not mean that you can plug in an HF digital USB interface. A USB interface draws more power than the iPad can provide, so the iPad will generate an error. An alternative is to use the Camera Connection Kit with a sound device designed for use with the iPad such as the Griffin iMic (**store.griffintechnology.com**).

The headphone/microphone jack another option. This jack requires an unusual four-conductor plug. You can use this diagram along with a four-conductor plug to make your own transmit/receive audio adapter. The alternative is to purchase one premade from companies such as KV Connection at **www. kvconnection.com**. (Note that cables for iPhones will work for iPads as well.)

Now that you've solved the audio problem, what about keying the radio? The iPad provides no means whatsoever to attach any kind of keying device. The solution is to use the iPad's transmit audio to do the job. In March 2011 *QST*, Skip Teller, KH6TY, described a sound-activated digital interface that will key your radio when it receives audio from the iPad ("Digital VOX Sound Card Interface," page 34).

TigerTronics makes a device that operates on the same principle. Their SignaLink SL-1+ interface also uses a VOX keying circuit. The SL-1+ is available from TigerTronics at **www.tigertronics.com**.

1.3.3 Digital Modes

What can you do with your new HF digital station? More than you might imagine. There are more than a dozen different HF digital modes on the air today, but only a handful are used extensively. Let's concentrate on the modes you're most likely to encounter.

RTTY

Good old radioteletype (RTTY) is still holding its ground on the HF bands. In fact, it is still the most popular digital mode for contests and DXpeditions (where groups of hams travel to rare locations to operate).

As with so many aspects of Amateur Radio,

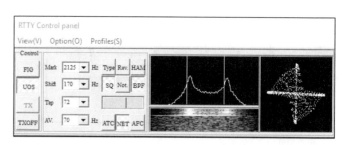

MMTTY software for decoding RTTY signals includes this control panel and tuning indicators. For a properly tuned signal. MARK and SPACE tones line up with the vertical bars in the indicator in the center. To the right, the display simulates an oscilloscope screen. One line is perfectly vertical and the other horizontal when the signal is properly tuned. Note that both tuning aids indicate that the received signal is mistuned slightly.

Don't Overdrive Your Transceiver!

When you're setting up your rig for your first PSK31 transmission, the temptation is to adjust the output settings for "maximum smoke." This can be a serious mistake because overdriving your transceiver in PSK31 can result in a horrendous amount of splatter, which will suddenly make your PSK31 signal much wider than 31 Hz — and make you highly unpopular with operators on adjacent frequencies.

As you increase the transmit audio output from your sound card or multimode processor, watch the ALC indicator on your transceiver. The ALC is the automatic level control that governs the audio drive level. When you see your ALC display indicating that audio limiting is taking place, you are feeding too much audio to the transceiver. The goal is to achieve the desired RF output with little or no activation of the ALC.

Unfortunately, monitoring the ALC by itself is not always a sure bet. Many radios can be driven to full output without budging the ALC meter. You'd think that it would be smooth sailing from there, but a number of rigs become decidedly nonlinear when asked to provide SSB output beyond a certain level. (Sometimes this nonlinearity can begin at the 50% output level.) We can ignore the linearity issue to a certain extent with an SSB voice signal, but not with PSK31 because the immediate result, once again, is splatter.

So how can you tell if your PSK31 signal is really clean? Unless you have the means to monitor your RF output with an oscilloscope, the only way to check your signal is to ask someone to give you an evaluation on the air. The PSK31 programs that use a waterfall audio spectrum display can easily detect "dirty" signals. The splatter appears as rows of lines extending to the right and left of your primary signal. (Overdriven PSK31 signals may also have a harsh, clicking sound.)

If you are told that you are splattering, ask the other station to observe your signal as you slowly decrease the audio level from the sound card or processor. When you reach the point where the splatter disappears, you're all set. Don't worry if you discover that you can only generate a clean signal at, say, 50 W output. With PSK31 the performance differential between 50 W and 100 W is inconsequential.

Table 1.6
Popular HF Digital Frequencies

Band (Meters)	Frequencies (MHz)
10	28.070 – 28.120
12	24.920 – 24.930
15	21.070 – 21.110
17	18.100 – 18.110
20	14.070 – 14.099
30	10.130 – 10.140
40	7.080 – 7.125
80	3.570 – 3.600
160	1.800 – 1.810

---

it is best to begin by listening. **Table 1.6** shows where to find digital mode activity on the various HF bands. There's almost always something happening on 20 meters, so try there first. Tune between 14.080 and 14.095 MHz and listen for the long, continuous *blee-blee-blee-blee* signals of RTTY. What you are hearing are the two alternating *mark* and *space* signals that RTTY uses in its binary *Baudot* coding scheme.

Depending on your transceiver and interface, you may use *audio frequency shift keying* (*AFSK*) or *frequency shift keying* (*FSK*) to transmit RTTY. The end result sounds the same on the air.

In AFSK, the audio tones for mark and space are generated by the computer and/or interface and fed into your transceiver's microphone input. For AFSK, make sure your transceiver is set for lower sideband (LSB). That is the RTTY convention.

Your rig may have an FSK mode (sometimes labeled DATA or RTTY). Many hams prefer operating this way because on most radios it allows them to use the transceiver's narrow IF filters to screen out interference. Just like on CW, with RTTY you can use 500 Hz or narrower filters to get rid of nearby signals. When you operate in FSK mode, your computer is not generating the mark and space tones. It is merely sending data pulses to the radio and the radio is creating its own mark and space signals. (This often requires a special connection to the transceiver. Consult your manual.)

A good time to observe RTTY activity is during a contest. There is at least one RTTY contest every month. With your software in the RTTY mode, tune across a RTTY signal. Your software likely includes some kind of tuning indicator to help you line up the mark and space signals correctly so that the software can start decoding. The tuning indicator may be part of a waterfall display. It might consist of two parallel lines that line up with mark and space, or it could even be a simulated oscilloscope display. Check your software manual and experiment with any variable settings. With some experience, you will be able to correlate the sound of the RTTY signal with the visual indicator and quickly tune in a new signal.

As you tune in the signal, you should see letters marching across your screen. If you've stumbled across a contest, you may see something like this...

AA5AU 599 CT CT 010 010 WB8IMY

In this instance, AA5AU is receiving a 599 signal report from WB8IMY in the state of Connecticut. This is also WB8IMY's tenth contact during the contest (that's the repeated "010").

Most contest operators create "canned" messages, called *macros*, in their software. A macro can be set up to place your radio in the transmit mode, send a string of text, then return the radio to receive. Macros eliminate the need to type the same thing over and over, which comes in handy in a contest where you may be making hundreds of contacts.

Let's assume that you have a contest CQ stored in a macro right now. Tap the appropriate key (or click your mouse on the designated button) and your RTTY macro will do the rest...

(The radio enters the transmit mode)

CQ TEST DE WB8IMY WB8IMY CQ

(The radio returns to receive)

Most RTTY contest operators set up additional macros to send the exchange, ask for repeats, acknowledge the received information and so forth.

Of course hams still enjoy chatting on RTTY, just like they do on SSB or CW, and you may see them exchanging names, locations, antenna descriptions and other items of interest. RTTY DXing is popular too, and so you may run across "pileups" on DX stations. If the DX station is rare, the QSOs may just be rapid-fire exchange of signal reports and call signs, just like on voice or CW.

Occasionally a rare DX station will operate split — receiving above or below the transmit frequency. That makes it easier to separate signals when many are calling. As always, it's a good idea to listen for a few minutes to determine the DX station's operating style and respond accordingly.

PSK31

PSK31 is the most widely used HF digital communications mode on the HF bands today. Most PSK31 activity involves casual conversation.

PSK stands for *phase shift keying*, the modulation method used to generate the signal; *31* is the bit rate. Where RTTY uses two specific frequencies to communicate the binary data, PSK31 does the same thing by creating an audio signal that shifts its phase 180° in sync with the 31.25 bit-per-second data stream. A 0 bit in the data stream generates an audio phase shift, but a 1 does not. The technique

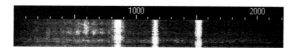

In this waterfall display, three strong PSK31 signals are represented by vertical lines. The transceiver is tuned to 14.070 MHz USB, and the display shows all signals in the 2200 Hz passband.

of using phase shifts (and the lack thereof) to represent binary data is known as *binary phase-shift keying*, or *BPSK*. If you apply a BPSK audio signal to an SSB transceiver, you end up with BPSK modulated RF. At this data rate the resulting PSK31 RF signal is only about 50 Hz wide, which is actually narrower than the average CW signal.

With such a narrow bandwidth, PSK31 makes the most of a very small amount of spectrum. Transmit power is highly concentrated, meaning that you don't need a lot of power to communicate over great distances. (Most PSK31 operators use less than 50 W output.) At the receiving end, the PSK31 software uses digital signal processing to detect the phase changes, even in very weak signals. The result is that PSK31 rivals or exceeds the weak-signal performance of CW.

Its terrific performance notwithstanding, PSK31 will not always provide 100% copy; it is as vulnerable to interference as any digital mode. And there are times, during a geomagnetic storm for example, when ionospheric propagation will cause slight changes in the frequency of the signal you're trying to copy. (When you are trying to receive a narrow-bandwidth, phase-shifting signal, frequency stability is very important.) This effect is almost always confined to the polar regions and it shows up as very rapid flutter, which is deadly to PSK31.

If you are operating your transceiver in SSB without using narrow IF or audio-frequency filtering, the bandwidth of the receive audio that you're dumping to your sound card is about 2000 to 3000 Hz. With a bandwidth of only about 50 Hz, a lot of PSK31 signals can squeeze into that spectrum. Your software acts like an audio spectrum analyzer, sweeping through the received audio from 100 to 3000 Hz and showing you the results in a waterfall display that continuously scrolls from top to bottom. What you see on your monitor are vertical lines of various colors that indicate every signal the software can detect. Bright yellow lines represent strong signals while blue lines indicate weaker signals.

Most of the PSK31 signals on 20 meters are clustered around 14.070 MHz. You'll also find PSK31 activity on 3.580, 7.070, 21.070, and 28.120 MHz. Start by putting your radio in the USB (upper sideband) mode and parking it on or near a PSK31 frequency (tune until

you see a number of lines in the waterfall). Do not touch your rig's VFO again. Just boot up your software and get ready to have fun.

It is not at all uncommon to see several strong signals (the audible ones) interspersed with wispy blue ghosts of very weak "silent" signals. Click on a few of these ghosts and you may be rewarded with text (not error free, but good enough to understand what is being discussed).

As you decode PSK31 signals, the results will be a conversation on your monitor…

Yes, John, I'm seeing perfect text on my screen, but I can barely hear your signal. PSK31 is amazing! KF6I DE WB8IMY K

I know what you mean, Steve. You are also weak on my end, but 100% copy. WB8IMY DE KF6I K

If you find a station calling CQ and you want to reply, don't worry about tuning your radio. The software will use your sound card to generate the PSK31 transmit signal at exactly the same audio frequency as the received signal. When applied to your radio, this audio signal will create an RF signal that is exactly where it needs to be.

Some PSK31 programs and processor software offer type-ahead buffers, which allow you to compose your response "off line" while you are reading the incoming text from the other station. Just type what you wish to send, then press the keyboard key or click on the software "button" to transmit. Some software includes memories for storing CQ messages, name, location and other common QSO elements.

A similar mode, PSK63, is growing in popularity.

MFSK16

An MFSK signal consists of 16 tones, sent one at a time at 15.625 baud, and they are spaced only 15.625 Hz apart. Each tone represents four binary bits of data. With a bandwidth of 316 Hz, the signal easily fits through a narrow CW filter. MFSK16 has a distinctive musical sound that some compare to an old-fashioned carnival calliope.

MFSK16 can be tricky to tune. You must place the cursor at exactly the right spot on the signal pattern in the waterfall display. It takes

some skill and patience to tune MFSK, but the results are worth the effort. MFSK offers excellent weak-signal performance and is a conversational mode like PSK31. Listen for the "music" of MFSK just above the PSK31 frequencies.

PACTOR

Unlike the sound card modes we've discussed so far, PACTOR is a burst mode. That is, it sends and receives data in segments or bursts rather than in a continuous stream. When a burst of data arrives, the receiving station quickly checks for errors caused by noise, interference or fading. If the data is corrupted, the receiving station transmits a brief signal known as a NAK (nonackowledgment) and the data burst is repeated. If the data arrives intact, or if the receiving station has enough information to "repair" any errors, an ACK (acknowledgment) is sent and the next block of data is on the way. This system of rapid-fire data bursts, ACKs and NAKs guarantees a 100% error-free information exchange between stations.

PACTOR AND WINLINK 2000

More than 50 HF digital stations worldwide have formed a remarkably efficient Internet information exchange network, including e-mail, binary file transfer, and global graphic weather reporting as part of a full-featured Internet-to-HF gateway system known as Winlink 2000 or "WL2K" (see **www.winlink.org**). Running Winlink 2000 software and using PACTOR, PACTOR II or PACTOR III protocols, these facilities transfer information between HF stations and the Internet. They also share information among themselves using Internet forwarding.

Winlink 2000 is a network of participating stations (PMBOs), all connected to a central server (CMBO), which is the "hub" for Internet connectivity to Internet e-mail and position reporting. Currently *RMS Express* is the preferred Winlink 2000 radio e-mail client.

Thanks to these advancements, an HF digital operator at sea, for example, can now connect to a Winlink 2000 participating network station using *RMS Express*, and exchange Internet e-mail with non-ham friends and family. He can also exchange messages with other amateurs by using the Winlink 2000 network stations as a traditional global "mailbox" operation.

Most Winlink 2000 participating stations scan a variety of HF digital frequencies on a regular basis, listening on each frequency for about two seconds. By scanning through frequencies on several bands, the Winlink 2000 stations can be accessed on whichever band is available to you at the time. To participate, in addition to your HF SSB transceiver you'll need a multimode processor that is capable of communicating in binary mode with either PACTOR I, PACTOR II or PACTOR III. At the time this book was published, only the SCS PTC series of multimode communications processors mentioned earlier in this chapter met this requirement.

Detailed information about operating procedures may be found at **www.winlink.org** or within the *RMS Express* help files. *RMS Express* can operate your radio if you set it up properly. Just choose a station, pick a frequency and push SEND. All information transfer is automatic and would be set up prior to the actual transmission just like any other e-mail agent. A continually updated list of stations and a catalog containing weather as well as other helpful information may be automatically maintained through *RMS Express*.

Remember that Winlink 2000 stations usually scan through several frequencies. If you can't seem to connect, the Winlink 2000 station may already be busy with another user, or propagation conditions may not be favorable on the frequency you've chosen. Either try again later or use the built-in propagation feature to connect on another band.

SENDING E-MAIL TO AND FROM THE INTERNET

From the Internet side of Winlink 2000, friends and family can send e-mail to you just as they would send e-mail to anyone else on the Net. In fact, the idea of Winlink 2000 is to make HF e-mail exchanges look essentially the same as regular Internet e-mail from the user's point of view. Internet users simply address their messages to **<your call sign>@winlink.org**. For example, a message addressed to **wb8imy@winlink.org** will be available when WB8IMY checks into *any* Winlink 2000 station.

JT65

By now amateurs are used to the sounds most digital modes create. JT65 is unique. As you tune across a JT65 signal you'll hear tones of varying pitch that "play" slowly, like someone lazily pecking on an electronic keyboard. Cryptic and strange as the tones may be, they carry call signs, signal reports and other bits of information that can be extracted from a JT65 signal even when it is extremely weak.

JT65 debuted as part of the *WSJT* software suite created by Dr Joe Taylor, K1JT. With just a sound card or sound chipset and a transceiver interface, *WSJT* makes it possible for hams with modest stations to enjoy VHF meteor scatter communication and even moonbounce, where signals are literally bounced off the surface of the Moon and returned to Earth. In the beginning, JT65 was embraced by some members of the moonbounce com-

munity and it was an instant success. It wasn't long before someone wondered what would happen if JT65 were used on the HF bands. Using a variant of JT65 known as JT65A, even a few watts of JT65 modulated RF to a wire dipole antenna resulted in transcontinental and even global communication.

SO WHAT IS JT65?

The short and simplified answer to this question is that JT65 is a weak-signal digital mode that uses one-minute transmit/receive sequences, meaning that you transmit within a one-minute window and then listen for one minute. Transmission actually begins 1 second after the start of a UTC minute and stops precisely 47.7 seconds later. There is a 1270.5 Hz synchronizing tone and 64 other tones. This combination gives JT65 its unusual musical quality.

Time synchronization is critical to JT65. If you are running *Windows 7* or newer, you can synchronize your computer time with Internet time servers. Just explore the DATE AND TIME menu under the *Windows* Control Panel. You may also want to investigate free software such as *Dimension4* (**www.thinkman.com/dimension4/**) to keep accurate time automatically.

JT65 is not a "conversational" mode like, say, PSK31. Instead, the idea is to exchange only the basic information required for a valid contact: call signs and signal reports. *JT65-HF* measures the actual received signal strength and incorporates it into the exchange. When you receive a report during a *JT65-HF* exchange, you'll know exactly how strong your signal is (in dB) at the other end. It is amazing to see who you can contact with JT65

while using miniscule amounts of power. Some JT65 enthusiasts are using output levels in the *milliwatt* range. In fact, 50 W is considered "high power" in the JT65 world.

JT65 SOFTWARE

As of mid-2016, JT65 software choices included:

• *WSJT-X* by Dr Joe Taylor, K1JT. Available free for *Windows*, *Linux* and *Mac OS* computers at **physics.princeton.edu/pulsar/K1JT/wsjtx.html**.

• *JT65-HF* by Joe Large, W6CQZ. Available free for *Windows* only and for JT65 only at **http://jt65-hf.com**. Although W6CQZ has stopped supporting JT65-HF, it remains one of the most popular programs for JT65 operating. Other variations include *JT65-HF-Comfort* and *JT65-HF-HB9AQX-Edition*. Use your favorite Internet search tool to find out more about these programs.

THE JT65-HF MAIN SCREEN

Let's take a quick look at the *JT65-HF* main screen, section by section, starting at the top. *WSJT-X* has similar features.

The waterfall display dominates most of the top portion of the *JT65-HF* main screen. Whenever *JT65-HF* is running, it sweeps through your receive audio spectrum from 0 to 2000 Hz. Every signal it detects appears in this window.

You'll notice that the waterfall is divided into two halves to the right and left of the center "zero" point. The display markers are positive to the right of the zero (0 to 1000) and negative to the left of the zero (0 to –1000). Along the top of the waterfall you'll see a red bracket. If you click your mouse cursor within

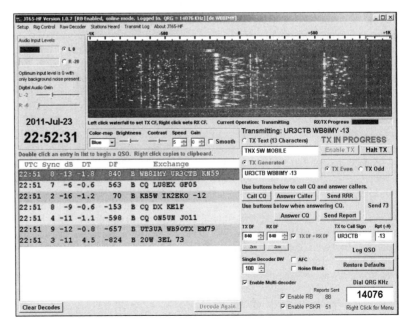

The *JT65-HF* software by Joe Large, W6CQZ.

The *JT65-HF* signal decoding window (see text)

the waterfall the red bracket will move to the position you just clicked. The bracket represents your 200 Hz transmit/receive window.

JT65-HF can operate in simplex (transmitting and receiving on the same frequency) and split (transmitting and receiving on different frequencies). Most of your contacts will be simplex, but it is worthwhile to know that *JT65-HF* has split-frequency capability. Two brackets appear when operating split — red for the transmit frequency and green for the receive frequency.

On the left side of the waterfall, you have the right and left channel audio input controls. When the band is quiet (when there are no signals), you should adjust the right and left channel controls to achieve 0 dB on both channels. Too much or too little audio makes it difficult to decode signals.

Below the waterfall you'll see controls for color, brightness, contrast, speed and gain. You're safe leaving all these at their default settings. There is little need to change them unless you're having difficulty viewing the waterfall or unless you are running *JT65-HF* on a slow computer.

Moving to the lower right section we have a number of check boxes and buttons. These may seem confusing but their functions will become more apparent when we make our first contacts.

Message to TX is the text you are sending to the other station. You can send text manually in the TX Text window, but you are limited to 13 characters. Immediately below this window you see the red-labeled TX Generated window. This window is for transmitted text that *JT65-HF* generates automatically, either when you click on one of the buttons below, or when you click on a line in the decoding window. Again, the function of this window will become clear as we step through your first contact.

To the right of the message windows are buttons to enable or halt transmission. Below these buttons is the section that allows you

to choose whether you wish to transmit on even or odd minutes. With JT65 you transmit and receive in turns — during one minute you transmit and during another minute you receive. Therefore, one minute will be an odd-numbered minute (such as 2105 UTC) and the next minute will be an even-numbered minute (such as 2102 UTC).

In most instances *JT65-HF* will make the choice for you. However, when calling CQ you get to choose when you will begin transmitting — on an even or odd minute. You definitely don't need to worry about even and odd minutes when you are answering someone else's call. That station has already selected which minute (even or odd) he will use. When you respond, *JT65-HF* will automatically choose the opposite minute.

Below the text-generating buttons you'll find several other interesting sections. The TX DF and RX DF sections are for split-frequency applications. For the vast majority of your JT65 contacts you will work simplex, so you want to leave the TX DF = RX DF box checked. An exception to the rule is when you are calling CQ, which we'll address later.

Below the TX DF and RX DF sections you'll find the controls for Single Decoder BW (Bandwidth) and Multi Decoder Spacing. This is another set of controls you'll rarely have a reason to change from their default values. Normally you'd never disable the multiple-signal decoder unless you are using a particularly slow computer. The default of 100 Hz for single bandwidth is usually adequate.

Put a checkmark in the AFC (automatic frequency control) box so that *JT65-HF* can compensate for stations that may be drifting a bit. If you live in an area with frequent storms or other sources of noise, put a checkmark in the Noise Blank box as well.

Enable Multi does exactly that. When enabled the decoder will attempt to find and decode all possible JT65 signals within the 2 kHz passband. Unless you are using a slow computer that has difficulty processing so

much information at once, always leave this box checked.

To the right you'll find the Log QSO button. When you click this button *JT65-HF* will save your contact information (who you worked, when, etc) to the file *jt65hf_log.adi* in the *JT65-HF* directory in a standard ADIF format that you can import into your computer logging software.

Finally, at the bottom of the lower right portion of the *JT65-HF* window you'll find two checkboxes labeled Enable RB and Enable PSKR, along with a sizeable window labeled Dial QRG kHz. If you are using transceiver-control software to read the transceiver frequency, the frequency will appear in this window. If you're not, you can right click your mouse cursor in this window and select from the list of common JT65 frequencies.

Why would you bother showing your operating frequency in the QRG window? The answer is that if you've checked the Enable RB and Enable PSKR windows *JT65-HF* will automatically access your home Internet connection and share your data (the stations you've heard and how strong they were) with the PSKReporter (PSKR) website at **pskreporter.info/pskmap.html** — if you've enabled this feature in the station setup screen. The information is extremely helpful to your fellow amateurs who study propagation, experiment with new antennas and so on. To make the information useable, however, they need to know your listening frequency; that's what the QRG window is all about.

WATCH THE ACTION

As is the case so often in Amateur Radio, when trying a new operating mode the best practice is to spend plenty of time listening *first*.

Start by looking at the list of JT65 frequencies in **Table 1.7**. Select a frequency and place your transceiver in the USB mode. Tune to that frequency and start the *JT65-HF* software. If there are stations transmitting, you'll see them in the waterfall display right away. You may notice that their signal traces seem to curve somewhat before settling into a regular pattern. That's a symptom of *JT65-HF* running its sample correction routine on your sound device. Depending on what sort of sound device you are using, a couple of minutes may pass before you are able to begin decoding transmissions.

When everyone stops transmitting at about the 48 second mark, use the opportunity to quickly adjust the audio gain controls to achieve 0 dB on both channels.

As the next minute begins, you should hear or see other stations starting their transmissions. Just sit back and watch. You'll notice that each transmission is comprised of a line — possibly a broken line — with several dots

Table 1.7
Common JT65 Frequencies

(All frequencies assume a transceiver display in USB mode.)

1838 kHz
3576 kHz
7039 kHz (European stations)
7076 kHz
14076 kHz
10139 kHz
18102 kHz
21076 kHz
24920 kHz
28076 kHz

appearing to the immediate right. The line represents the synchronizing tone and the dots are all the remaining tones.

When the clock reaches the 48 second point, everyone should stop transmitting automatically. Within the next few seconds you should see text appear in the window at the lower left.

Some of the text may be highlighted in green. These are stations calling CQ. You'll see other text shaded in gray. When you're involved in a conversation, the transmissions intended for you are highlighted in red.

Look at the sample decoding screen. First, let's decipher the headings along the top of the window, beginning at the far left.

UTC: The time the signal was decoded in UTC.

Sync: This is a measurement of the strength of the synchronizing tone. The higher the number, the better the sync signal.

dB: The strength of the JT65 signal in decibels. The lower the number, the stronger the signal. Zero dB is the strongest possible.

DT: How much the decoded station's time deviated from your time, measured in seconds or fractions of seconds. Ideally the decoded stations should be within 2 seconds of your computer's time, preferably less than 1 second.

DF: How far the signal frequency deviates, in hertz, above or below the zero center point of the waterfall display. A negative number is a signal to the left of zero; a positive number is a signal to the right of zero.

Exchange: The text the transmitting station actually sent. If you see two call signs, the transmitting station is the *second* call sign.

Just to the left of the exchange text you'll see either a B or a K. This is a reference to the kind of error correction algorithm that *JT65-HF* used to validate the text. B stands for *BM*, a simple Reed Solomon algorithm. K means *KVASD*, a much more complex algorithm. One way to think about this is to imagine that a K means that *JT65-HF* had to work particularly hard to make sense of the signal. If so, this station may present a challenge if you attempt to complete a contact.

As you observe the exchanges you'll probably see a pattern emerging. JT65 exchanges usually, though not always, follow a strict sequence. It goes like this, starting at 2102 UTC …

2102   CQ WB8IMY FN31
WB8IMY has begun sending CQ on an even minute from grid square FN31.

2103   WB8IMY N1NAS EN72
N1NAS replies and tells WB8IMY that he is located in grid square EN72.

2104   N1NAS WB8IMY -11
WB8IMY replies with a signal report of –11 dB.

2105   WB8IMY N1NAS R-15
N1NAS acknowledges the signal report from WB8IMY with an "R" followed by a signal report (–15).

2106   N1NAS WB8IMY RRR
WB8IMY sends "RRR," which means "Roger, roger, roger." Everything has been received and the exchange is complete.

2107   WB8IMY N1NAS 73
N1NAS sends 73 — best wishes.

2108   N1NAS WB8IMY 73
WB8IMY sends his 73 as well. The contact has ended.

Instead of sending 73, you'll often see stations sending bits of "free hand" text instead. They are doing this by typing the text into the TX Text window. You may see something like 40W LOOP ANT, which is shorthand for "I'm running 40 W to a loop antenna."

1.3.4 WSPR

WSPR (pronounced "whisper") is an acronym for "Weak Signal Propagation Reporter." It is a worldwide network of low power stations exchanging beacon-like transmissions to probe potential propagation paths. Most participating stations transmit as well as receive, although short wave listener (SWL) activity is also common. In principle, and with the propagation gods willing, everyone can copy and be copied by everyone else who is currently active with WSPR on the same band.

When a global picture of all these connections becomes available, things get especially interesting — and that's the purpose of WSPRnet. Most stations using WSPR are configured to automatically upload their reception reports to a central database at **WSPRnet.org**, in real time. By pointing your browser to WSPRnet you can get nearly

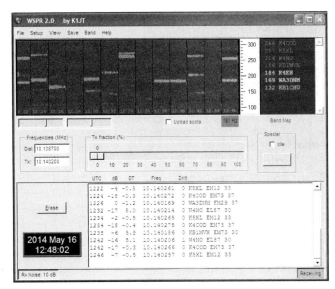

Main window of the WSPR program.

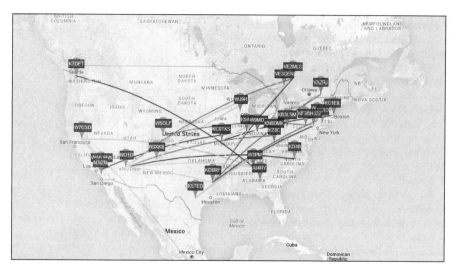

A WSPR 10 meter propagation snapshot taken during a band opening in mid-December.

instantaneous reports of where and at what signal strength you're being received, and view the results plotted on a world map.

WSPR is *sound card mode with* setup requirements similar to those described earlier in this section. WSPR transmits and receives, but it does not support normal types of on-the-air conversation. Instead, it sends and receives specially coded, beacon-like transmissions aimed at establishing whether particular propagation paths are open. Transmissions convey a call sign, station location, and power level using a compressed data format with strong forward error correction (FEC) and narrow-band, four-tone frequency-shift-keying (FSK). The FEC greatly improves chances of copy and reduces errors to an extremely low rate. The signal bandwidth is only 6 Hz, which together with randomized time-sharing assures that dozens of WSPR signals can fit into a tiny 200 Hz segment of each amateur band. The WSPR protocol is effective at signal-to-noise ratios as low as –28 dB in a 2500 Hz bandwidth, some 10 to 15 dB below the threshold of audibility. On most bands, typical WSPR power levels are 5 W or less — sometimes a *lot* less. You will be amazed to discover that these very low power signals can be copied in distant corners of the world.

WSPR Operation

WSPR software can be freely downloaded from **www.physics.princeton.edu/pulsar/ K1JT/**. Packaged installation files are available for *Windows* and *Linux*; the program can also be compiled for *Macintosh*, *FreeBSD* and other operating systems. *WSPR* is "open source" software, and its source code is maintained in a public repository at **developer. berlios.de/projects/wsjt/**.

As with all sound card modes, WSPR re-

quires audio connections between your computer and radio transceiver (described earlier in this section). Your SSB transceiver should be set to use upper sideband.

Even though FCC rules require you to be present at your station to operate WSPR, the operation itself is largely automated. Time-synchronized transmissions last for slightly less than two minutes, nominally starting one second into an even UTC minute. Reception and transmission intervals alternate in a pseudo-random fashion such that on average, a specified percentage (typically 20 to 25%) of the two minute intervals are used for transmitting. It's important for your computer's clock to be accurate to within a second or so.

Conventional operating frequencies for WSPR are summarized in **Table 1.8**. Many additional details of WSPR operation, including step-by-step startup instructions, are given in the *WSPR 2.0 User's Guide* which is available at **www.physics.princeton.edu/ pulsar/K1JT/wspr.html**.

In normal operation, at the end of each two minute reception interval the software decoder looks for all detectable *WSPR* signals

in a 200 Hz passband and displays the results in a waterfall spectrogram, a scrolling text window, and a scrolling Band Map. The spectrogram covers a frequency range of about 220 Hz; the last three digits of the received frequency, in Hz, are displayed on the vertical scale at right. Time runs from left to right in the spectrogram, the full width spanning about half an hour. On a typical computer screen each two-minute interval corresponds to a strip about 1 cm wide in the spectrogram. The times of your own transmissions are denoted by thin green vertical lines.

Each decoded WSPR signal produces text showing the UTC, signal-to-noise ratio in dB (in a 2500 Hz reference bandwidth), time offset DT in seconds, frequency in MHz, drift rate in Hz/minute, and the decoded message. Time offsets greater than about ±2 seconds indicate a significant clock error at transmitter or receiver, or possibly both. Apparent frequency drifts greater than ±1 Hz per minute can usually be traced to the transmitter, and should be corrected if possible. (Of course, receiver drift can also contribute to measured drifts, but this condition is easily recognized because nearly all signals will appear to drift by the same amount.) Good frequency stability is essential to WSPR's remarkable sensitivity, because the software filters used for decoding are only about 1.5 Hz wide.

WSPRnet

The **WSPRnet.org** website provides a central repository for WSPR reception reports ("spots") and offers a simple user interface for querying the database, a mapping facility, and many other handy features. By default, the worldwide map shows all WSPR stations reporting or decoded over the past hour, and illustrates the open propagation paths between them. The map can be zoomed and panned, and you can set various criteria to determine exactly which spots are included. The WSPRnet database represents a rich source of experimental data for propagation studies.

Table 1.8
Conventional Frequencies for WSPR Activity

Band (meters)	Dial Frequency (MHz)	Actual Transmitting Frequency (MHz)
160	1.836.600	1.838.000 – 1.838.200
80	3.592.600	3.594.000 – 3.594.200
40	7.038.600	7.040 000 – 7.040 200
30	10.138.700	10.140.100 – 10.140.300
20	14.095.600	14.097.000 – 14.097.200
17	18.104.600	18.106.000 – 18.106.200
15	21.094.600	21.096.000 – 21.926.200
12	24.924.600	24.926.000 – 24.926.200
10	28.124.600	28.126.000 – 28.126.200
6	50.293.000	50.294.400 – 50.294.600

1.3.5 HF Digital Resources

ARRL website: **www.arrl.org/digital-data-modes**
ARRL website: **www.arrl.org/digital-modes**
AA5AU RTTY pages: **www.aa5au.com/rtty**
Identifying digital modes:
    www.w1hkj.com/FldigiHelp-3.21/Modes/index.htm

Winlink 2000 amateur email system:
    www.winlink.org
WSJT Home Page:
    physics.princeton.edu/pulsar/k1jt/

You can also find more technical information in *The ARRL Handbook* as well as *Get on the Air with HF Digital* and *Work the World with JT65 and JT9*, all available from your favorite ham radio dealer or the ARRL website.

1.4 VHF/UHF FM, Repeaters, Digital Voice and Data

First, what exactly is a *repeater*? And why do we use one?

Without repeaters, the communication range between amateur VHF FM mobile and handheld radios at ground level is limited — about 5 to 15 miles between mobiles, and just a couple of miles between handhelds. The distance you can communicate is commonly referred to as *line-of-sight* — you can talk about as far as you can see. That's not technically true. VHF/UHF range is a little better than that, and there are some really significant exceptions, but the underlying principle that the higher the antenna, the greater the range, is valid. It's just hard to get a mobile or handheld antenna very high off the ground.

So extend our range, we use *repeaters*. A repeater is a specially designed receiver/transmitter combination. Repeater antennas are located on tall towers, buildings, or mountains, giving repeaters much greater range than radios with antennas near the ground. When you're in range of a repeater, you can talk to everyone else in range of that repeater.

When you operate through a repeater, its receiver picks up your signal on the *input* frequency, and the transmitter retransmits —

Joe Hamm, KC1BAQ, uses his VHF FM handheld transceiver while assisting with communications during a marathon in Wallingford, Connecticut.

or repeats — you on the *output* frequency. Those two frequencies are called a *repeater pair*, and the space between them is called the *offset*. Repeater pairs and offsets for each VHF/UHF band were standardized by the hams who developed repeaters in the 1970s, although there are some regional differences around the country.

Using a real-world example, one common 2 meter repeater pair is 146.34 and 146.94 MHz. In the shortcut language of FM, this would be called 34/94 (pronounced three-four, nine-four) or just simply 94 (nine-four). In this pair, 34 is the input frequency, and 94 is the output frequency. The offset for this and most 2 meter repeaters is 600 kHz, and nearly every radio manufactured for 2 meters since 1980 is pre-programmed for this offset. Given all the standards and the shortcut language, it's *almost* enough to say, "Meet me on the 94 repeater," without specifying the other details. Almost, but keep reading. Something called *tone* may get in the way. We'll explain shortly.

A repeater's range depends on a variety of factors, but primary are antenna height, terrain and output power. Those three factors

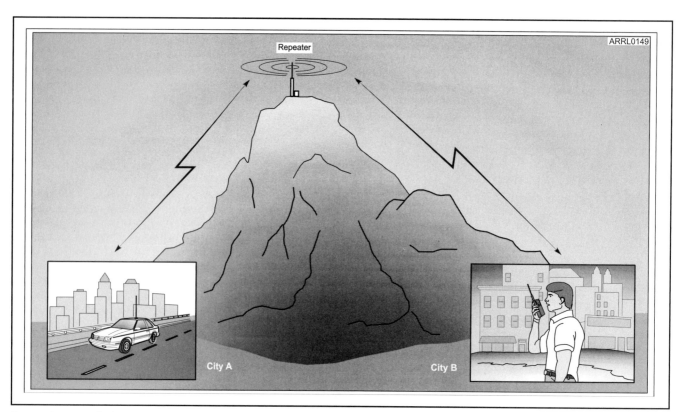

A repeater extends the range of its users, allowing them to communicate over longer distances.

apply not only to the repeater, but also your station and the station you want to talk to. You have to factor all sides of this equation if you want to know how far you might be able to talk through a repeater. But it's not that complicated in practice.

Here's another real world example: level ground, a repeater antenna at 500 feet, and two mobiles running 50 W. Reliable coverage from such a system would extend about 30 miles from the repeater. "Fringe" coverage — distances where you can probably use the repeater but signals will be weak and may drop out — can extend another 20 miles or so. If one mobile is near the southern limit of the repeater's coverage area, and the other mobile is near the northern end, that could be almost 100 miles between them, *much* better than the 5 to 15 miles they could talk without a repeater.

Put that repeater on a mountaintop, and the coverage jumps to a radius of 100 miles or more — 200 miles between mobiles at opposite ends of the coverage area. Except that mountains usually come bunched together,

and if you drive around the back side of the next mountain, it'll block your signal from the repeater.

When you ask about the coverage of a particular repeater, keep in mind that hams tend to think in terms of *maximum* range, not *reliable* range. If a ham heard someone hit a repeater from 120 miles out using a handheld once, they might tell you that repeater's range is 120 miles, when the realistic, everyday coverage is more like 40 miles.

Additional Features

Repeaters can have many features beyond just extending the range of mobile or handheld radios. Before cell phones became ubiquitous, the most popular feature was *autopatch* (*auto*matic telephone *patch*). A telephone line and special control equipment at the repeater allow you to make local phone calls from your radio.

Other common repeater features include voice announcements of the time, club meetings and activities; a talking S meter or voice recorder to let you know how well the repeater is hearing you; and a NOAA weather receiver to rebroadcast storm alerts. Now, the most commonly used feature is *linking*. The local repeater's coverage can be extended across the region, the state, even the world, via radio or the Internet, a topic we'll cover in more detail later.

1.4.1 How Do You Use Repeaters?

There are literally thousands of repeaters across the US (and the world). Each one can have its own peculiarities and unique operating procedures, but there are some basics that apply to almost all of them.

Mostly, you're here to get on the air and talk to people, right? So first you set your radio for the repeater you want to use. Don't know how to find a local repeater frequency? The *ARRL Repeater Directory* or RFinder app (**www.rfinder.net**) are great for that. And in most areas, somebody has posted a listing of local repeaters on a website. They're great resources, but there's a problem you'll run into sooner or later: not all the repeaters listed are actually on the air. *Most* of the repeaters listed, though, will be available.

Once you've selected a repeater and dialed it up on your radio, the first thing you should do is... *listen* for a while. There are two reasons for just listening.

First, listen to observe operating procedure. Learn how the locals do it. But don't assume everyone you hear is doing it right. You'll hear good procedure and bad. Over time you'll sort it out.

Second — and this applies every time you flip on the radio — listen for a while because repeaters are party lines. Lots of people use them on and off throughout the day, and the one you've selected may be busy with another conversation right now. So listen first.

If the repeater isn't busy, you can see if someone out there wants to talk. Key your transmitter and say something like "This is KN4AQ, listening." (Use your own call, not mine, please). There's no need to call CQ, the traditional method for generating a contact on the HF bands. On a repeater, your audience is already there, waiting with squelched receivers.

When you release your transmit button, most repeaters will stay on the air for a few seconds (called *hang time*), and many will send some kind of beep (a *courtesy tone*). Then, the repeater transmitter drops off the air. The beep is there to remind everyone to leave a pause between transmissions in case someone wants to break in. Even if there's no beep, leave a pause. Somebody may have just come across a traffic accident and needs the repeater to report it. If nobody leaves a pause between transmissions, they can't break in.

If somebody answers you, then have a good time! You can talk about anything you want that's allowed by FCC rules. Just remember that you're not having a private conversation — you may have lots of listeners, some of them children. Keep that in mind as you choose language and subject matter.

How long do you talk? It depends on the time of day, and who else might want to use the repeater. Rush hours are prime time for mobiles, evening is also a busy time, while 2 AM is probably pretty empty. Learn the local procedures and rules set down by the repeater's sponsor. For a long time, the conventional wisdom has been that repeaters are for mobiles, and base stations should stay off of them during drive-time. Ask the locals about that, too.

Not all conversations are strictly two-way. Three, four or five or more hams can be part of a roundtable conversation (five or more will be pretty unwieldy). A freewheeling roundtable is a lot of fun ... and it poses a problem: When the person transmitting now is done, who transmits next? Too often, the answer is *everybody* transmits next, and the result is a mess. The solution is simple. When you finish your transmission in the roundtable, specify who is to transmit next. "... Over to you, Rick. KN4AQ."

We Pause for Station Identification

The FCC rules say you must ID once every 10 minutes. Most repeater owners are big on clear identification when you use their repeaters, but you don't have to overdo it. Give your call sign when you first get on (this isn't required by the rules, but it's common practice), then about every 10 minutes, and again when you sign off. You don't have to give anyone else's call sign at any time, although sometimes it's a nice acknowledgment of the person you're talking to, like a handshake.

Breaking In

Since repeaters are shared among many hams, there are some times and reasons that a conversation in progress might be interrupted. You might break in to join the group and add your comments on the subject at hand. Someone might break in on you to reach someone else who is listening to the repeater. You might have to report an emergency. How to break in is an area of debate and disagreement. Here are some suggestions:

1) Pick a good time. If you have an emergency, a good time is *now*. That's why there's a pause between transmissions. Otherwise, listen a bit. Read the ebb and flow of the conversation. One of the fastest ways to establish a reputation as a jerk is to frequently butt your way onto the air without regard for the people already talking.

2) Give your call sign, and say what you want. When you've listened and decided it's okay to break in, transmit quickly when one station stops, before the beep, and say something like this: "KN4AQ, can I make a short call?" or "KN4AQ, can I add my 2 cents?"

3) What about saying "break?" Some hams will tell you that's the way to break in. The problem is that we don't all agree on exactly what "break" means. In some areas, "break" means "I just want to join in or make a call." "Break-break" means "I have very important traffic," and "break-break-break" means "I have a dire emergency." Other areas don't use "break" at all. If your area uses some version of "break," go with the flow. But plain English works everywhere.

Maybe somebody's breaking in on you. What do you do? Easy — let them transmit, right now, unless you know absolutely and for sure that they do not have an emergency. Maybe somebody just says "break" or drops in their call, when what they really mean is "HELP!" So let them talk. Say "go ahead," and give your call sign. And if they're interrupting your perfectly good conversation for no reason but to hear themselves talk, well, bite your lip and be glad you know better.

The exception is when someone actually announces an emergency. Say something like "Go ahead, emergency." Then CLEAR THE DECKS! The station that declared the emergency then has the frequency, and unless they ask for your help, don't give it. Unless... always an unless... they obviously *don't* know how to handle the situation... and you *do*.

DX!

Well, you probably won't be hearing Europe on 2 meter FM anytime soon (except via Internet linking), but VHF does have its own form of DX. Earlier we talked about a repeater that had about a 30-mile range. Usually. Sometimes, though, VHF/UHF "opens up," and stations can be heard for hundreds of miles. This weather-related phenomenon is a book-length subject, but just know that VHF/UHF band openings are a double-edged sword.

It's exciting to talk to someone 200 miles away, and it's okay, too. But keep in mind that repeaters were designed to cover local territory, not half the country. So when the band opens up, there is the potential for lots of interference as well as lots of fun. Repeaters on the same frequency, 120 miles apart, will suddenly seem too close together. You

Table 1.9
Simplex Channels

Simplex channels in 15 kHz channel step areas*:

146.43
146.46
146.49
146.52
145.55
146.58
147.42
147.45
147.48
147.51
147.54
147.57

Simplex channels in 20 kHz channel step areas:

146.42
146.44
146.46
146.48
146.50
146.52
146.54
146.56
146.58
147.42
147.44
147.46
147.48
147.50
147.52
147.54
147.56
147.58

*This chart for the *15 kHz channel step areas* leaves out the "15 kHz" channels (for example, 146.445 between 146.43 and 146.46) for a good reason. You need physical separation of many miles between stations using 15 kHz channel steps to avoid interference. With repeaters, this physical separation is part of the coordination process. But simplex channel use is not coordinated, so to reduce interference, avoid using the "15 kHz" channels.

could very easily be keying up two or more of them at once, even from a handheld! To be responsible, get to know where your signal is going (the *ARRL Repeater Directory* or RFinder app will help). Use a directional antenna, minimum power, and keep your conversation short.

Almost every repeater is ringed by co-channel neighbors — repeaters using the same frequency — between 100 and 200 miles away. You'll want to be sensitive to those neighbors as you decide how much power and antenna to use when talking on your local machine.

How much power is too much? Within the local coverage area of most repeaters, 5 W into a mobile antenna is all you need. Some mobile radios can do 50 W, and that's excessive until you reach the fringe. At home, with an antenna up on the roof, 50 W is *really* excessive for talking through a local repeater. When the band is open, even a 5 W mobile signal can travel to the neighboring co-channel repeater. At those times, patience and courtesy will help a lot.

Simplex

You don't have to use a repeater to communicate on FM! You can use simplex, which means your radio talking to my radio directly. We do have that five to 15 mile range — much more if we're using our home stations. So with that range, why not use simplex?

But don't just pick any old frequency your radio can generate to talk simplex! You may end up on the input of a repeater and interfere with people you can't hear. Use the simplex channels shown in **Table 1.9**, beginning with 146.52 MHz, the national simplex channel. On the higher bands, 223.5 and 446.0 are the primary simplex channels.

Timers

Almost all repeaters have a timer in the controller that starts counting down when you begin to transmit through the repeater. Typically this clock starts from about three minutes, though some can be shorter. If you transmit continuously through the repeater past its timer length, the repeater will go off the air (we call it "timing out"). Repeater timers usually reset when you, the user, stop transmitting. If the repeater has a courtesy beep, the timer may reset when you hear the beep. So to avoid being dumped by the repeater timer, you have to keep your transmissions under the timer length and always wait for the beep. The three-minute timer is one way to comply with the FCC rules for stations being operated by remote control (most repeaters are remotely controlled).

1.4.2 Band Plans

There is a plan organizing frequency use for the VHF and UHF bands (and, for that matter, every Amateur Radio band). For the most part, band plans are voluntary. The FCC regulates only a few modes and band segments. There's a lot more going on than FM and repeaters. The 2 meter and 70 cm bands have space for CW and SSB, beacons, packet, satellite operation and even EME (Earth-Moon-Earth) operation. The 70 cm band also includes fast-scan television. See the sidebar, "Band Plans" for a look at how one regional group has made sense of 2 meters.

The complete 2 meter band plan is even more detailed than that list shows. The repeater input and output segments are divided into more than 100 individual channels for repeaters and simplex operation. This channelized operation is also voluntary, but FM and repeaters wouldn't work if hams followed the HF practice of operating on any empty frequency they wanted to use.

To make things even more confusing, within the FM and repeater segments of 2 meters, there are two different channel steps: 15 kHz and 20 kHz. East of the Mississippi River, most states use 15 kHz steps for the repeater segment above 146 MHz, and 20 kHz steps below 146 MHz, for reasons discussed later. Many western states, along with Michigan and Alabama, use 20 kHz steps throughout the band. Look up your local plan in the *Repeater Directory*.

The 2 meter offset, though, is consistent nationwide at 600 kHz for almost every repeater. Below 147.0 MHz, most repeater offsets are "negative" (the input frequency is the lower frequency), and above 147.0 MHz more offsets are "positive" (the input frequency is the higher frequency).

The 440 MHz band is more regular, with all channel steps being 25 kHz (though some areas are in the process of dividing those in half — to 12.5 kHz — to make room for more repeaters). Everyone uses a 5 MHz offset, but some regions put the repeater transmitter on the higher frequency (much of the northeast, most of the west, and southern California), and some regions putting it on the lower frequency (the southeast, Midwest, Texas, the Pacific northwest and northern California,). That difference persists today.

The band is huge, running from 420 to 450 MHz. FM and repeaters fill the top 10 MHz (that's why it's called "440"). CW and SSB take a small sliver at 432 MHz, and a

Band Plans

The term *band plan* refers to an agreement among concerned VHF and UHF operators and users about how each Amateur Radio band should be arranged. The goal of a band plan is to reduce interference between all the modes sharing each band. Aside from FM repeater and simplex activity, CW, SSB, AM, satellite, amateur television (ATV) and radio control operations also use these bands. (For example, a powerful FM signal at 144.110 MHz could spoil someone else's long-distance SSB contact.) The VHF and UHF bands offer a wide variety of amateur activities, so hams have agreed to set aside space for each type.

When considering frequencies for use in conjunction with a proposed repeater, be certain both the input and output fall within subbands authorized for repeater use, and do not extend beyond the subband edges. FCC rules define frequencies available for repeater use.

Here is an example of the ARRL 2 meter band plan as modified for local use by SERA, the Southeastern Repeater Association. The band plan accommodates many different uses. Note that the band plan in your area may be different from this one. It's best to check with your local frequency coordinator if you have any questions.

Frequency (MHz)	Operation
144.000-144.050	EME CW
144.050-144.100	General CW Operation
144.100	CW National Calling Frequency
144.100-144.200	EME and Weak Signal SSB
144.200-144.300	General SSB Operation
144.200	SSB National Calling Frequency
144.275-144.300	Propagation Beacons
144.300-144.500	Multi-Mode Operation
144.390	APRS Nationwide (Mode = 1200 Baud FM Packet)
144.510-144.890	FM and D-STAR Repeater Inputs
144.910-145.090	FM Digital/Packet Simplex and D-STAR Repeater Outputs
145.110-145.490	FM and D-STAR Repeater Outputs
145.510-145.790	FM Digital/Packet Simplex (Auxiliary)
145.800-146.000	Satellite Sub-Band
146.010-146.385	FM and APCO P25 Repeater Inputs
146.400-146.585	FM Voice Simplex and Alternate Repeater Inputs
146.420-146.480	D-STAR Voice Simplex and Repeater Inputs
146.520	FM National Calling Frequency
146.610-147.390	FM and APCO P25 Repeater Outputs
147.405-147.585	FM Voice Simplex and Alternate Repeater Inputs
147.420-147.480	D-STAR Voice Simplex and Repeater Inputs
147.600-147.990	FM and APCO P25 Repeater Inputs

satellite band takes a bit more. The bulk of the band is reserved for ATV (amateur television) that requires 6 MHz per channel.

Six meter FM also has regular channel steps — 20 kHz — but regional differences in offset, with some areas using 1 MHz and some using 500 kHz. Check your local listing. The 6 meter FM calling frequency is another aberration. At 52.525 MHz, it does not conform to the 20 kHz channel step plan.

The 222 MHz band is the most regular of all. That band was the last to be occupied by FM and repeaters, and it was planned after

the other bands were hashed out or left in an "agree to disagree" state. It uses 20 kHz channel steps and a 1.6 MHz offset throughout the band and throughout the country.

Now, check out the frequency coverage of your shiny new 2 meter FM handheld. It covers the whole band, doesn't it? But if you use it any-old-where, you might interfere with someone — maybe an SSB operator, or a satellite station or a repeater input. Please stick to the band plan channels. If we all do that, we'll all get maximum use and enjoyment out of our bands.

1.4.3 Public Service

Repeaters are excellent tools for emergency communication. That's why we leave a pause between transmissions — you never know when someone (you) will need the repeater in an emergency. Beyond local incidents, repeaters are in regular use by our Amateur Radio emergency organizations (ARES, RACES, SKYWARN and others) for training and during disasters. These services are discussed in detail in Section 2 of this book.

ARES® is the Amateur Radio Emergency Service, sponsored by the ARRL. During any kind of emergency, ARES operators will be using repeaters for local coordination and passing traffic. During these operations, the active repeater will probably be closed to regular conversations. But unless a major disaster has hit the area, there will be other repeaters available for regular activity. Ask the net control station for the status of the repeater.

Radio Amateur Civil Emergency Service (RACES) is a parallel program under the control of federal, state, and local emergency managers. In many areas, hams have dual membership in RACES and ARES programs, and they are integrated and share the same leadership.

We also use repeaters to help the National Weather Service (NWS) in an operation called SKYWARN. Most areas of the country are covered by repeaters dedicated to SKYWARN during bad weather. When severe weather threatens your area, listen to your local SKYWARN repeater, and follow instructions from the net-control station. Weather spotter reports fill in what the NWS calls "ground truth" — the actual conditions on the ground that Doppler radar can't detect directly. Many NWS offices have Amateur Radio stations that are activated for direct reports during severe weather. SKYWARN is a program of the NWS, but in many areas the Amateur Radio component is run by the local ARES leadership.

Carl, K8BBT, and Strait, KY4YA, helped provide communications during the Mount Dora Bicycle Festival in Florida. [Ted Luebbers, K1AYZ, photo]

Events

Hams across the country regularly help charitable organizations with communications during fundraising events such as bike-a-thons, marathons, triathlons and walks. This activity can keep a repeater very busy, so it isn't compatible with other hams chatting on the same channel. During the event a repeater will again be closed to routine operation. If you need to make a call, ask the net control station and most likely you can use the repeater for a minute with no problem. Participation in these events is good training for emergency communications. They carry a lot of traffic and give you practice communicating on busy channels, and all the traffic means something.

Nets

Repeaters are great places for nets, and there are lots of nets. A net, short for "network

of stations," is an organized on-the-air activity. We've mentioned a few already, including SKYWARN and ARES, but there can be many other types: traffic nets, rag-chew nets, specialty topic nets, club information nets and more. Most nets meet on a specific frequency or repeater, on a regular schedule — some daily, and some weekly. When a net is active on a repeater, the repeater is closed to other activity. The net control station (NCS) is in charge of the frequency, and all communication should be directed to that station first.

You might be a little nervous the first time you check into a net. Listen carefully to see how it works, and when the net control station calls for check-ins, tell them it's your first net. They'll take some extra time with you to help figure it out. Many new hams find that checking into a net is the *easiest* way to make their first contact. You can find many local nets online at **www.arrl.org/arrl-net-directory-search**.

1.4.4 About Those Tones

Squelch is the circuit in FM radios that turns off the loud rush of noise that you would hear when there is no signal on the channel you're listening to. Most of the time, hams use *noise squelch*, also called *carrier squelch*, a squelch circuit that lets any signal at all come through. But there are ways to be more selective about what signal gets to your speaker or keys up your repeater. That's generically known as *coded squelch*, and more than half

of the repeaters on the air require you to send coded squelch to be able to use the repeater.

CTCSS

The most common form of coded squelch has the generic name *CTCSS* (continuous tone coded squelch system), but is better know by Motorola's trade name PL (Private Line), or just the nickname "tone." It adds a "subaudible" tone to your transmitted audio,

one of 50 very specific frequencies between 67 and 254 Hz. Yes, humans can hear these frequencies quite well, so they're *sub*audible only because your receiver's audio circuit is supposed to filter them out. A receiver with CTCSS will remain silent to all traffic on a channel unless the transmitting station is sending the correct tone. Then the receiver sends the transmitted audio to its speaker.

In commercial radio service, this allows

(A)

(B)

Setting squelch codes in a Kenwood handheld. (A) shows the menu for setting a CTCSS code, while (B) shows setting a DCS code. With most radios, selecting DCS sets the radio in encode and decode mode, while CTCSS allows an encode-only mode, or encode-decode.

Jane's Taxi Company and Bob's Towing Service to use the same channel without having to listen to each other's traffic. In Amateur Radio, some repeaters require users to send the correct CTCSS tone to use the repeater. This may mean the repeater is *closed*, for use only by members, but more likely it is simply being used to avoid being keyed up by users of their co-channel neighbor 100 miles away. Most radios built since the early 1980s have a CTCSS *encoder* built in, and most radios built since the early '90s also have a CTCSS *decoder* built in.

If your local repeater sends a CTCSS tone, you can use your decoder to monitor just that repeater, and avoid signals from other sources.

DCS

A newer form of coded squelch is called *DCS* (digital-coded squelch). DCS appeared in commercial service because CTCSS didn't provide enough tones to keep everyone out of each other's hair, so DCS adds another hundred or so code options. DCS started showing up in ham radios around 2000. It's safe to say that few open repeaters (repeaters open to any and all users) use DCS, since older

radios don't have it.

Don't confuse DCS with the new DV digital voice modes. DCS is added to ordinary analog FM voice — it doesn't make the voice signal digital in any way.

DTMF

DTMF (Dual Tone Multi Frequency) can also be used as a form of squelch, to turn a receiver on, though it's more often used to control various functions such as autopatch and talking S meters. Some repeaters that require CTCSS have a DTMF "override" that puts the repeater into carrier-squelch mode for a few minutes if you send the proper digits.

Tone Trouble

Repeater tone requirements are listed in the *ARRL Repeater Directory*, so they're not hard to find. Newer radios have a "tone scan" feature that will hunt the tone, *if* the repeater is sending tone. Most repeaters that require tone also transmit their tone, but they don't have to. Some helpful repeaters announce their tone along with their voice ID. In some areas of the country, most of the repeaters use the same tone, so if you know one, you know them all.

1.4.5 Linking and Crossband Repeaters

Most repeaters are standalone devices, providing their individual pool of coverage and that's it. But a significant number of repeaters are linked — connected to one or more other repeaters. Those other repeaters can be on other bands at the same location, or they can be in other locations, or both. This lets users communicate between different bands and across wider geographic areas than they can on a single repeater.

There are many ways to link repeaters. Sometimes 2 meter and 440 repeaters are on the same tower and can just be wired together, or they may even share the same controller. Repeaters within a hundred miles or so of each other can use a radio link — separate link transmitters and receivers at each repeater, with antennas pointed at each other. Repeaters farther apart can "daisy-chain" their links to cover even wider territory. There are a few linked repeater systems in the country that cover multiple states with dozens of repeaters, but most radio-linked repeater systems have more modest ambitions, covering just part of one or two states.

VoIP and the Internet have taken repeater linking to a new level, creating the ability to tie repeaters together around the world and in nearly unlimited number.

There are several ways linked repeaters can be operated, coming under the categories of *full-time* and *on demand*. Full-time linked repeaters operate just as the name implies — all the repeaters in a linked network are connected all the time. If you key up one of them, you're heard on all of them, and you can talk to anyone on any of the other repeaters on the network at any time. You don't have to do anything special to activate the network, since it's always there.

In an on-demand system, the linked re-

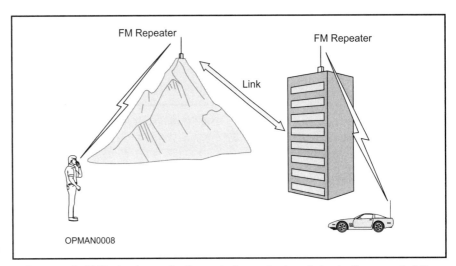

OPMAN0008

A diagram of a VoIP simplex node. If a control operator is not physically present at the station location and the node is functioning with wireless remote control, the control link must follow the rules for *auxiliary* operation.

peaters remain isolated unless you take some action, usually by sending a code by DTMF digits, to connect them. Your DTMF sequence may activate all the repeaters on the network, or the system may let you address just one specific repeater, somewhat like dialing a telephone. When you're finished, another DTMF code drops the link, or a timer may handle that chore when the repeaters are no longer in use.

Crossband Repeat

Dual-band mobile radios — radios that cover two ham bands, usually 2 meters and 70 cm — are often designed to be mini-repeaters. Yes, you can run a little repeater right out of your car! This can be helpful if you want to operate a handheld radio but need the oomph of a mobile radio to reach a distant repeater. For example, you're on the lower level of the mall with your handheld. You can't reach the local repeater from down there, but you can reach your car in the parking lot. With a crossband repeater in your car, you can relay your signal from the mall to the main repeater.

Crossband repeat operation in most mobile radios is simple. When the crossband function is turned on, anything the radio hears on one band is retransmitted on the other. When the signal stops, the radio goes into receive on both bands and waits for the next signal, on either band, to repeat.

There are some problems that limit the utility of crossband repeat. The biggest problem is *hang-time* on the main repeater — the time after somebody stops talking, but the repeater stays on the air, beeps, and then finally drops. On many repeaters that's several seconds, and when two hams are in conversation, the repeater *never* drops until they're done. Your crossband repeater can't tell the difference between a ham's transmission through the repeater and the hang time afterward. It's all just one long signal being received. So if you, down in the mall, are listening to two hams talk, you can't break in until they're done. As long as they're talking, your mobile never stops sending a signal to you, and never listens for you. (Something else to keep in mind here is that your mobile is now transmitting a lot, and it is not designed for continuous transmission. Keep it in low power.)

A few notes of caution: First, be very care-ful in configuring your crossband repeater. Choose frequencies wisely — your coordination group may have identified band segments for crossband repeat operation, so don't just plunk down anywhere you want. Do some research. And guard the "local" side of your crossband mobile with CTCSS or DCS. If you don't, and the squelch opens on your mobile, it will spew noise out to the main repeater. Crossband operation is particularly useful for emergency and public-service event work, but a noise-spewing, out-of-control crossband mobile can render a vital repeater useless.

Second, maintain control. The FCC rules require you to be in control of the transmitter, but are not specific about how you do that. If you can reach the car in a few minutes from inside the mall, that's probably good enough. But don't stop paying attention to it or leave the area.

Finally, you are required to ID *both* of your mobile's transmitters with your call sign. How do you ID the transmitter that's sending the main repeater signal back to you? None of the crossband repeaters on the market has an ID system built in. So it isn't easy.

1.4.6 Internet Linking

The Internet has expanded repeater linking exponentially, making worldwide communication through a local repeater commonplace. There are three Internet linking systems in common use. Two of them, IRLP and Echo-Link, have reached critical mass in the US and are available almost everywhere.

Internet Radio Linking Project (IRLP)

IRLP is the most "radio" based linking system. User access is only via radio, using either simplex stations or repeaters, while linking is done using VoIP on the Internet. An IRLP system operator establishes a *node* by interfacing his radio equipment to a *Linux* based computer with an Internet connection, and then running IRLP software. Once that's set up, repeater users send DTMF tones to make connections, either directly to other individual repeater or simplex nodes, or to *reflectors* — servers that tie multiple nodes together as one big party line.

The direct connections work like on-demand linked repeaters. You dial in the node number you want to connect to (some systems have you add an access code first), and you are connected to the distant repeater (or simplex node, but repeaters greatly outnumber simplex nodes). Once connected, everyone

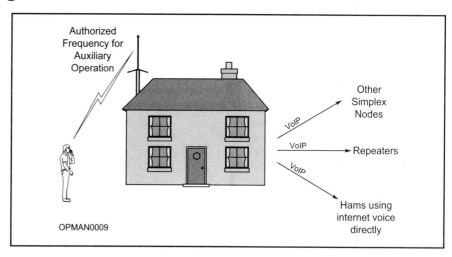

Two FM repeaters linked via VoIP.

on both ends can communicate. When you're finished, you usually take the link down with another DTMF sequence. Someone from a distant repeater can make a connection to you as well. Most nodes have a voice announcement that confirms the connection, and sometimes boasts a bit about the local system.

Reflectors work like a hybrid between on-demand and full-time linked repeaters. You can connect your local repeater to a reflector and leave it there all day, or you can connect for a special purpose (such as a net), and drop it when the event is over. Some reflectors are popular, busy places to connect and hear the world. Some are used for special events such as weather nets, and some just wait quietly for a connection.

If you have an underutilized repeater in your area, connecting it to a busy IRLP reflector will bring it to life during much of the day.

There are a couple thousand IRLP nodes online and working worldwide. There are about 30 reflectors operating, each of which has 10 independent "channels," so essentially 300 reflector paths are available. You can find more information at **www.irlp.net**.

EchoLink

EchoLink is the 800 pound gorilla of Internet linking, with thousands of users worldwide actively connected at any time, and tens of thousands more who could connect but are offline at the moment. EchoLink allows repeater connections as does IRLP, and has Conference Servers, similar to IRLP reflectors that permit multiple connections. The big difference, and the reason EchoLink is so much bigger, is that it allows individuals to connect to the network from their computers. You can download EchoLink client software from **www.echolink.org** (for *Windows,* and see the FAQ for *MacOS, Linux, iOS*, and Android), register yourself, and then connect to any repeater, individual or conference. Many of your connections won't go over the air at all, but proof of a ham license is required to register, so you'll be talking only to other hams.

The EchoLink conference servers all have more or less specific functions. Some are just regional gathering places, while some are topic or activity based.

To use EchoLink with a computer, you need a sound card, a headset (or a microphone and speaker), and an Internet connection. EchoLink will work with a good dial-up connection, but broadband is better. The software presents you with a list of every "station" on the system (a bit overwhelming), and each Conference. You double-click on a station to connect, and push your spacebar to talk. Your initial setup will include getting audio levels set correctly, and, if you use a router with a firewall, you may need to open some ports to allow the outbound EchoLink connection to pass through. Software and instructions are provided on the **www.echolink.org** website.

You can connect your EchoLink-enabled computer to your base station radio fairly easily through a sound card, and create an on-air node. If you do, pick your frequencies carefully. Don't pipe EchoLink to a local repeater without permission from the repeater owner. Watch your power output level — your base station isn't meant for continuous duty, but a busy EchoLink connection could have it transmitting a lot. And if you decide to create a full-time link from a computer to a repeater, consider using a dedicated UHF link frequency rather than just a base station on the repeater input. Same goes for IRLP connections.

WIRES-X

WIRES-X — Wide-coverage Internet Repeater Enhancement System — is a VoIP network created by Yaesu that works with Yaesu's C4FM digital radios as well as analog radios as part of System Fusion. The WIRES-X node software runs under *Windows* and the system has nodes throughout the world. The hardware portion of WIRES-X uses an interface that connects to the node radio and a PC, which in turn is connected to the Internet.

Like IRLP, WIRES-X is entirely radio based; you cannot access a WIRES-X node directly from the Internet. A WIRES-X host server maintains a continuously updated list of all active nodes. System Fusion users can search and connect to local node stations by pressing a button. The system will automatically obtain node station information and set up the required frequency and digital code parameters. Node station ID, city name, as well as distance and bearing are indicated on the display of the transceiver, and can be checked at a glance.

Internet linking on both IRLP and Echo-Link have become popular for emergency communications, with repeaters tied together for ARES and SKYWARN activity. The National Hurricane Center has been using both systems to take reports from hams as hurricanes approach landfall, and hams have been enthusiastic about participation. Of course, the Internet is infrastructure dependent, and both power and Internet access tend to disappear when storms reach their peak. Not surprisingly, stations along the coast also tend to disappear from the nets as Internet connections are lost. But in many cases Internet linking does provide another valuable tool in the emergency communications toolbox.

1.4.7 Digital Voice (DV) — The New Horizon

APCO-25, D-STAR, DMR, and System Fusion are digital voice systems making inroads into VHF/UHF Amateur Radio repeater operation. While all are digital, they are incompatible systems. Each has its own advantages and disadvantages.

APCO-25

Sometimes called just P-25, APCO-25 is a commercial system that's been in use in public-safety (police, fire, EMS) long enough that equipment is being "aged out" of commercial service and the old radios, often in very good condition, are cheap. Hams in some areas of the country have put P-25 repeaters on the air on the VHF and UHF ham bands. P-25 equipment was first marketed by Motorola under the brand Astro, but now P-25 is available from most commercial two-way radio manufacturers, including Icom, Kenwood and Vertex Standard. None of them, though, make P-25 equipment specifically

for Amateur Radio or put P-25 capability into their ham radio lines.

Commercial P-25 equipment is not hard to modify for Amateur Radio. The right models can be reprogrammed for ham operation with software — no retuning required. And most models (and most repeaters) are dual-mode, analog and digital. So a repeater owner can convert an analog repeater to digital without leaving the analog users out in the cold. (Analog users will want to use CTCSS decode to avoid hearing the growl that P-25 makes in an analog receiver).

There are positives and negatives to operating a radio designed for commercial service. It'll probably be quite rugged, a plus if you're prone to dropping your handheld. And it may be more immune to intermod and other RF junk. To program it, though, you'll need to visit your local radio shop, or a local ham who's purchased the software and cables needed. You could buy them

yourself, but they're expensive, and for some radios, they're available only to licensed service shops. You won't have the flexibility of adding and changing frequencies and memories on the fly that you do with true ham equipment. And there are no dual-band radios available. To those hams who prefer commercial equipment, this is a worthwhile tradeoff.

On the air, APCO-25 radios work much like conventional analog FM radios. The audio is a bit "metallic" or "robotic," but there is no noise or mobile flutter. The signal stays full-quieting until it drops off at the weak-signal threshold. P-25 radios send a bit of data at the beginning of a transmission that you can program to include your call sign. That will show up on the display of the receiving station. They can also send this data at the beginning of an analog transmission.

In public safety systems, P-25 radios are often part of linked systems. The linking is done by external equipment that has not found its way into Amateur Radio systems. Most P-25 repeaters are standalone, or part of limited networks like their analog cousins. There's no reason they can't be linked to analog repeaters, or use IRLP or EchoLink.

D-STAR

The all-amateur digital voice mode for VHF-UHF is called D-STAR. It was developed by the Japan Amateur Radio League (JARL), and it was designed from the ground up to be a networked system. The repeaters have an Ethernet port for connection to the Internet through a *Gateway* computer located at the repeater site, though the repeaters can be operated standalone with no Internet connection.

Icom offers a broad line of VHF, UHF and dual band mobiles, handhelds, and repeaters. D-STAR handheld and mobile transceivers are all dual-mode, analog and digital, but the current Icom repeaters are only digital. Recently FlexRadio Systems has added D-STAR capability to its 6000 series software defined radios (SDRs).

D-STAR shares P-25's slightly robotic sound, and its clarity and freedom from noise and picket-fencing. Both systems have a bit of "garble" as signals hover at the weak-signal threshold, but most of the time a signal is either perfectly clear, or it's gone. Some D-STAR repeater operators report slightly better range with D-STAR than with analog FM, though they'll admit that at the threshold when a D-STAR signal disappears, you might be able to pick some audio out of a very noisy analog signal.

The basic D-STAR operating experience is similar to analog — push to talk, release to listen. But the Icom repeater controllers have a minimal design. There's no hang-time, no courtesy tone. When you stop transmitting, usually you hear nothing. It's a little hard to tell if you've been heard until the station you're talking to returns and acknowledges your transmission. The repeater will send a short burst of data (its ID) after you let go. It's not audible, but you can see it on your S meter. Some of the "extras" of other repeater controllers such as voice ID, announcements and self-recording and replay (EchoTest), have been developed to run on the Gateway computer using an auxiliary program called *DPLUS*.

There's more to *see* with D-STAR. Your radio displays the call sign of the station you're listening to, and sometimes the call sign of the repeater you're talking through. Users can program a short text message that is sent with each transmission and scrolls through listener's displays. In addition, D-STAR's voice signal always carries with it a 1200 bit/s data signal that can be used for

text, small files — anything that fits in that low-speed connection. To use that data signal, you connect a computer with a special data cable. It can't be accessed from the radio directly. One program has taken the lead in using this data — D-RATS (**www.d-rats.com**). Originally a messaging program, D-RATS has expanded to include sending files, pictures, mapping, forms and its own networking.

D-STAR is designed to network using the Internet. Repeaters can be linked to each other, or to reflectors, similar to IRLP and EchoLink. And since most D-STAR repeaters have a limited number of local users, the reflectors help keep the repeaters busy and the local users entertained. This capability is actually an add-on, part of the *DPLUS* utilities package.

There are some additional devices on the market that help extend D-STAR's reach and usability. The two most popular are the DV Dongle and the DV Access Point Dongle (DVAP), USB connected devices from Internet Labs. Both are small slabs of plastic that allow the user to connect to D-STAR repeaters via the Internet, running a software app on a computer (PC, Mac, Linux). The DV Dongle uses the computer audio system (mic/speakers or headset), and does the D-STAR encoding and decoding. The software lets the user pick a repeater or reflector to connect to and converse with anyone else on the repeater or reflector. The DVAP also uses the computer's Internet connection, but instead of doing its own vocoding, it has a little 10-mW 2 meter transceiver that lets a ham use a handheld D-STAR radio to talk through the network, even if there is no D-STAR repeater in the vicinity. Note that the DVAP does not convert analog FM to D-STAR! It requires the user to be operating a D-STAR radio.

D-STAR's DV (voice) signal is part of a 4800 bit/s data stream. Of that, 2400 bit/s are used for the actual digitized voice, 1200 bit/s are used for "overhead" including forward error correction, and 1200 bit/s are going along for the ride as a data stream, called "low speed data," available to the user. D-STAR repeaters and Gateways pass the entire 4800 bit/s stream, so the data goes wherever the voice signal goes. You can send data while talking, just talk, or just send data — it's all the same signal. To take advantage of this data stream, you need a computer and an optional interface cable, and some software. The low-speed data mode is not accessible from the radio front panel. The D-RATS multi-function program has become the go-to software for D-STAR data operation.

DMR

DMR (Digital Mobile Radio) is the generic name for a system developed for business/

commercial use as a less expensive alternative to P-25. The most familiar brand name is Motorola's MotoTrbo, but there are many manufacturers making DMR compatible radios.

Not surprisingly, hams have adapted DMR to the ham bands. There is some surplus equipment available, but much new DMR equipment is affordable enough for hams. As with P-25 equipment (and, for that matter, any commercial FM equipment adapted for ham radio use), the DMR radios brought in from the commercial arena are not user- or field-programmable. You need software and cables to set them up.

In commercial service, DMR permits repeater networking and has the capability to devote some of its data to text/files, as does D-STAR. Hams have extended the commercial networking capability already, and we can expect more innovation to adapt the system to Amateur Radio's unique needs and capabilities. The commercial radios do *not* permit the individual user to control networking functions the way D-STAR systems do.

System Fusion

Yaesu has entered the Amateur Radio VHF/UHF digital voice fray in a big way with its System Fusion mobile and handheld radios and repeaters. This system maintains compatibility between conventional FM and Yaesu's choice of digital voice modulation, C4FM. In the *automatic* mode, a System Fusion repeater or transceiver system will select whatever mode is being received, and set the transmitter for that mode (except for AM, which is receive-only). Like the other digital voice modes, C4FM offers high clarity and near zero background noise down to the threshold.

Yaesu designed the DR-1 System Fusion repeater to be a drop-in replacement for an existing VHF or UHF repeater. It will interface to existing controllers and run analog FM, and then there are some options for integrating C4FM. One option is that users who have a C4FM radio can transmit to the repeater in digital, while the repeater continues to output analog FM — it simply demodulates the digital signal and applies the decoded voice to the FM modulator. Analog and digital users can talk to each other in the same conversation. Another option is to repeat analog signals as analog, and digital signals as digital. They occupy the same frequency, and it's one-at-a-time, or first-come, first-served. The repeater can't do both analog and digital at the same time, though. When the DR-1 is used in fully-digital mode, the analog-only users will not be able to listen to the conversation.

Yaesu's digital signal is 12.5 kHz wide, and the data rate is 9600 bits per second. DN is a simultaneous voice/data communication mode, and VW is a voice full-rate mode. In

DN mode, the voice audio isn't as full fidelity as VW because it's sharing the bits with error correction and a data field. VW uses the whole 12.5 kHz for voice with better quality. Yaesu lets you send text messages (80 characters max) with their on-screen keyboard and the receiving station reads the text message right on their screen. You can also do group messaging and send small images.

Will your analog radio become obsolete anytime soon? Only time will tell. There's no question that with an analog-only radio you will be missing out on the leading edge of new technology, but nobody expects analog repeaters to disappear anytime soon.

1.4.8 VHF/UHF Digital Data Modes

Let's move on to the VHF/UHF data modes, and keep in mind that with the advent of digital voice, our language must now change. We can no longer assume that "digital" means just text or files in Amateur Radio. Icom splits their D-STAR nomenclature into DV (digital voice) and DD (for 128 kbit/s digital data). We'll ignore for now the question of whether digitized voice is actually "data," but that question does bedevil our attempts to fit digital voice into the framework of Part 97.

Over the years, packet radio in the VHF/UHF spectrum has been its own roller-coaster ride. First developed in the 1980s and wildly popular in the 1990s, the Internet and its seemingly inexhaustible e-mail capabilities arrived and we all but abandoned the packet bulletin board (PBBS) network. But packet didn't die. Some PBBSs are still around, and packet radio is being used for other applications. APRS (the Automatic Packet Reporting System) inherits most of the packet radio legacy of equipment, tower sites and interest. And Winlink 2000 on VHF/UHF is giving new life to packet for ARES and emergency applications.

THE PACKET SYSTEM

The other end of packet communication can be a direct connection to another ham, just like voice simplex, but it's more likely to be a "node," also called a "digipeater." Examples of nodes are the PBBSs, DX PacketClusters or APRS nodes, but there can also be simple standalone nodes whose only function is to relay signals. There aren't many full-fledged repeaters dedicated to packet, partly because by the time packet got popular there wasn't much spectrum available for more repeaters, and partly because with digipeaters, we don't really need them.

Digipeaters are simplex devices that receive a packet, then re-send it more or less immediately after it's been received, all on one channel. A central PBBS might be ringed by digipeaters that help outlying users who can't reach the PBBS directly. Those digipeaters don't have to be on the same frequency as the PBBS. They can use a link radio, preferably on another band, to forward packets between you and the PBBS. It takes more

hardware, but it eases congestion on a busy packet channel.

WHAT FREQUENCY?

PBBS activity on 2 meters started on 145.01 MHz, and much of it remains there. So if you're looking for local activity, that's a good place to start. Other popular packet channels are 145.03, .05, .07 and .09. In some areas, packet systems can be found on channels between 144.91 and 144.99 MHz, and between 145.51 and 145.77 MHz. If you listen on those channels, you may hear the "braaap" of 1200 bit/s packet, or the "psssssh" of 9600 bit/s packet. APRS is almost exclusively on 144.39 MHz. You'll have to search local resources to see what's on the air in your area.

Assembling a VHF Packet Station

Most packet stations need a computer and a radio. Then they need a way to create and control the data packets and the audio tones that carry them. There are several ways to do this:

1) *A terminal node controller (TNC)* — a separate box containing the hardware and firmware that does most of the work. The TNC includes a modem, and the computer mostly acts as a "dumb terminal" — just a keyboard and display.

2) *A standalone modem*, and TNC emulation software in the computer.

3) *A sound card* and computer control software, which puts all the work on the computer. Most of the software is written for the *Windows* operating system, but there are programs for *Mac OS* and *Linux* as well. Some programs are freeware, and some are shareware. A web search for "Amateur Radio packet software" will yield a wealth of resources. *AGWPE* (AGW Packet Engine — www.sv2agw.com) is a free *Windows* programs that's popular today.

4) *A "built-in,"* with the TNC built into the radio and integrated into the radio operation to some degree. Some Kenwood and Yaesu models can operate APRS on one "side" of the radio, and voice on the other. Of course,

they can't be transmitting and receiving in the same band at the same time, so if you're operating 2 meter voice and packet, they stop receiving packets during voice transmissions, and when they send a packet beacon, the voice channel receiver drops out for a moment. On the other hand, if you're talking on UHF and using packet on VHF, it's like having independent radios.

RADIO EQUIPMENT

Most 25 W to 50 W radios made since the mid '80s will work fine for 1200 bit/s packet. Most modern radios will have dedicated packet connections so you don't have to plug into the mic connector and come out of the speaker jack. Many radios made since the late '90s have 9600 bit/s capability as well.

You shouldn't compromise on the radio or antenna. A bunch of transmitters will be sharing the channel with you. TNCs are designed to wait until a channel is clear before transmitting, but if other stations can't hear you, they might begin transmitting while you're on the air, clobbering you at the receiver you're trying to reach. If you can't hear them, your TNC might initiate a transmission while they're on the air. The more stations that can hear each other in a geographic area, the better the system works. A signal in your geographic area that you can't hear is called a *hidden transmitter.*

Automatic Packet Reporting System (APRS)

Just as packet systems in general were succumbing to competition from the Internet, APRS appeared, leading to a resurgence of interest. Some handheld and mobile radios include APRS capabilities or built-in TNC options.

When operating APRS, you, or a device at your station (GPS, weather monitor), send a bit of information to your TNC, which sends it to your radio for transmission on 144.39 MHz. An APRS digipeater relays your packets to all local stations, and to all surrounding digipeaters, which in turn relay your packet to all *their* local stations. That puts your data in the hands of stations for a hundred or so

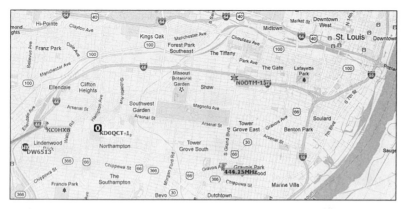

This is a screen-capture from www.aprs.fi of APRS activity around St. Louis, Missouri. It shows many stations, and the tracks of several GPS equipped mobiles. The site is highly customizable, and it has a history function that goes back years.

miles around. One of those stations also puts your information on the Internet, where it can be seen worldwide.

What information do you send? Many hams think of APRS first as a position reporting system, based on sending GPS location, speed, and altitude data via packet to be displayed on a map. The system can handle text messages, weather info, traffic reports, repeater, event, EchoLink and IRLP node location and info and more, in addition to location data for fixed and mobile stations.

On the receive end of things, you generally see some kind of map on your display, showing the location of all the area APRS stations. For moving stations, the display can show the direction, speed and altitude as well. Other windows or boxes display the text notes, weather information and other data being sent.

APRS SOFTWARE AND HARDWARE

At home, the hardware you need is standard packet-system stuff — computer, TNC, radio, antenna. If you have an old TNC, or buy a used one, check to see if its firmware supports GPS data. You may need a firmware upgrade. In the US and Canada, all routine APRS traffic is on 144.39 MHz at 1200 bit/s. Special event traffic can be handled on other frequencies.

Mobile APRS is another story. You can run a full APRS station with a laptop computer and APRS software, or you can have a transmit-only system that beacons your location, called a "tracker." Either way, you add a GPS to the mix.

For a full mobile station, you need a computer with two ports — one for the TNC and one for the GPS — or a TNC that accepts GPS information directly. Newer GPS receivers have USB connections, but some TNCs are built to connect to serial ports. If you have a

newer laptop without a serial port, you can use a USB-to-serial adapter. The software will forward the GPS information to the TNC. The program will beacon your location as you move. How often it beacons is one of several parameters you'll need to set. Some programs get very detailed, allowing you to send a beacon when you've turned a corner, and send more beacons when you're moving at high speed, fewer when going slowly or stopped.

With a tracker, you have the GPS, the TNC and the radio, but no computer except to initially set things up. The GPS plugs into the TNC directly. There are some special, small TNCs on the market designed just to be trackers, and some TNC/radio combinations. The only receiving they do is to make sure they don't transmit when a channel is busy. With a tracker, you drive down the road, letting the world (including family and friends) know where you are. They don't need APRS to find you — there are several websites that will display your location.

You can use the Internet to view APRS operation worldwide. One of the most popular is **aprs.fi**. This is an easy-to-use site that uses Google Maps to display all the APRS activity worldwide (which is too much to absorb). It lets you zoom into any area you want, and filter a variety of parameters until you see what you're looking for. It includes years of historical data, letting you look into the past for a specific station's APRS activity.

This Internet connectivity allows you to send text messages from any APRS station to any APRS station, anywhere in the world covered by a digipeater and an IGate. And you can send a message to any e-mail address by addressing an APRS message to EMAIL, then putting the e-mail address as the first "word" of the message, and then the short text message. It would look like this:

EMAIL
then
kn4aq@arrl.net Hello, Gary. Are you going to the hamfest this weekend?

The APRS e-mail server will send you an acknowledgement, which you'll probably receive, but no guarantees.

Propagation Network (PropNET)

Participating PropNET stations beacon signals using packet and PSK31 (with location information) on some HF and VHF bands, including 160, 30, 10, 6 and 2 meters. Receiving stations automatically forward the data to a PropNET server, and the results are available instantly on a series of maps on the PropNET website. PropNET needs all the receiving stations it can get. Perhaps you'd like to help. In any case, it's interesting to see band-opening information real-time. For more information, visit **www.propnet.org.**

Winlink and VHF/UHF Packet

Winlink 2000, discussed earlier in the HF Digital Communications section, is often thought of as a PACTOR based HF e-mail system for sailboats and RVers. But the developers of Winlink 2000 eager for you to know that it is growing on VHF and UHF as well, primarily as a vehicle for ARES and served agency related emergency communications. On VHF/UHF, the Winlink 2000 system uses packet, D-STAR, or IEEE 802.11 Wi-Fi, but not PACTOR.

A VHF/UHF Winlink 2000 system can restore e-mail operation to an EOC that has lost its Internet connection or e-mail server, if there's a TELPAC Gateway within range. (VHF/UHF stations equipped to transfer *Paclink MP* messages to the Internet are called TELPAC [TELnet-to-PACket] Gateways.) If there is no VHF/UHF system in range, or if a widespread disaster has knocked the local TELPAC out, a Winlink HF system can handle the traffic. It won't be a 5 Mbit/s connection, to be sure, but it will get e-mail moving, with limited size attachments.

In practice, a Winlink 2000 equipped EOC, Red Cross office or any other emergency venue that has lost its Internet connection from a disaster or broken e-mail server, and that is equipped with a laptop computer with *Paclink*, a TNC, and a VHF radio and antenna, may continue their emergency e-mail operation using the Winlink 2000 radio e-mail domain. *Paclink MP*, running on the agency local area network (LAN), acts like any other e-mail server. However, on the outbound side, *Paclink MP* sends the data through an automatic hierarchical routing scheme — including Telnet, IEEE 802.11 links, D-STAR, packet, or HF PACTOR — via a TNC and radio, depending on the priority set for each of the five output levels available. For the level of priority set to packet, the TNC and radio will communicate to the Winlink 2000 network through the TELPAC Gateway, which forwards it for processing to one of the Winlink 2000 PMBOs. If the agency has an 802.11 based wireless network, a ham can provide the link from a mobile station parked outside.

As useful as this is, not enough hams know about it, and it's sometimes been hard to "sell" it to emergency management officials. But ARES groups around the country are beginning to experiment with or implement the system, as documented in articles published in *QST*. For more information, see the main Winlink 2000 website at **www.winlink. org**.

Are you digital yet? Right now, there's a pretty good chance that you are an "all-analog" ham. And analog isn't going away anytime soon. But more digital is on the way.

1.4.9 VHF/UHF FM and Digital Resources

ARRL Band Plans: **www.arrl.org/band-plan**
Auxiliary stations: **www.arrl.org/auxiliary-station-faq**
Automatic Packet Reporting System (APRS):
    www.aprs.org
    www.arrl.org/aprs-mode
D-STAR:
    www.icomamerica.com/amateur/dstar
EchoLink: **www.echolink.org**

Internet Radio Linking Project (IRLP): **www.irlp.net**
RFinder Worldwide Repeater Directory: **www.rfinder.net**
TAPR: **www.tapr.org**
WIRES-X: **www.yaesu.com**

You can also find more information in *The ARRL Handbook*, *ARRL Repeater Directory*, and *VoIP: Internet Linking for Radio Amateurs*, all available from your favorite ham radio dealer or the ARRL website.

1.5 VHF/UHF Beyond FM and Repeaters

The radio spectrum between 30 and 3000 MHz is one of the greatest resources available to the radio amateur. The VHF and UHF amateur bands are a haven for rag chewers and experimenters alike; new modes of emission, new antennas and state-of-the-art equipment are all developed in this territory. Commercial transceivers or transverters are available for the bands through 10 GHz, and building your own gear is very popular as well. Propagation conditions may change rapidly and seemingly unpredictably, but the keen observer can take advantage of subtle clues to make the most of the bands. Most North American hams are already well acquainted with 2 meter or 440 MHz FM. For many, channelized repeater operation is their first exposure to VHF or UHF. However, FM is only part of the VHF/UHF story! A great variety of SSB, CW and digital activity congregates on the low ends of the bands from 6 meters all the way to the end of the radio spectrum — and even to light beyond.

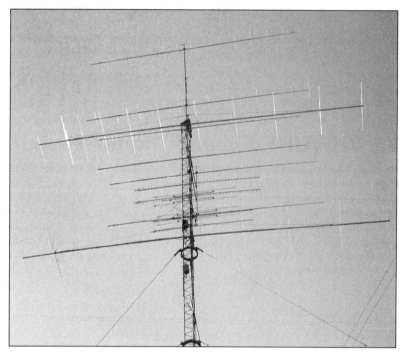

Bob, K2DRH, owns this impressive collection of VHF/UHF antennas in Illinois. [Bob Streigl, K2DRH, photo]

1.5.1 Overview

How are the Bands Organized?

One of the keys to using this immense resource properly is knowing how the bands are organized. Each of the VHF and UHF bands is many megahertz wide, huge in comparison to any HF band. Different activities take place in separate parts of each. Even in the low ends of each VHF and UHF band, where SSB, CW and digital activities congregate, there is a lot of space. Thus established and widely known *calling frequencies* help stations find each other.

By knowing the best frequencies and times to be on the air, you will have little trouble making plenty of contacts, working DX, and otherwise enjoying the world above 50 MHz. By far the two most popular bands are 6 and 2 meters, followed by 70 cm. The 1.25 meter (222 MHz) and 33 cm (902 MHz) bands are not available worldwide. For that reason, commercial equipment is more difficult to find for these bands, and thus they are less popular. The next two higher UHF bands at 23 cm (1296 MHz) and 13 cm (2304 MHz) are attractive, in part due to more commercial equipment being offered to meet the demands of amateur satellite operators.

There is plenty of space on the VHF and higher bands for rag chewing, experimenting, working DX and many other activities unknown to the HF world. This means that whatever you like to do — chat with your friends across town, test amateur television or bounce signals off the moon — there is plenty of spectrum available. VHF/UHF is a great resource!

The key to enjoyable use of this resource is to know how everyone else is using it and to follow their lead. Basically, this means to listen first. Pay attention to the segments of the band already in use, and follow the operating practices that experienced operators are using. This way, you won't interfere with ongoing use of the band by others, and you'll fit in right away.

When there is little happening on the band, the calling frequencies (see **Table 1.10**) are where operators will call CQ. For that reason, these are also the frequencies they are likely to monitor most of the time. Many VHF operators have gotten into a habit of tuning to one or more calling frequencies while doing something else around the shack. If someone wants a contact, you will already be on the right frequency to hear the call and make a contact.

The most important thing to remember about the calling frequencies is that they are not for rag chewing. In most areas of the country, everyone uses the calling frequency to establish a contact, and then the two stations move up or down a few tens of kHz to chat. You can easily tell if the band is open by monitoring the call signs of the stations

Table 1.10
North American Calling Frequencies

Band (MHz)	Calling Frequency
50	50.090 general CW
	50.110 DX only
	50.125, general SSB
	50.260 Digital/WSJT
144	144.110 CW
	144.140 Digital/WSJT
	144.200 SSB
222	222.100 CW, SSB
432	432.100 CW, SSB
902	902.100 CW, SSB
	903.100 CW, SSB
	(East Coast)
1296	1296.100 CW, SSB
2304	2304.1 CW, SSB
10,000	10,368.1 CW, SSB

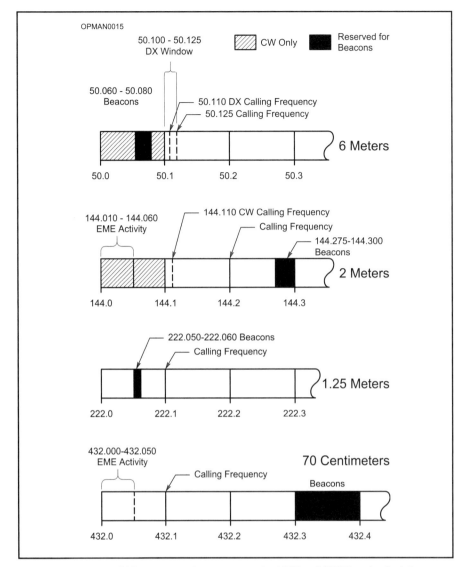

Suggested CW and SSB usage on the most popular VHF and UHF bands. Activity on 144 MHz and higher centers around the calling frequencies.

making contact on the calling frequency — you sure don't need to hear their whole QSO!

On 6 meters, a *DX window* has been established in order to reduce interference to DX stations. This window, which extends from 50.100 to 50.125 MHz, is intended for DX QSOs only. The DX calling frequency is 50.110 MHz. If you make a DX contact and expect to rag chew, you should move up a few kHz to clear the DX calling frequency. US and Canadian 6 meter operators should use the domestic calling frequency of 50.125 MHz for non-DX work.

Activity Nights

Although it is possible to scare up a QSO on 50 or 144 MHz almost any evening (especially during the summer), in some areas of the country there is not always enough activity to make it easy to make a contact. Therefore, informal *activity nights* have been established so you will know when to expect some activity. Each band has its own night. **Table 1.11** shows the most common activity nights, but there is some variation in activity nights from place to place. Check with someone in your area to find out about local activity nights.

Local VHF/UHF nets often meet during activity nights. Nets provide a regular meeting time for hams on 6 and 2 meters primarily, although there are regional nets at least as high as 1296 MHz. Several regional VHF clubs sponsor nets in various parts of the country, especially in urban areas. For information on the meeting times and frequencies of the nets, inquire locally.

Where Am I?

One of the first things you are bound to notice on the low end of any VHF band is that most QSOs include an exchange of grid locators. For example, instead of trying to tell a distant station, "I'm in Canton, New York," I say instead "My grid is FN24." It may sound strange, but FN24 is easier to locate on a grid locator map than my small town.

So what are these grid locators? They are 1° latitude by 2° longitude sections of the Earth. A grid locator in the center of the US is about 68 by 104 miles, but grids change size and shape slightly, depending on their latitude.

Each locator has a unique two-letter/two-number identifier. The two letters identify one of 324 worldwide fields, which cover 10° latitude by 20° longitude each. There are 100 locators in each field, and these are identified by the two numbers. Exactly 32,400 grid locators cover the entire Earth. Two additional letters can be added for a more exact location, as in FN24kp. The extra two letters uniquely identifies a locale within a few miles.

There are several ways to find out your own grid square identifier. The best place to start is the ARRL website (**www.arrl.org/grid-squares**) which has links to articles, online grid square calculators and other resources. You will need your latitude and longitude, readily available from Google Maps and other sources.

The ARRL publishes a colorful, 27 × 39-inch Amateur Radio Map of North America that shows grid squares for the continental United States and most populated areas of Canada. This map is available from ARRL online at **www.arrl.org/shop**. If you are keeping track of grids for VUCC (the VHF/UHF Century Club award), you can mark each grid as you work it. The ARRL also publishes a *World Grid Locator Atlas*, available from the web catalog as well.

Table 1.11
Common Activity Nights

Band (MHz)	Day	Local Time
50	Sunday	6:00 PM
144	Monday	7:00 PM
222	Tuesday	8:00 PM
432	Wednesday	9:00 PM
902	Friday	9:00 PM
1296	Thursday	10:00 PM

1.5.2 Propagation

What sort of range is considered normal in the world above 50 MHz? To a large extent, range on VHF is determined by location and the quality of the stations involved. After all, you can't expect the same performance from a 10 W rig and a small antenna on the roof as you might from a kilowatt and stacked beams at 100 feet.

On 2 meter SSB, a typical station probably consists of a low-powered multimode rig (SSB/CW/FM), followed by a 100 W amplifier, or one of the HF/VHF/UHF transceivers that includes SSB/CW at 50 to 100 W on this band. The antenna might be a single long Yagi at around 50 feet, fed with low-loss coax.

How far could this station cover on an average night using SSB? Location plays a big role, but it's probably safe to estimate that you could talk to a similarly equipped station about 200 miles away almost 100% of the time. Naturally, higher-power stations with tall antennas and low-noise receive preamps will have a greater range than this, up to a practical maximum of about 350 – 400 miles in the Midwest, less in the hilly West and East. It is almost always possible to extend your range significantly by switching from SSB to CW or a digital mode.

On 222 MHz, a similar station might expect to cover nearly the same distance, and perhaps 100 miles less on 432 MHz. This assumes normal propagation conditions and a reasonably unobstructed horizon. This range is a lot greater than you would get for noise-free communication on

FM, and it represents the sort of capability the typical station should seek. Increase the height of the antenna to 80 feet and the range might increase to 250 miles, probably more, depending on your location. That's not bad for reliable communication!

Band Openings and DX

The main thrill of the VHF and UHF bands for most of us is the occasional band opening, when signals from far away are received as if they are next door. DX of well over 1000 miles on 6 meters is commonplace during the summer, and the same distance at least once or twice a year on 144, 222, and 432 MHz in all but mountainous areas.

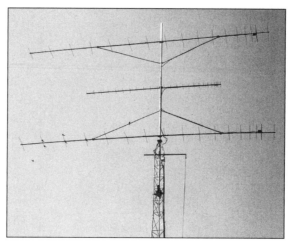

These Yagis for 144 and 432 MHz belong to Gedas, W8BYA, in grid EN70 (Indiana).

DX propagation on the VHF/UHF bands is strongly influenced by the seasons. Summer and fall are definitely the most active times in the spectrum above 50 MHz, although band openings occur at other times as well.

There are many different ways VHF and UHF signals propagate over long distances. These can be divided between conditions that exist in the troposphere (the weather-producing lowest 10 miles of the atmosphere) and the ionosphere (between 50 and 400 miles high). The two atmospheric regions are quite distinct and have little effect on each other.

Propagation Indicators

The Internet is a great resource for keeping abreast of VHF/UHF band openings. In addition to the DX Cluster spotting network, there are several VHF-specific websites such as the ON4KST chat rooms (**www.on4kst.com**) and DX Maps (**www.dxmaps.com**).

Active VHFers keep a careful eye on various propagation indicators to tell if the VHF bands will be open. The kind of indicator you monitor is related to the expected propagation. For example, during the summer it pays to watch closely for sporadic E because openings may be very brief. If your area only gets one or two per year on 2 meters, you sure don't want to miss them!

Many forms of VHF/UHF propagation develop first at low frequency and then move upward to include the higher bands. Aurora is a good

Owen, K3CB, is an active VHF/UHF operator from Maryland. The racks at the left house high power amplifiers that are helpful for contacts over marginal paths. [Andy Zwirko, K1RA, photo]

Rich, K1HTV, and Chuck, W4XP, operate a VHF contest with the K8GP team. [Andy Zwirko, K1RA, photo]

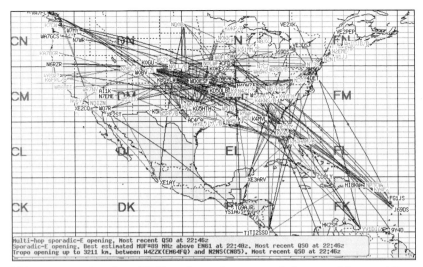

This screen capture from DX Maps (www.dxmaps.com) shows a widespread 6 meter sporadic opening in near real-time.

activity levels on the higher bands. It may be true that ducting affects the higher bands before the lower ones, but it is more likely to be noticed first on 2 meters, where many more stations are normally on the air. Six meter tropo openings are very rare because few inversion layers ever develop sufficient thickness to enhance such long-wavelength signals.

How can you monitor for band openings? The best way is to take advantage of commercial TV and FM broadcast stations, which serve admirably as propagation beacons. Television Channels 2 through 6 (54 – 88 MHz) are great for catching sporadic E. As the E opening develops, you will see one or more stations appear on each channel. First, you may see Channel 2 get cluttered with stations 1000 miles or more away, then the higher channels may follow. If you see strong DX stations on Channel 6, better get the 2 meter rig warmed up. Channel 7 is at 175 MHz, so you rarely see any sporadic E there or on any higher channels. If you do, however, it means that a major 2 meter opening is in progress!

The gap between TV Channel 6 and 7 is occupied partly by the FM broadcast band (88 – 108 MHz). Monitoring that spectrum will give you a similar feel for propagation conditions.

example. Usually it is heard first on 10 meters, then 6 meters, then 2 meters. Depending on your location and the intensity of the aurora, the time delay between hearing it on 6 meters and its appearance on 2 meters may be only a few minutes, to as much as an hour, later. Still, it shows up first at low frequency. The same is true of sporadic E; it will be noticed first on 10 meters, then 6, then 2.

Tropospheric propagation, particularly tropo ducting, acts in just the reverse manner. Inversions and ducts form at higher frequencies first. As the inversion layer grows in thickness, it refracts lower and lower frequencies. Even the most avid VHF operator may not notice this sequence because of lower

1.5.3 How Do I Operate on VHF/UHF?

The most important rule to follow on VHF/UHF, like all other amateur bands, is to listen first. Even on the relatively uncrowded VHF bands, interference is common near the calling frequencies. The first thing to do when you switch on the radio is to tune around, listening for activity. Of course, the calling frequencies are the best place to start listening. If you listen for a few minutes, you'll probably hear someone make a call, even if the band isn't open. If you don't hear anyone, then it's time to make some noise yourself!

Stirring up activity on the lower VHF bands is usually just a matter of pointing the antenna and calling CQ. Because most VHF beams are rather narrow, you might have to call CQ in several directions before you find someone. Several short CQs are always more productive than one long-winded CQ. But don't make CQs too short; you have to give the other station time to turn the antenna toward you.

Give your rotator lots of exercise; don't point the antenna at the same place all the time. You never know if a new station or some DX might be available at some odd beam

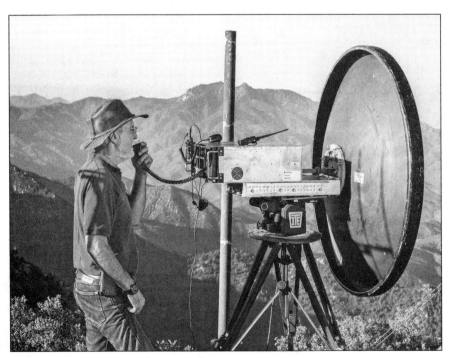

Kevin, AD7OI, operated the ARRL 10 GHz and Up Contest from Haydon Peak in Arizona and worked stations 400 km away. [Tammy Jackson, photo]

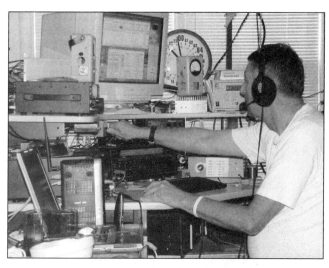

Dave, K1RZ, is a perennial top scorer in the VHF contests. [Andy Zwirko, K1RA, photo]

Ionospheric Forward Scatter

Scattering from the D and lower reaches of the E layers propagate VHF signals from 500 to a maximum of about 1000 miles. Signals at 50 MHz are apt to be very weak and fade in and out of the noise, even for the best equipped pairs of stations. Forward scatter contacts are much rarer at 144 MHz. SSB usually is not effective. The best times are at mid-day.

This mode is not used to its full potential, probably because forward scatter signals are often weak and easily overlooked. The best chances are for cooperating stations using CW in a quiet portion of the 50 or 144 MHz bands. Schedules may enhance the chances of success, but in any case, patience and a willingness to deal with weak fluttery signals is required. Contacts are sometimes completed via meteor scatter enhancement that by chance occurs at the same time.

Meteor Scatter

When meteors enter the Earth's atmosphere, they ionize a small trail through the E layer. This ionization typically lasts only a few seconds at 50 MHz, and for even shorter periods at higher frequencies. Before it dissipates, the ionization can scatter, or sometimes reflect, VHF radio waves. Meteor scatter signals may not last long, but they can be surprisingly strong, popping suddenly out of the noise and then slowly fading away.

Meteor scatter is very widely used on 50 and 144 MHz, and it has been used on 222 and 432 as well. Operation with this exciting mode of DX comes under two main headings: prearranged schedules and random contacts. Either SSB or CW may be used, although SSB is more popular in North America. The popular digital modes used for meteor scatter, based on *WSJT* software, are discussed in the next section.

Most SSB and CW meteor scatter work is done during major meteor showers, and stations often arrange schedules with stations in needed states or grid locators. In a sked, 15 second transmit-receive sequences are the norm for North America (Europeans use longer sequences). One station, almost always the westernmost, will take the first and third 15 second periods of each minute and the other station takes second and fourth. This is a very simple procedure that ensures that only one station is transmitting when a meteor falls. See accompanying sidebar.

A specific frequency, far removed from local activity centers, is chosen when the sked is set up. It is important that both stations have accurate frequency readout and synchronized clocks, but with today's technology this is not the big problem that it once was. Schedules normally run for 1/2 hour or 1 hour, especially

heading. VHFers in out-of-the-way locations, far from major cities, monitor the bands in the hope of hearing you.

Band Openings

How about DX? What is the best way to work DX when the band is open? There's no simple answer. Each main type of band opening or propagation mode requires its own techniques. This is natural, because the strength and duration of openings vary considerably. For example, you wouldn't expect to operate the same way during a 10 second meteor burst QSO as during a three-day tropo opening.

The following is a review of the different main types of propagation and descriptions of the ways that most VHFers take advantage of them.

Tropospheric Ducting

Ducts are responsible for the most common form of DX-producing propagation on the bands above 144 MHz. Ducts are like natural waveguides that trap signals close to the Earth for hundreds of miles with little loss of signal strength. They come in several forms, depending on local and regional weather patterns. This is because ducts are caused by the weather. Ducts may cover only a few hundred miles, or they may include huge areas of the country at once.

Tropospheric ducts, whatever their causes, affect the entire VHF through microwave range, although true ducting is rarely observed at 50 MHz. Ducts often persist for hours at a time, sometimes for several days, so there is usually no panic about making contacts. There is time to listen carefully and determine the extent of the opening and its likely evolution.

Ducts are most common in the Mississippi Valley during late summer and early fall, and they may expand over much of the country from the Rocky Mountains eastward. Sprawling high-pressure systems that slowly drift southeastward often create strong ducts. The best conditions usually appear in the southwestern quadrant of massive highs.

Along the East Coast, ducting is more common along coastal paths of up to 1000 miles and sometimes longer. Stations in New England have worked as far as Cuba on 2 meters this way. The mountainous west rarely experiences long-distance ducting.

This void is partially made up by one of the most famous of all ducting paths, which creates paths from the West Coast to Hawaii. The famous trans-Pacific duct opens up several times a year in summer, supporting often incredibly strong signals over 2500 miles on 144 MHz and up. Several world distance records have been made over this path. Other common over-water ducts appear across the Gulf of Mexico, mostly in early spring.

Ducts can be anticipated by studying weather maps and forecasts. Many VHFers also check television stations, especially in the UHF range, for early warnings of enhanced conditions. Check beacons on 144 MHz and higher, especially those you cannot ordinarily hear. Keep in mind that most forms of ducting intensify after sunset and peak just after sunrise. All of these techniques can enhance your chances of catching a ducting opening.

The APRS reporting network can show in real time the presence of and extent of tropospheric openings on 144 MHz (**aprs. mountainlake.k12.mn.us/**). There is an early warning system for the California to Hawaii duct at **dx.qsl.net/propagation/ tropo.php**.

SSB/CW Meteor Scatter Procedure

This sidebar covers SSB/CW meteor scatter procedures. See the text for information on digital mode meteor scatter operation with WSJT.

In a meteor scatter QSO, neither station can hear the other except when a meteor trail exists to scatter or reflect their signals. The two stations take turns transmitting so that they can be sure of hearing the other if a meteor happens to fall. They agree beforehand on the sequence of transmission. One station agrees to transmit the 1st and 3rd 15 seconds of each minute, and the other station takes the 2nd and 4th. It is standard procedure for the western-most station to transmit during the 1st and 3rd.

It's important to have a format for transmissions so you know what the other station has heard. This format is used by most US stations for CW and SSB:

Transmitting	Means you have copied
Call signs	nothing, or only partial calls
Call plus signal report (or grid or state)	full calls-both sets
ROGER plus signal report (or grid or state)	full calls, plus signal report (or grid or state)
ROGER	ROGER from other station

Remember, for a valid QSO to take place, you must exchange full call signs, some piece of information, and acknowledgment. Too many meteor QSOs have not been completed for lack of ROGERs. Don't quit too soon; be sure the other station has received your acknowledgment. Often, stations will add 73 when they want to indicate that they have heard the other station's ROGER.

Until a few years ago, it was universal practice to give a signal report which indicated the length of the meteor burst. S1 meant that you were just hearing pings, S2 meant 1-5 second bursts, and so on. Unfortunately, virtually everyone was sending S2, so there was no mystery at all, and no significant information was being exchanged.

Grid locators have become popular as the piece of information in meteor scatter QSOs. More and more stations are sending their grid instead of S2. This is especially true on random meteor scatter QSOs, where you might not know in advance where the station is located. Other stations prefer to give their state instead.

---

on 222 and 432 MHz where meteor scatter QSOs are well earned!

The best way to get the feel for the meteor scatter QSO format is to listen to a couple of skeds between experienced operators. Then, ask around for the call sign of veteran meteor scatter operators in the 800 – 1000 mile range from you (this is the easiest distance for meteor scatter). Contact them and arrange a sked. After you cut your teeth on easy skeds, you'll be ready for more difficult DX.

A lot of stations make plenty of meteor scatter QSOs without the help of skeds. Especially during major meteor showers, VHFers congregate near the calling frequency of each band. There they wait for meteor bursts like hunters waiting for ducks. Energetic operators make repeated and brief CQs, hoping to catch an elusive meteor. When meteors blast in, the band comes alive with dozens of quick QSOs. For a brief time, normally five seconds to perhaps 30 seconds, 2 meters may sound like 20 meters! Then the band is quiet again... until the next meteor burst!

The quality of shower-related meteor scatter DX depends on three factors. These three factors are well known or can be predicted. The most important is the radiant effect. The radiant is the spot in the sky from which the meteors appear to fall. If the radiant is below the horizon, or too high in the sky, you will

hear very few meteors. The most productive spot for the radiant is at an elevation of about 45° and an azimuth of 90° from the path you're trying to work. The second important factor is the velocity of the meteors. Slow meteors cannot ionize sufficiently to propagate 144 or 222 MHz signals, no matter how many meteors there are. For 144 MHz, meteors slower than 50 km/s are usually inadequate (see accompanying sidebar detailing major meteor showers). Third, the shower will have a peak in the number of meteors that the Earth intercepts. However, because the peak of many meteor showers is more than a day in length, the exact time of the peak is not as important as most people think.

It takes a lot of persistence and a good station to be successful with random meteor scatter. This is mainly because you must overcome tremendous interference in addition to the fluctuations of meteor propagation. At least 100 W is necessary for much success in meteor scatter, and a full kilowatt will help a lot. One or two Yagis, stacked vertically, is a good antenna system. Antennas with too much gain have narrow beamwidths, and so often cannot pick up many usable meteor scatter bursts.

In populated areas, it can be difficult to hear incoming meteor scatter DX if many local stations are calling CQ. Therefore, many areas

observe 15 second sequencing for random meteor scatter QSOs, just as for skeds. Those who want to call CQ do so at the same time so everyone can listen for responses between transmissions. Sometimes a bit of peer pressure is necessary to keep everyone together, but it pays off in more QSOs for all. The same QSO format is used for scheduled and random meteor scatter QSOs.

Meteor Scatter with WSJT

It may come as a surprise to learn that meteors are plunging into Earth's atmosphere around the clock, not just during annual meteor showers. Dust-grain meteors leave so-called *underdense meteor trails* that will reflect VHF radio signals, albeit briefly (seconds or fractions of seconds). Even in this narrow window of time, it is possible to communicate with bursts of digital data over distances of more than 1000 miles.

Joe Taylor, K1JT, set out to design a digital encoding scheme and software package to enable amateur QSOs using the brief *pings* (signal reflections) from underdense meteor trails. The result led to a computer program called *WSJT* (for "Weak Signal Communication, by K1JT") that implements a signal protocol called FSK441. The mode works so well that it has been rapidly embraced by the VHF fraternities in Europe and North America, and is now making inroads in Africa and the South Pacific as well.

If your station is capable of weak signal SSB work on the 6 meter or 2 meter bands — say, if you have 100 W or more to a modest Yagi up at least 40 feet — then with the help of *WSJT* you should be able to work similarly equipped stations in the 500 – 1100 mile range at nearly any time of the day or year. (On the minimum end of the scale, *WSJT* QSOs have been made with as little as 10 W.) With a higher antenna and more power, QSOs out to 1300 or 1400 miles become possible. QSOs have already been made with *WSJT* on 222 MHz as well, and contacts on 432 MHz might be possible near the peak of a major meteor shower.

WHAT DO YOU NEED?

WSJT requires an SSB transceiver, a computer running the *Windows* operating system, and a soundcard interfaced to the radio's "microphone in" and "speaker out" ports. *Mac OS* and *Linux* versions are also available. You will, of course, need a station capable of weak signal work on one or more VHF bands. The *WSJT* program is available for download free of charge at the website **physics.princeton. edu/pulsar/K1JT**.

You will need a sound card interface. The DTR or RTS line of one of the computer's serial communication (COM) ports is used to key your transmitter's push-to-talk (PTT)

Meteor Showers

Every day, the Earth is bombarded by billions of tiny grains of interplanetary debris, called meteors. They create short-lived trails of E-layer ionization which can be used as reflectors for VHF radio waves. On a normal morning, careful listeners can hear about 3 – 5 meteor pings (short bursts of meteor reflected signal) per hour on 2 meters.

At several times during the year, the Earth passes through huge clouds of concentrated meteoric debris, and VHFers enjoy a meteor shower. During meteor showers, 2 meter operators may hear 50 or more pings and bursts per hour. Here are some data on the major meteor showers of the year. Other showers also occur, but they are very minor.

Major Meteor Showers

Shower	Date range	Peak date	Time above quarter max	Approximate visual rate	Speed km/s	Best Paths and Times (local)
Quadrantids	Jan 1-6	Jan 3/4	14 hours	40-150	41	NE-SW (1300-1500), SE-NW (0500-0700)
Eta Aquarids	Apr 21-May 12	May 4/5	3 days	10-40	65	NE-SW (0500-0700), E-W (0600-0900), SE-NW (0900-1100)
Arietids	May 29-Jun 19	Jun 7	?	60	37	N-S (0600-0700 and 1300-1400)
Perseids	Jul 23-Aug 20	Aug 12	4.6 days	50-100	59	NE-SW (0900-1100), SE-NW (0100-0300)
Orionids	Oct 2-Nov 7	Oct 22	2 days	10-70	66	NE-SW (0100-0300), N-S (0100-0200 & 0700-0900), NW-SE (0700-0800)
Geminids	Dec 4-16	Dec 13/14	2.6 days	50-80	34	N-S (2200-2400 and 0500-0700)

line. Connections are also required between the transceiver audio output and computer sound card input, and vice versa. If your computer is already set up for sound-card-based HF digital modes as described in the HF Digital Communications section, you already have everything you need to operate *WSJT*.

Timing is critical when it comes to *WSJT* meteor scatter because stations typically transmit for 30 seconds and then listen for 30 seconds. You will need a method of synchronizing your computer clock with UTC to an accuracy around one second or better. If you have an Internet connection and you are using *Windows*, look under Date and Time in the Control Panel. There you will find a function that will synchronize your PC. Otherwise, try a synchronizing utility program called *Dimension 4* that you can download from the web at **www.thinkman.com/dimension4/**.

HOW DOES IT WORK?

The encoding scheme used in *WSJT* was designed to make the best use of signals just a few decibels above the receiver noise, exhibiting rapid fading and Doppler shifts up to 100 Hz, and typically lasting from 20 to a few hundred milliseconds. One *WSJT* protocol uses a four-tone frequency shift keying at a rate of 441 baud. The adopted scheme was been given the technical name FSK441, although most people seem to be calling it simply "the *WSJT* mode."

An FSK441 transmission contains no dead spaces between tones or between characters; the typical short messages exchanged in meteor scatter QSOs are sent repeatedly and continuously, usually for 30 seconds at a time.

At the top of the *WSJT* screen are two graphical areas. The larger one displays a "waterfall" spectrogram in which time runs left to right and audio frequency increases upward. The smaller graphical window at the right displays two spectral plots, also on a dB scale. The purple line graphs the spectrum of audio-frequency noise, averaged over the full 30 seconds; in the absence of any strong signal, it effectively illustrates the receiver's passband shape. The red line displays the spectrum of the strongest detected ping. Yellow tick marks at the top of this plot area (and also at the left, center, and right of the larger area) indicate the nominal frequencies of the four FSK441 tones.

The large text box in the middle of the *WSJT* screen displays decoded text from any pings detected in the receiving interval. One line of text appears for each validated ping.

Meteor scatter is not a communication mode well suited to rag chewing. QSOs can

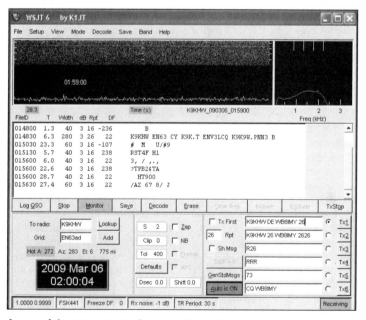

A powerful meteor scatter burst received with *WSJT* software during the Geminids meteor shower.

be completed much more easily if you adhere to a set of standard procedures. A standard message format and message sequence helps the process considerably. *WSJT* generates standard messages automatically, as illustrated in the text boxes at the lower right of screen. The formats of the messages are designed for efficient transfer of the most essential information: the exchange of both call signs, a signal report or other information, and acknowledgments of same. Timed message sequences are necessary, and *WSJT* defaults to 30 second transmitting and receiving periods. Although other intervals can be selected, it helps to minimize QRM from nearby stations if everyone adheres to one standard. According to the procedures used by common consent in North America, the westernmost station transmits first in each minute.

At the start of a QSO, you should send the other station's call and your own call alternately. Then, as the QSO proceeds…

1. If you have received less than both calls from the other station, send both calls.

2. If you have received both calls, send both calls and a signal report.

3. If you have received both calls and a report, send R plus signal report.

4. If you have received R plus signal report, send RRR.

5. If you have received RRR — that is, a definite acknowledgment of all of your information — your QSO is officially complete. However, the other station may not know this, so it is conventional to send 73 (or some other conversational information) to signify that you are done.

Signal reports are conventionally sent as two-digit numbers chosen from nonoverlapping ranges. The first digit characterizes the lengths of pings being received, on a 1 – 5 scale, and the second estimates their strength on a 6 – 9 scale. The most common signal reports are "26" for weak pings and "27" for stronger ones, but under good conditions reports such as "38" and higher are sometimes used. Whatever signal report you decide to send to your QSO partner, it is important that you do not change it, even if stronger pings should come along later in the contact. You never know when pings will successfully convey fragments of your message to the other end of your path, and you want your received information to be consistent.

The 6 and 2 meter calling frequencies in common use for *WSJT* in North America are 50.270 and 144.140 MHz. Typical practice for calling CQ is to send something like CQ U5 K1JT or CQ D9 K1JT, indicating that you will listen for replies up 5 kHz or down 9 kHz from your transmitting frequency, and will respond on that frequency. However, the easiest way to initiate a QSO is to post an on-line invitation on a web page known as

Ping Jockey Central at **www.pingjockey.net**. Someone at a suitable range from you will likely reply to such a posting, suggesting a specific frequency, and your QSO can begin. The ranges of frequencies now being used for *WSJT* in North America are 50.270 – 50.300 and 144.100 – 144.150 MHz.

Sporadic E

This type of propagation is the most spectacular DX-producer on the 50 MHz band, where it may occur almost every day from late May to early August. A less intense E_s season also occurs during December and January. Sporadic E is most common in mid-morning and again around sunset during the summer months, but it can occur any time, any date. E_s occurs on 2 meters several times a summer somewhere across the US.

E_s is the result of the formation of thin but unusually dense clouds of ionization in the E layer. These clouds appear to move about, intensify, and disappear rapidly and without warning. The causes of sporadic E are not fully understood.

Reflections from sporadic-E clouds make single-hop contacts of 500 to 1400 miles possible on 50 MHz and much more rarely on 144 MHz. Sporadic E contacts are possible but very rare on 222 MHz. Multi-hop E_s contacts commonly provide several coast-to-coast openings on 6 meters each summer and even opportunities to work Europe and Japan! The longest sporadic-E contacts are in excess of 6000 miles, but these are rare.

Sporadic-E signals are generally so loud and openings last long enough that no special operating techniques are necessary to enjoy this mode. On 6 meters, 10 W stations with simple antennas can easily make contacts out to 1000 miles or so. The band may open for only 15 minutes, or for many hours on any summer day, with signals constantly shifting, disappearing and reappearing. A sporadic-E opening on 2 meters is much less common and typically lasts for less than an hour. Signals out to 1000 miles or so can be unbelievably strong, yet there is reason to be more alert. E-skip openings on 2 meters are rare and do not usually last long.

The main question for those hoping for sporadic E is when the band will open. Aside from knowing sporadic E is more common in summer mornings and early evenings than any other times, there is no satisfactory way to predict E-skip. It can appear any time.

Sporadic E affects lower frequencies first, so you can get some warning by listening to 10 meters. When E-skip shortens to 500 miles or so, it is almost certain that there is propagation somewhere on 6 meters. Some avid E-skip fans monitor TV channel 2 or 3 (if there is no local station) for signs of sporadic E.

Aurora and Auroral E

The aurora borealis, or northern lights, is a beautiful spectacle which is seen occasionally by those who live in Canada, the northern part of the USA and northern Europe. Similar southern lights are sometimes visible in the southernmost parts of South America, Africa and Australia. The aurora is caused by the Earth intercepting a massive number of charged particles thrown from the Sun during a solar storm. These particles are funneled into the polar regions of the Earth by its magnetic field. As the charged particles interact with the upper atmosphere, the air glows, which we see as the aurora. These particles also create an irregular, moving curtain of ionization which can propagate signals for many hundreds of miles.

Like sporadic E, aurora is more evident on 6 meters than on 2 meters. Nevertheless, 2 meter aurora is far more common than 2 meter sporadic E, at least above 40° N latitude. Auroral propagation is also possible on 222 and 432 MHz, and many tremendous DX contacts have been made on these bands. Current record distances are over 1000 miles on 144, 222, and 432 MHz.

Aurora can be predicted to some extent from current reports of solar and geomagnetic activity, which can be found on most DX clusters, on websites sponsored by the National Oceanic and Atmospheric Administration, and on WWV broadcasts. At 18 minutes past each hour, WWV transmits a summary of the condition of the Earth's geomagnetic field. If the K index is 4 or above, you should watch for Au. Many VHFers have learned that a high K index is no guarantee of an aurora. Similarly, K indices of only 3 have occasionally produced spectacular radio auroras at middle latitudes. When in doubt, point the antenna north and listen!

Several websites provide information for early warning of auroral propagation. Space Weather (**www.spaceweather.com**) and Aurora Sentry (**www.aurorasentry.com**) are two good resources for this.

Aurora (Au) favors stations at high latitudes. It is a wonderful blessing for those who must suffer through long, cold winters because other forms of propagation are rare during the winter. Aurora can come at almost any time of the year. New England stations get Au on 2 meters about five to 10 times a year, whereas stations in Tennessee get it once a year if they're lucky. Central and Southern California rarely hear aurora.

The MUF of the aurora seems to rise quickly, so don't wait for the lower-frequency VHF bands to get exhausted before moving up in frequency. Check the higher bands right away.

You'll notice aurora by its characteristic hiss. Signals are distorted by reflection and scattering off the rapidly moving curtain of ionization. They sound like they are being transmitted by a leaking high-pressure steam vent rather than radio. SSB voice signals are so badly distorted that often you cannot understand them unless the speaker talks very slowly and clearly. The amount of distortion increases with frequency. Most 50 MHz Au contacts are made on SSB, where distortion is the least. On 144, 222 and 432 MHz, CW is the only really useful means of communicating via Au.

If you suspect Au, tune to the CW calling frequency (144.110) or the SSB calling frequency (144.200) and listen with the antenna to the north. Maybe you'll hear some signals. Try swinging the antenna as much as 45° either side of due north to peak signals. In general, the longest-distance DX stations peak the farthest away from due north. Also,

it is possible to work stations far south of you by using the aurora; in that case your antenna is often pointed north.

High power isn't necessary for aurora, but it helps. Ten-watt stations have made Au QSOs but it takes a lot of perseverance. Increasing your power to 100 W will greatly improve your chances of making Au QSOs. As with most short-lived DX openings, it pays to keep transmissions brief.

Aurora openings may last only a few minutes or they may last many hours, and the opening may return the next night, too. If WWV indicates a geomagnetic storm, begin listening on 2 meters in the late afternoon. Many spectacular Au openings begin before sunset and continue all evening. If you get the feeling that the Au has faded away, don't give up too soon. Aurora has a habit of dying

and then returning several times, often around midnight. If you experience a terrific Au opening, look for an encore performance about 27 to 28 days later, because of the rotation of the Sun.

Auroral-E propagation is nearly a nightly occurrence in the auroral zone, but it may accompany auroras at lower latitudes. Do not be surprised to hear rough-sounding auroral signals on 6 meters slowly turn clear and strong! Auroral E is probably more common after local midnight after any evening when there has been an aurora. Auroral E propagation can last until nearly dawn. Six meter contacts up to 2500 miles across northern latitudes (such as Maine to Yukon Territory) are not uncommon. Two meter auroral E may also be commonplace in the arctic, but it is very rarely observed south of Canada.

1.5.4 EME: Earth-Moon-Earth

EME operators use the Moon as a passive reflector for their signals, and QSO distance is limited only by the diameter of the Earth. Any two stations who can simultaneously see the Moon may be able to work each other via EME. QSOs between the USA and Europe or Japan are commonplace on VHF and UHF by using this mode. That's DX!

Improvements in technology — low-noise preamplifiers, better antenna designs and DSP-based digital modes — have made it easier to get started. Also, several individuals have assembled gigantic antenna arrays, which make up for the inadequacy of smaller antennas. The result is that even modestly equipped VHF stations (150 W and one or two Yagis) are capable of making moonbounce contacts on CW with the large stations.

Moonbounce using CW requires larger antennas than most terrestrial VHF/UHF work. In addition, you must have a high-power transmitting amplifier and a low-noise receiving preamplifier to work more than the biggest guns. A modest CW EME station on 144 MHz consists of four long boom Yagi antennas on an azimuth-elevation mount (for pointing at the Moon), a kilowatt amplifier and a low-noise preamplifier mounted at the antenna. On 432 MHz, the average antenna for EME stations is eight long Yagis. You can make contacts with a smaller antenna, but they will be with only larger stations on the other end. Some UHFers have also built large parabolic dish antennas.

With the introduction of DSP-based digital modes, the hardware requirements for

Digital modes and improvements to antennas and receivers have made EME with a small station possible. Paul, K4MSG, uses a pair of 18 element Yagis and 170 W for his 432 MHz EME contacts. [Paul Bock, K4MSG, photo]

EME are much simpler. The JT65 mode in the *WSJT* software package allows decoding of signals 10 dB or more weaker than the humans can detect. That opens the world of EME to stations with 50 to 100 W and a single antenna.

EME, or moonbounce, is available any

time the Moon is in a favorable position. Fortunately, the Moon's position may be easily calculated in advance, so you always know when this form of DX will be ready. It's not actually that simple, of course, because the Earth's geomagnetic field can play havoc with EME signals as they leave the Earth's atmosphere and as they return. Not only can absorption (path loss) vary, but the polarization of the radio waves can rotate, causing abnormally high path losses at some times. Still, most EME activity is predictable.

The most popular band for EME is 144 MHz, followed by 432 MHz. Other bands with regular EME activity are 1296 and 2304/2320 MHz. You will find many more signals off the Moon during times when the Moon is nearest the Earth (perigee), when it is overhead at relatively high northern latitudes (positive declination), and when the Moon is nearly at full phase. The one weekend per month which has the best combination of these three factors is informally designated the activity or skeds weekend, and most EMEers will be on the air then. This is particularly true for 432 EME; 144 MHz EME is active during the week and on non-skeds weekends as well.

CW EME Procedures

The majority of CW EME QSOs are made without any prearranged schedules and usually without rigid transmitting time-slot sequencing. Just as in CW QSOs on HF, you transmit when the other station turns it over to you. This is particularly true during EME contests, where time-slot transmissions slow down the exchange of information. Why take 10-15 minutes when two or three will do?

Moonbounce procedure for scheduled CW QSOs is different on 144 and 432 MHz. On 144 MHz, schedule transmissions are

Table 1.12
CW EME Signal Report and Meaning

Report	144 MHz	432 MHz
T	Signal just detectable	Portions of calls copyable
M	Portions of calls copyable	Complete calls copied
O	Both calls fully copied	Good signal, easily copied
R	Both calls and O signal report copied	Calls and report copied

2 minutes long, whereas on 432 they are 2½ minutes long. In addition, the meaning of signal reports is different on the two bands (see **Table 1.12**). Note that M reports aren't good enough for a valid QSO on 2 meters but they are good enough on 432. On both bands, if signals are really good, then normal RST reports are exchanged.

On 144 MHz, each station transmits for 2 minutes, then listens as the other station transmits. Which 2-minute sequence you transmit in is agreed to in advance. During the schedule, at the point when you've copied portions of both calls, the last 30 seconds of your 2-minute sequence is reserved for signal reports; otherwise, call sets are transmitted for the full 2 minutes.

On 432 MHz, sequences are longer. Each transmitting slot is 2½ minutes. You either transmit first or second. Naturally, first means that you transmit for the first 2½ minutes of each 5 minutes.

On 222 MHz, some stations use the 144 MHz procedure and some use the 432 MHz procedure. Which one is used is determined

in advance. On 1296 and above, the 432 procedure is always used.

EME operation generally takes place in the lowest parts of the VHF bands: 144.000 – 144.070; 222.000 – 222.025; 432.000 – 432.070; 1296.000 – 1296.050. Terrestrial QSOs are strongly discouraged in these portions of the bands. Activity on 10 GHz EME, which requires only a few watts when used with dish antennas 10 feet or more in diameter, is becoming increasingly popular.

Digital Modes for EME

As with meteor scatter, digital modes have appeared for EME as well. The *WSJT* software suite includes a mode known as JT65. This software has made moonbounce contacts possible using sound-card-equipped PCs, single Yagi antennas and 150 W or less — a feat that seemed impossible just a few years earlier. JT65 has finally put EME communication within the grasp of amateurs with limited antenna space and equally limited bank accounts.

1.5.5 Hilltopping and Portable Operation

One of the nice things about the VHF/UHF bands is that antennas are relatively small, and station equipment can be packed up and easily transported. Portable operation, commonly called hilltopping or mountaintopping, is a favorite activity for many amateurs. This is especially true during VHF and UHF contests, where a station can be very popular by being located in a rare grid. If you are on a hilltop or mountaintop as well, you will have a very competitive signal.

Hilltopping is fun and exciting because hills elevate your antenna far above surrounding terrain and therefore your VHF/UHF range is greatly extended. If you live in a low-lying area such as a valley, a drive up to the top of a nearby hill or mountain will have the same effect as buying a new tower and antenna, a high-power amplifier and a preamplifier, all in one!

The popularity of hilltopping has grown as

Mike, KD7TS, with his multiband VHF/UHF/microwave van on Burley Mountain, Washington. Another van belonging to Dale, KD7UO, can be seen in the background. [Mike Reed, KD7TS, photo]

The "portable extreme" 6 and 2 meter antennas used by Mike, K7ULS, take hilltopping to a higher level. [Mike White, K7ULS, photo]

equipment has become more portable. There are many high power, good performing HF + 6 meter radios on the market. Other models offer 25 W up to 75 or 100 W on 144 and 432 MHz, and a couple even cover 1296 MHz with optional modules. You need no other power source than a car battery, and even with a simple antenna your signals will be outstanding.

Many VHF/UHFers drive to the top of hills or mountains and set up their station. A hilltop park, rest area, or farmer's field are equally good sites, so long as they are clear of trees and obstructions. You should watch out for high-power FM or TV broadcasters who may also be taking advantage of the hill's good location; their powerful signals may cause intermodulation problems in your receiver.

Antennas, on a couple of 10-foot mast sections, may be turned by hand as the operator sits in the passenger seat of the car. A few hours of operating like this can be wonderfully enjoyable and can net you a lot of good VHF/UHF DX. In fact, some VHF enthusiasts have very modest home stations but rather elaborate hilltopping stations. When they notice that band conditions are improving, they hop in the car and head for the hills. There, they have a really excellent site and can make many more QSOs.

In some places, there are no roads to the tops of hills or mountains where you might wish to operate. In this case, it is a simple (but sometimes strenuous) affair to hike to the top, carrying the battery, rig, and antenna. Many hilltoppers have had great fun by setting up on the top of a fire tower on a hilltop, relying on a battery for power.

Some VHF/UHFers, especially contesters, like to take the entire station, high power amplifiers and all, to hilltops for extended operation. They may stay there for several days, camping out and DXing. Probably the most outstanding example of this kind of operation is seen during VHF contests, from stations operating in the multioperator category. Dozens of operators and helpers bring equipment for 6 meters through microwaves to the highest mountaintops and contact everyone within range.

1.5.6 Contests

The greatest amount of activity on the VHF/UHF bands occurs during contests. VHF/UHF contests are scheduled for some of the best propagation dates during the year. Not only are propagation conditions generally good, but activity is always very high. Many stations come out of the woodwork just for the contest, and many individuals and groups go hilltopping to rare states or grids.

There are quite a few contests for the world above 50 MHz. Some are for all the VHF and UHF bands, while others are for one band only. Some run for entire weekends and others for only a few hours. Despite their differences, all contests share a basic similarity. In most North American contests, your score is determined by the number of contacts (or more precisely, the number of QSO points) you make, times some multiplier, which is most often grid locators. In most of the current major contests, you keep track of QSOs and multipliers by band. In other words, you can work the same station on each band for separate QSO and multiplier credit.

One interesting aspect to VHF/UHF contests are "rover" stations with one or two

Bruce, W9FZ, is a frequent "rover" in VHF contests. [Bruce Richardson, W9FZ, photo]

operators that move among two or more grid locators during the contest. Rovers may contact the same stations all over again from a different grid. Most rovers operate from a car, van or truck specially equipped for convenience and efficiency. Hilltops in rare grids are favored rover sites. Rovers must move the entire station, antennas and power supply to qualify. Special scoring rules apply to rovers.

The major VHF through microwave contests in North America include the ARRL January, June and September VHF Contests, the *CQ* Worldwide VHF Contest, the ARRL UHF Contest, the ARRL 10-GHz and Up Cumulative Contest, and the ARRL EME Contest. Detailed rules for each contest are published by the sponsoring organizations and available online.

Awards

Several awards sponsored by ARRL help stir activity on the VHF and higher bands. Many of those originally designed for HF operators, including Worked All States (WAS), Worked All Continents (WAC) and DX Century Club (DXCC) are also coveted by operators on 6 meters and higher. The VHF/UHF Century Club (VUCC) is designed only for the world above 50 MHz. See Section 3 of this book for more information on contests and awards.

1.5.7 VHF/UHF Resources

ARRL website:
www.arrl.org/the-world-above-50-mhz
ARRL website:
www.arrl.org/vhf-uhf-microwave-weak-signal
ARRL website:
www.arrl.org/weak-signal-vhf-dx-meteor-scatter-eme-moonbounce
Central States VHF Society:
www.csvhf.org
Grid locators:
www.arrl.org/about-grid-squares
www.arrl.org/grid-locator
M. Owen, W9IP, "VHF Meteor Scatter: an Astronomical Perspective," *QST*, Jun 1986.
E. Pocock, W3EP, "The Weather That Brings VHF DX," *QST*, May 1983, pp 11-16.
J. Reisert, W1JR, "Improving Meteor Scatter Communications," *Ham Radio*, Jun 1984.

Meteor scatter: **www.pingjockey.net**
Northeast Weak Signal Group: **www.newsvhf.com**
Mt Airy VHF Radio Club (Packrats): **www.packratvhf.com**
San Bernardino Microwave Society:
www.ham-radio.com/sbms/
Southeastern VHF Society: **svhfs.org/wp/**
WSJT and JT65 for EME and terrestrial VHF/UHF:
physics.princeton.edu/pulsar/k1jt
www.dxmaps.com/jt65bintro.html
www.bigskyspaces.com/w7gj/6memetips.htm.
144 MHz EME Newsletter: **www.df2zc.de**
432 MHz and Above EME Newsletter:
www.nitehawk.com/rasmit/em70cm.html

You can also find more technical information in *The ARRL Handbook* and *The ARRL Antenna Book*, as well as *Amateur Radio on the Move* and *Your Mobile Companion*, all available from your favorite ham radio dealer or the ARRL website.

1.6 Amateur Satellites

Hams created the first amateur satellite in 1961, and we've been active ever since. Even so, satellite-active hams compose a relatively small segment of our hobby, primarily because of an unfortunate fiction that has been circulating for many years — the myth that operating through amateur satellites is difficult and expensive.

As with any other facet of Amateur Radio, satellite hamming is as expensive as you allow it to become. If you want to simply communicate with a few low-Earth-orbiting birds using less-than-state-of-the-art gear, a satellite station is no more expensive than a typical HF or VHF setup.

What about difficulty? Computers do all of the satellite orbit calculations for you and display the results in easy to understand formats (more about this later). Satellite equipment also has become much easier for the average ham to use.

Sean, KX9X, (foreground) and Mike, W5MPC, listen to an amateur satellite pass.

1.6.1 Satellite Orbits and Tracking

When this section was written, there were no amateur satellites traveling in *geostationary* orbits. The speed of a satellite in geostationary orbit matches the speed of the Earth's rotation at the equator. As a result, it remains fixed at a single point in the sky 24 hours a day. There is never any doubt about where the satellite is located. You simply aim your antenna at the bird and communicate. Home satellite TV systems are good examples of this concept. Their rooftop parabolic dish antennas never move — they don't need to. Their target is always in the same place.

Amateur satellites — often known as *OSCARs*, Orbiting Satellite Carrying Amateur Radio — usually travel in orbits close to the Earth, or in oblong, elliptical orbits that take them far into space (beyond where geostationary birds reside) before bringing them back toward Earth for a close, slingshot pass. The speeds of these satellites do not match the speed of the Earth's rotation, so they do not remain at fixed points in the sky. Instead, amateur satellites rise above the horizon, soar

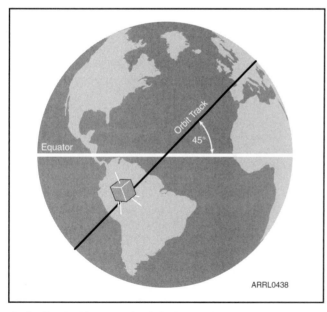

An *inclined* orbit is one that is inclined with respect to the Earth's equator. In this example, the satellite's orbit is inclined at 45° to the Equator.

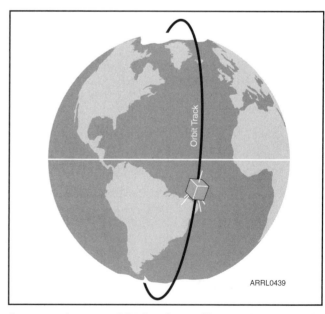

A *sun-synchronous* orbit takes the satellite over the north and south poles. A satellite in this orbit allows every station in the world to enjoy at least one high-elevation pass per day.

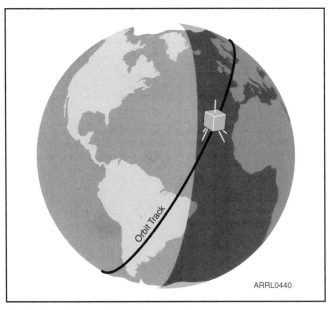

A *dawn-to-dusk* orbit is a variation on the sun-synchronous model except that the satellite spends most of its time in sunlight and relatively little time in eclipse.

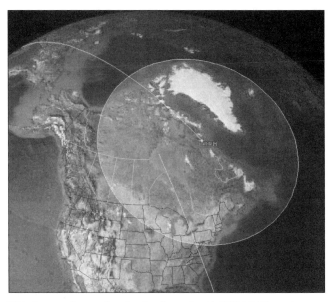

This image shows the circular footprint of OSCAR 52 as depicted by *NOVA* satellite-tracking software. The footprint indicates the area of the Earth that is visible to the satellite at any given time.

to a certain altitude (elevation) and then set below the horizon once again. Depending on the nature of the orbit, a satellite may be above the horizon for hours or for only a few minutes. The satellite may appear several times each day, but each pass will be at a different maximum elevation and will follow a different track across the heavens. To add to the confusion, a satellite may not appear at the same times each day, although it will follow predictable arrival patterns when plotted over days or weeks.

To enjoy an Amateur Radio satellite you need to know where it is, when it will arrive and how it will move across the sky. You need a basic understanding of satellite orbits and a computer program that will take the information about a satellite's orbit and turn it into accurate predictions of when it will appear.

Types of Orbits

Most active amateur satellites are in various types of *Low Earth Orbits* (LEOs). Let's take a brief look at several of the most common orbits.

An *inclined* orbit is one that is inclined with respect to the Earth's equator. A satellite that is inclined 90° would be orbiting from pole to pole; smaller inclination angles mean that the satellite is spending more time at lower latitudes. The International Space Station, for

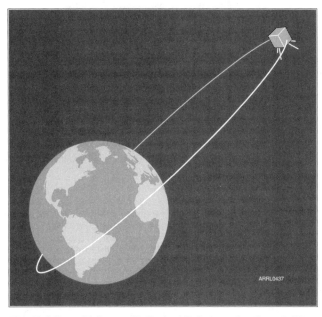

The *Molniya* orbit is an elliptical orbit that carries the satellite far into space at its greatest distance from Earth (apogee). To observers on the ground, the satellite at apogee appears to hover for hours at a time before it plunges earthward and (often) sweeps within 1000 km at its closest approach (perigee).

example, travels in an orbit that is inclined about 50° to the equator. Satellites that move in these orbits frequently fall into the Earth's shadow (eclipse), so they must rely on battery systems to provide power when the solar panels are not illuminated. Depending on the inclination angle, some locations on the Earth will never have good access because the satellites will rarely rise above their local horizons.

A *sun-synchronous* orbit takes the satel-

lite over the north and south poles. There are two advantages to a sun-synchronous orbit: (1) the satellite is available at approximately the same time of day, every day and (2) everyone, no matter where they are, will enjoy at least one high-altitude pass per day.

A *dawn-to-dusk* orbit is a variation on the sun-synchronous model except that the satellite spends most of its time in sunlight and relatively little time in eclipse.

The *Molniya* High Earth Orbit was pioneered by the former Soviet Union. It is an elliptical orbit that carries the satellite far into space at its greatest distance from Earth (apogee). To observers on the ground, the satellite at apogee appears to hover for hours at a time before it plunges earthward and sweeps to (sometimes) within 1000 km or so of the Earth at its closest approach (perigee). One great advantage of the Molniya orbit is that the satellite is capable of "seeing" an entire hemisphere of the planet while at apogee. Hams can use a Molniya satellite to enjoy long, leisurely conversations spanning thousands of kilometers here on Earth.

SATELLITE FOOTPRINTS

Speaking of how much of our planet a satellite sees, it is important to understand the concept of the satellite's *footprint*. A satellite footprint can be loosely defined as the area on the Earth's surface that is "illuminated" by the satellite's antenna systems at any given time. Another way to think of a footprint is to regard it as the zone within which stations can communicate with each other through the satellite.

Unless the satellite in question is geostationary, footprints are constantly moving. Their sizes can vary considerably, depending on the altitude of the satellite. The footprint of the low-orbiting International Space Station is about 600 km in diameter. In contrast, a higher orbiting OSCAR satellite might have a footprint that is nearly 1500 km across. The amount of time you have available to communicate depends on how long your station remains within the footprint. This time can be measured in minutes, or in the case of a satellite in a Molniya orbit, hours.

Understanding Your Place in the World

Before you can track an amateur satellite and communicate with it, you must first determine your own location with reasonable accuracy and understand your orientation to the expected path of the satellite.

Determining your location on the globe in terms of latitude and longitude coordinates is much easier today than it used be. If you own a Global Positioning System (GPS) receiver, you can use it to determine your coordinates almost instantly. If you don't own a GPS receiver, the Internet is your next best option. There are a number of mapping websites such as Google Maps where you can enter your street address and see a map that includes your latitude and longitude.

How precise do you need to be? If you plan on using movable directional "beam" antennas for your satellite station, the more precision the better. Your satellite tracking software will determine this direction for you, but its ability to give you accurate aiming information is highly dependent on it "knowing" where you are located in the first place. On the other hand, if you are using omnidirectional antennas that create broad radiation patterns, or directional antennas that don't move, the need for precision is less critical. In fact, the latitude and longitude of the nearest city will suffice.

Azimuth and Elevation

Once the tracking software knows your approximate position, it can predict a satellite's path across your local sky. The software will indicate the satellite's predicted position in terms of its *azimuth* and *elevation* relative to your station.

Azimuth describes the satellite's position in degrees referenced to true north. Imagine your station in the center of a giant compass circle that is divided in degree increments from 0 to 360. North is 0° (it is also 360°), east is 90°, south is 180° and west is 270°. If your tracking software indicates that you need to point your antenna to an azimuth of 135° to intercept the satellite, for example, you're going to point the antenna southeast.

Let's take a look at a more detailed example. Once again, your station is in the center of the compass circle. According to your satellite tracking program, the International Space Station (ISS) is scheduled to rise above your local horizon at precisely 03:57:30 UTC. The program may describe the satellite's azimuth path like this:

Time	Azimuth (degrees)
03:57	307
03:58	350
03:59	0
04:00	11
04:01	20
04:02	30

When you plot these azimuth points on the circle, you can quickly see the horizontal path the satellite is going to take. The bird is going to rise in your northwestern sky and quickly move toward the east, finally dipping below your northeast horizon at about 30°. If you have rotating antennas, you can see that they'll need to be pointing northwest at the beginning of the satellite's pass. As the satellite moves across the sky, your antennas will need to track around the circle from 307°, to 0° and so on until they are pointing at 30° azimuth when the satellite finally disappears.

Let's add another dimension to our satellite track — *elevation*. Elevation is simply the angle, in degrees, between your station and the satellite, referenced to the Earth's surface. The elevation angle begins at 0° with the satellite at the horizon and increases to 90° when the satellite is directly overhead. Elevation is every bit as critical as azimuth if you are using directional antennas. Not only do your antennas need to be pointed at the satellite as it appears to move in the horizontal plane, they must also tilt up and down to track

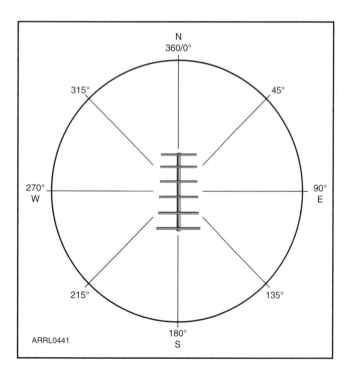

ARRL0441

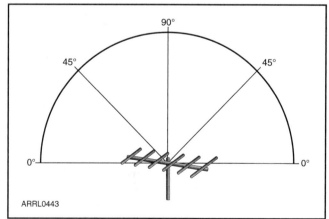

ARRL0443

Azimuth is the direction, in degrees referenced to true north, that an antenna must be pointed to receive a satellite signal. Imagine your station in the center of a giant compass circle that is divided in degree increments from 0 to 360. North is 0° (actually, it is also 360°), east is 90°, south is 180° and west is 270°.

Elevation is simply the angle, in degrees, between your station and the satellite, referenced to the Earth's surface.

the satellite as it moves in the vertical plane. Many amateur satellite stations use devices known as *az/el* (azimuth/elevation) *rotators* to move their directional antennas in both planes as the satellite streaks across the sky.

Even if you are not using movable antennas, knowing a satellite's elevation track is important for another reason. Unless you live in a flat location, chances are you do not have a clear view to the horizon in every direction. Perhaps there are serious RF obstacles such as mountains, hills or buildings blocking the way. If you are trying to receive a microwave signal from a satellite, the RF absorption properties of trees can present serious obstacles, too. The elevations of these objects represent your true *radio horizons* in whichever direction they may lie. If you have a ridge to the north with a maximum elevation of 30° above the horizon as viewed from your station, your northern radio horizon *begins* at 30° elevation. You can't communicate with a satellite in your northern sky until it rises above 30°, so you'll have to take that fact into account when you view the information provided by your satellite tracking software. Your software may tell you that the AOS (acquisition of signal) time is 0200 UTC as the satellite rises in the north, but you won't be able to receive the bird until it reaches 30°, which may be a few minutes later.

Usually — and particularly for satellites in low Earth orbits — as the satellite's elevation angle increases, its distance from you decreases. This is a good thing since the closer the satellite, the stronger the radio signal. With that idea in mind, the higher the elevation of a satellite pass, the better, right? Well…yes and no. Remember that satellites are moving at high speeds relative to your position. As they move closer to you (move higher in elevation), the *Doppler Effect* increasingly comes into play.

THE DOPPLER EFFECT

The Doppler Effect, named after scientist Christian Doppler (1803 – 1853), is the apparent change in frequency of sound or electromagnetic waves, varying with the relative velocity of the source and the observer.

Thanks to the Doppler Effect, as a satellite moves toward your location, its signal will *increase* in frequency; as it moves away from you, its signal will *decrease* in frequency.

When considering the Doppler Effect, it is important to realize that the satellite's transmit frequency is *not* changing. What is changing is the frequency of its signal *at your station*. You probably experience the Doppler Effect almost every day. When a fire truck approaches at high speed on a nearby freeway, you hear its siren blaring at a higher pitch, shifting downward as the truck passes and speeds off into the distance. The same thing happens with satellites, but unlike an earthbound fire truck that is moving at 60 MPH, the satellite is screaming by at thousands of miles per hour. The proportional difference between your speed and the speed of the satellite is enormous — high enough to shift the received frequency of a radio wave!

On a practical level, a high-elevation satellite pass can be problematic because the frequency shift caused by the Doppler Effect can be considerable. The effect also increases the higher you move in frequency. It can be quite a juggling act to adjust your receiver while trying to carry on a conversation.

Azimuth and Elevation Combined

Let's combine azimuth and elevation for a truly realistic satellite track, using our previous example of the International Space Station. We'll add the station's downlink frequency so we can see the Doppler Effect in action.

Time	Azimuth (degrees)	Elevation (degrees)	Frequency (MHz)
03:57	307	0	145.804
03:58	350	10	145.803
03:59	0	18	145.800
04:00	11	9	145.798
04:01	20	5	145.797
04:02	30	0	145.795

In this example, the International Space Station rises to an elevation of 18° at 03:59 UTC before sinking back down to the

horizon at 04:02 UTC. This is considered a low-elevation pass. If you have objects in your northern sky that rise above 18° elevation, you won't be able to communicate with the space station during this pass. The space station is transmitting at 145.800 MHz, but you'll notice that the frequency change caused by the Doppler Effect is minimal because the distance and relative velocity between you and the space station doesn't change dramatically.

Now we'll modify our example, making it a high-elevation pass.

Time	Azimuth (degrees)	Elevation (degrees)	Frequency (MHz)
03:57	307	0	145.810
03:58	350	10	145.808
03:59	0	25	145.806
04:00	11	40	145.804
04:01	20	65	145.802
04:02	30	80	145.800
04:03	36	60	145.798
04:04	41	45	145.796
04:05	50	29	145.794
04:06	55	15	145.792
04:07	59	0	145.790

There are several interesting things to note in this example. Did you notice that this high-elevation pass (topping out at 80° at 04:02 UTC) had a longer overall duration than the previous low-elevation pass? The low-elevation pass lasted only 5 minutes; this pass was a full 10 minutes in length. Obviously, when an object is tracking to a high elevation in the sky (almost directly overhead in this example), it is in the sky for a longer period.

Did you also notice what the Doppler Effect did to the downlink signal frequency at your station? Because the distance and relative velocity between you and the space station changed substantially during the pass, the Doppler Effect was very much in play. The result was a receive frequency that began at 145.810 MHz, shifted down to 145.800 MHz at maximum elevation, and then continued downward until it reached 145.790 MHz as the station slipped below the horizon. That's a 20 kHz frequency shift throughout the pass!

1.6.2 Satellite Tracking Software

You'll find satellite software programs written for *Windows*, *MacOS*, and *Linux* operating systems. Several popular applications are listed on the AMSAT website at **www.amsat.org/amsat-new/tools/software.php**. Modern applications provide the basic information: when the satellite will be available (AOS, acquisition of signal), how high the satellite will rise in the sky and when

the satellite is due to set below your horizon (LOS, loss of signal), plus many more features such as:

• The spacecraft's operating schedule, including which transponders and beacons are on.

• Predicted frequency offset (Doppler shift) on the link frequencies.

• The orientation of the spacecraft's anten-

nas with respect to your ground station and the distance between your ground station and the satellite.

• Which regions of the Earth have access to the spacecraft; that is, who's in QSO range?

• Whether the satellite is in sunlight or being eclipsed by the Earth. Some spacecraft only operate when in sunlight.

• When the next opportunity to cover a

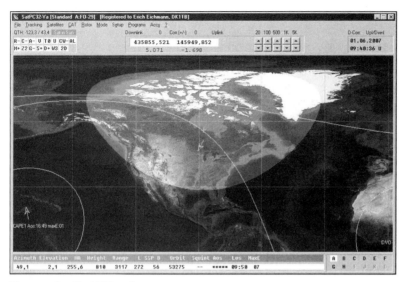

The popular *Sat32PC* software.

selected terrestrial path (mutual window) will occur.

• Changing data can often be updated at various intervals such as once per minute… or even once per second.

A number of applications do even more. Some will control antenna rotators, automatically keeping directional antennas aimed at the target satellite. Other applications will also control the radio to automatically compensate for frequency changes caused by Doppler shifting.

Adding additional spacecraft to the scenario suggests more questions. Which satellites are currently in range? How long each will be accessible? Will any new spacecraft be coming into range in the near future?

There are also several Internet sites where you can do your tracking on line. This eliminates all the hassles associated with acquiring and installing software. The currently available online tracking sites are not as powerful or flexible as the software you can install on your PC, however. One interesting site of this type is maintained by AMSAT-NA and you'll find it at **www.amsat.org/amsat-new/tools/**.

Getting Started With Software

There are a number of aspects of satellite-tracking software common to most programs. For example, we spent some time discussing how to determine your location with sufficient accuracy to be useful for satellite tracking. The next step is to get that information into your chosen program.

Most programs will ask you to enter your station location as part of the initial setup process. Some applications use the term "observer" to mean "station location." Some programs will provide you with a list of cities that

you can select to quickly enter your location. Other programs will ask you to enter your latitude and longitude coordinates manually.

When entering latitude, longitude (and other angles), make sure you know whether the computer expects degree-minute or decimal-degree notation. Following the notation used by the on-screen prompt usually works. Also make sure you understand the units and sign conventions being used. For example, are longitudes may be specified in negative number for locations west of Greenwich (0° longitude). Latitudes in the southern hemisphere may also require a minus sign. Fractional parts of a degree will have very little effect on tracking data so in most cases you can just ignore it.

Dates can also cause considerable trouble. Does the day or month appear first? Can November be abbreviated Nov or must you enter 11? The number is almost always required. Must you write 2016 or will 16 suffice? Should the parts be separated by colons, dashes or slashes? The list goes on and on. Once again, the prompt is your most important clue. For example, if the prompt reads "Enter date (DD:MM:YY)" and you want to enter February 9, 2016, follow the format of the prompt as precisely as possible and write 09:02:16.

When entering numbers, commas should never be used. For example, if a semi-major

axis of 20,243.51 km must be entered, type 20243.51 with the comma and units omitted. It takes a little time to get used to the quirks of each software package, but you'll soon find yourself responding automatically.

Once you have your coordinates entered, you're still not quite done. The software now "knows" its location, but it doesn't know the locations of the satellites you wish to track. The only way the software can calculate the positions of satellites is if it has a recent set of *orbital elements*.

Orbital Elements

Orbital elements are a set of six numbers that completely describe the orbit of a satellite at a specific time. Although scientists may occasionally use different groups of six quantities, radio amateurs nearly always use the six known as Keplerian Orbital Elements, or simply *Keps*.

These orbital elements are derived from very precise observations of each satellite's orbital motion. Using precision radar and highly sensitive optical observation techniques, the North American Aerospace Defense Command (NORAD) keeps a very accurate catalog of almost everything in Earth orbit. Periodically, they issue the unclassified portions of this information to the National Aeronautics and Space Administration (NASA) for release to the general public. The information is listed by individual catalog number of each satellite and contains numeric data that describes, in a mathematical way, how NORAD observed the satellite moving around the Earth at a very precise location in space at a very precise moment in the past.

Without getting into the complex details of orbital mechanics (or Kepler's laws!) suffice it to say that your software simply uses the orbital element information NASA publishes that describe where a particular satellite was "then" to solve the orbital math and make a prediction (either graphically or in tabular format) of where that satellite ought to be "now". The "now" part of the prediction is based on the local time and station location information you've also been asked to load into your software.

Orbital elements are frequently distributed with additional numerical data (which may or may not be used by a software tracking program) and are available as NASA Two-Line

---

Table 1.13
Orbital Elements

NASA Two-Line Elements for OSCAR 27

AO-27

1 22825U 93061C 08024.00479406 -.00000064 00000-0 -86594-5 0 8811
2 22825 098.3635 349.6253 0008378 336.4256 023.6532 14.29228459747030

Elements (see **Table 1.13** for an example). Satellite tracking programs read these elements and use them to generate predictions. One method of entering orbital elements is to grab the latest set from the AMSAT-NA website at **www.amsat.org** (look under "Keplerian Elements Resources" in the Satellite Info menu). You can download the element set as a text file and then tell your satellite-tracking program to read the file and create the database. Another excellent site is CelesTrak at **celestrak.com**.

If you're fortunate to own sophisticated tracking software such as *Nova*, and you have access to the Internet, the program will reach into cyberspace, download and process its Keps automatically. All it takes is a single click of your mouse button. Some program can even be configured to download the latest Keps on a regular basis without any prompting from you.

1.6.3 Satellite Operating

Satellite operating is unlike any other Amateur Radio activity. It is more than a matter of sitting down before your radio and making a contact. As you've learned in previous chapters, you have to know when the satellite is available, what path it will take from horizon to horizon, what uplink/downlink bands are in use and how you will deal with the Doppler Effect. All this amounts to a high-tech juggling act as you attempt to communicate with a spacecraft hurtling through the vacuum of space at many thousands of miles per hour.

But the challenge of satellite operating is part of the enjoyment. If it was as easy as making a contact on your local FM repeater, it wouldn't be nearly as fun. Even veteran operators will tell you that there is nothing like the thrill of making contact through a satellite. Even in our highly technical age, the sheer wonder of what you're doing never fails to inspire.

Several satellites with Amateur Radio uplinks and downlinks reach orbit every year. Some are research satellites that use amateur frequencies to relay telemetry data to Earth. Others are full-fledged ham satellites that sport uplink/downlink transponders. The transponders are labeled according to their uplinks and downlinks. See the list in **Table 1.14**. For instance, a Mode U/V transponder has an uplink on the 70 cm band (U) and a downlink on the 2 meter band (V).

Even under the best circumstances satellites are temporary things. Active satellites become inactive. Spacecraft in low orbit eventually re-enter our atmosphere. Satellites in higher orbits succumb to the hostile environment of space and become silent. It is impossible for a printed book to remain up to date with the status of the Amateur Radio satellite. With that in mind, your best source for current satellite information is the AMSAT website at **www.amsat.org**. In particular, check the Satellite Status page at **www.amsat.org/status**.

Single-Channel "Repeater" Satellites

The single-channel repeater satellites are among the easiest birds to work, not just from an equipment standpoint, but also from an operational perspective.

You can make contacts through these low-Earth orbiting satellites with little more than a dual band (2 meter/70 cm) FM mobile transceiver and an omnidirectional antenna — even a dual-band mobile whip will do. You can use a dual-band handheld radio as well, but don't expect success with its compact flexible antenna. Instead, you'll need something more substantial such as a dual-band Yagi.

Unfortunately, the popularity of FM repeater satellites is a handicap. Many stations attempt to use them, but only one station at a time can be repeated. Thanks to the "capture effect" inherent in FM receiver design, the strongest station at any given moment is the station that is demodulated and repeated. If several stations are received at nearly the same signal level, the result on the output is an unintelligible squeal.

When an FM repeater satellite is experiencing heavy use you'll hear stations in the clear, separated by screeches and sentence fragments. They tend to be congested during weekend passes when hams have more opportunities to take to the airwaves. Unless you have plenty of uplink power on 2 meters (50 W or more) and a directional antenna, your best bet is to try FM repeater satellites during less popular times. Passes during weekday mornings are significantly

Jerry, VE6AB, using a handheld transceiver and a tiny antenna to make contact through an FM repeater satellite.

less crowded. Weekday evening passes offer another worthwhile opportunity, although they can be crowded as well.

Because of the wide FM signal bandwidth (about 5 kHz), it is relatively easy to compensate for Doppler frequency shifting. There is no need to monitor your own downlink signal, which makes it possible to use ordinary dual-band FM transceivers that do not have full-duplex capability. In fact, you can exploit the *memory channels* in your radio to make Doppler compensation as simple as pushing a button.

Nearly all modern dual-band transceivers allow you to program memory channels for split-band operation, but consult the manual on how to go about doing it. For each channel you will need to program an uplink transmit frequency on 2 meters and a corresponding downlink receive frequency on 70 cm. Note that some FM repeater satellites may use CTCSS tones to control access, just like earthbound repeaters. If so, you'll need to program the correct CTCSS tone in each memory slot as well.

When the satellite pops above the horizon

Table 1.14
Satellite Uplink/Downlink Mode Designators

Satellite Band Designations

10 meters (29 MHz): H
2 meters (145 MHz): V
70 cm (435 MHz): U
23 cm (1260 MHz): L
13 cm (2.4 GHz): S
5 cm (5.6 GHz): C
3 cm (10 GHz): X

Common Operating Modes (Uplink/Downlink)

V/H (2 meters/10 meters)
H/V (10 meters/2 meters)

(acquisition of signal, AOS), select memory channel 1. Three minutes later, switch to memory channel 2 as the Doppler Effect begins to influence the uplink and downlink signals. You don't have to keep an eye on your watch. You'll know it is time to switch when the downlink signals become distorted and noisy. As the satellite reaches its maximum elevation (zenith), switch to channel 3. A minute later, select channel 4 and remain there until nearly the end of the pass (loss of signal, LOS) when you switch to channel 5. Note how memory channels are programmed to increment the uplink frequency *upward* throughout the pass while the downlink frequency ratchets *downward*. This guarantees Doppler compensation on your uplink signal for the satellite's receiver as well as on the downlink for your receiver.

Many transceivers allow you to substitute alphanumeric "tags" for the displayed memory channel frequencies. If your radio offers this feature, you can use it to label each memory in a distinctive manner. That way, you won't forget which memory to choose as the satellite is streaking overhead.

Here are some general FM repeater satellite operating tips…

If you hear nothing on the downlink frequency, do not transmit. It is quite possible that the satellite can hear *you* at times when you cannot hear *it*. By transmitting "in the blind," you'll cause unnecessary interference to everyone else. You can hear an FM repeater satellite coming into range by turning off your squelch and listening as the noise suddenly "quiets" and voices emerge.

Do not call "CQ." Operate the satellite as you would an FM repeater. Simply state your call sign and wait for a response, or answer someone else who has transmitted their call sign. A longwinded "CQ CQ CQ CQ…" merely ties up the satellite (and makes you very unpopular).

Keep it short and don't hog the satellite. If you establish contact, good for you! Just keep the conversation as short as possible. Always remember that passes last only 10 or 15 minutes and there are many other hams waiting for their chance. Avoid lengthy discussions of weather, antennas and so on. Of course, you may be lucky and find that the satellite is nearly empty. If that's the case, go ahead and chat but make sure you leave gaps between your transmissions in case someone else wants to make contact.

If there is a conversation in progress, don't interfere. Wait until it is complete before you begin throwing in your call sign.

A typical FM repeater satellite exchange might sound like this:

"KI1U"
"KI1U this is N9ATQ."
"N9ATQ this is KI1U near Hartford, Connecticut. Fox Nancy 31. Name is Mike."
"Good morning! I'm in Quincy, Illinois. Echo Nancy 40. Name is Craig. You're putting an excellent signal into the satellite."
"That's great. I'm just running 10 watts in my car."
"Sounds perfect to me, Mike. Hope to catch you on again. 73! N9ATQ clear."
"73, Craig. KI1U clear."

Notice how short the conversation is. Did you also notice the cryptic references to "Fox Nancy 31" and "Echo Nancy 40?" Those are *grid square* designations, which are a shorthand description of a station's general location. In the previous example, "Fox Nancy 31" translates to FN31, an imaginary rectangle centered on the state of Connecticut. Grid squares were discussed earlier, in the VHF/UHF Beyond FM and Repeaters section. The ARRL website at **www.arrl.org/grid-squares** offers more information and resources.

Linear Transponder Satellites

Single-channel satellites are attractive because of the minimal ground station equipment required to work them. Their major shortcoming, however, is their inability to support more than one conversation at a time. As a single-channel satellite operator, you're under constant pressure to make short-dura- tion contacts so that others can use the bird.

In contrast, linear transponder satellites relay an entire range of frequencies at once, not just a single channel. A linear transponder can, as a result, support many simultaneous conversations. There can still be interference issues, but once you've established contact you can chat for as long as you wish — or at least as long as the satellite is available to you. For low-Earth orbiting satellites, conversations can span 10 or 15 minutes. If the satellite in question is a high-Earth orbiter (HEO), conversations can last for *hours*.

Linear transponders are either *inverting* or *non-inverting*. An inverting transponder relays a mirror image of the uplink passband. This means that a *lower* sideband signal on the uplink becomes an *upper* sideband signal on the downlink. At the same time, a signal at the *high end* of the uplink passband will appear at the *low end* of the downlink passband. A non-inverting transponder relays the uplink signals exactly as they appear in the passband — sidebands remain unchanged and the relative position of an uplink signal in the downlink passband remains the same.

For engineering design reasons, most linear transponders are of the inverting variety. This presents a challenge when you're on the air. As you're *increasing* your uplink frequency, for example, you have to remember that your downlink frequency is *decreasing* — "heading the other way," as it were. For-

These 2 meter and 70 cm satellite antennas are mounted on an azimuth/elevation (AZ/EL) rotator system so they can track satellites across the sky. [Peter Budnik, KB1HY, photo]

tunately, a number of transceivers designed for satellite use have *reverse VFO tracking* among their features. This locks the uplink and downlink VFOs in a reverse arrangement. If you tweak the uplink VFO to increase your signal frequency by, say, 5 kHz, the downlink (receive) VFO will automatically shift downward by the same amount.

Finding Yourself...and Others

Full duplex operation is strongly recommended for linear transponder satellites. Because of the relatively narrow bandwidths of SSB and CW signals, the Doppler Effect will be more pronounced. You need to be able to hear your own signal while you are transmitting so that you can make frequent adjustments to the downlink receiver to maintain the tone (CW) or voice clarity (SSB).

It is possible to use a computer to estimate Doppler frequency shifts and apply receiver correction automatically (assuming your radio is under computer control). This is high-tech guesswork at best, though. The better, more accurate, solution is to slip on a pair of headphones and correct for Doppler by listening to your own downlink signal. (Headphones are necessary to help you avoid creating feedback through the satellite.)

Before you attempt your first conversation on a linear transponder satellite, it's best to gain some practice at receiving your own signal during a pass. For this example, let's use a LEO bird with an inverting linear transponder. Let's also assume that you are operating SSB. If you pick 435.230 MHz, for instance, as your uplink frequency, you might expect to hear yourself somewhere in the vicinity of 145.920 MHz. For SSB, the convention is to transmit lower sideband on the uplink, which inverts to upper sideband on the downlink.

If you are using separate transmitters and receivers, set your transmitter for 435.230 MHz LSB and leave it there. If you are using a multiband satellite-capable transceiver with a VFO tracking feature, "unlock" (disable) the tracking and set the transmitter VFO for 435.230 MHz LSB.

As the satellite climbs above the horizon, start sweeping your receive VFO through the 2 meter downlink passband, listening for signals as you go. (Another technique is to listen for a satellite's beacon, if available.) As soon as you hear activity, tune your receiver to 145.920 MHz. If the frequency is

clear, begin transmitting your call sign and perhaps the word "testing." As you speak, tune your downlink receiver back and forth from 145.920 to about 145.930 MHz. It may take a couple of minutes, but with luck you'll soon hear your own voice rising out of the noise. When you do, tune it in quickly until your voice sounds normal. Congratulations! You've just heard your own signal being relayed by a spacecraft!

This is a good time to experiment. Stop tuning your receiver and note how Doppler Effect changes the sound of your voice. Practice retuning to keep your voice sounding normal. If you are using a satellite transceiver, try locking the uplink and downlink VFOs and observe how the reverse tracking affects your signal.

CALLING CQ

Once you've become comfortable with finding your own signal, try calling CQ. Tune your uplink transmitter and downlink receiver to the frequencies of your choice. (If your radio has a VFO tracking feature, make sure it is unlocked.) When the satellite comes into range, start calling CQ as you listen for your voice on the downlink. Once you hear it, tweak your receiver as necessary to keep your voice sounding normal.

Don't be surprised if you suddenly hear a string of CW beeps. That's good news — it's the sound of someone who has heard your CQ and is quickly adjusting their uplink transmitter while sending a continuous series of Morse "dits" with a CW keyer. They are trying to hear their own signal and bring it to approximately the same frequency as your own. Alternatively, you may hear an off-frequency, high-pitched voice that suddenly "swoops" into your CQ. Once again, that is another station that has heard you and is preparing to answer.

Once the conversation is underway, all you have to do is adjust your uplink frequency to keep your voice, and the voice of the other operator, sounding normal. If your conversational companion is operating properly, he is doing the same thing.

ANSWERING A CQ

A duplex transceiver with a VFO tracking feature comes in handy when you're answering someone else's CQ. Once you've set the uplink and downlink VFOs, activate the tracking function to keep them locked together. Now all you have to do is tune through

the downlink passband with the receive VFO while the uplink (transmit) VFO follows you automatically. If you discover someone calling CQ, tune him in and then unlock the tracking. With your uplink VFO now operating independently, begin answering the other station as you gently adjust the *uplink* VFO to bring your signal on frequency. Once your frequency matches his (when your voice or CW tone sounds normal on the downlink), enjoy the conversation and compensate for Doppler by adjusting the uplink VFO.

If you are using separate rigs for the uplink and downlink, you'll need to tune in the station calling CQ, then make a quick estimate of the correct corresponding uplink frequency. Begin answering and adjust your uplink radio until your signal matches his on the downlink.

How Much Power is Enough?

The issue of uplink power and linear transponders has always been controversial. Obviously, you want to use enough power to generate a listenable signal on the downlink. For low-Earth orbiting satellites, that may amount to only 30 or 50 W, depending on the type of antenna you are using. For the high-Earth orbiters, uplink power levels of 100 to 150 W are common.

Unfortunately, there is a "more-is-better" obsession among some amateurs. A listenable downlink signal is not sufficient — they want a *loud* signal. Some of these operators, for example, are working the low-Earth orbiters by using directional antennas *and* 100 W of output power or more. The result can be an effective radiated power level in excess of *1 kW!*

The net effect of such a powerful signal on a linear transponder is to swamp its receiver. All signals weaker than the high-power station will be dramatically reduced in strength on the downlink; some may disappear altogether. This is because the satellite is dedicating the lion's share of its output to relaying the loud uplink signal while starving everyone else.

To be a good neighbor on a linear transponder satellite, the rule of thumb is to use only the uplink power necessary to keep your signal about as strong as everyone else's. If the satellite has a telemetry beacon, another technique is to use the beacon as the standard for downlink signal strength. In other words, your downlink signal should never be louder than the beacon.

1.6.4 Satellite Resources

ARRL website: **www.arrl.org/space-communication**
AMSAT: **www.amsat.org**
Amateur satellite tracking: **www.n2yo.com**

You can also find more technical information in *The ARRL Handbook* and *The ARRL Antenna Book*, as well as *The ARRL Satellite Handbook*, all available from your favorite ham radio dealer or the ARRL website.

1.7 Image Communications

As Amateur Radio operators, we communicate via radio. That's what our hobby is about. A natural extension to voice, CW, or data communication is television or image communication. We can also transmit and receive still pictures or full motion video on the ham bands. In the first part of this section, we will concentrate on fast scan amateur television (FSATV), usually just called ATV. Later we will explore slow scan television (SSTV).

Marty, N6VI, giving a report during a meeting of the San Bernardino Microwave Society being sent via ATV. [Courtesy Tom O'Hara, W6ORG]

1.7.1 Amateur Television (ATV) Overview

Are you interested in public service communications? You can assist by transmitting video of local events such as parades, marathons, various disaster drills, and so forth back to aid stations and operation centers. Maybe you'd like to share home videos with fellow ATVers or transmit the local ham club meeting with live color video and sound. You can record meetings and events and transmit them later for those who could not attend in person.

In general, ATV is like the analog television that broadcasters transmitted for more than 50 years. However, much simpler equipment is used. For ATV, you may already own two of the three main components in a basic station — the camera and receiver. The required camera can be the same camcorder that you use to record your family and vacation memories or it can be an inexpensive security camera. The audio and video (AV) cable from the camera is plugged directly into the ATV transmitter. Receiving your first ATV picture can be as easy as connecting your broadcast TV set to a rooftop 70 cm amateur band antenna (more on this later). The antenna should use the polarization (vertical or horizontal) common in your area.

You'll find most ATV activity on the 70 cm (420 – 450 MHz) band, but 33 cm (910 – 920 MHz), 23 cm (1250 – 1280 MHz) and 13 cm (2410 – 2450 MHz) are also used. Check the *ARRL Repeater Directory* to see if there is a local ATV repeater in your area and contact the owner or sponsoring group to find the most used frequencies, antenna polarization, and information on ATV nets or other regular activity.

Before transmitting, it is good practice to find out the local band plan and which frequencies are used in your area for ATV. Analog AM ATV channels are about 6 MHz wide, so basically there is only room for two 70 cm ATV frequencies to be used.

Setting up an ATV contact often involves calling "CQ ATV" on the local 2 meter FM voice ATV calling and talk-back frequency — typically 144.340 or 146.430 MHz simplex. "Talk back" means that during the ATV contact, the stations use 2 meter voice to allow the receiving stations to talk back at the same time as the 70 cm ATV transmitting station talks on the sound subcarrier which is heard from the TV speaker. It's much like talking on the telephone.

1.7.2 The ATV Station

Here we'll present a brief overview of a basic ATV station. For much more information on setting up an ATV station, see the Image Communications supplemental chapter on the *ARRL Handbook* CD and the ARRL website (**www.arrl.org/atv-fast-scan-amateur-television**).

Receivers

The frequency of cable channels 57 to 61 are actually within the 420 – 450 MHz (70 cm) ham band so the TV receiver is able to tune them directly — here is a great way to get some use from your old analog-only TV.

Cable channel 57 is 421.25 MHz and is popular for ATV repeater outputs. Cable channel 60 (439.25 MHz) is often used for ATV repeater inputs and for simplex DX. Due to technical band plan considerations for sharing with other modes, cable channel 61 (445.25 MHz) is not used because all local band plans use this part of the band for FM and digital voice repeaters. Usually 434.0 MHz is used rather than 433.25 MHz, which is cable channel 59, to keep the sound subcarrier out of the satellite subband. In most areas, 426.25 MHz is used instead of cable channel 58 (427.25 MHz) which keeps the sound subcarrier out of the weak signal subband. It is not a problem to receive these offset signals given that analog cable TV channels are 6 MHz wide and the TV sets automatic frequency control (AFC) can lock on to ATV stations that are up to 1 MHz off the exact cable video carrier frequency.

An ATV downconverter that mixes the 70 cm ham band down to TV channel 3 can also be used between the antenna and TV. Older TV sets that do not have cable tuners need a downconverter for ATV because the old broadcast UHF TV channels from 14 up are not the same as cable TV channels and do not cover the 70 cm ham band. ATV transceivers actually don't have a receiver in them, but instead have a downconverter. The

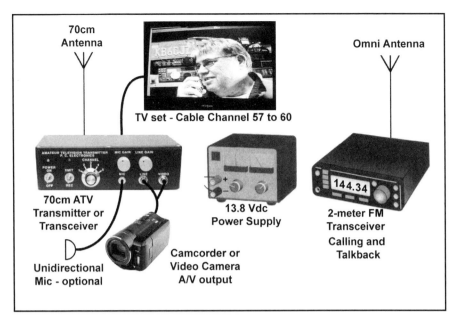

TV set - Cable Channel 57 to 60

70cm Antenna

Omni Antenna

70cm ATV Transmitter or Transceiver

Unidirectional Mic - optional

13.8 Vdc Power Supply

Camcorder or Video Camera A/V output

2-meter FM Transceiver Calling and Talkback

Here is the block diagram of a basic 70 cm ATV station. Any television with an analog cable tuner can be the receiver. The ATV transmitter provides TR switching to shift the antenna between it and the receiver. A 2 meter transceiver is commonly used to make initial contact and also for talking back to the ATV transmitting station. Audio either from the camera mic or an external directional mic is transmitted with the video.

TV is the actual receiver that does most of the system amplification, filtering, detection and processing of the video you see on its screen.

Downconverters can tune the exact ATV frequency and generally have a lower noise preamp stage for better sensitivity than the average TV. Downconverters are also used for analog ATV on the 33 and 23 cm ham bands and mix down to TV channel 3 or 8 respectively.

Antennas

Most stations use a 70 cm beam antenna rather than an omnidirectional antenna to receive ATV. The beam has gain to help with received signal levels and directivity to minimize multipath ghosting in the picture. But rather than rotating the 70 cm beam searching for activity on the air, it is more efficient to monitor a 2 meter ATV calling and talk-back frequency with a 2 meter omnidirectional antenna. If you can work someone on 2 meter FM voice with an omni antenna, it is a good indication that you have a chance to see them on 70 cm ATV using a 70 cm beam.

Once 2 meter contact is made, 70 cm beams can be aligned roughly toward each other, the ATV transmitter turned on and then the beam headings adjusted for least snow in the received picture. Running full duplex audio is also a real interactive advantage with this image mode for moving the camera or zooming in on objects in the picture being discussed or asking immediate questions.

If you have a 70 cm antenna on the roof

already, it is worth connecting it to the TV and giving it a try. However, if ATV stations in your area use the opposite antenna polarization, you can expect about 20 dB less signal. Ideally, ATV should be cross polarized to nearby users of other modes to reduce potential interference. But in many areas the polarization — horizontal for weak signal CW and SSB and vertical for FM voice repeaters — was determined by the earliest users and what they already had up on the tower.

Antennas designed for ATV are broader in bandwidth than ones used for FM voice repeaters, satellite and weak signal CW or SSB. Depending on how your existing antenna was designed, it may not have the same gain across the band or at the ATV frequency. Still, the signal might be strong enough to see that first picture so give it a try with whatever antenna you already have. Later, especially if you want to transmit ATV, you can add an antenna for the correct polarization and frequency. Some hams like to use circular

polarization or cross polarized antennas to enable working all modes with one antenna if tower space is limited. Low loss coax, N connectors and attention to weatherproofing all connections are a must on the 70 cm band and higher frequencies.

Transmitters

Now let's look at transmitting. Amplitude modulated analog 70 cm is the most popular for ATV as mentioned earlier because most people already have two of the three basic components. Also, the lower the frequency, the farther the signal goes given the same transmit power, transmit and receive antenna gains and coax loss factors.

Most all ATV transmitters are standalone units designed specifically for this mode. ATV transmitters accept the standard composite video signal and line level audio from camcorders, cameras and other video devices with AV outputs. Basically, any consumer video device you have been using that is plugged into a TV, home theater or VCR AV input can also be plugged into an ATV transmitter.

In addition, many ATV transmitters also have a low level mic input that is handy for using a separate unidirectional low-impedance dynamic mic. The directional mic is useful to avoid a feedback loop with the 2 meter radio speaker, cut down on extraneous noise, or to do voice-over commenting when transmitting a recording.

In addition to adjusting the audio gain control or the distance from the mic that you are probably used to with voice modes, ATVers quickly find that they must be concerned with focus and lighting of the scene. In the shack, you don't want the bags under your eyes to appear larger than they are! Placing a light behind the camera helps to minimize the shadows you might get from only having an overhead room light.

ATV transmitters are available at various RF power output levels from 50 mW to 20 W PEP. An alternative is to use a cable TV modulator if your local band plan allows for activity on the exact frequency of 427.25 MHz (channel 58) or 439.25 MHz (channel 60). They typically range in power output

A 5 W, 70 cm transmitter and optional companion downconverter is a good plug and play combination for public service events or the home station. [Courtesy of PC Electronics]

from 0.1 to 13 mW.

For higher power, both types of transmitters would add linear amplifiers designed for class A or AB operation and wide band amplitude modulation. Care must be taken to drive an amplifier strictly within its linear range which is often half its Amateur Radio maximum output power rating. Keeping the amplifier in its linear range is necessary to keep the video signal sync tip from compressing. Many ATV transmitters have a "sync stretcher" or "blanking pedestal" adjustment to compensate for a linear amplifier's gain compression at higher output levels. Sync stretchers allow driving linear amplifiers to higher output levels, but cable modulators don't have this feature.

On the 70 cm band, for a basic home station running 5 W PEP and 5 element beams at both ends, you can expect snow-free video over a line-of-sight path of up to 25 miles. That may be enough to work a local ATV repeater. To double the distance for the same picture quality or raise one P unit at the same distance, you will need to raise the effective radiated power (ERP) by 6 dB. (On ATV, signal reports are given in P units — P0 is barely recognizable, while P5 is snow-free.)

Antenna gain and placement for a line-of-sight path are the keys to reliable ATV communications. The antenna system should be your first improvement project, and it will help both transmitting and receiving.

Digital ATV

Digital cable modulators are available if you want to try your hand at digital ATV (D-ATV) transmission. This mode requires even more attention to lightly driving true linear amplifiers and preventing sideband growth and intermodulation distortion.

Unlike analog TV, where the picture is snowy but visible if signals are weak, digital TV is all or nothing. Above a signal-to-noise ratio of around 15 dB you get a perfect picture, but below that you get nothing. This is known

A complete DVB-T digital ATV transmitter system including a Hi-Des modulator (left), 70 cm linear amplifier (right) and a high-definition camcorder. [Jim Andrews, KH6HTV, photo]

as the *cliff effect* and occurs around the same signal level as a P1 or P2 AM or FM analog ATV picture. Also with D-ATV you do have to get used to a little time delay when talking back on 2 meters.

You'll find more information online in the D-ATV Yahoo Group at **groups.yahoo.com/group/DigitalATV** and in the Image Communications chapter on the *The ARRL Handbook* CD-ROM.

ATV Accessories

Whether you are using an analog or digital cable modulator plus linear amplifier or a standalone ATV transmitter module, you will need to add a transmit/receive (TR) antenna relay with enough isolation (40 dB typically) to put no more than 1 mW into the TV or

downconverter antenna input. Manufactured ATV transceivers and some transmitters have antenna TR relays built-in, and they also switch off the dc power to the downconverter in transmit.

When using just a TV set to receive, it is difficult to switch off the TV power when going to transmit, so be prepared to turn down the volume before flipping the transmit switch. Don't be surprised that your picture looks a mess in transmit — your transmitted signal is going to overload the TV.

Receiving your own transmitted signal on a TV in the shack is most often distorted from the overload and multipath signals. A diode detector in the antenna line with a 75 Ω line driver set to 1 V p-p and connected to a video monitor or the AV input of another TV will show your true transmitted picture.

1.7.3 Licensing, Limits, Repeaters, Identifying

ATV can be transmitted by any ham with a Technician license or higher on any ham band 420 MHz and above. Some regional limitations exist for frequency and power levels in parts of the United States, so check the *ARRL Repeater Directory* and FCC §97.303 or local sources before operating. Activity concentrates on different frequencies in different parts of the USA. However, most ATV activity can be found in the 420 – 440 MHz portion of the 70 cm band. Once you become involved with the people using the

ATV repeater or 2 meter ATV coordination and talk back frequency, you'll find that help with equipment selection, troubleshooting and all-around technical information will be plentiful.

ATV Repeaters

ATV repeaters usually transmit on 421.25 or 426.25 MHz (cable channel 57 or 58) and receive on 434.0 or 439.25 MHz (cable channel 59 or 60) and have VSB filters in the

antenna lines. An in-band ATV repeater needs at least 12 MHz separation and special duplexers and VSB filters to prevent the 6 MHz wide channels from desensing the repeater receiver. A few ATV repeaters transmit on 439 MHz and receive on 426 or 427 MHz.

Areas with many active FM voice repeaters below 444 MHz have opted to use 434.0 upper or 439.25 MHz lower VSB for their ATV repeater to avoid interference. Most ATV stations transmit both sidebands which makes them compatible with repeaters receiving either VSB. Upper VSB is standard, the same as cable TV. Some areas elected to go crossband with the repeater input or output on a higher band so as to free up one of the two possible 70 cm ATV channels for simplex.

Station Identification

Identifying on ATV has the same requirements of any other mode—you must transmit your call sign after 10 minutes of continuous operation and at the end of a transmission. On ATV, you can do that by speaking on the sound subcarrier or making your call sign plainly visible in the picture. Some operators use a QSL card. Others use something as simple as a felt-tip pen scribble on a piece of paper, while others use an automatic video overlay board.

Signal Reports

When you watch an ATVer's picture, you want to tell the sender how well it is being received. You could say, "Your picture is 20% snow." But that terminology is vague and wordy. The only exceptions are "I can't see it at all," or "You're perfectly snow-free," which we all understand. It's analogous to the digital 1s or 0s indicating on or off, but it's the shades of gray that become a bit more arbitrary. To solve this problem, the *P system* was developed for AM ATV signal reception. It goes like this: P stands for picture level and is divided into six levels from P0 to P5.

Crisp, clear digital ATV through the ATCO WR8ATV repeater.

A signal received as P0 is recognizable as to its existence only. No detail is discernible and usually only sync bars can be seen in the snow. Since the minimum recognizable signal change is about 3 dB, 6 dB steps are easily recognized and they represent a convenient increment. The numbers continue in 6 dB steps from P0 to P5. P5 is a snow-free signal and is 30 dB stronger than P0. Beyond that, ATVers tend to say

"P5 plus," or "broadcast quality."

P-unit reporting is universal across the USA and in other countries as well. This system is accurate only for AM because of the near-linear levels. P-unit reporting of FM signals can be used as long as it's understood that it will not be 6 dB per P unit because of the nonlinear nature of the receiver limiter and detection system.

1.7.4 UHF to Microwaves

While most ATV activity is on the 70 cm band, the higher bands can be fun to experiment with and offer some advantages. Full duplex video can expedite communications with each end transmitting on a different band at the same time.

For example, hams support the Angeles Crest 100 Mile Endurance Run. Hams at a remote, hard-to-get-to mountain aid station transmit on 70 cm to the next aid station 6 miles distant, and the other station transmits back at the same time on 23 cm. This allows medical personnel to make much better runner assessments and treatment suggestions than if they communicated by voice alone. It also lets a runner's crew and friends see and talk to him or her and to find out what assistance or support might be needed later.

The higher bands are often used for point-to-point links between ATV repeaters; for alternate inputs, outputs or modulation types; for short links to an emergency communications van; for simultaneous multiple camera operations; or any time 70 cm gets too active.

FM ATV Operation

Experimentally, using the US standard, FM ATV gives increasingly better picture-to-noise (snow) ratios than AM analog ATV at receiver input signals greater than 5 µV. Because of the wider noise bandwidth and FM threshold effect, AM analog video can be seen in the noise well before FM ATV or digital ATV. For DX work, it has been shown that AM signals are recognizable in the snow at up to four times (12 dB) greater distance than FM or DTV signals, with all other factors equal. Above the FM threshold, however, FM rapidly overtakes AM. FM snow-free pictures occur above 50 µV, or four times farther away than with AM signals. The crossover point is near the signal level where sound and color begin to appear for all three systems.

Occupied bandwidth is almost 19 MHz using the narrow FM ATV standard of 4 MHz

deviation and 5.5 MHz sound subcarrier. Therefore, FM ATV is only used in the bands above 902 MHz and not on 70 cm where interference with the many voice repeaters, satellite and weak signal stations would make it impractical. You will find some areas that run AM ATV on the 33 or 23 cm bands if they favor having more channels available in the band versus just one or two FM ATV channels. Consult your local band plan.

FM ATV requires using a complete receiver with an AV output connected to a monitor or re-modulated AM to channel 3 and a TV set. There a few manufactured AM or FM ATV transmitters and receivers in the USA but most of the imported gear is FM. Hams have modified low-cost, license-free FCC Part 15 wireless video transmitters and receivers for use on the 900 MHz, 2.4 GHz and 5.6 GHz ham bands and then added amplifiers.

Care must be taken that the selected FM center frequency is at least 8 MHz inside the band edges. Half of the 2.4 GHz Part 15 band is outside of the ham band and some of the imports are potentially not compliant for amateur use because they have channels way outside the bands. Check the channel switch often to make sure it has not been accidently changed and is set for inside the ham band.

Many amateurs have used old C band satellite TV receivers that tune 950 – 1450 MHz — covering the 23 cm band. Some even tune down to the amateur 33 cm band directly. On the 3.3 GHz band and above, these C band satellite receivers are used directly with antenna-mounted low noise downconverters or LNBs.

There is some ATV activity on the 10 GHz band. Gunnplexers are easily modulated with video on the Varicap input for 10.4 GHz ATV.

1.7.5 ATV Applications and Activities

Here's where it gets fun. After the station is built and a number of contacts have been made, the imagination starts to roam. "What else can I get involved in?" After all it's great talking with and seeing the ATVers but sometimes that's not enough. Many other activities could use ATV involvement — but they sometimes just don't know it! That helps form groups and then clubs dedicated to helping other activities. After all, it's a hobby so it's supposed to be fun. Get involved and make it just that.

Emergency Communications and Public Service Events

ATV can add remote eyes and ears to an emergency operation center (EOC) to more efficiently allocate and use resources. It can provide an early warning at parades and races with a view of the event back to event operations or aid stations. At public service events you can establish a video link up to a mile line-of-sight using 5-element beams and a 50-mW ATV transmitter. A 5-element 70 cm beam is less than 3 feet long and easy to transport.

Transmitting at races and parades on city streets, you can expect many reflections from buildings, street light and traffic signal posts, cars and other metal objects. If a reflected signal arrives with not much attenuation at the receive site, its amplitude and phase with some delay will mix with the direct signal — resulting in ghosting or sync tearing. Using beams will not only give gain in the desired direct path, but also, compared to an omni antenna, reduce the power to and from the sides and rear of the antennas toward the RF reflecting objects.

Tripod speaker stands with two or three 5-foot mast sections make a good portable antenna setup and allow you to easily move them around for best signal strength. Having the antennas 10 to 15 feet above the ground can reduce blockage to the line-of-sight path when people or vehicles pass between the two antennas (this could make the picture jump). A 2 meter voice link using handhelds is a good way for the receiving station to give the transmitting station instructions for fine-tuning antenna placement. The 2 meter link can also be used to communicate where to point the camera during the event.

Emergency communications and public service operations tend to have long transmit times unless multiple camera sites are used. You have to remember to identify every 10 minutes, and it's a good idea to use that as a reminder to also check that the transmitter is properly ventilated and the temperature has not risen to the "too hot to touch" level. Sun angles are an important consideration for transmitter heat dissipation, camera and TV placement, and they should be checked in advance during the hours of the event. As with photographs, having the sun at your back will give the best picture contrast and least shadowing. Similarly, the TV screen can be washed out if facing the sun. The TV receiver is best placed in the shade if possible without compromising the viewing ability of those using the information from the video. Brightness and contrast levels are going to be different in the field than they are in the home. Familiarize yourself with how to make these adjustments using the manual controls as well as the remote before the event.

ATV DX

For some hams the thrill of making far-away contacts drives them to make station improvements and ATVers are no exception.

A portable ATV transmitter sends live video to the finish area from a critical traffic intersection during a 10K run.

An ATV camera view from a balloon at 93,399 ft shows the blackness of space, the curvature of the earth and hazy clouds below. Note that the standard NMEA altitude data output from GPS receivers is in meters. [Courtesy Tom O'Hara, W6ORG]

DXers looking for ATV stations hundreds of miles away during periods of temperature inversion skip that typically occurs in the early summer months will put up large horizontally polarized arrays as high as possible and optimized for 439.25 MHz, the prime ATV DX frequency.

Instead of QSL cards to commemorate a DX ATV contact, the receiving station will take a photograph of the TV screen and then email it to the transmitting station. A contact is deemed valid if the call letters can be seen in the snow.

Radio Controlled Vehicles

ATV transmitters can be carried by radio controlled (RC) vehicles including airplanes, helicopters, cars and boats. Radio controlled airplanes with a camera and ATV transmitter aboard can give you a pilot's eye view. A 50 mW on 70 cm transmitter with a ground plane antenna works well for about a half mile around a flying field. Modified 900 MHz and 2.4 GHz license-free wireless AV transmitters with the cases stripped off to minimize size and weight can also be used for short range RC video in aircraft, cars and boats.

The RC control transmitter must not be in the same band as the ATV transmitter so that the ATV signal does not overload the RC receiver in the vehicle. Antenna, transmitter placement and possibly high and low pass filters can keep the ATV transmitter from overloading and capturing the RC control receiver. It is a good idea to test for positive control at the farthest distance on the ground before flying.

Balloons

High altitude balloon launches are popular. Hams fill up a 6-foot (or larger) weather balloon with helium, hang a foam box below it. The box can carry a video camera, 1 W transmitter and battery with an omnidirectional antenna hung below it. Some add a GPS receiver with video overlay to put the location, altitude and direction on the video. The payload might also include a 2 meter transmitter with APRS to track the location on a map over the Internet — **www.aprs. fi**. These balloons can reach heights beyond 100,000 feet (19 miles) and usually send back spectacular pictures of Earth's curvature and near outer space. Also, at that altitude the reception distance extends beyond 500 miles, so it provides an exciting show for many viewers.

Weather Spotting

ATVers and ham members of SKYWARN frequently provide video and audio to assist weather spotters. For example, the ATV group in central Ohio (ATCO) provides this service by retransmitting local TV station radar on the ATV repeater upon command to assist the weather spotters with up-to-date video of an incoming storm. When not in service, any ATVer can bring up the radar signal on command to check on weather conditions.

Computer Graphics

The same video adapters that are used to connect your computer to a video projector or video monitor can be plugged into the ATV transmitter and shown to other hams. Have a contest on net night for the one that comes up with the best computer generated call ID. Show the pictures stored in your computer of the family, vacations or ATV DX. Cable TV tuners that plug into the computer's USB port enable watching and even recording ATV or screen grabbing a photo to play back later. A laptop with a cable TV USB dongle makes a nice portable ATV receiver for viewing or documenting emergency communications, public service events, RC, rockets and balloon launches.

1.7.6 Slow-Scan Television (SSTV)

The previous sections discussed fast-scan amateur television, used to send wide-bandwidth full-motion video in the 420 MHz and higher bands. In contrast, slow-scan television (SSTV) is a method of sending still images in a narrow bandwidth and is widely used on the HF bands, although SSTV is sent via FM repeaters and amateur satellites too.

work, but sample rate accuracy is important for some SSTV modes (more on this later).

Within *Windows*, the sound mixer controls set the levels for the transmitted and received SSTV audio. All unused inputs should be muted. *Windows* sounds should be disabled to prevent them from going out along with the transmitted SSTV audio.

Interfacing the transceiver to the PC sound card can be as simple as connecting a couple of audio patch cables. Sound cards generally have stereo miniature phone jacks. Only one audio channel is required or desired — the left channel. This is the tip connection on the plug. Use shielded cable with the shield connected to the sleeve (ground) on the plug. Ground

SSTV Basics

Traditional SSTV is an analog mode, but in recent years several digital SSTV systems have been developed. All make use of standard Amateur Radio transceivers — no special radio gear or antennas required. SSTV transmissions require only the bandwidth of SSB voice, and they are allowed on any frequencies in the HF and higher bands where SSB voice is permitted. SSTV does not produce full motion video or streaming video.

A computer with sound card is required to use most of the software popular for SSTV. Software for the *Windows* operating system is the most popular, but other choices are available. Hardware and software setup is similar to that described for sound card modes presented earlier in the section on HF Digital Communications. Most sound cards will

Color SSTV image received from International Space Station in Martin 1 mode on 145.800 MHz FM.

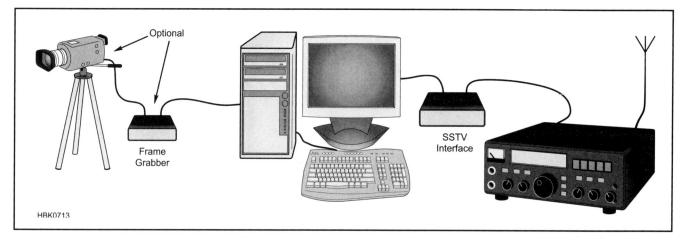

Modern stations need only a sound card equipped PC and simple interface to send and receive SSTV.

loop problems may be avoided by using an audio isolation transformer.

The connection for receiving SSTV audio from the transceiver may be made anywhere that received audio is available. The best choice is one that provides a fixed-level AF output. This will ensure that sound card levels will not have to be adjusted each time the volume on the transceiver is adjusted. You can use a headphone or speaker output if that's all that is available. If the received output level is enough for the LINE IN input on the sound card, use it, otherwise use the MICROPHONE input. If the level is too high for LINE IN, an attenuator may be required.

Use the LINE OUT connection on the sound card for the transmitted SSTV audio output. The cable for transmitted SSTV audio should go to the transceiver's AFSK connection. If the transceiver does not have a jack for this, then the microphone jack must be used — requiring a more elaborate interface. TR keying can be provided using the transceiver's VOX. Other methods for activating transmit include manual switching, a serial port circuit, an external VOX circuit and or a computer-control command.

Most of the commercially made sound card interfaces for the digital modes are suitable for SSTV. The microphone will be used regularly between SSTV transmissions, so consider its use along with the ease of operation when setting up for SSTV.

An SSB voice transceiver with a stable VFO is necessary for proper SSTV operation. The VFO should be calibrated and adjusted to be within 35 Hz of the dial frequency (more on this later). The transceiver's audio bandwidth should not be constrained so as to infringe on the audio spectrum used by SSTV. Optional filters should be turned off unless they can be set to 3 kHz or wider. SSTV software has its own DSP signal processing tools, so they are not needed in the transceiver. Most of the other transceiver settings should turned

be off, including transmit or receive audio equalization, noise blanker or noise reduction, compression or speech processing, and passband tuning or IF shift.

Adjust your transmitter output for proper operation with the microphone first, according to instructions in your manual. Then adjust the sound card output for desired drive level. For SSB operation, receiving stations should see about the same S meter reading for the SSTV signal as for voice. Properly adjusted levels and clean audio quality will improve the reception of the transmitted signal as well as reduce interference on adjacent frequencies. The SSTV signal is 100% duty cycle. If your transceiver is not designed for extended full-power operation, reduce the power output using the *Windows* volume control.

SSTV may be transmitted using AM, FM, or SSB. Use the same mode as you would use for voice operation on a given frequency. On HF, use the same sideband normally used for voice on that band. SSTV activity can be found on HF, VHF, UHF, repeaters, satellites, VoIP on the Internet and almost anywhere a voice signal can get through.

SSTV Operating Practices

Analog SSTV images are, in a sense, broadcast. They arrive as-is and do not require the recipient to establish a two-way connection. Most SSTV operation takes place on or near specific frequencies. Common analog SSTV frequencies include 3.845, 3.857, and 7.171 MHz in LSB and 14.230, 21.340, and 28.680 MHz in USB. Establish a contact by voice first before sending SSTV. If no signals can be heard, on voice ask if there is anyone sending. It may be that someone is sending but you cannot hear them. If there is no response, then try sending a "CQ picture." Note that on popular frequencies, weak signals can often be heard. In this case, wait for traffic to finish before sending SSTV even if you got

no response to your voice inquiry.

Receiving SSTV pictures is automatic as long as your software supports the mode used for transmission. Once a picture is received, it will be displayed and may be saved.

When selecting images to send, consider appropriateness, picture quality, and interest to the recipient. Choose an SSTV mode that suitable for the image to be sent, band conditions, signal strengths and the recipient's receive capability. Announce the SSTV mode prior to sending. Avoid sending a CW ID unless required by regulations. Describe the picture only after it is confirmed that it was properly received.

To send SSTV, use your software to select and load a picture to send. It will be displayed in a transmit screen. Next, select the SSTV transmission mode. Click the transmit button, and your transceiver will go into transmit and send the SSTV audio. When the SSTV transmission is over, the transceiver returns to receive. Be sure to send the full frame or the next picture sent may not be received properly because it may not start scanning from the top.

SOURCE FOR IMAGES

The Internet is a popular source for images. With the unlimited number of images available, it is surprising how often the same Internet pictures keep popping up on SSTV. Use a little imagination and come up with something original.

A digital camera is one of the best ways to create an original picture of your own. The subject matter could be almost anything that you might have available. Pictures of the shack, equipment and operator are always welcomed. Any image editing program can be used to make your own CQ picture, test pattern, video QSL card or 73 picture. Include your own personal drawings. Make your images colorful with lots of contrast to make them really stand out. You can also transmit pictures of your home, areas of local interest, other hobbies, projects, maps, cartoons and funny pictures.

It is common to have call sign, location and perhaps a short description as text on the pictures. If two calls are placed on an image, it is understood that the sender's call is placed last. Signal reports may also be included. Once the images are saved, they provide a convenient confirmation of contact.

Analog SSTV

SSTV signal characteristics are discussed in detail in the Image Communications chapter on *The ARRL Handbook* CD-ROM. Two popular modes for sending and receiving color SSTV pictures are called Martin and Scottie (named after their developers). Within each family are several different modes (Martin 1, Martin 2 and so forth). The various modes have different resolutions and scan rates.

Information about the size or resolution for each mode is generally available in the SSTV software. Better quality images will result when the source image is sized and cropped to the same dimensions used by the mode with which it is transmitted. Slower scan rates can provide better quality; those are the modes that take longer to send for the same resolution.

Each mode has a vertical interval signaling (VIS) code that identifies the mode being sent. When these codes are received, it readies the system to receive in the proper SSTV mode. For VIS detection to work, the receiver must be tuned within 70 Hz of the transmitted frequency. Two stations tuned exactly on the SSTV frequency but with VFO errors of +35 Hz and –35 Hz could successfully pass the VIS codes. As mentioned previously, each

transceiver must have the VFO and display calibrated within 35 Hz to ensure VIS code detection with the transceiver set to the SSTV frequency.

Received images are displayed in near real time as they are decoded. Almost any SSTV signal that is heard can produce an image, but it is rare to receive an image that is perfect. Changes in propagation or transceiver settings will become apparent as the image continues to scan down the screen. Noise will damage the lines received just as it occurs. Interference from other signals will distort the image or perhaps cause reception to stop. Signal fading may cause the image to appear grainy. Multipath will distort the vertical edges. Selective fading may cause patches of noise or loss of certain colors.

Images that are received with staggered edges are the result of an interruption of the sound card timing. Check with other operators to see if they also received the image with staggered edges. If not, then it may be your computer that has the problem and not the sending station. Some possible solutions are to close other programs, disable antivirus software and reboot the computer.

Under good conditions, images may come in "closed circuit." This means that the quality appears nearly as good as a photograph. SSTV has a reporting system similar to the RST reporting system used on CW. For analog SSTV it is RSV — readability, signal strength and *video*. Video uses a scale of 1 to 5, so a report of 595 would be the same as closed circuit.

ANALOG SSTV SOFTWARE

A variety of software programs are available for SSTV. Some multimode programs include SSTV and digital modes, while

others are dedicated to SSTV. One very popular SSTV package is the *Windows* program *MMSSTV* by Mako Mori, JE3HHT. For more information or to download a copy, visit **ham-soft.ca/pages/mmsstv.php**. Other SSTV software has similar features.

Sound card sample rate accuracy is important for some modes. Analog SSTV is one of them: pictures will appear *slanted* if the clock is off. The *MMSSTV* Help file includes detailed information on several ways to do a quick and easy calibration (see the Slant Corrections section). The best method is the one that uses a time standard such as WWV. (Before performing this calibration procedure, you must have the sound card interface connected so *MMSSTV* can detect received audio.) After performing the clock calibration, chances are, the timing will also be correct for transmit. If not, *MMSSTV* provides a means for making a separate adjustment for transmit.

Digital SSTV

Several forms of digital SSTV have been developed, but the modulation method most widely used for digital SSTV as of 2016 is derived from the shortwave broadcast system Digital Radio Mondiale (DRM). *HamDRM* by Francesco Lanza, HB9TLK, is a variation of DRM that fits in a 2.5 kHz bandwidth and is used in various programs.

The DRM digital SSTV signal occupies the bandwidth between 350 and 2750 Hz. Digital SSTV using DRM is not a weak signal mode like the narrow bandwidth data modes such as PSK31. An S-9 or better signal with little or no noise may be required before the software is able to achieve a sync lock and receive data.

(A)

(B)

If the sound card clock is inaccurate, analog SSTV images may appear slanted (A). The same image is shown at (B) after calibrating the clock.

DIGITAL SSTV SETUP

A popular DRM digital SSTV program is *EasyPal* by the late Erik Sundstrup, VK4AES (available from **www.vk3evl.com**). Digital SSTV uses the same type of PC and sound card setup described in the SSTV Basics section. As soon as the *EasyPal* software is installed, it is ready to receive pictures.

Unlike analog SSTV, the software detects and compensates automatically for clock timing differences so sound card calibration is not required. Software will also automatically adjust ±100 Hz for mistuned frequency.

With DRM SSTV the call sign is sent continuously. This may allow others to identify the transmitting station and perhaps turn an antenna in the right direction for better reception. Many sub modes are available, with various transmission speeds and levels of robustness. The sub mode is automatically detected and receiving starts automatically. Decoding is done on the fly, so there is no waiting for the computer to finish processing before the image appears.

Power output may appear low as measured by a conventional wattmeter. The actual signal strength as seen by others should be about the same as the SSB voice signal. Avoid capacitors in the audio lines as they may interfere with the phase of the digital signal.

DRM audio levels are low, so there may be problems getting the signal to trigger a VOX circuit. Set the transceiver for full RF output. Then adjust the sound card VOLUME CONTROL output until the transmitter shows little or no ALC indication. With an FM transmitter, keep the output level low to avoid overdeviation.

OPERATING DIGITAL SSTV

Before jumping into digital SSTV, try analog SSTV first. Copy some pictures to see if the sound card setup works. The level adjustments for analog SSTV are not as critical as those for DRM.

Common DRM SSTV frequencies include 3.847, 7.173, 7.228 MHz in LSB and 14.233 MHz in USB. Tune your VFO to the whole number in kHz (for example, 14,233.0). If a sending station is far off frequency, use the pilot carriers as seen in the software spectrum display as a guide. Adjusting the VFO while receiving an image is not advised as it will delay synchronization.

The signal-to-noise ratio (SNR) as displayed in the software is a measure of the received signal quality. The higher the SNR the better — decoding will be more reliable. Under very good band conditions this number may exceed 18. In that case, a higher speed mode may work. Because of the way the software measures the SNR, the peak value displayed for SNR may require 20-30 seconds of reception. Adjustments made on either end may change the SNR. Sub modes with less data per segment take longer to send, but they are more robust and allow for copy even if the SNR is low.

GETTING THE WHOLE PICTURE

Noise and fading may prevent 100% copy of all the segments. Any missing segments may be filled in later. Your software can send a *bad segment report (BSR)* that lists all the missing segments for a file that has only been partly received. In response, the other station can send a *FIX* should complete the file transfer. If not, the BSR and FIX process may be repeated.

EasyPal has a feature to provide a higher level of error correction so that 100% copy of all the segments is not necessary to receive the complete file. The transmitted file is encoded with redundant data so that the original file may be recreated even though not all the segments were received. The receiving station must also be running *EasyPal*.

Propagation only becomes a factor as it may take longer for the data to get through during poor conditions. The images received will be identical to the ones sent because the data in the files will also be identical. Replays will always be an exact copy. Multipath propagation does not disrupt DRM transmissions unless it is severe or results in selective fading.

IMAGE SIZE

Pictures of any size or resolution may be sent over digital SSTV. The sending station must pay careful attention to file size, though, or the transmission time may become excessively long. Compressing image files is necessary to get the transmit time down to a reasonable amount. Most images will be converted into JPEG 2000 (JP2), a lossy compression method that shows fewer artifacts. A slider varies the JP2 compression level, and a compromise must be made between image quality and file size. The smaller the file, the more visible the artifacts, but the faster it is sent.

Small image files may be sent without using compression. Some file types such as animated GIF files cannot be compressed, so they must be sent "as is."

A "busy picture" is one that shows lots of detail across most of the image area. This type of picture can be challenging to compress into a file size small enough to send that still maintains acceptable quality. Reducing the resolution by resizing and creating a much smaller image is the solution. Just about any busy picture can be resized down to 320 × 240 pixels, converted into JP2, and still look good when displayed on the receiving end.

About 2 minutes transmission time is the acceptable limit for the patience of most SSTV operators. A typical DRM digital SSTV transmission will take about 105 seconds for a file 23 KB in size, RS1 encoded and requiring 209 segments.

SENDING DIGITAL SSTV IMAGES

The ideal DRM signal will have a flat response across the 350 to 2750 Hz spectrum. The transceiver should be allowed to pass all frequencies within this bandwidth. In order to maintain the proper phase relationships with all the subcarriers, the signal must be kept linear. Avoid overdriving the transmitter and keep the ALC at the low end of the range. Eliminate hum and other stray signals in the audio.

The process of transmitting an image

EasyPal DRM digital SSTV software is used to exchange high quality, color images. Several levels of error correction and various transmission speeds are available.

starts with selecting an image and resizing or compressing it if needed, as described in the previous section. Within *EasyPal*, when the transmit button is clicked, the image file will be RS encoded if that option is selected. Then the resulting file will be broken down into segments and sent using DRM.

In receiving DRM, the audio is decoded and segments that pass the error check will have their data stored in memory. When enough of the segments are successfully received, the RS file is decoded and the JPEG 2000 image file is created. The content of this file should be identical to the JPEG 2000 image file transmitted.

It can be quite gratifying to receive your first digital SSTV picture. A lot has to go just right, and there is little room for errors. Propagation and interference always play havoc. There is no substitute for a low noise location and good antenna when it comes to extracting the image from the ether. Be patient and when the right signal comes by you will see the all the lights turn green and the segment counter will keep climbing. You won't believe the quality of the pictures!

1.7.7 Image Communication Resources

ATV Websites

Columbus, Ohio ATCO Group: **www.atco.tv**
Amateur Television Network: **atn-tv.org**
Baltimore, Maryland BRATS Group: **bratsatv.org**
Amateur Television Directory: **atv-tv.org**
WB8ELK Balloons: **fly.hiwaay.net/~bbrown/**
ATV at a trail race: **www.foothillflyers.org/hamtvac100.html**
ARRL website: **www.arrl.org/atv-fast-scan-amateur-television**
Ham TV Application Notes: **www.hamtv.com/info.html**

SSTV Websites

MMSSTV Yahoo Group: **groups.yahoo.com/group/MM-SSTV**
Digital SSTV Yahoo Group (DIGSSTV):
  groups.yahoo.com/group/digsstv
CQ SSTV de KB4YZ: **www.qsl.net/kb4yz/**
ARRL website: **www.arrl.org/sstv-slow-scan-television**

You can also find more technical information in *The ARRL Handbook* and *The ARRL Antenna Book*, available from your favorite ham radio dealer or the ARRL website.

1.8 Portable and Mobile Operation

Although Amateur Radio has traditionally been a home based activity, challenges such as deed restrictions, limited space, and urban noise levels have prompted hams to look for alternatives. This section discusses ways to get the most out of a portable or mobile station.

A suitable portable location can be as close as your nearest public park. Here Stuart, KB1HQS, is operating 20 meter SSB with a battery powered KX3 and magnetic loop antenna. [Stuart Thomas, KB1HQS, photo]

1.8.1 Portable Operating

Portable radio operation has taken off in the last decade with the introduction of smaller radios, lightweight accessories (antennas, batteries), and the increase in outdoor operating activities including Summits on the Air (SOTA), Islands on the Air (IOTA), and National Parks on the Air (NPOTA — an ARRL program during 2016). More operators are taking to the outdoors and operating away from their home stations. Other operators operate exclusively portable.

Portable operating can be divided into three different categories:

Operating from your vehicle. This differs from mobile operation where the vehicle is underway. Portable operation from your vehicle uses the vehicle as a temporary ham station and offers a power source for your radio. Setup can be quick, depending on the installation of your radio and antenna. Often additional power cables are necessary depending on your power needs.

Close to vehicle (less than 200 yards). There are times when operating from your vehicle may not be comfortable (low/high temperatures), parking access, and other factors. In these scenarios, your gear will be relocated from your vehicle to a spot less than 200 yards or so away. This location may be a picnic table, an overlook, or perhaps right outside your car. Beyond 200 yards you have to start to consider more efficient ways to carry your gear (for example, lugging around

a fifty pound car battery may no longer be an option!).

Backcountry hiking (> 200 yards). In this scenario weight and portability are the primary factors in successful portable operations.

Equipment

Unlike the desktop setup where your gear is permanently installed and configured, working portable requires flexibility and the ability for your gear to be carried, set up, and used efficiently.

Preparing for a hike to activate several summits in North Carolina. Radio, wire antenna, and accessories fit into the backpack along with other supplies. [Stuart Thomas, KB1HQS, photo]

STORING AND TRANSPORTING YOUR GEAR

How will you carry your gear? Most operators use a backpack to transport everything to their operating site. Considering you will be outside, you need to protect your expensive radio gear from environment — rain, wind, and hard surfaces such as rocks and the ground are all potential hazards.

One recommendation is to store your radio in a Pelican, Nanuk, or similar hard shell case, which is a waterproof and crushproof storage case designed for carrying sensitive gear. This ensures protection from the elements and gives you padded storage and organization. A useful item to include in your case is a reusable moisture absorber, especially in the winter when going from drastic cold to warm inside temperatures may cause condensation in your equipment. This is a cheap investment for protecting your radio. Finally, don't forget to include a laminated copy of your FCC license and some ARRL Get On The Air information handouts for visitors.

What kind of bag should you get to transport your gear on a hike or if you are going to operate some distance from your car? Unlike a Radio Go Kit mounted in a hard shell case, portable radio gear that will be carried any distance should be stored in a backpack, allowing your hands to be free. A backpack also distributes the weight better on your shoulders. For longer distances, be sure to get a comfortable pack with a waist strap.

If your setup area is nearby, you may get by with just carrying the gear by hand. If you operate portable a lot, you may find it necessary to use different bags depending on your operating environments and distances.

Another important factor is modularity. By having your gear set up in gear modules, you can easily move items between bags based on your needs. Different modules may include HF and VHF radios, feed line, or tools. Also be sure to include a checklist to verify you have everything you need. Forgetting a key piece of gear (such as a microphone or coax or an antenna) can ruin your trip!

Another important consideration is to store each piece of equipment in its own location to increase familiarity and ease of locating it in time of need. Moving gear around just makes it more difficult to locate it when you have no designated spot for it.

RADIO

What kind of radio do you need to operate portable? HF, VHF/UHF, or both?

In the past two decades manufacturers have produced smaller portable radios with efficient power requirements. Depending on the distance you will be traveling with your gear, the mode, band, and power requirements will dictate what kind of radio you should use. If the distance is short, using a heavy radio and battery may not be an issue. However if you are traveling by foot to a summit of a mountain, you will want a different gear setup.

In the backcountry, weight is everything. With small radios comes low RF power output and smaller batteries (meaning less weight). This leads to CW being a mode often

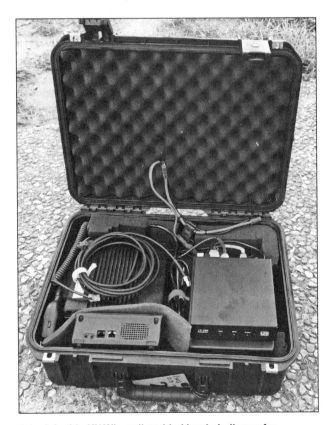

Ian, KI9W, traveled with his portable station to all call areas for more than 100 activations during ARRL's National Parks on the Air event in 2016. Radio, batteries, mast, antenna and accessories are all easily carried on a small cart and set up in about 15 minutes. [Ian Kuhn, KI9W, photo]

A look inside KI9W's well padded hard shell case for transporting his portable station. The contents include a 100 W HF/VHF transceiver, power supply, antenna tuner, and all necessary cables. [Ian Kuhn, KI9W, photo]

Elecraft's KX3 is extremely popular with portable operators. It covers 160 – 6 meters (plus 2 meters with an optional module) with 10 W output and works on SSB, CW, AM, FM, and data modes. [Stuart Thomas, KB1HQS, photo]

Operating from a summit greatly improves coverage with a typical VHF/UHF handheld transceiver. [Stuart Thomas, KB1HQS, photo]

employed with success. Propagation is also a factor and should be considered with the mode and antenna employed. Which bands offer the highest probability of success at the time when you will be operating? Knowing propagation data before entering the field is important — you may not have access to it once you set up depending on cell phone reception in the area.

What about the desktop radio you have at home? These radios, while bulky and having higher power requirements, can be used. However, weight and power source are issues in the field. Desktop radios often don't operate well with lower voltage inputs and don't pack well in backpacks.

Another key factor in operating radios in the outdoors is durability and ability to withstand environmental exposure (rain, snow, wind). In general, most amateur transceivers are not well suited for outdoor use, although some handheld FM radios are weatherproof. Having an additional waterproof case to store them in is advisable. Unlike the military radios that are built for harsh environments, amateur transceivers are usually not designed with these requirements in mind.

In addition to your radio, what kind of accessories should the portable operator carry? One useful item is a paint brush to use as a dust brush to sweep dirt, dust, and sand off your radio. Other items to include are spare power leads, headphones, and a microphone. In certain noisy environments, noise cancelling headphones might be useful. Carrying extra coax, connectors, and spare wire is a good idea. While in the field, don't forget to flag your antenna guy wires with high visibility flagging tape to prevent others from tripping and getting tangled up in your antennas. This is especially important in public parks.

POWER SOURCES

Along with your radio you will need a power source. If you are in your vehicle, you can use the car battery with the appropriately sized and fused power cable to power your radio (see the Mobile Stations section below). You may have to run the car to allow the alternator to keep the battery voltage topped off.

Once you leave the confines of your car, battery weight and radio wattage demands will determine how much battery you decide to carry. To determine the size of battery you need, first determine the amp-hours (Ah) your radio requires. You can calculate your Ah needs using this website: **www.4sqrp.com/ Battery_Capacity/index.php**.

Once you figure out the battery size, you will need to decide what kind of battery to buy. Battery technology is constantly changing. Currently there are three types of batteries being used in the field.

• *Sealed lead acid (SLA)*. Sealed lead acid batteries have been around for a long time. They are inexpensive and widely available, but are heavy and require maintenance. A "deep cycle" or "marine" battery is best for powering amateur equipment because it is designed to be deeply discharged on a regular basis. Starter batteries (as found in your car) are designed to deliver short bursts of very high current. Absorbed glass mat (AGM) batteries are spill proof.

• *Lithium ion phosphate (LiFePO4)*. A relatively recent development, LiFePO4 battery technology offers amateurs a safer, lightweight alternative to SLA batteries. For example, a popular 12 V, 20 Ah LiFePO4

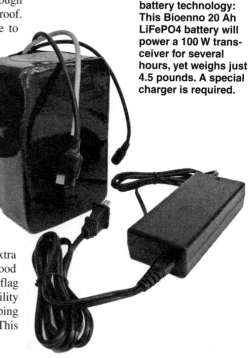

The magic of modern battery technology: This Bioenno 20 Ah LiFePO4 battery will power a 100 W transceiver for several hours, yet weighs just 4.5 pounds. A special charger is required.

battery weighs just 4.5 pounds, about a third of the weight of a comparable 20 Ah SLA battery. However the downside is that LiFRPO4 batteries come at a much higher cost and require a special charger.

In the field you may not have standard 120 V ac available to charge your batteries. Other options are portable ac generators and solar power. Generators such as the Honda EU1000i and EU2000i have been popular with amateurs because they offer clean sine wave output (radio friendly), fuel efficiency, reliability, and quiet operation.

Generators are often heavy and not something you would want to carry any amount of distance. There is also a carbon monoxide concern. Be sure to operate your generator outside and away from your operating position. They also require a fuel source to operate.

A less expensive and more lightweight charging source is solar power. Solar power is useful when you will be stationary for long periods of time and sunlight is available. Solar is quiet and easy to set up — no extra fuel or other items need to be operated. A downside of solar is the high cost per watt and the radio hash (RFI) produced by some charge controllers. Not all solar is radio friendly.

Also be aware, that if you are operating low power for a short duration, it may be more beneficial to carry extra battery capacity (a higher Ah battery or a spare) than to carry a solar power system. Ultimately it depends on your power requirements, available sunshine, and operating duration.

ANTENNAS

The third component in your field operating system is the antenna. To determine what antenna to use, consider how you plan to secure the antenna in the air and what bands you are interested in operating. Some areas may have plenty of trees to hang an antenna while others (summits, for example) may not.

The Pack Tenna Mini is a random wire antenna with a 9:1 balun that works on several bands, yet winds up into a tiny package. An antenna tuner is required. [Stuart Thomas, KB1HQS, photo]

In those situations, a collapsible fishing pole can be vertical as a temporary support to get your antennas aloft. For areas with trees, a throw line with a small weight can be used to get support lines aloft. Use mason twine initially as it has low resistance and allows the weight to fall easily. Then follow it with a heavier line that will hold your antenna aloft.

Going portable will often require small, lightweight antennas. This, along with QRP power levels, will require antennas that are efficient. Common HF antennas used in the field are dipoles, end-fed half wave wires, and magnetic loops. In the backcountry, ideally you want to be able to deploy your antenna and get on the air within 10 minutes. As with everything, it is a compromise between getting your antenna high up and getting on the air.

Popular VHF/UHF antennas include the J-pole, vertical and small Yagi. When it comes to VHF/UHF antennas and line-of-sight communication, elevation is key. You might be surprised at how far you can communicate from a summit with commanding views.

KI9W's antenna in the air. The ends of the dipole are secured with cement blocks on the ground. This system avoids any damage to property where the antenna is set up. Note the flagging tape to make the antenna visible to passersby. [Ian Kuhn, KI9W, photo]

For operating close to a vehicle, KI9W's easy-to erect portable antenna system includes a 22 foot collapsible mast, a base for the mast secured by driving a car tire over it, and a G5RV antenna for multiband operation. [Ian Kuhn, KI9W, photo]

ON THE AIR (OTA) ACTIVITIES

The day has arrived. You have your gear packed and your operating location selected. What techniques can you use to help increase your chances in making contacts while portable?

First there are several On the Air (OTA) activities you can participate in. Popular programs include including Summits on the Air (SOTA), Amateur Lighthouses on the Air (ARLHS), and Islands on the Air (IOTA) among others. Activating different summits, islands, or lighthouses will attract "chasers" who are hungry for your contact. These programs have websites or email lists for sharing information about upcoming operations. Before you leave home, be sure to register your upcoming activation announcing the details of your trip. These "alerts" give the details to those chasers interested in contacting you.

What if you are not participating in an OTA activity? If you have cell phone coverage, you can leverage your operating exposure by using spotting services such as DX Summit (**www.dxsummit.fi**) or Facebook group pages for the activity that you are participating in. In a remote area with no cell coverage? There is a network of "skimmers" that will pick up your CW CQ transmissions and spot you on the Reverse Beacon Network (RBN).

When calling CQ, mentioning that you are operating portable and your location may attract hams you who may not otherwise answer you. Everyone enjoys speaking with someone who is experiencing an adventure!

You have announced your upcoming trip, set up your gear and spotted yourself. You have a flood of amateurs calling you. How do you log them in the field? The traditional way is with pencil/pen and paper. If you use this method, using rain proof paper is preferred. Rite in the Rain notebooks (**www. riteintherain.com**) are low cost and handy for amateur portable operations. Other ways to log contacts include using smartphones or tablets with logging apps. Look for a logging app that will export the common ADIF file format so you can upload your contacts to Logbook of The World after your trip.

1.8.2 Mobile Stations

Mobile operation — from cars, RVs, boats and even bicycles — has experienced a renaissance in the past few years. The reason? Excellent, compact equipment and antennas! Hams have operated VHF and UHF from their vehicles for a long time, but with the advent of "all-band" radios that operate on everything from 160 meters through 70 cm, the mobile station no longer has to take a back seat to home operating.

This section introduces the most common mobile installation — for VHF/UHF FM operation. Then we'll extend the conversation to HF operating. Both types of installations have many aspects in common. While the vehicle is assumed to be a car, much of the information applies directly to other types of conveyance. Hamming while in motion places some extra requirements on the operator, too. If mobile operation sounds attractive to you, follow up with some of the resources listed at the end of the section.

When planning your mobile installation, the radio needs to be somewhere convenient. Transceivers with detachable control heads or faceplates are a great choice for modern cars. It's easier to find a home for a compact control head, and the main body of the radio can go under a seat or in the trunk.

Mobile Safety

Modern vehicles feature dozens of electronic gadgets and features for their owners, more than ever. A lot of work goes into making sure they are safe to use in a vehicle, especially on the road. When installing your mobile station, be sure to make safety your top priority.

Let's start with electrical safety. A vehicle moves and vibrates continuously while in motion. Your radio will also experience wide swings in temperature nearly every day. Any connection that's not secure is going to work its way loose in short order. If it's a radio signal connection — such as a cable or antenna — you'll experience erratic signals and possibly damage the radio.

Loose power connections can be much more dangerous. A vehicle's electrical system (and that includes any vehicle with batteries of any size) packs a lot of energy. An accidental short circuit will rapidly heat wire to the point where connectors oxidize and insulation melts. A vehicle fire is an expensive proposition! Make sure that all wiring is secure, protected against chafing or pinching by metal surfaces, and properly fused.

A common source of electrical problems is using wire or circuits that aren't adequately rated for the power requirements of the radio. Your radio's manual will specify the correct gauge wire to use. Follow that recommendation! At the very least, your radio may not operate properly if the resistance in the power wiring causes voltage at the radio to drop below the specified minimum. Overloaded wiring and connectors will also get quite hot and could start a fire.

Expect the worst to happen and protect yourself against it with proper fusing. Follow the recommendations of the manufacturer of your vehicle for installing a radio or other device. *Never* connect power leads directly to the vehicle's power system without proper fusing!

To minimize noise and voltage drops in the power wiring, connect the fused power leads directly to the battery, if possible. It may be

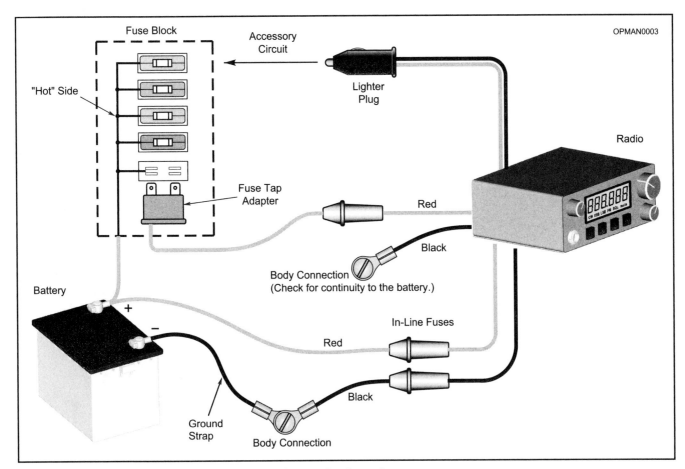

There are several ways to power your mobile station. See text for discussion.

more convenient to connect the negative lead to the vehicle battery ground strap where it is attached to the body or engine block. Fuses in *both* the positive and negative power leads will protect your radio's power wiring in case a positive wire comes in contact with the radio body or positive lead.

MECHANICAL SAFETY

It's important to mount or constrain your radio so that it cannot become a hazard to you or your passengers. Even in normal driving, a radio sliding around on a seat, underfoot, or on a dashboard can be a distraction at the minimum and an injury hazard at worst. Some states do not allow drivers to have any equipment mounted on the dashboard. Check your local regulations about requirements for mounting radios, then follow them. Your radio's user manual may also have some suggestions and recommendations.

In most cars, there is a place on the console where a radio might be installed. If so, and it will look acceptable to you, that's a good place to mount the radio. You'll be able to see the radio's front panel and the radio can look professionally installed. It will generally be secure, even in an accident.

If there's no convenient location for the whole rig, consider a radio with a detachable front panel and mount the radio under a seat or in the trunk. You'll probably need a *separation cable* or *separation kit* so that the microphone and *control head* (the panel with the operating controls and display) can be mounted up front and convenient where you are while the body of the radio is elsewhere. Wherever you mount the radio, be sure it can't come loose in a crash and become an injury-causing projectile.

Cables can also get tangled in control wiring, springs, levers and all the other gadgetry in a car. Be very sure that the microphone, antenna, power and any other accessory cables are secure or that they can't wrap themselves around something or jam a pedal.

DRIVING SAFETY

You've heard about driving and talking on mobile phones and the hazards of inattention. Maybe you've observed it firsthand because it's very common! Operating a mobile ham radio doesn't seem to be such a distraction because of the "push-to-talk" nature of ham communications. You're either talking or listening — never simultaneously as in a telephone conversation.

Nevertheless, don't hesitate to terminate a contact whenever you think you might need extra concentration on the road. You'll often hear a ham say, "I have to drive here" or "Time for both hands on the wheel" and sign off. That's a good idea. Don't compromise your safety or that of other drivers for a contact. If the contact is that important, pull over and devote your full attention to it.

Another driving distraction is having the radio controls placed where you have to take your eyes off the road to use them. Stuffing a radio between a seat and the console is a good example of how *not* to mount a radio. You'll have to turn your head and look down to turn knobs or press buttons if your microphone doesn't have duplicate controls. Be sure the radio or control head is mounted where you can pay attention to your number one job — driving!

VHF/UHF Mobile

The most common mobile installation for VHF and UHF mobile is a dual-band radio. They come with all the necessary mounting hardware, microphone, and power cabling for a proper installation. Many have a detachable front panel that can serve as a control head as described above. All have adequate power

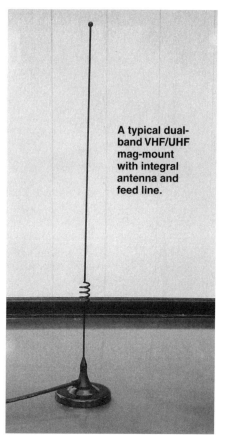

A typical dual-band VHF/UHF mag-mount with integral antenna and feed line.

Many HF mobile stations use the single-band helically wound whip antennas. Often called "hamsticks" these antennas were made popular by the Lakeview Company, which is no longer in business. Similar antennas are available from other sources. A hefty, multiple-magnet mount is required both to hold the large antenna on the car at driving speeds and to provide enough coupling to the car's metal surfaces.

output. Choosing one is largely a question of picking the secondary features that you want — automatic CTCSS tone detection, number of memories, scanning, receiving outside the amateur bands and so forth.

The antenna for VHF and UHF mobile should be a vertically-oriented "whip" solidly mounted on a flat metal surface of the vehicle such as the roof or trunk. Removable antennas with a magnetic mount (*mag mounts*) are very popular and work well — if your vehicle has steel exterior surfaces, which not all vehicles do. If your vehicle has plastic or aluminum body surfaces, consult the vehicle dealer about mounting antennas on the vehicle. You may wish to use a mount-on-glass antenna that does not require a ground plane to function.

Running the antenna cable into the interior of the car can be a challenge. Mag mount antennas are usually temporary, so the cable may be run through a door seal. If so, make sure the cable is not pinched hard enough to be deformed. Another problem is water getting in around the cable and you may have to experiment to find a spot where a cable will not give water a way in.

Trunk and hood mounts require a hole in the engine firewall or between the trunk and rear seat to run the cable. You may have to run the cable before installing the coax connector

in order to fit through the existing holes. Engine firewalls often have spare holes plugged with a grommet or the cable can be squeezed in alongside an existing wire bundle. In the trunk, look under the trunk liner and around the rear decking for ways into the passenger compartment. Regardless of which way you run the cable, be sure it won't be chafed or cut by the edges of brackets or other protruding metal.

HF Mobile

While you'll occasionally see a full-blown HF transceiver mounted in a larger car, truck or RV, the most common HF mobile rig is one of the "all-band" radios. These rigs typically put out 100 W on all HF bands through 6 meters and sometimes include 2 meters and 70 cm. (222 MHz is not covered because this is not an amateur band in most places outside of the US.)

All-band radios are a little larger than most VHF/UHF FM mobile radios and also draw considerably more current at full power. This makes them a little more difficult to mount in the passenger compartment. Most can be operated with the front panel mounted as a control head. At least two antenna cables are required for these radios — one is dedicated to HF or HF and 6 meters. VHF and UHF

may be combined into a single connection or they may be separate. All of the same cautions apply to installing HF radios as for VHF and UHF gear.

HF antennas bring their own special needs to the vehicle environment. A quarter-wave whip for 2 meters is less than 20 inches long, but the same antenna on 10 meters, the highest HF band, is approximately 8 feet long. On lower-frequency bands, the length of a full-size antenna rapidly becomes impractical for mobile operation. Most HF mobile antennas are coiled up, or *loaded*, to get the full electrical length crammed into a mobile-sized package. While this enables the antennas to be used while in motion, it also cuts their efficiency dramatically.

The ground connection to the vehicle is also critical on HF because the entire vehicle usually serves as the ground for the antenna. With the antenna efficiency already compromised, it becomes more important to avoid unnecessary ground losses. Many hams get good results using the "hamstick" style mobile whips. You can see that multiple magnets are used, not only because the antennas are larger and require additional holding power, but because the extra surface area of the magnets makes a better electrical connection to the vehicle surface. Whip style antennas can also be used with bumper or trailer-hitch mounts with good results. The key is to keep the base of the antenna, where current is the highest, in the clear and as high on the vehicle as possible.

Another type of HF mobile antenna that has become increasing popular is the "screwdriver" antenna. So-named because the initial designs used an electric screwdriver motor to adjust the antenna length, the antenna is a fixed-length whip tuned by moving sliding contacts along a coil at its base. Fixed mobile antennas, such as the Hamsticks, are relatively narrow-banded and must be retuned or changed in order to operate on greatly different frequencies within one band — for example 40 meter phone and 40 meter CW. The screwdriver type of antenna is tuned by the motor and can be used over a wide frequency range.

Operating SSB or CW on HF, the VHF/UHF operator will be surprised at how noisy the bands sound compared to the higher bands and noise suppression of FM. At HF, there is a lot more atmospheric noise. Noise is also generated in abundance by nearby motors, electrical lines, and even the vehicle's own ignition and accessory systems. The noise blankers found in the mobile radios can take out the worst of noise, but the HF operator typically just develops an "ear" for copying through it. The resources listed at the end of this section list numerous techniques for identifying and reducing or eliminating "mobile noise."

Keeping any kind of log while in motion is awkward at best and unsafe at worst, unless you train yourself to take notes without looking away from the road. A better idea is to just pull over and write the information in the log. Some operators use a digital voice recorder if they want to keep moving but still log the stations they work. The information is transcribed later.

MOBILE ACCESSORIES

As in the home shack, there are a number of useful accessories that can make radio easier on the road. One of the most useful is the communications speaker. The speaker in mobile radios is not very effective if the radio is installed under a seat, in the trunk or in a console. The external speaker can be mounted where sound is directed at the driver. (Most states do not allow the use of headphones while driving; check your local motor vehicle laws before doing so.) The frequency response of these speakers is tailored to the mobile environment, as well.

Antenna tuners are another common addition to the mobile HF station, allowing a fixed antenna to be used over a wider range. Auto-tuners are particularly popular, especially among boaters who use a single length of wire as their antenna for all bands. Several manufacturers offer tuners intended for use with mobile stations.

Even CW can be used on the road! Most operators prefer using a paddle due to the inconvenience of trying to use a straight key in a car. Paddles can be mounted on leg clips that hold them steady. Shops that sell aviation accessories often have lapboards or kneeboards that are quite suitable for mobiling, since pilots share many of the same concerns with hams.

Mobiling Activities

What can you do on the air while you're also on the road? Quite a bit! For starters, you can ragchew on any band just as well in motion as from home. In fact, the contacts tend to be longer because there are no interrupting phone calls or chores. Hilltopping on VHF and UHF is a popular practice, particularly during VHF+ contests.

If you like the idea of being the sought-after station, you may enjoy participating in the County Hunters program. Yes, people have actually made contact with all of the 3077 counties in the United States! A lot of those contacts are made with mobile stations, some of which have made a special trip to activity a lightly populated county or even two, transmitting from astride a county line. Your state QSO party probably encourages mobile operating, too, and out-of-state stations will be anxiously looking for you to increase their scores.

1.8.3 Portable and Mobile Resources

Portable Operation

Amateur Radio Lighthouses on the Air (ARLHS): **arlhs.com**
Batteries in a Portable World by Isidor
    Buchmann, **www.buchmann.ca/buchmann**
Islands on the Air (IOTA): **www.rsgbiota.org**

Summits on the Air (SOTA): **www.sota.org.uk**
Real time SOTA spotting: **www.sotawatch.org**
US Islands Award Program: **www.usislands.org**
World Wide Flora and Fauna in Amateur Radio: **wwff.co**

Mobile Operation

ARRL website: **www.arrl.org/hf-mobile**
AC6V, Operating Modes: **www.ac6v.com/opmodes.htm**
County Hunters: **www.countyhunter.com**
DX Zone's Mobile Page:
    www.dxzone.com/catalog/Operating_Modes/Mobile
KØBG website for mobile operators:
    www.k0bg.com
Mobile Amateur Radio Awards Club (MARAC):
    www.marac.org

You can also find more technical information in *The ARRL Handbook* and *The ARRL Antenna Book*, as well as *ARRL's Portable Antenna Classics*, *Amateur Radio on the Move* and *The Amateur Radio Mobile Handbook* (from RSGB), all available from your favorite ham radio dealer or the ARRL website.

Contents

2.1 Group Activities for the Radio Amateur
2.1.1 Local Activities
2.1.2 National and Online Groups and Activities

2.2 Preparing the Next Generation
2.2.1 Ham Radio Classes and Exams
2.2.2 Mentoring or "Elmering"
2.2.3 Educational Outreach

2.3 ARRL Field Day
2.3.1 Field Day Overview
2.3.2 Something for Everyone
2.3.3 Field Day Outreach
2.3.4 How to Get Started
2.3.5 Field Day Resources

2.4 Public Service Operating
2.4.1 Let's Get Started
2.4.2 Get on the Train — Training is a Must!
2.4.3 Basic Principles of Incident and
       Event Operating
2.4.4 Processing and Handling Messages
2.4.5 Emergency and Disaster Operations
2.4.6 Get with the Program
2.4.7 Public Service Operating Resources

Radio Clubs and Public Service

T.J. "Skip" Arey, N2EI, wrote the Group Activities for the Radio Amateur and Preparing the Next Generation sections. Rick Palm, K1CE, wrote the Public Service Operating section. The ARRL Field Day section was written by Dan Henderson, N1ND.

2.1 Group Activities for the Radio Amateur

Some people might see Amateur Radio as a solitary activity. Their image is of someone sitting alone in a room playing with radios. Nothing could be further from the truth! The number of opportunities for hams to interact with other folks could be a book in itself.

In addition to face-to-face gatherings (often called *eyeball* meetings), the Internet allows hams to gather via social media to discuss specific topics and share ideas about how to enjoy this hobby better. While most local clubs tend to be general interest organizations, you can also find groups that are dedicated to a specific area of amateur interest such as contesting or VHF/UHF operation. Interacting with other hams who share your interests is not only enjoyable, but can help you to learn from their experiences.

Radio club meetings often include a presentation on an interesting aspect of Amateur Radio or a guest speaker. Here, retired FCC Special Counsel for Enforcement Riley Hollingsworth, K4ZDH, addresses the Forsyth Amateur Radio Club in Winston-Salem, North Carolina. [Courtesy *HamRadioNow*]

2.1.1 Local Activities

Getting the Most Out of Your Local Club

If you have not yet become a licensed Amateur Radio operator, your local club will be the best place to get your start. In addition to the encouragement of a group of people who really want to see you succeed, many clubs offer formal training sessions to help you learn what you need to pass the test. Clubs may also have their own Volunteer Examiner (VE) testing programs or they often affiliate with one nearby.

It is quite easy to locate nearby ARRL Affiliated Clubs. The search function at **www.arrl.org/find-a-club** allows you to search for clubs and even learn a little bit about their activities and meeting times. Many of the listed clubs will include e-mail contact

Information on more than 2300 ARRL Affiliated Clubs and Special Service Clubs is available with the search function on the ARRL website.

information and even a club website. Both of these resources can serve to give you an understanding of what the hams in your area are up to and how you might join in the fun. ARRL Affiliated Clubs all take an interest in promoting the hobby and encouraging new folks to get the most out of their Amateur Radio experience.

Many of these clubs have taken the additional step of becoming Special Service Clubs (SSC). These clubs have established themselves as exceptional proponents for Amateur Radio training, public service, technical expertise, and operating skill. Special Service Clubs can help both the newcomer and the experienced ham to grow in their understanding and enjoyment of Amateur Radio.

While most clubs are general interest groups, some lean more toward certain activities such as contesting or public service. Don't let that discourage you! You will still meet hams in your area and you will quickly discover that, while the club might travel a particular path, its members are usually much more eclectic in their interests. If you live in a more populated area, you are likely to find more than one club to support your interest. Don't be surprised if you run into some of the same people wherever you go. Hams tend to enjoy each others' company.

If you are new to the hobby and attending your first meeting, you will more than likely hear a few things that you don't understand. Don't be afraid to ask questions. Amateur Radio has a long history of helping folks starting out in the hobby learn and grow. We were all beginners once. And if we have tried

to learn about a new operating mode or radio skill, we've been *newbies* more than a few times.

Most clubs have formal or informal *Special Interest Groups*. These are people who gravitate to a particular aspect of the hobby. If, for instance, you are interested in DXing or the CW mode or PSK31, it shouldn't take long to figure out which club members share those interests and are likely to help you develop your skills and abilities. Likewise, if you want to try something new, you will probably run across a group of people who can help you discover the best way to move forward in that new area of interest. You might even be the one who is the expert in a certain area and offer to help others in the group to give it a try.

Club meetings vary greatly, but you will usually find the following activities:

Business Meeting: This is where the club discusses particular aspects of their general operation. It can include upcoming events and projects or recent accomplishments of individual members such as upgrading their license or achieving an award. Reports from various committees such as DX or VE Testing might also be shared and discussed. Many clubs include a few moments to discuss the health and welfare of members who might be under the weather.

Informal Discussion: Usually done around the club coffee pot. This is where a new person can learn who is who and what their personal interests in the hobby might be. This is also the place to let folks know a little bit about who you are, what you're interested in, and

what your goals might be for advancing your ham radio interests.

Presentation: Many clubs will have one or more of their members or a guest give a formal presentation on some unique aspect of the hobby. It might be a lecture on a particular ham radio skill or a slide show about someone's recent portable operation. The topics are nearly endless with a hobby as wide ranging as ours. These presentations are always opportunities to discover new ways of enjoying the hobby. Consider offering a presentation on something you are interested in.

In addition to the regular meeting activities, some clubs might hold special events at specific meetings. These might include Swap and Sell sessions or Build-a-Thons where members work on club-supported kits or projects. Many clubs will also hold annual holiday or awards dinners. Some clubs make it a point to meet periodically for breakfast at a local restaurant. All these additional activities build friendship and camaraderie among the membership.

Once you get your feet wet and get to know a few folks, don't be surprised if you are invited to volunteer to help out with some aspect of the club's activities. Every ham club appreciates *new blood*. Helping out with a club activity or project is a great way to learn new things and meet new people.

If your club has some older, more experienced hams, take time to get to know them and hear their stories. Amateur Radio has grown and changed in so many ways over the years, it is always interesting and informative to hear about how things were done "back in the day." Old Timers have a lot of time in the log and a lot of experience to share.

Joining and becoming an active member of your local Amateur Radio club is the gateway to many years of ham radio fun and learning.

Special Interest Clubs

As mentioned previously, you may find that some of your local clubs center their interest around a single activity.

Contest clubs concentrate their efforts at logging big scores in many of the well-known on-air competitions. The members usually work together to set up multioperator stations that work all the bands. Such clubs also make serious efforts during activities such as ARRL Field Day. If you have a competitive spirit and want to build up your skills at fast paced operating, these clubs are a great place to learn and grow.

You will also find clubs that concentrate on public service and emergency communications (emcomm). These clubs are usually affiliated with the ARRL Amateur Radio Emergency Service® (ARES®), the National Weather Service SKYWARN program, and the Radio Amateur Civil Emergency Service (RACES). Their members might also join other support organizations such as the local Community Emergency Response Team (CERT) or the Red Cross. Many have affiliations with local public service agencies. Such clubs hold regular drills to build skills and practice specific operating protocols. They often give local support to community activities such as charity bike rides and walk-a-thons. If you have a strong interest in using your hobby to *give back* to your community, you may find a club like this is just for you.

Hamfests

Many clubs will make an effort to hold a *hamfest*, usually once a year. These gatherings serve many purposes. First and foremost, they are great places to meet fellow hams from your area.

Usually a hamfest will include a flea market or swap meet where hams can bring their equipment to sell or trade. Many times commercial vendors will also show up. A hamfest is a great place to find a reasonably priced used transceiver, antenna, or accessories to start your on-air activities or to improve your station. Hamfests are also a source for cables, parts, and other hard-to-find equipment that would otherwise need to be tracked down online.

Many hamfests also offer VE testing for people who want to get licensed or upgrade to a higher ticket. Some hamfests offer ARRL Worked All States (WAS) or DX Century Club (DXCC) *card checking* for people who are looking to add those awards to their wall.

Hamfests often offer forums where experienced hams speak about skills and practices.

Many clubs hold an annual hamfest, providing an opportunity for area hams to buy and sell equipment, attend presentations, and renew acquaintances.

These are great opportunities to learn new ways to enjoy the hobby.

In addition to hamfests offered by local clubs, ARRL Sections and ARRL Divisions regularly hold conventions that provide even more opportunities for hams to get together and enjoy each others' company. Also, every year the ARRL holds a National Convention. This event moves around the country to give hams all over the nation the chance to attend.

You can find details of local, regional, and national events in the pages of *QST* magazine each month. You can also search online at **www.arrl.org/hamfests-and-conventions-calendar**.

Join the ARRL Field Organization

What keeps Amateur Radio as vital and active as it is are the many folks who volunteer formally to help other hams enjoy the hobby. The ARRL Field Organization recruits and coordinates the efforts of dedicated volunteers in a number of areas of interest. The ARRL is organized into 71 Administrative areas known as Sections. These Sections are guided and directed by an elected Section Manager who facilitates programs and procedures within your local area. Any ARRL member can offer their services by seeking a Station Level appointment.

OFFICIAL OBSERVER ADVISORY NOTICE

calling

Radio: _____ your call was heard working _____ at _____ UTC.

Date: _____ 20 ___ Frequency: _____ MHz. Mode: _____ Your RST: _____

The following is noted in the interest of maintaining Amateur Radio's reputation for good operating and technical practices:
1 [ ] FREQUENCY INSTABILITY 2 [ ] CHIRP 3 [ ] SPURIOUS 4 [ ] HARMONIC 5 [ ] HUM 6 [ ] KEY CLICKS 7 [ ] BROAD SIGNAL 8 [ ] DISTORTED AUDIO 9 [ ] OVERDEVIATION 10 [ ] OUT OF BAND 11 [ ] IMPROPER ID 12 [ ] LANGUAGE 13 [ ] CAUSING INTERFERENCE 15 [ ] CARRIER 20 [ ] OTHER

Remarks: _____
_____

Please refer to FCC Regulation 47 CFR 97 _____. Please take a few minutes to determine what equipment factors or operating practices might have contributed to this apparent departure from the rule or the good amateur practice standard. The intent of this notice is to alert you to the above noted operating condition. NO REPLY IS NECESSARY. The undersigned ARRL Official Observer has fulfilled this helping role by simply alerting you, and is not *required* to reply to any correspondence. Thank you for your attention and any cooperative efforts to enhance the high standards of the Amateur Radio Service which we all share with pride.

FSD-213(1-04) Signature _____ Call _____

Good Operator Report

Radio: _____ ,your call was heard (calling)(working) _____ at _____ UTC.

Date: _____ 20 ___ Frequency: _____ MHz Mode: _____ . Your RST _____

We thought you would like to know ....

That this Official Observer has noted your EXCELLENT radio signal quality/operating procedure as a fine example for all radio amateurs.

Remarks: _____
_____

This observation by the undersigned ARRL Official Observer is a function of the Amateur Auxiliary to the FCC. This Observer thanks you for your excellent example of good amateur practice for others in the amateur Radio Service. Keep up the good work.

FSD-15(7-04) Signature _____ Call _____

As an ARRL Official Observer (OO) appointee, you may send an Advisory Notice (left) to remind an amateur to use good operating procedures, or a Good Operator Report (right) to recognize a ham heard operating in an exemplary manner.

You can offer to volunteer to be a:

Local Government Liaison (LGL). The LGL monitors local government dockets consistently, offers local, organized support quickly when necessary, and is known in the local amateur community as the point person for local government problems.

Official Emergency Station (OES). The Official Emergency Station appointee sets high standards of emergency preparedness and operating and makes a deeper commitment to the ARES program. Working with the appropriate Emergency Coordinator or District Emergency Coordinator, the OES appointee develops a detailed responsibility plan that makes the best use of his or her skills and abilities. During drills and actual emergency situations, the OES appointee is expected to implement his/her function with professionalism and minimal supervision.

Official Observer (OO). The object of the Official Observer program is to notify amateurs of operating and technical irregularities before they come to the attention of the FCC and to recognize good operating practices. The OO program is the backbone of the Amateur Auxiliary. OOs are certified in the Auxiliary by passing a mandatory written examination. OOs monitor the bands for such things as poor signal quality or out-of-band operation and send a notification card to the station involved.

Official Relay Station (ORS). This is a traffic-handling appointment for traffic handlers, regardless of mode employed or part of the spectrum used. The ORS participates regularly in traffic activities and is able to handle all communications speedily and reliably and set the example in efficient operating procedures.

Public Information Officer (PIO). The PIO is the contact for local media outlets. He or she establishes and maintains personal contacts with appropriate representatives of the media to provide information about Amateur Radio and activities of local hams. The PIO also works with the LGL to establish personal contacts with local government officials where possible and explain to them, briefly and non-technically, about Amateur Radio and how it can help their communities.

Technical Specialist (TS). The TS serves as a technical advisor to local hams and clubs. In addition to helping with general technical questions, the TS serves as advisor in radio frequency interference (RFI) issues. The TS may also be asked to speak at local clubs on popular tech topics.

Full details and requirements for these positions and how to go about volunteering can be found at **www.arrl.org/field-organization**.

2.1.2 National and Online Groups and Activities

National and International Clubs and Organizations

Access to the World Wide Web has allowed many Amateur Radio organizations to vastly expand their activities and provide service, support, and fellowship to hams all over the world. Many special interest clubs have taken advantage of setting up shop on line. Below is a list of some of the most popular groups currently just a few keystrokes away.

10 10 International (www.ten-ten.org) — For hams interested in operating on the 10 meter band.

Adventure Radio Society (arsqrp. blogspot.com) — Devoted to combining ham radio and outdoor activities.

ARHAB (www.arhab.org) — Amateur Radio High Altitude Ballooning, amateurs who launch radio balloons as a method of space exploration.

Amateur Radio Lighthouse Society (arlhs.com) — A group devoted to operating from lighthouses and lightships.

AMSAT (www.amsat.org) — The Radio Amateur Satellite Corporation, designs, builds, and arranges for the launch and operation of amateur satellites.

BMHA (www.bmha-hams.org) — Bicycle Mobile Hams of America, a group of hams who take their hobby mobile via bicycle.

CWops (www.cwops.org) — This organization is dedicated to the use of CW on the ham bands and promotes improved CW skills through its CW Academy and on-air activities.

FISTS (www.fists.org) — The International Morse Preservation Society, this group promotes building CW operating skills through training and on air events.

Flying Pigs QRP Club (www.fpqrp.org) — Low power operating group with an emphasis on monthly contests.

Handihams (www.handiham.org) — Courage Kenney Handiham Program, an organization for the support of amateurs with disabilities.

Homing In (www.homingin.com) — A site covering regional groups interested in the sport of radio direction finding (RDF).

IOTA (www.rsgbiota.org) — Islands on

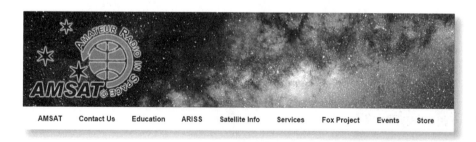

the Air, an awards program developed by the Radio Society of Great Britain (RSGB) to offer awards for contact with the world's islands.

MARAC (marac.org) — Mobile Amateur Radio Awards Club, a group of hams devoted to county hunting.

MARCO (marco-ltd.org) — Medical Amateur Radio Council, promotes fellowship between ham radio operators who are also involved in the healing arts.

NAQCC (www.naqcc.info) — North American QRP CW Club, devoted to using CW at low power levels of 5 W or less.

Old Old Timers Club (www.ootc.us) — A group for hams who have been involved in radio communications 40 or more years ago.

QCWA (www.qcwa.org) — Quarter Century Wireless Association, an organization for people licensed as radio amateurs for 25 years or longer.

QRP ARCI (www.qrparci.org) — QRP Amateur Radio Club International, devoted to operating with 5 W or less power.

SKCC (www.skccgroup.com) — Straight Key Century Club, promotes the sending of CW over the air using hand keys and other non-electronic mechanical keys such as semiautomatic *bugs*.

SMIRK (www.smirk.org) — Six Meter International Radio Klub, for hams with an interest in operating on the 6 meter band.

TAPR (www.tapr.org) — Tucson Amateur Packet Radio, dedicated to the development of all aspects of digital radio communications.

USPS Amateur Radio Club (www.usps. org/national/Ham/RadioClub.html) — A group for hams who are boaters affiliated with the United States Power Squadrons.

YLRL (www.ylrl.org) — Young Ladies Radio League, dedicated to promoting the efforts of female Amateur Radio operators. They hold regional conventions and on air contests.

Social Media

The growth of social media in the last few years has provided even more opportunities for hams to gather online and share ideas. These various Internet watering holes are growing and changing almost daily. It is well worth the effort to become familiar with these web based resources as references and places to find like-minded hams near and far.

Facebook (www.facebook.com). If you type the words Amateur Radio into Facebook's search field, you will discover literally hundreds of Facebook *groups*. You could spend hours just searching through the list. A better path might be to narrow your search by adding an area of interest (for example, Amateur Radio portable). If you are looking for ham activity in your area you could try adding your city or state to the search pattern (such as Amateur Radio New Jersey). If you search regionally, you will probably discover that some of the local clubs in your area have a Facebook page that you can "Like." If you are already on Facebook you may have already had a number of your Facebook friends suggest ham radio pages to you.

Facebook also has a messaging system built in that can be used in real-time if the other user is logged on, or it can be used to send short notes similar to e-mail. Facebook also provides mobile "apps" for most smartphones so you can have it as a tool wherever you go.

Often, DXpeditions or special event stations will set up Facebook pages to let you know when and where they might be on the air.

Instagram (www.instagram.com). This site allows users to share pictures and short videos. It interfaces with other social media platforms such as Facebook and Twitter. Mobile phone versions are most popular as many smartphones now have excellent cameras.

Twitter (twitter.com). This online service allows users to send and receive 140 character messages known as *tweets*. You can set your account to follow the tweets of other users. You can also forward (re-tweet) the message of another user to people in your group. You can label your messages with a *hashtag* (for example, #HamRadio) to allow others to see and search on your messages. One very useful way this service works for hams is exchanging up-to-date information

ARRL established a special Facebook group for the year-long National Parks on the Air (NPOTA) operating event in 2016. The social media site allowed thousands of NPOTA "activators" and "chasers" to share stories, photos, videos, tips, and real-time on-air spots — greatly enhancing the experience for everyone involved.

Yahoo Groups such as this one devoted to discussion of software defined radio (SDR) offer a wealth of information on a wide variety of topics. There are few questions that group members can't help with.

about what you are hearing on the bands. For example, if I hear HH2XX operating, I might Tweet out to my friends: "HH2XX Haiti on 14.020 simplex. Loud in PA #DX". This would alert anyone following my Twitter feed to listen and see if they can get the station in their log. Twitter offers a mobile app for most phone platforms.

Pinterest (www.pinterest.com). This is a photo sharing site that allows users to sort their pictures by subject matter. This site works well for sharing photos related to club activities or operating events.

Yahoo Groups (groups.yahoo.com). Yahoo is best known for its search and news services. However, the site has a large and active *Groups* section that contains countless Amateur Radio related resources. For example, if you own a particular brand or model of transceiver, you will more than likely find an active group that shares information, files, support documentation, and other information that will help you make best use of your equipment. You will also find groups that trade ideas and information about particular operating practices such as DXing or QRP. You can set up your group membership to deliver messages from the group to your e-mail account in real time or in a single daily digest.

YouTube (www.youtube.com). This site is used by hams to offer short educational and informational videos about many aspects of the hobby. A search will bring up information about how to get started in the hobby, documentaries about DXpeditions, equipment reviews, how-to articles on subjects such as antenna building and much more.

Ham Oriented Websites

In addition to pure social media platforms, there are a few traditional radio hobby web pages that have a strong social media aspect to them.

eHam.net (www.eham.net). Long before the current general interest social media sites became popular, hams had their own online gathering space. eHam presents users with articles of interest to the Amateur Radio community, a calendar of ham related events, classified ads, a call sign lookup service, a DX spotting network, and much more. It has a Forum section that allows hams to exchange views on a wide range of subjects. A very useful tool is its Reviews section where hams post their personal experience with just about any new or used piece of equipment you can imagine.

RadioReference.com (www.radioreference.com). This site is primarily devoted to the monitoring and scanning aspects of the radio hobby. That said, it also maintains a very large and active Amateur Radio series of Forums that can provide many opportunities for discussion and learning.

QRZ.com (www.qrz.com). Most hams use this site to search call signs in order to obtain QSL information or find out more about a station they have contacted. The site also has many other features, including up-to-date ham radio news services and a swap meet section where you can buy and sell equipment. It also has a large and very active Forums section where hams get involved in discussion about all aspects of the hobby.

ARRL website (www.arrl.org/forum). This section of the ARRL website is the place to discuss and ask questions about a number of League programs. Topics include Awards, Contesting, Technology, Education, and Amateur Radio in the Classroom.

Far from being a solitary hobby, Amateur Radio offers innumerable opportunities for hams to share their experiences and build lifelong friendships.

2.2 Preparing the Next Generation

Almost any activity you can think of is only one or two generations from extinction unless the participants actively seek ways keep the flame alive. Amateur Radio has survived and thrived through multiple technological and social upheavals. This is because of the ongoing efforts of dedicated volunteers who choose to give back to the hobby by helping new people, often younger people, discover the fun and excitement of ham radio.

Studying with a class offers a chance for interaction with instructors and other students, as well as a forum to ask questions or see demonstrations to help with understanding the material.

2.2.1 Ham Radio Classes and Exams

Studying for Your License

While it is possible to go it alone in seeking your ham ticket, most people benefit from attending training classes. Many local ham clubs (especially designated ARRL Special Service Clubs) periodically offer classes to assist folks in learning the theory and regulations necessary for passing their first license exam. Many also offer upgrade classes to help hams earn their General or Extra tickets.

If you're looking for a nearby class, start by going to the ARRL website and using the search function found at **www.arrl.org/find-an-amateur-radio-license-class**. If you don't find a nearby class, try contacting nearby ARRL Affiliated Clubs (**www.arrl.org/find-a-club**) and asking about upcoming classes.

The online ARRL Store at **www.arrl.org/shop** offers license manuals that include study material based upon the latest examination question pool. These books can be used to study on your own or as the essential texts for classes that are offered for any level of amateur license.

Helping Others Study

Perhaps you've been licensed and active for a while and want to help others learn what they need for their first license or an upgrade. Explaining the principles of radio science, FCC rules and regulations, operating practices, safety, and all of the other topics covered on Amateur Radio exams in a classroom setting class takes hard work and dedication. ARRL offers support and resources for those who participate in license training. Consider becoming an ARRL Reg-

istered Instructor — you can find out how, and what resources are available at **www.arrl.org/volunteer-instructors-mentors**

Clubs that want to offer classes can also find all the necessary resources for organizing and promoting classes at **www.arrl.org/volunteer-instructors-mentors**. The site includes teaching and study aids, lesson plans, and exam practice aids as well as the most current exam question pools to assure your class is sharing up-to-date information.

Additional Training Opportunities

Clubs that are oriented toward public service are likely to offer additional training including the ARRL Introduction to Emergency Communication course. This instruction provides essential skills for hams who want to serve their community with their radio skills.

In addition to licensing and certification

Amateur Radio licensing test sessions are administered by volunteer examiners (VEs) who grade the exams and take care of all the paperwork.

training, some clubs may offer training in specific Amateur Radio skills that help increase the enjoyment of the hobby. For example, while no longer required to obtain an FCC license, many hams still enjoy using the CW mode. Clubs can offer CW training classes to teach the code and improve speed and skill. The CWops club (**www.cwops.org**) offers the CW Academy program for amateurs who wish to improve their proficiency in Morse code.

For those interested in learning about contesting or improving their skills, Contest University (**www.contestuniversity.com**) is held in conjunction with the annual Dayton Hamvention and other events during the year. The website features past presentations on a number of topics. Similar opportunities and resources for those interested in DXing are available at DX University (**www.dxuniversity.com**).

Volunteer Examination

Since the 1980s, the process of Amateur Radio license testing has been performed by ham radio operators who volunteer to administer the exams that were traditionally offered only at FCC offices. These Volunteer Examiners (VEs) receive accreditation by way of the Volunteer Examiner Coordinator (VEC) system. This process assures fairness and integrity. Potential hams, and active hams who are seeking to upgrade their license, can take the necessary exams locally, usually through a local ham club or at a hamfest. However, VEs can self-organize and offer other testing opportunities as well.

VE exam sessions are held very regularly around the country. The easiest way to find a VE testing session near you is the check the ARRL website at **www.arrl.org/find-an-amateur-radio-license-exam-session**. You might also ask your local ham club to refer you to VE sessions in your area.

Would you like to get involved in giving exams in your area? Any ham over the age of 18 who holds a General Class or higher license and who has never had his or her license suspended or revoked can become a Volunteer Examiner. You can find information about how to become a VE at **www.arrl.org/become-an-arrl-ve**.

Setting up and offering regular VE sessions is a great way to bring new members into a local club.

2.2.2 Mentoring or "Elmering"

Most people who have been involved in Amateur Radio for any length of time can point to one or more experienced hams who helped them get started in the hobby. The name "Elmer" is believed to have first appeared in the March 1971 issue of *QST* in a column by Rod Newkirk, W9BRD. Since that time, the term Elmer has been used to refer to any ham who formally or informally aids a newcomer in the hobby. Passing the license exam is just the first step — helping other hams in putting together a station, getting on the air, feeling comfortable making contacts, and getting involved in interesting aspects of ham radio are the keys to growing our hobby.

Every ham has the opportunity, and some would say the responsibility, to be an Elmer. It can be as simple as showing a new ham your radio shack and giving them a few pointers about how to get on the air. An Elmer can share experiences and skills that will give a new ham a leg up on getting the most out of the hobby. It can even be as simple as providing a good example of on-air practice during a QSO. The assistance and encouragement you can give a new ham benefits the individual and the whole hobby. To have someone refer to you as their Elmer might very well be the highest praise in ham radio.

ARRL's Affiliated Club Mentor Program (**www.arrl.org/mentor-program**) offers clubs a place to share ideas and techniques that they have used to "Elmer" newer hams. As the program web page says, "...the local radio club is where the learning takes place. The local radio club is where the newcomer begins the journey of discovery and the seasoned veteran keeps informed of the latest technology. Regardless of where we are on our ham radio journey our local radio club is where we find our friends."

Field Day — For the Future of the Hobby

ARRL Field Day is the primary time of year when ham clubs actively seek to operate in a public space and encourage non-hams to discover the fun of Amateur Radio. While Field Day has aspects of a contest (making lots of contacts on various bands and modes), clubs get bonus points for such things as setting up in a public area, having a public information table, media publicity, educational activity, and using social media. There is also a bonus for offering a GOTA (Get On The

Nothing builds confidence better than gaining hands-on experience under the watchful eye of a mentor. Here, Chris Courson, KC4CMR, works with members of the Williamsburg Area Amateur Radio Club in their Builder's Group workshop. [Courtesy Dino Papas, KLØS]

This Field Day Station would not be able to operate without the volunteer efforts of many hams performing tasks large and small. [T.J. Arey, N2EI, photo]

Air) Station where non-hams and new hams can try out communicating with ham radio, as well as for youth participation. Field Day is often the experience that leads a person to consider joining the Amateur Radio community, and for new hams to mingle with experienced hams and gain on-the-air experience. Field Day is discussed in detail later in this section.

2.2.3 Educational Outreach

School Programs

In addition to Amateur Radio being a fun hobby, it can be used as a teaching tool for many different disciplines. The recent emphasis on Science, Technology, Engineering and Math (STEM) is a great entry point for our hobby. Amateur Radio can be a dynamic way of getting young people excited about STEM subjects. It can also be a way to help students develop verbal and social skills. Of course, ham radio operators who enjoy DXing will probably be able to easily pass any geography test.

Helping traditional educators understand the value of Amateur Radio is a great project for individual hams or clubs. Schools are often looking for programs and demonstrations that can enhance the learning experience, especially if they can make subjects more fun and interesting.

The ARRL has created an educational outreach program designed to introduce how ham radio can be used as an instructional resource. The Educational & Technology Program provides curriculum and resources to build a strong foundation related to wireless technology literacy. The ARRL can provide resources, grants, and professional development training to schools at no cost. These resources can lead to a school being designated an Educational & Technology Program (ETP) School. To date, more than 500 schools and teachers have become involved in ETP. This program is supported by donations from individuals, clubs, and equipment vendors. For more information, visit **www.arrl.org/ amateur-radio-in-the-classroom**.

Once a month Bill McCord, KC2ONQ, representing the Southern Counties Amateur Radio Association (SCARA), hosts a Hands-On Learning Experience at the Jersey Shore Children's Museum. He helps the kids learn about radio communication and they get to play a game of Fox Hunt. [T.J. Arey, N2EI, photo]

After giving a motivational speech to students, TV personality Ariel Tweto called CQ from the Pilot Station School Radio Club (WL7CXM) in Alaska during the School Club Roundup. [Donn Gallon, KL7DG, photo]

Geoff Haines, N1GY, helps a Scout get on the air at K4BOY, the club station of the Camp Flying Eagle Southwest Florida Scout Council. [Courtesy Ken Settlemyer, WW4KS]

School Club Roundup

Many schools and colleges have active Amateur Radio clubs. To celebrate and encourage these clubs, the ARRL sponsors the School Club Roundup (**www.arrl.org/school-club-roundup**) twice a year, during the Winter/Spring Term and Fall Term periods. During the Roundup, schools get points for communicating with each other. The schools can receive certificates in recognition of their efforts. Non-school clubs and individuals are also encouraged to lend their support by contacting the school stations. In addition to having fun with ham radio, these schools often are able to share information about the event through local press and social media. This gives a boost to the hobby for non-hams.

ARISS — Amateur Radio on the International Space Station

In a joint venture between the ARRL, NASA, and AMSAT, a program has been developed to allow educational institutions and organizations to contact and communicate with astronauts on the International Space Station (ISS). School Clubs or schools with the assistance of local hams and ham clubs, are given the opportunity to experience space communications. In addition to talking with the ISS crew, the students can learn many facets of radio communication and master skills that will lead them toward becoming licensed and developing as hams. Find out how to get involved at **www.arrl.org/amateur-radio-on-the-international-space-station**.

Youth Programs

Almost any place where young people gather can be an entry point for Amateur Radio. If your community has any youth group activities or community youth programs, you or your club might contact them to see where you can fit in to their programs. It can be something as simple as setting up an information table or as formal as giving a presentation. The ARRL provides ideas about how to engage young people at **www.arrl.org/outreach-to-youth**.

Many local schools, libraries, and colleges offer community based learning experiences. Offering a demonstration of ham radio or even a basic license class through one of these venues can draw in young people to the hobby.

Youth today are extremely comfortable with computers and smartphones. Demonstrating how Amateur Radio activity is enhanced by computers and mobile devices is something that many young people are attracted to. Demonstrating digital mode communication and cross platform systems such as D-STAR, System Fusion, DMR, IRLP, and EchoLink, especially how these might be used with mobile devices, should be interesting to many young folks.

If your local club holds a hamfest, consider setting up a Youth Lounge with information and activities that can draw in their interest. The ARRL offers resources to help develop this idea at **www.arrl.org/youth-lounge**.

Scouting

Amateur Radio and Scouting have a long and prosperous relationship. Historically,

many young folks first learned about the ham radio hobby through their Scouting experiences. This continues today and Scouting programs continue to grow the ranks of active amateurs. Boy Scouts can achieve a Merit Badge for Radio and another for Signals and Codes. They can also achieve the privilege of wearing a special Interpreter Strip if they master basic CW skills.

Recently Girl Scouts have also joined in the fun by offering a Radio and Wireless Technology patch program.

Individual hams and ham clubs can offer their assistance to local scout leadership and councils to provide support and training for

Adam Nathanson, N4EKV, of Lafayette, California, turned the shack over to his daughters Amber (front) and Audrey for Kid's Day.

young people entering into the hobby through Scouting.

The third weekend in October is the time for the annual Jamboree on the Air (JOTA). This annual on-air get together encourages Boy Scouts and Girl Scouts around the world to communicate by way of Amateur Radio. With over one million participants in this event, it is clear that ham radio and Scouting go together. If you hear a JOTA station on the air, give them a call and chat with the Scout at the other end for a bit.

For more information, visit **www.arrl.org/amateur-radio-and-scouting.**

Kid's Day

Twice each year, in January and June, the ARRL offers an event called Kid's Day (**www.arrl.org/kids-day**). During Kid's Day, hams are encouraged to invite young people into their home or club stations to get on the air and communicate with other young people around the world. Children are shown how to talk on the radio and make an exchange of information, sharing their name, age, and favorite color. Everyone who participates is eligible to receive a colorful certificate. They are also encouraged to share a bit about themselves. This initial exposure to Amateur Radio, even for the youngest kids can be a door into a future filled with the wonders of Amateur Radio.

Most of us are in this hobby today because someone showed us the way and gave us support and encouragement. It is incumbent upon us to pass our skills on to the next generation of young amateurs.

2.3 ARRL Field Day

"Elsewhere in this issue is announced the plan for a Field Day test of portable equipment... The idea of a local, national and international outing ought to be popular. If a sufficient volume of results of portable station work is reported, perhaps we can make it an annual affair. At any rate, we hope this announcement will serve as a test of the emergency availability of portable stations and equipment, and be just as valuable as local Fire Prevention Week or like endeavors, in its own special field of focusing attention on the subject of 'preparedness' for communications emergencies of course." — F.E. Handy, W1BDI, ARRL Communications Manager, *QST* 1933

With these words and from that humble beginning has emerged what has become the most time-honored tradition in Amateur Radio in the United States — ARRL Field Day. This operating event is always held the fourth full weekend in June and once you experience it, you will quickly understand its popularity.

Each year's ARRL Field Day has a unique logo that can be found on shirts, pins, mugs, and other items to promote the event.

2.3.1 Field Day Overview

More operators participate in Field Day than any other on-the-air activity during the year. On average, more than 35,000 people representing more than 2500 entries get involved with the premier operating event annually. During the brief 27-hour time frame of the event, well over 1,000,000 contacts will be made. Field Day entrants use most of the major bands and modes authorized for the Amateur Service.

What began as a short exercise for licensees to test their ability has morphed into an operating event that is part on-the-air contacts, part public relations event, part community outreach, part educational opportunity, part social event, and much more. Field Day is not an adjudicated contest; rather it is a multifaceted operating event that allows amateurs to showcase their talents and community service capabilities. It is also one of the best recruiting opportunities by which thousands of non-hams will experience the many dimensions of radio for the first time.

ARRL Field Day can be experienced by someone operating solo from the comfort of the home station; by a large group operating

from a public location putting on a demonstration of what they can do; by a solitary hiker at a remote campsite in the mountains; at a county emergency operations center; or by almost any imaginable combination of operating conditions and locales.

What Kind of Stations Operate?

Field Day entries are not classified by whether there is a single operator or multiple operators on the air at a station during the event (which is the standard for true contest events). The basic categories for a Field Day station are determined by where the operation is taking place and what power source is being used to run the equipment. Stations that are set up away from homes (including club stations or places where an amateur station is usually operated) are identified as either Class A or B. The difference between these two groups is that a Class A station will be organized, set up and run by a club or group of three or more participants, while in a Class B station only one or two persons are responsible for

the entire operation. During a typical Field Day event, approximately 55% of all stations operate as Classes A or B. These stations are set up in a wide range of places accessible to the public — parks, community centers, shopping mall parking lots, and school yards (to name a few common locales). Clubs and groups set up in these public spaces to be visible to passersby. Many licensees first became aware of Amateur Radio by noticing a club's Field Day setup and stopping by to see what was happening.

About one-third (37%) of Field Day operations are Class D or Class E, taking place from the existing home station of an individual or a club. The distinction between Class D and E stations is what they use to power their equipment. A home station using the commercial power grid would be Class D. Many home stations will use some type of emergency power (generator, solar units, or batteries) to go "off the grid" for the event. Stations operating with emergency power are Class E stations.

Though they constitute a small number of entries (about 1%), you will always find

Filling the logs in the HF tent at the St Charles Amateur Radio Club in Missouri are (front to back) WØLON, KDØEIA, KE5WXD, and KGØIGO. [Ward Silver, NØAX, photo]

erated power. The type of power source used for your total setup will serve as the final determinant of your operating class. A group operating in Class A using a gas-powered generator is still Class A. If they are operating with 5 W RF output or less and using a battery or renewable power source, they would qualify as Class AB. If the group uses commercial power mains, they will be classified as Class AC. Don't get too concerned about the subdivision of the categories though — the final classifications are determined by the ARRL when they process your entry.

How Do All Those Stations Get on the Air at Once?

A good question… After you decide which class (A – F) best suits your capabilities and interests, your next challenge is to decide how many transmitters you want to put on the air at once. This can be a major decision that takes lots of planning. Remember, the more transmitters you use at once, the more RF at your site and a greater possibility that stations will interfere with each other to some degree. About half of all Field Day entries operate using a single transmitter so the impact is minimal. But what about those that use two or more stations simultaneously?

The rules are that you can only have one transmitted signal on a frequency band/mode at any time. That means you can only have one station doing 20 meter phone at any one time. However, you are also allowed to have a 20 meter CW station and a 20 meter digital station operating at the same time as the 20 meter phone station. You can also have a 20 meter phone and a 40 meter CW station operating at the same time, for example. In the early 2000s, six clubs around Ottawa,

stations operating mobile during Field Day. These Class C station operators frequently have quite effective capabilities, able to use all three of the principle modes of Field Day communications — CW (Morse code), phone and digital. Their stations must be capable of operating while "in motion," including their antennas and whatever power source they utilize. Setting up and operating Class C stations can be a true challenge — but many Amateurs choose to step up and participate mobile.

The sixth broad operating classification for Field Day includes those stations that set up in conjunction with their local or state emergency management operations center. They make up about 7% of the entries. Known as Class F, the groups in this category are generally clubs or ARRL Amateur Radio Emergency Service (ARES) operators who have established a working relationship with local emergency officials and use the event to test some aspects of their operation's plan to support those organizations.

After the broad categories (Classes A through F), entries are next categorized by the number of transmitters in simultaneous operation. For example, a club operating in Class A that is using three transmitters would be classified as 3A. A group of friends operating two transmitters from a home station using commercial power would be 2D. The

local ARES group operating one transmitter from the county EOC would be 1F.

You will find that groups will use a variety of power sources during Field Day. Stations typically are using either a petroleum fueled generator (gas, diesel, propane); a natural, renewable power source such as solar or wind power; battery power; or commercially gen-

Members of the Ski Country ARC of Carbondale, Colorado, had a great time on the Western Slope during Field Day. [Peter Buckley, NØECT, photo]

Canada joined together to put a total of 35 stations on the air simultaneously, all within the required 1000-foot diameter circle! While that type of effort is not the norm for Field Day, but it is a good example of the kind of fun and experimentation that any group can have over the course of the event.

It takes a lot of effort and planning to reduce interference to your group's own stations from other transmitters at your site. It can be done but is a challenge. A good place to start is physically separating as much as possible antennas for stations that will be operating on the same band or on harmonically related bands (40 meters and 20 meters, for example). Bandpass filters and/or stub filters may be needed as well.

2.3.2 Something for Everyone

Field Day truly offers something for everyone when it comes to getting on the air. Many groups have a dedicated pool of long-time operators who enjoy making CW contacts and volunteer to staff the CW station or stations throughout the event. Almost every club has a cadre of good phone operators, and a Field Day phone station is an excellent place for a newer operator to get his or her feet wet.

With readily available software and sound cards in virtually every recent computer, digital mode contacts using popular modes such as RTTY and PSK31 are easily mastered through a desktop or laptop computer. The potential for contacts has never been greater. Some groups will have two stations (one phone and one CW/digital) on the "bread and butter" bands such as 40 or 20 meters. Other groups will put only one station on a band and alternate between the modes.

Remember that all US licensees have access to at least some HF spectrum. If the propagation is good, many groups will make a special effort to have a phone station operating on the 10 meter Novice/Technician phone subbands of 28.300 to 28.500 MHz. Technicians may also participate in other

HF phone bands under the supervision of a control operator with the appropriate license class. Clubs often have two people at an operating position, one handling the radio and the other logging the contacts. This is a great way

Rohan Agrawal, KJ6LXV (left) and Judy Halchin, KK6EWQ, ready a portable packet radio station for the Cupertino Amateur Radio Emergency Services Field Day operation. [Steve Hill, KK6FPI, photo]

to improve skills by observing how another operator handles the contacts and listening along to pick out call signs and reports.

All licensees Technician and above have full privileges on all frequencies above 50 MHz. VHF and up enthusiasts are quick to point out that certain propagation enhancements are common at the time of year when Field Day is held. One good sporadic-E opening on 6 meters (the "magic band") during a Field Day weekend has turned many casual operators on to the fun and challenges of the VHF spectrum! In addition, the rules also allow many groups to deploy a "free" VHF/UHF station without changing its operating category — yet another incentive and challenge for licensees just getting started.

Speaking of newcomers, several Field Day categories have the option of setting up a station dedicated to encourage newly licensed amateurs to start building their skills. Known as the Get On The Air (GOTA) station, groups are encouraged to team experienced operators with those just getting started and learning about good operating practices. The GOTA station is an opportunity for a "newbie" to make some contacts and gain some practical

Members of the Navarre CERT ARC prepare to launch a tethered weather balloon to support a long wire antenna. While providing a unique method of antenna support, the balloon also attracted visitors to the site. [Steve Van Den Akker, W4SJV, photo]

RheaAnn Crowe, KD5HTJ, took advantage of the NE7WY group's Get On The Air (GOTA) station to contact a station in Hawaii. [Garth Crowe, WY7GC, photo]

experience with using the various transceiver functions, logging contacts with computer software, or simply getting comfortable making contacts.

Field Day also has opportunities for those who would rather be "technical support" than full-bore operators. Many groups use Field Day to do hands-on learning. A group may be cutting, soldering, and raising their own antennas — valuable skills that can be passed on from each generation of amateurs. Actually setting up equipment, including interfacing computers to control radios and log contacts, adds an element of "high tech" learning. This may be something that younger participants can help teach the older operators who are not quite as comfortable with a keyboard as they might be with a key. Hang around a Field Day site for long and you will quickly see the free exchange of ideas and knowledge being openly shared.

Getting the Message Through

Another element that has existed in Field Day since its early years has been the concept of using the event to practice passing formal traffic using the ARRL's National Traffic System™ also known as the NTS™. The development of this skill set helps make the participant better trained if they are asked to assist with passing formal messages as part of a real-life emergency or disaster relief situation.

The Field Day rules allow these formal pieces of traffic to be passed either using the ARRL Radiogram™ or the ICS-213 General Message form, which is commonly used by most emergency service agencies. (See Public Service Operating later in this section for more information on message forms.) Passing these messages qualifies your operation to claim yet another set of bonus points — and hopefully helps encourage the operators to continue participating in this area of the public service communications.

2.3.3 Field Day Outreach

While getting on the air and contacting stations across the continent and beyond is certainly one of the key components to this event, that isn't its only impact. Field Day is truly the best opportunity for amateurs to reach out to their communities and lay the groundwork for a solid working relationship. To encourage this, Field Day has numerous extra "bonus point" opportunities that can be achieved by a group without the use of the radio.

Public relations and publicity for local clubs and Amateur Radio in general are at the forefront of these bonus activities. Amateurs at almost every club-sponsored Field Day operation reach out to their local and state governmental elected officials, such as the mayor and town councils, in order to demonstrate the volunteer resource available to supplement existing telecommunications infrastructures should the need arise. Groups can earn bonus points when an invited elected official shows up at their site.

Beyond the elected officials bonus, a second bonus can be earned if an official from a served agency visits your Field Day site. Be sure to invite your local police department, fire and rescue department, or emergency management official to visit your Field Day operation and learn more about your capabilities. The entire Amateur Radio community is strengthened when there are strong, vibrant relationships between the local Amateur Radio clubs or groups and the "clients" with which they interact when called upon. Though Amateur Radio is not designated as an emergency communications service, it does work with local and state officials to provide support when emergency or disaster relief communications are needed in our communities.

Never undersell the power of the press!

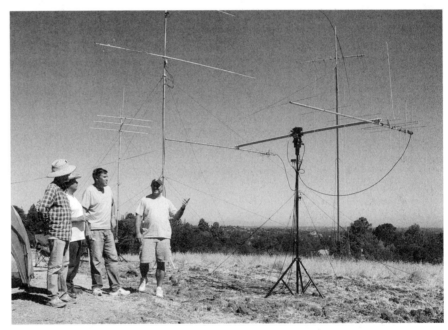

The West Valley Radio Association used a satellite communications tutorial to take advantage of the Field Day Educational Activity bonus. [Jim Peterson, K6EI, photo]

Amateur Radio has a good story to tell, and local media outlets (newspapers, television, community websites, and broadcast radio stations) are always looking for good stories to print or air. People involved with Field Day and Amateur Radio are encouraged to reach out to the media. Send them a short press release about what your group will be doing during Field Day and how your efforts fit into the national scope of the event — and invite them to visit the site to see for themselves. Remember, the more activity you have going on at your site — especially things that highlight youth participation and education — the more likely it is that your group's efforts will be recognized with a little ink or a short story during the weekend news. That exposure not only helps your club's visibility but also helps raise community awareness of what Amateur Radio is all about.

In the 21st century, Amateur Radio faces the challenge of reaching a population that is more connected than ever before. How to get people's fingers off their smartphones and into the magic of Amateur Radio is a challenge Field Day can help resolve. In these times it seems everyone is into social media — Facebook, Twitter, and Snapchat just to name a few. Field Day offers an opportunity to encounter and engage the millions of people who daily use these and other social media platforms, inviting them to check out what has in some circles been called the original "social media" — Amateur Radio. A social media post that leads someone to check out what this "radio stuff" is about by visiting a group's Field Day operation is how our community starts to connect with the potential next generation of amateurs. Put some of your social media skills to work helping find and recruit the next generation of licensees and earn bonus points at the same time!

Youth and Field Day

Ask at any radio club meeting or gathering how the attendees got interested in Amateur Radio and the odds are that a good number of them got involved as a youngster, many by attending a Field Day operation. Whether attending with your parent or grandparent who was already licensed, or as part of a Girl or Boy Scout field trip, or with a church youth excursion, many amateurs got their start as part of Field Day. That is why another of the central components to this annual event is activities designed to get youth involved.

Any Field Day group can earn bonus points for having young people attend and participate in your operation. Many groups use the

Sylvia Riddell and her father Tim stopped by the Williamsburg (VA) ARC site to investigate Field Day operation. Sylvia made about 30 contacts at the GOTA station, thanks to coach Don Johnson, N4DJ (pictured). Sylvia and Tim had so much fun that they went on to earn their Technician licenses and are now KF5WZF and KF5WZG. [Dan Ewart, WG4F, photo]

GOTA station with a mentor/GOTA coach to allow these youths to have a firsthand experience with Amateur Radio. Not every kid who visits the site is going to immediately become a licensee, but plant that potential spark. Who knows what may happen down the road?

Keep in mind that nothing will turn off a

young person more than being shuffled off to the side and not brought into the group as a participant. Have activities for all ages to do as part of your Field Day operation. Many groups use the special Educational Activity bonus to make sure certain visitors, especially young people, are actively engaged and not just passive observers. Groups may have a hands-on activity, such as learning how to solder a connector, in order to teach a simple skill to the youthful visitors. If your club has some younger members, get them involved as peer-teachers with some aspect of the hobby that interests them.

Kids (and adults too) get excited about things new and different. Many Field Day groups will utilize the special Satellite QSO bonus to help spark activity and interest with younger generations. This aspect will usually require special preparation beforehand, and probably a seasoned satellite operator working with them, but imagine the story a young person will have to tell! And keep in mind that most years astronauts living on the International Space Station will turn on their ham gear and participate in Field Day. Nothing will energize a group of students — or a club for that matter — like completing a Field Day QSO through an amateur satellite or with the ISS.

2.3.4 How to Get Started

The first thing to remember with ARRL Field Day is that it is not a contest: it is a non-adjudicated operating event. Don't get too anxious about trying to maximize your score, especially at the expense of maximizing the fun of the experience. There is no single right way to operate during Field Day. What works for an average radio club in the mountains of

western North Carolina may not work for a club located in the suburbs of Chicago. That is exactly what makes this event so popular and challenging. The more times you participate in the event, the more things you will add to your personal operating skill set.

Planning for Field Day generally starts months before the event. If you are partici-

pating with an established club, they will probably have a general plan of action that has served them in the past. Jump in and work with the club members planning the event, offering your unique experience and talents. Ask questions — that's the best way to learn. Don't be afraid to volunteer to tackle a job in the planning of the event. If you are a good writer, offer to create a press release to

The Nashoba Valley ARC set up their 1A station in a quiet location in Pepperell, Massachusetts. Note the portable tower at the right. [Ralph Swick, KD1SM, photo]

be distributed to local media or write letters of invitation to elected officials and served agencies. If you are a computer expert, offer to work with the team that is getting the logging computers loaded and working. What you bring to the group is as important as what you will take from the experience.

Don't be intimidated by the lengthy set of rules. Because of the nature of the event, there is a lot of explanatory information in them that will help you participate success-fully. Each year the ARRL makes available a substantial *Field Day Packet* with information such as the latest rules, entry submission forms, and dozens of pages of information as well as FAQs on almost every aspect of the event. Included in the packet you will find things such as a sample press release that you can modify to send to your local media outlets, explanatory information on the scoring system, and such operational tools as the list of ARRL sections that you will hear as part of the required on-the-air exchange of information. And the staff at the ARRL Contest Branch is ready with answers to help you maximize your Field Day efforts.

Finally, remember that while the event may be similar to a contest and has elements of public service communications and community public relations as key components, it really all boils down to one basic premise: ARRL Field Day is fun! See you on the air the fourth full weekend of June!

2.3.5 Field Day Resources

- ARRL website: **www.arrl.org/field-day**
- *ARRL Handbook* — portable power sources such as batteries and generators.
- *ARRL Antenna Book* — building and optimizing stub filters
- *Managing Interstation Interference* by George Cutsogeorge, W2VJN, available from Vibroplex (**www.vibroplex.com**).

You can also find more technical information about portable stations and antennas in *The ARRL Handbook* and *The ARRL Antenna Book*, as well as *ARRL's Portable Antenna Classics*, *Amateur Radio on the Move* and *The Amateur Radio Mobile Handbook* (from RSGB), all available from your favorite ham radio dealer or the ARRL website.

2.4 Public Service Operating

Operating your station for providing disaster response, emergency, and public event communications is a major function of Amateur Radio and a major justification of our access to the limited, valuable frequency spectrum. Hams are engaged in these activities for many reasons, including giving back to society through public service, to be part of a team, or for excitement, adventure, and meeting new friends. They work side-by-side with disaster relief agency officials from the Red Cross, Salvation Army, government emergency management and other entities, supplementing their communication by handling potentially life and property saving messages. It is a historic function, dating back to the beginnings of radio and Amateur Radio. Hams develop a sense of deep camaraderie and team spirit that results from working with their peers in what sometimes are desperate circumstances.

The ARRL's Amateur Radio Emergency Service® (ARES®) program is the primary platform upon which Amateur Radio disaster response and emergency communications is conducted in this country, and it has been the backbone of public service since 1935. In this section, you will learn the basics of emergency communications operating, plans, and procedures under the premier program in the United States — ARES.

Walter Paluch, KA2CAQ, at the Babylon, Long Island (New York) EOC station during the Great South Bay Hurricane Sandy response in 2012. [Robert Myers, K2TV, photo]

2.4.1 Let's Get Started

Getting started down the public service pathway is not done in a vacuum: Public service operating is almost always performed in concert with others, many of whom are experienced veteran operators who can serve as mentors for you. You will learn from them, and serve apprenticeships with them until at some point in the future — depending on your level of practice and experience — you will be working side-by-side with them as peers. Then, it will be your turn to mentor someone new.

You will want to be an *asset* to an effort — be it as a communicator/operator at a road rally safety checkpoint or past the roadblocks in a major disaster area — not a *liability*. The difference is manifested in your positive, professional attitude and appearance, and the breadth and depth of training you take and experience you have. This chapter will offer basic public service operating information and time-tested tips to get you started, but no book like this can replace the value of

hands-on mentoring/training/practicing with your peers found in your neighborhood and community Amateur Radio clubs and ARES or Radio Amateur Civil Emergency Service (RACES) groups. Seek them out, and your path to public service operating will run straight and true.

First Things First: Get a Simple, Field-Ready Radio

Most hams new to public service operating begin their efforts on-the-air through a local 2 meter or 70 cm FM repeater (see Section 1 of this book for basic repeater operating information). Area hams tend to congregate there for sundry activities: traffic and ARES nets, swap nets, weather spotter nets, club meetings, training nets, informal chats and discussions, and weather report exchanges. You will quickly learn the protocols, courtesies, and nuances of repeater and net operating, which, along with simplex (direct

A dual band (2 meter/70 cm) handheld transceiver is essential for participation in public service activities in the field.

Personal, Family Safety First!

Prepare yourself and your family to ensure their safety and the protection of your property well in advance of any possible activation; you may be required to report to your assignment immediately without being able to stop at home first. Here are a few things to keep in mind:
- Your family needs at least three days of non-refrigerated food and bottled water available.
- Have a medical kit available and make sure your family knows how to use it.
- Have fire extinguishers at home; make sure your family knows how to use them.
- Make your family aware of escape routes from the immediate area. Give them a map.
- Pre-designate a place for them to go: a friend's house or alternate agreed-upon meeting place.
- Have phone numbers in your wallet/purse for your family's alternate shelter(s).
- Have alternate means of communication should cell/landline phone systems go down.
- Consider registering with the Red Cross's "Safe and Well" service: **safeandwell. communityos.org**.
- Keep valuable documents in a safe place or take them with you.
- Have cash on hand for you and your family as ATMs will likely be down.

These are just a few ideas; there are many more. Study FEMA's Ready website for more. The above list was adapted from the excellent reference guide *Auxiliary Communications Field Operations Guide* (AUXFOG) produced by the Department of Homeland Security — Office of Emergency Communications. You can download a copy from **www.publicsafetytools.info**.

communication without repeaters) operation, form the bedrock of public service operating. Listen at first, and don't transmit until you feel that you have a basic idea of how communications are conducted on your local repeater nets. It could take listening to several nets over the course of many evenings before you should feel comfortable transmitting and checking in.

To do it, you'll need a radio, of course! Start with a simple-to-operate 2 meter/70 cm FM handheld with a short, flexible rubber-coated antenna, or better yet, a simple "whip" antenna that will yield more gain. The marketplace has a plethora of choices available from many manufacturers and advertised in *QST*. Browse the ads and check out *QST*'s Product Review column for reviews of radios that interest you. Search for past reviews on the ARRL's website at **www.arrl.org/product-review**. Ask local hams for their recommendations, and see if you can try several different models to find one that is comfortable for you.

You will be taking your radio into the field for public events, emergencies and disasters, so *portability* is a critical feature. You will have to operate "off the grid" — away from commercial mains — so you will need alternative power sources such as extra batteries, portable generators, and solar panels. The same goes for antennas: you will want to find a balance between getting antenna gain sufficient to initiate and maintain communications from potentially remote locations, and the ability to easily transport and erect them in the field.

Keep power output as low as possible: Just

a watt or two should be enough power to talk across your neighborhood or community on simplex and through your local repeater. Higher power output translates to faster battery discharge and depletion. Most handhelds come with a basic rechargeable battery pack and wall charger. Look for optional larger capacity battery packs and higher-power desktop "drop-in" chargers that will charge your batteries faster. Buy a second battery pack to use when you're charging your first battery. Buy the optional alkaline battery holder, if available, as a back-up in the event your standard rechargeable battery pack(s) fails or power is not available for a charger. The use of batteries for handhelds and other types of radios was addressed in the Public Service column for March 2015 *QST*. The use of portable generators is discussed in the Public Service column for October 2015 *QST*. (ARRL members may view past *QST* articles online at **www.arrl.org/qst**.)

For enhancing your reception and transmitted signal, forego higher power in favor of a better antenna. Consider purchasing a telescoping ⅝ wave whip antenna that replaces the rubber-coated short antenna that your radio came bundled with. The longer antenna will give you higher gain, and hence, wider coverage for your signals and better "copy" on weak or distant stations. (Don't toss out the flexible rubber antenna, however: it's useful for close-in communications.)

Mobile Operation

The next step is to operate your handheld

from your car or pickup truck, which you'll need to be able to do for working public events, emergencies and disasters. Install an antenna on the roof of your vehicle, which makes for a great ground plane. The easiest way to start is to "stick" a magnetically-mounted antenna "mag mount" on the roof and screw on a coil and ⅝ wavelength whip antenna; then run the cable through an opening in your window. You can use your handheld's internal battery pack for power, of course, but more efficient is the use of a dc power adapter and cable that can be connected to the vehicle's battery and run to the handheld, giving you a robust power source that can run your transceiver for a long time.

After some experience with this setup, you may decide to purchase a radio that is designed specifically for mobile applications. A "mobile rig" has more RF power output, on the order of 50 W or more, versus the minimal few watts of the typical handheld. Mobile rigs are usually hard wired into the vehicle's 12 V battery, with a fixed whip antenna/coil/mount mounted through a hole drilled into the roof of your vehicle. (If you are uncomfortable with the idea of drilling and installing such a mount yourself, find a local 2-way radio shop that caters to the community public safety fleet — the shop has the experience and tools to install your mount for you at a nominal cost). See Section 1 of this book for more information on setting up a mobile station.

Don't transport your valuable, expensive gear in cardboard boxes. Protect and transport it in a well padded hard-shell case. See the sidebar.

Other Radio Tips

"Slow charge" your batteries. Fast chargers can heat batteries and shorten their life spans. It is less expensive and more efficient to have several batteries on hand and rotate them through a slow charger. Number each battery and keep a log, just a simple piece of paper, at your battery charging station. If you charge your batteries on the fly, such as in your car, then just put a sticker on the battery and write the charging date/time on the sticker.

Avoid a short circuit. Always use the terminal cap (if provided) to cover the positive battery terminal, or better yet, house your battery in a protective plastic case to keep any conductive material from falling across the terminals.

Check and test your gear. Murphy's Law dictates that some part of your gear won't work — at the worst possible time. Check and test your gear well before a deployment, and mark a piece of tape with the date you checked it — stick it on the item.

Weatherproof connectors. Anywhere you have connectors, you will likely need weather sealant to keep moisture out. Putty-

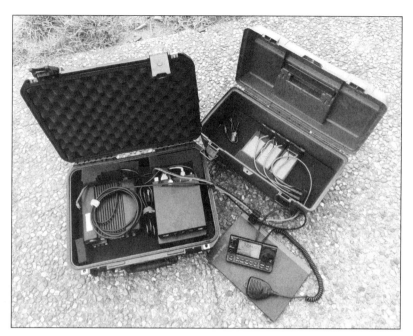

Ian, KI9W, transports a 100 W HF/VHF transceiver, power supply, antenna tuner, and all necessary cables in one well padded hard-shell case made by SKB (in the iSeries line). Several deep-cycle, spill proof AGM batteries and charger fit in another case for times when power from a vehicle battery or commercial mains is not available. [Ian Kuhn, KI9W, photo]

like sealant is fine for permanent installations, but for temporary in-the-field operations consider using stretchable plastic weather sealant tape instead. It's much easier to remove.

Headphones/headsets. A set of headphones may be an absolute necessity in a disaster scene deployment. You may be deployed in an area where other operators are working on different bands, you may be out in the open, or you may even be in the middle of a noisy shelter. A headset, perhaps with an attached boom microphone, should be a vital part of your kit. You can't communicate if you can't hear.

Pack carefully. When securing from a disaster scene, don't just throw everything in a box and leave. Coil up your cords, bag loose items and put everything back in its place so it will be ready next time. In particular, take time to wipe off your coaxial cable. Use a little silicone spray on it to help protect it and keep it supple.

Safety first! When deploying your equipment in the field, think *safety first*. Ask yourself: Can it fall on anyone's foot? Have I created an electrical hazard? Could anyone trip over my feed line or get poked in the eye

Transport and Store Your Gear in Hard-Shell Cases

By Rick Palm, K1CE

How many times have you witnessed operators transporting their radios to Field Day, checkpoint stations at road rallies, or even disaster sites/stations in the radios' original cardboard boxes, usually old and water stained? There is a much better way: store and transport your radios and other gear in a hard-shell case. I have found Pelican brand cases to be airtight, waterproof, and almost indestructible. Foam inserts can be sculpted to fit your gear snugly, protecting it from rough handling in the field.

Pelican cases are expensive, but there are less-expensive alternatives, too numerous to list here. A simple Google search for "inexpensive alternatives to Pelican cases" will result in lots of possibilities. For example, Nanuk brand equipment cases are available from DX Engineering, a *QST* advertiser. Also, look for older, used Halliburton cases, which were the leaders for camera cases when cameras still used film! Try searching Internet auction sites for Halliburton or other good quality used cases that can save you money.

To store/transport my radios, I use four different cases. A Pelican model 1600, a large suitcase-size case with four heavy duty latches and handle, handles my compact HF/VHF transceiver with dc power cable and mic, wattmeter, antenna tuner, and a 30 A switching power supply and cord. The manuals fit under the foam. A Pelican model 1300 case transports and protects my VHF FM/digital radio with cord and mic, and manual. My handheld 2 meter transceiver and flexible rubber antenna packs perfectly into a Pelican model 1030 Micro Case. And, finally, identification cards, credit cards, cash, driver's license, Amateur Radio license, and ARES identification cards go neatly into a Pelican model 1010 Micro Case for protection and ease-of-access in the field. Don't keep those cards in your wallet on a major disaster scene — that's just asking for them to be lost, soiled, or stolen.

The bottom line is this: You paid a lot of money for your radios,

K1CE's radios in their Pelican cases. At the rear left is the 1300 case next to the 1600 on the right. In the foreground is the 1030 mini case. [Rick Palm, K1CE, photo]

so spend a little more to protect your investment in good cases. Don't transport your good radios in rickety old cardboard boxes with the cables looking like they're trying to escape! Plus, transporting your gear in good cases lends you and your gear a professional look.

ARES/RACES Groups Use Anderson Powerpole Connectors

The ARES/RACES organizations have standardized on use of Anderson Powerpole connectors for dc power connections to radio equipment. Establishing a standard power connector offers the same benefit to the public service operator as the standard PL-259/SO-239 connector for antennas — interoperability. With all of your radios' dc power cables terminated with Powerpole connectors, you will be able to switch radios and power supplies instantly, giving portability and transferability between your home, mobile, and portable stations. In the field, your radios and power supplies will be interoperable with the radios and supplies of your colleagues.

The Powerpole connector housings are genderless with basically only two parts, greatly simplifying assembly. With a little practice, they can be assembled efficiently even in demanding field environments. They are stackable modular housings that easily slide together but are difficult to accidentally pull apart. They take almost all standard wire sizes used in amateur applications, yet use the same housing for all wires sizes, lending interchangeability.

The housings are color-coded red (+) and black (–), helping to ensure that the connectors are assembled and mated correctly. Internal stainless steel spring contacts are strong enough to hold the connectors together in the mated condition, but allow them to be quickly disconnected.

There is a wealth of information, videos and guidance for terminating your dc power cables with Powerpoles. Make modifying your station to an emergency-ready state a hobby within a hobby; converting your dc power cable connectors to Powerpoles is an integral part of this process.

These two Anderson Power-pole connectors are set up in the ARES configuration (red on the left, black on the right). The wide section on top is the hood and the narrow section on the bottom contains the clip that holds the connector. Installed are the 45 A contacts. [Steve Sant Andrea, AG1YK, photo]

by my antenna? Make sure your antenna is a safe distance away from your operating location and that its emissions are not directed at anyone. Make sure your equipment cannot harm you or anyone else.

Public Service Nets: Listen, Learn, Then Check In

After listening to the locals on the repeater or on simplex frequencies as recommended above, try checking into the nightly or weekly traffic or ARES net. By participating in the net you will further learn the critical importance of net protocol and discipline, as well as how to properly originate, send, receive, and deliver formal written messages (traffic handling). These are baseline competencies that form the heart of every public service operator's skill set. You will make mistakes, but you will also find a patient, friendly community of hams on frequency ready to help you gain more confidence and skill, because they need you for their ARES or RACES team as much as you need them!

To find public service nets, check the on-line ARRL Net Search page from the links at **www.arrl.org/arrl-net-directory-search**. More information on message handling is presented later in this section. Also study the ARRL NTS Manual, available from **www.arrl.org/nts-manual**. The NTS Manual will teach you how to properly format and handle messages in the ARRL National Traffic System™ and other nets.

2.4.2 Get on the Train — Training is a Must!

You simply cannot be a viable public service operator unless you are properly trained. Since operating in a net is the first skill any public service operator should have, let's start with some basic net operating protocols.

Net Operator Training

Net discipline, control, liaison and message-handling procedures are fundamentals. Training should involve as many different operators as possible in all of these functions. Don't let the same operator perform the same function repeatedly or you will lose valuable training experience for yourself and the other members of the group. Step up to the plate and volunteer to try these functions. Good liaison and coordination with other nets requires versatile operators, and those who also can operate different modes. Even though phone operators may not feel comfortable on digital modes, and vice versa, encourage yourself and other net operators to gain familiarity

on all modes through proper training and experience. You and your peers can learn by following along with or logging for an operator who regularly uses that mode.

As a net operator, you have a duty to be self-disciplined. A net is only as good as its weakest link (the worst operator). You can be an exemplary net operator by following a few easy guidelines:

1) **Make sure you're on exactly the same frequency as the net control station (NCS)**. Check your VFO! Even on an FM repeater, you could be 5 kHz off frequency and sound distorted to the other check-ins and NCS.

2) **Don't be late.** Liaison stations are sometimes on a tight timetable. Don't hold them up by checking in 10 minutes late with traffic.

3) **Speak only when spoken to by the NCS**. Unless it is a bona fide emergency situation, you don't need to help the NCS unless specifically asked. If you need to contact the NCS, make it brief. Resist the urge to help

clear the frequency for the NCS or to advise the NCS. The NCS, not you, is boss.

4) **Unless otherwise instructed by the NCS, transmit only to the NCS**. Side comments to another station in the net are out of order.

5) **Stay until you are excused**. If the NCS calls you and you don't respond, the NCS may assume you've left the net, and net business may be stymied. If you need to leave the net prematurely, contact the NCS and simply ask to be excused.

6) **Be brief** when transmitting to the NCS. Don't waste valuable net time.

7) **Know how the net runs**. The NCS doesn't have time to explain procedure to you while the net is in session. Ask questions before or after the net!

8) **Before the net begins, get yourself organized**. Have all the materials you will need to receive traffic at hand. If you have messages to send, have them grouped by com-

mon destination according to the procedure of the net you're participating in. Nothing is more frustrating to the other operators — especially the one waiting to take your traffic — than being told "Wait a minute, I've got it here somewhere."

9) When receiving traffic and you have a question about the accuracy of anything passed in the message, **don't tie the net up with discussions** about ZIP codes, telephone area codes, and so on. Just tell the NCS that you would like to discuss message number 123 with the sending station after the net, or request to be allowed to move off frequency to clear up the matter. Remember, only the originating station can change the message — with the exception of the word count — between the number and the signature. Any suggested changes can be added as an operator note if necessary.

10) **Don't freelance your traffic**. Wait your turn to pass your messages as directed by the NCS.

Finally, have a current copy of the *Public Service Communications Manual* and other references available and refer to them as needed.

Other Net Operating Tips

Give a simple answer. During an emergency/public event net, either real or practice, if you are asked a question, do your best to give a short, simple answer. Try not to add a lot of qualifiers or exceptions. When asked for a simple "yes" or "no," if you can't answer, your only other response should be, "I don't know."

Pay attention. One of the most common mistakes on nets is that operators think they know what the net controller is going to say, and stop listening. They miss the instructions and wind up giving inappropriate responses. One way to develop the habit of paying attention is to write down the key elements of what the net controller is saying.

Refrain from over-explaining things, engaging in personal greetings and chats, and anything else that might prevent important traffic from getting through. Air time is precious, especially when there are numerous operators on the same frequency as in a net.

Only transmit information you know to be factual. Consider the following exchange: Station 1: "Does anyone know where the fire chief is?" Station 2: "It's pretty close to noon. He might have gone to lunch." The operator at Station 2 is just speculating, but his statement may be taken as accurate. Leave the guesswork off the air.

Avoid words or phrases that carry strong emotions. Most emergency situations are emotionally charged already, and we do not need to add to the problem. For instance, instead of saying, "horrific dam-

age and people torn to bits," we might say "significant physical damage and serious personal injuries."

Do not use Q-signals on voice. Q-signals are useful if you are sending Morse code, but may lead to confusion when used verbally. The notion that "everyone knows" certain Q-signals is a fallacy.

Talk slower. The biggest cause of errors during voice communications is an operator talking too fast. The receiving operator either misunderstands or misses parts of the message.

Keep complaints off the air. "Okay, I'll do it. But it's not actually my job. The guy who's supposed to do that is always away from the table doing something else." The other operator doesn't want to hear any of that and it ties up the frequency. Make a note of your complaints in your log and bring them up at the after-action debriefing, but keep them off the air.

Do not alter a message, even to correct a typographical error. What you think is right may actually be wrong. Moreover, any change you make might subtly alter the meaning of the message. Send or write it exactly as you receive it.

Don't use VOX (voice activated transmitter). Ambient noise might activate the transmitter and tie up the frequency. Also, you do not want your casual comments to go out over the air.

Net Control Station Best Practices

There are net discipline/protocols for net control stations, too. For example, the net control station says, "When checking in, tell me in the following order your physical location, tactical call sign, if you have any traffic to pass, your call sign and then your name. I will take check-ins by call sign suffix. If the suffix of your call sign begins with A through I, call now." The net controller has given instructions that make it easier for him to log responses, but almost impossible for anyone to grasp quickly and efficiently. No one will follow the instructions. **Keep instructions simple and easy to understand**. Never give instructions that require a lot of mental arithmetic.

Pause long enough for answers. Another example: the NCS asks, "Are there any other stations wishing to check in?" You push-to-talk and give your call sign, but when you release your mic key all you hear is a truncated statement that ends with, ". . . no more check ins, I will now close the net." The NCS has not paused long enough for answers. When a net controller calls for a response of any kind, he or she should wait at least five seconds before continuing.

Identify the net regularly. Some net control operators make the mistake of identifying the net only once, just as they begin it. For the benefit of those just tuning in, the name of the net and the net control station's call sign should be transmitted regularly.

Other Training and Resources

The modern emergency/disaster and public event operator has an enormous amount of training, operating aids, and other support services available on paper hard copies or through the keypad of mobile devices and laptops. Many resources are portable and can be toted easily into the field for immediate consultation at a road side checkpoint or remote station site in a large disaster area. Let's look at a few online assets that may help you perform on your deployment assignments, starting with the comprehensive array of ARRL offerings.

The League develops, publishes, and regularly updates a large section on its website devoted entirely to resources and training for public service operators — **www.arrl.org/public-service**. A good place to start — and a must-have — is the *ARES Manual*, which was revised by a panel of experts in 2015 with updates to several chapters on ARES organization, RACES, operating guidelines, and more. You can download a copy from **www.arrl.org/files/file/Public%20Service/ARES/ARESmanual2015.pdf**

Also highly recommended is the *ARES Field Resources Manual*, a summary and companion volume to the *ARES Manual*, which is easily printed and toted into the field in a go-kit or backpack. It contains reference information and templates for populating with your own local data and may be downloaded from **www.arrl.org/files/file/**

The monthly ARRL ARES E-Letter is a great way to keep up to date on what is happening in the world of emergency/disaster/event operating.

ARES_FR_Manual.pdf. (Hard copies are also available from the ARRL store at **www.arrl.org/shop**.)

To keep up to date on new ARES, RACES, and emergency/disaster/event operating knowledge, protocols and after action reports on activations across the country, subscribe to the popular monthly ARRL *ARES E-Letter*. ARRL members can sign up to receive each copy by e-mail. Simply log in to the Members area on the ARRL website and edit your profile's e-mail subscriptions by selecting the *ARES E-Letter*.

The ARRL publishes a wide array of operating aids and forms indispensable to the field operator. You can find them at **www.arrl.org/public-service-field-services-forms.**The ARRL has entered into formal agreements with partner agencies such as the American Red Cross and Federal Emergency Management Agency (FEMA). Known as *memoranda of understanding*, these agreements set forth principles and guidelines to facilitate working with the leadership and staffs of our service partners. These documents are helpful in opening the doors to these agencies at the local level. See **www.arrl.org/served-agencies-and-partners**.

ARRL INTRODUCTION TO EMERGENCY COMMUNICATION COURSE

The League's popular, comprehensive *Introduction to Emergency Communication* course lends broad knowledge that instills in students competency well-recognized in the field by emergency coordinators and partner agency officials. Trained operators are much more valuable to leaders than spontaneous or "out of the woodwork" volunteer-operators who just show up. The course is rigorous and demanding for the student who is willing to make a serious commitment. The course is mentored, and features six sections with 29 lesson topics, including required student activities, concluding with a 35-question final assessment. Allow approximately 45 hours over a 9-week period to complete it. This ARRL gold standard course comes highly recommended. Read more about it at **www.arrl.org/online-course-catalog**.

The course graduate will be better prepared to serve as an emergency/disaster/public event communicator when called up, and ready to take advanced training (the ARRL's *Public Service and Emergency Communication Management for Radio Amateurs* course, for example) leading to ARES and other groups' leadership positions.

ARRL on-line education on technical topics such as Powerpole connector installation, emergency power sources, NVIS and J-pole antennas, and much more is available in a series of articles written by field experts and available from **www.arrl.org/public-service-**

equipment. Operating topics such as popular digital modes EchoLink, Winlink, APRS, and NBEMS systems of excellent utility to the field operator are also discussed online. See **www.arrl.org/public-service-operating**.

FEMA TRAINING

One of the best models of online emergency/disaster training is found on the popular FEMA Independent Study website, **www.training.fema.gov/is/**.The ever-expanding catalog of course offerings are of special interest to public service operators. Most courses can be completed in a few hours. Passing a final exam yields a handsome certificate of completion e-mailed to you within minutes. Browse the extensive list of courses, and take the ones of interest to you as an emergency/disaster communicator.

Last but not least, and quite possibly the best, consult your ARRL local, Section and Division websites for ARES-specific training and resources provided by your own area's Emergency Coordinators, District ECs, and Section ECs. They provide a wide array of operating and equipment resources and training *based on their personal experience*, having served in the trenches of emergencies/disasters. They often post "lessons learned" and after action reports (AAR), which are often more valuable than any academic study. Start by looking at your and other sections' pages and websites linked from the ARRL website at **www.arrl.org/sections**.

On the Air Training Exercises

Practical on-the-air activities, such as ARRL's Field Day and Simulated Emergen-

cy Test offer additional training opportunities on a nationwide basis for individuals and groups. Participation in such events reveals weak areas where discussion and more training are needed. Also, drills and tests can be designed specifically to check dependability of emergency equipment or to rate training in the local area.

ARRL FIELD DAY

The ARRL Field Day (FD — **www.arrl.org/field-day**) gets more amateurs out of their cozy shacks and into tents on hilltops than any other event. Someday you may be operating from a tent in a disaster area; the training you will get from FD is invaluable.

In ARRL Field Day, a premium is placed on sharp operating skills, adapting equipment that can meet challenges of emergency preparedness and flexible logistics. Amateurs assemble portable stations capable of long-range communications at almost any place and under varying conditions. Alternatives to commercial power in the form of generators, car batteries, solar power, and other sources are used to power equipment to make as many contacts as possible. FD is held on the fourth full weekend of June. Field Day is discussed in detail earlier in this section.

ARRL SIMULATED EMERGENCY TEST

The ARRL Simulated Emergency Test (SET) offers volunteers an opportunity to build disaster response competencies. The purposes of SET are to:

• Help amateurs gain experience in communicating using standard procedures under simulated emergency conditions, and to ex-

---

Emergency Management Institute

FEMA

This Certificate of Achievement is to acknowledge that

RICHARD PALM

has reaffirmed a dedication to serve in times of crisis through continued professional development and completion of the independent study course:

IS-00100.b
Introduction to Incident Command System
ICS-100

Issued this 9th Day of August, 2012

Tony Russell
Superintendent
Emergency Management Institute

0.3 IACET CEU

IACET

FEMA courses are an excellent resource for emergency communications volunteers.

Mike Powloka, KT1Q, maintains contact through the K1SV repeater as part of his group's annual Simulated Emergency Test exercises in Bennington, Vermont. [Robin Conway, N1WWW, photo]

Assistant Emergency Coordinator Tom Olley, KG4VUB, operates from a shelter location in the Cherokee County, Georgia, Simulated Emergency Test. [James Millsap, WB4NWS, photo]

periment with new modes, equipment, and concepts.

• Identify strengths and weaknesses in individual operators and groups for post-SET training and troubleshooting.

• Provide a demonstration to served agencies and to the public through the news media, of the value of Amateur Radio, particularly in times of emergency and disaster.

The goals of SET are to:

• Strengthen VHF-to-HF links at the local level, ensuring that ARES and traffic nets work in concert for efficient, reliable, accurate message handling.

• Encourage greater use of digital modes for wider capability.

• Implement the Memoranda of Understanding between the ARRL, the users and

A Portable VHF/UHF Antenna Mount and Support

By Rick Palm, K1CE

A portable antenna mounting assembly and pole, easily assembled and deployed and easily disassembled for transport, is a good asset for your emergency-prepared portable/mobile station. Here is one way to make a heavy duty support that can withstand the rigorous physical demands of a disaster area.

Start with the Larsen Base Conversion Kit (BSAKIT) from Larsen Antennas. It converts an NMO (Motorola style) mobile whip antenna into an omnidirectional base station ground plane antenna, with a frequency range of 144 to 512 MHz, good for the popular amateur VHF and UHF bands. Four radials extend from the small base, and are held in place with Allen screws and easily removable. The feed connection is an SO-239 (UHF female). The mount comes with two adjustable hose clamps for connecting to a variety of masts, but you can use the two screw holes to secure the metal bracket to a wood post. The antenna is wind rated to 100 MPH.

One way to mount the antenna is to use a pressure treated 4×4 wood post and a medium-duty 4×4 post ground spike from a home improvement store. Insert a small piece of 4×4 wood into the receptacle on top of the spike so it can be hammered into the ground without damaging the metal receptacle. Screw in an NMO series antenna — a ⅝ wave 2 meter whip and coil/base, for example — connect the coax and you're ready to roll. Be aware of any underground conduit and pipes before banging the spike into the ground!

John Bowser, NØYXG, Project Facilitator/Utility Cut Inspector for the City of St. Joseph, Missouri, notes that it is prudent to check local laws before driving in a ground spike. With all of the fiber optic and plastic lines being bored in, it would be dangerous to drive the ground stake in without checking with an appropriate local notification system such as Call Before You Dig, DigSafe, or OneCall.

A standard 32 inch post base provides a solid support for ground mounting the ground plane. [Rick Palm, K1CE, photo]

The Larsen mount is secured to a section of wood post and converts a mobile whip into a ground plane antenna. [Rick Palm, K1CE, photo]

cooperative agencies, testing and cementing local relationships.

• Focus energy on ARES communications at the local level.

• Increase use and recognition of tactical communication on behalf of served agencies; use less amateur-to-amateur formal ARRL Radiogram traffic.

Help promote the SET on nets and repeaters with announcements or bulletins, at club meetings, and in club newsletters. SET is conducted on the first full weekend of October. However, some groups have their SETs any time between September 1 and November 30, especially if an alternate date coincides more favorably with a planned communications activity and provides greater publicity. Specific SET guidelines are announced in *QST*.

OTHER DRILLS AND TESTS

An ad hoc drill or test that includes interest and practical value makes a group glad to participate because it seems worthy of its efforts. Formulate training around a simu-lated disaster such as a tornado or a vehicle accident. Elaborate on the situation to develop a realistic scenario or have the drill in conjunction with a local event. Many ARRL Section Emergency Coordinators (SECs) have developed training activities that are specifically designed for your state, section or local area. County professional emergency managers are often well practiced in setting up exercises that can help you sharpen your communications and general emergency response skills. Consult with them, or better yet, coordinate drills and exercises *with* them!

During a drill:

1) Announce the simulated emergency situation. Activate the emergency net and dispatch mobiles and portables to served agencies' offices, shelters, and other critical locations/sites.

2) Originate and relay messages and requests for participating served agency managers by using formal and tactical communications as indicated. (Preface and close each message with a "this is a drill only" statement, no matter what mode is used to transmit it.)

3) Use emergency-powered repeaters and employ digital modes. Use and test a simplex frequency.

4) As warranted by traffic loads, assign liaison stations to receive traffic on the local net and relay to wider coverage nets. Be sure there is a representative on each session of the wider area nets to receive traffic coming to your area.

After a drill:

1) Gather hard data and feedback from all participants to study and cover in after action reports. Share the results with all.

2) Critique the drill, and derive a "lessons learned" summary for review and changes to procedures and protocols for the next drill or real incident.

3) Report your efforts, including any photos, clippings and other items of interest, to your SEC or ARRL HQ.

Use Portable Scaffolding as an Operating Platform

By Rick Palm, K1CE

Scaffolding that painters use to walk on and reach high places to paint makes a perfect platform for mounting and operating radios. The Metaltech Scaffolding unit, which cost $100, has a frame made of 1-inch steel tubing, and folds flat to 4 inches thickness for ease in transporting and storing. It's four feet tall, with two height-adjustable heavy duty steel anti-slip shelves that are moveable within the frame, and four heavy duty casters with locks for easy portability and maneuverability (allowing for ease of access to both front and back panels of radios). The manufacturer's weight capacity rating is 500 pounds, more than enough for even the heaviest amateur components. It takes only two minutes to set it up (it's an intuitive process).

Drill mounting holes in the steel shelf and screw in your radios' mounting brackets. After a deployment for a public service event or disaster incident, you can simply put your radios back in their cases for safe transportation, fold up the scaffolding, throw it all in the back of your communications van or pickup truck and you're on your way within minutes.

How many times have you seen amateur stations at Field Day, checkpoints on road races, and in disaster or drill theaters of operation where radios are set up on wobbly card tables, or in fashions that minimize access to radio rear panels? Elevate your game with the greater utility of scaffolding!

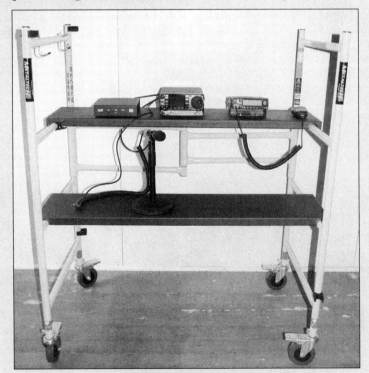

K1CE's radios mounted on the Metaltech scaffold, a good platform for a sturdy, easily transportable station that is simple to set up and take down. [Rick Palm, K1CE, photo]

2.4.3 Basic Principles of Incident and Event Operating

It is impossible to state exact rules that will cover every situation that arises, but there are general principles that should guide the public service operator when communicating in an emergency or disaster, or for a public event. These rules should be part of your training in ARES.

1. **Keep transmissions to a minimum, or even not at all**. In any incident, planned or unplanned, many of the most crucial stations will be weak in signal strength. It is essential that all other stations remain silent unless they are called upon. If you're not sure you should transmit — don't. Instead, study the situation by listening. Don't ever break into a disaster net just to inform the control station you are there if needed.

2. **Monitor established disaster frequencies**. Many areas have pre-established disaster frequencies where someone is always (or nearly always) monitoring for possible calls. Listen on such frequencies, especially during periods of potential emergency or disaster (for example, during a hurricane or tornado situation) for weak stations operating with marginal resources (low power, downed antennas, or other issues). Monitor for potentially weak distress calls: on CW, SOS is universally recognized. On voice, one can use "Mayday" (universal, the phone equivalent of SOS) or break into a net or conversation with the word "emergency."

3. **Don't spread rumors**. During and after a disaster situation, especially on the phone bands, you may hear almost anything. Unfortunately, much misinformation is transmitted. Rumors are started by expansion, deletion, amplification or modification of words, exaggeration, or interpretation. All addressed transmissions should be officially authenticated as to their source. These transmissions should be repeated word for word, if at all, and only when specifically authorized. In a disaster/emergency situation, with everyone's nerves on edge, it is little short of criminal to make a statement on the air without foundation in authenticated fact.

4. **Authenticate all messages**. Every message that purports to be of an official nature should be written and signed. Whenever possible, amateurs should avoid initiating disaster or emergency traffic themselves. We do the communicating; the agency officials we serve supply the content of the communications.

5. **Strive for efficiency**. Whatever happens in an emergency, you will find hysteria and some amateurs who are activated by the thought that they must be "sleepless heroes." Instead of operating your own station full time at the expense of your health and efficiency, it is much better to serve a shift at one of the best-located and best-equipped stations. This station will be suitable for the work at hand, and staffed by relief shifts of the best-qualified operators. This reduces interference and secures well-operated stations.

6. **Select the mode and band to suit the need**. It is a characteristic of all amateurs to believe that their favorite mode and band is superior to all others. For certain specific purposes and distances, this may be true. However, the merits of a particular band or mode in a communications emergency should be evaluated impartially with a view to the appropriate use of bands and modes. There is, of course, no alternative to using what happens to be available, but there are ways to optimize available communications.

Long experience has developed the following advantages:

CW Mode

1) Less interference in most amateur bands.

2) More secure communications — contents of communications are much less likely to be intercepted by the general public to start rumors or undue concern.

3) Simpler transmitting equipment.

4) Greater accuracy in "for the record" communications.

5) Longer range for a given amount of power.

Voice Mode

1) More practical for portable and mobile work.

2) More widespread availability of operators.

3) Faster communication for tactical or "command" purposes.

4) More readily appreciated and understood by the public.

5) Official-to-official and phone-patch communication.

Digital Modes

1) Less interference in most amateur bands.

2) More secure communications — contents of communications are much less likely to be intercepted by the general public to start rumors or undue concern.

3) More widespread availability of operators.

4) Greater speed in record communication than some of the other modes.

5) Error correction (in most but not all digital modes).

6) The potential for message store and forward capability, and for "digipeating" messages from point A to point Z via numerous automatically controlled middle points.

The well-balanced disaster organization

Public service events are excellent training for emergency communications. Amateurs in Michigan provided communications for an annual dog sled race using a variety of Amateur Radio modes and technologies. At left, an ATV station at the Start/Finish line was used to monitor teams' progress about 2 miles away. At right, Webster, W8QBX, collected and recorded times called in from various crossings, and Marv, KC8MLD, passed them to the Start/Finish line via digital modes. [Dale Johnson, KC8JLH, photos]

will have CW, phone, and digital mode capabilities available in order to promote efficiency and effectiveness. Of course, one must make the best use of whatever is available, but a great deal of efficiency is lost when there is lack of coordination between the different types of operation in an emergency. Absolute impartiality and a willingness to let performance speak for itself are prime requisites if we are to realize the best possible results.

7. **Use all communications channels intelligently**. While the prime object of emergency communications is to save lives and property, Amateur Radio is a secondary communications means; normal channels are primary and should be used if available. Emergency channels other than amateur that are available in the absence of amateur channels should be utilized without fear of favoritism in the interest of getting the message through.

8. **Don't broadcast**. Some amateur stations in an emergency situation have a tendency to emulate broadcast techniques. While it is true that the general public may be listening, our transmissions are not and should not be made for that purpose. Broadcast stations are well equipped to perform any such service. Our job is to communicate *for*, not *with* the general public.

9. **Communication support**. When disaster strikes, the first priority of those operators who live in or near the disaster area is to make their expertise and radio assets available to their Emergency Coordinator where and when they are needed. For timely and effective response, this means that operators need to talk to their ECs *well in advance* of the time of need so that they will know how to best respond.

10. **Use plain language**. It's readily understood by all entities supporting a special event or emergency/disaster response, and thus promotes interoperability. If, however, a special event turned into a terrorist incident as what occurred at the Boston Marathon in 2013, tactical language is occasionally warranted.

11. **Arrive at your assignment on time; inform the net**. Allow plenty of time to negotiate traffic, barriers, detours, and potentially bad weather. Get to your first obligation, usually a staging area, or even a restaurant for a pre-event briefing by your team leaders, early. Showing up late is bad form at best, and at worst, ratchets up the stress levels of your team leaders and fellow operators unnecessarily (they're already anxious), and undermines the possibility of a good, efficient start to a long day of operating in the field. Your leader and teammates are counting on you.

12. **Observe net protocols**. As mentioned earlier, transmit only when directed to do so by net control. Keep transmissions brief for efficiency and conservation of battery capacity. Listen carefully to net control; respond quickly to roll calls. Have at least two operators at each field location — switch operators for frequent relief breaks and to avoid physical and mental fatigue, which can reduce operation efficiency and effectiveness. You don't want to miss an important piece of information from net control, or worse, provide an erroneous report. *Stay on task!* If the net is quiet, do not "tune around," keep your ears glued to the net frequency, so you won't miss some critical traffic.

Don't make negative statements on the air. Such statements serve no purpose, undermine morale of weary volunteers, and interrupt interoperability — the ability of all responders across all agencies/disciplines to work together from the same playbook. Don't transmit sensitive information such as fatality counts, locations of staging areas, or fuel areas. Only transmit messages given to you by the proper authority. Log your messages passed and received.

In order to make your communications plan, you'll need to know what you have to work with: Be familiar with the amateur and other radio frequencies of your community, region and state, including HF and VHF/UHF frequencies and assets such as repeaters.

Don't force yourself or your organization

on the emergency/public safety professional management community. Don't self-ID your personal vehicle without proper authority, nor deploy to an area without permission — never self deploy.

When idle on a deployment, don't just sit there and wait for the next assignment! Always look for other opportunities to help, with permission. Observe other responders — study and learn their functions to enable you to better support them in the future.

Never express local politics. Maintain a professional appearance and behave like a professional. Leave your call sign badges, hats, club jackets, and ham bumper stickers at home. Don't wear public safety type uniforms without consent of the officials and staff you are serving. Don't bring any communications equipment into an EOC unless it is authorized.

And perhaps most important of all: Don't make a negative impression. We all are familiar with incidents where one operator acts or speaks in a negative way, resulting in sometimes years of disenfranchisement with the local emergency management agencies. One ham/one incident can spoil a good relationship for the rest of us.

During every deployment or exercise, think about the next time. You will always find that something is missing, broken, doesn't work as expected, wasn't planned for and so forth. Keep a mental record, or better still a written one of everything that is wrong. Be sure to look it over carefully after the event so you will be better prepared next time.

For Amateur Radio communications planners and leaders, don't promise event or incident managers services you can't supply: The key is to under-promise and over-deliver. Have extra operators on standby as fill-ins when the inevitable occurs — there will be no-shows, and worse, no calls saying they will be no-shows. Establish contact with other entities' leadership immediately upon arrival at the staging area for a smooth start to management of the incident or event.

2.4.4 Processing and Handling Messages

Message handling is the essence of public event/emergency/disaster communications by radio amateurs. Following a disaster, the potential clients for Amateur Radio services include both official organizations communicating among themselves, and citizens-potential victims who are without the conventional means to contact their friends and family. It is difficult for the amateur service provider to place an exclusive priority on one or the other, particularly if the means exist to serve both

customer groups. Regardless of the method used, the customer being served, or who is providing the service, effective communications requires the successful completion of all three major communications phases of *origination*, *transport*, and *delivery*. Originating messages from within a disaster area requires a minimum of one Amateur Radio operator, is often the primary focus, and can usually be accomplished. Without the concurrent provision for the transport and delivery phases,

however, originated messages cannot get to their destinations/addressees.

Traditional Amateur Radio networks consist of at least two Amateur Radio operators on a common mode and frequency, which satisfies all three communications phases. As the distance between the origination and destination locations increases, additional operators are required to relay the messages: the transport and delivery phases. Irrespective of the mode and frequency used, these are referred to as manual networks, and all function similarly.

Semiautomatic networks require an Amateur Radio operator to originate a message, but use automatic systems to execute the transport and sometimes delivery phases. These systems provide speed and accuracy, but they require specific and detailed addresses, and additional equipment at the origination point. One of the best known of these systems is Winlink 2000, which treats all messages as having the same priority and delivers messages to e-mail addresses through a hybrid RF/Internet interface. Semiautomatic networks are ill-suited for high priority, immediate warning/tactical communications, and should never be used to the exclusion of real-time networks, such as voice. *The greatest value to the customer is provided when all available communications networks are used.*

Tactical Traffic

Whether traffic is tactical, by formal message, or otherwise, success depends on knowing which type to use, and how to use it. Tactical traffic is usually fast, first-response, often point-to-point or peer-to-peer communications in an emergency/disaster/public event situation involving a few operators in a small area. It may be urgent instructions or inquiries such as "send an ambulance" or "who has the medical supplies?" Tactical traffic, even though unformatted and seldom written, is particularly important in localized communications when working with government and law-enforcement agencies. Note, however, that logs should be kept by hams passing tactical traffic. A log may be relevant later for law enforcement or other legal actions, and can even serve to protect the Amateur Radio operator in some situations.

The 146.52 MHz FM simplex calling frequency — or VHF and UHF repeaters — are typically used for tactical communications. This is a natural choice because FM mobile, portable and fixed-station equipment is so plentiful and popular, and VHF/UHF offers reliable line-of-sight local coverage. The 222 and 440 MHz bands may provide better communications from steel or concrete structures, have less interference, and be more secure for sensitive transmissions.

One way to make tactical communication and net operation efficient is to use tactical identifiers — words that describe a function, location, or agency. Their use prevents confusing listeners who are monitoring. When operators change shifts or locations, the set of tactical identifiers remains the same; that is, the tactical identifier remains with the position even if the operators switch. Examples include: "Parade Headquarters," "Finish Line," "Red Cross," "Net Control" or

"Weather Center." However, amateurs must still identify with their FCC-assigned call sign at the end of a transmission or series of transmissions and at intervals not to exceed 10 minutes, per the FCC rules.

Another tip is to use the military standard 24 hour time, or even UTC if the event or incident theater of operation crosses time zones, when working with relief agencies.

In some incident relief activities, tactical nets become resource or command nets. A resource net is used for an event that goes beyond the boundaries of a single jurisdiction and when mutual aid is needed. A command net is used for communications between EOCs, and Incident Command System officials. Yet with all the variety of nets, sometimes the act of simply putting the parties that need to communicate with each other together directly on the radio — instead of trying to interpret their words — is the best approach.

Formal Message Traffic

Formal message traffic is written and signed, and tends to be longer term and distance communications that involve more radio amateurs as traffic handlers and more people (potential message clients) over a larger area — across a state or even the country, for example. It's generally cast in standard ARRL message format (see sidebar) and handled on well-established traffic nets. Nets operate primarily on 75 and 40 meter SSB, 80 meter and 40 meter CW, linked 2 meter FM repeater systems, and semiautomatic digital systems. Formal messages can be used for disaster and weather situation reports not requiring immediate relay/delivery, for example, when more documentation, authentication, and record keeping is needed. These types of messages, already familiar to many agency officials and to the public, avoid message duplication while ensuring accuracy. Messages should be read back to the originators before sending them, since the originators are responsible for their content. When accuracy is more important than speed, getting the message on paper before it is transmitted is an inherent advantage of formal traffic.

Make sure to understand equivalent forms in ICS formats, as these will also be a very familiar to Incident Commanders and other ICS personnel. The General Message (ICS 213, see sidebar) format is used by the incident dispatchers to send any message or notification to incident personnel that requires hard-copy delivery.

Emergency, Priority, and Health-and-Welfare Traffic

There can be a tremendous amount of radio traffic to handle during a disaster. Handling

messages by radio frees phone lines and cell service that remain in working order for official emergency use and by those citizens caught in the disaster area in peril.

Shortly after the onset of a major disaster, *emergency* messages within the disaster area often have life-and-death urgency. Of course, they receive first priority handling. Much of the emergency traffic will be handled locally on VHF or UHF frequencies for many of the reasons cited earlier. Next in order of priority, after the emergency traffic is handled, is *priority* traffic — messages of a disaster-related nature but not having the utmost urgency of emergency traffic (*immediate* safety of life/property). Then, only when the emergency and priority traffic is handled, *health and welfare* traffic is originated by evacuees at shelters or by the injured at hospitals and sent/relayed to the outside world by Amateur Radio. It flows only one way, and that is out of the disaster area for reasons of efficiency. Just one outgoing message to a family member outside of the disaster area, distributed to other family and friends by the recipient, can potentially head off numerous inquiry messages coming into the shelters and disaster areas that can clog communication channels.

Incoming health-and-welfare traffic/inquiries should be handled last, if at all. So, don't solicit traffic addressed to someone inside the disaster area. Welfare inquiries are also inefficient for other reasons: they can take time to process and to discover hard-to-find answers. An advisory back to the inquirer uses even more time and channel occupancy. Meanwhile, some questions might have already been answered through restored circuits.

Sometimes shelter stations, acting as net control stations, can exchange information on the HF bands directly with destination areas as propagation permits. Or, they can handle traffic through a few outside operators via VHF FM channels who, in turn, can communicate to HF stations for relaying messages for delivery down the line. By having many trained traffic handlers, it's easy to adapt to whatever communications are required.

Another good way of heading off more health-and-welfare traffic potentially clogging critical channels is to encourage the use of the Red Cross "Safe and Well" online utility at **safeandwell.communityos.org/cms/ index.php.**

Message Relaying Systems

While VHF repeater, simplex, and HF voice nets are by far the most prevalent means of handling traffic on the air, there are numerous other modes and conduits for traffic handling. We will discuss examples, but let's start with the more traditional models

How to Fill Out the ARRL Message Form

The ARRL Radiogram™ has four parts: the *preamble*, the *address* block, the *text* and the *signature*. The preamble is analogous to the return address in a letter and contains the following:

1) The *number* denotes the message number of the originating station. Most traffic handlers begin with number 1 on January 1, but some stations with heavy volumes of traffic begin the numbering sequence every quarter or every month.

2) The *precedence* indicates the relative importance of the message. Most messages are Routine (R) precedence — in fact, about 99 out of 100 are in this category. You might ask, then why use any precedence on routine messages? The reason is that operators should get used to having a precedence on messages so they will be accustomed to it and be alerted in case a message shows up with a different precedence. A Routine message is one that has no urgency aspect of any kind, such as a greeting. And that's what most amateur messages are — just greetings.

The Welfare (W) precedence refers to either an inquiry as to the health and welfare of an individual in the disaster area or an advisory from the disaster area that indicates all is well. Welfare traffic is handled only after all emergency and priority traffic is cleared. The Red Cross equivalent to an incoming Welfare message is a Disaster Welfare Inquiry (DWI).

The Priority (P) precedence is getting into the category of high importance and is applicable in a number of circumstances: (1) important messages having a specific time limit, (2) official messages not covered in the emergency category, (3) press dispatches and emergency-related traffic not of the utmost urgency, and (4) notice of death or injury in a disaster area, personal or official.

The highest order of precedence is EMERGENCY (always spelled out, regardless of mode). This indicates any message having life-and-death urgency to any person or group of persons, which is transmitted by Amateur Radio in the absence of regular commercial facilities. This includes official messages of welfare agencies during emergencies requesting supplies, materials or instructions vital to relief of stricken populace in emergency areas. During normal times, it will be very rare.

3) *Handling Instructions* are optional cues to handle a message in a specific way. For instance, HXG tells us to cancel delivery if it requires a toll call or mail delivery, and to service it back instead. Most messages will not contain handling instructions.

4) Although the *station of origin* block seems self-explanatory, many new traffic handlers make the common mistake of exchanging their call sign for the station of origin after handling it. The station of origin never changes. That call serves as the return route should the message encounter trouble, and replacing it with your call will eliminate that route. A good rule of thumb is never to change any part of a message.

5) The *check* is merely the word count of the text of the message. The signature is not counted in the check. If you discover that the check is wrong, you may not change it, but you may amend it by putting a slash bar and the amended count after the original count. Another common mistake of new traffickers involves ARL checks. A check of ARL 8 merely means the text has an ARL numbered radiogram message text in it, and a word count of 8. It does not mean ARL numbered message 8. ARL numbered radiograms are abbreviations for common messages — refer to form FSD-3 at **www.arrl.org/public-service-field-services-forms**.

6) The *place of origin* can either be the location (City/State or City/Province) of the originating station or the location of the third party wishing to initiate a message through the originating station. Use standard abbreviations for state or province. ZIP or postal codes are not necessary. For messages from outside the US and Canada, city and country is usually used.

7) The *filing time* is another option, usually used if speed of delivery is of significant importance. Filing times should be in UTC time.

8) The final part of the preamble, the *date*, is the month and day the message was filed — year isn't necessary.

Next in the message is the *address*. Although things such as ZIP code and phone number aren't entirely necessary, the more items included in the address, the better its chances of reaching its destination. To experienced traffic handlers, ZIP codes and telephone area codes can be tip-offs to what area of the state the traffic goes, and can serve as a method of verification in case of garbling. For example, all ZIP codes in Minnesota start with a 5. Therefore, if a piece of traffic sent as St Joseph, MO, with a ZIP of 56374 has been garbled along the way, it conceivably can be re-routed. So, when it comes to addresses, the adage "the more, the better" applies.

The *text*, of course, is the message itself. You can expedite the counting of the check by following this simple rule — when copying by hand, write five words to a line. When copying with a keyboard, or when sending a message via a digital mode, type the message 10 words to a line. You will discover that this is a quick way to see if your message count agrees with the check. If you don't agree, nine times out of 10 you have dropped or added an X-ray (a break), so copy carefully. Another important thing to remember is that you never end a text with an X-ray — it just wastes space and makes the word count longer.

When counting words in messages, don't forget that each X-ray (instead of period), Query (question mark) and initial group counts as a word. Ten-digit telephone numbers count as three words; the ARRL-recommended procedure for counting the telephone number in the text of an ARRL Radiogram message is to separate the telephone number into groups, with the area code (if any) counting as one word, the three-digit exchange counting as one word, and the last four digits counting as one word. Separating the telephone number into separate groups also helps to minimize garbling. Also remember that closings such as "love" or "sincerely" (that would be in the signature of a letter) are considered part of the text in a piece of amateur traffic.

Finally, the *signature*. Remember, complementary closing words such as "sincerely" belong in the text, not the signature. In addition, signatures such as "Dody, Vanessa, Jeremy, Ashleigh, and Uncle Porter," no matter how long, go entirely on the signature line.

Sample message properly entered on the ARRL message form.

IC-213 General Message Form

Most public service operators, especially ARES and National Traffic System members, will be very familiar with the ARRL Radiogram message form, a time-tested and proven method of originating, sending, receiving, and delivering messages, sometimes referred to as the formal message form for formal message handling. See the sidebar elsewhere in this section on how to draft an ARRL Radiogram and perform these functions.

Sooner or later, however, the public service operator will be deployed to an event or incident that is conducted under the government's template for emergency or incident response — the Incident Command System (ICS). The system provides a means for all jurisdictions (local, county, state agencies), and disciplines (fire, EMS, search and rescue, law enforcement, and other emergency support functions) to communicate and work together seamlessly — called *Interoperability*. Toward this end, the ICS drafters/managers in the federal government publish a wide array of forms to be used by all responders for uniform familiarity, efficiency, and effectiveness. They can be found readily through an Internet search engine, but a great place to find the forms repository is in the Department of Homeland Security's Office of Emergency Communications publication Auxiliary Communications Field Operations Guide (AUXFOG) — available on-line at **www.publicsafetytools.info** or at the FEMA ICS Resources page at **training.fema.gov/emiweb/is/icsresource/icsforms.htm**

Every public service operator should be familiar with these forms, especially the ICS-213 General Message Form, which will be used by Incident Commanders and all ICS personnel in all incident responses. Specifically, the form is used by Incident dispatchers to record incoming messages that cannot be orally transmitted to the intended recipients; EOC and other incident personnel to transmit messages via radio or telephone to the addressee; and Incident personnel to send any message or notification that requires hard-copy delivery to other incident personnel.

The form is simplified for maximum

The ICS-213 General Message form.

efficiency, yet retains the "paper trail" information blanks including the To, From, Authorized By and Reply By, with space for names/positions and date/time of events in the chain from origination to delivery and reply back. The message should be concise. The ICS-213 is a three-part form, typically using carbon paper. The sender will complete Part 1 of the form and send Parts 2 and 3 to the recipient. The recipient will complete Part 2 and return Part 3 to the sender. A copy of the ICS-213 should be sent to and maintained within the Documentation Unit. Contact information for the sender and receiver can be added for communications purposes to confirm resource orders.

NATIONAL TRAFFIC SYSTEM

When you check into your local net or section net, chances are good that the net may be part of the National Traffic System™ (NTS™), or at least will have NTS representatives called liaison stations to give and take ARRL Radiogram formatted messages for further relay, even across the country, all via Amateur Radio (see **www.arrl.org/nts**).

The National Traffic System includes four different net levels (Local, Section, Region, and Area) that operate in an orderly time sequence to effect a definite flow pattern for traffic from origin to destination. A message flows through NTS like an airline passenger who starts out in a small residential town with a destination across the country in another small town. He or she has to change carriers many times in the process, starting with a local ground conveyance to a feeder airline, to a transcontinental airline, to another feeder airline, then local transportation for delivery to the passenger's final destination. Similarly, a message addressed to a recipient across the country starts with the originating station in a local net, is carried to the section net, the region net, the area net, then via a transcontinental traffic handler to a distant area net and then back down the line to delivery.

Of course the message, like the passenger, can "get on" or "get off" at any point if that's its origin or destination. Trained, designated liaison operators relay the messages to and from the various levels of NTS nets. Voice and CW modes are typically used to convey messages among the various NTS levels and nets, but messages may also be passed through NTS-affiliated local and section digital traffic nodes with store-and-forward capabilities and bulletin board systems. To learn more about getting involved with NTS, check with your local ARRL officials for NTS nets serving your local area and Section. See also the online net directory and search function on the ARRL website at **www.arrl.org/arrl-net-directory-search**.

PACKET RADIO

Packet radio is a powerful tool for traffic handling, including ARRL Radiogram messages, especially with detailed or lengthy text messages that need to be handled more securely than those transmitted by voice. The first step is to prepare and edit messages off line as text files. Then, they can be sent error free in just seconds, an efficient timesaver for busy traffic channels. Packet Bulletin Board systems (PBBS) add utility to the mode, such as dropping off messages for routing and delivery, and picking up messages for the same functions. Packet BBSs have been in use for ARRL Radiogram message routing since the 1980s. Public service agencies are impressed by fast and accurate printed messages. Packet radio stations can even be mobile or portable. Relaying might be supplemented by Winlink 2000, the system equipped to handle e-mail messages among HF stations, the Internet and packet radio VHF stations.

IMAGE COMMUNICATIONS

Image communication offers "messages" as live video or still pictures of an area to allow, for example, damage assessment by authorities. Amateur television (ATV) in its public service role usually employs portable fast-scan television (FSTV), which displays full motion, has excellent detail, can be in color and has a simultaneous sound channel. Although a picture is worth a thousand words, an ATV system requires more equipment, operating skill, and preparation than using a simple FM radio.

Slow scan TV (SSTV) is also popularly used for damage assessment. Portable SSTV operations can use a digital still image camera, laptop computer and handheld or mobile transceiver. Signals may be relayed through a repeater to increase their range. More information on these modes may be found in Section 1 of this book.

A potentially new tool for image communi-

cation is a drone equipped with a small video camera and a transmitter, which is destined to become a more popular utility for damage assessment: ARES members can "fly" their drones from safer locations, out of potentially unstable ground conditions, and their ground stations can relay imaging to emergency managers and other clients. Note that anyone who owns a small unmanned aircraft that weighs more than 0.55 pound and less than 55 pounds must register with the Federal Aviation Administration's UAS registry before they fly outdoors. "Pilots" who do not register could face civil and criminal penalties.

AUTOMATIC PACKET REPORTING SYSTEM (APRS)

APRS® is a well-established, ever evolving and proven Amateur Radio technology that incorporates Global Positioning System (GPS) receiver tracking, weather instrumentation stations, digital cartography mapping, radio direction finding, and comprehensive messaging utilities in one package. APRS has been adopted by some SKYWARN and ARES organizations as frontline technology for severe weather operations. Such a system provides accurate, real-time weather telemetry that SKYWARN operators and National Weather Service meteorologists use to issue severe weather warnings and advisories. A combination of APRS and Emergency Management Weather Information Network (EMWIN) can be used to transmit warnings to field spotters to help track a storm's movement as well as report tornadoes or hail. A mobile APRS with GPS capability can be an essential tool during and following a large scale disaster to pinpoint critical locations in an area void of landmarks, such as forest fires or search and rescue activities. New APRS-friendly radios put tactical messaging capability in the palm of your hand. See Sec-

tion 1 of this book for more information on these modes.

OTHER DIGITAL TECHNOLOGIES

D-STAR (Digital Smart Technologies for Amateur Radio) is a digital voice and data protocol developed for Amateur Radio. While there are other digital on-air technologies such as APCO's P25 being used by amateurs that have come from other services, D-STAR is designed specifically for amateur service use. D-STAR offers voice communication and slow data transfer, using half-duplex, digitized voice transmissions, with digitized voice/audio signals and short data messages being supported. Voice and audio streams are transmitted synchronously to support communications quality reproduction. Data and voice/audio transmissions are interleaved, and routed via an international network of repeaters and reflectors connected via the Internet. D-STAR has been around for a while and is well-established in some regions of the US. In northeast Florida, for example, D-STAR has seen extensive use in disaster response and emergency communications.

The newer Fusion and DMR systems involve other data protocols based on similar hybrid Internet/RF voice/data models.

NBEMS AND THE *FLDIGI* SUITE OF UTILITIES

Narrow Band Emergency Messaging Software (NBEMS) is an Open Source software suite that allows amateurs to reliably send and receive data messages using nearly any computer with soundcard and any analog radio with interface without requiring a dedicated digital infrastructure or specialized modem hardware. NBEMS works on both VHF/UHF FM and on HF. It's easy to send and receive verified files and forms using *flmsg*. You can integrate NBEMS with a high-speed

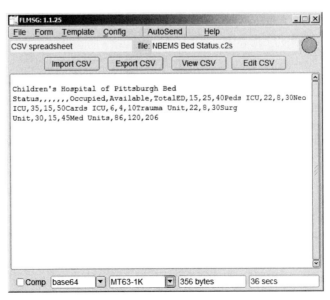

Flmsg, one of the NBEMS suite of programs, uses this form to send spreadsheet data. The data is entered using the comma separated value (CSV) format. [Courtesy Harry Bloomberg, W3YJ]

mesh network. NBEMS is a very popular digital emergency communications package for many ARES groups around the country.

RMS EXPRESS

RMS Express is a Winlink 2000 (WL2K) radio e-mail program that supports a wide array of TNCs and multimode controllers, the sound card mode WINMOR, HF PACTOR, VHF/UHF AX.25 packet radio, and direct telnet to other networks. *RMS Express* is also a very popular program set for emergency/disaster communications. It has some special features such as forms/message templates creation and formless content transport, plus a growing library of pre-created forms to use. Before adopting *RMS Express* as a program for your ARES group, check with your local leadership for their plans.

AMATEUR BROADBAND HIGH SPEED MULTIMEDIA (HSMM)

One of the most recent and exciting developments is hams making their own high speed digital multimedia microwave networks. Using commercial off-the-shelf equipment and developing their own software, groups of hams have created high speed wireless Amateur Radio digital networks with wide area coverage.

The uses for these high speed data networks for Amateur Radio and public service are endless. Virtually any service that works on the regular Internet can be adapted to an Amateur Radio high speed multimedia (HSMM) network, including video conferencing, instant messaging, voice over Internet protocol (VoIP), network sensors and cam-

---

San Diego ARES Showcases High Speed Networking and Data Transfer
By Ed Sack, W3NRG

A recent San Diego, California ARES (SDGARES) drill featured a remarkable microwave link established between the city's Sharp Coronado Hospital and the *Club de Radio Experimentadores de Baja California* (CREBC) club headquarters in Baja through the efforts of the CREBC club, the Coronado Emergency Radio Operators (CERO) and the High Data Rate Emergency group (HDRENS). Mike Burton, N6KZB, at CREBC HQ, and the Coronado Hospital ARES group (WW6RB, N6QKE, KK6DKW and W3NRG) working from the hospital conference room were in high speed video/audio contact extensively such that in effect the two sites were working in tandem: There was no waiting for voice channels to be free or typing and accessing data messages. It was just like having both groups in the same room all the time. The reliability of the link and connection was outstanding — the video definition was excellent as was the audio such that one could follow the voice exchanges between CREBC and ARES at the Coronado hospital just by listening to the speaker in the CREBC club room in Mexico. In addition, the software gave the groups the ability to send files of any size back and forth and to connect to the commercial Internet if needed. The Sharp headquarters visitors and hospital staff who passed through could be seen at CREBC, and vice versa. The drill garnered good public relations for SDGARES.

---

eras, remote station control, and many other services. With the capability to send real-time video and data files, the public service and disaster support utility of Amateur Radio is expanded tremendously. See the sidebar on San Diego (California) ARES use of this technology for hospital communications.

OTHER SYSTEMS

Winlink 2000, IRLP, EchoLink and WIRES-X, APCO25, HF sound card modes and Automatic Link Establishment (ALE) are all additional modes and tools to help emer-

gency communications operators answer questions such as: Can you transfer supply lists or personnel assignments between emergency operations sites? Can you get critical e-mails to the Internet if a connection goes down? Can you relay digital images of damage at specific locations? Can you track the locations of emergency personnel and display them on computer maps?

With these modes and others, the above critical questions can be answered by ARES operators with "yes."

2.4.5 Emergency and Disaster Operations

Emergency Operations Plan (EOP)

More than any other facet of Amateur Radio, public event, disaster response, or emergency communication activity requires a *plan* — an orderly arrangement of time, personnel, and actions that ensures that performance is efficient and effective and objectives are met. Lack of a plan could hamper execution of urgent operations or delay crucial decisions and delivery of critical services and supplies, undermining achievement of goals. Start drafting your plan by identifying the types of hazards that may occur in your area, defining specific responsibilities and actions to be taken by specific personnel for each type of incident, and developing objectives to be covered and met. For example, a major portion of your plan will be to specify

radio assets and frequencies available for accomplishing the mission, and assigning them to the various nets that will be run to meet function and communication needs. Use a successful plan from another ARES group as a model or template for yours. Start with a small plan, then test the plan a piece at a time, and redefine it if it is unsatisfactory. Testing involves activating and implementing the plan under simulated disaster scenarios, and then revising it as indicated. Drilling on the plan also helps teach communicators what to do in a real emergency, without a great deal of risk. Finally, prepare a few contingency plans just in case the original plan fails.

ARES groups are among the most likely to have well-evolved emergency operations plans coordinated with their served agency partners, where members train and prepare constantly in an organized way. Communi-

cations plans must take into consideration the sometimes unique characteristics of the environments operators are serving in: urban versus suburban or rural versus wilderness, for example. Topography also dictates how some plans must be crafted. Cities may have paid emergency management and public safety professionals, while smaller towns may rely more on volunteers, with more territory to cover. The rural public then, with few volunteers spread over a wide area, may be isolated, unable to call for help or incapable of reporting all of the damage. The point is, "no size fits all" — careful consideration of all the factors that come into play in the operating environment must result in a customized emergency operations plan. And, train, test and drill on the plan, revise it accordingly, and train, test and drill again, over and over!

Procedures

Aside from having plans, it is also necessary to draft protocols and procedures — the time-tested, best methods or ways to do a job. Procedures become habits, independent of a plan, when everyone knows what happens next and can tell others what to do. Actually, the size of a disaster affects the size of the response, but not the procedures.

Procedures that should be widely known before disasters occur include how to coordinate or deploy people, equipment, and supplies. There are procedures to use a repeater and an autopatch, to check into a net and to format or handle traffic. Because it takes time to learn activities that are not normally used every day, excessively detailed procedures will confuse people and should be avoided.

Your EC will have developed a procedure to activate the ARES group, but he or she will need your help to make it work. A telephone alerting "tree" call-up, even if based on a current list of phone numbers, might fail if there are gaps in the calling sequence, or members are not near a phone, or there is no phone service. Consider alternative procedures. Use alerting tones and frequent announcements on a well monitored repeater to round up many operators at once. An unused 2 meter simplex frequency can function for alerting; instead of turning off radios, your group would monitor this frequency for alerts without the need of any equipment modifications. Since this channel is normally quiet, any activity on it would probably be an alert announcement.

During an emergency, report to the EC so that up-to-the-minute data on operators will be available. Don't rely on one leader; everyone should keep an emergency reference list of relief-agency officials, police, sheriff and fire departments, ambulance service and ARES and other nets. Be ready to help, but stay off the air unless there is a specific job to be done that you can handle efficiently. Always listen before you transmit. Work and cooperate with the local civic and relief agencies as the EC suggests. During a major emergency, copy special W1AW bulletins for the latest developments.

Afterward, let your EC know about your activities, so that a timely report can be submitted to ARRL HQ. These reports are critical in helping ARRL maintain up to date and complete records of Amateur Radio service in emergencies. Help maintain this record.

Working with Served Partner Agencies

Amateur Radio affords public-safety agencies and local police and fire officials with an extremely valuable resource in times of

---

Why Public Service Operators Should Participate in Contests

By Marty Woll, N6VI

Contesting helps prepare us for demanding communication environments and tasks such as might be encountered during a major disaster. Contesting hones important emergency/disaster communications skills:

- Hearing, understanding, and recording information quickly and accurately.
- Extracting information from weak signals or through interference and noise.
- Establishing and completing contacts with rapid efficiency.
- Finding workarounds when the unexpected happens, rather than giving up.
- Knowing how to get the most out of your equipment and antennas.
- Understanding propagation and making those tough long-haul contacts.

Each contest has its own unique rules that define the challenge. There are specific starting and ending times, encompassing operating periods as short as four hours or as long as two days. Eligible stations (those with whom contacts count for contest credit) may be confined to a specific state or country or may include all hams worldwide.

There is a defined exchange, a set of information that must be sent, received, and logged accurately. Exchanges can be as simple as three or four characters or as complicated as a lengthy data set that simulates the message header in a formal Radiogram.

Each contact adds points, and often there is a "multiplier" for each geographic area contacted. The sum of contact points times the sum of multipliers yields the final score. Participating operators usually submit their contest logs to the sponsoring organization in electronic form, which enables rigorous cross-checking for accuracy and facilitates timely publishing of the results.

Contests are not limited to the HF bands that are primarily the domain of many General-class and higher licensees. There are VHF, UHF, and even microwave contests, all available to holders of every class of license. If you think that the 2 meter or 70 cm band is limited to supporting nearby and repeater contacts, you're in for a surprise! Communication over hundreds of miles and more is possible with suitable antennas and equipment. By participating in these competitions, you will learn what works best and how your station's effectiveness can be improved.

You don't have to be in it to win it; just take part, and have fun while you're learning to enhance your and your station's performance. We can identify and correct weaknesses in our stations, evaluate the impact of equipment and antenna changes, and push ourselves to solve real-time communication problems as efficiently as possible, as would be demanded in emergency/disaster situations.

---

emergency. Once initial acceptance by the authorities is achieved, an ongoing working relationship between amateurs and safety agencies is based on the efficiency of our performance. Officials tend to be very cautious and skeptical about those who are not members of the public-safety professions. At times, officials may have trouble separating problem solvers from problem makers, but they often accept communications help if it is offered in the proper spirit.

Here are several image-building rules for working with served agencies:

• *Maintain group unity.* Work within ARES, RACES, or local club groups. Position your EC as the direct link with the agencies.

• *Be honest.* If your group cannot handle a request, say so and explain why. Safety personnel often risk their lives based on a fellow disaster worker's promise to perform.

• *Equip conservatively.* Do not have more signs, decals, and antennas than used by the average police or fire vehicle. Safety pro-

fessionals are trained to use the minimum resources necessary to get the job done.

• *Look professional.* In the field, wear a simple jump suit or jacket with an ARES patch to give a professional image and to help officials identify radio operators.

• *Respect authority.* Only assume the level of authority and responsibility that has been given to you.

• *Publicize Amateur Radio.* If contacted by members of the press, restrict comments solely to the amateurs' role in the situation. Emergency status and names of victims should only come from a press information officer or from the government agency concerned.

The public service lifeline provided by Amateur Radio must be understood by public-safety agencies before the next disaster occurs. Have an amateur representative meet with public-safety officials in advance of major emergencies so each group will know the capabilities of the other. The representative should appear professional with a calm, businesslike manner and wear conservative attire. It is up to you to invite the local agencies to observe or cooperatively participate with your group.

If the agency offers training in its particular operations, sign up to learn its mission, history, protocols, and rules. It shows your interest, and will help you serve them more effectively.

Do not bring your group's problems (personnel, hardware, radios/antennas, or other issues) to agency officials to sort out. Work through your group's issues internally. Your job is to listen to agency officials' problems and needs, and offer well-conceived plans for solving and meeting them.

If invited to play in an exercise, accept the invitation, and show them what you can do! Pre-plan your group's role and participation, but your members should be prepared to think and react on their feet, too. Exercise evaluators will be looking at your abilities to do just that.

Other tips:

• *Don't "self-dispatch"* to agency offices and facilities; you're just asking to be a liability, not an asset, to an incident or exercise. At an assignment, ARES operators should be seen and seldom heard. *Dress appropriately* for the assignment in clean, neat attire. Do *not* smoke.

• *Come prepared to be self-contained.* Though an agency will likely provide food and possibly a place to sleep (for example, a Red Cross shelter provides food for all and would likely provide the radio operator an off-duty place to sleep), be prepared with your own food and sleeping bag, cot, and other basic supplies. When checking in to an assigned site, inquire with whom you need to sign in and out with. Ask to whom you report at the site. Ask for a "who's who" briefing — it helps to know from whom you may accept messages.

• *Be flexible.* Be prepared to use agency equipment such as their radios and to talk over *their* circuits, not just amateur frequencies.

• *Never tell an agency official or staffer that your way is better.* They have established protocols and procedures — work within them. You may politely suggest changes at an appropriate time *after* the incident/event is over, perhaps during the "hot wash" (after action review and critique).

• *Accuracy counts.* When accepting a verbal message, listen to what the message originator wants passed, and then read back the message to double-check for accuracy before transmitting, or delivering it.

Even though our radio service is titled "Amateur," above all, present a *professional* posture! The difference between "amateur" and "professional" should only be a paycheck.

Madison County (Florida) Emergency Coordinator Pat Lightcap, K4NRD, a 30 year veteran, at the HF position in the Madison County EOC communications room. [Rick Palm, K1CE, photo]

Emergency Operations Center (EOC)

The Emergency Operations Center (EOC) is a central, usually hardened location and facility where government at any level can provide interagency and emergency support function (ESF) coordination and execute decision making to support incident response. The emergency manager keeps the elected officials informed for any policy decisions necessary. The EOC typically does not command or control the boots on the ground, on-scene response. Those are functions usually reserved for the incident commander. The EOC is involved with strategy, and tactical decisions are left to the incident commander and his/her command and general staff.

The EOC is involved with information collection and evaluation, priority setting, and resource management. Communications is the key to effective operations and interface, and Amateur Radio has historically had an important, longstanding role in this regard. The EOC is often organized based on the various ESFs: for example, the Communications function is ESF#2. Physically, each ESF manager has a desk or seat at the main table in the central room with a placard with the name of his/her function. Amateur Radio operators often provide alternate communications between the ESF managers and the field, and between the emergency manager and his/her counterparts at the incident command post and/or other locations.

Incident Command System

Amateur Radio emergency communications and message handling are frequently involved with the Incident Command System (ICS), and emergency operations center (EOC) functioning. The ICS is a way to control initial and subsequent activities in emergency and disaster situations, and is the standard management model used by all levels of government for disaster response.

Consider an automobile accident where a citizen or an amateur, first on the scene, becomes a temporary Incident Commander (IC) when he or she calls for or radios a message for help. A law enforcement officer is dispatched to the accident scene in a squad car and, upon arriving, takes over the IC tasks. Relief efforts, like those in this simple example of an automobile accident, begin when someone takes charge, makes a decision and directs the efforts of others.

The EOC responds to the IC through message communications and subsequent dispatching of equipment and emergency support function staff, anticipating needs and assistance. It may send more equipment to a staging area to be stored where it can be available almost instantly or send more people to react quickly to changing situations. All of this depends on message handling — in many instances, by radio amateurs.

If the status of an accident changes (a car hits a utility pole, which later causes a fire), the IC sends a message to the EOC with an updated report then keeps control even after the support agencies arrive and take over their specific responsibilities: Injuries — medical; fires — fire department; disabled vehicles — law enforcement or tow truck; and utility poles — utility company. The ICS can be expanded as conditions dictate, but there is still a unified command. By being outside the perimeter of a potentially unstable disaster area, the EOC can use the proper type of radio communications for the task at hand, concentrate on gathering data from other agencies, and then provide the right support to the ICS personnel in the affected area.

Whether there is a minor vehicle accident or a major disaster operation, the effectiveness of the amateur effort in an emergency depends mainly on handling information, often within the framework of the Incident Command System.

TEMPLATES FOR SUCCESS

The Incident Command System (ICS) also works well for radio amateurs engaged in a special event project. To easily remember the four main functions or *sections*, use the mnemonic *flop*, for the Finance section, Logistics section, Operations section, and Planning section. The Amateur Radio special event team leader should choose a chief for each. A safety officer should also be appointed, as well as a public information officer. These official titles largely speak for themselves, but essentially cover the waterfront for prepa-

When Is ICS Used?

ICS can be used to manage:

- Natural hazards.
- Technological hazards.
- Human-caused hazards.
- Planned events.

FEMA

Visual 2.5
ICS Overview

An understanding of the Incident Command System (ICS) is fundamental to all FEMA operations. The principles can be applied to local activations and even Field Day. [Courtesy FEMA]

ration for support of the event: How much money will be needed — what do we need to buy in terms of hardware (radios, repeaters, laptops, battery and/or generator power, antennas, and so forth) and software such as APRS (discussed above), which provides an excellent medium for reporting positions and other data from field teams, for example.

Logistics include transportation to and from the staging area and field locations (at participant rest stops, for example), and food and supplies for operators. Planning should involve all Amateur Radio team members, with their input and feedback eagerly sought, resulting in "ownership" or "buy-in" to the communications plan, and consequently a higher morale and team spirit going in.

Operations, of course, refers to the time frame of when the event is actually being run, with roll calls, communications messages being passed, and problems being referred to the chain of command in real time for immediate fixes to keep things running smoothly. The public information officer monitors the

Amateur Radio operations and informs the media outlets of the role of radio amateurs in the event. The safety officer (preferably a health care professional) monitors the health and welfare of members of the Amateur Radio team and coordinates medical assistance as needed — from the use of a small First Aid kit, to a full-blown medical emergency and evacuation.

Another advantage of using the ICS template is that it is universally accepted and used by emergency management and other entities such as special event coordinators, and thus a level playing field is achieved when Amateur Radio teams use it, too — in many cases, dovetailing nicely with the other entities' own planning and operations.

Shelter Operations

A shelter or relief center, often managed by the Red Cross (an ARRL partner entity), is a temporary place of protection where rescuers can bring disaster victims and where supplies

can be dispensed. Many displaced people can stay at the homes of friends or relatives, but those searching for family members or in need are housed in shelters.

Whether a shelter is for a few stranded motorists during a snowstorm or a whole community of homeless residents after a disaster, it is an excellent location to set up an Amateur Radio communication base station. A good alternate station location would be an ARES mobile communications van, if available, next to the shelter.

Once officials designate the locations for shelters, radio operators can be assigned to set up equipment and check into the appropriate nets from those sites. With the authorization of the shelter manager, the amateur station operators could share a table with shelter registration workers. Make sure you obtain permission for access to the shelter to assist and respect the privacy and needs of the shelter evacuees/residents.

Damage Assessment

Damage caused by natural disasters can be sudden and extensive. Responsible officials in the area affected by the disaster will need communications channels to contact appropriate officials outside the affected areas to give damage reports and solicit assistance, potentially for the safety of life and property. Such data will be used to initiate and coordinate disaster relief. Amateur Radio operators can provide communications in support of agency officials, but can also perform sweeps of the affected areas if safe to do so, and provide their own damage assessments to officials as well.

Amateurs coming into the disaster areas sometimes are unable to cross roadblocks established to limit access by sightseers and po-

Amateurs in Arkansas provided support for search and rescue operations following a flash flood that claimed 20 lives. [John Luther, W5LED, photo]

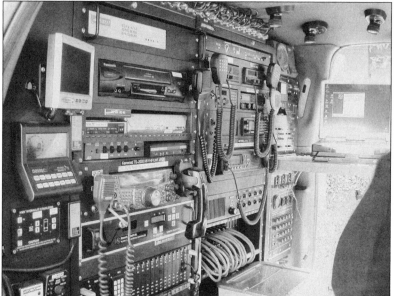

This American Red Cross Emergency Communications Vehicle carries many different kinds of communications gear, including Amateur Radio. Increasingly, amateurs must be familiar with the various communications systems used by served agencies in addition to Amateur Radio. [Elizabeth Leslie, photos]

modern VHF handheld and mobile radios to activate a repeater autopatch, call 9-1-1 and report directly to law enforcement.

Autopatch protocol: Don't transmit continuously! Talk in short sentences, releasing your push to talk switch after each one, so the operator can ask you questions. When you report a vehicle accident, remain calm and get as much information as you can. This is one time you certainly have the right to break into a conversation on a repeater. Use plain language, say exactly what you mean, and be brief and to the point. Do not guess about injuries; if you don't know, say so. Some accidents may look worse than they really are; requesting an ambulance to be sent needlessly could divert it away from a more serious accident injury occurring at the same time elsewhere. And besides, police cruisers are generally only minutes away in an urban area.

Search and Rescue (SAR)

Amateurs supporting search efforts for an injured hiker or climber use repeaters to coordinate the rescue. A small airplane crashes, and amateurs help direct the search by tracking signals from its Emergency Locator Transmitter. No matter what the situation, radio amateurs often join local search-and-rescue teams who have familiarity with the search area. Once a victim is found, the hams can radio the status, autopatch for medical information, guide further help to the area, and plan for return transportation. If the victim is found in good condition, Amateur Radio can bolster the hopes of base camp personnel and the family of the victim with direct communications.

Even in cities, searches are occasionally necessary, called urban SAR. An elderly person out for a walk gets lost and doesn't return home. After a reasonable time, a local search team plans and coordinates a search.

Search and rescue consists of three separate operations: *Size-up* involves assessing the situation and determining a safe action plan. *Search* involves locating victims and documenting their location. *Rescue* involves the procedures and methods required to extricate the victims. Well-intentioned but untrained searchers/rescuers can become victims themselves, compounding problems. Many radio amateurs are trained in search and rescue and have a history of serving searchers/rescuers with radio communications. There are numerous environments for SAR, and one size does not fit all. The person in charge should be aware of, and trained specifically for, the kind of SAR environment he/she will face: urban or wild land SAR, for examples.

tential looters; proper emergency responder identification will be required to gain access into these areas. Secure proper credentials from relevant officials well in advance of any potential responses! During the emergency is not the time to deal with the administrative aspects of disaster response. In some instances, call sign license plates on the front of the car or placards inside windshields may help.

It's important for amateurs to keep complete and accurate logs for use by officials to survey damage, or to use as a guide for replacement operators.

Accidents and Hazards

Accidents and hazardous situations arise suddenly, are unpredictable, and can happen anywhere. Historically, an emergency *autopatch* has been used to report incidents that pose threats to life or personal safety, such as vehicle accidents, disabled vehicles or debris in traffic, injured persons, criminal activities, and fires. With the ubiquity of cell phones, accident reporting by amateurs has diminished, but when cell service is not available, hams can use the keypad on most

Hospital Communications

Hospitals are among the critical institutions in emergency and disaster situations when victims are hurt, whether in a crash on the Interstate, or during a mass casualty incident such as an earthquake, tornado, hurricane, hazmat spill, or terrorist attack. The hospital can be involved in taking in casualties from its own region, or from afar when the situation is so large that it overwhelms the local healthcare systems' ability to care for them. In the latter scenario, the government's National Disaster Medical System (NDMS) was designed to evacuate and airlift patients to distant medical facilities, diffusing the caseload throughout the entire country if necessary. Amateur Radio was involved in planning and exercises for NDMS back in the mid-80s.

Hospitals are organized by department: the ER, ICU, OR, the medical/surgical floors, radiology, pharmacy, and laboratories, and so on. They can't fulfill their functions without fast, error-free accurate and effective communications. In several areas of the country, hospitals have used the services of Amateur Radio operators at key communication points throughout their campuses to provide critical back-up communications.

During a disaster or emergency the need may arise for patient information to be sent via Amateur Radio. Patient privacy is a serious concern of health care and public health professionals and is protected through the Health Insurance Portability and Accountability Act (HIPAA). In the rare case that patient information is requested to be sent via Amateur Radio, while it is not the role of the radio operator to determine what is and is not permitted under HIPAA, it may be appropriate for the operator to remind their immediate supervisor or the originator of the message that there can be no expectation of privacy because encryption of information sent via Amateur Radio is not permitted under Part 97 rules. See the sidebar on an Orange County, California hospital ARES group.

Toxic-Chemical Spills and Hazardous Materials

A toxic-chemical spill suddenly appears when gasoline pours from a ruptured bulk-storage tank. A water supply is unexpectedly contaminated, or a fire causes chlorine gas to escape at an apartment swimming pool. On a highway, a faulty shut-off valve lets chemicals leak from a truck, or drums of chemicals fall onto the highway and rupture. Amateur communications have helped in all of these situations, but special caution is mandated: Treat a known or suspected hazardous material like a *STOP* sign — do not go any closer. Instead, ARES members should evaluate the situation from a safe distance: Don't touch anything, position yourself uphill and upwind, and warn others to stay away. When safe, call 9-1-1, preferably by landline, avoiding use of a cell phone.

Vehicles carrying 1000 pounds or more of a HAZMAT are required by Federal regulations to display a placard bearing a four-digit identification number. From a safe distance radio the placard number to the authorities and they will decide whether to send HAZMAT experts to contain the spills.

Follow directions from those in command. Provide communications to help them evacuate residents in the immediate area and coordinate between the spill site and the shelter facilities. Hams also assist public service agencies by setting flares for traffic control, helping reroute motorists and so on. We're occasionally asked to make autopatch calls for police or fire-department workers on the scene as they try to determine the nature of the chemicals.

Severe Weather

Radio amateurs are heavily invested in observing and reporting severe weather events to the National Weather Service offices, EOCs, emergency managers and other public safety officials, collecting reports from amateurs in the field via a weather net. The Net Control Station of the net, typically using a VHF repeater or simplex frequency, directs and maintains control over traffic being passed on the net. The NCS also collates reports, relates pertinent material to the Weather Service and organizes liaison with other area repeaters. The NCS might start the net upon hearing a NOAA radio alert, or upon request by NWS or the EC. The NCS should keep in mind that the general public or government officials might be listening to net operations with scanners.

Here are some guidelines an NCS might use to initiate and handle a severe weather net on a repeater:

1) Activate alert tone on repeater.
2) Read weather-net activation format.
3) Appoint a backup NCS to copy and log all traffic — and to take over in the event the NCS goes off-the-air or needs relief.
4) Ask the National Weather Service (NWS) for the current weather status.
5) Check in all available operators.
6) Assign operators to priority stations and liaisons.
7) Give severe-weather report outline and updates.
8) Be apprised of situations and assignments by EC.
9) Periodically read instructions on net procedures and types of severe weather to report.
10) Acknowledge and respond to all calls immediately.
11) Require that net stations request permission to leave the net.
12) During periods of inactivity and to keep the frequency open, make periodic announcements that a net is in progress.
13) Close the net after operations conclude.

AT THE WEATHER SERVICE

The NCS position at the National Weather Service office, when practical, can be handled by the EC and other ARES personnel. Operators assigned there must have 2 meter handheld radios with fully charged batteries. The station located at the NWS office may also be connected to other positions with an off-the-air intercom system. This allows some traffic handling without loading up the repeater. Designate a supplementary radio channel in anticipation of an overload or loss of primary communications circuits.

If traffic is flowing faster than you can easily copy and relay, NWS personnel may request that a handheld radio be placed at the severe-weather desk. This arrangement allows them to monitor incoming traffic directly. Nevertheless, all traffic should be written on report forms.

Hospital Disaster Support Communications System Works with California Hospitals

By April Moell, WA6OPS,
District Emergency Coordinator,
Orange Section, ARES

The Hospital Disaster Support Communications System (HDSCS) is a special ARES group of about 80 radio amateurs who have volunteered for more than 30 years to provide backup internal and external communications for critical medical facilities in Orange County, California whenever normal communications are interrupted for any reason. The HDSCS antenna team follows up with hospitals that exhibit problems during regular drills and also helps to determine the best locations for antennas and feed lines during renovations or relocation of command centers.

Huntington Beach Hospital has hosted HDSCS for ARRL Field Day for many years to showcase what Amateur Radio can do in setting up emergency communications in a major area-wide disaster by making use of existing structures, such as flag poles and exterior stairways. In addition, hospital staff deploys surge capacity tents and portable generators for HDSCS use. With this collaborative effort the hospital can show accrediting agencies how they work with resources from the community.

REPEATER LIAISONS

Assign properly equipped and located stations to act as liaisons with other repeaters. Two stations should be appointed to each liaison assignment. One monitors the weather repeater at all times and switches to the assigned repeater just long enough to pass traffic. The second monitors the assigned repeater and switches to the weather repeater just long enough to pass traffic. If there aren't enough qualified liaison stations, one station can be given both assignments.

WEATHER WARNINGS

NWS policy is to issue warnings only when there is absolute certainty, for fear of the "cry wolf" syndrome (premature warnings cause the public to ignore later warnings). Public confidence increases with reliable weather warnings. When NWS calls a weather alert, it will contact the local EC by phone or voice-message pager, or the EC may call NWS to check on a weather situation. The National Weather Service's SKYWARN program is discussed in more detail below. SKYWARN provides expert training on how to spot and report severe weather — a must for anyone checked into a weather net.

Special Event Communications

Planning, preparedness, and practice for providing radio communications at special events such as running races, bike-a-thons, walks for special causes, competitions and parades demand the best from Amateur Radio operators in efficiency and effectiveness. There is much at stake in terms of safety of not only the event participants, but also the public watching the event, and the "machine" of behind-the-scenes officials and workers making the event run smoothly.

Radio amateurs are cogs in the machine, with a profound responsibility for ensuring officials and workers are able to communicate with one another as needed. Our reputations are also at stake as an effective communications plan carried out flawlessly results in us being asked to return next year, and also asked to serve in sometimes even more demanding situations such as disaster responses.

All of the discussion above on emergency/disaster operating principles, net discipline/

Olympic Peninsula ARES Supports Statewide Exercise, then Marathon

A fine example of execution of good operating practice and principles is found in the effort of ARES operators on the Olympic Peninsula of Washington State who recently participated in the Washington State Emergency Department's statewide *Fifth Saturday Exercise*. The exercise presents an opportunity to assess the area, which features unique terrain over logging roads and other challenging conditions, and as a dry run for a trail marathon conducted the following week in the same area. Information concerning road conditions, hazards, and radio communications coverage at critical field waypoints was garnered and provided to government and race officials in After Action reports. Great Olympic Adventure Trail Marathon officials had provided an outline of the event, and expressed concerns about lack of cell phone coverage, and hence reliable safety and security communications.

The exercise (a wildfire scenario) was managed under the Incident Command System (ICS) and began with operators contacting the Resources net for check-in. They proceeded to a staging area where they received instructions and a safety briefing for deployment. Assignments and maps were issued to the two-person teams and Operations took control of the exercise from Resources. The teams were then dispatched to their assigned locations.

Upon reporting arrival at their locations, teams awaited net roll calls on repeater and simplex channels. When Operations found that they could not maintain contact with all of the deployed elements from the Incident Command Post, control was passed to the only station that could. The teams assessed road conditions and reported locations and signal strengths to the net. All then returned to the staging area for the hot wash and were released to the Resources net control for final check-out. Findings were reported to the marathon event coordinator and necessary changes were made to the communications plan.

For the marathon, after contacting Resources, ARES personnel deployed directly to the locations they had manned during the exercise. The Operations net received check-ins as members arrived on location. ARES members manned the start locations, the finish line and all critical points along the trail where cell phone communications were impossible because of terrain. Aside from minor glitches, radio communications ran smoothly the entire day. ARES members were readily identifiable with communications vests and radios. "Our demonstrated professionalism was not lost on event organizers, and ARES was able to practice and become familiar with our unique geography for incidents and events in the future," said a coordinator, Bruce Reiter, KD7WBM.

Analysis of a Winning Team Effort

There are many things the group did right, starting with an assessment of terrain and its related challenges to be met — in a government emergency response exercise no less — with special attention paid to communications coverage and gaps. They coordinated and planned with exercise and event officials, as well as their own leadership. An initial net took check-ins and roll call, a staging area provided the forum for instructions and safety briefing, and two-person teams (wisely providing a back-up operator) were deployed to assigned positions, checked in to another net upon arrival. Operators were already aware of the terrain and hazards, communications coverage and gaps, thanks to their participation in the previous week's exercise. The result was a professionally-run, efficient and successful communications service.

procedures/protocols, message handling and systems applies to special or public event operating and will not be repeated here, but see the sidebars on the Olympic Peninsula ARES and Virginia Beach ARES efforts for excellent examples of public event communications.

ARES Effort Supports Shamrock Marathon in Virginia Beach

By Steve Isenmann, WØJTC

The Virginia Beach Amateur Radio Emergency Service (VBARES) supports the Shamrock Marathon and Half-Marathon, with amateur volunteers placed at each mile marker along the course, at all water stops, and at the medical tent. They run supplies in vans, track the last runners on the course, provided a liaison with the local emergency operations center, and transport runners who drop out or request minor medical attention. The organizers provide a hotel room for the VBARES team to manage ARES operations and control the net. The Net Control team consists of six volunteers who spend the entire weekend at the hotel monitoring radio traffic and relaying information to the organizers.

Planning for the event starts well before the March races. Recruiting volunteers starts in September with pitches at VBARC meetings. A Standard Operating Procedure (SOP) handbook is used for training. Once the volunteers have signed up for the Marathon/Half-Marathon, individuals are assigned to specific locations on the course: 26 operators are needed for the mile markers for the full marathon and 13 for the half marathon. Others are assigned to the water stops, the EOC, as drivers and riders for two pick up vans, two supply vans, and the "Tail End Charlie" vehicle, which follows the last runner. Two operators are assigned as shadows for the race directors. Rounding out the assignments is an operator at the start and finish lines, and the operators who serve as net control stations and run the APRS assets. A total of 66 volunteer operators support the marathons.

On the Thursday before the race,

the mile markers and timing clocks are gathered from the race organizers and distributed to the hams per their assignments. A pre-race meeting is held that evening to deliver materials such as maps, safety vests and clock instructions, along with a briefing on last minute changes. Volunteers also receive green jackets with their name and call sign sewn on for identification.

On Friday morning, the vans are equipped for the race. The tail-end Charlie van and the two pick up vans are fitted with mobile dual-band radios and an APRS radio. Warning lights are attached to the vans, and water, blankets and gloves are put inside. The two supply vans are also fitted with radios. The lead vehicles have a radio and APRS unit installed on Saturday night. All vans are secured for pick up on race day. On Sunday morning, the marathon course is inspected for the proper locations of the mile markers and clocks. Operators then head to the hotel room to set up the net control function.

The net control station equipment consists of two dual-band mobile radios supplied by the local ARES group, with two antennas strapped to the upper floor balcony. Two repeaters are used: one for the north end of the course and the other for the south end. The net control station is located in the center of the course, yielding good coverage for the mobile and handheld units. The APRS receiver is set up and tested; several computers are booted up. Organizers give the hams a flash drive with runners' data to be loaded onto the net control computer.

Sunday activity starts at 5 AM with the operators and net control finalizing

details, and troubleshooting. Then, roll is called and on-course stations are checked in. The start of the Half Marathon is 7 AM with up to 10,000 runners, followed by the full marathon at 8:30 with up to 4000 runners. As the runners are on the course, net control and the on-course operators track the runners, report injuries, watch for problems, and try to resolve any issues that arise. As the day wears down, radio traffic is mainly runners' needs, supply issues at water stops, location of the vans and securing a mile marker or clock location when the last runner has passed through. The volunteer operator is free to leave once his station has been secured.

Once the last runner has crossed the finish line, net control operators secure their station, pack up and leave. Radios, lights and APRS gear are removed from the vans, stowed, and the vans are returned. Race data is collected for the hot wash and planning for next year, and the operators head home.

ARES leaders compile the collected data and file a report with the race organizers. The leaders accept emails from the volunteers with recommendations for changes for next year. Every suggestion is considered, and results in the Shamrock Marathon radio communications being conducted and coordinated very efficiently by the members of VBARES. ARES leaders spend hundreds of hours planning, talking to volunteers, and using the best in Amateur Radio practice and communication gear, to help the city of Virginia Beach successfully pull off the Shamrock Marathon and other races and runs through the entire year.

2.4.6 Get with the Program

ARRL Amateur Radio Emergency Service (ARES)

The Amateur Radio Emergency Service®, or ARES® for short, has been around for a long time, since before World War II. The mission hasn't changed that much: to provide a cadre of trained, disciplined and registered amateur operators capable of using their stations — fixed, mobile and portable as dictated by conditions — for the provision of alternative, backup communications services to a panoply of emergency/disaster,

public safety, and relief entities. Examples of "served agencies" include local, county, and state government emergency management agencies, and local Red Cross chapter facilities. (A longstanding function of ARES has been to establish networks among Red Cross shelters, and offices, during major disasters.)

It's not all about emergencies and disasters, however: ARES operators also provide communications support for public safety at events such as bicycle races and parades. These operations serve both sides of this

equation well: the public's safety, and the exercising of the operators' skills and station assets to keep them sharp for when emergencies or disasters strike, a win-win scenario.

OFFICIAL EMERGENCY STATION (OES)

After you get some ARES training and practice, you might want to refine your skills in emergency communications. If you possess a full ARRL membership, there are several opportunities available. The first is the OES appointment, which requires regular participation in ARES including drills, emergency nets and, possibly, real disaster

The Madison County (Florida) ARES members work closely with Madison County EOC personnel and have participated in the program for more than 20 years. All are trained SKYWARN spotters.

situations. An OES aims for high standards of activity, emergency preparedness and operating skills.

EMERGENCY COORDINATOR (EC)

Next, when you feel qualified enough to become a team leader of your local ARES group, consider the EC appointment, if that position is vacant in your area. An EC, usually responsible for a county or similar geographic area, is the person who can plan, organize, maintain response-readiness and coordinate for emergency communications.

Much of the work involves promoting a working relationship with local government and agencies. The busy EC can hold meetings, train members, keep records, encourage newcomers, determine equipment availability, lead others in drills or be first on the scene in an actual disaster. Some highly populated or emergency-prone areas may also need one or more Assistant Emergency Coordinators (AEC) to help the EC. The AEC is an appointment made by an EC. The AEC position can be held by a ham with any class of license.

DISTRICT EMERGENCY COORDINATOR (DEC)

If there are many ARES groups in an area, a DEC may be appointed. Usually responsible for several counties, the DEC coordinates emergency plans between local ARES groups, encourages activity on ARES nets, directs the overall communication needs of a large area or can be a backup for an EC. As a model emergency communicator, the DEC trains clubs in tactical traffic, formal traffic, disaster communications and operating skills.

SECTION EMERGENCY COORDINATOR (SEC)

Finally, there is one rare individual who can qualify as the top leader of the emergency structure in each ARRL Section — the SEC. Only the Section Manager can appoint a candidate to become the SEC. The SEC does some fairly hefty work on a section-wide level: making policies and plans and establishing goals, selecting the DECs and ECs, promoting ARES membership and keeping tabs on emergency preparedness. During an actual emergency, the SEC follows activities from behind the scenes, making sure that plans work and section communications are effective.

ARRL FIELD ORGANIZATION

The overall leader of the ARRL Field Organization in each section is the Section Manager, who is elected by the ARRL membership in that section. For further details on the Field Organization, visit these ARRL web pages for more information: **www.arrl. org/field-organization** and **www.arrl.org/ sections**.

SIGN UP!

It's easy to get started. Simply fill out the ARES registration form and submit it to your local Emergency Coordinator (EC). The form is available online at **www.arrl. org/files/file/ARESRegistrationForm9-15. pdf.** To find your local ARES officials, refer to your ARRL Section leadership (see **www. arrl.org/sections**). They will help you get your application form into the hands of your EC. As for requirements, an amateur service license is needed, and emergency power is an asset, but not a requirement.

SKYWARN

Severe weather impacts all of us in this country. In Florida, for example, citizens keep an eye on advisories from the National Hurricane Center. Hurricanes often spawn tornadoes. "Tornado alley," mostly in the Midwest and Central states, is often ground zero for these lethal storms. Other forms of severe weather and flooding are found in other portions of the country. Weather events have become more severe with climate change.

Meteorological data gathering technology has improved dramatically over the past twenty years, but no technology can match the eyes of trained weather spotters on the ground, volunteers in the SKYWARN® program sponsored by the National Weather Service (NWS). To obtain critical "ground truths," the NWS, an ARRL partner under a long-held memorandum of understanding, established SKYWARN with partner organizations. There are currently almost 300,000

SKYWARN Recognition Day at National Weather Service Taunton, Massachusetts, station WX1BOX. [Mike Corey, KI1U, photo]

trained severe weather spotters who provide timely and accurate reports of severe weather to the National Weather Service. In an average year, 10,000 severe thunderstorms, 5000 floods and more than 1000 tornadoes occur across the United States. Storm spots help NWS offices improve their public advisories, saving lives and property.

Volunteer spotters include police and fire personnel, dispatchers, EMS workers, public utility workers, and the average citizen. The staffs of hospital, school, church, nursing home, and other public facilities are encouraged to become spotters. We as radio amateurs make ideal SKYWARN spotters owing to our ability to communicate with efficiency and accuracy by Amateur Radio, especially when cell phone and other means of public communication are down in a storm. Many NWS offices have amateur stations and many NWS meteorologists and other staff have become licensed to take advantage of radio communication efficacies. Every December, the ARRL and National Weather Service sponsor SKYWARN Recognition Day®, when NWS offices and amateurs make contacts with other offices across the country in celebration of the relationship, but also exercise stations and personnel. There are 122 Weather Forecast Offices, each with a Warning Coordination Meteorologist.

Formal training is conducted in the form of classes at these local offices, which are free and typically are about two hours long. To find a class in your area, contact your local Warning Coordination Meteorologist (see **www.stormready.noaa.gov/contact.htm**).

Although radio amateurs/trained spotters take positions near their community and report wind gusts, hail size, rainfall, and cloud formations that could signal a developing tornado, another aspect of their participation is the receipt and effective distribution of National Weather Service warnings and advisories on weather nets and for county emergency management agencies, and neighborhood and community CERTs.

Much more information about storm spotting and Amateur Radio's role in SKYWARN may be found in *Storm Spotting and Amateur Radio* (2nd ed) by Mike Corey, KI1U, and Victor Morris, AH6WX, published by ARRL.

Radio Amateur Civil Emergency Service (RACES)

The Radio Amateur Civil Emergency Service (RACES) was set up in 1952 as a special sub-service of the Amateur Service conducted by volunteer licensed amateurs. It is currently designed to provide emergency communications to local or state governmental agencies during times when normal communications are down or overloaded.

While RACES was originally based on potential use during wartime, it now encompasses all types of emergencies and natural disasters. RACES is usually administered by a state-level Office of Emergency Management.

Amateurs operating in a local RACES organization must be officially enrolled (registered). RACES operation is conducted by amateurs using their own primary station licenses, and by existing RACES stations. The FCC no longer issues new RACES (WC prefix) station call signs. Operator privileges in RACES are dependent upon, and identical to, those for the class of license held in the Amateur Service. All of the authorized frequencies and emissions allocated to the Amateur Service are also available to RACES on a shared basis.

When operating in a RACES capacity, RACES stations and amateurs registered in the local RACES organization may not communicate with amateurs not operating in a similar capacity. See FCC regulations for further information.

Although RACES and ARES are separate entities, the ARRL advocates dual membership and cooperative efforts between both groups whenever possible. The RACES regulations make it simple for an ARES group whose members are all enrolled in and certified by RACES to operate in an emergency with great flexibility. Using the same operators and the same frequencies, an ARES group also enrolled as RACES can "switch hats" from ARES to RACES or RACES to ARES to meet the requirements of the situation as it develops. For example, during a "non-declared emergency," ARES can operate under ARES, but when an emergency or disaster is officially declared by a state or federal authority, the operation can become RACES with no change in personnel or frequencies.

In an area without a RACES program, it would be a simple matter for an ARES group to enroll in that capacity, after a presentation to the civil-preparedness authorities. For more information on RACES, contact your State Emergency Management.

For more information on RACES, see the comprehensive discussion in the *ARRL ARES Manual*, **www.arrl.org/ares**.

Community Emergency Response Teams (CERT)

The Community Emergency Response Team (CERT) program educates people about disaster preparedness for hazards that may impact their area and trains them in basic disaster response skills, such as fire safety, light search and rescue, team organization, and disaster medical operations. Using training learned in the classroom and during exercises, CERT members can assist others in their neighborhood or workplace following an event when professional responders are not immediately available to help. CERT members also are encouraged to support emergency response agencies by taking a more active role in emergency preparedness projects in their community.

The basic CERT course offerings include *Introduction to Community Emergency Response Teams*, IS-317, a FEMA independent study course that serves as an introduction to

Reviewing the online CERT course will give you an overview of the CERT program and the kinds of useful knowledge the CERT program has to offer. [Courtesy FEMA]

CERT for those wanting to complete training or as a refresher for current team members. Topics include an introduction to CERT, fire safety, hazardous material and terrorist incidents, disaster medical operations, and search and rescue. It takes between six and eight hours to complete the course. Those who successfully finish it will receive a certificate of completion. IS-317 can be taken by anyone interested in CERT. However, to become a CERT volunteer, one must complete the classroom training offered by a local government agency such as the emergency management agency, fire, or police department. If your home area has the program, you can contact your local emergency manager to learn about the local education and training opportunities available to you. Let this person know about your interest in taking CERT training. Amateur Radio is a natural fit for a CERT as all teams will need good, reliable radio communications for safety and functioning.

Final Notes

When operating, have fun! There is no thrill in Amateur Radio like being in the field with a radio and team of fellow amateurs performing together like a well-oiled machine. There is nothing as beautiful as a fast, efficient and effective net of experienced, expert operators trading messages, being led by an inspiring net control! Take a "time-out" to savor the moment!

2.4.7 Public Service Operating Resources

GENERAL ARRL RESOURCES

Amateur Radio Emergency Service:
www.arrl.org/ares
ARES e-mail newsletter: **www.arrl.org/ares-e-letter**
Media resources: **www.arrl.org/media-and-public-relations**
Public service: **www.arrl.org/public-service**
ARRL NTS Manual: **www.arrl.org/files/file/Public%20
Service/NTS_Manual2015.pdf**
M. Corey and V. Morris, *Storm Spotting and Amateur Radio* (2nd ed, 2016), available from Amateur Radio dealers or **www.arrl.org/shop.**

TRAINING

ARRL training courses:
www.arrl.org/emergency-communications-training
FEMA training courses: **training.fema.gov**
FEMA National Incident Management System:
www.fema.gov/national-incident-management-system
IARU Emergency Communications:
www.iaru.org/emergency-communications.html
Red Cross training: **www.redcross.org/ux/take-a-class**

MAJOR AMATEUR RADIO EMERGENCY COMMUNICATIONS NETS

Hurricane Watch Net: **www.hwn.org**
Maritime Mobile Service Net: **www.mmsn.org**
Salvation Army (SATERN) Net: **www.satern.org**
VoIP SKYWARN/Hurricane Net: **www.voipwx.net**
Waterway Net: **www.waterwayradio.net**

SERVED AGENCIES AND OTHER ORGANIZATIONS

American Red Cross: **www.redcross.org**
ARRL/Served Agency Memoranda of Understanding:
www.arrl.org/served-agencies-and-partners
Association of Public-Safety Communications Officials — International: **www.apcointl.org**
Department of Homeland Security — Citizen Corps, FEMA:
www.ready.gov/citizen-corp, www.dhs.gov, www.fema.gov
National Volunteer Organizations Active in Disaster:
www.nvoad.org
National Weather Service: **www.weather.gov**
National Communications System: **www.ncs.gov**
iNARTE (International Association for Radio, Telecommunications and Electromagnetics): **inarte.org**
Quarter Century Wireless Association: **www.qcwa.org**
Radio Emergency Associated Communication Teams:
www.reactintl.org
Salvation Army: **www.salvationarmyusa.org**
Society of Broadcast Engineers: **www.sbe.org**
SKYWARN: **www.nws.noaa.gov/skywarn/**

Contents

3.1 Awards — Measuring Operating Achievements
3.1.1 Classic Awards — the Basics
3.1.2 VHF/UHF Awards
3.1.3 Other Awards

3.2 DXing — Contacting Those Faraway Places
3.2.1 Getting Started in DXing
3.2.2 Intermediate DXing
3.2.3 DXpeditions
3.2.4 Unusual Propagation
3.2.5 Developing Good Operating Practices
3.2.6 Advanced DXing
3.2.7 VHF DXing
3.2.8 Resources for DXers

3.3 Confirming the Contact — QSLing
3.3.1 Electronic QSO Confirmation
3.3.2 Paper QSLs

3.4 Contesting — Competitive Wireless
3.4.1 Types of Contests
3.4.2 Contesting Basics
3.4.3 Contest Equipment
3.4.4 Operating Basics: Your First Contests
3.4.5 Intermediate Contest Operating
3.4.6 Contest Strategy
3.4.7 After the Contest
3.4.8 Computers and Contesting
3.4.9 Multioperator Contesting
3.4.10 Glossary
3.4.11 Resources for the Contester

On-Air Activities and Radiosport

The material in this section is edited and updated by Doug Grant, K1DG. It draws upon material by Ward Silver, NØAX, and Steve Ford, WB8IMY prepared for previous editions of the ARRL Operating Manual.

3.1 Awards — Measuring Operating Achievements

Why Awards?

Awards hunting is a significant part of Amateur Radio operating. It's a major motivating force behind many of the contacts that occur on the bands day after day. It takes skillful operating to qualify, and the reward of having a beautiful certificate or plaque on your ham shack wall commemorating your achievement is very gratifying. If you've been on the air for a while, you can probably get a good start by pulling out your shoebox of QSLs to see what gems you already have on hand, and which awards you may already qualify for.

Aside from expanding your Amateur Radio-related knowledge, chasing awards is also a fascinating way to learn about the geography, history, or political structure of another country, or perhaps even your own. It also gives you a basis for measuring your accomplishments on the air against those of other operators, and it may suggest ways to improve your station.

Award Basics

There are some basic considerations to keep in mind when applying for awards. Always read the rules carefully, so that your application complies fully. Use the standard award application if possible. Make sure your application is neat and legible, and that it indicates clearly what you are applying for. Official rules and application materials are available directly from the organization sponsoring the particular award. You can often find the needed information and forms on the web. Sufficient return postage should also be included when directing awards-related correspondence to awards managers. Many (if not most) are volunteers. Above all, be patient!

Most ARRL-sponsored awards (and a few others) do not require paper QSL cards to be submitted. The ARRL's Logbook of The World (LoTW) system provides a secure electronic way to confirm contacts quickly and without postal expense. Other electronic confirmation systems exist, such as eQSL.cc, and offer awards based on electronic confirmations. More on this later.

If QSL cards are required with your award application, send them the safest possible way and always include sufficient return postage for their return the same way. It is vital that you check your cards carefully before mailing them. Make sure each card contains your call sign and other substantiating information (band, mode, and so on). Never send cards that are altered or have information crossed out and marked over, even if such modifications are

Hams enjoy exchanging QSL cards and collecting them to count for various awards. Whether you're chasing DX countries, US states, grid locators, call sign prefixes or counties, the QSL card is the foundation upon which most awards are based. In recent years, hams have gravitated toward ARRL's electronic Logbook of The World to help bolster DXCC and WAS totals, but everyone loves to receive a colorful QSL card in the mail from a "rare one."

made by the amateur filling out the card. Altered cards, even if such alterations are made in "good faith," are not acceptable for awards. If you are unsure about a particular card, don't submit it. Secure a replacement.

Chasing awards is a robust facet of hamming that makes each and every QSO a key element in your present or future Amateur Radio success.

3.1.1 Classic Awards — the Basics

Worked All States — WAS

ARRL's most popular award is the Worked All States (WAS) Award. Thousands upon thousands of awards have been issued to hams around the world. In 2015, ARRL redesigned the certificates and the program in hopes of streamlining and improving the award. The WAS program has many options which are summarized below. Full details are available on the ARRL website.

The WAS Award is available to all amateurs worldwide who submit proof with written confirmation of contacts with each of the 50 states of the United States of America. Amateurs in the US and possessions must be members of ARRL to apply. Applicants from outside the US are exempt from this requirement.

Two-way communication with each state must be established on amateur bands. There is no minimum signal report required. Any or all bands may be used (with the exception of 60 meters). The District of Columbia may be counted for Maryland.

Contacts must be made from same location, or from locations no two of which are more than 50 miles (80 kilometers) apart. You may apply for and be granted multiple WAS awards, including WAS achieved from different, or multiple locations each of which are in different 50-mile circles (for example, from different home stations or portable locations).

Contacts may be completed over any period. Contacts must be confirmed in writing, preferably in the form of QSL cards, or via Logbook of The World (LoTW). Confirmations must show the applicant's call sign, band, mode, date and time, and indicate that the QSO was two-way.

Contacts made through repeaters or any other power relay method cannot be used for WAS credit, but a WAS award is available for Satellite contacts. All stations contacted must be "land-based stations." Contacts with ships, anchored or otherwise, and aircraft cannot be counted.

There are many types of WAS award available and they fall roughly into four categories:
• *Mixed bands and modes:* Mixed
• *Mode specific:* Phone, CW, Digital (any digital mode or combination of digital modes), RTTY, Satellite.
• *Band specific:* All contacts on 160, 80, 40, 30, 20, 17, 15, 12, 10, 6, 2, or 1.25 meters, and 70 or 23 cm.

Advanced WAS awards, including:
• *5BWAS* (for contacting all 50 states on each of the following five bands: 80, 40, 20, 15, and 10 meters); may be endorsed for other bands. This award is available as either a certificate or a plaque.
• *Triple Play WAS* (for QSOs with all 50 states on Phone, CW, and Digital modes made after 0000Z on January 1, 2009, on any band or combination of bands. Confirmations *via LoTW only*; paper QSLs are not accepted for this award.

You may apply for a WAS award in several ways. The easiest and fastest way is to use Logbook of The World. LoTW provides an easy way to track your progress toward completing WAS, and offers a convenient way to submit the application and fees online. It is also the only application method available for the Triple Play WAS award.

You may submit paper QSLs, application forms, and record sheets to an approved ARRL Special Service Club HF Awards Manager (via mail or in person, please contact the Manager for instructions). ARRL Special Service Clubs may appoint HF Awards Managers whose names are posted online at **www.arrl.org/was-card-checker-search**. Additionally, DXCC Card Checkers

WAS Award	New LoTW QSLs	LoTW QSLs in Process	WAS Credits Awarded	Total
Mixed	50	0	0	50
160M	27	0	0	27
80M	36	0	0	36
40M	45	0	0	45
30M	1	0	0	1
20M	46	0	0	46
17M	1	0	0	1
15M	49	0	0	49
12M	1	0	0	1
10M	50	0	0	50
6M	12	0	0	12
2M	6	0	0	6
CW	47	0	0	47
Phone	48	0	0	48
Digital	49	0	0	49
RTTY	49	0	0	49

Account Status

ARRL's Logbook of The World provides a convenient way to track progress toward the wide variety of WAS awards.

may, at their option, check WAS applications. DXCC Card Checkers can be found at **www.arrl.org/dxcc-card-checker-search**. Cards checked by an HF Awards Manager or DXCC Card Checker do not have to be sent to ARRL HQ. The Card Checker will send the edited and signed application form to HQ. The applicant should supply the postage and envelope to the Card Checker, at his/her instruction.

You may also send QSLs and applications to ARRL HQ for checking (except for the Triple Play WAS award). All such applications sent to HQ must include sufficient postage to provide for safe return of the QSLs via trackable shipping. Please ensure that your QSLs are sorted in the same order in which they appear on the record sheet(s) so the Card

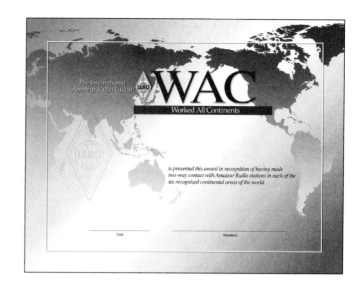

Checker will not have to struggle with your application.

It is okay to supplement a LoTW application with QSL cards. It is preferable to complete the LoTW application first, while noting in the application that the missing state confirmations will be checked from QSLs and sent separately. In such an application, the LoTW application will be used at HQ to finalize the charges and take payment.

Worked All Continents — WAC

In recognition of international two-way Amateur Radio communication, the International Amateur Radio Union (IARU) issues Worked All Continents (WAC) certificates to Amateur Radio stations around the world. WAC is issued for working and confirming two-way contacts with all six continents (North America, South America, Oceania, Asia, Europe and Africa) on a variety of bands and modes. The ARRL DXCC List includes a continent designation for each DXCC country.

To apply for WAC, US amateurs must have current ARRL membership. All other applicants must be members of their national Amateur Radio society affiliated with IARU and must apply through their Society only.

The following WAC certificates are available: Basic Certificate (mixed mode); CW Certificate; Phone Certificate; Image Certificate; Digital Certificate; Satellite Certificate.

The following WAC endorsements are available: QRP (5 W output or less); 1.8 MHz; 3.5 MHz; 50 MHz; 144 MHz; 430 MHz;

1270 MHz; any higher-band.

5 Band WAC: For the primary 5 Band WAC certificate, you must work six continents on each of these five bands: 10, 15, 20, 40, and 80 meters. Upon completion of these bands, endorsements are available for remaining amateur bands. A 6 Band WAC endorsement is available.

All contacts must be made from the same country or separate territory within the same continental area of the world. All QSL cards (no photocopies) must show the mode and/or band for any endorsement applied for.

Current rules and forms are available online at **www.iaru.org/wac/**. For amateurs in the US or countries without IARU representation, applications and QSL cards may be sent to the ARRL Awards Manager, 225 Main St, Newington, CT 06111. After verification, the cards will be returned, and the award sent

soon afterward. Sufficient return postage for the cards is required.

For amateurs in the United States, QSL cards can also be approved by an official ARRL DXCC Card Checker (see **www.arrl. org/dxcc-card-checker-search**). QSOs listed in an applicant's DXCC award account in the DXCC computer system may also be used for confirmation. In this case, on the application form applicants *must* fill in details of the QSOs they want to use for WAC confirmation in the space provided. QSO confirmations in ARRL's Logbook of The World (LoTW) system cannot be used for WAC confirmation.

Check **www.iaru.org/wac/** for the latest information about WAC and for the current fee schedule.

DX Century Club — DXCC

The ARRL DX Century Club, or DXCC award, is the premier operating award in Amateur Radio. The DXCC certificate is available to ARRL members in the US and possessions, and Puerto Rico, and all

amateurs in the rest of the world. The basic award requires confirmed contacts with stations in 100 entities on the DXCC List. Endorsements are available in specific increments beyond the 100 entity level.

The DXCC List is based on Clinton B. DeSoto's, W1CBD, landmark 1935 *QST* article, "How to Count Countries Worked, A New DX Scoring System." DeSoto's article discussed problems DXers had in determining how to count the DX, or entities, they had worked. He presented the solution that has worked successfully for succeeding generations of DXers.

In DeSoto's words, "The basic rule is simple and direct: Each discrete geographical or political entity is considered to be a country." This rule has stood the test of time — from the original list published in 1937, to the ARRL DXCC List of today. For more than 70 years, the DXCC List has been the standard for DXers around the world.

DeSoto never intended that all DXCC "countries" would be countries in the traditional sense of the word. Rather, they are the distinct geographic and political entities that DXers seek to contact. Individual achievement is measured by working and confirming the various entities comprising the DXCC List. This is the essence of the DXCC program.

Over time, criteria for the DXCC List have changed. The List remains unchanged until an entity no longer satisfies the criteria under which it was added, at which time it is moved to the "Deleted List." Thus, today's DXCC List does not fully conform with today's criteria since many entities are grandfathered under previous rules. As of mid-2016, there are 339 entities on the DXCC list, and 62 Deleted Entities.

There are several DXCC awards available and they fall roughly into four categories:
- *Mixed bands and modes:* Mixed
- *Mode specific:* Phone, CW, Digital, Satellite
- *Band specific:* All contacts on 160, 80, 40, 30, 20, 17, 15, 12, 10, 6, or 2 meters and 70 cm.

DXCC HONOR ROLL

The DXCC Honor Roll is awarded to those participants who are closing in on working all current entities. It is currently awarded for confirmed contacts with 330 or more entities, and the #1 Honor Roll plaque is available when you work them all.

5BDXCC

The 5BDXCC (Five Band DXCC) award is a formidable accomplishment. This award requires confirmed two-way contacts with 100 different DXCC entities on each of the 80, 40, 20, 15, and 10 meter bands. It encourages more uniform DX activity throughout the amateur bands, as well as the development of more versatile antenna systems and equipment. 5BDXCC is endorsable for additional bands: 160, 30, 17, 12, 6, and 2 meters. In addition to the 5BDXCC certificate, a 5BDXCC plaque is available at an extra charge.

DXCC CHALLENGE

The DXCC Challenge Award is earned by working and confirming at least 1000 DXCC band-entities on any amateur bands, 1.8 through 54 MHz (except 60 meters) and can be endorsed in increments of 500. Entities for each band are totaled to give the Challenge standing. Deleted entities do not count for this award. All contacts must be made after November 15, 1945. Contacts on bands with fewer than 100 confirmed entities are acceptable for credit for this award. Check **www. arrl.org/dxcc** for fees and more information.

QRP DXCC

In recognition of the popularity of QRP (low power) operating, the ARRL offers the QRP DX Century Club, or QRP DXCC. The award is available to amateurs who have contacted at least 100 DXCC entities using 5 W output or less. The QRP DXCC is a one-time award and is not endorsable. This award is separate and distinct from the traditional DXCC award program. Credits are not assigned to other DXCC awards.

The award is available to amateurs worldwide, and you do not have to be an ARRL member to qualify. To apply for the QRP DXCC, just send a list of your contacts including call signs, countries/entities and contact dates. Do *not* send QSLs. The list must also carry a signed statement from you that all of the contacts were made with 5 W RF output (as measured at the antenna system input) or less.

The ARRL Board of Directors voted in July 2016 to establish a Mobile DXCC award, for operators who contact 100 or more entities from their mobile stations. At press time, rules for this award are not available.

The complete DXCC rules are quite lengthy. You can download the most current rules and application forms, as well as search for the nearest DXCC Card Checker following the links from **www.arrl. org/dxcc**.

Chasing awards doesn't take a huge station. ARRL CEO Tom Gallagher, NY2RF, presents fifteen-year-old Matt Shea, AA1CT, with his DXCC and Worked All States (WAS) awards, earned in less than a year with a modest setup — 100 W with a 35-foot end-fed wire in the attic for his antenna.

Worked All Zones — WAZ

The Worked All Zones, or WAZ, award is offered by *CQ* magazine for confirmed two-way contacts with stations in all 40 *CQ* Zones of the world. (Note that these are different from ITU zones.) The originators of the WAZ award felt that the WAC award had become too easy, and there was no DXCC award at

the time. The WAZ map first appeared in *R/9* magazine (an ancestor of today's *CQ* magazine) in 1934 and was drawn more-or-less along boundaries of states or territories of the time. It was also drawn without regard to activity from certain areas. It was assumed that these areas would have more activity in the future. The WAZ map has been fine-tuned several times since then, and the latest map is available at **www.cq-amateur-radio. com/cq_awards/cq_waz_awards/cq_waz_ map.html**. You can see that some larger countries and DXCC entities, such as the

United States, Canada, Australia, and Asiatic Russia actually cover multiple zones.

The WAZ Award is offered in several categories:

• *Mixed Mode:* Contacts may be made on any mode or combination of modes.

• *Single Mode*: All contacts must be made on the same mode. Eligible modes are: AM, SSB, CW, RTTY, SSTV, Digital (any digital mode or combination of modes except RTTY), Satellite, and EME.

• *Single Band*: All contacts on the same band and mode on 80, 40, 30, 20, 17, 12, and 10 meters; contacts may be on any mode or combination of modes on 160 and 6 meters. The 160 meter award requires confirmations from 35 zones and is endorsable up to all 40, while the 6 meter award only requires confirmations from 25 zones.

• *5BWAZ (Five Band WAZ):* 5BWAZ is an extremely challenging award. It requires proof of contact with the 40 zones of the world on these five HF bands — 80, 40, 20, 15, and 10 meters (for a total of 200). The award is available for Mixed Mode only. The first plateau, where the initial certificate is issued, requires a total of 150 of the possible 200 zones on a combination of the five bands. The 5 Band WAZ Award is governed by the same rules as the regular WAZ Award and uses the same zone boundaries.

The WAZ Application Form and complete rules are available in PDF format at the *CQ* magazine website (**www.cq-amateur-radio. com**). This information is also available from either the WAZ Award Manager or *CQ* magazine in hardcopy.

3.1.2 VHF/UHF Awards

VHF/UHF Century Club — VUCC

The ARRL VHF/UHF Century Club (VUCC) is awarded for contacts on 50 MHz and above with stations located in Maidenhead 2° × 1° grid locators. Grid locators are designated by a combination of two letters and two numbers (for example, W1AW is in FN31 in central Connecticut). More information on grid locators can be found online at **www.arrl.org/grid-squares**.

The VUCC certificate and endorsements are available to amateurs worldwide. ARRL membership is required for hams in the US, possessions, and Puerto Rico. The minimum number of grid locators needed to qualify for a certificate is as follows:

• 50 MHz, 144 MHz, and Satellite: 100 credits
• 222 and 432 MHz: 50 credits
• 902 and 1296 MHz: 25 credits
• 2.3 GHz: 10 credits
• 3.4, 5.7, 10, 24, 47, 75, 119, 142, 241 GHz, and Laser (300 GHz): 5 credits.

Endorsements are available for additional contacts at these levels:
- 50 MHz, 144 MHz, and Satellite: 25 credits
- 222 MHz and 432 MHz: 10 credits
- 902 MHz and above: 5 credits

Contacts must be dated January 1, 1983, and later to count. Separate bands count for separate awards. Repeater and/or crossband contacts are not permitted except for Satellite awards. Contacts with aeronautical mobile stations do not count, but maritime mobiles are okay. For VUCC awards on 50 through 1296 MHz and Satellite, all contacts must be made from locations no more than 200 km apart. For SHF awards, contacts must be made from a single location, defined as within a 300 meter diameter circle.

You can download the most current rules and forms, as well as search for the nearest ARRL VHF Awards Manager, by following the links from **www.arrl.org/vucc**.

You can use the ARRL Logbook of The World (LoTW) system to confirm QSOs for the VUCC award or you may submit paper confirmations (QSLs) and application forms to an approved VHF Awards Manager (Card Checker) for certification. If a VHF Awards Manager is not available, cards may be checked by an ARRL DXCC Card Checker (see **www.arrl.org/dxcc-card-checker-search**). Foreign VUCC applications should be checked by the Awards Manager for the IARU Member Society in their respective country. Do not send cards to ARRL HQ, unless asked to do so.

Fred Fish Memorial Award — FFMA

The Fred Fish Memorial Award was created in April 2008 in honor of the late Fred Fish, W5FF, who was the first amateur to work and confirm all 488 Maidenhead grid squares in the 48 contiguous United States on 6 meters. The award is given to any amateur who can duplicate W5FF's impressive accomplishment. The FFMA also encourages operation on the VHF bands from rare grid squares (known as Grid DXpeditions) to help activate all 488 grids. Many of these grids have no resident amateurs (or none active on 6 meters) or present significant logistical challenges to Grid DXpeditioners. The inconsistent and unpredictable nature of 6 meter propagation makes this award especially challenging. As of mid-2016, only seven FFMA awards had been issued.

The rules of FFMA closely follow the VUCC rules. Complete rules, application forms and resources such as a list of all required grid squares and a survey of rare grids may be found at **www.arrl.org/ffma**.

3.1.3 Other Awards

The awards listed so far in this chapter require a reasonable amount of effort and represent significant achievement. After "checking the box" for most of these awards, you may want to move on to some that reward different accomplishments. Some of these are even more challenging and may take years to accomplish.

Working Prefixes: WPX

The *CQ* WPX Award is for working different Amateur Radio prefixes around the world (NN1, DL7, JA6, 9J2, and so on). For portable stations, the portable designator becomes the prefix. For example, WN5N/7 counts as WN7, while J6/WN5N counts as J6. New prefixes are allocated occasionally, so this award is essentially open-ended. The leaders have well over 3000 prefixes confirmed!

Certificates are issued for contacts on HF (160 – 10 meters) and 6 meters. Awards start at 400 prefixes for Mixed Mode and 300 prefixes for single-mode awards — CW, SSB and Digital. Cross-mode contacts are not eligible for single-mode awards. Endorsements are issued in increments of 50 prefixes. Band endorsements are available for 1.8 MHz (50 prefixes), 3.5 and 5 MHz (175 prefixes), 7 and 10 MHz (250 prefixes) and 14 – 50 MHz (300 prefixes). Continent endorsements are available as well — North America (160 prefixes), South America (95 prefixes), Europe (160 prefixes), Africa (90 prefixes), Asia (75 prefixes), and Oceania (60 prefixes).

High-achieving stations are eligible for inclusion in the WPX Honor Roll (600 prefixes minimum, available for Mixed, CW, SSB, and Digital modes) and the WPX Award of Excellence (requires all of the following: 1000 prefixes Mixed, 600 SSB, 600 CW, all six continental endorsements, and individual band endorsements for 80, 40, 20, 15, and 10 meters). As of mid-2016, only about 300 amateurs have received the WPX Award of Excellence.

CQ WPX Awards are supported by ARRL's Logbook of The World. LoTW users may track prefix confirmations and request credits toward *CQ* WPX awards. See **www.arrl.org/cq-awards** for details. eQSL.cc users may apply using the CQ Award section on eQSL.cc.

Paper applications (*CQ* Form 1051) and appropriate fees may also be sent to *CQ* WPX Award Manager Steve Bolia, N8BJQ, PO Box 355, New Carlisle, OH 45344. Complete rules, forms and other resources are available at **www.cq-amateur-radio.com** and **sites.google.com/site/cqwpxawards/**

County Hunting: USA-CA Program

The United States of America Counties Award (USA-CA), also sponsored by *CQ*, is issued for confirmed two-way radio contacts with specified numbers of US counties. Full rules, forms, and current fees are available from **www.cq-amateur-radio.com**. With a

Account Status					
WPX Award	New LoTW QSLs	LoTW QSLs in Process	WPX Credits Awarded	Total
WPX Mixed	2060	0	0	2060
WPX Mixed 160M	475	0	0	475
WPX Mixed 80M	773	0	0	773
WPX Mixed 40M	1140	0	0	1140
WPX Mixed 30M	428	0	0	428
WPX Mixed 20M	1420	0	0	1420
WPX Mixed 17M	544	0	0	544
WPX Mixed 15M	1312	0	0	1312
WPX Mixed 12M	577	0	0	577
WPX Mixed 10M	1227	0	0	1227
WPX Mixed 6M	285	0	0	285
WPX Mixed North America	822	0	0	822
WPX Mixed South America	134	0	0	134
WPX Mixed Europe	834	0	0	834
WPX Mixed Africa	83	0	0	83
WPX Mixed Asia	136	0	0	136
WPX Mixed Oceania	63	0	0	63
WPX CW	1667	0	0	1667
WPX CW 160M	435	0	0	435
WPX CW 80M	595	0	0	595
WPX CW 30M	351	0	0	351
WPX CW 40M	891	0	0	891

There are a lot of prefixes to work and apply toward a huge variety of WPX awards offered by *CQ* magazine. ARRL's Logbook of The World confirmations may be used to apply for any of the WPX awards.

Table 3.1
Counties and States Needed for USA-CA Award Levels

Class	Counties Required	States Required
USA-500	500	Any
USA-1000	1000	25
USA-1500	1500	45
USA-2000	2000	50
USA-2500	2500	50
USA-3000	3000	50
USA 3077	ALL	50

total of 3077 counties in the US, this award can take many years to accomplish.

The USA-CA is issued in seven different classes. Higher levels are awarded as endorsement seals on the basic certificate. Also, special endorsements will be made for all one band or mode operations subject to the rules. **Table 3.1** shows the counties and states required.

USA-CA is available to all licensed amateurs anywhere in the world. You can accumulate contacts toward the USA-CA Award with any call sign you have held, and from any operating locations or dates. All contacts must be confirmed by QSL, and such QSLs must be in your possession for examination by USA-CA officials. QSL cards must not be altered in any way. QSOs via repeaters, satellites, moonbounce and phone patches are not valid for USA-CA. So-called "team" contacts, where one person acknowledges a signal report and another returns a signal report, while both amateur call signs are logged, are not valid for USA-CA. Acceptable contact can be made with only one station at a time.

Unless otherwise indicated on QSL cards, the QTH printed on cards will determine county identity. For mobile and portable operations, the postmark shall identify the county unless other information is stated on QSL card to positively identify the county of operation In the case of cities, parks or reservations not within counties proper, applicants may claim any one of adjoining counties for credit (once).

The USA-CA program is administered by a *CQ* staff member acting as USA-CA Custodian, currently Ted Melinosky, K1BV, and all applications and related correspondence should be sent directly to the custodian. Decisions of the Custodian in administering these rules and their interpretation, including future amendments, are final.

The scope of USA-CA makes it mandatory that special Record Books be used for application. For this purpose, *CQ* provides a 64-page 4.25 × 11-inch Record Book that contains application and certification forms and provides record-log space meeting the conditions of any class award and/or endorsement requested.

A completed USA-CA Record Book constitutes the medium of the basic award application and becomes the property of *CQ* for record purposes. On subsequent applications for either higher classes or for special endorsements, the applicant may use additional Record Books to list required data or may make up an alphabetical list conforming to requirements. It is recommended that two be obtained, one for application use and one for personal file copy. See the USA-CA section of the *CQ* website for cost and ordering information.

County hunter activity may be found daily on these frequencies: 14.336 MHz SSB, and 14.056.5, 7.056.5, and 10.122.5 MHz CW.

Islands On The Air — IOTA

The IOTA Program was created by Geoff Watts, a leading British shortwave listener, in 1964. It was taken over by the Radio Society of Great Britain (RSGB) in 1985, and in 2016 management of the IOTA Program moved to

One of the rarer IOTA-listed islands is Rockall (EU-189). It is an uninhabited granite rock that extends about 60 feet above the sea, located about 270 miles northwest of Great Britain. Landing on Rockall in the always-rough seas and scaling its sheer vertical walls to make QSOs available for IOTA chasers is a challenge!

The Summits On The Air (SOTA) "Mountain Goat" award is earned by Activators who collect 1000 points. Not a mountain climber? No problem — you can go for the "Shack Sloth" award by collecting 1000 points as a Chaser.

a newly-created organization called Islands on the Air (IOTA) Ltd. The IOTA program's popularity grows each year and it is highly regarded among amateurs worldwide. The information given here is just a summary of the program. Full information, rules and forms may be found at www.rsgbiota.org.

Part of the fun of IOTA is that it is an evolving program with many new islands and island groups being activated for the first time. The IOTA program recognizes 1200 islands and island groups. All of the ocean islands of the world are included, with some islands grouped together for convenience. As of mid-2016, nobody has contacted all 1200, with the leaders slightly over 1100.

The basic award is for working stations located on 100 islands/groups. There are higher achievement awards for working 200, 300, 400, 500, 600, 700, 800, 900, and 1000 islands/groups. In addition there are seven continental awards (including Antarctica) and three regional awards — Arctic Islands, British Isles, and West Indies—for contacting a specified number of islands/groups listed in each area. The IOTA World Diploma is available for working 50% of the numbered groups in each of the seven continents. A Plaque of Excellence is available for confirmed contacts with at least 750 islands/groups. Shields are available for every 25 additional islands/groups. The IOTA 1000 Islands Trophy is available for contacting 1000 IOTA groups. Mini plates are available for additional IOTA groups in increments of 25.

Applicants must register and create an account on the IOTA website at www.rsgbiota.org. Electronic applications are strongly encouraged and award credits may be tracked

online. The rules currently require that QSL cards be submitted to nominated IOTA checkpoints for checking. These checkpoints are listed on the IOTA website and in the *RSGB IOTA Directory and Yearbook*. For those who prefer paperless confirmations, IOTA credits are now available for contacts matching in Club Log. See www.rsgbiota.org for more details.

The official source of IOTA information is the *RSGB IOTA Directory*. This publication lists thousands of islands, grouped by continent and indexed by prefix, details the award rules, and provides application forms and a wealth of information and advice for the island enthusiast. The colorful new IOTA certificates are also shown. The latest *RSGB IOTA Directory* is an essential purchase for those interested in island-chasing. Copies are available from the ARRL at www.arrl.org/shop or the RSGB at www.rsgbshop.org.

A similar award program exists for working US inland islands in rivers and lakes. See www.usislands.org for more information.

Summits On The Air — SOTA

The Summits on the Air (SOTA) program began in 2002 and has quickly become very popular. The purpose of the SOTA program is to encourage Amateur Radio activity from the summits of hills and mountains in countries around the world, including major mountains, and to provide an award system for radio amateurs in all DXCC entities (see www.sota.org.uk/). The program provides for participation by Activators who make QSOs from the summits, Chasers who make contact with the Activators, and short wave listeners.

Associations in each DXCC entity (or subdivisions of larger entities) are responsible for identifying qualifying summits and assigning reference numbers. Each mountain region in the association is assigned a unique two-character identifier. Individual summits within the region are assigned a number in the range 001 to 999.

Within an association, this creates a unique reference number, for example LD-003. Leading zeros are applied as shown where the number is less than 100. The reference number is used throughout the program to identify the summit.

SOTA reference numbers are created by prefixing the reference number with the Association identifier. This is either

• The ITU allocated prefix, in the event that subdivision has not occurred, such as G/LD-003

• The ITU allocated prefix plus the subdivision identifier, where Subdivision has occurred, for example W2/WE-003.

In general, summits are peaks or "prominences" of at least 150 meters. There are exceptions made for regions where there are no such peaks, in which case a 100 meter minimum is used. Each Association assigns a point value to each summit, from 1 to 10 points, depending on height. Some regions have only a few summits (W5 – Mississippi and 9V– Singapore each have only one), while others have many more (the two associations in Alaska each have more than 6000).

Awards include trophies for both "Shack Sloths" (Chasers with 1000 points or more) and "Mountain Goats" (Activators with 1000 points or more). As of mid-2016, the top Chasers in the SOTA program had contacted

Most QSL cards from Japanese hams include the JCC number.

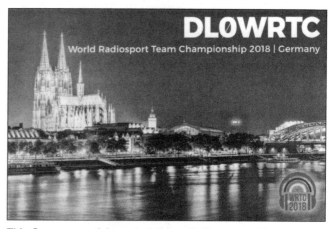

This German special event station with its unusual four-letter suffix celebrates the 2018 World Radiosport Team Championship (WRTC).

well over 25,000 Activators and amassed well over 100,000 points. The top Activators have operated from nearly 2000 summits.

You can find more information on the SOTA program at **www.sota.org.uk** . The program's database is extensively documented and awards tracked online at **www. sotadata.org.uk**.

Japan Century Cities — JCC

The Japan Century Cities (JCC) award is a popular award offered by the Japan Amateur Radio League (JARL). To earn this award, you must confirm QSOs with at least 100 of the 813 designated cities in Japan. Additional certificates are awarded for 200, 300, 400,

500, 600, 700 and 800 cities with endorsement stickers available for every additional 50. Each designated city is numbered, with the first two digits denoting the prefecture (47 total) except for the Tokyo area (prefecture 10), where the 23 individual Tokyo wards are numbered 100101 through 100123. Full details on the JCC award are available at **www.jarl.org/English/4_Library/A-4-2_ Awards/Award_Main.htm**.

Special Event Stations

Nearly every week, a group will organize a "special event station" to commemorate or celebrate an event of some kind. Most of these stations offer awards to stations that contact them. It can be great fun to collect them, and use them as a tool to learn something about the event being celebrated. Special event stations are promoted in the Amateur Radio magazines and newsletters and online, and very often are identifiable by their distinctive call signs.

In the US, the "1×1" series of call signs (for example, K1A, W6Z, N5Z) are reserved for short-term use by special event stations. When you hear a station using one of these call signs, it's a good idea to work it, since it could be a special event at a county fair or possibly a DXpedition to a rare US possession that counts for a DXCC entity.

Information on Other Awards

One of the handiest references for the awards chaser is *The K1BV DX Awards Directory* website at **www.dxawards.com**, maintained by Ted Melinosky, K1BV. This online directory contains information for thousands of long-term and short-term awards from 110 DXCC countries. The website also features sections with hints and suggestions for both the beginning and advanced collector of awards. The website is updated regularly.

3.2 DXing — Contacting Those Far Away Places

What is DX? An abbreviation for "distant station" or "signal from a distant station," DX is at the core of Amateur Radio. The excitement of contacting ever more distant stations has attracted amateurs of all types from the very earliest days of radio. The goal of spanning larger and larger distances has driven many technological advances. Whether DX means to you, as it does to HF DXers, a contact somewhere outside your own country, or to VHF DXers, a faraway grid square or hilltop, all of us get a thrill out of pushing the limits of our own skill and equipment. That's what "DXing" really means—extending your radio range and abilities.

Most amateurs don't begin their ham radio activity as DXers. We start by making local contacts with friends and club members and gradually become aware of radio's broader possibilities. Even experienced hams have discovered DXing after years of local

Martti Laine, OH2BH, is one of the world's top DXers and DXpeditioners. He describes himself as a globetrotter and restless soul at home wherever he hangs his hat. In his lengthy career, he has operated with more than 150 call signs in such exotic DX entities as Scarborough Reef, Pratas Island, Palestine, Temotu, Market Reef, Western Sahara, North Korea, Myanmar and Albania. He has often been involved in the first activity from a newly-created or opened DXCC entity. Here he is shown operating the CQWW DX Contest as ZA1WW in Albania. [Martti Laine, OH2BH photo]

and regional contacts. The spark may be a visit to a DXer's station or seeing a presentation on DX, but is most likely to be an unexpected contact over a long distance. Perhaps a DX station answers your CQ one evening or you encounter an unexpected call sign while tuning the band. Even bringing up your favorite repeater while far from home on a hike or drive is DXing! This is the "magic of radio" writ large and it has been known to take hold of one's ham radio interests with a lifetime's tenacity.

DXing is even more fun if you become skilled at it! That's the purpose of this section — to introduce beginners to DXing and help those with some experience at the DX game get better at it. We'll cover DXing for the beginner and then move on to more advanced techniques, followed by a section on DX activities. Propagation, so important to DXers, is covered on a band-by-band basis. See you in the pileups!

3.2.1 Getting Started in DXing

If you've made a few DX contacts (or would like to) and are interested in making DX a part of your regular ham radio diet, you've come to the right place! In many ways, this is the most exciting part of your DX career. Every time you turn on the radio, you'll experience something new and every contact is as exciting as it can possibly be!

As a beginning DXer, you will have the exalted title of "Little Pistol." Even if you have a lot of fancy equipment, you'll still be learning the ropes and getting used to the techniques and procedures of DXing. This section assumes that if you will be engaging in HF DXing, you have a General, Advanced, or Amateur Extra license. While it is possible to engage in DXing as a Technician licensee, the limited bands available make it challenging. However, in years of high solar activity, the 10 meter band offers excellent opportunities for chasing DX.

Basic DXing Equipment

Some amateurs seem to think that giant rotary beam antennas, state-of-the-art radios, and amplifiers are required to have fun in DXing. Relax! You don't have to take out a second mortgage to get into the world of DXing! In fact, you may have most of the gear

already. You may be surprised to learn that most of the DX stations you encounter on HF will be using equipment very similar to yours.

HF TRANSCEIVER

Almost any modern 100 W HF transceiver (160 – 10 meters) less than 20 years old will give perfectly adequate performance. If your radio doesn't use DSP (digital signal processing) for IF filters, the receiver should be equipped with both SSB (2.0 or 2.4 kHz) and CW receive (400 or 500 Hz) crystal or mechanical filters. You should invest in a comfortable set of communications quality (200 to 4000 Hz is sufficient) headphones—you'll be wearing them a lot — and a high-quality microphone. Headphones with an attached boom mike (called a *boom set*) are a good choice. The radio should support computer control. Radios with a second receiver are quite useful for DXing. The transceiver will likely have two VFOs (usually shown as VFO A and VFO B) that you should learn to access and select. If you are just learning CW, learn to use a *paddle* with your rig's internal keyer or use an external electronic keyer.

HF ANTENNAS

For the "high bands" above 10 MHz,

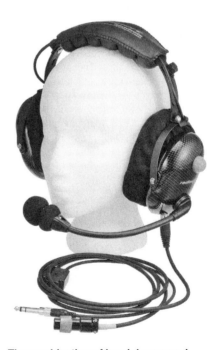

The combination of headphones and lightweight microphone makes extended hours of operating a breeze. Choosing a microphone element designed for maximum intelligibility and proper positioning of the boom really makes a difference on the other end of the QSO.

Learn to use a paddle and keyer to raise your code speed while reducing the effort required to send CW. The K1EL WK-USB keyer can also connect to your computer via USB, so your logging program can do the sending for you. [Steve Elliott, K1EL, photo]

Phil, K3UA, uses this simple station with modest antennas to work a lot of DX. He has accomplished DXCC Honor Roll and well over 300 DXCC entities on CW, SSB, and digital modes and all HF bands from 80 through 10 meters (289 so far on 160). [Phil Koch, K3UA, photo]

dipoles at least 20 feet off the ground will get you started. A multiband vertical (with plenty of radials for ¼-wavelength ground-plane antennas) will also work. On the low bands below 10 MHz, a vertical wire antenna (such as an inverted L), dipoles at heights of 40 to 50 feet or more, or multiband verticals will do the job. A copy of the *ARRL Antenna Book* with its many antenna designs and information on antenna systems is a valuable addition to your station reference materials. ARRL's *Simple and Fun Antennas for Hams* offers a variety of real world, practical antennas. For a wide selection of antenna projects, the series of antenna *Classics* books published by the ARRL has proven designs for wire antennas, verticals and beams. (All of the ARRL publications are available online from the ARRL Store — **www.arrl.org/shop**.)

Dipoles generally work best with both ends at about the same height although an inverted V configuration (a dipole with ends lower than the middle) is acceptable. They may also be mounted in a sloping position, with one end much higher than the other. This is often done for DXing on 40, 60, 80, and 160 meters. Many variations on the dipole and other similar wire antennas may be found in the ARRL book *ON4UN's Low-Band DXing* by John Devoldere, ON4UN.

If a ground-mounted vertical is used, install at least 16 radials and more if possible. If the vertical is elevated, such as on a roof or mast, it is best to provide at least four radials for each desired band. Excellent references for installation of radial systems for verticals may be found in the *ARRL Antenna Book* and *Vertical Antenna Classics* (available from the ARRL).

Use low-loss coax, such as RG-8 or RG-213 and trim the antennas to resonance near the bottom end of the General frequency allocations. If impedance matching (an antenna tuner, for example) is required, invest in good quality equipment.

It is also important to make sure that your station is capable of hearing well. The electronic entertainment devices pervading residential areas often create significant electronic noise which can cover up weak signals from DX stations. If you turn on your HF rig and hear mostly noise dominating the bands, you may have to re-orient or relocate your antenna.

REMOTE DXING

You may discover that your own QTH is unsuitable for DXing. Maybe you live in an apartment or an area where you cannot install an effective antenna. Maybe the local noise level prevents you from hearing any but the strongest signals. Don't let that stop you!

You may be able to operate remotely using the computer in your shack connected via Internet to a station located somewhere else. This remote station can be your own at another location, or a friend's station. There are also commercial businesses with multiple remote stations available for a fee. One such business is Remote Ham Radio (**www. remotehamradio.com**), which operates a network of well-equipped stations in locations around the United States and in several other countries.

You can count DX you work through a properly-licensed remote station for your DXCC awards as long as the remote station is located in the same country as your DXCC account. It is *never* okay to remotely use a station outside of your "home DXCC entity" to add to the home-entity DXCC totals — just as it is *never* okay for you to ask someone else at another station in another place to make QSOs for you. You can control the remote station from anywhere, but of course you must have a license that allows you to operate the remote station, wherever it is located. If the remote station is located in a different country than the control operator, make sure the local regulations permit cross-border operation.

COMPUTERS AND SOFTWARE

You'll find a lot of resources on the Internet, so you should be able to make use of your computer at the same time you're on the air. Most ham programs are not "resource hogs" so you won't need a top-of-the-line computer. The computer should have at least one USB or serial port available to connect to your radio's control port. If you plan to use the digital modes for DXing, you will want an interface between the computer's audio input and output ports and the audio inputs and outputs of the radio as discussed in the HF Digital Modes section earlier in this book. The majority of ham programs are *Windows*-based, but there is software available for *Linux* and Macintosh users too.

According to the Club Log database, the three most popular programs among both new and experienced DXers are *Logger32* (**www. logger32.net**), *DX Keeper* (**www.dxlabsuite. com/dxkeeper**), and *Ham Radio Deluxe* (**ham-radio-deluxe.com**). Try one of these or another program and choose whichever has the features and user interface you like best.

Most logging programs include features such as QSL label printing, award status tracking, interfaces to spotting networks, gray-line maps, and the ability to export log data as ADIF formatted files for electronic QSLing. Many also provide support for generating and decoding many digital modes using the PC's sound resources. It is not recommended that you write your own

ADIF Log File Format

Ever since software has become a part of Amateur Radio, there have been as many data formats as there have been ham radio software programmers. Hams have struggled with converting data among various formats. In early 1996, KK7A promoted the idea of a standard for exchange of ham data, and an internet reflector was set up for discussing such a standard. Ray, WF1B, and Dennis, WN4AZY, publishers of commercial ham radio software, took the best suggestions from this discussion and proposed the Amateur Data Interface Format (ADIF), which Ray introduced as ADIF 1.0 at the 1996 Dayton Hamvention. Within a year, this standard was adopted by most software publishers.

Starting in 2002, ADIF 2.0.0 initiated a period of upward-compatible expansion. During 2010, the need to support international characters led to a proposal to define a second file format (syntax) known as ADX that would introduce international data types. The complete ADIF specification can be found at **www.adif.org**.

An ADI file can contain all the details of a QSO, from the basic information required for most award applications (date, time, frequency, mode, call sign worked, and signal report) to extensive additional data such as name, address (which can be imported from a database), specific location details, propagation mode, contest, and much more.

Virtually all Amateur Radio logging programs can import and export ADI files, and most award programs that accept electronic submission require ADI files. The ARRL Logbook of The World accepts ADI files and can export a user's data in ADI format.

Creators of homebrew logging software should strongly consider complying with ADIF. Electronic logs in other formats may be converted to ADI using the *ADIF Master* program downloadable at **www.dxshell.com/adif-master.html**

ADI File Structure

An ADI file begins with an optional Header followed by one or more Records:

Header   (the end of the header section is designated by <eoh>)
Record   (the end of each record is designated by <eor>)
Record
...
Record
Here is a sample ADI file:
Generated on 2011-11-22 at 02:15:23Z for WN4AZY

<adif_ver:5>3.0.4
<programid:7>monolog
<EOH>

<qso_date:8>19900620
<time_on:4>1523
<call:5>VK9NS
<band:3>20M
<mode:4>RTTY
<sweatersize:1>M
<shoesize:2>11
<app_monolog_compression:3>off
<eor>

<qso_date:8>20101022

[Introduction and sample file excerpted from **www.adif.org**]

---

software or use a spreadsheet or word processor for logging since your log won't be compatible with other common programs. Besides, you should be spending your time on the air working stations, not writing and debugging software!

Basic DX Operating

As you begin to take DXing seriously, the most important thing is not to learn how to transmit but how to listen! Listen, listen, listen! Even in this age of computer networks and instantaneous worldwide connections, there is no substitute for being able to tune the band, understanding what you hear. As you become more experienced you'll learn what the bands sound like when they're open. You'll get to know the characteristic sound of a signal that originated far away, what a pileup sounds like, how to hear the DX station under all that interference, and so forth. If you jump right in and start transmitting you'll never get a chance to learn. The oldest DX saying in the book is, "You can't work 'em if you can't hear 'em!" The moral of that story is that if you want to make your transmissions count, learn how to receive.

Another important aspect of learning any activity is to have reasonable expectations.

After all, if you begin an exercise program you don't expect to start winning races right away, do you? It's important to expect you'll have successes — savor them! Expecting too much — such as working 200 different countries in a month or working more DX than the local Big Gun — is a sure recipe for disappointment. What DX you can expect to work depends a great deal on where you live and solar conditions but if you keep your expectations modest you'll find DXing will continue to be enjoyable day after day.

In line with reasonable expectations, it's also unreasonable to start DXing with too little power. A 100 W transceiver will generate a solid, mid-level signal capable of working many DX stations. QRP (5 W output or less on CW) places a premium on the operator skills that you are trying to acquire, so avoid the frustrations of QRP for the time being. Once you are more skilled, turn the power down and enjoy the pleasant challenges of QRP operating.

CHOOSING YOUR MODE FOR DXING

It is easy to start on SSB, right? Just plug in a microphone and talk. However, SSB is probably the least effective mode to use for DXing! If conditions are good, and signals are strong, SSB is a reasonable choice. However, the power of a phone signal is spread out over a wide bandwidth and the receiving filters are wider, allowing more interference from stations on adjacent frequencies. If you are new to HF operating, you will also find that it takes some practice to tune in SSB signals correctly, especially for DX stations who may speak with accented English. The HF bands (except for 60 meters) do not use fixed channels, so the tuning is continuous. While you may be able to understand a signal that is tuned a little off frequency, your signal may not be very intelligible to the other operator. If the voice sounds either muffled or high-pitched (like the Donald Duck cartoon character), then you don't have it tuned in quite correctly!

Sometimes, a DX station with many callers will operate "split." This means that he is listening and transmitting on different frequencies. Split-frequency operation makes it possible for callers to hear who the DX station is answering, and allows the DX station to spread out the callers over a range of frequencies. In order to work a DX station that is operating split, you need to know how to set your transceiver for split operation, and make sure you are set to transmit where the DX station is listening. It is common to hear beginners accidentally transmit on the wrong VFO, causing interference to the DX station.

What about CW? This is also a great time to start learning CW if you don't already use it. As a Little Pistol, you'll want to maximize the effectiveness of your station and CW allows

Alain, FR1GV, enjoys DXing using digital modes from his QTH on exotic Reunion Island.

you to do just that. Veteran DXers will confirm that it is a lot easier to make a contact on CW than on phone, regardless of power level. CW signals pack their power into a narrow bandwidth instead of spreading it out over a couple of kilohertz. This allows you to "get through" when conditions aren't good or noise levels are high, as they often are on the lower bands. While CW decoder programs are available, you should learn to copy CW by ear. Start now and you'll be knee-deep in the CW pileups before you know it!

Since most computers have audio input and output capabilities, a lot of software has been developed to allow the computer to generate and demodulate a wide range of digital signals that can be used for DXing. There are literally hundreds of different modes now in use, from legacy RTTY (Radio TeleTYpe) with simple two-level FSK modulation, to more modern modes such as PSK31, to advanced systems such as JT65 with 65-level FSK, error correction coding, and many more features built in. These systems use digital signal processing techniques and coding to enable successful DX contacts with low power and modest antennas. You can even complete a two-way contact with a station whose signal cannot be copied by ear. Digital modes are worth considering for the new DXer.

DX Propagation Characteristics of HF Bands

Now that you have chosen a mode to operate, it's time to figure out what band(s) to use. We have nine HF bands available, and while it is possible to work DX on all of them, some are easier than others.

10 METERS

If you're new to the HF bands, you may be wondering why there is such a fuss about 10 meters. As this book is being written (2016), we are on the downward slope of the 11-year solar activity cycle. This means that DX openings on the 10 meter band will become rarer, and you may hear no DX signals on the band for days or weeks at a time. In periods of high solar activity, 10 is a fantastic band for DXing, with long openings to many regions of the world and excellent signals.

During low solar activity periods, 10 meters occasionally opens with *sporadic E* as RF-reflecting E layer clouds form rather quickly and often break up just as fast. Openings can be from 1500 to 3000 miles, depending upon whether there are clouds in place to permit one or two hops. Sporadic E occurs most often during the summer, and sometimes in mid-winter. Openings can be as short as a few minutes or last as long as 24 hours.

During periods of high sunspots, the preferred propagation mode is via the F layer of the ionosphere. This produces the best long distance propagation of all.

North-south transequatorial propagation is available at almost any time in the sunspot cycle. From North America, it is possible to work Africa, New Zealand, Australia or South America this way. With its unique characteristics, 10 meters gets attention from amateurs of all interests. When 10 meters is open, DX stations will tend to operate here to take advantage of the opening because it is easy to find a clear frequency since it is our widest HF band.

12 METERS

As you might expect, 12 meters closely resembles 10 meters. It is lower in frequency so it is open more often than 10 but slightly less than 15 meters. If 15 is open, it is worthwhile to try 12. And if the 10 or 15 meter band is occupied by contest activity and you're not interested, 12 meters provides a safe haven since no contests are held on that band.

15 METERS

The 15 meter band has many of the characteristics of 20 meters at times, in addition to some of the characteristics of 10 meters. It often provides very long distance openings, and is a good choice for working Africa and the Pacific in the afternoon during times of moderate to good solar activity. At times of low sunspots it may not open at all on east-west paths but is usually open to the south.

Typically, 15 opens after sunrise — if it is going to open. At the bottom of the sunspot cycle, openings are likely to be of very short duration. During solar cycle peaks, openings are likely to last from sunrise to long after sunset. Propagation moves noticeably from east to west, with absorption around local noon often making signal levels drop for a while, only to return later in the afternoon.

At times of high solar activity, 15 meters will provide openings to Asia as late as local midnight. However, at times of low solar activity, the band isn't likely to open to Asia at all unless the DXer happens to live on the West Coast. When it is open, no band provides more access to exotic DX than 15 meters. Many beginning DXers use a 40 meter dipole successfully on 15 meters.

17 METERS

Sandwiched between 15 and 20, 17 meters has many of the characteristics of 15 meters. It's lower in frequency, so it's open more often and for longer periods, especially during times of low sunspots. Again, look for morning openings from the east and evening openings to the west. Tuning down the bands, you will begin to notice more atmospheric noise as you move from 15 to 17 meters. Like 12 meters, this band is a "contest-free zone."

20 METERS

The undisputed king of the DX bands is 20 meters which supports long distance propagation at any time of the sunspot cycle. During low sunspot periods, it's likely to be the *only* band open for DX during the daytime. At sunspot maximums, 20 will be open to somewhere almost 24 hours each day.

During the winter, 20 will open to the east at sunrise. The opening will last until stations at the eastern end of the path are past sunset. In the early afternoon, the opening will extend to the south and to the southwest. Early evening should find the band opening to the west to northwest.

In the spring and fall, long-path propagation exists with openings to the east coming from a southwesterly to westerly path just after sunrise and lasting for several hours. In the evening, long-path opens to the southeast. It is not unusual to find long-path openings to areas of the world that are actually stronger than the short-path opening.

Summertime often finds openings to the Far East in the mornings while European openings continue through the early evening and on into the night. There is always a southern path extending well into the night after other paths have closed. The band may seem to close, then open up again later, around midnight on certain paths.

This single band is so productive that more than a few serious DXers restrict their antenna choice to one large monoband 20 meter antenna. All DX operates on 20 meters at some

You'll want to be sure you are available and your station is in perfect condition when the rare DXCC entities such as Bouvet, North Korea, Howland Island, or Pratas Island come on the air. It may be many, many years before the next operation.

point; it's impossible to be a truly effective DXer without it.

30 METERS

If ever there was a DX band that provided 24-hour DXing at any stage of the sunspot cycle, 30 meters would be it. It shares many of the characteristics of 20 and 40 meters with long nighttime openings while providing DX throughout most of the daytime as well. Propagation is hard to describe as 30 meters can almost be open to anywhere at any time as the seasons change. US stations are limited to 200 W output, and most stations are using modest antennas so it can be easier to break through pileups on rare DX stations than other bands where you may be competing against stations running 1500 W and larger antennas. In addition, SSB is not allowed on the small (50 kHz wide) band, so the more-efficient CW and digital modes are used. There are no contests on this band.

40 METERS

If 20 meters is the king of DX bands, then 40 meters surely must be the queen. While affected by many of the same conditions as 80, absorption by the D layer in the daytime

is reduced because of the shorter wavelength, and it is possible to work intercontinental DX any time from late afternoon to a few hours after local sunrise. In fact, at the sunspot minimum it's possible to hear DX all day long and some of it may be worked if your signals are not too severely absorbed. In the late afternoon during the winter months, the band is likely to provide good long-path openings to the southeast along the gray line.

DXing on 40 meter phone historically was very difficult because of interference from shortwave broadcast stations located in Europe and Asia. These megawatt transmitters made sharing the band difficult, if not impossible. This situation changed in 2009 as broadcasters in most countries vacated their 40 meter frequencies, and a worldwide primary allocation for amateurs was created from 7 to 7.2 MHz. With the interference from the megawatt broadcasters gone in most of the band, it is common in the evenings to have excellent SSB DX QSOs in the 7.125 to 7.200 MHz band segment that is shared worldwide. In periods of high activity such as contests or DXpeditions, DX stations outside the US will operate "split," transmitting below 7.100 MHz on a frequency clear from interference,

and listening higher in the band for callers. You will need to learn how to use your radio's second VFO in order to work stations operating split on 40 meter SSB.

60 METERS

Just as 30 meters shares the characteristics of both 20 and 40 meters, 60 meters features aspects of its adjacent bands, 80 and 40 meters. This band is a relatively new allocation, first introduced in 2002, that was originally only available in a few countries. Over the years however, an increasing proportion of countries' telecommunications administrations — together with their government and military users — have permitted Amateur Radio operation in the 5 MHz area on a short or longer term basis, ranging from discrete channels to a frequency band allocation. The 2015 ITU World Radiocommunication Conference (WRC-15) created a worldwide frequency allocation of 5351.5 – 5366.5 kHz to the Amateur Service on a secondary basis. The ITU's allocation limits amateur stations to 15 W effective isotropic radiated power (EIRP); however, some locations will be permitted up to 25 W EIRP. The allocation will not come into effect until January 1, 2017.

Amateur stations will not be able to use this allocation until their national administration implements it.

The shared nature of this band, along with the secondary nature of the amateur allocation and the limited frequency range make this band generally unsuitable for DXing. In fact, many of the major awards are not applicable to contacts made on 60 meters and contests are not permitted in an effort to limit activity and minimize unnecessary interference to the primary users! The ARRL has published information on the 60 meter band at **www.arrl.org/60-meter-faq**. Check this page for updates in regulations and band planning.

80 METERS

Most amateurs think of 80 meters strictly as a band for local QSOs. DXing is possible here but can be challenging and is generally not for the beginner. Signals are generally much weaker than the higher-frequency bands, there is much more atmospheric noise, and effective antennas are very large. DX propagation is generally between locations that are both in darkness since daytime absorption in the D-layer of the ionosphere makes long-distance propagation impossible. There is a noticeable peak as one end of the path or the other experiences sunrise or sunset. DXing on 80 meters is seasonal, with better conditions in the wintertime due to longer periods of darkness and lower noise. DX is still available in the summer (especially to the southern hemisphere, where it is winter). In times of low sunspots, 80 (or 75, as the phone part of the band is commonly called) becomes the prime nighttime band as 20 and 40 both close. The band allocations vary across different regions. For example, stations in ITU Region 1 (Europe) are not allowed to transmit above 3800 kHz. During busy periods such as SSB contests, split-frequency operation is popular with stations in Europe transmitting below 3800 and listening for US callers above 3800 where there is less local interference.

Using Spotting Networks

Once (and still) simply referred to as "packet," or the "cluster," DX spotting networks have become a significant force in DXing. Since the early days of DXing, local DXers have banded together to share information about what stations are on the air. Before packet radio, DXers listened on a VHF frequency (usually on 2 meters) that was kept quiet except for announcements about DX stations. For example, you might hear, "TZ6ZZ is on 14024, listening up two, K6ABC clear" Helping each other has a long and honorable history in DXing.

Packet radio became popular in the early 1980s for digital communications and DXers naturally migrated to it. Bulletin board systems appeared, based on similar systems used over landline computer networks. Soon PacketCluster software adapted the bulletin board to the DX-centric format used today. Local stations connected via VHF or UHF and stayed connected, receiving a steady stream of information that could be stored and reviewed, if so desired. Instead of a voice announcement, the example above might have looked like "1530Z K6ABC TZ6ZZ 14.024 QSX up 2."

As the Internet became ubiquitous, the packet radio link gave way to a network connection. By that time, the format for data and commands for PacketCluster operating were in widespread use and so were replicated on web-based versions such as DX-Spider, and AR-Cluster. Today, a worldwide system incorporates users linked mostly by TELNET or web-based interfaces. Most logging programs can interface to these systems automatically. If desired, you can sit in your shack and watch a steady stream of DX station information and announcements flow by, posted by stations from all over the world!

This is a "good news, bad news" situation. The good news is, of course, that there is so much information for DXers. More DX QSOs and entities are being logged by more DXers than ever. What could be wrong with that? The bad news is that there is so much information that the need to actually tune the band yourself is reduced. Without putting your ears to work, you lose the opportunity to gain hard-won personal knowledge of propagation and band characteristics. You will also find that the posted information is not 100% reliable, as well, leading to the "busted call" or dreaded "not in the log" result. An operator who miscopies a call sign and thinks he is hearing a rare DX entity, then posts a spot to the entire world creates considerable ill will and looks like a fool when his error is revealed. Don't be that operator!

DX spots also create a version of a "flash mob," known as a "packet pileup" to DX operators. As information about the DX station filters out across the world's spotting networks, dozens to literally hundreds of DXers can descend on a single frequency, hoping for a QSO! It's important to remember that a DXer relying on spotting information to do his or her tuning will never be the first to find a DX station on the bands!

Nevertheless, as long as an appropriate amount of caution is applied and you remember that spotting networks are an aid and not an end in themselves, the information can be a great boon. Learn as much as you can about the spotting system you choose to use. Use the information to help you find the DX first instead of rushing madly about as spots pop up on your computer screen.

You can find local spotting networks by inquiring of your local or regional DX club. spotting systems worldwide, Internet spotting sites and many other useful spot-related links is available at **www.dxcluster.info** and at **www.ng3k.com**. Once connected, be sure to use the Help functions of the system to find out how to operate it correctly. Remember that the information you post will likely be seen around the planet within a few minutes!

A relatively new innovation in DX spotting technology is the Reverse Beacon Network, or "RBN." This system uses versions of the CW Skimmer and RTTY Skimmer software programs developed by VE3NEA that automatically decode all CW (and RTTY) signals across a band at a receiving site. With over 100 wideband receivers located around the world, this system provides a real-time snapshot of what bands are open and what signals are being heard. Instead of listening to a set of beacon transmitters like the NCDXF network, you can find out if your station is being heard on a band by simply calling CQ on a clear frequency and signing your call sign a few times. Within a minute or two, the RBN will show your call sign and report your CW speed and signal-to-noise ratio at any receivers that can hear you. If your signal is not being heard, try another band.

DX Summit is perhaps the best known Internet spotting site. Users can set a variety of filters to focus on spots that are of the most interest.

THE NCDXF/IARU Beacon Network

The Northern California DX Foundation (NCDXF), in cooperation with the international Amateur Radio Union (IARU), constructed and operates a worldwide network of high-frequency radio beacons on 14.100, 18.110, 21.150, 24.930, and 28.200 MHz. These beacons help both amateur and commercial high-frequency radio users assess the current condition of the ionosphere. The entire system is designed, built and operated by volunteers at no cost except for the actual price of hardware components, shipping costs, and so on.

The first beacon began transmissions from Northern California in 1979 and was so successful that the IARU proposed a worldwide network of beacons operating 24 hours a day. Over the next few years the network was expanded slowly. The current system of 18 beacons began operation in 1995 and has been in continuous operation ever since.

Stan Huntting, KW7KW, wrote, "There are at least two possible explanations for an apparently dead band: 1) propagation is poor, or 2) no one is transmitting. The NCDXF/IARU International Beacon Network addresses the second of these possibilities by insuring that reliable signals are always on the air, around the clock, from fixed locations worldwide." With three minutes of listening for the beacons, one can find out either where a particular band is open or which band has the best propagation to a particular part of the world.

In principle, you can simply listen on the beacon frequencies and copy the CW call signs of the various beacons to figure out where the band is open, but in practice, not every ham operator can copy calls at twenty-two words per minute and some beacons may be heard at too low a signal strength to catch the call. Because the beacons transmit at known times, it is easy to know which beacon you are hearing without actually copying the CW call sign. Since the beacons are running one hundred watts to a vertical antenna, even a weak beacon signal may indicate a path with excellent propagation for stations using higher power and directive antennas.

In order to know which beacon is transmitting at any particular time, one can either refer to the Beacon Transmission Schedule below, or use your computer and one of the many available programs listed on the NCDXF/IARU Beacon Project web page **www.ncdxf.org/beacon/**

The slot indicates the order of transmission. The beacons transmit on 5 frequencies: 14.100, 18.110, 21.150, 24.930, 28.200 MHz in a 3 minute cycle so that no two beacons transmit at the same time on the same frequency. Each beacon trans-

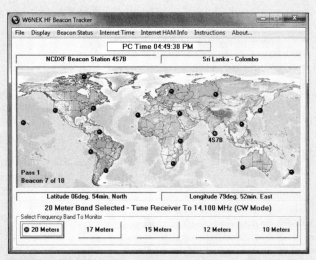

The W6NEK HF Beacon Tracker software provides a visual indication of which beacon is scheduled to be transmitting at any time and on which frequency.

mission lasts 10 seconds so that no two beacons are on the same frequency at the same time. After a beacon completes its transmission on a band, it steps to the next higher frequency band for the next time slot. After transmitting on the 10 meter frequency, the beacon starts its cycle again on the 20 meter frequency.

The free W6NEK HF Beacon Tracker software (available at **www.w6nek.com**) provides a visual indication of which beacon is scheduled to be transmitting at any time and on which frequency. More advanced software is also available, such as the FAROS program written by Alex, VE3NEA and available at **www.dxatlas.com/Faros/**. This software uses a connection to a computer-controlled radio and continuously monitors the 18 NCDXF beacons on five bands, automatically detects the presence of the beacon signals, even in QRM and noise, and can generate a real-time display of band conditions, long-term history of beacon observations and much more.

[Excerpted from text at **www.ncdxf.org**, used with permission.]

List of NCDXF/IARU Beacon Stations

Slot	DX Entity	Call	Location	Grid Square	Operator
1	United Nations	4U1UN	New York City	FN30as	UNRC
2	Canada	VE8AT	Eureka, Nunavut	EQ79ax	RAC/NARC
3	United States	W6WX	Mt. Umunhum	CM97bd	NCDXF
4	Hawaii	KH6RS	Maui	BL10ts	Maui ARC
5	New Zealand	ZL6B	Masterton	RE78tw	NZART
6	Australia	VK6RBP	Rolystone	OF87av	WIA
7	Japan	JA2IGY	Mt. Asama	PM84jk	JARL
8	Russia	RR9O	Novosibirsk	NO14kx	SRR
9	Hong Kong	VR2B	Hong Kong	OL72bg	HARTS
10	Sri Lanka	4S7B	Colombo	MJ96wv	RSSL
11	South Africa	ZS6DN	Pretoria	KG44dc	ZS6DN
12	Kenya	5Z4B	Kariobangi	KI88ks	ARSK
13	Israel	4X6TU	Tel Aviv	KM72jb	IARC
14	Finland	OH2B	Lohja	KP20	SRAL
15	Madeira	CS3B	Santo da Serra	IM12or	ARRM
16	Argentina	LU4AA	Buenos Aires	GFØ5tj	RCA
17	Peru	OA4B	Lima	FH17mw	RCP
18	Venezuela	YV5B	Caracas	FJ69cc	RCV

160 METERS

Often called the "Top Band," 160 offers one of the great DX challenges. Openings are sometimes very short in duration and signals are weaker than on other bands. Noise is higher than on any other amateur band. Even simple antennas are enormous: a half-wave dipole is over 250 feet long and should be installed very high (over 100 feet) to be effective. A full-size quarter-wave vertical is over 125 feet tall, and requires many radials to be effective (although an inverted-L-style antenna with 40 or 50 feet vertical and the top run out horizontally can be successful). It is not generally considered a good band for beginning DXers.

Like 80 meters, 160 meters is a nighttime band. DX propagation on 160 begins in the late afternoon to early evening, in the direction of the approaching darkness. As stations in the east approach their sunrise, there will likely be a short but noticeable increase in their signal strength called the *dawn enhancement*. This is your opportunity to span the longest distances. Propagation continues to flow east to west, as the DXer follows the Sun. As the Sun rises, the DXer can expect to work stations to the west until they finally sink into the noise as the D layer begins to absorb the signal again.

Shorter periods of sunlight and less thunderstorm activity make 160 meter propagation better in the fall and winter.

Collecting Information

Gathering information is as important to a DXer as any other facet of operating, because knowledge really is power. In fact, it's *better* than power because it doesn't matter how strong your signal is if you're operating on the wrong frequency or at the wrong time!

A DX newsletter, such as *Daily DX* (**www. dailydx.com**) or *QRZ DX* (**www.dxpub.net**) really helps the DXer in the search for new stations.

DX spotting networks are another important tool. In fact, many DXers owe their DXCC Honor Roll plaques to them. A "DX spot" is a short message that a particular station is being heard on a specific frequency — see the sidebar "Using Spotting Networks." Add spot filtering software that alerts the operator if a needed station comes on the air, and you have a most formidable tool.

The DX spotting network now stretches around the world through Internet connections. It's possible to see what's being worked in Italy or Japan. This is actually more useful than you may think. First, it's possible to know that stations from certain areas are actually on the air. It's also possible to identify these stations and even request schedules. Sometimes, depending on propagation, spots

from another area of the country can be useful. Spots can help you work stations at times that you would not have even listened and spots have tipped operators to band openings not thought possible before. Some sites allow you to search past spots to help determine the best bands or times to try.

Real-time spotting is the best method of intelligence gathering currently in use for ongoing operations. It is a truly amazing system and the hybrid radio/Internet system is one of the best forms of useful ham ingenuity.

The Northern California DX Foundation operates a network of beacons that provides useful information on propagation. A network of 18 synchronized stations in locations around the world cycle through the bands on the same frequency transmitting their call sign and a series of CW dashes at different power levels so you can determine how well a band is open between your location and the beacon's location.

Let's Work Some DX!

You've read this chapter, made a few notes, and now you have some free time to operate. Let's say it is a weekend morning and you'd like to try and work some DX. We know that the "low bands" (160 through 40 meters) are probably not open for long-distance contacts since it is daylight. There are a few options for determining the best band to start on.

The old-fashioned way is to put on the headphones and start on a higher band that is open, say 10 or 12 meters, and tune slowly through the band. It's easiest to tune through the phone segment of the band, especially if you are not yet comfortable with copying CW. As you tune slowly from the bottom edge of the phone band toward the top, you will

probably hear an assortment of signals. Loud signals, with the operator speaking American English, might not be very interesting since they are not DX. Keep tuning.

At some point, you may hear a signal speaking accented English (you may also hear other languages, but the majority of casual DX QSOs are conducted in English). The signal may be weaker than the loud American, and may fade in and out somewhat. At the end of the operator's transmission, he will probably sign his call sign. The call sign prefix will tell you the country where the station is located, since each country has its own ITU-assigned block of prefixes. Then you can determine if the station is DX, and whether it is a country you have not yet contacted.

If you do not hear any DX stations, perhaps the band is not open. Try switching to a lower band such as 15 or 17 meters. Start at the bottom again and tune higher until you find a DX station. If you have some patience, tune to the NCDXF/IARU beacon frequency on the band you want to use and listen for three minutes to see if you can hear any signals from the CW beacon stations. If there are no beacons audible, the band is probably not open.

If you are comfortable sending CW or have RTTY capability in your station, you can call CQ a few times on a clear frequency, sign your call, and watch the Reverse Beacon Network (**www.reversebeacon.net**) to see if any of that system's receivers are hearing your signal. If your signal is not reported, try another band.

Today, it is likely that you have the DX Cluster available on your computer or even your smartphone. This can save a lot of time, since you can quickly look at the screen and see if any DX stations have been spotted by stations in your area on the band of interest.

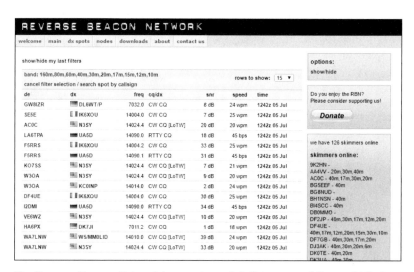

The Reverse Beacon Network is a system of stations around the world that monitor and decode CW, RTTY, and PSK signals on many bands at once and report signals heard on the Internet.

You can then tune to their frequency and be ready to make contact.

However you find a DX station, you should listen for a while to get the flow of the conversation. Is the DX station chatting, or is he moving quickly from one contact to the next? This will suggest how you should engage. Of course, you should wait until the current contact is complete and the DX station asks for new callers. If the DX station is calling CQ, feel free to call him right away! If he answers someone else (who may have a stronger signal), be patient and wait until the next opportunity. You may find that the DX station is in high demand and there are hundreds of very strong stations all calling at the same time, competing to be the next contact. This is called a pileup. In this situation, you may want to listen for a while to get the rhythm of the operator and listen to his technique (and those of the callers), then move on and find another station to work if you don't get through in a few calls. There's no point getting frustrated at not making a DX contact. There are a lot more stations on the band!

A Basic DX QSO

Basic DX contacts tend to be fairly simple. The basic format on most modes is shown below…let's say that you (W1AW for this example) have just tuned in GB2RS…

DX station: "CQ, CQ, CQ, this is GB2RS — Golf Bravo Two Romeo Sierra calling CQ and listening"

You: "GB2RS, this is W1AW, Whiskey One Alfa Whiskey. Over." (Of course, you would substitute your own call sign and corresponding phonetics in place of W1AW.)

GB2RS: "W1AW this is GB2RS. Good morning! Your signal is five by seven here near London, England, and my name is Clive, spelled Charlie Lima India Victor Echo, Clive. How do you copy? W1AW, this is GB2RS."

W1AW: "GB2RS this is W1AW. Thanks for the report, Clive. Nice to meet you. Your signal is very strong here today, five by nine. My name is Hiram, that's Hotel India Romeo Alfa Mike, and my QTH is the town of Newington, Connecticut. I'm running 100 watts and a vertical antenna here. How do you

Table 3.2
ITU Phonetic Alphabet

Letter	Word	Letter	Word
A	Alfa	N	November
B	Bravo	O	Oscar
C	Charlie	P	Papa
D	Delta	Q	Quebec
E	Echo	R	Romeo
F	Foxtrot	S	Sierra
G	Golf	T	Tango
H	Hotel	U	Uniform
I	India	V	Victor
J	Juliet	W	Whiskey
K	Kilo	X	X-Ray
L	Lima	Y	Yankee
M	Mike	Z	Zulu

copy? GB2RS this is W1AW."

Let's review these steps. First, note that each transmission is fairly short, which is important if conditions are not stable. A long transmission may be so long that signals fade out and the contact is not completed to anyone's satisfaction, like a dropped cell phone call.

Both stations use standard phonetic alphabets (**Table 3.2**) to clarify their call signs when they are initiating contact. They also use the same phonetic alphabet to spell out their names. If either one wants the full details of the other's city, they may ask for the place name to be spelled out phonetically also, but most of the time it is not needed. DX stations are usually mostly interested in what state you are in.

At this point, both stations have exchanged signal reports, names, and locations, and that may be all there is to the contact, especially if signals are weak or there is noise or interference. The contact could proceed in several different ways from there. One option is to wrap it up and move on. In that case, you'll hear something like…

GB2RS: "W1AW this is GB2RS. OK, Hiram, I copied everything OK. If you'd like a card, you can send one via the bureau or direct. I also use Logbook of The World if you'd like to confirm the QSO electronically. Thanks for the contact. W1AW this is GB2RS. 73."

At this point, you may offer a quick "73,"

then let GB2RS go back to working other stations.

On the other hand, the QSO may progress further. GB2RS may want to tell you more about his station, his weather, his recent vacation trip to your area, or anything else. If he wants to chat and signals are good, go for it! But be polite…if he doesn't want to chat, let him move on.

If the DX station wants to chat, you may find it interesting to look up his call sign on the QRZ.com website. Many DX stations post a short biography and often a photograph of themselves or their station. This can lead to an enjoyable QSO and possibly a new friendship.

Some DX stations, especially in rare DXCC entities, move very quickly from one QSO to the next. They are interested in making themselves available to the maximum number of stations possible while they have propagation so they often keep their contacts very short, exchanging only call signs and signal reports. In these cases, take your cue from their behavior and act accordingly.

When the QSO is complete, you'll want to record it, either on paper or preferably on the computer. Make sure you log all the details correctly, including date, time, frequency band, call sign, signal reports, and any other details you want to keep on record. This will be required when you attempt to get confirmation of the contact and apply for awards. We'll discuss confirming QSOs later in this chapter.

Now that you've worked one DX station, you'll probably want to work some more. You may want to set goals for your career as a Little Pistol DXer. For example:

• Learn to operate your transceiver well, tuning in stations accurately on all modes.

• Start computer logging and register for Logbook of The World (see the section on QSLing later in this chapter).

• Work 50 or more different DXCC entities, including contacts on at least three bands.

• Operate one session without using the DX Cluster or Reverse Beacon Network. See if you can find and work a DX station without any assistance.

3.2.2 Intermediate DXing

As you progress in experience, you will begin to develop a feel for working DX. You should begin to understand which bands work well at your station, and what time of day is best for you to contact certain regions. And you will encounter some new operating situations.

Pileup Operating

One situation mentioned previously is the "pileup." This is where a DX station has attracted a large number of stations all trying to make contact next. With some patience, and practice, you can learn to get through pileups without always having the biggest signal.

Once again, the key is to listen first. Are similarly-equipped stations in your area getting through the pileup? If not, maybe you need to wait a while for propagation to change and favor you. Store the DX station's frequency in memory and come back later.

If comparable stations are getting through, then you probably have a chance. When

Sometimes DX stations operate "split," transmitting on one frequency and listening on another. This helps prevent calling stations from covering up the DX station and can allow calling stations to spread out for more efficient pileup management. Double-check your radio settings before calling to be sure you are transmitting on the correct VFO.

calling in a pileup, give your call *one time* using phonetics (on phone…don't use phonetics on CW or digital!). If the DX station doesn't answer anyone, try again. Stop calling when he answers someone! It may be that the DX station only gets part of a call sign. If that fragment does not match part of your call sign, he is probably not answering you, so *don't call*!

If you're beaten in the pileup, wait until the next opportunity and call again. Perhaps you notice that the DX station tends to answer when only one station is calling. If so, wait until everyone in the pileup takes a breath, and give a quick call — once with phonetics. Careful timing is the difference between a good operator who gets through pileups quickly and a poor operator who goes away without a QSO.

Another technique that works sometimes is "tail-ending." Some DX operators will leave a small gap before between the end of a caller giving a signal report and their next transmission. You can take advantage of that short gap to send your call sign, once, quickly, with phonetics. However, use this technique only when the other operator is answering tail-enders…otherwise you may be transmitting when he transmits, and causing interference and confusion on the frequency.

If the DX station answers you, be quick about the QSO. Don't make others wait by giving your name and QTH, weather report, and other details. Give him a signal report, make sure he has your call correct, then let him go back to working others. Never ask the station for QSL information in this type of pileup — listen until it's given or look it up on the Internet.

Split-Frequency Operation

Occasionally you may encounter a situation when you hear a DX station working a pileup, but you don't hear anyone calling. Yet he keeps answering stations and the signal reports keep on coming! What is happening is that the DX station is probably working split with the callers transmitting on a different frequency. Listen for a while, and the DX station will announce where he is listening. Be patient — don't jump on top of the DX station and ask "Where is he listening?" That

will only create QRM on the DX station's frequency and likely launch an avalanche of unflattering comments about your lack of operating skill.

Usually, the DX station will announce he is "listening up 5 to 10," you should call between 5 and 10 kHz higher. On CW or RTTY, the DX station will say "QSX up 1" (Q signal for "I am listening up 1 kHz"), or simply "up."

You will have to learn how to operate your transceiver in split-frequency mode. Usually there is a button labeled SPLIT, and either a second VFO knob or a button to assign the tuning knob to one VFO or the other. Most radios also include a button to allow you to listen to your transmitting frequency momentarily so you can check the frequency where you are planning to call to make sure it is clear. All radios have different controls for split-frequency operation, so check the manual.

The biggest mistake newcomers make when they try to operate split the first time is calling on the wrong VFO and covering up the DX station. This is extremely embarrassing when the error is pointed out (and it *will* be pointed out!). However, even the most experienced DXers make mistakes sometimes.

Calling in a split pileup requires some additional technique. And once more, the key is to listen! When a DX station is operating split, he may use one of several methods to pick out a station to answer. Sometimes, the DX station tunes a bit higher after every contact. Sometimes, he tunes around until he finds a clear frequency and waits for a station to call on that frequency. Sometimes he hops randomly around trying to find a station that he can copy.

Listen for a bit and determine the DX station's tuning routine. If he is tuning smoothly up the band through the pileup, find the station he is working, set your transmitting frequency a bit higher, and call at the next opportunity. The DX station may find you there. If not, find out who he works, and move higher. Keep in mind that a skilled DX pileup operator will eventually stop going higher, and will then start again at the bottom of his listening frequencies. If you notice that he has shifted back to the bottom of his pileup, you may get through while others are still tuning up higher.

If the DX station is struggling, he may

spread the pileup out further. If he does, move up! The key is to figure out exactly where the DX station is likely to listen next — find a clear frequency where nobody else is calling and you will get through more quickly.

Another technique used often by inexperienced DX stations trying to manage a pileup is "going by the numbers." In this practice, the DX station will announce which call area he is listening for, identifying by the number in call sign. In principle, it should reduce the number of stations calling at any time by a factor of ten, making it easier to copy a call sign. It can work well if the operator moves quickly from one number to the next, but falls apart if he continues to work stations from a single area for too long and other areas lose propagation. Obviously it is rude and unacceptable operating practice to call out of turn.

Sometimes a DX station will ask for callers from a certain geographic area that has poor propagation compared to most of the callers in the pileup. Again, it is rude and unacceptable to call out of turn. For example, US stations should not call a DX station who is asking for South America only.

As you progress through the lessons that lead you into the Medium Gun level of DXer, you may want to set new goals. For example:

• Raise the total number of entities worked to 75 or more.

• Make QSOs on all modes: SSB, CW, and digital.

• Work at least one major DXpedition.

• Begin tracking your DXCC entity total and look for "easy" new ones.

• Identify ways you can improve your station and start planning the changes.

Adding to your DX entity total will require some planning. The first few dozen entities are easy. A lot of entities have lots of active stations, so they are easy to find. However, getting to 75 or more will require working stations in different areas and entities where there is not much activity.

It is interesting to see where the 339 DXCC entities are located geographically, as shown in **Table 3.3**.

This table takes some interpretation

Table 3.3
DXCC Entities by Continent

Continent	Entities
Africa	76
Asia	53
Antarctica	2
Europe	67
North America	50
South America	30
Oceania	59

Note: Two DXCC entities straddle continental boundaries. Maldives (8Q) is in both Oceania and Asia; and Turkey (TA) is in both Europe and Asia.

though. While there are indeed 76 entities in Africa, most of them do not have a sizable ham population and can be difficult to work. Asia and Oceania also have a lot of entities that are difficult to work for lack of activity.

Most of the easily-worked entities are located in Europe and North America (more specifically, the Caribbean/Central America area) and these areas should be your focus as you seek out new entities to add to your total. You should be on bands that are open to these regions as much as possible when you are on the air.

You should also consider subscribing to DX newsletters or checking online resources to be aware of when activity is expected from entities you need. Vacationing hams often bring a rig and antenna along when they travel to islands in the Caribbean, and this can be a good source of lots of new entities, especially if the island's residents are not active in DXing.

Now is also the time to attend a DX convention or a DX club meeting. Conventions include presentations on everything from operating technique to a review of a recent DXpedition. Club meetings are a great opportunity to learn from the experienced Big Gun DXers. If there are no DX clubs where you live, you have probably discovered the local Big Gun by hearing him on the air. Drop him an e-mail and see if he is willing to let you visit. You can ask Big Guns questions about operating technique, antennas, equipment optimization and more, and they are usually willing to help, since they were in your situation once upon a time.

3.2.3 DXpeditions

These short-term operations have been mentioned several times so far in this chapter. From the DXer's perspective, they provide an exciting change to the everyday bands and will be the only chance you will have to contact many entities that are uninhabited. Suddenly there are big pileups on different bands and modes — everyone wants a contact before they shut down! Their QSLs are often spectacular and there may be a video or convention presentation to enjoy. With radios and antennas more compact and efficient than ever, there are more DXpeditions on the air than ever, too! While most are active on HF, more and more DXpeditions take gear for 6 meters, even moonbounce!

Nigel Cawthorne, G3TXF, is a frequent DXpeditioner, usually making short trips with minimal equipment and simple antennas. Here he is shown operating as J79XF in Dominica, one of the 104 DXCC entities from which he has operated.

You'll find that there is a wide variety in the capabilities of DXpeditions. Some are one-operator holidays with operating time, bands and modes limited to the interests and schedule of the individual taking the trip. At the other end of the scale is the "mega" DXpedition with a dozen operators or more, lots of equipment, continuous operation, and loud signals wherever they choose to tune. Operations of this size often have supporting resources such as online logs and pilot stations that provide feedback and guidance to the expeditioners on band openings that they may otherwise miss.

Once the DXpedition is on the air, listen to the pileups and decide on a strategy. If your station has strong capabilities in that part of the world, you might enjoy jumping in at the beginning. If not, take the opportunity to listen and learn the operating styles being used. You can wait until the pile thins out or try to catch them as they change bands or modes. The risk of waiting is, of course, that something might go wrong — generator failure or a storm — and cause an early shutdown. Toward the end of even the largest expeditions, however, the pileups thin out and it becomes easier to make contact.

While Little Pistol DXers will be happy with one contact for an "all time new

Working DXpeditions

You won't be able to work DXpeditions unless you know they're on the air. Furthermore, you may have to make arrangements to be on the air at the right time for propagation to your area. After all, the expeditioners aren't going to wait for you to get home from work! Most DXpeditions are 24/7 operations, following the bands with the Sun.

The first thing is to learn about the trip and who is taking it. This is where newsletters and DX websites are most helpful. They'll alert you to upcoming expeditions and answer questions such as: When will the operation begin and end? Who are the operators? What bands and modes will they use? Will they be using specific frequencies or will you need to be looking for them? It's a good thing that there are websites and newsletters to provide the information. Write down all the necessary information on paper and post it at your station for easy reference. You might also want to let other family members know that you'll be operating at odd times in pursuit of these rare birds!

The 2016 VP8STI DXpedition to South Thule Island in the South Sandwich group was cut short when a major blizzard damaged the operating tents and many of the antennas. The operators were forced to return to the ship, but returned later to recover the equipment and continue to their next destination (VP8SGI, South Georgia Island). [David Collingham, K3LP, photo]

This is the crew that operated from Navassa Island in 2015. The uninhabited Caribbean island between Jamaica and Haiti is administered by the US Fish and Wildlife Service which limits visitors. K1N was the first Amateur Radio operation allowed there in more than 20 years.

one," Medium Gun DXers may take as a goal to have a single, solid contact in the DXpedition's log on each band and mode in which they have an interest. It's usually not necessary to make several "insurance" QSOs to be sure of having one good one. If the DX sent your call clearly and you were able to hear the entire QSO without confusion as to timing, you should be in the log. If not, make a second QSO. Avoid being one of the "DX hogs" who make duplicate QSOs just because they can. It denies other stations an opportunity to make possibly their first QSO with the expedition and maybe the first ever with that entity! Online logs that are available during the operation are particularly helpful in this regard. Once your call is confirmed, you can relax.

After the expedition is over, be sure to QSL according to the directions of the operators or their QSL manager. Manage your expectations for a quick confirmation. Most DXpeditions check their logs carefully before responding to QSL requests, and nearly all now use Logbook of The World to automate the process for electronic confirmation. Paper QSLs take longer, since they have to be printed and mailed and that may take weeks or months before your QSL request is processed. If patience is difficult to come by, get on the air and work some more DX!

During the days of chasing an elusive DXpedition QSO you may become frustrated. The operators may switch to another area just as propagation to yours is building. They may operate on bands with poor propagation to you or not spend time on your favorite mode. There may be times when the operator has a hard time controlling the pileup or working stations at a decent rate. At times like this, don't let your frustrations get the better of you. The expeditioners are likely operating under stress. They're hot, cold, thirsty, smelly, being bitten by insects or crabs, and

wondering why it was that they sailed, flew, or drove all the way to whatever bizarre location it is. It's your relatively easy job to remain calm and follow their instructions. Give them the benefit of the doubt, since they have gone to great lengths for your benefit.

Am I Really in the Log?

Sometimes you may be uncertain if your QSO with a DXpedition is complete. Perhaps the operator missed a letter of your call sign, and when you corrected it, QRM covered him up and you aren't sure if he got the correction. Or you thought he answered you, and gave a

signal report but he never acknowledged your report then he changed bands or modes and you lost the chance to confirm the contact. Or the DXpedition's log file could become corrupted or lost.

In the past, the only way to find out if you were definitely in a DXpedition station's log was to wait for the QSL card or LoTW upload. However, nowadays most DXpeditions bring a secondary means of communication with them and upload their logs to a safe place during the DXpedition, usually daily. This is a good way to find out if you are in the log. Generally the information only tells you which bands and modes that you are in the log, but not the details of the date or time. It is up to you to have the correct date and time when you send for confirmation.

The 2016 VKØEK DXpedition to remote Heard Island went one step further. Heard Island is uninhabited, so they brought a satellite-based Internet terminal with them, and used a program called *DXA* to report stations worked *every minute* so everyone could see who was in the log and what parts of the world were being worked on each band. If you were logged into the site and made a QSO with the DXpedition, a "Congratulations" message appeared within a minute or two of the QSO.

Of course, a real QSL or electronic confirmation is needed for award purposes, but knowing that you are in the log with a good QSO is a good feeling!

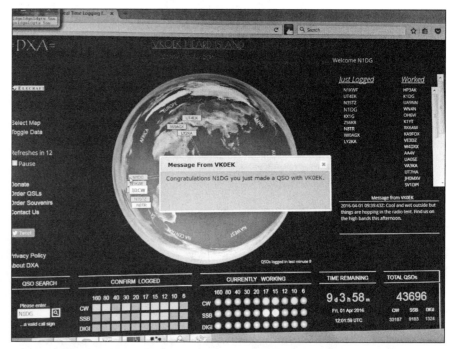

The VKØEK DXpedition uploaded their log in real-time and provided a website to track QSOs on a minute-by-minute basis. [Courtesy Don Greenbaum, N1DG]

3.2.4 Unusual Propagation

After operating for a while, you may be used to particular propagation patterns. Then one day you may notice a signal coming in at an unexpected time of day. Here are a few examples of interesting propagation effects that you may experience as you spend more time DXing.

Long-Path Propagation

Any of the HF bands can support long-path propagation at some point during the sunspot cycle. Because of the extra distance involved, signals are generally weaker and the openings much shorter. Making contacts via the long-path is exciting and worth the extra effort.

The conditions that support long-path propagation vary depending on the band. For the "low bands" (those below 10 MHz), long-path most often occurs along the gray line (see below) near sunrise and sunset. The openings are short — often just a few minutes. Because of atmospheric noise on these bands, working DX long-path usually requires a good location and capable station. Above 10 MHz, long-path requires solar illumination instead of darkness so that the MUF (maximum useable frequency) is high enough to support propagation all the way along the route. Watch for long-path openings to the southeast in the morning and to the southwest in the afternoon.

Long path most often occurs over paths that pass over the oceans because the lower losses of reflection by salt water keep signal strengths usable at longer distances. A special form of long-path is *round-the-world* (RTW) propagation. If you hear an echo of your signal delayed by about $\frac{1}{7}$ of a second, your signal may be traveling completely around the Earth!

Backscatter

Another source of echoes on signals is backscatter. If you are listening to a station on one of the high bands a few hundred miles or so away who has big antennas, a good location, and is running full power, you may observe an echo on the signal. This is caused by the signal being reflected both forward and backward as it impacts the reflecting layer of the ionosphere. The echo is usually delayed much less than $\frac{1}{10}$ of a second, so it is not traveling all the way around the Earth, but sounds very impressive.

Gray Line Propagation

Because the signal-absorbing D layer is the lowest layer of the ionosphere, it remains non-illuminated for longer than the higher layers. Thus, it forms after all the other layers and is the first one to dissipate. The result is a region along the *terminator* — the dividing line between light and dark areas — in which absorption from the D layer is reduced. Propagation along the terminator is called *gray-line* propagation. Gray-line propagation may be especially useful at the beginning of an opening and on the low bands. A good antenna system and output power will maximize the success of gray-line contacts. Your logging program may be able to generate gray-line maps for the different seasons and you can use the map to locate stations that are on the gray line at the same time as you are and make easy long-haul contacts.

DX Pileup Jammers

Whenever a DXpedition comes on the air, certain bad pileup behaviors emerge. Since most DXpeditions operate in split-frequency mode, inevitably a station will accidentally call on the wrong VFO, causing interference to the DX station. This is usually followed by self-appointed "policemen" informing the offender that he is on the wrong VFO. This of course, also causes interference to the DX station...and leads to even more policemen telling the first wave of policemen to stop transmitting. And on and on it goes, slowing everyone down in the process.

Sometimes a station will deliberately interfere with the DXpedition. Nobody seems to know why operators engage in this aberrant behavior...perhaps for attention, perhaps to prevent others from working the DX. Most of these deliberate QRMers believe they cannot be caught. The sidebar on the next page by Roger Western, G3SXW, a noted DXpeditioner himself, describes how one DQRMer was identified using a combination of technology and local investigation, giving hope that this problem will be reduced in the future.

3.2.5 Developing Good Operating Practices

As you operate more and more, you should begin to pay attention to your operating style. Good habits learned and put into practice early when you are a Little Pistol will pay dividends in the future in both DXing success and your reputation as an operator. The DX Code of Conduct is a good starting point. Many clubs and DXpeditions have endorsed this code and it is good advice.

DX Code of Conduct

• I will listen, and listen, and then listen again before calling.

• I will only call if I can copy the DX station properly.

• I will not trust the DX cluster and will be sure of the DX station's call sign before calling.

• I will not interfere with the DX station nor anyone calling and will never tune up on the DX frequency or in the QSX slot.

• I will wait for the DX station to end a contact before I call.

• I will always send my full call sign.

• I will call and then listen for a reasonable interval. I will not call continuously.

• I will not transmit when the DX operator calls another call sign, not mine.

• I will not transmit when the DX operator queries a call sign not like mine.

• I will not transmit when the DX station requests geographic areas other than mine.

• When the DX operator calls me, I will not repeat my call sign unless I think he has copied it incorrectly.

• I will be thankful if and when I do make a contact.

• I will respect my fellow hams and conduct myself so as to earn their respect.

Expanded commentary on each point of the Code and translation into various languages are at **www.dx-code.org**

Identifying DQRM

(The full version of this article by Roger Western, G3SXW, originally appeared in the May 2016 edition of the CDXC Digest)

A small number of stations generate *Deliberate QRM*, known as DQRM, by transmitting on the frequency of a rare station in order to disrupt the operation. They do so anonymously, not identifying with their licensed call sign and thereby contravening the terms of their transmitting license. They do not explain their motives for this anti-social behavior, so the rationale for DQRM is poorly understood and perhaps can be viewed as anarchy — just disruption for the sake of it. But it can cause considerable inconvenience, even anger, to legitimate DX Chasers and is deemed a serious nuisance. DQRM is becoming an ever bigger problem these days.

One such DQRMer has been identified by the content of his CW transmissions (usually resembling a call sign…not his!). Over a period of several years this station has caused prolific CW DQRM to DXpeditions on countless occasions and for long periods. His transmit frequency is fairly accurate and he often appears quickly on the frequency when a rare station starts to operate.

His CW sending is distinctive both in terms of his poorly constructed Morse code and the content of his messages. So he is easily identifiable, no matter which "call sign" he chooses to use on that day. His CW is hand-sent, not computer-derived, and is immediately identifiable.

Direction Finding

A small group of determined DXers therefore set out to identify this station, as the first step in identifying a number of persistent DQRMers. The first objective was to locate and identify this individual, then to arrange that he cease his disruptive activities. To achieve the first objective required DF. It was quickly established, some years ago, that the signal emanates on a beam heading of about 120 degrees azimuth from the UK. It was thought that this station was located in Southern Europe, possibly Italy, Greece or a Balkan country. Refining the beam headings we concluded that he was located somewhere in Italy.

A well-positioned radio amateur DXer is employed in the UK with access to professional HF direction-finding (DF) facilities. He joined our small, ad hoc investigative group and was permitted by his employer to track the interferer when not otherwise engaged in his professional duties. This facility is extremely accurate, determining a heading to within two degrees azimuth and may simultaneously take automated bearings from several different sources (countries). The headings are automatically drawn on a map and the lines converge on one point, indicating the location of the signal within the range of a very few miles. This facility was used, during 2014, to help locate the DQRMer.

The DF measurements converged on a point just West of Rome, Italy.

At this stage of the project two local radio amateurs living in Rome, who are DXers and who were well aware of the problem, were approached for help. Being keen to assist they collated a list of some sixty licensed radio amateurs in the local area. Within that list they identified a few possible sources of the DQRM by homing in on those who were heard regularly on the HF bands, using CW.

To define the target area to within say ten miles with the professional DF facility was the quicker part of the project. To home in on one address was more difficult and time-consuming. Our local helpers in Rome could hear the extremely strong DQRMer's signal. From their location they determined with directional antennas that it was emanating from West of Rome, which confirmed the earlier findings of the DF maps. In order to define the precise location of the station one member of the team then drove to the address of each possible suspect, one by one, while the DQRMer was transmitting. In the car was a receiver but only three feet of wire as the receiving antenna located inside the car. Our second helper in Rome stayed at his home station, monitoring the interferer's signal and communicating with the in-car operator by mobile telephone to report the precise moments when the DQRMer was transmitting.

They quickly determined, one by one, that the first two suspects were not transmitting at the times when the base station in Rome was hearing the signal because while parked outside the target house no signal could be heard with the tiny antenna. But the third target provided an extremely loud signal when the car was at the address. The signal was clearly identified as sending the usual content and the building at that address was seen to accommodate several large HF transmitting antennas. Our culprit had been identified, beyond any reasonable doubt. Great care was taken at this vital stage of the research, encompassing numerous car journeys over a period of many months.

Additionally, this station has been monitored over such a long period of time that on two occasions he was heard to send his own, real call-sign by mistake on CW and RTTY. He has also on several occasions been heard operating with his real call-sign and working a DXpedition in the normal pile-up manner of DX-chasing (transmitting on a different frequency to the DXpedition), but then proceeding immediately to commence his DQRM on the DXpedition transmit frequency. We conjectured that having made the contact himself, he then wished to prevent others from so doing.

Having identified the culprit with complete certainty the next step was to build the evidence to prove the case incontrovertibly so that our findings might be deemed legally valid.

Identifying Evidence

Log: A log had been kept of the DQRMer (and his various other "call signs") whenever he was heard on the air. This clearly is not a complete log of all his activities, only when we heard him. This demonstrates his persistence over a long period of time: a period of one year is described, starting from when it was decided that we would require a log. His DQRM is known to have started several years earlier.

Recordings: Audio and video recordings were made from the car, immediately outside the house which show the date, time, street name, house number, transmitting frequency and signal strength. With only a tiny antenna wire and by introducing 18 dB of receiver attenuation the signal is loud enough to be sure that the origin is very close indeed.

DX Cluster: Archives show that some DXers already believed that this was the identity of the station generating the DQRM, during a period of some 13 years! It is not known how they traced his real identity.

Action Taken

This is a serious case of DQRM which has persisted over such a long period and caused so much unprecedented levels of interference and inconvenience to many DX chasers. IARU Region 1 officials wrote to the operator explaining that the offending station had been located "very close to his address" and asking for his help to identify the culprit. The reply denied blame but we noted that this source of DQRM then completely ceased.

The final objective of dissuading others from causing DQRM may be partly achieved by publication of this story. We have shown that even anonymous signals can be identified.

Future

This case study shows that effective action can be taken to identify and locate DQRM. The work is made much more effective by the availability of local volunteers who can help with "the last mile." Based on this experience, the core team and IARU Region 1 intend to repeat the process on other "characteristic" DQRM. The long range DF takes only a second or two, and so a short carrier from a DQRMer can result in a trace to his location. Thereafter, the local volunteers will need to be willing to invest some serious time in local work to narrow the source down to a street and a house. But the experience of this case shows it can be done, and this should serve as a warning to others who may feel that DQRMing is a smart thing to do. IARU Member Societies will be encouraged to invoke the help of their national regulators once a DQRMer has been localized to a small area. In this way, we hope we open the way to prosecution of offenders and we hope that slowly, the scourge of DQRM will be eliminated.

3.2.6 Advanced DXing

At this point, you should feel confident on the bands, you have enough contacts for an award or two (even if you choose not to apply for them), and you begin to recognize the sounds of DXing. You can discern the bands opening and closing, identify the characteristics of DX signals, and know how to make DX QSOs. When a DXpedition comes on, your goal is to work it on several different bands and modes.

This is the busiest period of any DXer's "career" because there are plenty of "New Ones" to put in the log. You're now skilled enough to be successful on a regular basis, but not so experienced that you don't get surprised now and then! You should be at or above the 100 confirmed entities needed for the basic DXCC award and headed toward over-100 endorsements, with plans for how to get to the Honor Roll.

Going on a DXpedition

It's a rare DXer indeed who hasn't listened to a DXpedition and imagined being at the "other end" with the headphones on, picking out calls one by one from a sandy beach or mountaintop location. Surely, we've all thought, "I could do that!" as we listen to contacts stream by. The answer is that you can certainly give it a try! There is no guarantee of success, of course, but it's a lot easier to be the DX than you might think. Hundreds of stations calling, pileups around the clock day and night, thousands of contacts logged at high rates. This could be you! What's to stop you from putting together a small station and hopping on the next plane for somewhere with sandy beaches and not much radio activity? Not much, actually!

You need to start simple, of course. Good practice is surprisingly easy to come by — operate from an IOTA island or operate from a portable location in the next contest. Read articles or websites about the experiences of other DXpedition operators. Learn what gear you require and develop a package of equipment that works. Get used to operating away from your comfortable shack. Become skilled at packing, transporting, deploying, and repacking your equipment.

Once you're ready to become "real DX," choose a reasonable first location. You wouldn't want to try for a really difficult destination on the first time

out. Difficulty can mean transportation or licensing. Remember that you'll need all the proper permissions for your operation to count for most award programs! It's best to start with an easier location where licensing and transportation and accommodations are not a problem. After a couple of "shakedown cruises" you can set your sights higher. Is your passport up to date? Let's go then!

There are a number of websites that can assist you in finding the necessary information. The ARRL website has a good section on international licensing at **www.arrl.org/international-operating.** You can also reach out via email to operators who have operated from your chosen location before. Most are quite willing to help you out by answering questions and even making recommendations or introductions. Soon you'll have airline tickets and your gear packed for the trip!

An alternative to figuring it all out on your own is to join forces with a group making a trip of their own. If one of your club members has gone on DXpeditions, that's a good place to start your inquiries. They may be planning another trip, or know someone who is, and be willing to make an introduction. You can also contact DXpedition operators from teams that have made recent trips, perhaps by approaching them after a presentation. If you're enthusiastic and keep at it, you should

be able to eventually find a team in need of another operator. Here's where your practice trips will come in handy as experience the group will value. You'll have to fit in with their plans and style, contributing and assisting as requested. Nevertheless, the experience will be invaluable to you.

Describing the process of conducting a DXpedition is well beyond the scope of this book. Every trip is different but all require a lot of detailed and painstaking effort to be successful. Start small, work your way up, soak up information from every source available, and someday we'll see your face on the cover of our favorite magazine with a weathered but happy smile!

Supporting DXpeditions

As you will find out if you go on a DXpedition, they can be expensive undertakings! To put a team of operators on a rock in the middle of the ocean or on a bleak uninhabited island near one of the Earth's poles — and get them back home again safely — requires a lot of resources and planning. Recent DXpeditions to some of the rarest islands have operating budgets of more than $500,000! Needless to say, not all of this expense is borne by the operating team. Sponsors are required. Manufacturers often donate or loan equipment to DXpeditions but that won't pay for a boat!

DXers are encouraged to support the DXpedition by making a donation as requested and encouraging your DX club to do the same. While it is most helpful to donate before the DXpedition hits the airwaves, it is also acceptable to make a donation with your QSL request.

The following are just a few of the organizations that raise money to support DXpeditions and who are themselves supported themselves by the donations of individual DXers: European DX Foundation (EUDXF, **www.eudxf.de**); German DX Foundation (GDXF, **www.gdxf.de**); INDEXA (**www.indexa.org**); Northern California DX Foundation (**www.ncdxf.org**).

Many DXpeditions are low-key "holiday style" operations. Kai, KE4PT, brought along a magnetic loop antenna and QRP radio on a trip to New Zealand and enjoyed operating using the JT65 digital mode. [Courtesy Kai Siwiak, KE4PT]

DXing Equipment — The Next Step

As a DXer with some experience in the log, you'll have used your station enough to have found some of its weak spots

CQ DX Hall of Fame

The *CQ* DX Hall of Fame (started in 1967) recognizes those amateurs who have made major contributions to DXing. The activities and accomplishments that qualify one for membership in these elite groups involve both significant accomplishments as an operator or DXpeditioner, and considerable personal sacrifice that can usually be described by the phrase "above and beyond the call of duty." A maximum of two people may be inducted into the DX Hall of Fame each year.

CQ DX Hall of Fame Members as of June 2016, sorted by call sign:

9V1YC	James Brooks
DJ6SI	Baldur Drobnica
DJ9ZB	Franz Langner
Editor/Publisher	Geoff Watts
G3KMA	Roger Ballister
G3NUG	Neville Cheadle
G3SXW	Roger Western
G3TXF	Nigel Cawthorne
G7VJR	Michael Wells
I1JQJ/IK1ADH	Mauro & Valeria Pregliasco
JA1BK	Kan Mizoguchi
JA1DM	Masayoshi Ebisawa
JH1AJT	Yasuo "Zorro" Miyazawa
K3LP	David Collingham
K4MQG	Robert "Gary" Dixon
K4UEE	Robert Allphin
K5YY	Dr. Sanford Hutson
K6NRJ	Nigel Jolly and the crew of the RV Braveheart
K7LMU	Chuck Swain
K9AJ	Michael J. McGirr
KØIR	Ralph Fedor
KV4AA	Richard C. Spenceley
N1DG	Don Greenbaum
N2OO	Bob Schenck
N4AA	Carl Smith
N4MM	John Kanode
N4XP	Tom Harrell
N7NG	Wayne Mills
OH2BH	Martti Laine
ON4UN	John Devoldere
P29JS/VK9NS	Jim Smith
RAEM	Ernst Krenkel
SMØAGD	Eric Sjolund
UA4WHX/AC4LN	Vladimir Bykov
VP2VB	Danny Weil
W1BB	Stewart S. Perry
W1FH	Charlie Mellen
W1JR	Joe Reisert
W1WY	Frank Anzalone
W2CTN	John M. Cummings

W2GHK	Stuart Meyer
W3HNK	Joe Arcure
W4BPD	Gus Browning
W4DQS	H. Dale Strieter
W4DR	Robert Eshleman
W4KVX	Don Chesser
W4NL	Lynn Lamb
W4OPM	C. J. (Joe) Hiller
W6AM	Don C. Wallace
W6ISQ	John Troster
W6KG & W6QL	Lloyd & Iris Colvin
W6OAT	Rusty Epps
W6QD	Herb Becker
W6RGG	Robert Vallio
W6RJ	Robert Ferrero
W8OK	Frank Schwab
W9BRD	Rodney Newkirk
W9KNI	Robert Locher
WØGJ	Glenn Johnson
WA4JQS	Anthony W. DePrato
WA6AUD	Hugh Cassidy
WB2CHO/VP2ML	Chod Harris
WB4ZNH	Carl Henson
WØAR	Lee Bergren
XE1CI	Nellie de Lazard
ZL2AWJ	Ted Thorpe

Captain Nigel Jolly, K6NRJ, and the crew of the RV Braveheart were inducted into the *CQ* DX Hall of Fame in 2016 for their service providing transportation for DXpeditions to remote locations such as Campbell Island, South Orkney, Heard Island, Ducie Island, Kerguelen, South Sandwich, South Georgia and many others. Bob Allphin, K4UEE, a frequent passenger on Braveheart, presented the award. [Robert Pestinger, KC8RP, photo]

and have a list of features you need. Now's the time to upgrade, including obtaining the Amateur Extra license for the additional frequencies that are prime DX territory! Before you begin changing your equipment, make a list of what your station can and cannot do. Get the advice of more experienced DXers to see if you're missing something important or are yearning for a feature or gadget that really doesn't make much difference.

A cautionary note — there is no substitute for being on the air! All the gear in the world and all the Internet bandwidth won't put your call in the DX log. It's easy to get lost in the gadgetry of DXing. As you improve your station's capabilities, build for reliability. A fancy, but broken, amplifier or antenna doesn't make any QSOs! Your goal should be to put out a solid signal every time you operate and to get plenty of "chair time."

HF Transceiver

A transceiver with 100 W of RF output will generally remain adequate. Upgrade to one of the rigs that uses advanced DSP technology to create the IF filters or purchase a complete set of filters for your radio. Modern filtering designs can be a very powerful listening tool! Other DSP functions, such as several levels and styles of noise reduction and auto-notch filters will be useful, as well. You may want to consider a software-defined radio (SDR) for the flexibility it can offer.

Accessories, such as the microphone and paddle, should be selected to fit your operating preferences. Evaluate different types of microphone elements on the air to find the one that gives you punchy but crisp and clear audio. For DXing, high and low frequency response is secondary to intelligibility over difficult paths and in pileups. As your CW competency and speed increase you may want a paddle with a lighter touch. An external keyer with message memories or a computer interface may make operating more convenient. Don't be afraid to start trying different styles of these very important interfaces between you and the radio!

Sound interfaces and suitable software to enable digital mode operation will become useful as you pursue DX on those modes. Make sure you adjust the audio levels correctly to avoid overdriving your rig and causing interference to other stations.

As you pursue rarer DX over more difficult paths, or DX on the low bands, obtaining an amplifier will prove to be a good step. It needn't be a top-of-the-line, 1500 W continuous-duty auto-tune model. Amps that put out 500 or 1000 W or so are perfectly adequate. There are lots of used amplifiers that will give plenty of good service. Make sure your shack is wired for the additional power (most amplifiers require 240 V service), and that your coax is capable of handling the higher power.

HF Antennas

By far the biggest improvement you can make to your station is the antenna. You'll probably want to consider some sort of tower and beam antenna. This is a great investment, one of the best the DXer could ever make. A small *tribander* (a rotatable Yagi antenna that operates on 20-15-10 meters) at 40 to 50 feet will provide a noticeable improvement over wire antennas on both transmit and receive. Wires may still be used for the low bands or the tower itself may be fed as a vertical.

The 30, 17, and 12 meter bands become increasingly important as the DX becomes rarer. Be sure to at least have wire antennas for these bands, particularly for 30 and 17 meters. If you can obtain a beam antenna for 17 and 12 meters it will make a big difference because those bands often provide a contact with a DXpedition or rare station when 20, 15, and 10 meters are too crowded.

If you get interested in DXing on the low bands, you'll want to consider dedicated receiving antennas. Most low-band transmitting antennas pick up considerable noise and may make it difficult to copy weak DX stations. A Beverage receiving antenna can greatly improve your low-band capabilities at a very low investment. A Beverage is simply a long wire (more than one wavelength) a few feet above the ground, and can be terminated with a resistor to ground or left open for bidirectional operation. Signals received on a Beverage are weaker than they are on a transmitting antenna, but the noise is *much* weaker, yielding a net improvement in readability. Specialized arrays of short verticals or loops can also provide improvements in low-band receiving.

Pay particular attention to your feed lines and associated accessory equipment. Don't throw away your hard work and expense by using inferior cable, connectors, or construction techniques. Pay attention to the details and "do it right." Individual fractions of a dB saved by careful assembly of station components can add up to significant differences on the air. Proper assembly reduces station down time too!

Eventually you'll approach some rarefied air — 300 DXCC entities or 200 grids or band-mode-zone totals that seemed unattainable not so long ago. Remember? You may also begin chasing DXCC award endorsements for single bands or single modes, or the advanced DX awards such as 5BDXCC and 5BWAZ. At this point, you've become a Big Gun! Don't forget what it was like to be a Little Pistol and the magic spell of your first DX QSO. Your assignment? Be a mentor and a friend to an up-and-coming Little Pistol so that they will become a Big Gun someday, just like you!

3.2.7 VHF DXing

6 Meters

A DX band? Yes! As the nickname "The Magic Band" attests, 6 meters can provide some of the most exciting DXing of any band. Again, many modes of propagation are available, but sporadic E is probably the most common. Occurring in the spring and early summer and again in December, sporadic E can provide DX contacts up to 4000 miles and sometimes more. However, the use of "sporadic" is quite appropriate for this kind of propagation. You may listen to the 6 meter band for months and not hear any stations outside your local area, and then one day without warning, the band will fill up with stations. At the peak of the solar cycle, 6 meters provides intercontinental contacts via the F layer.

This band is the lowest practical frequency for EME (moonbounce) operations. Stations utilizing four or more high gain antennas and high power have been able to communicate internationally even though the band is closed for other propagation modes. No longer a curiosity, 6 meters is a legitimate DX band. Many stations have DXCC totals well over 100 on this band.

All modes are used on 6 meters. As on HF, SSB is the easiest mode to operate, but it is the least effective when signals are weak. CW skill will help considerably to add to your

This impressive collection of antennas at K5TR is quite effective on the 50, 144, 222, and 432 MHz bands. [George Fremin, K5TR, photo]

6 meter VUCC and DXCC total, as well as helping to identify beacon stations transmitting on the lower part of the band. Digital modes such as WSJT are very popular on 6 meters, especially for EME and meteor-scatter propagation.

2 Meters

While 2 meters is primarily used for local contacts, especially on FM repeaters, it is also a DX band. DX, or "weak-signal" work is concentrated in the lower segment of the band, from 144.000 to 144.200 or so. Through the use of meteor scatter (reflecting signals off the short-lived ionized trails of meteors as they enter the Earth's atmosphere and burn up) and tropospheric scatter propagation (relying on atmospheric anomalies to reflect or duct signals), contacts over multi-hundred-mile paths are achievable. While meteor scatter is possible virtually every day, veteran 2 meter operators mark their calendars with the dates of the major annual meteor showers to take advantage of the higher number of meteors during those periods. Websites such as **www.pingjockey.net** are used to coordinate schedules.

Sporadic-E propagation to 1000 miles or more is possible on rare occasions on two meters. Many Europeans have earned credits for their Mixed DXCC on 2 meters using terrestrial modes. However, most DXers who have earned DXCC on 2 meters have done so through the use of moonbounce (EME). This is most often done with the WSJT digital modes, which allow even modest stations to participate.

VHF Equipment

On VHF, one of the many fine 50 W or higher "all-band" rigs is more than sufficient to get you started. You will be primarily operating on 6 and 2 meters. A CW filter is a "nice to have" feature on the VHF bands but not critical. For antennas, you can get started with dipoles or loops but there are many inexpensive 2- or 3-element 6 meter beam antennas available. For 2 meters, a Yagi with five or more elements is easy to mount and rotate and will yield much better results than an omnidirectional antenna. You can try building your own antenna from the plans in *VHF and UHF Antenna Classics* or try some of WA5VJB's "Cheap Yagi" designs at **www. wa5vjb.com**.

Use horizontally polarized antennas because that is the standard on VHF. Low-loss coax is a must — every dB lost in the feed line is very hard to make up! And a higher antenna is usually a better antenna.

Height is important on VHF to increase the distance to your radio horizon. If you aren't in an advantageous location, consider an effective portable or "rover" installation that you can drive to a nearby hilltop — even the roof of a parking garage will do!

Once you've tried a bit of VHF/UHF operation, the biggest bang for your ham radio buck is to install bigger antennas mounted higher above ground. Propagation is often marginal on 6 and 2 meters, particularly after you've worked all of the nearby grids and those common on sporadic-E or whatever tropospheric propagation is common in your area. Antennas with longer booms and more elements — for example, a 4 or 5-element Yagi on 6 meters and 10 elements or more on 2 meters — often make the crucial difference in being heard when signals are weak and openings very brief. Fortunately such antennas are relatively small and easily turned by an inexpensive rotator.

Power amplifiers and mast-mounted preamps on the higher bands will pay dividends by increasing your ability to take advantage of marginal openings. You'll also begin to hear and work weaker stations, increasing the number of stations available for you to contact. Feed line and connector quality is crucial for VHF DXing so don't scrimp. Ask for advice from veteran VHF DXers.

Finding VHF DX Band Openings

VHF DX band openings can be few and far between, so you won't want to miss one! Many of the same resources used to determine if an HF band is open also apply to 6 and 2 meters. The DX Cluster covers both bands, and many of the stations in the Reverse Beacon Network have 6 meter receivers. There are also beacon stations around the world transmitting continuously on specific frequencies. They usually transmit a repeating CW message along the lines of "V V V DE W1AW W1AW FN31." Since these beacons are mostly privately owned and operated, they tend to come and go, so you should check on the web for a current list of active beacons.

Online chat rooms can provide real-time alerts when the bands open. One popular site among the VHF DX community is **www. on4kst.com**. It is free (donations are accepted), and includes band- and region-specific chat rooms as well as links to the DX Cluster. DX Maps (**www.dxmaps.com**) is another source of real-time information about VHF/UHF band openings.

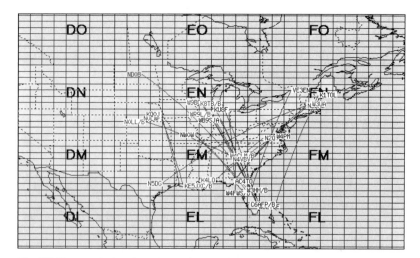

The DX Maps website shows at a glance where contacts have been made in the past few minutes, based on spots from users and from CW Skimmer stations. Here, a 6 meter sporadic E opening is in progress, with stations in the southeast working into the northeast and midwest.

3.2.8 Resources for DXers

Books and Magazines

• The ARRL Store (**www.arrl.org/shop**) offers a number of books and videos on DX and DXing — just enter "DX" into the search window for a list of available items.

• *The Complete DXer* by Bob Locher, W9KNI is an excellent tutorial to turn a Little Pistol into a Medium Gun. Bob's *A Year of DX* recounts his adventures pursuing the CQ DX Marathon's top spot over the course of a year. Both are available from the ARRL Store.

• *Up Two!* and *Contesting in Africa* by Roger Western, G3SXW — funny, engaging stories by G3SXW of his many one- and two-man DXpeditions to rare spots around the globe.

• *Nifty E-Z Guide to Adventures in DXing* by Jeff Cantor, K1ZN covers a wide range of topics related to DXing including antenna, transceiver, amplifiers, propagation prediction tools and radio operating protocols used for successfully making DX contacts.

• *DX Magazine* (**www.dxpub.com**) is a storied bi-monthly publication with a long history of stories about recent DXpeditions, large and small.

• DX columns are included each month in *QST*, *CQ*, and most other national amateur radio society magazines.

DX Clubs

• A list of links to DX club websites around the world is available at **www.ac6v.com**.

• To find local or regional DX clubs affiliated with the ARRL, check **www.arrl.org/find-a-club**.

DX Awards

• A website devoted to awards, including K1BV's directory of more than 3000 Amateur Radio awards, can be found at **www.dxawards.com**.

DX News Services and Websites

• 425 DX Bulletin, **www.425dxn.org**
• *Announced DX Operations*, **www.ng3k.com**
• *DX Coffee,* **www.dxcoffee.com/eng/**
• *DX News,* **dxnews.com**
• *DX World,* **www.dx-world.net**
• *OPDXA Bulletin,* **www.papays.com/opdx.html**
• *QRZ DX* and *DX Magazine*, **www.dxpub.com**
• *The Daily DX,* **www.dailydx.com**
• *W1AW DX Bulletin,* **www.arrl.org/bulletins**

3.3 Confirming the Contact — QSLing

For DXers who are pursuing awards, confirming the contact is almost as important as the contact itself. The paper QSL has been a part of Amateur Radio and DXing for as long as radio itself has existed. Electronic confirmation systems, such as ARRL's Logbook of The World, complement paper QSLs and are equally valid for awards. In either case, they provide the confirmation that actually proves the contact. After all, without a confirmation the DXer might never know that he or she had worked a pirate or a bootlegger!

3.3.1 Electronic QSO Confirmation

Why, in this 21st century age of instantaneous communication and digital information, are there not systems to confirm a QSO electronically? Why, there are! The two most-used systems are eQSL (**www.eqsl.cc**) and the ARRL's Logbook of The World (LoTW, **www.arrl.org/lotw** — discussed in more detail later in this section). Both systems require a registration process and that you upload an electronic copy of your logbook. Your logging program should support the Amateur Data Interface Format (ADIF — see the sidebar earlier in this section) in order to make it easy to upload your QSOs for confirmations and qualify for awards.

Not all awards programs accept all forms of electronic QSLs. For example, the ARRL does not accept eQSL confirmations for its awards while Logbook of The World confirmations are accepted for its major awards. Each system publishes a list of awards for

Hamad, 9K2HN is one of many DXers around the world using the Logbook of The World electronic contact confirmation system. Hamad has uploaded more than 300,000 QSOs made over many years.

which electronic QSLs are accepted. There are complete instructions for using the system and descriptions of how the system works on their respective home pages.

Most DXpeditions eventually upload their logs to LoTW so your QSOs can be confirmed automatically. If you want a paper QSL you'll have to request that separately by using one of the methods described below. The electronic LoTW confirmation may be used for ARRL awards and other award programs are being added to LoTW. As of 2016, LoTW supports DXCC, VUCC, WAS, and the CQ WPX award program. Check the LoTW website to see what other award programs are being

Logbook of The World (LoTW)

By the mid to late 1990s, as postage and printing costs rose and delivery difficulties and delays increased, many people were asking "why not the Internet?" for confirmations. In July 2000, the ARRL Board of Directors approved development of Logbook of The World (LoTW), a depository of QSO information that would allow participants to submit radio logs containing digitally signed QSO records. Logs from all participants would be collected in a secure, central database, where they could be scanned for matching confirmations. A pair of matching QSO records resulted in a confirmation that could be sent to the appropriate award system, where awards credit for both participants could be automatically recorded.

Logbook of The World went "live" in September 2003. By mid-2016, the system had almost 90,000 users worldwide, had received more than 750 million QSOs, and had made over 130 million confirmations. Using only QSOs confirmed in LoTW, users have confirmed DXCC on 9 bands and WAS on 10 bands. Some stations have LoTW-only Mixed DXCC totals over

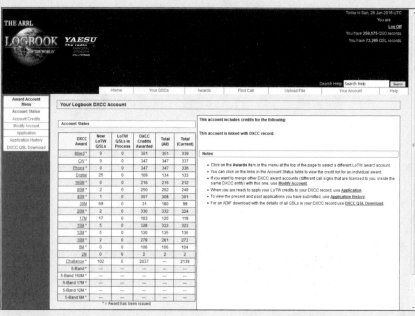

The DXCC credits of one active DXer as reported by LoTW. One more credit to go for 10BDXCC!

300! Of all current entities on the ARRL DXCC List, only Mount Athos does not have logs in LoTW.

Trustworthy Data

Logbook of The World is designed to generate QSO confirmations that can be used for awards credits. That is to say, when you submit a log, your data is compared to all of the existing data in the database. If the log data you submit matches that in another station's record, the result is a confirmed QSO record. Either you or the other operator may then apply that confirmed QSO credit to various awards. All of this data is handled electronically, from the submission of the original logs to placement of the credit in an award database.

LoTW goes beyond the concept of a paper QSL card. A single QSL card is a one-sided request for a confirmation from the other side of the QSO. LoTW begins by verifying that a QSO has occurred between two stations, based on the "signed" data submitted by each.

Participants must be assured that each confirmation submitted to the system is authentic — that it comes from the true owner of the associated call sign. With digital signature technology, it is possible for an amateur to indelibly "mark" QSO data with a signature connected to his/her call sign. The Logbook of The World system uses digital signatures to ensure the authenticity of every QSO record. Digital signatures utilize a technology called Public Key Infrastructure or PKI. These signatures cannot be forged, and the QSO data cannot be altered without detection. This not only ensures that we know the origin of the data, but also assures us that the data has not been altered anywhere along the way.

A Digital Certificate

In order to be able to submit your log to Logbook of The World, you must obtain a digital certificate. A digital certificate ties the identity of a participant to a digital key pair, which allows an electronic message to be signed.

For digital signatures to be trusted, we must be sure of the identity of each person to whom a certificate is assigned. We need to verify you are who you say you are. The security of the entire system depends heavily on the method used for verifying the user's identity. This process is called Authentication. Authentication for US call signs relies on a combination of information in the FCC license database and postal mail addresses. Authentication for non-US calls relies on photocopies of a radio license and an official identification document.

You'll need to apply for, receive and install the digital certificate on your system

to become a registered LoTW user and start submitting QSOs. The program *TQSL*, downloadable from the LoTW website, is for used generating requests for digital certificates and storing the resulting digital certificates that you receive from ARRL.

The Hows and Whens

To get started, visit the LoTW website at **www.arrl.org/ logbook-of-the-world** where you can find directions, updates, news, and tips. This system will be "always under construction" as we add software updates, additional capabilities and more user information. Once you have received and installed your digital certificate, *TQSL* can be used to prepare log data for submission to LoTW.

Anyone with a suitable computer can submit data to LoTW as soon as they have received a digital certificate from ARRL. LoTW accepts signed logs in either ADIF

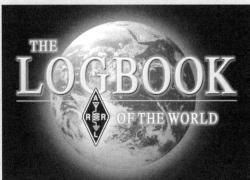

(Amateur Data Interchange Format) or Cabrillo (contest log) format, which are standard in most commercial logging software. Log files are "signed" using a digital certificate. The signing process is a mathematical operation that will work best on computers with a fast, modern processor, but older computers will work.

You may send in QSO information from your logs as far back in time as 1945. Computer logging really got going only in the late 1980s and early 1990s, so it is not going to be likely that you will find many confirmations for QSOs farther back than that. But many people have typed their old logs into logging programs, so one never knows. You can query the system to determine if a certain station has submitted a log.

Although there may be cases when you will want to use *TQSL*'s ability to manually enter a submission for a small group of QSOs (perhaps just the ones you need), the best method will be to submit all of your contacts to give others credit for your QSO even if you have no interest in theirs. The first time, submit your whole log. After that, submit that portion created since you last submitted (resubmitting all of your QSOs just slows down the system and is of no benefit to you).

A number of popular logging and con-

testing programs include built-in support for LoTW. That makes it easier to select a group of QSOs and prepare them for submission. Some logging programs automate the process completely, digitally signing the QSOs with your certificate, generating the appropriate file for submission, and calling up your e-mail program to send the file to ARRL.

How am I going to receive awards credit? Look for links to "Awards" on the LoTW website. Here you can find out what countries or states you have confirmed in the system and follow the directions to select the ones that you would like to use for credit for your DXCC, WAS, VUCC or CQ WPX award. (More awards may be supported in the future.) You can also link your existing DXCC or VUCC records to your Logbook account to see what credits you already have and where the new Logbook credits fit in.

One very important point: ARRL is not the "QSL Manager" for the stations submitting logs to Logbook of the World. If a contact is not in The log, you will need to work it out with the station involved. We will not search the log for your contact. If you can't submit a match, you won't be able to receive a credit. Broken calls and incorrect QSO information won't be acceptable. A time window allows some leeway to allow for variations in time keeping, however.

What does it cost? Everyone is invited to submit data — Logbook wants all logs! For this reason, there is no charge for submitting logs. This all takes time and money, of course, and LoTW is being paid for initially by ARRL members, so there is a per-QSO charge for each credit used toward an award. Check the LoTW website for the current fee schedule — you will be pleasantly surprised to see how much less expensive it is than the cost to print paper cards and exchange them via postal mail. Detailed instructions for using LoTW confirmations for award credit are shown on the website.

While we hope everyone will use and enjoy Logbook of The World, we realize that there will be those who cannot, or will not, use it. ARRL will always accept traditional QSL cards for its awards using the same applications and methods now in place. We do anticipate the nature of QSLing will change. We are confident that everyone will find their own "best" way to make use of this new technology. Most people use a combination of Logbook and traditional QSLing methods. Others have started "from scratch" and built credits for awards that in the past would have taken many years and hundreds or thousands of dollars in postage and printing costs to achieve. Some of those who have avoided operating because of the resulting QSL responsibilities have become more active. Will you be one of them?

supported, as new ones are added from time to time.

Electronic QSLs are unlikely to ever completely replace paper QSLs because the experience of exchanging QSLs remains very enjoyable. A collection of paper QSLs built up over a lifetime contains many beautiful souvenirs. It is likely that DXers will continue to exchange a paper card for initial contacts and use electronic QSLing for subsequent confirmations and for contest QSOs.

Online QSL Request System (OQRS)

Many DXpeditions have started using the Online QSL Request System (OQRS) created by Bernd Koch, DF3CB, in 2003. This system allows you, the DXer, to request a paper QSL and also make supporting donations to the expedition. This frees the expedition from handling all of your cards — which they rarely need for any reason — and allows you to cover postage and handling costs completely online. No stamps, envelopes, postal delays (or worse), and you still get a card!

Each DXpedition operates its own OQRS independently although most DXpeditions use the Club Log OQRS resource. This allows each expedition to tailor their QSLing practices as required. You'll need to follow the expedition's instructions for requesting a QSL and supporting the expedition.

Club Log

Club Log (**www.clublog.org**) is a free web-based application developed by Michael, G7VJR, and Marios, 5B4WN, that analyzes log files from radio amateurs all over the world. Using the logs, Club Log offers a wide range of reports for your own benefit, and identifies large scale trends from the sum of all activity in the database.

As of June 2016, there were 176 clubs, 40,002 users and 53,499 call signs registered in Club Log. Each day, an average of over 1000 new logs are uploaded and more than 360 million log entries are available for analysis. Most DXpeditions use Club Log and you can search for your QSOs and request direct or bureau QSLs through the site, using PayPal to cover the costs. You can also enable "Incoming OQRS" so other operators can request your direct or bureau card through the system.

Club Log sponsors competitions among clubs and creates Leaderboards for major DXpeditions to track which DXers have worked the DXpedition on the most bands/modes. It also includes a lot of tools for DXers, such as great circle maps, and even QSL label printing utilities.

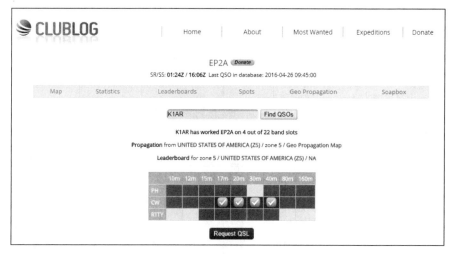

DXpeditions often upload their logs to Club Log while the DXpedition is still in progress. This allows DXers to be sure they are in the log, and to request QSL cards via the OQRS system after the expedition is over. Other useful information such as propagation charts based on actual contacts is available as well.

3.3.2 Paper QSLs

While online QSL requests and all-electronic QSLs are faster and cheaper than physically sending paper QSLs, some DX stations still like to receive them. But it's important to realize that a DX station receives a lot more incoming cards than he or she really needs. Therefore, it's really important for DXers to make it easy for their cards to be answered.

First, the card itself should be designed for the convenience of the DX station or QSL manager (see below). Having to process literally tens of thousands of QSLs, it's easy to understand how a manager could get a little upset with having to hunt for information around the card or on both sides. The QSL card should have all the information on one side only. It should be easy to read and in a logical order.

There is certain information required on a QSL card that is to be submitted for DXCC credit: the call signs of both stations, the DXCC entity, mode, date, time, and the frequency band used. For VUCC, the station's grid square should be included. Desirable information includes the county and if the DXer lives on an island, an Islands on the Air (IOTA) identifier. This way, if DX stations happen to be pursuing awards, they will be able to use the DXer's QSL card for their own purposes.

There are three ways to get a card to its destination: by bureau, by QSL service, and by direct mail. Each has its advantages, although there are some differences in the speed. There are also some differences in how a DX station will handle them. The method the DXer uses depends upon his or her own personal requirements.

The ARRL Outgoing QSL Service provides economical service to the countries that have incoming bureaus. Stations in the US receive cards through the ARRL Incoming Bureau System. Full details of both of these services are available at **www.arrl.org/qsl-service**. While the QSL bureau system is slow, with turnaround time sometimes exceeding a year or more, this may be considered an efficient and cost effective method for QSLing. This is especially true when compared with postal pilferage of direct QSLs in some parts of the world. The disadvantages of the bureau system are that in some countries served by bureaus, only the cards of members are delivered. The bureau system is highly recommended when QSLing to countries with large populations of hams.

The GlobalQSL system (**www.globalqsl.com**) bypasses a great deal of the paperwork by allowing you to upload your log (in ADIF format) directly to their service. Attractive two-sided color QSLs that you design using their online tools and (optionally) your own photos are then printed and include QSO data from your log data printed directly on each card. The cards are then sent to bureaus and managers directly. This is slower (and less

Front and back of a typical QSL card produced by GlobalQSL.com. Note that the QSO details are printed directly on the card.

expensive) than direct mailing individual cards but faster (and more expensive) than the bureau system.

Another QSL forwarding service is the K3FN QSL Service (**www.airmailpostage. com/k3fncustomqslservice.html**) formerly operated by WF5E for many years. For a small amount per card the QSL service will forward your cards to the bureau, by direct mail, or to a manager. Cards are returned via the DXer's own incoming bureau unless special arrangements are made.

Turnaround time via QSL services like this is reduced as cards are sent to bureaus in smaller quantities and cards are sent to managers with return postage. In most cases, it isn't even necessary to know the manager as the QSL service keeps track of managers and will get the card to the right place. The success rate of using a QSL service is very good.

QSL Managers

Some DX stations prefer to spend their time making QSOs and arrange for another ham to act as their "QSL Manager" and handle their QSLing. In some cases, mail service is unreliable in the DX station's country and a QSL manager is the only way to respond to QSL requests. All the advice in this section relating to sending paper QSLs applies equally to DX stations that do their own QSLing and QSL managers.

Direct QSLs

QSLing direct isn't cheap, so be prepared to spend some money if this method is used. Presentation is worth a lot when QSLing direct, so carefully prepare the card and envelopes to maximize the chance of a response. The bureau, if available, is often more convenient for amateurs who are permanent residents.

Direct QSLing starts with a good address. DX stations rarely give a complete address

Rose-Anne Lawrence, KB1DMW, sorts cards at the ARRL Outgoing QSL Bureau at ARRL HQ. During times of good propagation and high activity, the bureau handles a million or more cards from ARRL members destined for QSL bureaus in other countries.

over the air. Most stations are listed on the QRZ.com website, with complete QSL instructions. If the station is not listed, search the Internet for "QSL routes" and numerous sites will be found. At least one will have an address that you can use.

The envelopes themselves are important. The best size is a 4¾ × 6½ inch outer air mail envelope, and a 4½ × 6¼-inch inner air mail envelope for returns (some stations prefer the larger size for the return as well). If possible, the addresses should be typed directly on the envelope, or printed labels. It is important to

remember that *no* call signs should go on the outside of any envelope, again to avoid unwanted attention. The envelope should look as ordinary as possible.

Return Postage

The old saying "The final courtesy of a QSO is a QSL" should be changed to "It is discourteous to send a QSL card *without* return postage provisions." As this is written, the cost of a postage stamp in most countries to send a card in an envelope to another country is well over $1.00. Add the cost of the card itself and an envelope, and multiply it by a few thousand for an active DX station, and it should be easy to see why there is poor or no response to cards received without return postage. A word to the wise: If you really want that QSL card, be sure that return postage is provided in whatever form is necessary.

In the past, one popular way of providing return postage was the International Reply Coupon (IRC). IRCs could be purchased at a local post office and were redeemable for the lowest air mail rate in any Universal Postal Union (UPU) country. However, IRCs are no longer sold by the United States Postal Service, and while foreign IRCs are still redeemable at the USPS, most postal clerks are unfamiliar with the process. After a long run, the IRC is rapidly becoming obsolete.

Some DX stations will still accept IRCs. Some are able to redeem them for postage at their post office, but more often sell them to other DXers. Be aware that in some countries, the lowest air mail rate won't provide enough postage to return an envelope and QSL card. Sometimes it takes two IRCs to provide enough postage.

Another way to provide return postage is by sending unused stamps of the country of the DX station or QSL manager with sufficient value to provide return postage. This allows the manager to fill out the card and

put it in the envelope without converting money or redeeming IRCs. Purchase postage and affix it to the envelope. If this method is used, it's best to put the postage on the return envelope so that it may only be used for returning the DXer's cards. K3FN (**www.airmailpostage.com**) offers airmail stamps of many countries for sale as well as useful postal supplies for international QSLing.

Some DXers prefer to provide return postage by sending a ubiquitous "green stamp," the United States one dollar bill. There are several problems associated with using green stamps, not the least of which is mail pilferage. Even mail passing through the US is not immune and in some countries if the envelope is identified as going to an Amateur Radio operator it is almost certain to disappear. In addition to exchange problems at the country of destination, there are some countries around the world where it is illegal to have US currency.

One dollar no longer will buy sufficient postage in many countries. So two are required if the DXer expects to get a return. Green stamps are used mostly for convenience but the price paid may well be loss of the card.

Many DX stations now take advantage of online payment systems such as PayPal as a way to receive funds for return postage. Some even state that your paper QSL is not needed — all you need to do is send the QSO details in the notes section of the PayPal transaction, and a card will be sent to you. PayPal allows you to pay using a credit card if you don't have (or want) a PayPal account.

One word about QSL turnaround: Many DXers have far too high expectations of how quickly they should receive QSLs from DXpeditions. It depends upon the operation and whether a special effort is put into quick turnaround, but six months is very reasonable for QSL return. Allow a minimum of at least six months before even thinking about a second QSL, even if friends are receiving theirs. A card may just have been near the bottom of the pile.

3.4 Contesting — Competitive Wireless

It's natural in any activity for individuals to use competition to compare their abilities with their peers. Amateur Radio is no different. Contests have been organized almost since the beginning of wireless communications to allow operators to compare their skills and stations against others. In fact, it has been said that the first contest occurred when the third ham got on the air and the other two competed to see who could contact him first!

There are many reasons to engage in ham radio contests (also known as *radiosport*). Just as there are many levels of athletes, from the occasionally engaged to the devoted aficionado, contesting attracts many types of entrants. For some hams, contesting is their primary interest. They build highly capable stations, travel thousands of miles to desirable locations or assemble a skilled team of master operators. Others operate just a few minutes or hours to try to pick up some needed DXCC entities or states or to hand out some contacts from their own rare location. Most contesters, whether they are on the air for an hour or a weekend, operate just for the pleasure of reaching out and touching so many other hams in so many other places so quickly.

The World Radiosport Team Championship is often called the "Olympics of Ham Radio." Two-operator teams from around the world are invited to compete using identical antennas and power from the same geographic location to level the playing field. The 2014 WRTC medal winners were (l-r) Silver: OM3BH and OM3GI; Gold: N6MJ and KL9A; Bronze DL1IAO and DJ5MW [Bob Wilson, N6TV, photo]

3.4.1 Types of Contests

Along with the most common phone and CW contests, there are a growing number of digital-mode events. There are also plenty of specialty contests intended to foster interest and activity from a particular region or in a specific band, mode, or style of operating. Some follow a "world-works-world" format, while others are "world-works-target area" or even limited to stations in one country or area. Some contests are 48-hour marathon events, others are 24, 12, or even 4 hours long. And on both VHF+ and HF, even shorter contests known as *sprints* are becoming more popular all the time.

Contests are held throughout the year. A few of the more popular contests include:

North American QSO Parties in January and August, sponsored by the *National Contest Journal* (**www.ncjweb.com**); separate weekends for CW, SSB, and RTTY. Exchange name and state/province/country.

ARRL November Sweepstakes held on the first (CW) and third (Phone) weekends of November. The exchange is one of the more complicated, and includes the year the operator was first licensed.

ARRL International DX Contest with a CW weekend in February and Phone in

Contesting History

Contests have their genesis in the early days of message handling when the ability to relay messages quickly and accurately was the hallmark of a good operator. Even in the days of spark, there were a number of exercises that attempted to move messages across the country as quickly as possible. The signature of message handling is writ large across contesting today. Many of today's top operators got started as traffic handlers in the National Traffic System™ (NTS™). If you look at the information exchanged during the ARRL Sweepstakes — number, category, call, check and section — you'll recognize the header of an ARRL Radiogram. The characteristics of a good traffic handler remain the attributes of a top contester: accurate, efficient, flexible, capable.

The first formal on-the-air competition was the 1927 International Relay Contest, sponsored by the ARRL as an extension to the annual "Transatlantic Tests" in which stations attempted to make contact with stations outside the US and Canada (which explains why stations on CW traditionally call "CQ TEST" when soliciting contacts). This event has changed names several times, growing into the ARRL International DX Contest of today. The need also grew for a domestic contest emphasizing shorter distances within the North American continent. The result was the creation of the ARRL Sweepstakes contest in 1930. Contesting on the VHF and higher bands got its start in 1948 and the first radioteletype contest was held in 1957.

March. This is a "world-works W/VE" event, so DX stations may only work stations in the 48 states, District of Columbia, and Canadian provinces

CQ World Wide DX Contest (**www.cqww.** **com**) sponsored by *CQ* magazine. This is a world-works-world format and is the highest-participation contest of all. CQWW is held on the last full weekends of September (RTTY), October (SSB), and November (CW).

CQ WPX Contest (**www.cqwpx.com**) also sponsored by *CQ* magazine, held in February (RTTY), March (SSB) and May (CW). This is a world-works-world event.

VHF+ contests include the ARRL contests in January, June, and September and the CQ World Wide VHF Contest in July.

State QSO parties ("world-works-state" format) are great events for beginners. For example, the California and Florida QSO parties generate a lot of activity and those states are easy to work. If you are located in a state holding a QSO party, you will be in demand!

The World Radiosport Team Championship (WRTC, see **www.wrtc.info**) is generally regarded as the "Olympics of Ham Radio." It is an invitation-only event held every four years, and features the best operators in the world competing from the same geographic region with identical power and antennas so that the only remaining variable is operator skill and strategy.

One contest specifically aimed at newcomers is the ARRL Rookie Roundup. Amateurs licensed for three years or less are eligible to compete. This six-hour event is held three times per year (SSB in April, RTTY in August and CW in December). Rookies can contact anybody, while Old Timers make contact with only Rookies. Mentoring is a big part of this event!

Categories

Contest sponsors understand that it would not be fair for a megastation with multiple operating positions, kilowatt amplifiers, and operators working each band to compete against a station with just one operator and low power. That's why there are lots of different entry categories.

The main entry categories for contests include:

• Single-operator, where one operator performs all operating and logging functions

• Single-operator Assisted (or "Unlimited"), where the operator may use spotting networks to locate new stations to work.

• Multioperator, Single Transmitter (the rules for this category can get complicated, with limits on how often the station can change bands, and most of the competitive stations in this category actually have multiple transmitters available).

• Multioperator, Multi-transmitter, where a well-equipped station may be operating on two or more bands simultaneously.

There are also classes for High Power, Low Power (usually 100 W maximum), and QRP (usually 5 W output or less). Many contests also have single-band categories for single-operators.

VHF+ contests also have separate categories for "Rover" stations, which move to different grid squares during the contest and can be

It is a tradition on Aruba (P4) that after the contest, all of the visiting operators gather for dinner and relaxation. From the smiles, there are a lot of QSOs in the logs of (l-r) P49V (SK), P40A, P40P, P40YL, P43C, P43A, and P49Y. [John Bayne, KK9A, photo]

contacted again from the new location. Some also have separate categories for "Portable" stations. These are ideal categories for an operator with a disadvantaged home location.

Coexisting with Contests

Sometimes it sounds like a contest has taken over an entire band! In reality, there are plenty of kilohertz without contest activity. On the HF bands, by general agreement there is no contest activity on 60, 30, 17 or 12 meters. On the VHF+ bands, most contest activity takes place on SSB and CW in the so-called "weak signal" segments at the lower edge of the bands, although there is also some FM activity on 2 meters.

Most of the larger contests restrict operation to one mode on a given weekend so you'll just find normal or even lighter activity on the other portions of the bands. Even though there may be more than one contest scheduled during a weekend, most are small enough that activity is clustered around a handful of frequencies. If you choose not to participate, tune around or change bands or modes and you'll likely be able to avoid contest activity. If you have a rotatable antenna, you may be able to point it in a direction that minimizes QRM from stations in the contest but leaves plenty of signal for a comfortable QSO. Choosing frequencies toward the high end of the band segment, away from the lower portions where signals are stronger, will also help. There are usually plenty of opportunities to coexist with a contest.

German YL operators Sandy, DL1QQ, and Irina, DL8DYL, competed at WRTC2014. They are shown here with their on-site referee Rusty Epps, W6OAT. [Bob Wilson, N6TV, photo]

3.4.2 Contesting Basics

So what is a contest anyway? If you encounter someone calling "CQ Contest" on the air, what should you do? If you've found a contest that looks interesting, how can you determine the proper way of operating? Let's start with the basics.

The Contest QSO

A contest is a competition between stations to make as many contacts as possible according to the theme of the contest within the time period defined by the contest rules. Each contact will be as short as possible while still satisfying the rules of contest. Remember, this is a competition so what constitutes a contact is different than during regular day-to-day operating. During a contest, contacts include a minimum of non-contest information.

Each contact consists of five steps that are just like a regular contact but greatly abbreviated:
• One station calls CQ.
• Another station (the "caller") responds to the CQ.
• The CQing station responds with the call sign of the caller, then sends the required information.
• The caller acknowledges receiving the information and sends information back in return.
• The CQing station acknowledges receiving the caller's exchange and ends the contact, usually calling CQ again or otherwise announcing that he is available for a QSO. The caller tunes off to another frequency and works another station, or perhaps finds a clear frequency and calls CQ.

At any point, should one of the stations not receive a call sign or exchange properly, the information is repeated until received correctly. We'll go over that process later in this section.

The Contest Exchange

During each contact, specific information must be exchanged and logged. This information is called the *exchange*. In some contests, the exchange is very simple. For example, in the North American QSO Party, the exchange is your name and state, province, or country. Because "state, province, or country" is so commonly used in contesting, it is often abbreviated SPC or S/P/C. ARRL November Sweepstakes, mentioned earlier, has a lengthy exchange. Most contests keep the exchange simple, beginning with signal report (RS or RST) and adding other information in line with the contest's theme. Here are some common types of information you'll find in contest exchanges:
• *ITU or CQ Zone* — there are 88 ITU Zones (**www.iaru.org/regions.html**) and 40 CQ Zones (go to **www.cq-amateur-radio.com** and look for the *CQ WAZ Award* page).
• *Serial number* — the number of the contact in the contest. Your first contact would be serial number 1 (sometimes sent as 001 for clarity), the next would be 2, and so forth.
• *Name* — just your first or most common name. Nicknames are acceptable.
• *Power* — up to three digits specifying your transmitter power ("KW," "K" or "kilowatt" is sometimes sent instead of "1000").
• *Location code or abbreviation* — for contests that target a specific country or region, this is an abbreviation (such as "TN" for Tennessee in contests that use states) or numeric identifier. It can also be an abbreviated county name, ARRL section, or a grid square in VHF+ contests. The contest sponsor website will define these exactly.

There are other types of information that might be needed in a contest exchange but these cover most contests. When in doubt, check the contest sponsor's website.

If you encounter a contester calling CQ and you'd like to help him with a QSO but don't know the exchange information ask, "What do you need?". The CQing station will respond with something like, "I need your number and ARRL section" or on CW "PSE NR ES ARRL SEC." If it's your first contact in the contest and you live in the Pittsburgh, Pennsylvania, area you would respond with, "You're my number 1 in Western Pennsylvania" or on CW "NR 1 WPA." That's it! Contesters want and need your QSO so don't hesitate to ask them for help.

One common question from new contesters is, "Why are signal reports always 59 or 599?" During a non-contest QSO, accurate signal reports help both stations gauge the clarity of communications during the QSO. Since contest QSOs are so short, typically 10 seconds or less, there is little need for an accurate report. If the contester can hear you, 59 or 599 is just as good as any other report and removes uncertainty from what is sent. It also cues you to mentally prepare to copy the rest of the exchange. On CW, most contesters send 599 as 5NN. The "N" is a form of *cut number* where an abbreviation for a numeral is sent to save time. Other common cut numbers are "A" for 1 and a dash ("T") or "O" for zero. You are expected to convert the cut number character to a real numeral when you enter it into your log, even a computer log.

Contest Scoring

Your final score is based on the total number of contacts and the number of contacts with different locations or attributes, according to the theme of the contest. The usual calculation begins with adding up points from each contact, called *QSO points*. The total is then multiplied by the sum of the different

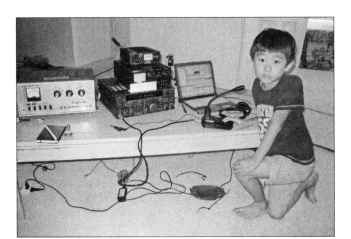

Yoshiki, JF1UCV/KHØUA, likes contesting more than Nintendo. He had eight years of contest experience by the age of 16 (yes...he began contesting at age 8!) [Kuniyoshi Nakada, W1FPU/7L1FPU, photo]

locations or attributes, called *multipliers*. Since each contest has a different system (*vive la difference!*), check the sponsor's rules to compute your score. If you are using a logging program, the software will compute the score for you.

All contacts may have the same QSO point value or the points may vary by band or distance or mode. Here are some examples:

• *North American QSO Party* — each contact counts for 1 point.

• *ARRL 10 Meter Contest* — phone contacts count for 2 points and CW contacts 4 points.

• *CQ World Wide DX* — contacts between stations on different continents are worth 3 points. Contacts between stations in different countries on the same continent count for 1 point, except contacts between stations in different North American countries count for 2 points. Contacts within one's own country do not count for points but can count for multiplier credit.

• *Stew Perry Topband Distance Challenge* — points for each contact are calculated based on the distance between the stations, determined by the grid square exchanged. In addition, QSO points for QSOs with Low Power and QRP stations are multiplied by 2 and 4 respectively.

Multipliers are really the spice of the contest! If contesting were just about working a large number of stations it would be a rather simple game and quickly lose its novelty. Adding the requirement to make contacts with special stations or locations makes things really interesting! You have to continuously balance the benefit of making easy QSOs or chasing multipliers. There are many aspects to consider, with the capabilities of one's station and propagation being the most important.

Check the rules for each contest to find out how multipliers are defined and then go hunting! You'll want to know if each multiplier counts only once or whether you can count multipliers from each band or mode. For example, in the ARRL Sweepstakes each section is counted once and only once — you can work a maximum of 83 section multipliers. In the ARRL DX Contest, though, each different DXCC entity counts as a separate multiplier on each band. There may be different types of multipliers besides locations. The IARU HF Championship also recognizes stations operating from the IARU radio society headquarters in each country as multipliers.

TYPICAL RULES

Now that you're familiar with the basic ideas behind contesting, let's take a close look at a typical contest rule summary.

1. Object. This is where the contest sponsor outlines the goals of the contest, who is eligible to participate, and the bands and/or modes to be used.

2. Date and Contest Period: This is always specified in UTC, and may include a limit on how many hours may be operated in the contest period.

3. Entry Categories: This will generally include single-operator and multioperator categories, power classes, and sometimes separate categories for different modes.

4. Contest Exchange: The sponsor specifies what information must be exchanged to define an acceptable contact.

5. Scoring: Defines how points are earned and the multiplier structure.

6. Miscellaneous: Some contests have unique rules and they are usually defined here.

7. Awards: Most contest sponsors offer awards for high-scoring stations. This defines what awards are available.

8. Log Submission: The contest sponsor will specify how you should send in your log, usually by e-mail or a web upload, and the deadline.

3.4.3 Contest Equipment

Just as a knowledgeable driver can't win a race without a good car, the radiosport operator will find it hard to make a good score without solid radio gear. Start by purchasing good-quality equipment and work your way up, learning how to make the most out of every item. Step by step, you'll build your way to a capable, effective station.

Basic Equipment

A good transceiver is needed for even the casual contester, and whatever you already have may be suitable. Most modern radios have good receivers that can handle the big signals you'll encounter on contest weekends. For non-DSP radios, a 500 Hz CW filter is a great investment. Headphones are a must, as you just can't catch all of the weak calls in the QRM without them. Others near your operating position will appreciate their use too.

The hand mike that came with your radio is not really suitable for contest operation, since you will have to pick it up to press the

John Dorr, K1AR, has posted some fine contest scores and works a lot of DX from this simple station and wire antennas. [Barbara Dorr, photo]

PTT button to transmit and put it down to log the contact. A boom mike mounted on the headset will leave your hands free for tuning the radio and typing QSOs in the logging program. You can use VOX or PTT via a footswitch to handle switching between transmit and receive...learn how to adjust your VOX properly! Make sure that you have your mike gain and compression settings adjusted correctly for SSB and digital modes using AFSK. Remember that overdriving your transceiver or amplifier is not only bad manners but also hurts your intelligibility on the air. It is important to have a crisp, clear signal.

A memory keyer or a computer with a keying interface is a must for CW. Configure the memories to send as much of the CQ and exchange information as possible. For digital mode contesting, use *function* keys that send pre-programmed messages.

You will also want a contest logging program on the computer in your station. There are lots of programs available, and they provide a lot of functions, from keeping the log straight and checking for duplicate

K9CT's operating positions all used state-of-the-art software-defined radios (FlexRadio FLEX-6000 series) in a very high-tech, fully-networked multiop station to win the Multi-2 category in the 2016 ARRL DX Phone Contest. The operators were (l-r): K9ZO, K9QQ, K3WA, and N0AX. [Craig Thompson, K9CT, photo]

contacts, to alerting when a new station has been spotted on the Cluster, calculating your score in real-time, and preparing your log for submission to the contest sponsor. More on this later.

You can start with whatever antennas you have now, but like DXing or any other operating, better antennas will be more effective. A dipole at modest height gives great "bang for the buck" performance. If you can't install it up high, try sloping it from as high as possible on one end toward a preferred direction. If you use a vertical antenna, make sure you install a good ground system and keep it clear of obstructions. Both antennas will probably work better than you'd expect — don't be afraid to call any stations you can hear. They'll probably hear you better than you can hear them. Tribanders (beams that operate on 20, 15 and 10 meters) and other gain antennas are more desirable.

Without recommending a specific type of antenna, one thing will always hold true: Proper installation is the key. Ultimately contesting is the true test of a station's potential. It doesn't do any good to have the best, highest antenna in the world if it's fed with inferior or poor-quality coaxial cable and unsoldered connectors. Make sure that the antenna is properly built and tuned, that you use good quality feed line, and all connectors are installed and waterproofed correctly.

Intermediate Equipment

As you become more engaged in contesting, take every opportunity to optimize your station as much as possible within your budget. A contest station can be as cheap or expensive as you want to make it but you will

never regret purchasing top quality equipment, new or used.

Receiver improvements at this level revolve around better performance in crowded conditions, not necessarily more memories or wider coverage. You'll want to take every opportunity to listen to different receivers. Can the receiver clearly reproduce a weak signal squeezed in between two domestic titans calling CQ? If many stations are calling, does the receiver allow you hear individual signals or do they merge into one big mess? How does the receiver sound when the DSP functions are operating? Most modern receivers are quite good and significant improvements are often subtle. Take the time to learn about them because you'll be using a receiver every time you're on the air!

The ability to hear through QRM makes the difference between good scores and great ones. The better you can hear, the better the results. Use the receive attenuator to prevent overload. A receiver's AGC can be overpowered by strong nearby signals — try reducing the RF gain as this often will help you hear weak signals through strong signals. Use the variable bandwidth or IF shift controls. Turn off the noise blanker (many noise blankers are overloaded by strong signals elsewhere on the band). Experiment with the settings in the face of QRM but remember the original settings so that you can return to them.

DSP filtering is the norm in contest-grade radios and can be tailored to suit almost any conditions. Just remember that while you're spending time experimenting with the filter settings, you're not making QSOs!

For analog receivers, install multiple filters if available, especially for CW. There are two schools of thought on wide and narrow CW

filters. One says that it is better to hear stations calling if they are not exactly on your frequency, while the other school feels that in crowded band conditions it's better to use the narrow filters. If you have both filters available, you can switch between them to suit the circumstances.

AMPLIFIERS

Adding an amplifier to a transceiver is definitely a way to reach a new layer or two of stations. A small amplifier with 500 to 1000 W output will make a big difference in your signal (going from 100 W to 1000 W is a 10 dB increase) and allow you to hold a frequency under challenging conditions. Going to a "full gallon" at 1500 W output is better yet. Remember that you may need to upgrade your antenna system and feed line components to handle the higher power level. You may also have to run a sufficiently heavy electrical service to the shack since most amplifiers use 240 V. Cooling is important, so don't block the fan. If you are buying a used amplifier, check availability and price of the amplifier tubes and components that may need to be replaced, such as the TR relays.

A few words of caution are in order regarding adding an amplifier to your station. Think about the last time you operated. If you were able to work every station you called on the first or second try, and were able to get answers to your CQs, you probably don't need an amplifier yet. Maybe you should consider improving your antennas first. On the other hand, if stations that you can hear are not answering your calls, then an amplifier will help fix that problem.

Planning Your Antennas

The place to start in planning a contest antenna system is the *ARRL Antenna Book*. The propagation chapter and the companion CD-ROM provide tables of radiation angles at which openings occur with maximum probability for most areas of the world. By using that information, you can develop an effective antenna strategy for your location and the types of contests you want to enter.

HIGH BAND ANTENNAS

Antennas for serious contesting are usually bigger, higher, and more efficient than for any other use in Amateur Radio. The antenna system is where more improvement can be made than anywhere else in the station.

This discussion will focus on the needs of the single-operator, all-band operator. Those needs are different from the single-band operator or multiop station. For example, the single-band or multi-multi operator needs antennas capable of getting through during band opening and closing times and marginal openings as well as providing good coverage

VHF+ Contesting

By Jon Jones, NØJK

VHF+ contests offer an exciting and challenging experience for the HF contester. Most of these events include VHF, UHF, and microwave bands but they're mainly just called "VHF or VHF+ contests." The single-band 10 meter and 160 meter contests are perhaps the most like VHF+ contests. At the solar minimum, 10 meters behaves a lot like 6 meters at the solar maximum. Ionospheric F2 propagation can make an appearance in the ARRL's September and January VHF contests. E-skip, aurora, and meteor scatter are propagation modes used both on 10 and 6 meters. Working weak signals on the higher VHF bands is much like digging out weak DX amid the static on 160 meters.

Station Equipment

You may already have a transceiver that will get you started in VHF+ contesting. HF/VHF/UHF "all-band" radios such as the ICOM IC-7100, the Kenwood TS-2000, and Yaesu's FT-991, FT-857D, and FT-817 allow casual participants to get their feet wet on 6 and 2 meters and even 70 cm with their current radios in the VHF contests. Most modern HF transceivers offer 6 meter coverage, which will get you started in VHF+ contesting as a single-band 6 meter entry. For higher bands and 222 MHz, transverters are usually necessary (222 MHz is not an amateur band outside North America, so manufacturers tend to not include it in their radios). Several transverter models are commercially available from manufacturers such as Down East Microwave and SSB Electronic and require only a little special knowledge to set up and use.

Although you can start with a dipole or your 2 meter FM antenna, you'll quickly find that the contest is more fun with a horizontally polarized Yagi of some sort. On 6 meters a dipole can work well, but a small 3-element Yagi is a significant improvement. The good news is that VHF/UHF antennas are compact so you can put them on a mast, roof tripod, or light-duty tower and turn them with a small rotator. You might even have some extra room in between your HF antennas. Be sure to use a good quality feed line — coaxial cables like RG-213 have quite a bit of loss at higher frequencies.

Portable operation is popular and encouraged in the VHF+ contests. For the antenna-restricted or apartment operator, the Single Operator, Portable and Rover categories let you operate on a competitive basis with many of the well-equipped home stations. A 10 W portable station on a mountaintop can be louder than a high power station down in a valley!

Multioperator teams set up high-power stations and large antennas for all bands on high mountaintops to extend their reach. They're like beacons, operating with big signals and sensitive receivers on several bands simultaneously and give many VHF+ operators their first far-away contacts.

Operating a VHF Contest

Grid locators, often called "grid squares," are usually the multipliers in VHF+ contests. For example, the grid square for W1AW in central Connecticut is FN31. In most VHF+ contests, grid squares are the only information (other than call signs) that must be exchanged. The VHF Sprints use a more precise "6-character" grid locator for more precision. My grid then becomes EM28ix. See **www.arrl.org/grid-square** for more information on grid locators.

VHF contests are often casual when conditions are slow. Operators work at a leisurely pace and may take several tries to finish a contact with a weak station. Things change if the band opens, though. During a tropo or E-skip opening, the VHF+ bands can be as busy as 40 meters on Saturday evening in the phone Sweepstakes! Several stations have reached more than 2000 contacts on 6 meters in a VHF contest, with peak rates of over 200 contacts per hour.

Strategy

Strategy is important to achieving a high score. Operating as many bands as possible and making sure to work stations on all available bands is the way to maximize your score. A 432 MHz QSO is worth twice as many points as one on 6 or 2 meters. On 1296 MHz a contact is worth three times as much, plus the grids are counted as new multipliers on each band. This means you can increase your score dramatically by moving stations from band to band for new QSOs. This is common practice so be sure to ask if a station has other bands available.

Just as in an HF contest, balance your efforts between working new grids and making more QSO points to maximize your score. If a band is open to an unusual area, stick with it to expand your multiplier and QSO count. It may not be open later. For example, operate on 6 and 2 meters in the ARRL June VHF Contest as long as they are open and work the higher bands at a later time. In the January VHF Contest, when 6 meters is often dead, changing bands frequently and moving stations to needed bands as you run across them is the way to maximize your score.

Always remember that on VHF and above, enhanced propagation can occur when you least expect it. For example, E-skip can appear in January. So stay alert and "expect the unexpected" in VHF+ contests — this is often what make them fun and interesting to operate in.

Recent ARRL VHF+ Contest Rule Changes

In 2015 and 2016, the ARRL made several changes to the rules regarding VHF+ contests. First, the use of spotting networks is now permitted for all entry categories, including single-operator. Furthermore, stations are allowed to "self-spot," announcing their presence on a particular frequency to alert other stations to possible band openings. Self-spotting is not permitted in HF contests, but can serve a useful purpose in VHF+ contests, where marginal openings can go unnoticed by stations using highly directional antennas pointed in the wrong direction.

Another major change dealt with the use of FM in VHF+ contests. Prior to the 2016 January VHF Contest, it was forbidden to make contest QSOs on the national FM calling frequency of 146.52 MHz. That rule was removed in order to attract more casual 2 meter operators to make contest QSOs.

VHF+ contesters can go on expeditions, too! Jon, NØJK, traveled to Bermuda (VP9) for the June ARRL VHF Contest. From this location, E-skip (E_s) propagation is common into the Eastern seaboard and even across the US on 6 meters if conditions are good. Other VHF+ contesters head for the Caribbean, beaming northwest across the entire US and Canada.

during the peak band openings. The single-operator all-band operator needs antennas that provide good coverage during the peak band openings but not necessarily during the marginal band openings and closings. The single operator needs to be working lots of QSOs on the best open band rather than chasing marginal openings.

Most contesters make their first big station improvement on their high-band (20, 15, and 10 meter) antenna systems with a large Yagi antenna at least 60 feet in the air. These antennas should have at least three elements active on each band, providing gain above that available from smaller or shortened three-element antennas. Front-to-back ratio will improve by an S unit or more, which is helpful in reducing interference from nearby stations. A station using an amplifier and such an antenna in an average or better location should be able to hold a run frequency under most conditions.

Higher is usually, but not always, better. You may find that raising an antenna actually hurts performance! Very high antennas produce their maximum signals at low takeoff angles and are best for working long distances, and may be less effective than low antennas for use in domestic contests where the takeoff angles are generally higher. Comparisons of antenna heights should be made based on the topography of the site. Antenna type also makes a difference in choice of heights. Using modeling programs and studying the angles can help with choice of antenna type and best height. Multiple antennas at different heights can be fed together or "stacked" to provide gain at different take-off angles. Many contest operators have successfully stacked triband Yagis. Using stacked tribanders can increase the flexibility and competitiveness of smaller contest stations.

LOW-BAND ANTENNAS

The low bands (160, 80, and 40 meters) require just as much study as the high bands. You may, however, have fewer practical options because of the physical size of antennas for these bands. Even if you're on a city lot rather than acreage out in the country, it is still possible to put out a decent signal if you pay attention to detail.

For 40 meters, the easiest solution these days seems to be the two-element shortened beam, often called the "shorty forty." Offered by several companies, these antennas work well at 70 feet or higher and will show a significant improvement over a ground-mounted vertical or low dipole or inverted-V. Rotatable dipoles are often quite effective at these heights.

Phased verticals can also be used and a simple vertical radiator can be made from aluminum tubing. If your property has suitable trees, a wire antenna such as an inverted-L or a wire Yagi are often excellent choices.

You'll find that 80 and 160 meters are similar — it's just the size of the antenna that's different. While a three-element 80 meter beam is nice to dream about, many serious contesters use arrays of phased verticals on these bands. Another popular option is a switched array of sloping dipoles suspended from a tower. You can be competitive with well-planned but simple arrays.

You would do well to buy a copy of *ON4UN's Low Band DXing* written by John Devoldere, ON4UN, and published by ARRL. This book has everything you need to know about low-band transmit and receive antennas.

Remote Contesting

If you are in a situation where it is impossible to build an effective contest station at your home, don't give up! It is now very possible to operate a contest using a remote station connected via Internet. In fact, the 2015 CQWW CW contest Single Operator All Band category was won with a record score by Kevin Stockton, N5DX, using a remote station in New York while he was at home in Arkansas.

Whether the remote station is at a different location that you own, or owned by a friend, or a "QTH-for-hire" (such as the Remote Ham Radio network — see **www.remoteham radio.com**), you will need to make sure your Internet connection is sufficiently fast and has low enough latency to provide minimal delays. Test it out thoroughly before the contest!

If you use a remote station, your score will count in the geographic region where the transmitting station is located. And make sure you are properly licensed and if you are operating a remote station in a different country, make sure that such cross-border control is permitted.

VHF/UHF Antenna Systems

A beginning VHF+ contester likely has a beam of several elements for 2 meters and possibly a dipole or small beam on 6 meters. Unlike FM antennas, those used for SSB/CW operation and contesting are horizontally polarized. It is easy to improve antenna gain and pattern at VHF+ in ways impossible at lower frequencies.

Big improvements in gain are available simply by increasing the number of elements on a long-boom Yagi antenna. It's not unusual to see Yagis with 20 elements or more at 2 meters and higher frequencies and 7 element Yagis are not uncommon on 6 meters. These antennas can have more than 10 dB of gain in free space — the same as an amplifier! Be careful around these antennas because of the increased levels of RF exposure at high power!

Beyond simply increasing the boom length and number of elements, arrays of multiple long-boom Yagis create some truly awesome gain and pattern performance. They take some careful planning to get the mechanical and electrical details right but the results are impressive.

Another area of improved antenna system performance at VHF+ frequencies is in feed line loss. For a feed line run of 100 feet, changing to hardline (½-inch or larger, and often available surplus at low cost) can reduce loss by several dB compared to flexible coax. For example, on 2 meters, 100 feet of RG-8X has about 4.7 dB of loss, and RG-213 has 2.8 dB. Replacing these with ½-inch hardline

Roving — operating on the move or from several choice locations — is a very popular operating style for VHF+ contesters. John, W1RT, is giving his rover antennas some "hands-on" attention from atop Mohawk Mountain in grid FN31 during the ARRL September VHF QSO Party. [Andy Zwirko, K1RA, photo]

(LDF4-50, for example, which has 0.85 dB of loss) has the same effect as increasing your transmitter power by 2.5× or 1.5×. Lower feed line loss means you'll also hear better.

One aspect of high-performance VHF+ antenna building not available to HF operators is for roving or portable operation. If you can't build a powerhouse antenna system at home, make one you can move and take it on the road! VHF+ antenna systems can be mounted on a vehicle or trailer and taken to a hilltop or other advantageous location. Veteran VHF+ contest rover John, W1RT, gives a lot of advice on getting started in roving on his website **w1rt.us.** His rover vehicle is equipped for 11 bands, from 50 MHz through 24 GHz!

An extreme case of roving occurred in the January 2016 ARRL VHF Contest. Andrea, N2EZ, activated a total of 27 grid squares, driving almost 1700 miles from Western Pennsylvania to Houston, TX.

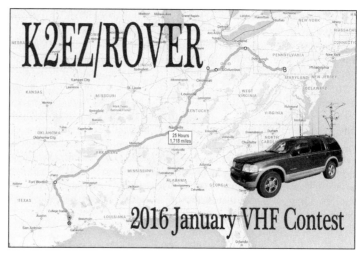

Andrea, N2EZ, roved through six states, four ARRL divisions, and seven ARRL sections in the ARRL January VHF Contest.

3.4.4 Operating Basics: Your First Contests

You may have happened upon several contests and even made a few contest QSOs. It was fun, wasn't it? Are you ready to try entering one for real? Let's go! Your QSOs will be welcomed by everyone, especially the serious participants. They are always looking for additional contacts and unless there are many callers will be glad to guide you through your first contest QSOs.

Making a Contest QSO

Let's start with a typical QSO in the Washington State QSO Party (also known as "The Salmon Run"). In this example, we'll assume you are operating from W1AW in Connecticut.

On voice, the contact sounds like this:
W7DX: CQ Washington State QSO Party from Whiskey Seven Delta X-ray
[W7DX is soliciting contacts and is identifying the contest he is entering.]
W1AW: Whiskey One Alfa Whiskey
[Just give your call once, phonetically.]
W7DX: W1AW you're five nine in Chelan county
[This identifies the caller and gives the exchange.]
W1AW: Thank you, you're five nine in Connecticut
[You acknowledge that you've received W7DX's information and give yours — no repeat is needed unless requested by W7DX.]
W7DX: Thank you, CQ Salmon Run from W7DX

[This acknowledges receiving W1AW's information and starts the cycle again. See how easy it is?]

Here's the same contact on CW (RTTY contest contacts are very similar):
W7DX: CQ SR DE W7DX
["SR" stands for Salmon Run; it could also be WAQP for Washington QSO Party. In a RTTY contest it's common to tack on another CQ after the call sign.]

W1AW: W1AW
[Again, just your call sign. No K or BK is required.]
W7DX: W1AW 5NN CHE
[Note the use of the cut number N to abbreviate 9 — this saves time on CW but is not recommended on RTTY. "CHE" is the abbreviation for Chelan County. Most QSO Party sponsors publish a list of approved abbreviations to make sure the contact is scored correctly.]

Ken, K4ZW (right) works with Halle, AB3OX, Tsegaya, KB3WWJ, and Adula, KB3WXC, at the ET3AA station in Ethiopia during the IARU Radiosport contest. [Ken Claerbout, K4ZW, photo]

Field Day — Not a Contest?

First held in 1933 as an emergency exercise Field Day is a *non-contest* in a contest-like environment. It incorporates all modes, including satellite communications and both HF and VHF/UHF bands — the only ARRL on-air event to touch so many parts of ham radio. More US licensed amateurs participate in Field Day annually than any other on-the-air operating event. It allows contacts with any station worldwide, on any mode and on all bands (except 60, 30, 17, and 12 meters). Even diehard non-contesters seem to enjoy participating in this all-inclusive operating event.

Field Day occupies a special place in the hearts of many contesters because it is during these outings that many get their first taste of competitive operating. Perhaps at the elbow of a more experienced operator, logging and listening, inexperienced operators gain valuable experience during a single operating shift.

If you are new to contesting, take advantage of Field Day's smorgasbord to sample different styles of operating. Make sure to listen as a contest veteran tunes the bands or holds a frequency. Take a turn yourself! If you're an experienced ham, be sure to return the favor of those that taught you by showing a new contester "how it's done." You'll make a lifetime friend and help keep radiosport going!

Field Day isn't a contest but you can't tell it from the focus of the night-time operators! Filling the logs in the HF tent at the St Charles Amateur Radio Club, KO0A Field Day operation are (front to back) W0LON, KD0EIA, KE5WXD, and KD0IGO. [Ward Silver, N0AX photo]

W1AW: R 5NN CT
[A simple "R" confirms that you received the information; then send yours. Again, no BK or repeats of the other station's exchange are needed.]
W7DX: TU CQ SR DE W7DX
[The TU (CW abbreviation for "Thank You") politely acknowledges receiving W1AW's information and starts the cycle again. If there are other callers W7DX might just send **TU** or **TU W7DX**.]

That's pretty snappy operating! No wasted characters or unnecessary information. If this were emergency traffic isn't that how you would want it to flow? Remember that even in a small contest, efficiency is important. You can ragchew with the station some other day although it's perfectly okay to quickly say hello if you know the operator. Just don't launch into a long-winded conversation in the middle of a contest QSO!

There is more to making contest QSOs than this simple example but that format will get you started. If you'd like to know more, the following sections are an introduction to real contest operating.

Search and Pounce

What a great term! *Search and pounce*

(S&P) describes exactly the technique of tuning up and down a band for new stations (searching) then working them (pouncing). As you tune, you'll hear some stations calling "CQ Contest" or simply "CQ Test." If you are using a DX spotting network, you can simply "click-and-pounce" but take the time to copy the CQing station's call sign yourself. Never ever assume that a spotted call sign is correct!

Practice giving your exchange along with a QSO being made on the air but without transmitting. Here's a tip: in a phone contest take a full breath before replying to a station. Give all of your exchange the same way every time in a single, uninterrupted statement. Your voice will be natural and unforced — you'll sound and feel much more confident.

Once you're ready, how do you give yourself the best chance of getting through? What's the best way to call? On phone, make the most of your transmissions by speaking clearly and distinctly without rushing or mumbling. Use standard phonetics that are easy to speak (remember, you'll be saying them a lot!) and easy to understand. If you're unsure about your technique, practice with a friend on a quiet band before the contest. On CW, send your call cleanly with the characters spaced properly. Using a computer program

or CW keyer is a good way to send your call correctly every time. Send at a speed you'll feel comfortable receiving.

Give your full call one time and one time only, using phonetics on phone. Sending only a partial call (such as the poor practice of giving only the "last two" letters) requires at least one extra set of transmissions to get your complete call sign. This slows down the running station — a breach of contest etiquette. And why only one time? Because if you're heard, you'll get through with only one call. If you're not heard, the extra calls are just interference. Listen for the running station's response and respond appropriately. If another station is called, wait until the contact is completed and try again. Or if you think too many other stations are calling, store the frequency in one of your rig's VFOs or memories or even write the frequency and call on paper so that you can come back later and try again.

Stick with standard or commonly used phonetics. You should eventually learn up to three common sets because in marginal conditions it pays to be able to change to a more easily understood word for better comprehension.

Another problem for operators new to

contesting is keeping up with the speed at which contacts are conducted. A running station may only listen for two seconds before starting another CQ. You have to start your call during that short window to be heard. Don't put the microphone down or take your hand off the key! By the time you get ready to transmit, it will be too late. Be ready to transmit as soon as the running station's transmission ends. You don't have to send your entire call in two seconds because the running station will pause as soon as your transmissions are heard. It's only important that you start in time to be heard. Just think of contesting as "DXing speeded up" and you'll quickly adapt.

Efficiency is the name of game in contesting. There's no need to give the running station's call before yours — after all, the other operator already knows his or her call! Don't append information to your call unless it's necessary to identify your station. Don't add "/QRP" or your location, for example. It adds nothing to identify you and just creates more work for the station you're calling.

If the running station hears you, be ready to copy the response. Most contacts will happen just as shown in the example given earlier. What happens if there is QRM, QRN, QSB or any number of other problems that cause errors? What if the running station gets your call sign wrong?

Let's start with correcting your call sign. The best time to fix it is as soon as the running station responds to you. Don't give your exchange — implying your acceptance of

the incorrect call — until your call is given correctly by the running station. Here's an example (imagine that both stations are using phonetics in this phone example):
OH8X: CQ contest from OH8X
KD8ABC: KD8ABC
OH8X: KD8AVZ you are 59 15
[OH8X has the call wrong and gave you the exchange 59 zone 15. Usually the word "zone" is omitted — it's understood.]
KD8ABC: KD8 Alfa Bravo Charlie KD8 Alfa Bravo Charlie
[Just say your call sign, phonetically, no exchange yet.]
OH8X: Is it KD8 Alfa Bravo Zulu?
KD8ABC: KD8 Alfa Bravo Charlie, the last letter is C for Canada
[Here's your chance to try a different phonetic for the difficult letter.]
OH8X: KD8Alfa Bravo Charlie QSL, 59 15
[Now that OH8X has your call sign and you have OH8X's exchange, give your exchange. KD8ABC is in zone 4.]
KD8ABC: Thank you, 59 4
OH8X: Thank you, CQ contest OH8X

What if part of the exchange is lost? Request a repeat immediately, before giving your information as shown in this CW example for a VHF+ contest:
W8XYZ: KD8ABC [static crash]
KD8ABC: GRID?
W8XYZ: KD8ABC EM99
KD8ABC: R EN81

There are many variations on making corrections. The important thing is to let the

other station know there is a problem before sending information back to them. If you implicitly accept the incorrect information by responding with your exchange, it's confusing and takes longer to correct the error.

As you give your exchange information, don't add any extra words or phrases. Just give the information in the same order used by the running station. There is no need for phrases such as "please copy" or "you are" or to name each bit of information. Do not repeat the exchange you've received. Just rattle off your information in one string and the running station will be perfectly happy.

Don't say or send anything twice. Don't repeat any information unless requested or you are absolutely sure the running station won't copy everything on the first try — you might be surprised! Just send your information — once — as smoothly and as efficiently as possible. You will be pleased with how effective this technique is and how it builds your confidence.

If you are asked for a repeat, give only the information requested. The receiving station already has most of what of the information or will confirm a full call sign after getting all of it. To send anything extra may cause confusion under marginal receiving conditions.

Now that you have all of the information, log the QSO including the complete exchange. Then continue to tune for more contest contacts. There's still a lot to learn but the basic fun of contesting has begun!

3.4.5 Intermediate Contest Operating

After you find out how easy it is to have fun in a contest, you may want to get a little more serious about participating. You don't have to go all-out as a serious contester to enjoy some success but it will take a little effort to get good results. You'll want to submit a log to the sponsors, see your standings in the final results and possibly even contribute your score to a contest club. Even if you never get more serious about radiosport than casual contesting, it will be amazing how much you learn about operating and propagation while simultaneously extending your station's capabilities.

Part of being successful lies in managing your expectations. Unreasonable expectations lead to frustration that can really diminish your enjoyment of contesting. Don't expect to place in the national Top Ten until you've spent some time gaining experience. If your QTH is challenging — such as a valley location, a high noise area or limited by antenna

restrictions — it will be difficult to make a big score from home. In any case, plan an operating strategy by which you could reach some reasonable goals. Get creative to develop your radio skills! Operating from a portable location or mobile or even a remote Internet-linked station is an option getting more popular every year.

Be prepared to handle the QRM that comes naturally in a contest. The bands will be much more crowded than during a weekday or non-contest weekend. Don't

Ana, CR7ADN, operated as CR6K in the ARRL 10 Meter Contest with Jose, CT1CJJ, and Filipe, CT1ILT.

expect quiet, clear frequencies in the middle of the activity. This is where your listening skills become very important. Contesting develops an operator's ability to copy information through noise, fading and interference from nearby signals. How you handle contest QRM is one of the most important contest skills.

Calling CQ

You may have tried an occasional CQ in a contest as a beginner but as a more serious participant you'll want to CQ or *run* as much as possible. Experienced contesters know that if they have a good signal, the overall rate at which they can make contacts will be as good or better than tuning the band. More importantly, they also know that many multipliers will eventually answer their CQs. Learning to call CQ and hold a run frequency effectively is an important contest skill.

To decide whether or not to call CQ you have to decide whether your signal is strong enough in the target area. One way to find out is to tune the band searching and pouncing. If you are working stations on the first call, you're probably loud enough to get answers to a CQ. You can also ask stations that you work about your signal strength. If you decide you're loud enough, the next step is to find an unoccupied frequency.

A good way to find a frequency is to tune from one end of the band (usually the high end) and look for "holes" between stations calling CQ. When you find one, ask if the frequency is in use (send "QRL?" or your call once on CW, although just "?" is common) and listen for responses. On phone, you will need to be at least 1.5 kHz from adjacent stations. On CW, at least 300 Hz. Don't expect a perfectly clear channel without QRM in a big contest. If you can hear just the high frequency crackle or low-frequency rumble of nearby signals, that's about as good as you can expect.

Assuming you got no response to your inquiry (and remember to listen for non-contest QSOs), it's time for a CQ. On phone or CW, leave two to three seconds between CQs. Short CQs work best on busy bands — too long a CQ and impatient contest stations will tune right by.

Here are some examples of reasonable contest CQs on phone. Note the use of phonetics at least once in each CQ:

CQ Contest CQ Contest from Whiskey One Alfa Whiskey, Whiskey One Alfa Whiskey, Contest

or

CQ CQ Contest this is Kilo Delta Seven Foxtrot Yankee X-ray, KD7FYX

And on CW:

CQ TEST VE7SV VE7SV TEST

or

Gator, N5RZ, and Deborah, K5RZA, traveled to the island of St. Croix in the US Virgin Islands and took top honors in North America in the 2013 CQ WPX RTTY contest Multi-2 category.

CQ SS CQ SS K4RO K4RO SS (SS is for Sweepstakes)

or

TEST K1TO (if QSOs are really moving along quickly)

And on RTTY:

CQ RU AA5AU AA5AU CQ (RU is for RTTY Roundup)

or

RU AA5AU CQ (if QSOs are really moving along quickly)

Instead of "Contest" you can substitute the name of the contest if you are participating in one of the smaller contests. That attracts the attention of stations tuning by.

Each CQ should be brisk and crisp, not slurred or tentative. Think of each CQ as a small advertisement for your station that makes another operator want to answer you. Your voice should be friendly but businesslike and your audio quality clean and punchy. Get together on a dead band with a friend between contests and adjust your mic gain and speech processor settings for good audio. If you use a voice keyer, do the same for its messages.

Let's assume that you find a frequency and you're calling CQ. If you get a steady stream of callers, there's nothing better in contesting! Be consistent and smooth in your responses. Make sure of the other station's call sign and exchange before calling CQ again. Remember that contest sponsors remove points for incorrectly logged call signs and exchanges.

You can improve your running rate by getting the full call sign sent to you the first time, every time. Repeats not only take time but stations waiting to work you may move on.

What if you don't get many callers? How long should you continue to call CQ? There is no set answer but you should be doing whatever maximizes your contact rate. Most contesters will try a reasonably clear frequency for two or three minutes without callers before tuning away. Sometimes contacts come in "clumps" — no contacts for a minute or two, then several callers at once. If in the past hour you were able to work stations by searching and pouncing at a rate of 30/hour (most contest logging software will display your "last hour" rate), then calling CQ should be expected to generate that rate or better. If your rate calling CQ is lower, then you should go back to S&P mode. As you gain experience, your intuition will begin to tell you when to CQ and when to tune.

If you're not getting answers to your calls or are being asked for repeats a lot, think about why this might be. Are you sending too fast on CW? Are you transmitting clean audio on SSB? Either can prevent you from making QSOs, so it's counterproductive to have poor audio or to send too fast. On CW, it's often more productive to slow down late in the contest when you've already worked most of the active contesters. Remember, you cannot win many contests by working only the hardcore, experienced contesters. You have to also work casual operators who turn on their radios, make a few contacts, then go off to enjoy other pursuits. Temper your voice or keying speed to what you're trying to accomplish at that minute. If you have a large pileup, go fast so callers will know they have a chance and stick around. If you're getting only one or two calls per minute, be slower and friendlier.

If you have multiple or directional antennas, don't forget to try different directions or antennas. As bands open and close, the vertical and horizontal angles at which signals arrive can change dramatically. An antenna that was hot as a pistol when the band first opened may be the wrong one an hour later. The band may also open to another area. For example, from the Midwest in a domestic contest such as Sweepstakes, fading rate to the 1-2-3 districts is a cue that it's time to turn your antennas west.

You might also lose your frequency to another station. Two stations in each other's skip zones can call CQ right on top of each other without ever hearing each other! You can tell this is happening when stations seem to be calling but the timing isn't "right." You may also hear the other station faintly via backscatter. When this happens, if you feel you're the louder station, you might want to stay and battle it out. If you think sticking around will hurt your contact rate too badly, by all means look for another frequency.

Occasionally another station will ask if the frequency is in use, not hear your reply and proceed to call CQ. You can try to convince them to move or you can move yourself. It depends on your interpersonal skills and signal strength. Another station may try to squeeze in between you and the next station up or down the band when there really isn't room. You'll just have to decide whether to hold your ground, slide up or down the band a little bit to accommodate the newcomer, or look for a new frequency. In any of these cases, don't lose your temper and get into an argument or worse, intentionally interfere with the other station. Life is too short for that stuff — if you're arguing with another station, you're not making QSOs!

Advanced Search and Pounce

As a more serious competitor, you'll want to make better use of the time you spend tuning around the band. A good operator can work stations at a rate of 60/hour on a "fresh" band with lots of stations calling CQ.

Don't just tune from loud signal to loud signal. Listen carefully where there seems to be a small gap or a weak signal. Stations with small antennas, such as temporary setups by operators on vacation or operating Field Day-style, may have weak signals and be unable to attract a large pileup. They can probably hear you just fine, however — if you don't tune past them!

Many logging programs offer a feature called a *band map*. This is a linear scale along one edge of the display showing call signs and frequencies. Call signs are added to the band map as you work them, by manually entering them into the band map or automatically from a spotting network. It's usually possible to configure the band map to show only multipliers, only stations not yet worked or even all stations. As you tune, some programs will even put the call of a station on the band map at the current frequency into the call window, ready for you to give your call and work them!

As you develop these quick-tuning skills, you'll find a quick scan of the band to be a valuable way to grab points quickly as you change bands or between periods of CQing.

Using Spotting Networks

By Charles Fulp, K3WW

Many contests have added a Single-Operator Assisted (SOA) or Unlimited (SOU) category. We'll just call it SOA here. This category usually has the same rules at the Single-Operator category with one major exception. The entrant may use spotting networks such as the DX clusters and the Reverse Beacon Network (**www.reversebeacon.net**). Spotting networks have opened up a whole new world for many contesters, allowing access to information about band conditions, available stations and multipliers during the contest like never before. Some contests now permit *all* single operators to use spotting networks, so the comments in this section apply to all single-operator entrants in those events.

The SOA category allows operators who enjoy monitoring their spotting network for new countries to participate in contests without missing anything. Other operators like working cooperatively with their friends, by sharing spots, while operating contests. Still others feel that the use of spotting networks can help them score more points for their club by increasing their multiplier totals. Being part of the network can keep some operators motivated to push on to bigger scores. Being "connected" in many ways makes SOA closer to a multiop category than single-op.

The only special equipment necessary to participate in the SOA category is a link to a spotting network. Most logging programs will accommodate packet and/or Internet connections and will interact with the radio, computer and logging in such a way that getting to a spot is only a mouse click or keystroke away.

SOA Station Setup

If you decide to try to make the best scores you can, some station design features can help you and make SOA much more fun. The first thing you should have is a transceiver that can be controlled by your contest logging program. This allows you to move quickly to work new multipliers and back to your original frequency, where you can resume your tuning or calling CQ.

If you choose to use high power, an auto-tuning amplifier and automatic antenna switch allows you to quickly jump from one band to another. Some operators just bypass the amplifier when making a quick contact on another band.

As in the Single-Op category, the use of a second radio can improve your performance as an SOA entrant. If your station is capable of running at good rates on some bands, you can use the second station to study spots. When the opportunity is right, make quick contacts between answers to your CQ. Since many SOA stations are not the biggest on the bands, being able to stay on a frequency and catch some extra multipliers without leaving for more than a few seconds at a time can help you get the most out of your station. Having a second radio also decreases the importance of auto-tuning amplifiers and rapid band change antenna switching. Of course the more automated everything is, the more flexible your station can be.

Too Much Information

Historically the top Single-Op entrants usually out-score the top SOA. There are several reasons for this. Traditionally the top operators with stations capable of winning at the highest levels enter the Single-Op category. After competing in the SOA category for a few years and watching the performance of other participants, I coined the term "Single-Op Distracted."

There are many elements involved in building a big score, and access to spotting information is only one. Being distracted by all the spots is the biggest nemesis of the serious SOA entrant. If you are actually trying to make the best score you can, reverting to being a DXer can ruin your effort. In order to chase spots, it is usually necessary to give up some of the other activities that can build a big score. Even if you work every spot with one call, you will lose running time chasing them.

Most operators will find it difficult to hold a run (CQ) frequency and simultaneously enter a lot of large pileups. It is very easy to become distracted by all of the information available on the spotting networks and end up forgetting to do all the other things that Single-Ops do to make big scores. At some point, you must be able to ignore exotic, hard-to-work multipliers and concentrate on making lots of easy-to-make contacts. On the other hand, you may set a goal of working the

Using Spotting Networks in Contests

As an intermediate contester, you'll be using your computer for contest logging as explained in more detail later in the section Computers and Contesting. Besides automating many of the housekeeping functions of logging, the computer can also connect you to information from other contesters. Some contests allow this "assistance" for all entry categories, while some require you to enter the Single Operator Assisted (SOA), or Single Op Unlimited category as it is known in some contests. DX spotting networks are sometimes called "packet" because the original computer-based spotting networks used *PacketCluster* software running over packet radio links.

Connecting your computer to the Internet and your radio is a powerful combination used through two features of the logging software, the *announce window* and the *band map*. The logging software can use information from

Chas, K3WW, operates from this well organized ham shack. You can count on him to finish in the Top Ten in the Single-Op Assisted category.

Information from the spotting network will let you know which bands are most active and should allow you to choose the best band at any given time. Nothing replaces knowledge of what is going on around you. It is wise to set up your RBN filtering so you can see spots of your own call from around the world. When you call CQ on a new frequency you can quickly see where you are being heard.

It is important to be patient, especially early in the contest when there are large numbers of spots for stations that will be active throughout the weekend and much easier to work later in the contest. Unless you especially like the challenge of entering pileups with many of the biggest stations in your area, you may find it easier to wait for the smoke to clear before you go after a new multiplier.

If a station in an area where you have long periods of propagation is spotted early and the pileup is large, don't waste time unless you have an incredible signal. Even if you do, it may be more productive to wait until later to pick up many of these stations.

Technology keeps changing — the VHF spotting voice nets gave way to Packet-Cluster, which has to a large degree been replaced by Internet-based DX clusters. The Reverse Beacon Network now provides more accurate CW and RTTY spots almost the instant a station begins to call CQ on a new frequency. This has permitted extended opportunities to chase spots at rates that often approach the rates of a typical run. For CW operators, there are now many times when chasing the RBN spots can be faster than running. Holding a run frequency has become less critical, as everyone is found by the RBN and will quickly get answers even if they have modest signals. It is amazing how quickly the serious multiop stations get to any new call that is found by the RBN.

More of the traditional top level Single-Op folks are going full bore into Single-Op Assisted, proving that the technology does offer the opportunity to make the bigger scores that have always been assumed, but rarely proven. Remember to spot stations that you find, that have not been spotted. On CW this is becoming unusual; however, on SSB it is very important that we all contribute with plenty of spots. If you want to maximize your enjoyment of the entire contest experience, give the Single-Op Assisted category a try.

most multipliers possible and not be concerned about optimizing your score.

Knowing your objective, regardless of your entry category, is important in establishing a game plan for any category. If you want to work some new countries or make a clean sweep, monitoring the spotting nets can improve your chances. If you want to make more points for your club, you will need a different strategy. Here's the most effective game plan for the SOA entrant: Do everything that you would do as a Single-Op, while judiciously picking up extra multipliers without detracting from your most efficient practices.

Calling CQ is still the fastest way to build a large QSO total for most operators. When we can't run effectively, searching and pouncing can produce good QSO totals. With spotting, S&P can be even more effective. As you tune the band, you can skip over duplicates quickly and the spots may help in identifying some of the stations you come to.

Making the Best Use of Spots

It pays to tune in an orderly manner, even if you do run off to a different portion of the band or even to another band to grab a new multiplier. Most software now displays a band map, which lets you see many of the calls as you tune your radio. This visual display permits you to know who you can probably skip and who you probably need to work. You can click your mouse or use keyboard shortcuts and go to new multipliers directly from the band map as well as from the window that lists the most recent spots.

Early in the contest I tend to just display new multipliers but use the band map to make tuning on my second radio, while running on my primary radio, a quicker job. Later in the contest it may be more productive to work through the band map jumping from one needed station to the next, especially if you cannot hold a good run frequency.

Listen carefully to be sure the spots are accurate! If you have already worked a lot of QSOs, the ones that show up as "needed" may well be bad calls. If you only have one radio but it has two receivers, you can still try to maintain a run and listen on the second receiver to the spots in your band map. I find this more efficient than trying to tune the second receiver on the same band that I am running with no help from the spotting network.

On some bands you will find stations working split. An unfortunate complication of spotting networks is that many stations now announce their listening frequency less often. For the SOA operator this information is often available from the network, making it faster to work these stations while Single-Ops have to wait for the DX station to announce the listening frequency.

Another situation involves stations that do not identify very often. There is a strong temptation to assume that the spot is correct and work these stations without ever hearing the call. This is a risky proposition as a fair percentage of spotted calls are incorrect. Even when spots are correct, sometimes a different station is on the frequency when you arrive.

the spotting network to populate the band map automatically, filling it with stations spotted around the world. It's like having the whole world tuning for you! As you tune, the computer senses the new frequency and scrolls the band map along with your receive frequency. Or you can just click on a spot when it appears and the logging program will send the radio to that frequency instantly.

The announce window shows each spot individually. This is important because additional information may be posted by the spotter, such as "listening up 2" or "QSX 7167" for a DX station on 40 meter phone who is transmitting below 7100 kHz and listening in the US phone band. The band map and announce window features can usually be configured to show only stations you haven't yet worked or only those that are new multipliers. It may be able to show the different types of information in different colors, to help you quickly make sense of it.

Spotting networks have had a big effect on contesting — not all of it good. The fun side of spotting is that casual participants have more fun by finding more stations to work. This increases their score, as well as their club's aggregate score, and they may work some new stations toward an award. The problem arises when the spotting information begins to *replace* tuning and operating skill instead of *assisting* the operator or the operator blindly trusts the spots.

The rush of stations to work a newly spotted station creates what are known as "packet pileups." DX operators know instantly when they've been "spotted" as their pileup grows suddenly from a handful of callers to dozens or more. The sudden rush of stations is confusing to everyone, causing the pileups to get out of sync with the DX station, reducing contact rate for everyone. Don't contribute to the mob mentality — if you grab a spot to work a station, wait until you can hear them before calling and use good pileup discipline. Sometimes it's more productive to wait a while before chasing a spot, giving the packet pileup a chance to subside.

Don't become dependent on spotting network assistance. Use it to aid you and your own abilities. Make sure that you copy each call sign you work. Spots are helpful but the call signs given may be — and frequently are — wrong or *busted*. For example, if you see a spot in a CW contest for "BY2T" at a time of day when there is no propagation to China, and you hear a strong signal sending fast CW, it is probably a busted spot for 6Y2T. By not copying the call sign and exchange for yourself, and simply trusting the spotting network, you run the risk of having the incorrect QSO removed from your log, along with a penalty!

CW Skimmer

CW contesting recently added a new operator — this one doesn't transmit though because it is completely automated! Alex, VE3NEA has developed the *CW Skimmer* (www.dxatlas.com/cwskimmer) that can decode up to 700 CW signals simultaneously (!) using the output of a wide-band receiver.

The output of a *CW Skimmer* is both a visual window showing where the stations are calling and also decoded call signs and frequencies that can be used as the input to your logging software or to send spots to the worldwide spotting networks.

Having this automated capability has been "turned around" by the Reverse Beacon Network or RBN (www.reversebeacon.net) into a "who's being heard where" service that listens to the HF and VHF+ bands continually. The RBN monitors the output from *CW Skimmers* located around the world, displaying the call signs and signal strengths of stations calling CQs that are heard and decoded by the skimmers. To find out if you're being heard and how well, get on the air and call CQ on CW a few times — unless your signal is really weak, within a minute your call sign will appear in the list.

Needless to say, this has had an impact on CW contesting! By reducing the need to tune the band looking for stations, more stations find the CQers. The bad news is that so many stations can tune to the CQer's frequency so quickly that the pileups can quickly become too unwieldy to handle. In the words of Yogi Berra, "Nobody goes there anymore — it's too crowded!" So use the *CW Skimmer* wisely — don't let it substitute for the radio "know-how" you need to become a skilled operator.

3.4.6 Contest Strategy

As an intermediate contester, you have progressed from struggling to tune the bands and work stations one by one to being able to quickly search and pounce your way through a thicket of stations. You're probably even calling CQ and holding your own! You're ready to start thinking about strategy. Make sure your station is in good working order. Check the SWR of all antennas, make sure the rotator is turning, then start thinking about the contest.

Pre-Contest Preparation

Start by making sure you know the contest rules well enough to perform properly during the contest. This includes knowing whom to work during the contest and how the scoring system works. All of these will play a part in strategic planning for the contest. The exchange should be memorized to the point that you could send the exchange while concentrating on some other contest chore, such as logging, checking multipliers, or monitoring equipment conditions. You should know your grid square, CQ zone, ITU zone, state, county, section or anything else required for any contest you might enter. A seasoned contester knows the exchange for all of the major contests.

Select an operating category based on your station capabilities, operating time available, and personal abilities. If propagation is good, you might want to try QRP or leave the amplifier off for the weekend and try low power. Single-band categories are often a great way to really learn about propagation and pursue single-band DXCC or other single-band awards.

Even if the category is one where you do not think you will win, you should still have some sort of plan and goals set before the contest. Find the results of last year's contest and see what it took to win your section, division or call area. Then see what the leaders in your chosen category did in last year's version of the contest. Evaluate this year's expected propagation. For example, on HF when sunspots are rising, expect 10 meters to be better than the year before. As sunspots decline, expect 10 meters to be worse.

Along with evaluating the probable propagation on each band, check previous contest *breakdowns* of other stations in your category — the number of multipliers and QSOs on each band. A *rate sheet* will show the number of QSOs on each band during each clock hour, giving you a picture of which hours were busy and slow. It's best to pick a station near to you and with similar equipment for this evaluation. Breakdown information can be found at the **3830scores.com** website or in the detailed online contest results from ARRL and other contest sponsors.

Breakdowns from last year's contest can be used to prepare for this year's contest.

These are some of the antennas at the station of Tim Duffy, K3LR. The station is active in major contests in the multi-multi category and is one of the better-equipped contest stations in the world. [Mark Haverstock, K8MSH, photo]

Use those breakdowns to set goals for this year's contest. It's often helpful to compare your own hourly QSO rate from the previous year to find out where you were and what you were doing as the contest progressed, especially if you made a wrong move last year. Some logging programs allow you to import a previous contest's log and set it as a goal, and track your progress hour-by-hour.

Finally, make the necessary plans to prevent interruptions to your contest effort. Be ready to go at the start of the contest period and stay at the station as much as possible during the contest. As described later in this chapter, food preparation should be such that there is sufficient food available but you should not plan on having a sit-down dinner away from the rig during the contest. Try to get as much rest as possible in the days leading up to the contest. Sleep time will be minimal and the sleeping area should be close by and comfortable. Be sure to have a good alarm clock (or two!) and be able to motivate yourself to get out of bed when it goes off.

Getting a Fast Start

Beginning on the highest band expected to be open at the start of the contest is generally the best thing to do. Working stations in the first few minutes of the contest is important to your overall success and can have a positive effect on your attitude for the whole weekend.

If you start by doing search-and-pounce, consider starting without using the spotting network. You'll have better results by making a quick sweep through the band. Since most stations tune from the bottom of the band to the top, sometimes you can outsmart the pileups by starting at the top and tuning down

instead. You may have to make a couple of band changes right away to find the best band for making contacts.

You may decide to start by trying to establish a run frequency. This is a good strategy if you know you have a good signal where the band is open. Unless you're a Big Gun, aim for higher in the band where the crowding won't be so intense. As you work the first few stations, assess what the conditions and activity will bear. If you're not getting answers, try another band or beaming a different direction, or go back to searching and pouncing.

QSO Rate Versus Multipliers

Any contest should be considered as something similar to a scavenger hunt. The object is to collect a lot of something (QSOs in this case) while also acquiring as many items from a list (multipliers) as possible. Each contest has a different theme (list) with different strategies as a result. For example, in working a DX contest from the US the most active, available multipliers are in Europe. From the eastern US, the most QSOs will also be found in Europe. Thus, if you live in the eastern US, you should concentrate your operating hours during times when the bands are open to Europe. If you live in the western US, you are likely to work the most QSOs in Asia, which has fewer active multipliers. So you would try to work European multipliers when possible but plan on making most of your QSOs by working Asia.

If a station calls you that would be a multiplier on another band and you think propagation would support a QSO on that band, you can ask the station to move to that band for a quick contact. This is called *moving*

Scott, ZF2SC, combined a vacation with some contest operating in the ARRL 10 Meter Contest. From the right location a simple station can make a lot of contacts! [Scott McDonald, ZF2SC, photo]

multipliers and can make a dramatic improvement in your score.

Whether you decide to S&P, call CQ, or change bands will depend on how far along the contest is. If it's the first day and other bands are open, you might want to S&P on another band, especially if you're running low power or the band is too crowded for you to hold a run frequency. The decision of whether to chase multipliers or to stay with calling CQ largely depends on both the contact rate and the point value of a new multiplier. Most contest logging programs will display the value of a new multiplier in both minutes at your current rate, and the equivalent number of QSOs each new multiplier is worth.

The ARRL November Sweepstakes Contest offers a mug each year for working all sections (a "Clean Sweep"). Some operators collect them.

Tracking Your Score Against the Competition

If you are curious about how you are doing compared to other stations in your category during the contest, you can connect your logging program to the **cqcontest.net** website. This site collects scores from connected stations in real time and allows you to see where you are doing well and where you need to work a little harder. This can be a great motivational tool for multiop stations. In some contests, use of this information is considered "outside assistance" which is not allowed for single-operator entrants. Check with the contest's sponsor before using it.

Ethics in Contesting

It is an unfortunate characteristic of human behavior that some individuals believe in winning at all costs, even to the point of breaking the rules. This is true in radiosport as well. Newcomers to contesting quickly discover that nobody is watching them during the contest, and assume that they can break the rules and nobody will know.

Bad Behavior in Contesting

There are several common infractions, and the contest sponsors are well aware of them, as are most experienced contesters. For example, in contests where single operators are not allowed to use spotting assistance, some operators use it anyway and expect that nobody will notice. Of course, when their score is published and shows a considerably higher multiplier total than their peers, people get suspicious. Some contest sponsors routinely download the logs of all the cluster networks and compare the times when multipliers are spotted to the times they are worked by suspected "cluster cheaters." A pattern soon emerges and violators may be disqualified.

Some operators use higher power than their entry category permits. For example, a QRP category entrant may actually run 100 W or a Low Power entrant may be running an amplifier. In extreme cases, even some high-power entrants choose to use higher power than their license allows. The Reverse Beacon Network (**www.reversebeacon.net**) includes a signal comparison tool which logs the signal strength of all signals received during a contest. Using this tool to compare a suspected power cheater with other stations often gives a indication that something is not right. Obviously, difference in location, local terrain, and antenna systems can affect signal strength, but local hams may choose to visit a suspected cheater during a contest to see how much power is really in use.

Sometimes an operator will insert contacts in his log that are not actually made, usually new multipliers. Sometimes an entrant will insert fake QSOs with friends who are not actually active in the contest. These are often detected as "Unique" contacts, and an unusually high percentage of such QSOs is a red flag for the log checkers.

Some operators also attempt to generate activity by spotting themselves, but using a spoofed call sign (maybe their local club, maybe a friend) as the source of the spot. These are also easy to detect in the log-checking process.

Stations in the multioperator single- and two-transmitter categories sometimes alter the times in their log to cover up band-change timing violations. Single-operators in contests with mandatory off-times sometimes alter the logged time of QSOs at the beginning and end of their operating periods (this is known as "rubber-clocking"). These are also easily detected by the log-checking software and are grounds for disqualification.

Some operators choose to intentionally transmit with wide signals in an effort to create a clear frequency for themselves. This is an example of very poor sportsmanship — we all share the same spectrum, and when one station takes more than his share, everyone suffers.

Some of the major contests now use a network of wideband receiving stations to record all bands for the entire contest. Today's technology allows a single low-cost hard disk drive to contain the recording of all six contest bands for 48 hours. Contest sponsors can listen to any frequency at the time of a reported suspicious QSO, and play it back to review exactly what transpired. Time violations, faked QSOs, intentional poor signal quality, and other types of violations are easily proven with this tool. The lesson is that you should operate with the expectation that Big Brother is indeed listening to you.

Fortunately, with the tools available to the log checkers and peer pressure from locals, cheating in contests is the exception rather than the rule. The vast majority of competitors, especially at the highest levels, play by the rules.

Contester's Code of Ethics

The World Wide Radio Operators Foundation (WWROF, **www.wwrof.org**) has created a Contester's Code of Ethics, patterned after the DX Code of Conduct, and adopted by many contesting clubs and organizations.
- I will learn and obey the rules of any contest I enter, including the rules of my entry category.
- I will obey the rules for amateur radio in my country.
- I will not modify my log after the contest by using additional data sources to correct call sign/exchange errors.
- I will accept the judging and scoring decisions of the contest sponsor as final.
- I will adhere to the DX Code of Conduct in my operating style.
- I will yield my frequency to any emergency communications activity.
- I will operate my transmitter with sufficient signal quality to minimize interference to others.

3.4.7 After the Contest

You've put a lot of effort into making contacts and working multipliers, so you should definitely submit your log to the contest sponsors! If you're a contest club member, you will want to be sure your club receives credit for your score, as well. Even if you've just entered the contest casually and made a handful of QSOs, go ahead and submit a log. The sponsor will appreciate your efforts and it allows them to more accurately gauge contest activity and score all the logs.

As soon as the contest is over, start the log preparation process by making a backup copy of the log file before you do anything else. You're probably tired and anxious to relax — this is when mistakes happen, so be careful about naming and storing the file! There is no feeling worse than losing your just-completed contest log.

If you're really tired, go no further! Wait until you're fresh to submit your computer log. Remember, the log you submit is the log that will be checked.

What about duplicate QSOs — should they be removed? No. Leave them in the log. The sponsor's software will only count one of the QSOs automatically. You won't be penalized for duplicate QSOs.

Each contest has a submission deadline found in the rules announcement on the sponsor's website. It's usually less than 30 days and sometimes much less, so submit your log as soon as possible after the contest ends so you won't miss the deadline or forget. The amount of work involved in processing and verifying your contacts is considerable so contest sponsors are strict about meeting the log submission deadlines. Make sure you get an acknowledgement that your log was received. Most contest sponsors will send an email acknowledging that your log was received, and many publish a list of all logs received on their web pages. If your log is not acknowledged in one of these ways, make sure you have the correct e-mail address, and send it again!

To Edit or Not to Edit

Should you edit your log after the contest and prior to submitting it to the sponsor? How much editing is appropriate? What should you do if the information you've logged "looks" wrong?

Most top contesters agree that the contest is over at the time the rules say it's over. Examples of post-contest log manipulation (not allowed) may include editing times, correcting band changes, checking calls against the call book, checking against cluster spots, looking through logs from other contesters, confirming calls and exchanges with your buddies, reading DX and contesting reflectors for news about rare calls and even posting questions such as, "did anyone get QSL info for that 8Q7?"

There are wide ranging opinions about the acceptability of editing your log after the contest. The most conservative (and always acceptable) view is that no editing of any sort is permissible. Most contesters would agree that if you made a note during the contest about an error, it's OK to fix it afterwards. Furthermore, it is generally OK to make a quick pass through the log immediately after the contest looking for "obvious" typos such

The Contest Club

If you've tried a contest or two and liked it, you might want to consider joining a contest club. What better way to improve your operating and contesting skills, to learn the tricks of the trade or to gain knowledge and experience in contesting than by joining together with other amateurs with the same interests? In every region of the country you will find solid contest clubs, all working toward a similar goal: being the best at radiosport.

Just as different hams have different interests, you will find a wide variety of contest clubs, each with a special focus. Most contest clubs concentrate on HF events and possibly have DXing as an additional focus of the group. Some of these clubs specialize in DX contests, while others specialize in domestic contests. More than a few of these clubs also sponsor some specialty contests of their own, such as state QSO parties. Meeting programs often show new and simple ideas for improving station or operator capabilities.

Some clubs concentrate their efforts on VHF+ events. These clubs often form portable multiop expeditions or seek to have rover stations active during the contest. They can often provide technical assistance, perhaps helping you to get on a new microwave band for the contest.

Meetings of a contest club, such as the Yankee Clipper Contest Club shown here, are excellent opportunities to pick up valuable operating and technical information, as well as providing the opportunity to meet other contesters from your area. [Jim Idelson, K1IR, photo]

Club Competition

What challenges these clubs to compete? The ARRL sponsors affiliated club competition in most operating events. Each year dozens of clubs — in Local, Medium or Unlimited categories depending on their size — enlist their members to "win one for the club." If your club isn't already competing, check out the criteria for the ARRL Affiliated Club Competition published on the ARRL website. Clubs may also compete against one another in other major contests, such as the CQ World Wide DX Contest.

Join the Group, Improve Your Score

At meetings of the contest club, you'll have the opportunity to meet individuals at all experience levels. Many clubs have some sort of program for helping new contesters. Most clubs have one or more multioperator stations that need a supply of operators. It's valuable to get onto a multiop crew to learn contesting from experienced individuals. Camaraderie in a contest club makes the contester feel like part of the group, and sharing contest experiences at meetings (official and otherwise) helps bring the contester along to new heights. The value of a contest club to the individual contester cannot be denied and it is rare that anyone is found in the Top Ten of any contest who is not a member of a recognized contest club.

You can find local and regional contest clubs by using the ARRL Club search web page at **www.arrl.org/find-a-club**. Enter "contest" in the keyword window. You can also contact your ARRL Division's representative on the Contest Advisory Committee (**www.arrl.org/arrl-staff-cac**).

as entering CT as CTT or changing "o" to "Ø". Correcting syntax errors reported by a log acceptance robot, such as improper dates or multiplier abbreviations is also acceptable. Once you step over the line into making changes to what you think you "should" have logged, that's going too far.

Log Submission

When you are satisfied with your log, it's time to send it to the contest sponsor. The rules will usually specify the format in which the log should be submitted. The log format is the arrangement of information in the submitted computer file. The most common is known as *Cabrillo* and most logging software can create log files in this format. Again, carefully check the rules to see what types of files are accepted. If you don't send the right one, chances are your log won't be accepted and your score won't show up in the results.

THE CABRILLO CONTEST LOG FORMAT

The most common file format used by contest sponsors is Cabrillo. All electronic files for ARRL (and many other) contests *must* be in the Cabrillo format. All of the major contest logging programs will generate a valid Cabrillo file.

Cabrillo files are composed of ASCII characters, and the log information is in fixed-position columns. Cabrillo also adds a number of standardized "header" lines that contain information about the log, such as the operator's name, call and location,

contest category, power and so forth. The Cabrillo format allows sponsors to automate the process of log collection, sorting, and checking even though entrants use many different programs to generate the log files. The Cabrillo log file should be named **yourcall.cbr** or **yourcall.log** (for example, **w1aw.cbr** or **w1aw.log**). You can read about the Cabrillo file format at **wwrof.org/cabrillo/**.

Most contest sponsors accept logs via e-mail attachment, and some allow direct upload to a website. The rules will provide instructions. The e-mail or uploaded log will most likely be processed by a software "robot" program that automatically scans the received log files. Details of submitting logs for ARRL contests may be found at **www.arrl.org/log-submissions** and the ARRL contest log upload web page is **contest-log-submission.arrl.org/**.

If a software robot accepts your log, it will scan the log immediately. The robot looks to be sure that it understands everything in the log. The robot does *not* perform any QSO crosschecks with other logs. The robot will tell you if your dates are wrong or if you've picked a category that doesn't exist for that contest or if your contest club isn't recognized, for example. You can then correct any problems in the log file, resubmit it to the robot and wait for the reply. You can send your log to the robot any number of times. Each subsequent version will overwrite the previous version.

When the robot is happy with the information in your log (remember, that doesn't mean your QSOs are okay, just that the information

is properly formatted) you will receive a message that the log has been accepted and you may be given a numeric "receipt" or confirmation number. Save the robot's e-mail and all confirmation numbers for possible later reference.

Most contesters also post their claimed score (and comments) to the **3830scores.com** website. This gives a quick indication of how the score stacks up against others in the same category. However, be aware that posting your score to 3830 does *not* enter your log in the contest! You must send the log to the sponsor!

LOG CHECKING

What happens next varies from contest to contest but the overall process is more or less the same. Your log is inspected to be sure that it has all the necessary information, that the dates are correct, and so forth. The logs are then sorted by category and crosschecking begins.

For larger contests, including those sponsored by the ARRL, the automated process is much more thorough. All logs, once accepted by the robot or checked by hand, are combined into a master database. Special software then compares each of the submitted QSOs with the log of the corresponding station and looks for errors. If there are errors, the appropriate penalties are assessed. Following the crosscheck of all QSOs, the scores for all participants are then computed and compiled for the sponsor, who then publishes the results. The results for larger contests are generally available a few months after the log-submission deadline. Some contests with smaller numbers of participants, such as the North American Sprint, have the results finalized in a week or so after the contest.

The automated log checking process also generates a report for each log containing information on what the process found. This is called a *log checking report* (LCR) or a *UBN report*, where "UBN" stands for Unique, Busted or Not-In-the-Log. (See the Glossary at the end of this section.) Log checking reports are full of valuable information, generally containing complete information on every QSO in which errors were found.

Errors that can be attributed to you (miscopying calls or exchange information or just not appearing in the other station's log) will result in penalties defined by the sponsors. In general, you'll lose credit for the QSO including any multiplier credit claimed (if you worked the multiplier again later in the contest, you'll still get credit for it). Some contests also assess an additional penalty to discourage fast-but-sloppy operating. You're not being accused of cheating, just penalized for making a mistake to reward better performance next time!

Errors not attributed to you (the other

```
START-OF-LOG: 2.0
ARRL-SECTION: NH
CALLSIGN: K1RO
CATEGORY: SINGLE-OP 160M LOW CW
CLAIMED-SCORE: 47320
CLUB:
CONTEST: ARRL-160
CREATED-BY: WriteLog V10.43F
NAME: Mark Wilson
ADDRESS: 77 Anderson Rd
ADDRESS: Newport, NH 03773
OPERATORS: K1RO
SOAPBOX:
QSO:  1836 CW 2006-12-02 0043 K1RO       599 NH    K0TV      599    NH
QSO:  1839 CW 2006-12-02 0045 K1RO       599 NH    K4ZA      599    MDC
QSO:  1840 CW 2006-12-02 0045 K1RO       599 NH    AA1SU     599    VT
QSO:  1805 CW 2006-12-02 0047 K1RO       599 NH    N8II      599    WV
QSO:  1806 CW 2006-12-02 0048 K1RO       599 NH    VE3MIS    599    ON
QSO:  1809 CW 2006-12-02 0049 K1RO       599 NH    K1EO      599    EMA
QSO:  1810 CW 2006-12-02 0050 K1RO       599 NH    N2MM      599    SNJ
QSO:  1812 CW 2006-12-02 0052 K1RO       599 NH    K1GU      599    TN
QSO:  1814 CW 2006-12-02 0052 K1RO       599 NH    K3ZO      599    MDC
QSO:  1815 CW 2006-12-02 0053 K1RO       599 NH    N4IR      599    TN
QSO:  1817 CW 2006-12-02 0053 K1RO       599 NH    W3BGN     599    EPA
QSO:  1864 CW 2006-12-02 0056 K1RO       599 NH    K1EP      599    EMA
QSO:  1860 CW 2006-12-02 0057 K1RO       599 NH    W4PM      599    VA
QSO:  1859 CW 2006-12-02 0057 K1RO       599 NH    NB1B      599    EMA
```

The header and first few QSOs from a typical Cabrillo file ready for submission to the contest sponsor. The header contains all the information that the sponsor needs to include the entry in the right category and send awards if earned. Each QSO is reported on a separate line in a consistent format. Because the Cabrillo format is the same no matter which logging program was used during the contest, log data can easily be loaded into a master database for crosschecking.

RTTY Contesting

By Ed Muns, WØYK

New hams as well as veteran CW and phone contesters are jumping into the fun on RTTY. Unlike RTTY operation a few decades ago, today you can set up this digital mode with a minimum of additional equipment beyond a basic CW/phone station. Transmitting and receiving can be easily done with most modern transceivers, an old PC and simple cables. Most contesters already have a computer integrated with their stations, so getting on RTTY can be very quick. The HF Digital Modes section earlier in this book shows how to do it.

Gearing Up

Don Hill, AA5AU developed and maintains a robust RTTY contesting website at www.rttycontesting.com. An experienced and successful RTTY competitor, Don gives an excellent overview of all aspects of RTTY contesting from getting started to choosing a logging program to operating hints. Although his website is mostly based on the *WriteLog* contest software, much of the information is equally applicable to setups using other programs. There are also links to many other sources of information for new and experienced RTTY contesters alike.

There are several choices for software, but most people starting out today choose *MMTTY*, a freeware RTTY PC program for receiving and transmitting. While the RTTY modulation and demodulation capability is superb, the contest logging aspect of *MMTTY* is far less than what most contesters will want. For RTTY contest logging, the three most popular programs are *Writelog*, *N1MM Logger* and *Win-Test*. *MMTTY* can be integrated with each of these so that RTTY encoding/decoding is available with contest logging in a single optimized package. Other popular decoding packages are *2Tone* and *GRitty*.

RTTY Operating Skills

In contrast to CW contesting where the operator's brain timeshares between decoding CW and other tasks, in RTTY contesting the computer does all the decoding for you. When a RTTY signal is properly tuned in on the receiver, the result is clear "printing" of the transmitted characters on the computer screen. The good news is that this frees up the operator to attend to other details of contest operation, including very effective use of SO2R (single-op, two-radio) operating. The bad news is that until the receiver is tuned very close to the correct frequency of the incoming signal, only gibberish is available on the screen. With practice, your ears will be able to help you tune in the signal to within a few hertz. RTTY decoding software and RTTY modems have tuning indicators to facilitate precise

Ed, WØYK/P49X is active and successful in all major RTTY contests.

tuning of the signal.

In normal RTTY ragchewing with little or no QRM from nearby signals, wide IF filtering in the receiver works best because the RTTY decoding software typically provides optimal filtering. However, in the typical contest environment with heavy QRM, many RTTY contesters use a narrow 250-Hz IF filter. Starting out, you may want to use a 500-Hz filter until you are accustomed to quickly tuning in a RTTY signal.

Once you have basic RTTY receiving and transmitting working and integrated with your choice of contest logging software, you will want to focus on making your system as streamlined as possible for the most efficient RTTY contest operation. Basic to this are the message buffers used almost exclusively for all RTTY contest transmissions. While it is easy to go into "keyboard mode" and be able to type free text, it is far more efficient to use message buffers, just as in CW contesting. Message buffers should be kept as short as possible to reliably convey the necessary information. Each message should be preceded with a Line Feed and ended with a Space. This sets off your transmission within the screen of the receiving station in the presence of gibberish characters generated from band noise.

You will soon learn that some "gibberish" is actually numbers that were falsely decoded as letters. For example, "TOO" becomes "599" when this occurs. If you suspect a letter group is really a number, as in a contest exchange, look at the keyboard and translate the letters to numbers by mapping the key above and to the left of each letter key.

Efficient RTTY contest operation for high rates also requires minimum keystrokes for each of (hopefully!) hundreds or thousands of contacts. Thus, it is

important to study your logging software features to understand how to accomplish each phase of a RTTY contest QSO with the fewest keystrokes.

In many loggers, each phase can be achieved with a single keystroke. For example, software using a call sign database will capture and highlight valid call signs out of incoming transmissions. Properly configured, the logger will grab the most recent call sign that is a new multiplier or a new band-station, drop it in the call sign field of the entry window, call the station and send your exchange…all as a result of pressing a single key on the keyboard! As the return exchange comes in, use the mouse to click on any part of the exchange that is not already pre-filled in the entry window. At the end of the station's transmission, you can press another key to send a TU, QRZ message.

Single Op, Two Radios

With the RTTY fixed speed of 60 WPM, it quite feasible to achieve hourly QSO rates in excess of 120/hour with a properly configured and tuned SO2R RTTY contesting station. Because the operator does not need to expend brainpower on decoding the signal, more attention can be given to tuning and operating each radio. In fact, this characteristic leads veteran CW contester K5ZD to point out that RTTY contesting is the ideal training ground for SO2R skill development in general.

So jump in and have a blast with RTTY contesting! While there are many similarities to CW and phone contesting, there are also a number of unique differences. This can add diversity and excitement to your overall contesting experience. Be aware of direct comparisons to your current favorite mode of contesting and keep an open mind while learning RTTY contesting.

station busting your call or information) are still valuable because they highlight possible shortcomings in your transmissions. For example, if a lot of stations are miscopying the H in your call as S or 5 in CW contests, you may be sending too fast for the conditions. Or perhaps you are using non-standard phonetics on phone and one letter in your call is frequently miscopied as a result. Fortunately, you are not penalized for errors by "the other guy" in most contests.

Once the log checking is complete, the scores are compiled and the sponsor determines the winners. Results are usually published on the web and sometimes in magazines such as *QST, CQ* or *National Contest Journal (NCJ)*. The highest scorers are recognized with plaques in most major events, and regional winners are awarded certificates, either mailed or downloadable from the sponsor's website.

RESULTS ANALYSIS

After the contest, results can be analyzed to see what might have been done differently. Comparing notes with friends is a good idea, as you will often find they did something totally different from you and it may come in handy to have the benefit of their experience in the future.

Assuming you used computer logging, you'll find that most programs have several post-contest features for use in log analysis. In addition, standalone log analyzer software such as *CBS by K5KA* (**www.kkn.net/~k5tr/cbs.html**) and *SH5* (**sites.google.com/site/sh5analyzer/**), can provide in-depth analysis of contest logs.

3.4.8 Computers and Contesting

Using software to log contacts, connect to worldwide networks, and control station equipment has taken a central role in contesting. This is a natural result of the power available in even low-end computers combined with low-cost or free software for day-to-day operating and special programs designed just for contesting.

Once just a tool for entering log information, the computer is integrated into nearly all phases of the modern contest station. The computer sends voice and CW messages. It reads and sets the operating parameters of the radio. Digital mode contesting is virtually impossible without it. Through interfaces, it can control nearly all of the station equipment. All this allows the operator to remain focused on making QSOs instead of fiddling with various pieces of equipment.

If you log DX and ragchew contacts on a computer or use a sound-card for digital mode operating, it's a short step to computer-based contesting, too.

The most popular contest logging program is *N1MM+*. It can be used for virtually any contest, offers many user-customizable features and provides all the information an operator can use during a contest. And its best feature is that it's free! [Courtesy Tom Wagner, N1MM]

Logging Software

If you are just getting started in contesting, you can get along just fine with a simple program and manual radio control. Take advantage of the logging software's ability to handle the "paperwork" so you can focus on operating. Most general-purpose software isn't really designed for efficient contest operating — you should begin with one of the simpler contest logging programs or "loggers" and learn how it works. Contest-oriented programs can generate files for importing by your general-purpose logging program so all of your contacts are tracked for awards and QSLing.

Once you've entered a station's call sign in the logger's call entry window, the software will check to see if the station is a duplicate or a possible new multiplier, whether the multiplier is needed on other bands, and provide similar call signs of active contest stations in case you're not sure of what you copied. Entering the other station's exchange is just as easy.

A logging program can send CW messages for you automatically, record and playback voice messages on phone, and both decode and send RTTY signals.

If you want to take advantage of the worldwide spotting networks, your contest logging program can interact directly with those websites to both capture the calls and frequencies of stations in the contest and send out spots from your contacts. The calls can be displayed on *band maps* that show you where stations are operating — you can click on the call signs and control your radio to go right to that frequency!

Most contest logging software and accessory programs are written for the *Windows* operating system. There a few programs for the Macintosh and *Linux* user, as well. Some of the more-popular programs include *N1MM+* (**n1mm.hamdocs.com**), *Win-Test* (**www.win-test.com**), and *WriteLog* (**writelog.com**).

SELECTING LOGGING SOFTWARE

Start your selection process by asking friends or club members what logging programs they use and which ones they started with. Pick a contest in which you have a bit of experience and try out the software without trying to automate your station. Another strategy is to guest-operate at a station already running the software you're interested in. Note what you like and don't like about it then go back to the club members with your questions. Most of the loggers have active user's groups to help newcomers, test new versions, and share experiences.

After you've gotten a little experience with two or three programs, you'll have a pretty good idea of what you want and need.

Upgrade to or purchase the latest version of the program and install it on your computer. Walk through the tutorial or practice sessions if the software offers them. Print out the user's manual or operating guide. Learn how to configure the software for your favorite contests — many loggers can store configuration files that can set up the program for specific contests individually.

After you use logging software a few times you'll develop preferences for how the software looks on the computer display. Programs that can open several windows for different functions allow you to resize and move the windows around the screen. Place the main contact entry window, call sign check window, and any spotting network windows where you can see them without swiveling your head around or having to use the mouse or keyboard to bring them to the "front." Move lesser-used windows that display contact rate, general information, score summaries and so forth to the edges of the display. If you have a second display, this would be a good place to put the supporting windows.

A detailed discussion of using and configuring contest-logging software is beyond the scope of this book but you will find many, many articles and posts on computer logging both online and in magazines such as the *National Contest Journal*. Again, rely on the experiences of club members to help you over the rough spots and don't be afraid to sit in and watch a skilled operator use the computer during a contest.

Computer Requirements

Since the demands of contest operating are modest for a computer (how fast can you possibly work stations, anyway?) you don't have to use top-of-the-line hardware. Check the logging software's minimum requirements for what you need. The used and reconditioned computers available at your local computer recycler will probably work just fine and at a fraction of a new computer's cost. They will also have lots of older interface cards and adapters that may work just fine in a ham shack. Save your budget for antennas and radios!

It is important to have a full-size keyboard. The smaller keyboards of laptops and ultrabooks are more difficult to use. You should probably learn to touch-type since that will allow you to focus on the contact and not on where the keys are! If you plan on doing much digital mode operating, make room for an external mouse or trackball on your desktop. Remember that any input device you use will need to operate with a minimum of distraction to the operator.

If you plan on using the spotting networks you'll need a full-time connection to the Internet.

RFI to and from computers (and their accompanying Internet connection hardware) can be an issue. Make sure your computer has a metal enclosure (laptops and tablets are often designed to be less RFI-prone because of their plastic cases) and that interface cards and cable shields can be securely grounded to it. When you're shopping for cables, the extra expense for shielded cables is usually worthwhile. You should purchase a selection of ferrite snap-on cores and toroids as well.

Don't scrimp on display quality — you'll be looking at it hour after hour. A mid-size display that you can place close to the operating position is more effective than a large display that you have to place further away.

Interfacing the Computer to the Station

Looking at photos and videos of competitive stations in the contest writeups, you'll find a large display (or two!) front and center at the operating position with radios and accessory gear to the sides. Behind the operating position it's not uncommon to find more computer cables for audio, data, and control than RF cables.

You'll need to connect the computer to the radio through its control port. Radio control interfaces can be anything from RS-232 to ICOM's CI-V interface to USB and Ethernet or even wireless interfaces. The data protocols used to control radios vary with manufacturer and model so be sure your logging software will support your radio and that your computer has the correct interface for it.

Keying interfaces for CW are usually based on a COM (RS-232) or USB port. Since most new laptop PCs do not have an RS-232 port, you may have to use a USB-to-RS-232

adapter or get a computer-to-transceiver interface designed for USB operation. Due to timing issues within *Windows*, most contesters use an external WinKey-based keyer (www.k1el.com) as a standalone keyer or as part of a more comprehensive control interface. The WinKey accepts ASCII characters one at a time over the USB port and creates perfectly-formed CW characters. You can use a standalone external keyer in conjunction with the logger-based keying by connecting them in parallel at the radio key input jack.

Audio and digital signal interfaces generally include transformer-isolation to minimize hum and RFI. The audio connection to the radio can be made through the microphone input or via an accessory connector. Direct FSK and CW keying is sometimes supported through an optically isolated solid-state switch. There are many variations of these interfaces so it is best that you list all of your operating needs and then start shopping. This is another area in which your contest club can be very helpful and there are number of construction articles in magazines and online to build them yourself.

Two-Radio Contesting (SO2R)

The use of two radios in a single-operator station (single-op, two-radios, or SO2R) has been around for many years but has spread significantly in recent years. Coupled with innovations in logging software, it is almost necessary for the winning single-op contester in either the Low Power or High Power category to use two radios.

The basic technique for SO2R is to call CQ on one radio on one band while tuning or chasing spots for new stations on the second radio on another band. This allows the SO2R

Bill, K2PO, uses this simple SO2R station to score at or near the top of the Low Power category in the ARRL November Sweepstakes contest every year. [Bill Conwell, K2PO, photo]

operator to effectively be in two places at once, but requires that the second radio be capable of hearing weak signals while the first radio is CQing at full power. The operator can pause his CQing on the first radio long enough to work a station on the second radio, then resume CQing. Over the course of a 48-hour contest, a neophyte to SO2R operation may add up to 100 QSOs. An accomplished operator can add as many as 400 QSOs, including multipliers that may not otherwise be worked. Some operators have learned how use their SO2R stations to CQ and run pileups on two bands at the same time (with only one radio transmitting at a time) Needless to say, this is a tremendous advantage over an operator with only one radio. As with any contesting skill, effective SO2R operation requires practice and you should not try it until you have mastered one-radio contesting!

The design of a station capable of two-radio contesting can be more complicated than the design of a multi-multi station. Like a multi-multi station, band-pass filters and harmonic suppression stubs are necessary to prevent damage to the second radio's receiver, especially during high-power operation. Unlike the multi-multi case where each band has a dedicated radio, an SO2R station must be able to access any band at any time, so the filters must be switchable.

Given the expense of repairing or replacing a blown filter, amplifier output, or receiver input, automating SO2R station switching tasks is a good investment once complexity begins to exceed the operator's ability to keep track of all the settings. You can tell when it has become time for automated interface control when you find yourself making mistakes in the heat of the contest or become confused when tired or busy. A receiver protection device such as the DX Engineering RG-5000 "Receiver Guard" is inexpensive protection compared to the cost of repairing a transceiver.

Most of the information to control antenna switching is available in the band and frequency information the radio can supply through its data and band ports. *Band decoders* are standalone devices that translate the band information generated by your radio into switch or relay closures that can control antenna switches, filters, and perform other station configuration tasks. Logging software can often read the radio's information and change antenna and filter settings through band decoders or other external interfaces.

Audio and CW keyer switching is necessary to allow the operator to listen to the active radio and transmit on the correct radio. All of this can be controlled by the logging program through suitable interface boxes. Articles in *National Contest Journal* and information in the *ARRL Antenna Book* and the *ARRL Handbook* show you how to build this equipment yourself, if you prefer.

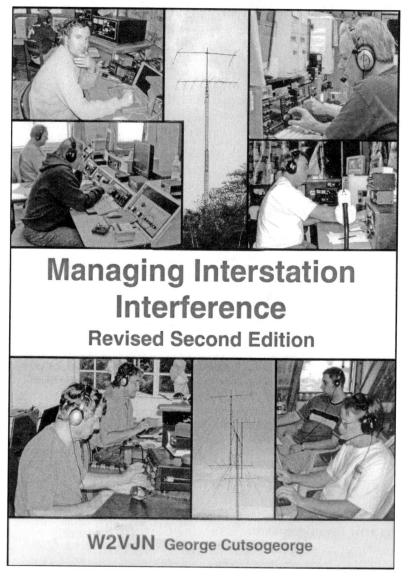

Managing Interstation Interference by George Cutsogeorge, W2VJN, is required reading for a multiop or SO2R station builder. It is available from Vibroplex (www.vibroplex.com).

As the number of interface functions has increased, several manufacturers have introduced SO2R controllers that bring many common functions into one piece of equipment — CW and voice keyers, audio switching, digital mode interfaces, accessory equipment control, and so on. Manufacturers offering SO2R controllers, switchable filters, and other interface boxes include microHam (**www.microham.com**), Top Ten Devices (**www.qth.com/topten**), 4O3A (**www.4o3a. com**), Dunestar Systems (**www.dunestar. com**) and the Yankee Clipper Contest Club (YCCC) club SO2R project with kits available at **k1xm.org/SO2R/**.

Ergonomics

Ergonomics is the study and practice of human engineering in station design. Simply put, if you're not comfortable, you won't stay in the chair and operate. If you don't stay in the chair, you won't be competitive. This section touches on some of the important aspects of station ergonomics but for more complete information and guidelines, read up on workplace ergonomics. The requirements are much the same as for a radio operating position. Enter "office ergonomics guidelines" into an Internet search engine for numerous references on placement of equipment, products, exercises and so forth. Over the course of a contest, ergonomics and the comfort factor can make a big difference in your alertness and energy!

Choose an office chair designed for someone who works at a computer keyboard all day. It should be firm but comfortable, adjustable for height and back support and sturdy enough to last. You'll find big, padded models too soft for long-term sitting. A firm, adjustable chair allows you to change positions for variety through the contest. If you spent hundreds (or thousands) of dollars on your radio — you shouldn't scrimp on another piece of equipment you'll be using every minute the rig is on!

ARRANGING YOUR OPERATING DESK

The operating desk's surface should be large enough to hold all of your operating equipment, usually with multiple tiers for holding the various items in their most convenient locations. Arrange equipment so that everything used frequently during the contest is immediately at hand or in front of you. The keyboard, radio, and monitor should be central, with all peripheral equipment surrounding the operator in accordance with how it will be used. Place the keyboard, radio, and CW paddle short distances apart to minimize unnecessary hand and arm movement. In general, if you're uncomfortable while operating move the equipment around until you are comfortable. Place the computer case completely off the desktop since it shouldn't have to be touched during contest.

Your desk or table will usually be 29 inches (about 74 cm) high. That's the standard for office furniture in the US and an ideal height for a working surface. The standard height for a typing surface is 26 inches. That's the height you would want for a computer keyboard, and you may want to consider a separate shelf below the desk to hold the keyboard. Remember to use a pad to support your wrists and forearms if the keyboard is on the desktop.

Place the computer display directly in front of the operating chair, since that's where you will be looking most of the time. Don't place the display to the side or so high that you have to raise your head to look at it. The display should be at the right distance for comfortable viewing. If you wear glasses, to reduce eye strain consider a pair of single-lens glasses specifically for viewing a computer display at that distance.

Rotator control boxes and antenna switches should be easy to reach, although consideration should be given to having these items controlled by the radio or computer. Wattmeters should be placed in visual range so that you can monitor the functions of the transmitter and antennas during the course of the contest. Dual-needle wattmeters are helpful since they give an instant indication of high SWR if you accidentally try to transmit on the wrong antenna or if something has gone wrong with the antenna.

Unless your amplifier has automatic band switching, mark the dials so that you can quickly set the controls when you make band changes. Amplifiers should be placed where you can see the meters and indicator lights to check for proper operation and where you can reach the controls for occasional adjustments. Since the adjustments and band changes aren't made frequently, amps can be placed off to the side or above the radios and monitor. Make sure it is easy to see warning and overload indicators from your operating position.

To save wear and tear on your voice, phone operators should definitely consider a voice keyer of some sort — particularly for calling CQ. The best option might be using the computer's sound card to record messages that can be replayed from the computer keyboard under control of the logging software.

Personal Preparation

Whether you are just making contest QSOs now and then, for a few hours at a time, or spending the whole weekend at it, you need to be alert and clear-headed to make and record QSOs accurately and operate your equipment properly. To do so means that you should also take care of that very important piece of equipment — the operator!

SLEEP

The number one consideration to taking care of yourself during long contest weekends is getting enough sleep. Some contesters can "do 48 in the chair" but they have to prepare themselves first. They stock up on sleep throughout the week before the contest and often try to sleep during the hours just before the contest starts. That means no tower or antenna work on contest day! By building up a reserve of sleep they start the contest refreshed, making it a lot easier to get through that first 24 hours. The second night is tough for everybody and about impossible if you were running on empty during the first night.

How many operators actually operate all 48 hours? Not many! Look at the contest results to see if hours of operation are listed. Most of the top scorers in a 48 hour contest put in between 40 and 46 hours of operating time. They grab short periods of sleep during slow hours, trading the loss of a few QSOs against mental acuity the following day. Again, look at logs and ask other operators to find out when you should do the same.

How long should you sleep? The answer varies from person to person but there are a number of references that indicate the brain works best with a 90-minute sleep cycle. According to those researchers, sleeping for one such cycle leaves you more refreshed and satisfied than one hour or two hours. Two 90-minute naps every 24 hours results in 42 hours of operating time. (See "Sleep — A Contest Prescription," by T. Scott Johnson, KC1JI, in Nov/Dec 1988 *NCJ* and "A Sleep Strategy for DX Contesting," by Randall A. Thompson, K5ZD, in Sep/Oct 1994 *NCJ* and updated at **www.contesting.com/articles/37**) The archives of the CQ-Contest reflector have numerous posts on the subject, as well.

Another popular strategy is to catnap for a few minutes right at the operating position whenever you need a bit of sleep. The trick is to wake back up before too much time goes by.

When should you sleep? Analysis of your hourly rate from previous contests shows when it is most productive to sleep if you don't play to stay awake for the entire contest. For example, if your rate went to 5 QSOs per hour at 0800 UTC and only one of those contacts was a multiplier, perhaps an hour's rest would have helped you more the next day.

FOOD AND FITNESS

There as many opinions about the right food for contesting as there are contest operators. In general, contesters prefer light fare during the contest that's easy to digest and keeps blood sugar levels topped off. Some operators like to "carbo-load" before the contest, just like for a bike race. Experiment with different favorites to see what keeps you nourished without making you drowsy. Eat lightly to avoid a post-meal "low" and remember that what goes in must eventually come out.

What about coffee and energy drinks? Caffeine and herbal "boosters" do pick up your mental energy for a while but the fall off afterwards can be worse than not having the beverage in the first place. Many contesters try not to use any kind of stimulant until the

Braco, OE1EMS/E77DX, maintains his intense focus in contests by staying fit doing CrossFit workouts and tower work. [Braco Memic, E77DX, photo]

second day of a contest when the boost is really needed. Try to go into a contest refreshed and caught up on sleep. Don't try to coffee or cola your way through.

While contesting doesn't require a lot of physical activity — just the opposite — it certainly does burn a lot of calories. Being physically fit does have a measurable effect on one's stamina and the ability to remain alert and focused. Prepare for big contest efforts with regular exercise and attention to your diet. You'll be more comfortable and able to maintain high performance levels longer.

BREAKS

Would you subject yourself to a 48-hour airplane flight without breaks or the opportunity for some activity? Of course not, so why do it in the ham shack? Sitting in one position for long periods of time is not healthy. You need to get up every once in a while and stretch. A short walk is recommended but even operating from a standing position can help. Use headphones with a cord long enough to permit bending and stretching.

There are very few contests in which you can't take a few minutes every few hours to get a little exercise. Activity is often the perfect tonic when you're dragging with a slow QSO rate.

Bathroom breaks can be managed by managing your liquid intake. Be sure to stay hydrated but avoid having a continuously full beverage glass. You'll wind up visiting the facilities way too often! Note that leaving the keyer in "auto-repeat" mode while you take a pit stop is considered bad contest manners!

3.4.9 Multioperator Contesting

Nowhere else in Amateur Radio will you find the camaraderie that exists in operating a multiop station. Shared experiences are always more enjoyable and there's no better way to share the contest experience than with a group of enthusiastic friends.

Multiops provide an ideal training ground for operators new to contesting, allowing the new operator to learn from contesters having years of experience. Multiops also allow those who have the desire and skills but not the time or energy to participate as a competitive single-op entry.

There are three categories of multiops in most contests: Multiop, Single-transmitter (MS), Multiop, Two-transmitter (M2), and Multiop, Multi-transmitter (MM). In VHF+ contests, multiop categories sometimes include "Limited" (where up to four bands are used) and "Unlimited."

Multi-Single and Multi-Two

The multi-single class was originally conceived as a way to keep a single station on the air for the entire contest by allowing more than one operator to take a turn. It has evolved over time into a very competitive category. In many cases more than one station is used during the course of the contest — a "run station" that strives for the maximum of QSOs and a "mult station" that searches for multipliers. Strategy plays an important part in the planning and operation of the multi-single station. The key is to determine how a second station and additional operator(s) can be used for maximum effectiveness.

Multi-single stations are generally limited to a certain number of band changes per hour or are required to spend a minimum amount of time on a particular band before changing bands. The multi-single participant must use those band changes strategically. For example, before a band change is made for purposes of working a multiplier, the operator manning the multiplier station should

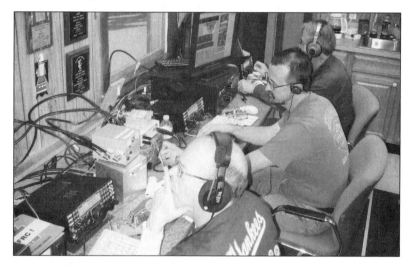

Multioperator contesting can be a lot of fun. (l-r) W2RQ, W2NO and W1GD were part of the W2GD team during the ARRL 160 Meter Contest. They operated from the facilities of radio station WYRS-FM in West Creek, New Jersey. [Craig Thompson, K9CT, photo]

The call sign WB9Z has been heard in contests for many years. In this contest the multiop crew included (l-r) Jerry, KE9I; Don, K9NR; Val, NV9L; Mike, K9XZ; and Carl, K9CS.

CQ Contest Hall of Fame

The *CQ* Contest Hall of Fame (started in 1986) was established by *CQ* magazine to recognize those amateurs who have made major contributions to contesting. The activities and accomplishments that qualify one for membership include both proven skill as an operator, demonstrated by high scores in contests, but also contributions to the contest community usually described by the phrase "above and beyond the call of duty." A maximum of two people may be inducted into the Contest Hall of Fame each year.

Rich Strand, KL7RA (left photo), was posthumously inducted into the CQ Contest Hall of Fame at a ceremony in Dayton, Ohio, in May 2016. Accepting the award were his son Jeff and wife Jyl. CQWW Contest Director Randy Thompson, K5ZD, presented the award. [Bob Wilson, N6TV, photo]

CQ Contest Hall of Fame Members as of June 2016, sorted by call sign:

AA5AU	Don Hill	K6NA	Glenn Rattmann	S52AA	Tine Brajnik
AD1C	Jim Reisert	K6SSS	Frederick Capossela	S59AA	Franc Bogataj
AI6V	Carl Cook	KH6IJ	Katashi Nose	VE3EJ	John Sluymer
DJ6QT	Walter Skudlarek	KL7RA	Richard Strand	VE7SV	Dale Green
DL3TD	Lothar Wilke	LU8DQ	Jorge Humberto Bozzo	WØAIH	Paul Bittner
G3FXB	Al J. Slater	LY2NK	Algis Kregzde	WØYK	Ed Muns
G3SXW	Roger Western	NØAX	Ward Silver	W1BIH/PJ9JT	John Thompson
I2UIY	Paolo Cortese	N2AA	Eugene Walsh	W1WY	Frank Anzalone
KØDQ	J. Scott Redd	N3RS	Ron Sigismonti	W2GD	John Crovelli
KØTO	Tod Olson	N5KO	Trey Garlough	W2PV	Jim Lawson
K1AR	John Dorr	N6AA	Dick Norton	W3AU	Ed Bissell
K1DG	Doug Grant	N6RO	Ken Keeler	W3GM	W. Gerry Mathis
K1EA	Ken Wolff	N6TJ	Jim Neiger	W3GRF	Leonard Chertok
K1TO	Dan Street	N6TR	Larry "Tree" Tyree	W3LPL	Francis Donovan
K1ZM	Jeffrey Briggs	N6TW	Larry Weaver	W4AN	Bill Fisher
K2GL	Hazzard "Buzz" Reeves	N6ZZ	Phil Goetz	W4KFC	Vic Clark
K3EST	Bob Cox	N8BJQ	Steve Bolia	W6OAT	Charles "Rusty" Epps
K3LR	Tim Duffy	OH2BH	Martti Laine	W6QD	Herb Becker
K3WW	Charles "Chas" Fulp	OH2MM	Ville Hiilesmaa	W6RR	Gordon Marshall
K3ZO	Fred Laun	ON4UN	John Devoldere	W7RM	Rush Drake
K4VX	Lew Gordon	OZ1LO	Leif Ottosen	W8IMZ	Bernie W. Welch
K5RC	Tom Taormina	PY5EG	Atilano de Oms	WA2AAU	Richard Frey
K5ZD	Randy Thompson				

make a band map of stations to work before changing bands to maximize the benefit of the band change.

While the limitations on the multi-single stations (and multi-two) may seem somewhat restrictive, multi-single has been a popular category over the years and competition at the highest level is fierce. Recent winners in multi-single categories actually use three or more independent stations at one QTH with elaborate lockouts to prevent transmitting on two frequencies on the same band simultaneously. In recent years, many contests have added a Low Power Multi-single category.

Multi-two category rules are very similar to multi-single, with the addition of a second run station and a single multiplier station trading off band changes between the two run stations. The strategy to maximize output of a multi-two station is an interesting challenge and often requires four complete stations to really maximize the score.

Multi-Multi

The multi-multi station consists of exactly what the name implies: many operators and many transmitters with only one transmitting on any band at one time. High-end multi-multi stations often have two-station capability on each band. One chases multipliers or other unworked stations on the band while the other one calls CQ throughout the contest. Only one transmitted signal per band at any time is allowed but that's easy to ensure with an interlock circuit or software function that prevents both transmitters from being keyed at once. It's no wonder that these stations make very high scores in the contests where the category is permitted.

These stations provide excellent training grounds for new operators as staffing a multi-multi is one of the more difficult tasks in contesting. You can frequently get "chair time" at one if you make the acquaintance of one of the regular operators and have the opportunity to watch and hear the operators go about their business at a top multiop.

The multi-multi is also useful to the beginning operator for learning what is possible on each band. The successful multi-multi is required to work all bands almost all the time. By doing so, one can learn about those midnight over-the-pole openings on 15 or 20, how early 40 meters opens to Asia, how 80 meters opens before sunset and stays open an hour or two after sunrise, and what contacts might be possible at those times. It's a great way to gain useful experience in every phase of contesting by operating with experienced teachers of the contest art.

Remember, Contesting is Fun!

Of course there are many good reasons for contest participation; improving station and operator capability foremost among them. But the main reason it is so popular (and when did you ever hear as much activity on the bands as during a contest?) is that it's *fun*. Over the years, you'll find that you work a lot of the same people regularly and it's fun to say hello by giving them a contact. You'll develop new topics of conversation as you run into them on the air between contests. Meeting other contesters in person adds another dimension to contesting. It provides the opportunity to see the faces of your on-air friends and builds a special camaraderie. Try it and see!

3.4.10 Glossary

10-minute rule — refers to a limit on the number of band changes permitted in an hour or how long a station is required to operate on a band after making a band change

3830 — a popular website and e-mail reflector for reporting scores after the contest (**www.3830scores.com** and **lists. contesting.com/_3830**)

Alligator — a station whose signal is loud but cannot hear calling stations well

Assisted — obtaining information about other stations in the contest from other stations or the Internet (does *not* refer to physical assistance in operating), also called Unlimited

Band map — a display of call signs received from the spotting network organized by frequency

Bonus — extra points added to a score for making a specific type of QSO, for contacting specific stations or operating in a specified way

Breakdown — a table showing the QSOs and multipliers worked on each band

Busted — an incorrect spot, call sign or exchange

Cabrillo — a format standard for contest logs

Check partial — compare the logged call to calls already logged in the contest; Super Check Partial uses a database of calls known to be active

Checklog — submitted logs that are only used in the log checking process and are not listed in the results for competitive purposes

Claimed score — the score based on the logged contacts before log checking

Confirmation number — a receipt number generated by an automated log submission process

Cut numbers — letter abbreviations for Morse numerals, such as N for 9, A for 1, T for zero, and so forth

Deadline — closing date for score and log submissions for a contest

DQ — disqualified, the result of rules violations

Dupe — duplicate contact, a station that has been worked before and can't be contacted again for point credit

Exchange — the information that must be exchanged in a contest QSO

Golden log — a log in which all contact information has been copied correctly

Grid square — the grid locator as defined by the Maidenhead Locator system, can be either 4- or 6-character

Hired gun — a guest operator, usually referring to someone highly skilled

Hold — in reference to a frequency, to maintain a presence on a frequency by calling CQ

LCR — Log Checking Report, the output of the log checking process for a submitted log

Lockout — a device or software that prevents two transmitters from being keyed on the same band at the same time

MO, MS, MM, M2 — Multioperator; Multioperator Single-Transmitter; Multioperator Multi-Transmitter; Multioperator Two-Transmitter

Move —to coordinate a change to another band to contact a station for additional multiplier credit

Mult — shorthand for multiplier

Not in the log (NIL) — a QSO that cannot be cross-referenced to an entry in the log of the station with which the QSO is claimed

Off-time — required periods of non-operation during a contest

Packet — a general term now referring to the worldwide spotting networks

Penalty — points removed during the log checking process in response to errors

QSO B4 — "QSO before" meaning a duplicate contact

QSO points — the point credit for a specific QSO

Rate — the equivalent number of stations that would be worked in an hour, based on various time periods (last hour, last 10 minutes, last 10 stations, last 100 stations, and so forth)

Robot — a software program that processes logs submitted by e-mail

Rover — a mobile station that operates while in motion or from multiple locations in a contest

Run — to work stations by calling CQ; a run also means a steady stream of callers in response to CQs

S&P — search-and-pounce, the technique of tuning for stations to work instead of calling CQ

Schedule — arrange to make a contact later in the contest

Serial number — the sequential number of the contact in the contest — first contact, second contact, 199th contact, and so on

SO, SOAB, SOSB — Single Operator; Single-Operator All-Band; Single-Operator Single Band

SOA, SOU — Single-Operator Assisted, Single-Operator Unlimited (see **Assisted**)

SO2R — Single-Operator, Two Radio; a technique of listening to two radios at once in order to run on one band while tuning on a second to find multipliers and other unworked stations.

SPC or S/P/C — State, Province, Country, the most common three location-based types of multipliers

Spot — an announcement of a station's call and frequency via a spotting network

Sprint — a short contest, usually six hours or less

Summary sheet — an entry form provided by contest sponsors containing information about the operator and the submitted log

Sunday driver — casual operators who appear late in the contest (usually Sunday afternoon) to make a few QSOs

UBN — Unique, Busted, Not In Log; the three ways in which a QSO can be declared invalid

Unique — a call sign that was not in any other submitted log

Unlimited — see Assisted

Zones — either ITU or CQ zones, used frequently as part of contest exchanges

3.4.11 Resources for the Contester

Magazines and Newsletters

ARRL *Contest Update* — **www.arrl.org/the-arrl-contest-update**

National Contest Journal — **www.ncjweb.com**

Contest columns appear regularly in *CQ* Magazine — **www.cq-amateur-radio.com**

Websites and E-mail Reflectors

ARRL Contest Branch — **www.arrl.org/contests** (part of the On The Air section of the ARRL website)

Contesting.com — **www.contesting.com** — a general site about contesting (part of the eham.net website)

3830 score reporting — **www.3830scores.com**

CQ-Contest reflector — **lists.contesting.com/mailman/listinfo/cq-contest**

Contest University — **www.contestuniversity.com** — contest training organization

World-Wide Radio Operators Foundation — **wwrof.org** — an organization that supports contesting and contest sponsors

RTTY Contesting — **www.rttycontesting.com** — a comprehensive website on RTTY contesting with plenty of information for beginners

Online Contest Calendars

ARRL Contest Corral — **www.arrl.org/contests** (also monthly in *QST*)

SM3CER Contest Service — **www.sk3bg.se/contest**

WA7BNM Contest Calendar — **www.hornucopia.com/contestcal**

Resources for the Active Ham

Contents

US Amateur Radio Bands	4.1
Allocation of International Call Sign Series	4.2
Morse Code Character Set	4.4
Morse Abbreviated ("Cut") Numbers	4.4
ARRL Procedural Signals (Prosigns)	4.5
Q Signals	4.5
CW Abbreviations	4.6
ITU Recommended Phonetics	4.7
Alternative Phonetics	4.7
Spanish Phonetics	4.7
The RST System	4.7
ARRL Message Form and Handling Instructions	4.8
ARL Numbered Radiograms	4.9
ICS-213 General Message Form	4.10

Amateur Radio Emergency Service (ARES) Registration	4.12
ARRL Worked All States (WAS) Map	4.13
ARRL Grid Locator Map for North America	4.14
WAC Award Application	4.15
ARRL DXCC Award Application	4.16
ARRL VUCC Award Application	4.18
ARRL WAS Award Application	4.20
ARRL 5 Band WAS Application	4.22
ARRL Incoming QSL Bureau System	4.24
ARRL Outgoing QSL Service	4.24
Characteristics of Common Feed Lines	4.26
PL-259 (UHF) Connector Assembly	4.26
ARRL DXCC List	4.27

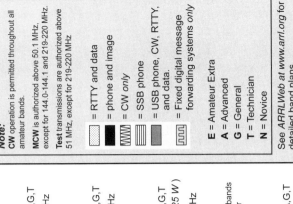

US Amateur Radio Bands

Effective Date March 5, 2012

US AMATEUR POWER LIMITS

FCC 97.313 An amateur station must use the minimum transmitter power necessary to carry out the desired communications. (b) No station may transmit with a transmitter power exceeding 1.5 kW PEP.

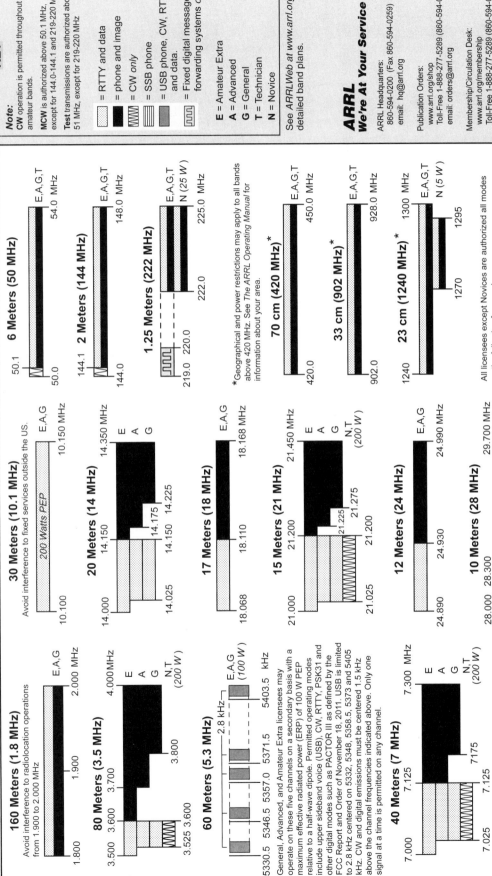

KEY

Note:
CW operation is permitted throughout all amateur bands.

MCW is authorized above 50.1 MHz, except for 144.0-144.1 and 219-220 MHz.

Test transmissions are authorized above 51 MHz, except for 219-220 MHz

- ▨ = RTTY and data
- ■ = phone and image
- ▥ = CW only
- ▦ = SSB phone
- ▦ = USB phone, CW, RTTY, and data.
- ▦ = Fixed digital message forwarding systems only

E = Amateur Extra
A = Advanced
G = General
T = Technician
N = Novice

See *ARRLWeb* at *www.arrl.org* for detailed band plans.

ARRL
We're At Your Service

ARRL Headquarters:
860-594-0200 (Fax 860-594-0259)
email: hq@arrl.org

Publication Orders:
www.arrl.org/shop
Toll-Free 1-888-277-5289 (860-594-0355)
email: orders@arrl.org

Membership/Circulation Desk:
www.arrl.org/membership
Toll-Free 1-888-277-5289 (860-594-0338)
email: membership@arrl.org

Getting Started in Amateur Radio:
Toll-Free 1-800-326-3942 (860-594-0355)
email: newham@arrl.org

Exams: 860-594-0300 email: vec@arrl.org

Copyright © ARRL 2012 rev. 6/3/2016

---

160 Meters (1.8 MHz)
Avoid interference to radiolocation operations from 1.900 to 2.000 MHz
E,A,G
1.800 — 1.900 — 2.000 MHz

80 Meters (3.5 MHz)
E / A / G / N,T (200 W)
3.500 3.600 3.700 3.800 4.000 MHz
3.525 3.600

60 Meters (5.3 MHz)
2.8 kHz
E,A,G (100 W)
5330.5 5346.5 5357.0 5371.5 5403.5 kHz

General, Advanced, and Amateur Extra licensees may operate on these five channels on a secondary basis with a maximum effective radiated power (ERP) of 100 W PEP relative to a half-wave dipole. Permitted operating modes include upper sideband voice (USB), CW, RTTY, PSK31 and other digital modes such as PACTOR III as defined by the FCC Report and Order of November 18, 2011. USB is limited to 2.8 kHz centered on 5332, 5348, 5358.5, 5373 and 5405 kHz. CW and digital emissions must be centered 1.5 kHz above the channel frequencies indicated above. Only one signal at a time is permitted on any channel.

40 Meters (7 MHz)
E / A / G / N,T (200 W)
7.000 7.125 7.175 7.300 MHz
7.025 7.125

Phone and Image modes are permitted between 7.075 and 7.100 MHz for FCC licensed stations in ITU Regions 1 and 3 and by FCC licensed stations in ITU Region 2 West of 130 degrees West longitude or South of 20 degrees North latitude. See Sections 97.305(c) and 97.307(f)(11). Novice and Technician licensees outside ITU Region 2 may use CW only between 7.025 and 7.075 MHz and between 7.100 and 7.125 MHz. 7.200 to 7.300 MHz is not available outside ITU Region 2. See Section 97.301(e). These exemptions do not apply to stations in the continental US.

30 Meters (10.1 MHz)
Avoid interference to fixed services outside the US.
E,A,G
200 Watts PEP
10.100 10.150 MHz

20 Meters (14 MHz)
E / A / G
14.000 14.025 14.150 14.150 14.175 14.225 14.350 MHz

17 Meters (18 MHz)
E,A,G
18.068 18.110 18.168 MHz

15 Meters (21 MHz)
E / A / G / N,T (200 W)
21.000 21.025 21.200 21.200 21.225 21.275 21.450 MHz

12 Meters (24 MHz)
E,A,G
24.890 24.930 24.990 MHz

10 Meters (28 MHz)
E,A,G / N,T (200 W)
28.000 28.000 28.300 28.500 29.700 MHz

6 Meters (50 MHz)
E,A,G,T
50.0 50.1 54.0 MHz

2 Meters (144 MHz)
E,A,G,T
144.0 144.1 148.0 MHz

1.25 Meters (222 MHz)
E,A,G,T / N (25 W)
219.0 220.0 222.0 225.0 MHz

70 cm (420 MHz)*
E,A,G,T
420.0 450.0 MHz

33 cm (902 MHz)*
E,A,G,T
902.0 928.0 MHz

23 cm (1240 MHz)*
E,A,G,T / N (5 W)
1240 1270 1295 1300 MHz

*Geographical and power restrictions may apply to all bands above 420 MHz. See *The ARRL Operating Manual* for information about your area.

All licensees except Novices are authorized all modes on the following frequencies:

2300-2310 MHz	10.0-10.5 GHz *
2390-2450 MHz	24.0-24.25 GHz
3300-3500 MHz	47.0-47.2 GHz
5650-5925 MHz	76.0-81.0 GHz
122.25-123.0 GHz	
134-141 GHz	
241-250 GHz	
All above 275 GHz	

* No pulse emissions

ITU TABLE OF ALLOCATION OF INTERNATIONAL CALL SIGN SERIES ━━━━━━━━

Call Sign Series	Allocated to
AAA-ALZ	United States of America
AMA-AOZ	Spain
APA-ASZ	Pakistan
ATA-AWZ	India
AXA-AXZ	Australia
AYA-AZZ	Argentina
A2A-A2Z	Botswana
A3A-A3Z	Tonga
A4A-A4Z	Oman
A5A-A5Z	Bhutan
A6A-A6Z	United Arab Emirates
A7A-A7Z	Qatar
A8A-A8Z	Liberia
A9A-A9Z	Bahrain
BAA-BZZ	China (People's Republic of)
CAA-CEZ	Chile
CFA-CKZ	Canada
CLA-CMZ	Cuba
CNA-CNZ	Morocco
COA-COZ	Cuba
CPA-CPZ	Bolivia
CQA-CUZ	Portugal
CVA-CXZ	Uruguay
CYA-CZZ	Canada
C2A-C2Z	Nauru
C3A-C3Z	Andorra
C4A-C4Z	Cyprus
C5A-C5Z	Gambia
C6A-C6Z	Bahamas
C7A-C7Z	World Meteorological Organization
C8A-C9Z	Mozambique
DAA-DRZ	Germany (Federal Rep of)
DSA-DTZ	Korea (Rep of)
DUA-DZZ	Philippines
D2A-D3Z	Angola
D4A-D4Z	Cape Verde
D5A-D5Z	Liberia
D6A-D6Z	Comoros
D7A-D9Z	Korea (Rep of)
EAA-EHZ	Spain
EIA-EJZ	Ireland
EKA-EKZ	Armenia
ELA-ELZ	Liberia
EMA-EOZ	Ukraine
EPA-EQZ	Iran (Islamic Rep of)
ERA-ERZ	Moldova
ESA-ESZ	Estonia
ETA-ETZ	Ethiopia
EUA-EWZ	Belarus
EXA-EXZ	Kyrgyz Republic
EYA-EYZ	Tajikistan
EZA-EZZ	Turkmenistan
E2A-E2Z	Thailand
E3A-E3Z	Eritrea
E4A-E4Z	Palestine
E5A-E5Z	New Zealand - Cook Islands
E6A-E6Z	New Zealand - Niue
E7A-E7Z	Bosnia and Herzegovina
FAA-FZZ	France
GAA-GZZ	United Kingdom of Great Britain and Northern Ireland
HAA-HAZ	Hungary
HBA-HBZ	Switzerland
HCA-HDZ	Ecuador
HEA-HEZ	Switzerland
HFA-HFZ	Poland
HGA-HGZ	Hungary
HHA-HHZ	Haiti
HIA-HIZ	Dominican Republic
HJA-HKZ	Colombia
HLA-HLZ	Korea (Rep of)
HMA-HMZ	Korea (Dem People's Rep of)
HNA-HNZ	Iraq
HOA-HPZ	Panama
HQA-HRZ	Honduras
HSA-HSZ	Thailand
HTA-HTZ	Nicaragua
HUA-HUZ	El Salvador

Call Sign Series	Allocated to
HVA-HVZ	Vatican City State
HWA-HYZ	France
HZA-HZZ	Saudi Arabia
H2A-H2Z	Cyprus
H3A-H3Z	Panama
H4A-H4Z	Solomon Islands
H6A-H7Z	Nicaragua
H8A-H9Z	Panama
IAA-IZZ	Italy
JAA-JSZ	Japan
JTA-JVZ	Mongolia
JWA-JXZ	Norway
JYA-JYZ	Jordan
JZA-JZZ	Indonesia
J2A-J2Z	Djibouti
J3A-J3Z	Grenada
J4A-J4Z	Greece
J5A-J5Z	Guinea-Bissau
J6A-J6Z	Saint Lucia
J7A-J7Z	Dominica
J8A-J8Z	St. Vincent and the Grenadines
KAA-KZZ	United States of America
LAA-LNZ	Norway
LOA-LWZ	Argentina
LXA-LXZ	Luxembourg
LYA-LYZ	Lithuania
LZA-LZZ	Bulgaria
L2A-L9Z	Argentina
MAA-MZZ	United Kingdom of Great Britain and Northern Ireland
NAA-NZZ	United States of America
OAA-OCZ	Peru
ODA-ODZ	Lebanon
OEA-OEZ	Austria
OFA-OJZ	Finland
OKA-OLZ	Czech Republic
OMA-OMZ	Slovak Republic
ONA-OTZ	Belgium
OUA-OZZ	Denmark
PAA-PIZ	Netherlands
PJA-PJZ	Netherlands (Kingdom of the)
PKA-POZ	Indonesia
PPA-PYZ	Brazil
PZA-PZZ	Suriname
P2A-P2Z	Papua New Guinea
P3A-P3Z	Cyprus
P4A-P4Z	Netherlands (Kingdom of the) - Aruba
P5A-P9Z	Korea (Dem People's Rep of)
RAA-RZZ	Russian Federation
SAA-SMZ	Sweden
SNA-SRZ	Poland
SSA-SSM	Egypt (Arab Rep of)
SSN-STZ	Sudan (Republic of the)
SUA-SUZ	Egypt (Arab Rep of)
SVA-SZZ	Greece
S2A-S3Z	Bangladesh
S5A-S5Z	Slovenia
S6A-S6Z	Singapore
S7A-S7Z	Seychelles
S8A-S8Z	South Africa (Rep of)
S9A-S9Z	Sao Tome and Principe
TAA-TCZ	Turkey
TDA-TDZ	Guatemala
TEA-TEZ	Costa Rica
TFA-TFZ	Iceland
TGA-TGZ	Guatemala
THA-THZ	France
TIA-TIZ	Costa Rica
TJA-TJZ	Cameroon
TKA-TKZ	France
TLA-TLZ	Central African Rep
TMA-TMZ	France
TNA-TNZ	Congo (Rep of the)
TOA-TQZ	France
TRA-TRZ	Gabon
TSA-TSZ	Tunisia
TTA-TTZ	Chad

Call Sign Series	Allocated to
TUA-TUZ	Cote d'Ivoire
TVA-TXZ	France
TYA-TYZ	Benin
TZA-TZZ	Mali
T2A-T2Z	Tuvalu
T3A-T3Z	Kiribati
T4A-T4Z	Cuba
T5A-T5Z	Somalia
T6A-T6Z	Afghanistan
T7A-T7Z	San Marino
T8A-T8Z	Palau
UAA-UIZ	Russian Federation
UJA-UMZ	Uzbekistan
UNA-UQZ	Kazakhstan
URA-UZZ	Ukraine
VAA-VGZ	Canada
VHA-VNZ	Australia
VOA-VOZ	Canada
VPA-VQZ	United Kingdom of Great Britain and Northern Ireland
VRA-VRZ	China (People's Republic of) - Hong Kong
VSA-VSZ	United Kingdom of Great Britain and Northern Ireland
VTA-VWZ	India
VXA-VYZ	Canada
VZA-VZZ	Australia
V2A-V2Z	Antigua and Barbuda
V3A-V3Z	Belize
V4A-V4Z	Saint Kitts and Nevis
V5A-V5Z	Namibia
V6A-V6Z	Micronesia (Federated States of)
V7A-V7Z	Marshall Islands
V8A-V8Z	Brunei Darussalam
WAA-WZZ	United States of America
XAA-XIZ	Mexico
XJA-XOZ	Canada
XPA-XPZ	Denmark
XQA-XRZ	Chile
XSA-XSZ	China (People's Republic of)
XTA-XTZ	Burkina Faso
XUA-XUZ	Cambodia (Kingdom of)
XVA-XVZ	Viet Nam
XWA-XWZ	Laos (People's Dem Rep)
XXA-XXZ	China (People's Republic of) - Macao
XYA-XZZ	Myanmar
YAA-YAZ	Afghanistan
YBA-YHZ	Indonesia
YIA-YIZ	Iraq
YJA-YJZ	Vanuatu
YKA-YKZ	Syrian Arab Rep
YLA-YLZ	Latvia
YMA-YMZ	Turkey
YNA-YNZ	Nicaragua
YOA-YRZ	Romania
YSA-YSZ	El Salvador
YTA-YUZ	Serbia
YVA-YYZ	Venezuela
Y2A-Y9Z	Germany (Federal Rep of)
ZAA-ZAZ	Albania
ZBA-ZJZ	United Kingdom of Great Britain and Northern Ireland
ZKA-ZMZ	New Zealand
ZNA-ZOZ	United Kingdom of Great Britain and Northern Ireland
ZPA-ZPZ	Paraguay
ZQA-ZQZ	United Kingdom of Great Britain and Northern Ireland
ZRA-ZUZ	South Africa (Rep of)
ZVA-ZZZ	Brazil
Z2A-Z2Z	Zimbabwe
Z3A-Z3Z	The Former Yugoslav Republic of Macedonia
Z8A-Z8Z	South Sudan (Republic of)
2AA-2ZZ	United Kindom of Great Britain and Northern Ireland
3AA-3AZ	Monaco
3BA-3BZ	Mauritius
3CA-3CZ	Equatorial Guinea
3DA-3DM	Swaziland
3DN-3DZ	Fiji
3EA-3FZ	Panama
3GA-3GZ	Chile
3HA-3UZ	China (People's Republic of)
3VA-3VZ	Tunisia
3WA-3WZ	Viet Nam
3XA-3XZ	Guinea

Call Sign Series	Allocated to
3YA-3YZ	Norway
3ZA-3ZZ	Poland
4AA-4CZ	Mexico
4DA-4IZ	Philippines
4JA-4KZ	Azerbaijani
4LA-4LZ	Georgia
4MA-4MZ	Venezuela
4OA-4OZ	Montenegro
4PA-4SZ	Sri Lanka
4TA-4TZ	Peru
4UA-4UZ	United Nations
4VA-4VZ	Haiti
4WA-4WZ	Timor-Leste
4XA-4XZ	Israel
4YA-4YZ	International Civil Aviation Organization
4ZA-4ZZ	Israel
5AA-5AZ	Libya
5BA-5BZ	Cyprus
5CA-5GZ	Morocco
5HA-5IZ	Tanzania
5JA-5KZ	Colombia
5LA-5MZ	Liberia
5NA-5OZ	Nigeria
5PA-5QZ	Denmark
5RA-5SZ	Madagascar
5TA-5TZ	Mauritania
5UA-5UZ	Niger
5VA-5VZ	Togolese Rep
5WA-5WZ	Samoa
5XA-5XZ	Uganda
5YA-5ZZ	Kenya
6AA-6BZ	Egypt
6CA-6CZ	Syria
6DA-6JZ	Mexico
6KA-6NZ	Korea (Rep of)
6OA-6OZ	Somalia
6PA-6SZ	Pakistan
6TA-6UZ	Sudan
6VA-6WZ	Senegal
6XA-6XZ	Madagascar
6YA-6YZ	Jamaica
6ZA-6ZZ	Liberia
7AA-7IZ	Indonesia
7JA-7NZ	Japan
7OA-7OZ	Yemen
7PA-7PZ	Lesotho
7QA-7QZ	Malawi
7RA-7RZ	Algeria
7SA-7SZ	Sweden
7TA-7YZ	Algeria
7ZA-7ZZ	Saudi Arabia
8AA-8IZ	Indonesia
8JA-8NZ	Japan
8OA-8OZ	Botswana
8PA-8PZ	Barbados
8QA-8QZ	Maldives
8RA-8RZ	Guyana
8SA-8SZ	Sweden
8TA-8YZ	India
8ZA-8ZZ	Saudi Arabia
9AA-9AZ	Croatia
9BA-9DZ	Iran
9EA-9FZ	Ethiopia
9GA-9GZ	Ghana
9HA-9HZ	Malta
9IA-9JZ	Zambia
9KA-9KZ	Kuwait
9LA-9LZ	Sierra Leone
9MA-9MZ	Malaysia
9NA-9NZ	Nepal
9OA-9TZ	Congo (Dem Rep of)
9UA-9UZ	Burundi
9VA-9VZ	Singapore
9WA-9WZ	Malaysia
9XA-9XZ	Rwanda
9YA-9ZZ	Trinidad and Tobago

Morse Code Character Set[1]

A	didah	• —
B	dahdididit	— •••
C	dahdidahdit	— • — •
D	dahdidit	— ••
E	dit	•
F	dididahdit	•• — •
G	dahdahdit	— — •
H	didididit	••••
I	didit	••
J	didahdahdah	• — — —
K	dahdidah	— • —
L	didahdidit	• — ••
M	dahdah	— —
N	dahdit	— •
O	dahdahdah	— — —
P	didahdahdit	• — — •
Q	dahdahdidah	— — • —
R	didahdit	• — •
S	dididit	•••
T	dah	—
U	dididah	•• —
V	didididah	••• —
W	didahdah	• — —
X	dahdididah	— •• —
Y	dahdidahdah	— • — —
Z	dahdahdidit	— — ••

1	didahdahdahdah	• — — — —
2	dididahdahdah	•• — — —
3	didididahdah	••• — —
4	dididididah	•••• —
5	didididit	•••••
6	dahdidididit	— ••••
7	dahdahdididit	— — •••
8	dahdahdahdidit	— — — ••
9	dahdahdahdahdit	— — — — •
0	dahdahdahdahdah	— — — — —

At [@]	didahdahdidahdit	• — — • — •	$\overline{AC}$
Period [.]:	didahdidahdidah	• — • — • —	$\overline{AAA}$
Comma [,]:	dahdahdididahdah	— — •• — —	$\overline{MIM}$
Question mark or request for repetition [?]:	dididahdahdidit	•• — — ••	$\overline{IMI}$
Error:	didididididididit	••••••••	$\overline{HH}$
Hyphen or dash [–]:	dahdidididahdah	— •••• —	$\overline{DU}$
Double dash [=]	dahdidididah	— •••• —	$\overline{BT}$
Colon [:]:	dahdahdahdidididit	— — — •••	$\overline{OS}$
Semicolon [;]:	dahdidahdidahdit	— • — • — •	$\overline{KR}$
Left parenthesis [(]:	dahdidahdahdit	— • — — •	$\overline{KN}$
Right parenthesis [)]:	dahdidahdahdahdidah	— • — — • —	$\overline{KK}$
Fraction bar [/]:	dahdididahdit	— •• — •	$\overline{DN}$
Quotation marks ["]:	didahdididahdit	• — •• — •	$\overline{AF}$
Dollar sign [$]:	didididahdididah	••• — ••• —	$\overline{SX}$
Apostrophe [']:	didahdahdahdahdit	• — — — — •	$\overline{WG}$
Paragraph [¶]:	didahdidahdidit	• — • — ••	$\overline{AL}$
Underline [_]:	dididahdahdidah	•• — — • —	$\overline{IQ}$
Starting signal:	dahdidahdidah	— • — • —	$\overline{KA}$
Wait:	didahdididit	• — •••	$\overline{AS}$
End of message or cross [+]:	didahdidahdit	• — • — •	$\overline{AR}$
Invitation to transmit [K]:	dahdidah	— • —	K
End of work:	didididahdidah	••• — • —	$\overline{SK}$
Understood:	didididahdit	••• — •	$\overline{SN}$

Notes:

1. Not all Morse characters shown are used in FCC code tests. License applicants are responsible for knowing, and may be tested on, the 26 letters, the numerals 0 to 9, the period, the comma, the question mark, $\overline{AR}$, $\overline{SK}$, $\overline{BT}$ and fraction bar [$\overline{DN}$].

2. The following letters are used in certain European languages which use the Latin alphabet:

Ä, Ą	didahdidah	• — • —
Á, Å, À, Â	didahdahdidah	• — — • —
Ç, Ć	dahdidahdidit	— • — ••
É, È, Ę	didahdidit	•• — ••
È	didahdahdidah	• — ••—
Ê	dahdididahdit	— •• — •
Ö, Ő, Ó	dahdahdahdit	— — — •
Ñ	dahdahdidahdah	— — • — —
Ü	dididahdah	•• — —
Ź	dahdahdidit	— — ••
Z	dahdahdididah	— — •• —
CH, Ş	dahdahdahdah	— — — —

3. Special Esperanto characters:

Ĉ	dahdidahdidit	— • — ••
Ŝ	didididahdit	••• — •
Ĵ	didahdahdahdit	• — — —•
Ĥ	dahdidahdahdit	— • — — •
Ŭ	dididahdah	•• — —
Ĝ	dahdahdidahdit	— — • — •

4. Signals used in other radio services:

Interrogatory	dididahdidah	•• — • —	$\overline{INT}$
Emergency silence	dididididahdah	•••• — —	$\overline{HM}$
Executive follows	dididahdididah	•• — •• —	$\overline{IX}$
Break–in signal	dahdahdahdahdah	— — — — —	$\overline{TTTTT}$
Emergency signal	didididahdahdahdididit	••• — — — •••	$\overline{SOS}$
Relay of distress	dahdidididahdidididahdidit	— •• •• — ••	$\overline{DDD}$

Morse Abbeviated ("Cut") Numbers

Numeral		Long Number			Abbreviated Number	Equivalent Character
1	didahdahdahdah	• — — — —	didah	• —	A
2	dididahdahdah	•• — — —	dididah	•• —	U
3	didididahdah	••• — —	didididah	••• —	V
4	dididididah	•••• —	dididididah	•••• —	4
5	didididit	•••••	didididit	••••• or •	5 or E
6	dahdidididit	— ••••	dahdidididit	— ••••	6
7	dahdahdididit	— — •••	dahdididit	— •••	B
8	dahdahdahdidit	— — — ••	dahdidit	— ••	D
9	dahdahdahdahdit	— — — — •	dahdit	— •	N
0	dahdahdahdahdah	— — — — —	dah	—	T

Note: These abbreviated numbers are not legal for use in call signs. They should be used only where there is agreement between operators and when no confusion will result.

ARRL Procedural Signals (Prosigns)

In general, the CW prosigns are used on all data modes as well, although word abbreviations may be spelled out. That is, "CLEAR" might be used rather than "CL" on radioteletype. Additional radioteletype conventions appear at the end of the table.

Situation	CW	Voice
check for a clear frequency	QRL?	Is the frequency in use?
seek contact with any station	CQ	CQ
after call to specific named station or to indicate end of message	AR	over, end of message
invite any station to transmit	K	go
invite a specific named station to transmit	KN	go only
invite receiving station to transmit	BK	back to you
all received correctly	R	received
please stand by	AS	wait, stand by
end of contact (sent before call sign)	SK	clear
going off the air	CL	closing station

Additional RTTY prosigns

SK QRZ—Ending contact, but listening on frequency.
SK KN—Ending contact, but listening for one last transmission from the other station.
SK SZ—Signing off and listening on the frequency for any other calls.

Q Signals

These Q signals most often need to be expressed with brevity and clarity in amateur work. (Q abbreviations take the form of questions only when each is sent followed by a question mark.)

QRA   What is the name of your station? The name of your station is _____.

QRG   Will you tell me my exact frequency (or that of _____)? Your exact frequency (or that of _____) is _____ kHz.

QRH   Does my frequency vary? Your frequency varies.

QRI   How is the tone of my transmission? The tone of your transmission is _____ (1. Good; 2. Variable; 3. Bad).

QRJ   Are you receiving me badly? I cannot receive you. Your signals are too weak.

QRK   What is the intelligibility of my signals (or those of _____)? The intelligibility of your signals (or those of _____) is _____ (1. Bad; 2. Poor; 3. Fair; 4. Good; 5. Excellent).

QRL   Are you busy? I am busy (or I am busy with _____). Please do not interfere.

QRM   Is my transmission being interfered with? Your transmission is being interfered with (1. Nil; 2. Slightly; 3. Moderately; 4. Severely; 5. Extremely.)

QRN   Are you troubled by static? I am troubled by static _____ (1-5 as under QRM).

QRO   Shall I increase power? Increase power.

QRP   Shall I decrease power? Decrease power.

QRQ   Shall I send faster? Send faster (_____ WPM).

QRS   Shall I send more slowly? Send more slowly (_____ WPM).

QRT   Shall I stop sending? Stop sending.

QRU   Have you anything for me? I have nothing for you.

QRV   Are you ready? I am ready.

QRW   Shall I inform _____ that you are calling on _____ kHz? Please inform _____ that I am calling on _____ kHz.

QRX   When will you call me again? I will call you again at _____ hours (on _____ kHz).

QRY   What is my turn? Your turn is numbered _____

QRZ   Who is calling me? You are being called by _____ (on _____ kHz).

QSA   What is the strength of my signals (or those of _____)? The strength of your signals (or those of _____) is _____

(1. Scarcely perceptible; 2. Weak; 3. Fairly good; 4. Good; 5. Very good).

QSB   Are my signals fading? Your signals are fading.

QSD   Is my keying defective? Your keying is defective.

QSG   Shall I send _____ messages at a time? Send _____ messages at a time.

QSK   Can you hear me between your signals and if so can I break in on your transmission? I can hear you between my signals; break in on my transmission.

QSL   Can you acknowledge receipt? I am acknowledging receipt.

QSM   Shall I repeat the last message which I sent you, or some previous message? Repeat the last message which you sent me [or message(s) number(s) _____].

QSN   Did you hear me (or _____) on _____ kHz? I did hear you (or _____) on _____ kHz.

QSO   Can you communicate with _____ direct or by relay? I can communicate with _____ direct (or by relay through _____).

QSP   Will you relay to _____? I will relay to _____

QST   General call preceding a message addressed to all amateurs and ARRL members. This is in effect "CQ ARRL."

QSU   Shall I send or reply on this frequency (or on _____ kHz)? Send or reply on this frequency (or _____ kHz).

QSV   Shall I send a series of Vs on this frequency (or on _____ kHz)? Send a series of Vs on this frequency (or on _____ kHz).

QSW   Will you send on this frequency (or on _____ kHz)? I am going to send on this frequency (or on _____ kHz).

QSX   Will you listen to _____ on _____ kHz? I am listening to _____ on _____ kHz.

QSY   Shall I change to transmission on another frequency? Change to transmission on another frequency (or on _____ kHz).

QSZ   Shall I send each word or group more than once? Send each word or group twice (or _____ times).

QTA   Shall I cancel message number _____? Cancel message number _____

QTB   Do you agree with my counting of words? I do not agree with your counting of words. I will repeat the first letter or digit of each word or group.

QTC	How many messages have you to send? I have _____ messages for you (or for _____).
QTH	What is your location? My location is _____
QTR	What is the correct time? The correct time is _____
QTV	Shall I stand guard for you? Stand guard for me.
QTX	Will you keep your station open for further communication with me? Keep your station open for me.
QUA	Have you news of _____? I have news of _____.

ARRL QN Signals

QNA*	Answer in prearranged order.
QNB	Act as relay between _____ and _____.
QNC	All net stations copy. I have a message for all net stations.
QND*	Net is Directed (Controlled by net control station.)
QNE*	Entire net stand by.
QNF	Net is Free (not controlled).
QNG	Take over as net control station
QNH	Your net frequency is High.
QNI	Net stations report in. I am reporting into the net. (Follow with a list of traffic or QRU.)
QNJ	Can you copy me?
QNK*	Transmit messages for _____ to _____.
QNL	Your net frequency is Low.
QNM*	You are QRMing the net. Stand by.
QNN	Net control station is _____. What station has net control?
QNO	Station is leaving the net.
QNP	Unable to copy you. Unable to copy _____.
QNQ*	Move frequency to _____ and wait for _____ to finish handling traffic. Then send him traffic for _____.
QNR*	Answer _____ and Receive traffic.
QNS	Following Stations are in the net.* (follow with list.) Request list of stations in the net.
QNT	I request permission to leave the net for _____ minutes.
QNU*	The net has traffic for *you*. Stand by.
QNV*	Establish contact with _____ on this frequency. If successful, move to _____ and send him traffic for _____.
QNW	How do I route messages for _____?
QNX	You are excused from the net.*
QNY*	Shift to another frequency (or to _____ kHz) to clear traffic with _____.
QNZ	Zero beat your signal with mine.

*For use only by the Net Control Station.

Notes on Use of QN Signals

These QN signals are special ARRL signals for use in amateur CW nets *only*. They are not for use in casual amateur conversation. Other meanings that may be used in other services do not apply. Do not use QN signals on phone nets. *Say it with words.* QN signals need not be followed by a question mark, even though the meaning may be interrogatory.

CW Abbreviations

AA	All after	HI	The telegraphic laugh; high	SKED	Schedule
AB	All before	HR	Here, hear	SRI	Sorry
AB	About	HV	Have	SSB	Single sideband
ADR	Address	HW	How	SVC	Service; prefix to service message
AGN	Again	LID	A poor operator		
ANT	Antenna	MA, MILS	Milliamperes	T	Zero
BCI	Broadcast interference	MSG	Message; prefix to radiogram	TFC	Traffic
BCL	Broadcast listener	N	No	TMW	Tomorrow
BK	Break; break me; break in	NCS	Net control station	TNX-TKS	Thanks
BN	All between; been	ND	Nothing doing	TT	That
BUG	Semi-automatic key	NIL	Nothing; I have nothing for you	TU	Thank you
B4	Before	NM	No more	TVI	Television interference
C	Yes	NR	Number	TX	Transmitter
CFM	Confirm; I confirm	NW	Now; I resume transmission	TXT	Text
CK	Check	OB	Old boy	UR-URS	Your; you're; yours
CL	I am closing my station; call	OC	Old chap	VFO	Variable-frequency oscillator
CLD-CLG	Called; calling	OM	Old man	VY	Very
CQ	Calling any station	OP-OPR	Operator	WA	Word after
CUD	Could	OT	Old timer; old top	WB	Word before
CUL	See you later	PBL	Preamble	WD-WDS	Word; words
CW	Continuous wave (i.e., radio-telegraph)	PSE	Please	WKD-WKG	Worked; working
		PWR	Power	WL	Well; will
DE	From	PX	Press	WUD	Would
DLD-DLVD	Delivered	R	Received as transmitted; are	WX	Weather
DR	Dear	RCD	Received	XCVR	Transceiver
DX	Distance, foreign countries	RCVR (RX)	Receiver	XMTR (TX)	Transmitter
ES	And, &	REF	Refer to; referring to; reference	XTAL	Crystal
FB	Fine business, excellent	RFI	Radio Frequency Interference	XYL (YF)	Wife
FM	Frequency modulation	RIG	Station equipment	YL	Young lady
GA	Go ahead (or resume sending)	RPT	Repeat; I repeat; report	73	Best regards
GB	Good-by	RTTY	Radioteletype	88	Love and Kisses
GBA	Give better address	RX	Receiver		
GE	Good evening	SASE	Self-addressed, stamped envelope		
GG	Going				
GM	Good morning	SED	Said		
GN	Good night	SIG	Signature; signal		
GND	Ground	SINE	Operator's personal initials or nickname		
GUD	Good				

Although abbreviations help to cut down unnecessary transmission, make it a rule not to abbreviate unnecessarily when working an operator of unknown experience.

ITU Recommended Phonetics

A — Alfa (**AL** FAH)
B — Bravo (**BRAH** VOH)
C — Charlie (**CHAR** LEE OR **SHAR** LEE)
D — Delta (**DELL** TAH)
E — Echo (**ECK** OH)
F — Foxtrot (**FOKS** TROT)
G — Golf (GOLF)
H — Hotel (HOH **TELL**)
I — India (**IN** DEE AH)
J — Juliet (**JEW** LEE ETT)
K — Kilo (**KEY** LOH)
L — Lima (**LEE** MAH)
M — Mike (MIKE)
N — November (NO **VEM** BER)
O — Oscar (**OSS** CAH)
P — Papa (PAH **PAH**)

Q — Quebec (KEH **BECK**)
R — Romeo (**ROW** ME OH)
S — Sierra (SEE *AIR* RAH)
T — Tango (**TANG** GO)
U — Uniform (**YOU** NEE FORM or **OO** NEE FORM)
V — Victor (**VIK** TAH)
W — Whiskey (**WISS** KEY)
X — X-Ray (**ECKS** RAY)
Y — Yankee (**YANG** KEY)
Z — Zulu (**ZOO** LOO)

Note: The **Boldfaced** syllables are emphasized. The pronunciations shown in the table were designed for speakers from all international languages. The pronunciations given for "Oscar" and "Victor" may seem awkward to English-speaking people in the U.S.

Alternative Phonetics

Although the ITU standard phonetics are always preferred, occasionally you may have trouble getting through. In that case, try another word. Here are some alternatives commonly heard on the amateur bands.

America	France	Kentucky	Queen	Victoria
Boston	Germany	London	Radio	Washington
Canada	Honolulu	Mexico	Santiago	X-ray
Denmark	Italy	Ontario	Tokyo	Yokohama
England	Japan	Pacific	United	Zanzibar

Spanish Phonetics

The syllables in capital letters are emphasized.

America	ah-MAIR-ika	Norvega	nor-WAY-gah	W	DOE-bleh-vay	
Brazil	brah-SIL	Ontario	on-TAR-eeoh	0	cero	SEH-roe
Canada	cana-DAH	Portugal	portu-GAL	1	uno	OO-no
Dinamarca	dina-MAR-ka	Quito	KEY-toe	2	dos	DOS
Espana	es-PAHN-yah	Roma	ROW-mah	3	tres	TRAYCE
Francia	FRAHN-seeah	Santiago	santee-AH-go	4	cuatro	KWAT-roe
Grenada	gre-NAH-dah	Toronto	tor-ON-toe	5	cinco	SINK-oh
Holanda	oh-LONN-dah	Uniforme	oonee-FORM-eh	6	sels	SAYCE
Italia	i-TAL-eeah	Victoria	vic-TOR-eeah	7	siete	see-AY-teh
Japon	hop-OWN	Washington	washingtone	8	ocho	OCH-oh
Kilowatio	kilo-WAT-eeoh	Xilofono	see-LOW-phono	9	nueve	new-AY-veh
Lima	LIMA	Yucatan	yuca-TAN	(courtesy John Mason, EA5AXW)		
Mejico	MEH-heeco	Zelandia	see-LANDeeah			

The RST System

Readability

1—Unreadable.
2—Barely readable, occasional words distinguishable.
3—Readable with considerable difficulty.
4—Readable with practically no difficulty.
5—Perfectly readable.

Signal Strength

1—Faint signals, barely perceptible.
2—Very weak signals.
3—Weak signals.
4—Fair signals.
5—Fairly good signals.
6—Good signals.
7—Moderately strong signals.
8—Strong signals.
9—Extremely strong signals.

Tone

1—Sixty-cycle ac or less, very rough and broad.
2—Very rough ac, very harsh and broad.
3—Rough ac tone, rectified but not filtered.
4—Rough note, some trace of filtering.
5—Filtered rectified ac but strongly ripple-modulated.
6—Filtered tone, definite trace of ripple modulation.
7—Near pure tone, trace of ripple modulation.
8—Near perfect tone, slight trace of modulation.
9—Perfect tone, no trace of ripple of modulation of any kind.
If the signal has the characteristic steadiness of crystal control, add the letter X to the RST report. If there is a chirp, add the letter C. Similarly for a click, add K. (See FCC Regulations §97.307, Emissions Standards.) The above reporting system is used on both CW and voice; leave out the "tone" report on voice.

ARRL — *the national association for Amateur Radio*™

RADIOGRAM

NUMBER	PRECEDENCE	HX	STATION OF ORIGIN	CHECK	PLACE OF ORIGIN	TIME FILED	DATE

TO

THIS RADIO MESSAGE WAS RECEIVED AT

AMATEUR STATION _____ PHONE _____

NAME _____ E-MAIL _____

PHONE NUMBER

STREET _____

E-MAIL

CITY, STATE, ZIP _____

_____	_____	_____	_____	_____
_____	_____	_____	_____	_____
_____	_____	_____	_____	_____
_____	_____	_____	_____	_____
_____	_____	_____	_____	_____

FROM		DATE	TIME	TO		DATE	TIME
REC'D				**SENT**			

This message was handled at no charge by a licensed Amateur Radio operator, whose address is shown in the box at right above. No compensation can be accepted by a "ham" operator. A return message may be filed with the "ham" delivering this message to you. Further information on Amateur Radio may be obtained from ARRL Headquarters, 225 Main Street, Newington, CT 06111 or **www.arrl.org**.

The ARRL is the national association for Amateur Radio and the publisher of *QST* magazine. One of its functions is promotion of public service communication among Amateur Radio operators. To that end, the ARRL has organized the National Traffic System for daily nationwide message handling.

1320 2/11

ARRL Message Form

The ARRL Radiogram™ has four parts: the *preamble*, the *address* block, the *text* and the *signature*. The preamble is analogous to the return address in a letter and contains the following:

1) The *number* denotes the message number of the originating station.

2) The *precedence* indicates the relative importance of the message. Routine (R) — has no urgency aspect of any kind, such as a greeting. Welfare (W) — an inquiry as to the health and welfare of an individual in the disaster area or an advisory from the disaster area that indicates all is well. Welfare traffic is handled only after all emergency and priority traffic is cleared. Priority (P) —high importance, for example important messages having a specific time limit, official messages not covered in the emergency category, press dispatches and emergency-related traffic not of the utmost urgency, and notice of death or injury in a disaster area, personal or official. EMERGENCY (always spelled out, regardless of mode) — any message having life-and-death urgency to any person or group of persons, which is transmitted by Amateur Radio in the absence of regular commercial facilities. This includes official messages of welfare agencies during emergencies requesting supplies, materials or instructions vital to relief of stricken populace in emergency areas.

3) *Handling Instructions* are optional cues to handle a message in a specific way (see Table).

4) *Station of origin* is the call sign of the station that originated the message and never changes.

5) The *check* is merely the word count of the text of the message. The signature is not counted in the check. When counting words in messages, don't forget that each X-ray (instead of period), Query (question mark) and initial group counts as a word. Ten-digit telephone numbers count as three words; the ARRL-recommended procedure for counting the telephone number in the text of an ARRL Radiogram message is to separate the telephone number into groups, with the area code (if any) counting as one word, the three-digit exchange counting as one word, and the last four digits counting as one word. Separating the telephone number into separate groups also helps to minimize garbling. Also remember that closings such as "love" or "sincerely" (that would be in the signature of a letter) are considered part of the text in a piece of amateur traffic. A check of ARL 8 means the text has an ARL numbered radiogram message text in it, and a word count of 8.

6) The *place of origin* can either be the location (City/State or City/Province) of the originating station or the location of the third party wishing to initiate a message through the originating station.

7) The *filing time* is another option, usually used if speed of delivery is of significant importance. Filing times should be in UTC time.

8) The *date*, is the month and day the message was filed — year isn't necessary.

The *address* is the intended recipient. The more items included in the address, the better its chances of reaching its destination.

The *text* is the message itself. The term X-ray indicates a break, query a question mark.

Finally, the *signature*. Remember, closing words such as "sincerely" belong in the text, not the signature. Signatures such as "Jeremy, Ashleigh, and Uncle Porter," no matter how long, go entirely on the signature line.

Handling Instructions

HXA — (Followed by number.) Collect landline delivery authorized by addressee within ____ miles. (If no number, authorization is unlimited.)

HXB — (Followed by number.) Cancel message if not delivered within ____ hours of filing time; service originating station.

HXC — Report date and time of delivery (TOD) to originating station.

HXD — Report to originating station the identity of station from which received, plus date and time. Report identity of station to which relayed, plus date and time, or if delivered report date, time and method of delivery.

HXE — Delivering station get reply from addressee, originate message back.

HXF — (Followed by number.) Hold delivery until ____ (date).

HXG — Delivery by mail or landline toll call not required. If toll or other expense involved, cancel message and service originating station.

An HX prosign (when used) will be inserted in the message preamble before the station of origin, like this: NR 207 R HXA50 W1AW 12 . . . (etc).

If more than one HX prosign is used, they can be combined if no numbers are to be inserted, like this: NR 207 R HXAC W1AW . . . (etc).

If numbers are inserted, the HX should be repeated: NR 207 R HXA50 HXC W1AW . . . (etc).

On phone, use phonetics for the letter or letters following the HX, to ensure accuracy.

ARL NUMBERED RADIOGRAMS

Group One—For Possible "Relief Emergency" Use

ONE	Everyone safe here. Please don't worry.
TWO	Coming home as soon as possible.
THREE	Am in _____ hospital. Receiving excellent care and recovering fine.
FOUR	Only slight property damage here. Do not be concerned about disaster reports.
FIVE	Am moving to new location. Send no further mail or communication. Will inform you of new address when relocated.
SIX	Will contact you as soon as possible.
SEVEN	Please reply by Amateur Radio through the amateur delivering this message. This is a free public service.
EIGHT	Need additional _____ mobile or portable equipment for immediate emergency use.
NINE	Additional _____ radio operators needed to assist with emergency at this location.
TEN	Please contact _____. Advise to standby and provide further emergency information, instructions or assistance.
ELEVEN	Establish Amateur Radio emergency communications with _____ on _____ MHz.
TWELVE	Anxious to hear from you. No word in some time. Please contact me as soon as possible.
THIRTEEN	Medical emergency situation exits here.
FOURTEEN	Situation here becoming critical. Losses and damage from _____ increasing.
FIFTEEN	Please advise your condition and what help is needed.
SIXTEEN	Property damage very severe in this area.
SEVENTEEN	REACT communications services also available. Establish REACT communication with _____ on channel _____.
EIGHTEEN	Please contact me as soon as possible at _____.
NINETEEN	Request health and welfare report on _____. (State name, address and telephone number.)
TWENTY	Temporarily stranded. Will need some assistance. Please contact me at _____.
TWENTY ONE	Search and Rescue assistance is needed by local authorities here. Advise availability.
TWENTY TWO	Need accurate information on the extent and type of conditions now existing at your location. Please furnish this information and reply without delay.
TWENTY THREE	Report at once the accessibility and best way to reach your location.
TWENTY FOUR	Evacuation of residents from this area urgently needed. Advise plans for help.
TWENTY FIVE	Furnish as soon as possible the weather conditions at your location.
TWENTY SIX	Help and care for evacuation of sick and injured from this location needed at once.

Emergency/priority messages originating from official sources must carry the signature of the originating official.

Group Two—Routine Messages

FORTY SIX	Greetings on your birthday and best wishes for many more to come.
FORTY SEVEN	Reference your message number _____ to _____ delivered on _____ at _____ UTC.
FIFTY	Greetings by Amateur Radio.
FIFTY ONE	Greetings by Amateur Radio. This message is sent as a free public service by ham radio operators at _____. Am having a wonderful time.
FIFTY TWO	Really enjoyed being with you. Looking forward to getting together again.
FIFTY THREE	Received your _____. It's appreciated; many thanks.
FIFTY FOUR	Many thanks for your good wishes.
FIFTY FIVE	Good news is always welcome. Very delighted to hear about yours.
FIFTY SIX	Congratulations on your _____, a most worthy and deserved achievement.
FIFTY SEVEN	Wish we could be together.
FIFTY EIGHT	Have a wonderful time. Let us know when you return.
FIFTY NINE	Congratulations on the new arrival. Hope mother and child are well.
♦SIXTY	Wishing you the best of everything on _____.
SIXTY ONE	Wishing you a very Merry Christmas and a Happy New Year.
♦SIXTY TWO	Greetings and best wishes to you for a pleasant _____ holiday season.
SIXTY THREE	Victory or defeat, our best wishes are with you. Hope you win.
SIXTY FOUR	Arrived safely at _____.
SIXTY FIVE	Arriving _____ on _____. Please arrange to meet me there.
SIXTY SIX	DX QSLs are on hand for you at the _____ QSL Bureau. Send _____ self addressed envelopes.
SIXTY SEVEN	Your message number _____ undeliverable because of _____. Please advise.
SIXTY EIGHT	Sorry to hear you are ill. Best wishes for a speedy recovery.
SIXTY NINE	Welcome to the _____. We are glad to have you with us and hope you will enjoy the fun and fellowship of the organization.

♦Can be used for all holidays.

Note: ARL numbers should be spelled out at all times.

GENERAL MESSAGE (ICS 213)

1. Incident Name (Optional):		
2. To (Name and Position):		
3. From (Name and Position):		

4. Subject:	**5. Date:** Date	**6. Time** HHMM

7. Message:

8. Approved by: Name: Signature: _____   Position/Title: _____

9. Reply:

10. Replied by: Name: Position/Title: Signature: _____

ICS 213   Date/Time: Date

ICS 213
General Message

Purpose. The General Message (ICS 213) is used by the incident dispatchers to record incoming messages that cannot be orally transmitted to the intended recipients. The ICS 213 is also used by the Incident Command Post and other incident personnel to transmit messages (e.g., resource order, incident name change, other ICS coordination issues, etc.) to the Incident Communications Center for transmission via radio or telephone to the addressee. This form is used to send any message or notification to incident personnel that requires hard-copy delivery.

Preparation. The ICS 213 may be initiated by incident dispatchers and any other personnel on an incident.

Distribution. Upon completion, the ICS 213 may be delivered to the addressee and/or delivered to the Incident Communication Center for transmission.

Notes:
- The ICS 213 is a three-part form, typically using carbon paper. The sender will complete Part 1 of the form and send Parts 2 and 3 to the recipient. The recipient will complete Part 2 and return Part 3 to the sender.
- A copy of the ICS 213 should be sent to and maintained within the Documentation Unit.
- Contact information for the sender and receiver can be added for communications purposes to confirm resource orders. Refer to 213RR example (Appendix B)

Block Number	Block Title	Instructions
1	**Incident Name** (Optional)	Enter the name assigned to the incident. This block is optional.
2	**To** (Name and Position)	Enter the name and position the General Message is intended for. For all individuals, use at least the first initial and last name. For Unified Command, include agency names.
3	**From** (Name and Position)	Enter the name and position of the individual sending the General Message. For all individuals, use at least the first initial and last name. For Unified Command, include agency names.
4	**Subject**	Enter the subject of the message.
5	**Date**	Enter the date (month/day/year) of the message.
6	**Time**	Enter the time (using the 24-hour clock) of the message.
7	**Message**	Enter the content of the message. Try to be as concise as possible.
8	**Approved by** • Name • Signature • Position/Title	Enter the name, signature, and ICS position/title of the person approving the message.
9	**Reply**	The intended recipient will enter a reply to the message and return it to the originator.
10	**Replied by** • Name • Position/Title • Signature • Date/Time	Enter the name, ICS position/title, and signature of the person replying to the message. Enter date (month/day/year) and time prepared (24-hour clock).

Amateur Radio Emergency Service®

ARES® Registration Form

Name:	
Call Sign:	
Mailing Address:	
City, State, ZIP code:	
e-mail address(es):	
Home phone number:	
Work phone number:	
Cell phone number:	
License Class:	

Check bands and modes that you can operate:

MODE	HF	6 meters	2 meters	222 MHz	440 MHz	Others	
SSB							
CW							
FM							
DATA							
PACKET							
Other modes (specify below)							
Mobile Operation							

Can your home station be operated without commercial power? Yes [   ]   No [   ]

Signature_____ Date _____

Contact ARES® and ARRL Section Leaders in your area: www.arrl.org/sections/.
Learn about ARRL-sponsored Amateur Radio Emergency Communications Courses:
www.arrl.org/online-course-catalog

FSD-98 (07/12)

Complete this form and submit it to your local Emergency Coordinator. For more information, visit www.arrl.org/ares.

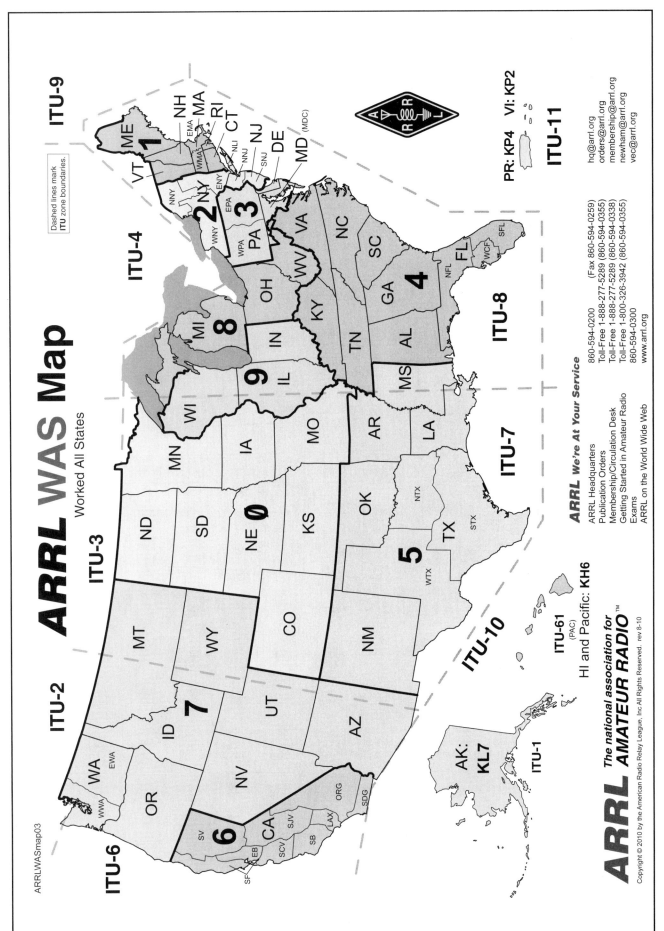

ARRL WAS Map

Worked All States

ARRLWASmap03

Dashed lines mark ITU zone boundaries.

ITU-9

ITU-2

ITU-3

ITU-4

ITU-6

ITU-8

ITU-7

ITU-10

ITU-11

PR: KP4   VI: KP2

ITU-61 (PAC)
HI and Pacific: KH6

AK: KL7

ITU-1

hq@arrl.org
orders@arrl.org
membership@arrl.org
newham@arrl.org
vec@arrl.org

ARRL *We're At Your Service*

ARRL Headquarters	860-594-0200	(Fax 860-594-0259)
Publication Orders	Toll-Free 1-888-277-5289 (860-594-0355)	
Membership/Circulation Desk	Toll-Free 1-888-277-5289 (860-594-0338)	
Getting Started in Amateur Radio Exams	Toll-Free 1-800-326-3942 (860-594-0355)	
ARRL on the World Wide Web	860-594-0300	
	www.arrl.org	

ARRL The national association for **AMATEUR RADIO**™

Copyright © 2010 by the American Radio Relay League, Inc All Rights Reserved. rev 8-10

A map showing US states, ARRL Sections and ITU zones

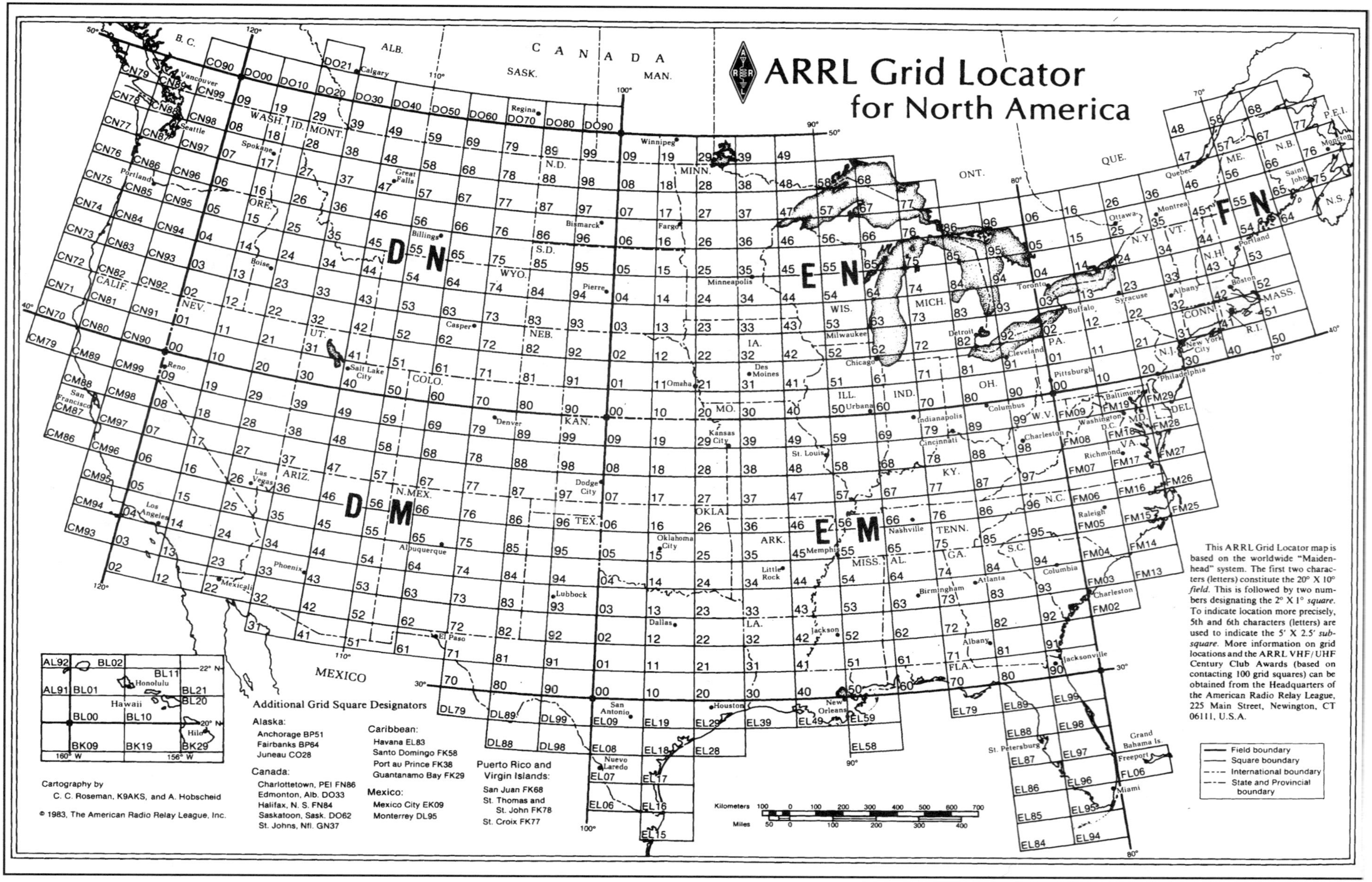

ARRL Grid Locator Map for North America. This map and the World Grid Locator Map are available from ARRL.

ARRL Grid Locator
for North America

This ARRL Grid Locator map is based on the worldwide "Maidenhead" system. The first two characters (letters) constitute the 20° X 10° *field*. This is followed by two numbers designating the 2° X 1° *square*. To indicate location more precisely, 5th and 6th characters (letters) are used to indicate the 5' X 2.5' *subsquare*. More information on grid locations and the ARRL VHF/UHF Century Club Awards (based on contacting 100 grid squares) can be obtained from the Headquarters of the American Radio Relay League, 225 Main Street, Newington, CT 06111, U.S.A.

— Field boundary
— Square boundary
- - - - International boundary
- · - · - State and Provincial boundary

© 1983, The American Radio Relay League, Inc.

Cartography by
C. C. Roseman, K9AKS, and A. Hobscheid

Additional Grid Square Designators

Alaska:
Anchorage BP51
Fairbanks BP94
Juneau CO28

Canada:
Charlottetown, PEI FN86
Edmonton, Alb. DO33
Halifax, N. S. FN84
Saskatoon, Sask. DO62
St. Johns, Nfl GN37

Caribbean:
Havana EL83
Santo Domingo FK58
Port au Prince FK38
Guantanamo Bay FK29

Mexico:
Mexico City EK09
Monterrey DL95

Puerto Rico and
Virgin Islands:
San Juan FK68
St. Thomas FK78
St. John FK78
St. Croix FK77

Hawaii

Kilometers
Miles

WAC Award Application
Please print clearly and complete all sections

Name _____ Callsign _____
(Name as to appear on certificate)

Mailing Address _____

City/Town_____ State_____ Zip Code _____

Country: _____ Email Address: _____

Award(s) applied for:
__ Basic certificate
__ CW certificate
__ Phone certificate
__ Image certificate
__ Digital certificate
__ Satellite certificate

Endorsement(s) Applied for:
__ QRP endorsement (5 watts output or less)
__ 1.8 MHz endorsement
__ 3.5 MHz endorsement
__ 50 MHz endorsement
__ 144 MHz endorsement
__ 432 MHz endorsement
__ 1296 MHz endorsement
__ Other Endorsement(s) _____

☐ *Cards listed below can be found in my DXCC account.*

You must list the callsigns of the QSOs from your DXCC (not LoTW) account that you want to claim.

Special Note: Contacts in LoTW are currently not eligible for WAC credit

I am claiming credit for the following stations. Enter MHz and callsigns:

Note Band Info ⇒	( ) MHz	( ) MHz	( ) MHz	( ) MHz	( ) MHz
North America					
South America					
Oceania					
Asia					
Europe					
Africa					

I have read all of the program rules and have complied with all program rules and governmental regulations regarding amateur radio in my country.

Signature_____ Callsign _____ Date _____

For non-USA applicants, applications should be presented to the local IARU awards manager for verification. The awards manager will handle all WAC applications. Approved DXCC card checkers can also verify application for WAC. (See http://www.arrl.org/dxcc-card-checker-master-list for the complete listing of approved DXCC card checkers).

I am a member of _____ **IARU member society (membership is required)**

Postage fee is not part of application fees. Applicant is responsible for return postage for cards. US card return is $3.00 and international mailing is $8.00.
Application forms with cards credited in a DXCC account can be sent to WAC by e-mail or fax along with payment noted on the form.

Card Checker Signature_____ Callsign _____ Date _____

Send application form, fees and QSL cards to:
ARRL Awards Branch/WAC
225 Main Street
Newington, CT USA 06111
Send comments and questions to wac@arrl.org
Fax: (860) 594-0346
WAC Web Site: www.arrl.org/wac

WAC Award Fees (per certificate) multiple awards/endorsements can be placed on one certificate:
WAC Certificate (Per Certificate) - $16.00 (US Mail); $18.00 (International mail)
Endorsements (Multiple endorsements on one form is one-time $7.50 fee) - $7.50

Check or Money Order Enclosed in the amount of _____

Credit Card # _____ Exp Date _____

_____
Awards Manager Verification Signature

_____
Date

2016

DXCC AWARD APPLICATION
(Required with Each New Submission and Endorsements)

I am applying for the following DXCC award(s)/
Endorsement(s):

New Award(s) _____

Endorsement(s) _____

# of QSL cards enclosed_____

# of QSOs _____

**Use post-it note on multiple QSO cards if you do not
need all QSOs. Cards must be sorted as noted on the
guidelines on the Record Sheet.**
See http://www.arrl.org/dxcc-faq/) for complete
Application instructions

Current DXCC fees are shown at: www.arrl.org/dxcc

- The use of a current DXCC application form is
  required.
- Return postage is required for the return of cards,
  paperwork returns and all written requests.
- DXCC accepts most credit cards. If you are not
  sure of the correct charges, you should use a credit
  card. This will allow us to charge the exact
  amount. You must clear previous balances (per
  your last credit slip) with this submission in order
  to avoid delays. **DXCC cannot bill you.**
  Current fee schedule located at:
  http://www.arrl.org/dxcc-awards-fees

"I affirm that I have observed all DXCC rules as well
as all governmental regulations established for
Amateur Radio in my country. I understand that
ARRL is not responsible for cards handled by DXCC
Card Checkers and will not honor any claims. I
agree to be bound by the decisions of the ARRL
Awards Committee and that all decisions of the ARRL
Awards Committee are final."

Call Sign: _____

Ex Calls:_____

Name: _____
           First   Last

Mailing Address:

_____

_____

_____
           (City, State/Zip, Country)

↑ **This is where your cards, paperwork, & certificates will be shipped** ↑

___ Check here if this is a new address

Name as to Appear on Certificate:

_____
(Print name exactly as you want it to appear on certificate)

Telephone #: _____
Email: _____

Return My QSL Cards Via:
United States Shipping: **Foreign Shipping:**
__ First Class (non-traceable)   __ First Class International (non-traceable)
__ First Class Priority (recommended; __ First Class Int Priority (traceable)
   traceable)   __ Fedex International Economy
__ FedEx (recommended; traceable)   (traceable)

For a printout of your DXCC matrix: __ $2.00 US __ $5.00 Foreign
(This is available for free if you have a DXCC account via LoTW)

_____
Applicant Signature (REQUIRED)   **Callsign**   **Date**   **ARRL Membership Expiration Date**

Send application forms, QSL cards, fees, and return postage to: DXCC Desk, ARRL HQ, 225 Main Street, Newington, CT 06111, U.S.A. For
questions or clarifications, please write to the DXCC Desk at the above address, or via e-mail to **dxccadmin@arrl.org** To confirm the
receipt of your application, go to this link: **http://www.arrl.org/dxcc-applications-received%20**The DXCC Desk can also be contacted as
follows: Telephone: 860-594-0200, Fax: 860-594-0346 (24 hour direct line to ARRL HQ). For complete program information, please visit the
DXCC web site at: http://www.arrl.org/dxcc

Click **here** to locate your nearest DXCC card checker. Only those in red can check 160 Meters.
For ARRL DXCC Card Checker Use Only
I affirm that I have personally inspected the confirmations and verify that this application is accurate.

_____
Card Checker Signature   **Callsign**   **Date**

DXCC Card Checkers must forward the application and fees to HQ within 2 working days.
FIELD CHECKED APPLICATIONS MUST BE SUBMITTED ONLY BY CARD CHECKERS.
Payment Details

Check or Money Order Enclosed in the Amount of $_____

Credit Card # _____ Expiration Date: _____

Name as it appears on credit card: _____

2015

DXCC Record Sheet

_____
Your Call

Note: Cards may be submitted directly to ARRL or checked by an approved DXCC Card Checker. This form *must* be completed if a Card Checker checks the application. In *either* case, the cards or listed credits must be sorted first by band then by mode. If you fill out the form, supply all information as requested. Be sure to use the Entity name, not just the prefix. Cards indicating multiple contacts must be placed together. If cards with multiple credits are submitted direct to ARRL, a notation must be made on each card indicating which credits are to be entered. If no indication is made on a card, all credits will be entered into your record.

	CALL	QSO DATE (DD| MM |YY)		BAND	MODE	ENTITY/ COUNTRY NAME
1		|	|			
2		|	|			
3		|	|			
4		|	|			
5		|	|			
6		|	|			
7		|	|			
8		|	|			
9		|	|			
10		|	|			
11		|	|			
12		|	|			
13		|	|			
14		|	|			
15		|	|			
16		|	|			
17		|	|			
18		|	|			
19		|	|			
20		|	|			
21		|	|			
22		|	|			
23		|	|			
24		|	|			
25		|	|			

This side of form may be photocopied if more pages are needed.

ARRL VUCC AWARD APPLICATION FORM
This form is required with each submission new or endorsement

Please print or type **clearly** and use a separate application for **each** award.

Callsign:_____ → from Grid Locator → (_____)
↑ *Required* ↑

Ex Callsigns:_____

Name: _____
Print exactly as you want your name and call to appear on certificate

Address:_____

City:_____ State:_____ Zip Code:_____

Email Address: _____ Telephone: _____

ARRL Membership ID Number: _____ Expiration Date: _____

Band: (please check only one):   Use One (1) Application Per Band

☐ 50 MHz   ☐ 144 MHz   ☐ 222 MHz   ☐ 432 MHz
☐ 902 MHz   ☐ 1296 MHz   ☐ 2.3 GHz   ☐ 3.4 GHz
☐ 5.7 GHz   ☐ 10 GHz   ☐ 24 GHz   ☐ 47 GHz
☐ 75 GHz   ☐ 119 GHz   ☐ 142 GHz   ☐ 241 GHz
☐ Laser (300 GHz) ☐ Satellite   ☐ Other _____ (Specify)

Initial Applicant's _____ Number of Grid Locators

Endorsements:

_____ + _____ = _____
Previous Total   Number added with this endorsement   New Total

"I affirm that I have observed all the VUCC rules as well as all pertinent government regulations established for Amateur Radio in my country. I agree to be bound by the ARRL Awards Committee (Decisions of the ARRL Awards Committee are final)."

Signature:_____ Callsign:_____ Date:_____

VHF Awards Manager Verification: "I have verified these contacts as set forth by the rules of the VUCC Program."

_____ _____ _____
Signature   Callsign   Date
Traditional QSL Application Directions

1) Complete **ALL** fields above.
2) Enclose award fees. Certificate w/postage is $17 in the US; $27 outside the US. Pin w/postage is $7 in the US; $8 international mailings. Sticker w/postage is $1 in the US; $2 international mailings.
3) Enclose application fee: $5 for ARRL members or $10 for non-members outside the US.
4) Enclose fifteen cents for each QSO ($0.15).
5) Sort cards alpha-numerically by grid locator and list on the record sheet(s).
6) Contact your VHF Awards Manager before sending cards to assure they are available to make arrangements for checking.
7) Give your Awards Manager all fees and mailing costs. They are responsible for sending paperwork to ARRL.
8) If you prefer, you may send cards to ARRL HQ. Enclose sufficient funds to return cards via traceable mail.

Payment Details

Check or Money Order: _____

Credit Card # _____ Exp Date: _____

(2014)

ARRL VUCC Award Field Sheet

Callsign: _____

☐ 50　☐ 144　☐ 222　☐ 432　☐ 902　☐ 1296　☐ 2.3　☐ 3.4　☐ 5.7　☐ 10
☐ 24　☐ 47　☐ 75　☐ 119　☐ 142　☐ 241　☐ Laser (300 GHz)　☐ Satellite

Directions: This sheet is good for **ONE** field.
1. Enter your callsign and check band
2. Enter two-letter field
3. Enter the callsign of the stations worked next to the appropriate square below
4. Total grid locators for each field

Field: _____ (First 2 letters of locator)

Sq	Callsign	Sq	Callsign	Sq	Callsign	Sq	Callsign
00	_____	25	_____	50	_____	75	_____
01	_____	26	_____	51	_____	76	_____
02	_____	27	_____	52	_____	77	_____
03	_____	28	_____	53	_____	78	_____
04	_____	29	_____	54	_____	79	_____
05	_____	30	_____	55	_____	80	_____
06	_____	31	_____	56	_____	81	_____
07	_____	32	_____	57	_____	82	_____
08	_____	33	_____	58	_____	83	_____
09	_____	34	_____	59	_____	84	_____
10	_____	35	_____	60	_____	85	_____
11	_____	36	_____	61	_____	86	_____
12	_____	37	_____	62	_____	87	_____
13	_____	38	_____	63	_____	88	_____
14	_____	39	_____	64	_____	89	_____
15	_____	40	_____	65	_____	90	_____
16	_____	41	_____	66	_____	91	_____
17	_____	42	_____	67	_____	92	_____
18	_____	43	_____	68	_____	93	_____
19	_____	44	_____	69	_____	94	_____
20	_____	45	_____	70	_____	95	_____
21	_____	46	_____	71	_____	96	_____
22	_____	47	_____	72	_____	97	_____
23	_____	48	_____	73	_____	98	_____
24	_____	49	_____	74	_____	99	_____

TOTAL number of grid locators worked in this field:_____

msd-259(11/12TV)

 **ARRL** The national association for **AMATEUR RADIO®**

ARRL WAS APPLICATION FORM

Please print or type your name and callsign **CLEARLY**:

Name: _____ Call: _____
(Print exactly as you want it on certificate)

List any ex-calls used on any cards: _____

Address: _____

_____
(City)   (State)   (Zip)   (Country)
Email Address: _____

I have submitted an application via LoTW -   **Yes**   **No**   **(Circle One)**

☐ I am applying for ONE or TWO of the following WAS Awards (each is numbered separately/use
additional form[s] to order more awards). **Circle One or Two:**

Basic Mixed Award	**Phone**	**Digital**	**RTTY**	**CW**	
6 Meters	144 MHz	432 MHz	160 Meters	222 MHz	1296 MHz
	Satellite	SSTV	5-Band		

☐ I am applying for the following band endorsements and indicate which award (circle all that apply):

6   10   12   15   17   20   30   40   80   160 (Meters)   for my _____ award

6   10   12   15   17   20   30   40   80   160 (Meters)   for my _____ award

Power Endorsement: ☐ QRP for my _____ award
                   ☐ QRP for my _____ award

☐ I am applying for the following mode endorsements:

Circle One: PSK31   JT65   FSK441   HELL   CLOVER   OLIVIA   RTTY   Other _____ for my _____ award

                PSK31   JT65   FSK441   HELL   CLOVER   OLIVIA   RTTY   Other _____ for my _____ award

I have read, understood and followed all the rules of WAS:

_____   _____
Applicant's Signature   Date

HF AWARDS MANAGER/CARD CHECKER VERIFICATION

I have personally inspected the confirmations with all 50 states and verify that this application is correct and true. This
application is for the following SPECIALTY awards or ENDORSEMENTS: _____ (Write **NONE** if none)

_____   _____   _____
Signature   Callsign   Date

DIRECTIONS TO APPLICANT

1. Fill out this Application Form.
2. Sort cards by state as listed on the Record Sheet and fill in Record Sheet.
3. Present application and cards to your ARRL HF Awards Manager for verification. Applications from DX stations may
be certified by the Awards Manager of your IARU member-society.
4. Send application to ARRL HQ with the appropriate fee(s): $12 for **each** WAS certificate. Shipping is $5 for one or
two certificates if mailed in the US or $15 for one or two certificates if mailed internationally. $2.00 for any number of
endorsement stickers mailed in the US, and $3.00 for any number of endorsement stickers mailed internationally.
Pins are $7.50.

PAYMENT DETAILS

Return QSLs Via :   ☐ US Priority ($8)   ☐ International Priority without tracking ($11)
☐ International Priority with tracking ($40)

For Certificate(s) $ _____ + Shipping $ _____   For Endorsement(s) $ _____ For Pin(s) $ _____

Total Payment:
Check or Money Order Enclosed $ _____ or

Credit Card # _____ Exp Date _____

Mar 2016

WAS RECORD SHEET

Applicant's callsign _____

List any ex-calls used on any cards submitted: _____

STATE	CALL	DATE	BAND	MODE
Alabama				
Alaska				
Arizona				
Arkansas				
California				
Colorado				
Connecticut				
Delaware				
Florida				
Georgia				
Hawaii				
Idaho				
Illinois				
Indiana				
Iowa				
Kansas				
Kentucky				
Louisiana				
Maine				
Maryland (D.C.)				
Massachusetts				
Michigan				
Minnesota				
Mississippi				
Missouri				
Montana				
Nebraska				
Nevada				
New Hampshire				
New Jersey				
New Mexico				
New York				
North Carolina				
North Dakota				
Ohio				
Oklahoma				
Oregon				
Pennsylvania				
Rhode Island				
South Carolina				
South Dakota				
Tennessee				
Texas				
Utah				
Vermont				
Virginia				
Washington				
West Virginia				
Wisconsin				
Wyoming				

Mar 2016

ARRL 5 BAND WAS APPLICATION FORM

Please print or type your name and callsign **CLEARLY**:

Name: _____ Call: _____
(Print exactly as you want it on certificate)

List any ex-calls used on any cards: _____

Address: _____

_____
(City)   (State)   (Zip)   (Country)

Email Address: _____

☐   I have submitted an application via LoTW.

I am applying for: ☐   5BWAS Certificate   ☐   5BWAS Plaque   ☐   5BWAS Pin

I have read, understood, and followed all the rules of WAS:

_____   _____
Applicant's Signature   Date

HF AWARDS MANAGER/CARD CHECKER VERIFICATION
I have personally inspected all the confirmations that were submitted to me with this application, unless otherwise marked, and verify that this application is correct.

_____   _____   _____
Signature   Callsign   Date

•••••••••••••••••••• 5 Band WAS Rules ••••••••••••••••••••

1. The 5BWAS certificate and plaque (see #4) will be issued for having submitted confirmations with each of the 50 United States for contacts dated January 1, 1970, or after, on the 80, 40, 20, 15, and 10 Meter bands. Phone and CW segments of a band do not count as separate bands.
2. WAS Rules that do not conflict with these 5BWAS rules also apply to the 5BWAS Award.
3. There are no specialty 5 Band awards or endorsements.
4. A 9 x 12 personalized plaque is available for a fee of $60.00 US (payable by check, money order, or credit card), or $80.00 International (payable by international money order, or credit card), including shipping.
5. 5BWAS certificates are $12.00. Shipping is $5.00 USA / $15.00 International.
6. 5BWAS pins are $7.50 USA / $7.50 International, including shipping.

•••••••••••••••••••• Directions to Applicant ••••••••••••••••••••

1. Read the 5BWAS and WAS Rules carefully.
2. Fill out both pages of this application.
3. Sort cards by state as listed on the record sheet.
4. Present application and cards to your ARRL HR Awards Manager for verification. Applications from DX stations may be certified by the Awards Manager of your IARU member-society.
5. Send applications to ARRL HQ. Send cards ONLY if there is no local HF Awards Manager to verify your application.
6. If mailing cards, enclose the appropriate fee(s) and sufficient postage for the return of your cards. You can find postage pricing at the following site: http://www.arrl.org/was
7. Enclose $60.00 USA / $80.00 International if also requesting a plaque.

PAYMENT DETAILS

Return QSLs Via : _____ US Priority ($8) _____ International Priority without tracking ($11)

_____ International Priority with tracking ($40)

For 5BWAS Certificate $ _____   For 5BWAS Pin $ _____   For 5BWAS Plaque $ _____

Total Payment:

Check or Money Order Enclosed $ _____ or

Credit Card # _____ Exp Date _____

June 2015

Applicant's callsign:

List any of your previous calls used on any cards submitted:

5 BAND WAS RECORD SHEET

Place the call sign of the station worked in the boxes below

STATE	80 Meters	40 Meters	20 Meters	15 Meters	10 Meters
Alabama					
Alaska					
Arizona					
Arkansas					
California					
Colorado					
Connecticut					
Delaware					
Florida					
Georgia					
Hawaii					
Idaho					
Illinois					
Indiana					
Iowa					
Kansas					
Kentucky					
Louisiana					
Maine					
Maryland (D.C.)					
Massachusetts					
Michigan					
Minnesota					
Mississippi					
Missouri					
Montana					
Nebraska					
Nevada					
New Hampshire					
New Jersey					
New Mexico					
New York					
North Carolina					
North Dakota					
Ohio					
Oklahoma					
Oregon					
Pennsylvania					
Rhode Island					
South Carolina					
South Dakota					
Tennessee					
Texas					
Utah					
Vermont					
Virginia					
Washington					
West Virginia					
Wisconsin					
Wyoming					

June 2015

The ARRL Incoming QSL Bureau System

Within the US and Canada, the ARRL DX QSL Bureau System is made up of numerous call area bureaus that act as central clearing houses for QSLs arriving from other countries. These incoming bureaus are staffed by volunteers. The service is free and ARRL membership is not required. (Canadian amateurs can use the Radio Amateurs of Canada's incoming QSL bureau.)

How it Works

Most countries have "outgoing" QSL bureaus that operate in much the same manner as the ARRL Outgoing QSL Service. The members send cards to the outgoing bureau where they are packaged and shipped to the appropriate countries.

A majority of the DX QSLs are shipped directly to the individual incoming bureaus where volunteers sort the incoming QSLs by the first letter of the call sign suffix. An individual may be assigned the responsibility of handling one or more letters of the alphabet.

With the many vanity calls on the air, what bureau should you use? The answer is to use the bureau that handles QSLs for the district represented by the number in your call sign. If your call is NØAX, use the tenth district bureau no matter where you operate from. If you operate portable or mobile from another district, QSLs will still be sent to your home district's bureau — don't use the "portable" bureau. If you operate from an entity outside the US and it has a bureau, make the necessary arrangements for your QSLs to be mailed to you, otherwise they may be discarded.

Claiming Your QSLs

Check with your incoming bureau to see what procedure they follow. Some incoming bureaus prefer that you send them a supply of self-addressed, stamped envelopes (SASEs), while others prefer that you send money which will be used for envelope and postage credits. Check with your bureau for the preferred method. The incoming bureaus occasionally change managers or addresses or web addresses. Their requirements and services may change. For this reason, you should check the ARRL website at **www.arrl. org/qsl-service** for the latest information and addresses for each incoming bureau.

In the absence of instructions to the contrary, SASEs should be 5 × 7.5 or 6 × 9 inches. Neatly print your call sign in the upper left corner of the envelope. Place your mailing address on the front of the envelope. A suggested way to send envelopes is to affix First Class postage for 1 ounce and clip extra postage to the envelope. Then, if you receive more than 1 ounce of cards, they can be sent in a single package. (Check with your local post office for the correct rates.)

Helpful Hints

Good cooperation between the DXer and the bureau is important to ensure a smooth flow of cards. Remember that the people who work in the area bureaus are volunteers. They are providing you with a valuable service. With that thought in mind, please pay close attention to the following DOs and DON'Ts.

DO

• Do keep self-addressed 5 × 7½ or 6 × 9 inch envelopes or money credit on file at your bureau, with your call sign in the upper left corner, and affix at least one unit of first-class postage.

• Do send the bureau enough postage to cover SASEs on file and enough to take care of possible postage rate increases.

• Do respond quickly to any bureau request for SASEs, stamps or money. Unclaimed card backlogs are the bureau's biggest problem.

• Do notify the bureau of your new call sign as you upgrade. Please send SASEs with your new call, in addition to SASEs with your old call.

• Do include your call sign on any correspondence with the bureau.

• Do include a SASE with any information request to the bureau.

• Do notify the bureau in writing if you don't want your cards.

• Do notify the bureau of a change of address.

DON'T

• Don't send domestic US to US cards to the various call area bureaus.

• Don't expect DX cards to arrive for several months after the QSO. Overseas delivery is very slow. Many cards coming from overseas bureaus are over a year old.

• Don't send your outgoing DX cards to your call area bureau.

• Don't send SASEs to your "portable" bureau. For example, NUØX/1 sends SASEs to the WØ bureau, not the W1 bureau.

• Don't send SASEs or money credits to the ARRL Outgoing QSL Service.

• Don't send SASEs larger than 6 × 9 inches. SASEs larger than 6 × 9 inches require additional postage surcharges.

For the latest information on the ARRL Incoming QSL Bureau system, check **www. arrl.org/qsl-service**.

The ARRL Outgoing QSL Service

One of the greatest bargains of ARRL membership is being able to use the Outgoing QSL Service to conveniently send your DX QSL cards to overseas QSL Bureaus. You just need to provide proof of ARRL Membership and include payment. Your cards are sorted and on their way overseas usually within a week of arrival at HQ. Sending QSL cards via the Bureau takes longer than mailing them directly, but it is easier and much less expensive than addressing and mailing each QSL card separately.

Note that the ARRL QSL Service *cannot be used to exchange QSL cards within the 48 contiguous states*. QSLs from the 48 states to and from Alaska and Hawaii may be sent through the ARRL QSL Service. And you may send QSLs via the Service to any QSL manager who manages a non-US call sign. However, you must clearly indicate the QSL manager's call sign on your outgoing card — for example: 8P8P via NN1N. Sort this card in with other cards going to US managers. There are many sources of QSL information online.

For the latest information on the ARRL Outgoing QSL Service and the current fee schedule, check **www.arrl.org/qsl-service** or e-mail **buro@arrl.org**

How to Use the ARRL Outgoing QSL Service

1. Presort your DX QSLs alphabetically by parent call sign prefix (AP, CE, DL, ES, EZ, F, G, JA, LY, PY, UN, YL, 5N, 9Y and so on). Canadian and Australian cards should be sorted by numerical call sign (VE1, VE2, VE3 or VK1, VK2, VK3 etc). Note: Some countries have a parent prefix and use additional prefixes. For example, G is the parent prefix for M, 2E, and many other prefixes. When sorting countries that have multiple prefixes, keep that country's prefixes grouped with the parent prefix in your alphabetical stack. Addresses are not required.

2. Do not separate the country prefixes by use of paper clips, rubber bands, slips of paper, or envelopes.

3. Please enclose proof of your current ARRL membership. This can be in the form of a photocopy or cut-out of the address area from your current copy of *QST*. You can also write the information from the label on a slip of paper and use that as proof of membership.

A copy of your current membership card is also acceptable.

4. Members, including those who are international members, QSL managers, or managers for DXpeditions, should enclose payment.

For the latest information on the ARRL Outgoing QSL Service fee schedule, check **www.arrl.org/qsl-service** or e-mail **buro@arrl.org**.

5. Please pay by check (or money order) and write your call sign on the check. Send cash at your own risk. DO NOT send postage stamps or IRCs. Please make checks payable to: "The ARRL Outgoing QSL Service." If you would like to know that your cards were received at the ARRL QSL Bureau, enclose an SASE in with your cards and we will return that to you as receipt.

6. DXCC credits cannot be used towards the QSL Service fee.

7. Include only the cards, proof of membership, an SASE (if desired) and the appropriate fee in the package. Wrap the package securely and address it to the ARRL Outgoing QSL Service, 225 Main Street, Newington, CT 06111-1494.

8. Family members may also use the service by enclosing their QSLs with those of the primary member. Include the appropriate fee and indicate "family membership" on the primary member's proof of membership.

9. Blind members who do not receive *QST* need only include the appropriate fee along with a note indicating the cards are from a blind member.

10. ARRL affiliated-club stations may use the service when submitting club QSLs for its members in bulk ("pooling" their members cards together in one package) by indicating the club name inside the package. Club secretaries should check club affiliation on the ARRL website to ensure that their affiliation is current. In a "pooled" package, each club member using this service must also be an ARRL member. Cards should be sorted "en masse" by prefix and a proof of membership should be enclosed for each ARRL member. QSLs for unaffiliated club calls may also be sent via the outgoing bureau to foreign destinations if the trustee of the club call is a member in good standing. The trustee's proof of membership must be included with the club call-QSLs.

Recommended QSL Card Dimensions

Cards of unusual dimensions, either much larger or much smaller than normal or printed on thin paper (ie, copier paper), slow the work of the bureaus, most of which is done by unpaid volunteers. A review of the cards received by the ARRL Outgoing QSL Service indicates that most fall in the following range: Height = 2¾ to 4¼ in. (70 to 110 mm) and Width = 4¾ to 6¼ in. (120 to 160 mm). IARU Region 2 (which includes the United States) has suggested the following dimensions as optimum: Height 3½ in. (90 mm) and Width 5½ in. (140 mm). Cards in this range can be easily sorted, stacked and packaged. Cards outside this range create problems. In particular, the larger cards often cannot be handled without folding or otherwise damaging them.

Countries Not Served By the Outgoing QSL Service

Approximately 225 DXCC entities are served by the ARRL Outgoing QSL Service. This includes nearly every active country. Cards are forwarded from the ARRL Outgoing Service to a counterpart bureau in each of these countries. In some cases, there is no Incoming Bureau in a particular country and cards, therefore, cannot be forwarded. However, QSL cards can be forwarded to a QSL manager, such as ZB2FX via G3RFX. Most operations from places without a QSL bureau have a QSL manager.

DXCC Entities Not Served by the ARRL Outgoing QSL Service

As of August 2016

A3	Tonga	P2	Papua New Guinea	XZ	Myanmar
A5	Bhutan	P5	North Korea	YA	Afghanistan
A6	United Arab Emirates	PZ	Suriname	Z2	Zimbabwe
C2	Nauru	SØ	Western Sahara	ZA	Albania
C5	Gambia	S7	Seychelles	3B	Agalega, Mauritius, Rodrigues
C6	Bahamas	S9	Sao Tome & Principe	3CØ	Pagalu Island
CN	Morocco	ST	Sudan	3CØ	Equatorial Guinea
D2	Angola	SU	Egypt	3DA	Swaziland
D4	Cape Verde	T2	Tuvalu	3W	Vietnam
E3	Eritrea	T3	Kiribati	3X	Guinea
E4	Palestine	T5	Somalia	4J, 4K	Azerbaijan
E5	North & South Cook Islands	T8	Palau	4W	Timor-Leste
ET	Ethiopia	TJ	Cameroon	5A	Libya
HH	Haiti	TL	Central African Republic	5R	Madagascar
HV	Vatican	TN	Congo	5T	Mauritania
J5	Guinea-Bissau	TT	Chad	5U	Niger
J8	St. Vincent	TU	Cote d'Ivoire	5V	Togo
KG4	Guantanamo Bay	TY	Benin	7O	Yemen
KHØ	Mariana Island	V3	Belize	7P	Lesotho
KH1	Baker & Howland Islands	V4	St. Kitts & Nevis	7Q	Malawi
KH4	Midway Island	V6	Micronesia	8Q	Maldives
KH5	Palmyra & Jarvis Islands	VP2E	Anguilla	9L	Sierra Leone
KH7K	Kure Island	VP2M	Montserrat	9N	Nepal
KH9	Wake Island	VQ9	Chagos Diego Garcia	9U	Burundi
KP1	Desecheo Island	XU	Cambodia	9X	Rwanda
		XW	Laos		

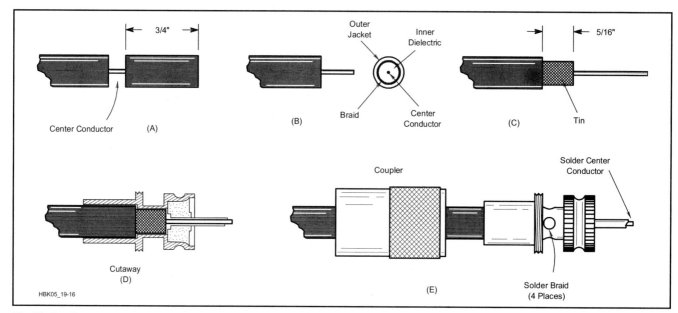

The PL-259 (also called "UHF") connector is almost universal for amateur HF work and is also popular for operating in the VHF range.

Characteristics of Common Feed Lines

Specifications vary. See manufacturers' websites for data on specific brands and part numbers.

RG or Type	Nominal Impedance (Ω)	Velocity Factor (%)	Dielectric Type*	Outer Diam (inches)	Max Voltage (RMS)	--Matched Loss (dB/100 feet)--			
						1 MHz	10 MHz	100 MHz	1000 MHz
RG-6	75	82	FPE	0.275	300	0.3	0.7	1.8	5.9
RG-6	75	66	PE	0.332	2700	0.4	0.8	2.7	9.8
RG-8	50	85	FPE	0.405	600	0.1	0.4	1.3	4.1
RG-8	52	66	PE	0.405	3700	0.2	0.6	1.9	7.4
RG-8X	50	82	FPE	0.242	300	0.3	0.9	3.2	11.2
RG-9	51	66	PE	0.42	5000	0.2	0.6	2.1	8.2
RG-11	75	84	FPE	0.405	300	0.1	0.4	1.3	5.2
RG-11	75	66	PE	0.405	300	0.2	0.7	2	7.1
RG-58	50	85	FPE	0.195	300	0.3	1	3	9.7
RG-58	52	66	PE	0.193	1400	0.3	1.1	3.8	14.5
RG-58A	53	73	FPE	0.195	300	0.4	1.3	4.5	18.1
RG-58A	50	66	PE	0.192	1400	0.5	1.5	5.4	22.8
RG-59	75	78	FPE	0.242	300	0.2	1	3	10.9
RG-59	75	66	PE	0.242	1700	0.6	1.1	3.4	12
RG-62A	93	84	ASPE	0.24	750	0.3	0.9	2.7	8.7
RG-142	50	69.5	TFE	0.195	1900	0.3	1.1	3.8	12.8
RG-174	50	73.5	FPE	0.11	300	0.6	2	6.5	21.3
RG-174	50	66	PE	0.11	1100	0.8	2.5	8.6	33.7
RG-213	50	66	PE	0.405	3700	0.2	0.6	2.1	8
RG-214	50	66	PE	0.425	3700	0.2	0.7	2.2	8
1/2" CATV hardline	50	81	FPE	0.5	2500	0.05	0.2	0.8	3.2
1/2" CATV hardline	75	81	FPE	0.5	2500	0.1	0.2	0.8	3.2
7/8" CATV hardline	50	81	FPE	0.875	4000	0.03	0.1	0.6	2.9
7/8" CATV hardline	75	81	FPE	0.875	4000	0.03	0.1	0.6	2.9
1/2 inch Heliax	50	88	FPE	0.63	1400	0.02	0.2	0.6	2.4
7/8 inch Heliax	50	88	FPE	1.09	2100	0.03	0.1	0.4	1.3
TV Twinlead	300	80	PE	0.4	n/a	0.1	0.3	1.4	5.9
Twinlead	300	80	PE	0.4	8000	0.1	0.2	1.1	4.8
Generic Window Line	450	91	PE	1	10000	0.02	0.08	0.3	1.1
Open-Wire Line	600	0.95-99**	none	n/a	12000	0.02	0.06	0.2	—

*PE = polyethylene; FPE = foamed polyethylene; ASPE = air spaced polyethylene; TFE = Teflon
**Velocity factor of open wire line varies with spacer material and spacing

Approximate Power Handling Capability (1:1 SWR, 40°C Ambient)

Specifications vary. See manufacturers' websites for data on specific brands and part numbers.

	1.8 MHz	7 MHz	14 MHz	30 MHz	50 MHz	150 MHz	222 MHz	450 MHz	1 GHz
RG-58 Style	1350	700	500	350	250	150	120	100	50
RG-59 Style	2300	1100	800	550	400	250	200	130	90
RG-8X Style	1830	840	560	360	270	145	115	80	50
RG-8/213 Style	5900	3000	2000	1500	1000	600	500	350	250
1/2 in Heliax	38000	18000	13000	8200	6200	3400	2800	1900	1200
7/8 in Heliax	67000	32000	22000	14000	11000	5900	4800	3200	2100

ARRL DXCC LIST

All entities shown here are on the current list are eligible for field checking.
*Indicates entities for which QSLs may be forwarded by the ARRL Outgoing QSL Service.
†Indicates entities with which US Amateurs may legally handle third-party message traffic.
Continent: AF = Africa; AN = Antarctica; AS = Asia; EU = Europe; NA = North America;
OC = Oceania; SA = South America
Zone notes: (A) 33, 42, 43, 44, 47, 48; (B) 67, 69-74; (C) 12, 13, 29, 30, 32, 38, 39; (D) 12, 13, 15;(E) 19, 20, 29, 30;
(F) 20-26, 30-35, 75; (G) 16, 17, 18, 19, 23; (H) 2, 3, 4, 9, 75; (I) 55, 58, 59

Prefix	Entity	CONTINENT	ZONE ITU	ZONE CQ	MIXED	PHONE	CW	DIGITAL	SAT	160	80	40	30	20	17	15	12	10	6
	Spratly Is.	AS	50	26															
1A[1]	Sov. Mil. Order of Malta	EU	28	15															
3A*	Monaco	EU	27	14															
3B6, 7	Agalega & St. Brandon Is.	AF	53	39															
3B8	Mauritius	AF	53	39															
3B9	Rodriguez I.	AF	53	39															
3C	Equatorial Guinea	AF	47	36															
3CØ	Annobon I.	AF	52	36															
3D2*	Fiji	OC	56	32															
3D2*	Conway Reef	OC	56	32															
3D2*	Rotuma I.	OC	56	32															
3DA†	Swaziland	AF	57	38															
3V*	Tunisia	AF	37	33															
3W, XV	Vietnam	AS	49	26															
3X	Guinea	AF	46	35															
3Y*	Bouvet	AF	67	38															
3Y*	Peter 1 I.	AN	72	12															
4J, 4K	Azerbaijan	AS	29	21															
4L*	Georgia	AS	29	21															
4O[47]*	Montenegro	EU	28	15															
4S*	Sri Lanka	AS	41	22															
4U_ITU†*	ITU HQ	EU	28	14															
4U_UN*	United Nations HQ	NA	08	05															
4W[44]	Timor - Leste	OC	54	28															
4X, 4Z†*	Israel	AS	39	20															
5A	Libya	AF	38	34															
5B, C4, P3*	Cyprus	AS	39	20															
5H-5I*	Tanzania	AF	53	37															
5N*	Nigeria	AF	46	35															
5R	Madagascar	AF	53	39															
5T[2]	Mauritania	AF	46	35															
5U[3]	Niger	AF	46	35															
5V	Togo	AF	46	35															

Prefix	Entity	CONTINENT	ITU	CQ	MIXED	PHONE	CW	DIGITAL	SAT	160	80	40	30	20	17	15	12	10	6
5W*	Samoa	OC	62	32															
5X*	Uganda	AF	48	37															
5Y-5Z*	Kenya	AF	48	37															
6V-6W4*	Senegal	AF	46	35															
6Y†*	Jamaica	NA	11	08															
7O[5]	Yemen	AS	39	21, 37															
7P	Lesotho	AF	57	38															
7Q	Malawi	AF	53	37															
7T-7Y*	Algeria	AF	37	33															
8P*	Barbados	NA	11	08															
8Q	Maldives	AS/AF	41	22															
8R†*	Guyana	SA	12	09															
9A[6]*	Croatia	EU	28	15															
9G[7]†*	Ghana	AF	46	35															
9H*	Malta	EU	28	15															
9I-9J*	Zambia	AF	53	36															
9K*	Kuwait	AS	39	21															
9L†	Sierra Leone	AF	46	35															
9M2, 4[8]*	West Malaysia	AS	54	28															
9M6, 8[8]*	East Malaysia	OC	54	28															
9N	Nepal	AS	42	22															
9Q-9T*	Dem. Rep. of Congo	AF	52	36															
9U[9]	Burundi	AF	52	36															
9V[10]*	Singapore	AS	54	28															
9X[9]	Rwanda	AF	52	36															
9Y-9Z†*	Trinidad & Tobago	SA	11	09															
A2*	Botswana	AF	57	38															
A3	Tonga	OC	62	32															
A4*	Oman	AS	39	21															
A5	Bhutan	AS	41	22															
A6	United Arab Emirates	AS	39	21															
A7*	Qatar	AS	39	21															
A9*	Bahrain	AS	39	21															
AP*	Pakistan	AS	41	21															
B*	China	AS	(A)	23,24															
BS7[11]	Scarborough Reef	AS	50	27															
BU-BX*	Taiwan	AS	44	24															
BV9P[12]	Pratas I.	AS	44	24															
C2	Nauru	OC	65	31															
C3*	Andorra	EU	27	14															

Prefix	Entity	CONTINENT	ZONE ITU	ZONE CQ	MIXED	PHONE	CW	DIGITAL	SAT	160	80	40	30	20	17	15	12	10	6
C5†	The Gambia	AF	46	35															
C6	Bahamas	NA	11	08															
C8-9*	Mozambique	AF	53	37															
CA-CE†*	Chile	SA	14,16	12															
CE0†*	Easter I.	SA	63	12															
CE0†*	Juan Fernandez Is.	SA	14	12															
CE0†*	San Felix & San Ambrosio	SA	14	12															
CE9/KC4▲*	Antarctica	AN	(B)	(C)															
CM, CO†*	Cuba	NA	11	08															
CN	Morocco	AF	37	33															
CP†*	Bolivia	SA	12,14	10															
CT*	Portugal	EU	37	14															
CT3*	Madeira Is.	AF	36	33															
CU*	Azores	EU	36	14															
CV-CX†*	Uruguay	SA	14	13															
CY0*	Sable I.	NA	09	05															
CY9*	St. Paul I.	NA	09	05															
D2-3	Angola	AF	52	36															
D4	Cape Verde	AF	46	35															
D6¹³†*	Comoros	AF	53	39															
DA-DR¹⁴*	Fed. Rep. of Germany	EU	28	14															
DU-DZ, 4D-4I†*	Philippines	OC	50	27															
E3¹⁵	Eritrea	AF	48	37															
E4⁴³	Palestine	AS	39	20															
E5	N. Cook I.	OC	62	32															
E5	S. Cook I.	OC	62	32															
E6*	Niue	OC	62	32															
E7²⁹†*	Bosnia-Herzegovina	EU	28	15															
EA-EH*	Spain	EU	37	14															
EA6-EH6*	Balearic Is.	EU	37	14															
EA8-EH8*	Canary Is.	AF	36	33															
EA9-EH9*	Ceuta & Melilla	AF	37	33															
EI-EJ*	Ireland	EU	27	14															
EK*	Armenia	AS	29	21															
EL†*	Liberia	AF	46	35															
EP-EQ*	Iran	AS	40	21															
ER*	Moldova	EU	29	16															
ES*	Estonia	EU	29	15															
ET*	Ethiopia	AF	48	37															
EU-EW*	Belarus	EU	29	16															
EX*	Kyrgyzstan	AS	30,31	17															

Prefix	Entity	CONTINENT	ZONE ITU	ZONE CQ	MIXED	PHONE	CW	DIGITAL	SAT	160	80	40	30	20	17	15	12	10	6
EY*	Tajikistan	AS	30	17															
EZ*	Turkmenistan	AS	30	17															
F*	France	EU	27	14															
FG, TO*	Guadeloupe	NA	11	08															
FH, TO13*	Mayotte	AF	53	39															
FJ, TO49*	Saint Barthelemy	NA	11	08															
FK, TX*	New Caledonia	OC	56	32															
FK, TX45	Chesterfield Is.	OC	56	30															
FM, TO*	Martinique	NA	11	08															
FO, TX16*	Austral Is.	OC	63	32															
FO, TX*	Clipperton I.	NA	10	07															
FO, TX*	French Polynesia	OC	63	32															
FO, TX16*	Marquesas Is.	OC	63	31															
FP, TO*	St. Pierre & Miquelon	NA	09	05															
FR, TO*	Reunion I.	AF	53	39															
FS, TO*	Saint Martin	NA	11	08															
FT/G, TO17*	Glorioso Is.	AF	53	39															
FT/J, /E, TO17*	Juan de Nova, Europa	AF	53	39															
FT/T, TO*	Tromelin I.	AF	53	39															
FT/W*	Crozet I.	AF	68	39															
FT/X*	Kerguelen Is.	AF	68	39															
FT/Z*	Amsterdam & St. Paul Is.	AF	68	39															
FW*	Wallis & Futuna Is.	OC	62	32															
FY*	French Guiana	SA	12	09															
G, GX, M*	England	EU	27	14															
GD, GT, MD*	Isle of Man	EU	27	14															
GI, GN, MI*	Northern Ireland	EU	27	14															
GJ, GH, MJ*	Jersey	EU	27	14															
GM, GS, MM*	Scotland	EU	27	14															
GU, GP, MU*	Guernsey	EU	27	14															
GW, GC, MW*	Wales	EU	27	14															
H4*	Solomon Is.	OC	51	28															
H4Ø18*	Temotu Province	OC	51	32															
HA, HG*	Hungary	EU	28	15															
HB*	Switzerland	EU	28	14															
HBØ*	Liechtenstein	EU	28	14															
HC-HD†*	Ecuador	SA	12	10															
HC8-HD8†*	Galapagos Is.	SA	12	10															
HH†	Haiti	NA	11	08															
HI†*	Dominican Republic	NA	11	08															

Prefix	Entity	CONTINENT	ZONE ITU	ZONE CQ	MIXED	PHONE	CW	DIGITAL	SAT	160	80	40	30	20	17	15	12	10	6
HJ-HK, 5J-5K†*	Colombia	SA	12	09															
HKØ†*	Malpelo I.	SA	12	09															
HKØ†*	San Andres & Providencia	NA	11	07															
HL, 6K-6N*	Republic of Korea	AS	44	25															
HO-HP†*	Panama	NA	11	07															
HQ-HR†*	Honduras	NA	11	07															
HS, E2*	Thailand	AS	49	26															
HV	Vatican	EU	28	15															
HZ*	Saudi Arabia	AS	39	21															
I*	Italy	EU	28	15, 33															
ISØ, IMØ *	Sardinia	EU	28	15															
J2*	Djibouti	AF	48	37															
J3†*	Grenada	NA	11	08															
J5	Guinea-Bissau	AF	46	35															
J6†*	St. Lucia	NA	11	08															
J7†*	Dominica	NA	11	08															
J8†	St. Vincent	NA	11	08															
JA-JS, 7J-7N*	Japan	AS	45	25															
JD1 19*	Minami Torishima	OC	90	27															
JD1 20*	Ogasawara	AS	45	27															
JT-JV*	Mongolia	AS	32,33	23															
JW*	Svalbard	EU	18	40															
JX*	Jan Mayen	EU	18	40															
JY†*	Jordan	AS	39	20															
K,W, N, AA-AK†	United States of America	NA	6,7,8	3,4,5															
KG4†	Guantanamo Bay	NA	11	08															
KHØ†	Mariana Is.	OC	64	27															
KH1†	Baker & Howland Is.	OC	61	31															
KH2†*	Guam	OC	64	27															
KH3†*	Johnston I.	OC	61	31															
KH4†	Midway I.	OC	61	31															
KH5†	Palmyra & Jarvis Is.	OC	61,62	31															
KH6, 7†*	Hawaii	OC	61	31															
KH7K†	Kure I.	OC	61	31															
KH8†*	American Samoa	OC	62	32															
KH8 48†*	Swains I.	OC	62	32															
KH9†	Wake I.	OC	65	31															
KL, AL, NL, WL*	Alaska	NA	1, 2	1															
KP1†	Navassa I.	NA	11	08															
KP2†*	Virgin Is.	NA	11	08															
KP3, 4†*	Puerto Rico	NA	11	08															

Prefix	Entity	CONTINENT	ZONE ITU	ZONE CQ	MIXED	PHONE	CW	DIGITAL	SAT	160	80	40	30	20	17	15	12	10	6
KP5[22†]	Desecheo I.	NA	11	08															
LA-LN*	Norway	EU	18	14															
LO-LW[†*]	Argentina	SA	14,16	13															
LX*	Luxembourg	EU	27	14															
LY*	Lithuania	EU	29	15															
LZ*	Bulgaria	EU	28	20															
OA-OC[†*]	Peru	SA	12	10															
OD*	Lebanon	AS	39	20															
OE[†*]	Austria	EU	28	15															
OF-OI*	Finland	EU	18	15															
OH0*	Aland Is.	EU	18	15															
OJ0*	Market Reef	EU	18	15															
OK-OL[23*]	Czech Rep.	EU	28	15															
OM[23*]	Slovak Rep.	EU	28	15															
ON-OT*	Belgium	EU	27	14															
OU,ON,OZ,5P,5Q*	Denmark	EU	18	14															
OX, XP*	Greenland	NA	5, 75	40															
OY, OW*	Faroe Is.	EU	18	14															
P2[24]	Papua New Guinea	OC	51	28															
P4[25*]	Aruba	SA	11	09															
P5[26]	Dem. People's Rep. Korea	AS	44	25															
PA-PI*	Netherlands	EU	27	14															
PJ2[50*]	Curacao	SA	11	09															
PJ4[51]	Bonaire	SA	11	09															
PJ5, 6[52]	Saba, St. Eustatius	NA	11	08															
PJ7[53*]	St. Maarten	NA	11	08															
PP-PY, ZV-ZZ[†*]	Brazil	SA	(D)	11															
PP0-PY0F[†*]	Fernando de Noronha	SA	13	11															
PP0-PY0S[†*]	St. Peter & St. Paul Rocks	SA	13	11															
PP0-PY0T[†*]	Trindade & Martim Vaz Is.	SA	15	11															
PZ	Suriname	SA	12	09															
R1/F*	Franz Josef Land	EU	75	40															
S0[1,27]	Western Sahara	AF	46	33															
S2*	Bangladesh	AS	41	22															
S5[6*]	Slovenia	EU	28	15															
S7	Seychelles	AF	53	39															
S9	Sao Tome & Principe	AF	47	36															
SA-SM, 7S, 8S*	Sweden	EU	18	14															
SN-SR*	Poland	EU	28	15															
ST	Sudan	AF	47, 48	34															
SU	Egypt	AF	38	34															
SV-SZ, J4*	Greece	EU	28	20															

Prefix	Entity	CONTINENT	ITU	CQ	MIXED	PHONE	CW	DIGITAL	SAT	160	80	40	30	20	17	15	12	10	6
SV/A*	Mount Athos	EU	28	20															
SV5, J45*	Dodecanese	EU	28	20															
SV9, J49*	Crete	EU	28	20															
T2²⁸	Tuvalu	OC	65	31															
T3Ø	W. Kiribati (Gilbert Is.)	OC	65	31															
T31	C. Kiribati (Brit. Phoenix Is.)	OC	62	31															
T32	E. Kiribati (Line Is.)	OC	61,63	31															
T33	Banaba I. (Ocean I.)	OC	65	31															
T5, 6O	Somalia	AF	48	37															
T7*	San Marino	EU	28	15															
T8²¹	Palau	OC	64	27															
TA-TC†*	Turkey	EU/AS	39	20															
TF*	Iceland	EU	17	40															
TG, TD†*	Guatemala	NA	12	07															
TI, TE†*	Costa Rica	NA	11	07															
TI9†*	Cocos I.	NA	11	07															
TJ	Cameroon	AF	47	36															
TK*	Corsica	EU	28	15															
TL³⁰	Central Africa	AF	47	36															
TN³¹	Congo (Republic of)	AF	52	36															
TR³²*	Gabon	AF	52	36															
TT³³	Chad	AF	47	36															
TU³⁴	Côte d'Ivoire	AF	46	35															
TY³⁵	Benin	AF	46	35															
TZ³⁶*	Mali	AF	46	35															
UA-UI1-7 - RA-RZ*	European Russia	EU	(E)	16															
UA2, RA2*	Kaliningrad	EU	29	15															
UA-UI8, 9, Ø RA-RZ*	Asiatic Russia	AS	(F)	(G)															
UJ-UM*	Uzbekistan	AS	30	17															
UN-UQ*	Kazakhstan	AS	29-31	17															
UR-UZ, EM-EO*	Ukraine	EU	29	16															
V2†*	Antigua & Barbuda	NA	11	08															
V3†	Belize	NA	11	07															
V4³⁷†	St. Kitts & Nevis	NA	11	08															
V5*	Namibia	AF	57	38															
V6³⁸†	Micronesia	OC	65	27															
V7†*	Marshall Is.	OC	65	31															
V8*	Brunei Darussalam	OC	54	28															
VA-VG, VO, VY†*	Canada	NA	(H)	1-5															
VK, AX†*	Australia	OC	(I)	29,30															
VKØ†*	Heard I.	AF	68	39															

Prefix	Entity	Continent	ZONE		MIXED	PHONE	CW	DIGITAL	SAT	160	80	40	30	20	17	15	12	10	6
			ITU	CQ															
VKØ†*	Macquarie I.	OC	60	30															
VK9C†*	Cocos (Keeling) Is.	OC	54	29															
VK9L†*	Lord Howe I.	OC	60	30															
VK9M†*	Mellish Reef	OC	56	30															
VK9N*	Norfolk I.	OC	60	32															
VK9W†*	Willis I.	OC	55	30															
VK9X†*	Christmas I.	OC	54	29															
VP2E37	Anguilla	NA	11	08															
VP2M37	Montserrat	NA	11	08															
VP2V37*	British Virgin Is.	NA	11	08															
VP5, VQ5*	Turks & Caicos Is.	NA	11	08															
VP6†*	Pitcairn I.	OC	63	32															
VP646*	Ducie I.	OC	63	32															
VP8*	Falkland Is.	SA	16	13															
VP8, LU*	South Georgia I.	SA	73	13															
VP8, LU*	South Orkney Is.	SA	73	13															
VP8, LU*	South Sandwich Is.	SA	73	13															
VP8, LU, CE9, HFØ, 4K1*	South Shetland Is.	SA	73	13															
VP9*	Bermuda	NA	11	05															
VQ9*	Chagos Is.	AF	41	39															
VR*	Hong Kong	AS	44	24															
VU*	India	AS	41	22															
VU4*	Andaman & Nicobar Is.	AS	49	26															
VU7*	Lakshadweep Is.	AS	41	22															
XA-XI†*	Mexico	NA	10	06															
XA4-XI4†*	Revillagigedo	NA	10	06															
XT39*	Burkina Faso	AF	46	35															
XU	Cambodia	AS	49	26															
XW	Laos	AS	49	26															
XX9*	Macao	AS	44	24															
XY-XZ	Myanmar	AS	49	26															
YA, T6	Afghanistan	AS	40	21															
YB-YH40*	Indonesia	OC	51,54	28															
YI*	Iraq	AS	39	21															
YJ*	Vanuatu	OC	56	32															
YK*	Syria	AS	39	20															
YL*	Latvia	EU	29	15															
YN, H6-7, HT†*	Nicaragua	NA	11	07															
YO-YR*	Romania	EU	28	20															
YS, HU†*	El Salvador	NA	11	07															
YT-YU*	Serbia	EU	28	15															

Prefix	Entity	CONTINENT	ZONE ITU	ZONE CQ	MIXED	PHONE	CW	DIGITAL	SAT	160	80	40	30	20	17	15	12	10	6
YV-YY, 4M[†*]	Venezuela	SA	12	09															
YVØ[†*]	Aves I.	NA	11	08															
Z2	Zimbabwe	AF	53	38															
Z3[41*]	Macedonia	EU	28	15															
Z8[54]	South Sudan (Republic of)	AF	47,48	34															
ZA	Albania	EU	28	15															
ZB*	Gibraltar	EU	37	14															
ZC4[42 *]	UK Sov. Base Areas on Cyprus	AS	39	20															
ZD7	St. Helena	AF	66	36															
ZD8	Ascension I.	AF	66	36															
ZD9	Tristan da Cunha & Gough I.	AF	66	38															
ZF*	Cayman Is.	NA	11	08															
ZK3*	Tokelau Is.	OC	62	31															
ZL-ZM*	New Zealand	OC	60	32															
ZL7	Chatham Is.	OC	60	32															
ZL8	Kermadec Is.	OC	60	32															
ZL9	New Zealand SubAntarctic Is	OC	60	32															
ZP[†*]	Paraguay	SA	14	11															
ZR-ZU[†*]	South Africa	AF	57	38															
ZS8*	Prince Edward & Marion Is.	AF	57	38															

Notes

[1] Unofficial prefix.
[2] (5T) Only contacts made June 20, 1960, and after, count for this entity.
[3] (5U) Only contacts made August 3, 1960, and after, count for this entity.
[4] (6W) Only contacts made June 20, 1960, and after, count for this entity.
[5] (7O) Only contacts made May 22, 1990, and after, count for this entity.
[6] (9A, S5) Only contacts made June 26, 1991, and after, count for this entity.
[7] (9G) Only contacts made March 5, 1957, and after, count for this entity.
[8] (9M2, 4, 6, 8) Only contacts made September 16, 1963, and after, count for this entity.
[9] (9U, 9X) Only contacts made July 1, 1962, and after, count for this entity.
[10] (9V) Contacts made from September 16, 1963 to August 8, 1965, count for West Malaysia.
[11] (BS7) Only contacts made January 1, 1995, and after, count for this entity.
[12] (BV9P) Only contacts made January 1, 1994, and after, count for this entity.
[13] (D6, FH8) Only contacts made July 6, 1975, and after, count for this entity.
[14] (DA-DR) Only contacts made with DA-DR stations September 17, 1973, and after, and contacts made with Y2-Y9 stations October 3, 1990 and after, count for this entity.
[15] (E3) Only contacts made November 14, 1962, and before, or May 24, 1991, and after, count for this entity.
[16] (FO) Only contacts made after 23:59 UTC, March 31, 1998 count for this entity.
[17] (FR) Only contacts made June 25, 1960, and after, count for this entity.
[18] (H4Ø) Only contacts made after 23:59 UTC, March 31, 1998, count for this entity.
[19] (JD) Formerly Marcus Island.
[20] (JD) Formerly Bonin and Volcano Islands.
[21] (T8) Valid prefix January 1, 1994 or after. (KC6 prior to this date.)
[22] (KP5, KP4) Only contacts made March 1, 1979, and after, count for this entity.
[23] (OK-OL, OM) Only contacts made January 1, 1993, and after, count for this entity.
[24] (P2) Only contacts made September 16, 1975, and after, count for this entity.
[25] (P4) Only contacts made January 1, 1986, and after, count for this entity.

[26] (P5) Only contacts made May 14, 1995, and after count for this entity.
[27] (SØ) Contacts with Rio de Oro (Spanish Sahara), EA9, also count for this entity.
[28] (T2) Only contacts made January 1, 1976, and after, count for this entity.
[29] (E7) New prefix for Bosnia-Herzegovina effective November 17, 2007. Contacts are valid for this entity effective October 15, 1991.
[30] (TL) Only contacts made August 13, 1960, and after, count for this entity.
[31] (TN) Only contacts made August 15, 1960, and after, count for this entity.
[32] (TR) Only contacts made August 17, 1960, and after, count for this entity.
[33] (TT) Only contacts made August 11, 1960, and after count for this entity.
[34] (TU) Only contacts made August 7, 1960, and after, count for this entity.
[35] (TY) Only contacts made August 1, 1960, and after, count for this entity.
[36] (TZ) Only contacts made June 20, 1960, and after, count for this entity.
[37] (V4, VP2) For DXCC credit for contacts made May 31, 1958 and before, see page 97, June 1958 QST.
[38] (V6) Includes Yap Islands January 1, 1981, and after.
[39] (XT) Only contacts made August 5, 1960, and after, count for this entity.
[40] (YB) Only contacts made May 1, 1963, and after, count for this entity.
[41] (Z3) Only contacts made September 8, 1991, and after, count for this entity.
[42] (ZC4) Only contacts made August 16, 1960, and after, count for this entity.
[43] (E4) Only contacts made February 1, 1999 and after, count for this entity.
[44] (4W) Only contacts made March 1, 2000, and after, count for this entity.
[45] (FK/C) Only contacts made March 23, 2000, and after, count for this entity.
[46] (VP6) Only contacts made November 16, 2001, and after, count for this entity.
[47] (4O) Only contacts made June 28, 2006, and after, count for this entity.
[48] (KH8) Only contacts made July 22, 2006, and after, count for this entity.
[49] (FJ) Only contacts made December 14, 2007, and after, count for this entity.
[50] (PJ2) Only contacts made October 10, 2010, and after, count for this entity.
[51] (PJ4) Only contacts made October 10, 2010, and after, count for this entity.
[52] (PJ5, 6) Only contacts made October 10, 2010, and after, count for this entity.
[53] (PJ7) Only contacts made October 10, 2010, and after, count for this entity.
[54] (Z8) Only contacts made July 14, 2011, and after, count for this entity.

▲Also 3Y, 8J1, ATØ, DPØ, FT8Y, LU, OR4, R1AN, VKØ, VP8, ZL5, ZS1, ZXØ, etc. QSL via entity under whose auspices the particular station is operating. The availability of a third-party traffic agreement and a QSL Bureau applies to the entity under whose auspices the particular station is operating.

Index

Editor's Note: Except for commonly used phrases and abbreviations, topics are indexed by their noun names. The letters "ff" after a page number indicate coverage of the indexed topic on succeeding pages.

10 10 International: 2.4
5 Band DXCC: 3.5
5 Band WAC: 3.4
5 Band WAS: 3.3
    Application: 4.22
5 Band WAZ: 3.6

A

AC and RF grounding: 1.10
ADIF (Amateur Data Interchange Format): 3.13
Adventure Radio Society: 2.4
Allocation of International Call Sign Series: 4.2
Amateur Radio Emergency Service
   (ARES): 1.38, 2.39ff
    ARES E-Letter: 2.23
    ARES Field Resources Manual: 2.22
    ARES Manual: 2.22
    Registration form: 4.12
Amateur Radio High Altitude Ballooning
   (ARHAB): 2.4
Amateur Radio Lighthouses on the Air
   (ARLHS): 1.80
Amateur television (ATV): 1.66ff
    Applications: 1.70ff
    Balloons: 1.71
    Computer graphics: 1.71
    Digital ATV: 1.66
    DX: 1.70
    Equipment: 1.66
    FM ATV: 1.69
    Identification: 1.69
    Radio control vehicles: 1.71
    Repeaters: 1.68
    Weather spotting: 1.71
AMSAT: 2.4
Anderson Powerpole connectors: 2.21
Antennas: 1.10ff
    HF dipole: 1.11
    Mobile: 1.82
    Portable operation: 1.79
    VHF/UHF ground-plane: 1.11
APCO-25: 1.42

ARES E-Letter: 2.23
ARES Field Resources Manual: 2.22
ARES Manual: 2.22
ARISS: 2.10
ARL Numbered Radiograms: 4.9
ARRL DXCC List: 4.27ff
ARRL Education & Technology Program: 2.9
ARRL Field Organization: 2.3
    ARRL Section Manager: 2.40
    Assistant Emergency Coordinator (AEC): 2.40
    District Emergency Coordinator (DEC): 2.40
    Emergency Coordinator (EC): 2.40
    Local Government Liaison (LGL): 2.4
    Official Emergency Station (OES): 2.4, 2.39
    Official Observer (OO): 2.4
    Official Relay Station (ORS): 2.4
    Public Information Officer (PIO): 2.4
    Section Emergency Coordinator (SEC): 2.40
    Technical Specialist (TS): 2.4
ARRL Grid Locator Map for North America: 4.14
ARRL Incoming QSL Bureau System: 4.24
ARRL Message Form: 2.29, 4.8
    Handling Instructions: 4.8
ARRL Outgoing QSL Service: 4.24
ARRL Procedural Signals (Prosigns): 4.5
ARRL Registered Instructor: 2.7
ARRL Section Manager: 2.40
ARRL website forums: 2.6
ARRL Worked All States (WAS) Map: 4.13
Assembling a station: 1.6ff
    Resources: 1.13
Assistant Emergency Coordinator (AEC): 2.40
Aurora: 1.53
Automatic Packet Reporting System (APRS): 1.43
    Public service: 2.31
Awards: 3.1ff
    5 Band DXCC: 3.5
    5 Band WAC: 3.4
    5 Band WAS: 3.3, 4.22
    5 Band WAZ: 3.6
    CQ WPX Award: 3.7
    DX Century Club (DXCC): 3.4, 4.16

DXCC Card Checker: 3.3
DXCC Challenge: 3.5
DXCC Honor Roll: 3.5
Fred Fish Memorial Award (FFMA): 3.7
Islands on the Air (IOTA): 3.8
Japan Century Cities (JCC) Award: 3.10
K1BV Awards Directory: 3.10
Logbook of The World (LoTW): 3.30ff
QRP DXCC: 3.5
Special event stations: 3.10
Summits on the Air (SOTA): 3.9
Triple Play WAS: 3.3
USA-CA (County) Award: 3.7
VHF/UHF Century Club (VUCC): 3.6, 4.18
Worked All Continents (WAC): 3.4, 4.15
Worked All States (WAS): 3.3, 4.20
Worked All Zones (WAZ): 3.6

B

Backscatter propagation: 3.23
Band plans
    Considerate Operator's Frequency Guide: ... 1.17
    US Amateur Radio Bands chart: 1.16, 4.2
    VHF/UHF: 1.37, 1.46
Beacons: 1.15, 3.17
Bicycle Mobile Hams of America (BHMA): 2.4

C

Cabrillo log format: 3.52
Calling frequencies: 1.46
Characteristics of Common Feed Lines: 4.26
Club Log: 3.32
Clubs: 2.1ff
    Contest: 3.51
    Contesting for training: 2.2
    National and online: 2.4
    Public service: 2.2
    Repeater: 1.35
    Special Service Club: 2.2
Community Emergency Response Team
    (CERT): 2.41
Considerate Operator's Frequency Guide: 1.17
Contesting: 3.35ff
    Antennas: 3.39
    Basic operating techniques: 3.37, 3.42
    Cabrillo log format: 3.52
    Calling CQ: 3.45
    Categories: 3.36
    Clubs: 3.51
    Computers: 3.54
    CQ Contest Hall of Fame: 3.59
    Equipment: 3.38
    Ergonomics: 3.56

Ethics: 3.50
Food and fitness: 3.57
Glossary: 3.60
History: 3.35
Intermediate operating techniques: 3.44
Log checking: 3.52
Log submission: 3.51
Multioperator: 3.58
Personal preparation: 3.57
Public service training: 2.33
QSO exchange: 3.37, 3.42
Remote operating: 3.41
Resources: 3.61
RTTY: 3.53
Rules: 3.38
Scoring: 3.37
Search and pounce: 3.43, 3.46
Sleep strategy: 3.57
SO2R (Single Op 2 Radio): 3.55
Software: 3.54
Spotting networks: 3.46
Strategy: 3.49
VHF/UHF: 1.56, 3.40
Continuous Tone Coded Squelch System
    (CTCSS): 1.38
CQ Contest Hall of Fame: 3.59
CQ DX Hall of Fame: 3.26
CQ WPX Award: 3.7
Crossband repeaters: 1.40
CW Abbreviations: 4.6
CW operating procedures: 1.19
CW Skimmer: 3.48
CWops: 2.4
    CW Academy: 2.8

D

D-STAR: 1.42
Deliberate QRM (DQRM): 3.24
Digital Coded Squelch (DCS): 1.39
Digital communications
    Accessory ports: 1.23
    Automatic Packet Reporting System
        (APRS): 1.43
    Equipment: 1.23
    HF: 1.23ff
    HF resources: 1.33
    Interface: 1.25
    JT65: 1.29ff
    MFSK16: 1.28
    Packet radio: 1.43
    PACTOR: 1.25, 1.28
    Propagation Network (PropNET): 1.44
    PSK31: 1.27

Radioteletype (RTTY): 1.26
Software: 1.25
Sound card: 1.24
Tablet: 1.24
USB ports: 1.23
VHF/UHF: 1.43
Winlink 2000: 1.28, 1.44
WSPR: 1.31ff
Digital voice: 1.41ff
   APCO-25: 1.41
   D-STAR: 1.42
   DMR: 1.42
   System Fusion: 1.42
District Emergency Coordinator (DEC): 2.40
DMR: 1.42
Dual Tone Multi Frequency (DTMF): 1.39
DX Century Club (DXCC): 3.4
   Application: 4.16
   ARRL DXCC List: 4.27ff
DX Code of Conduct: 3.23
DX Keeper: 3.12
DX Maps: 1.48, 3.28
DXCC Card Checker: 3.3
DXCC Challenge: 3.5
DXCC Honor Roll: 3.5
DXing: 3.11ff
   Advanced operating techniques: 3.25
   Basic operating techniques: 3.13
   CQ DX Hall of Fame: 3.26
   Deliberate QRM (DQRM): 3.24
   DX Code of Conduct: 3.23
   DX Maps: 3.28
   DXpeditions: 3.21ff, 3.25
   Equipment: 3.11, 3.26
   Intermediate operating techniques: 3.19
   Jammers: 3.23
   Logging software: 3.12
   NCDXF/IARU International Beacon Project: .. 3.17
   ON4KST chat room: 3.28
   Pileup operating: 3.19
   Propagation: 3.14ff, 3.23
   Remote operating: 3.12
   Resources: 3.29
   Reverse Beacon Network (RBN): 3.18
   Split frequency operation: 3.20
   Spotting networks: 3.16
   VHF/UHF: 3.28
DXpeditions: 3.21ff, 3.25

E

Earth-Moon-Earth (EME): 1.54ff
EchoLink: 1.41
eHam.net: 2.6

Elmering: 2.8
Emergency Coordinator (EC): 2.40
Emergency Operations Center (EOC): 2.34
Emergency Operations Plan: 2.32
eQSL.cc: 3.30
Equipment
   Accessories: 1.9
   Amateur television (ATV): 1.66
   Choosing a radio: 1.6
   Digital communications: 1.23
   HF: 1.8
   Portable operation: 1.76
   Slow-scan television (SSTV): 1.71
   Station setup: 1.9
   VHF/UHF: 1.7
Ethics
   Contesting: 3.50
   DXing: 3.23

F

Facebook: 2.5
FEMA Independent Study: 2.23
Field Day: 2.8, 2.12ff, 2.23, 3.43
   Community outreach: 2.15
   Entry classes: 2.12
   Get On The Air (GOTA): 2.14
   Resources: 2.17
   Traffic handling: 2.15
   Youth participation: 2.16
FISTS: 2.4
Flying Pigs QRP Club: 2.4
FM repeater satellites: 1.63
Fred Fish Memorial Award (FFMA): 3.7

G

Gray line propagation: 3.23
Greenwich Mean Time (GMT): 1.21
Grid locators: 1.47
Guest operators: 1.20

H

Ham Radio Deluxe: 3.12
Hamfests: 2.3
Handihams: 2.4
High Speed Multimedia (HSMM)
   Public service: 2.32
Homing In: 2.4

I

ICS-213 General Message: 2.30, 4.10
Image communications: 1.66ff
Incident Command System (ICS): 2.34
Instagram: 2.5

Internet Radio Linking Project (IRLP): 1.40
Introduction to Emergency Communications
    course: 2.7, 2.23
Ionospheric forward scatter: 1.50
Islands On The Air (IOTA): 1.80, 2.4, 3.8
ITU Recommended Phonetics: 4.7

J
Japan Century Cities (JCC) Award: 3.10
JT65: 1.29ff

K
K1BV Awards Directory: 3.10
Kid's Day: 2.11

L
License study classes: 2.7
Linear transponder satellites: 1.64
Linked repeaters: 1.39
Local Government Liaison (LGL): 2.4
Log (station log): 1.21
Logbook of The World (LoTW): 3.30ff
Logger32: 3.12
Logging software: 3.12
Long-path propagation: 3.23

M
Managing Interstation Interference: 3.56
Medical Amateur Radio Council (MARCO): 2.5
Memoranda of Understanding: 2.23
Mentoring: 2.8
Meteor scatter: 1.50
    WSJT: 1.51
Meteor showers: 1.52
MFSK16: 1.28
Mobile Amateur Radio Awards Club (MARAC): 2.5
Mobile operation: 1.80ff
    HF: 1.82
    Resources: 1.83
    Safety: 1.80
    VHF/UHF: 1.81
Morse Abbreviated ("Cut") Numbers: 4.4
Morse Code Character Set: 4.4

N
N1MM+: 3.54
Narrow Band Emergency Messaging
    Software (NBEMS): 2.31
National Weather Service: 2.37, 2.40
NCDXF/IARU International Beacon Project: 1.15, 3.17
Nets: 1.38
North American QRP CW Club (NAQCC): 2.5

O
Official Emergency Station (OES): 2.4, 2.39, 2.40
Official Observer (OO): 2.4
Official Relay Station (ORS): 2.4
Old Old Timers Club: 2.5
ON4KST chat room: 1.48, 3.28
Online QSL Request System (OQRS): 3.32
Operating techniques
    Basic procedures: 1.14ff
    CW procedures: 1.19
    Phone procedures: 1.17
    Picking a band: 1.14
    Repeater: 1.35
    Satellites: 1.63ff
    Slow-scan television (SSTV): 1.72
    VHF/UHF SSB and CW: 1.50

P
Packet radio: 1.43
    Public service: 2.31
PACTOR: 1.25, 1.28
Phone operating procedures: 1.17
Phonetic alphabet: 1.18, 3.19, 4.7
    Alternative: 4.7
    Spanish: 4.7
Pileup operating: 3.19
Pinterest: 2.6
PL-259 (UHF) Connector Assembly: 4.26
Portable operation: 1.76ff
    Antennas: 1.79
    On the air activities: 1.80
    Power sources: 1.78
    Resources: 1.83
    VHF/UHF: 1.55
Propagation: 1.14, 3.14ff, 3.23
    Backscatter: 3.23
    Beacons: 1.15
    Gray line: 3.23
    Long-path: 3.23
    VHF/UHF: 1.48ff, 1.50ff
Propagation Network (PropNET): 1.44
PSK31: 1.27ff
Public Information Officer (PIO): 2.4
Public service: 1.38, 2.18
    Accidents and hazards: 2.36
    Amateur Radio Emergency Service
        (ARES): 2.39ff
    Amateur television (ATV): 1.70
    Anderson Powerpole connectors: 2.21
    ARES E-Letter: 2.23
    ARES Field Resources Manual: 2.22
    ARES Manual: 2.22
    ARRL Field Organization: 2.39ff

ARRL Message Form: 2.29, 4.8
Automatic Packet Reporting System
    (APRS): 2.31
Community Emergency Response Team
    (CERT): 2.41
Contesting for training: 2.33
Damage assessment: 2.35
Drills and tests: 2.23
Emergency Operations Center (EOC): 2.34
Emergency Operations Plan: 2.32
Equipment: 2.18ff
FEMA Independent Study: 2.23
Field Day: 2.23
High Speed Multimedia (HSMM): 2.32
Hospital communications: 2.37
ICS-213 General Message: 2.30, 4.10
Incident Command System (ICS): 2.34
Introduction to Emergency Communications
    course: 2.23
Memoranda of Understanding: 2.23
Message traffic: 2.27
Narrow Band Emergency Messaging Software
    (NBEMS): 2.31
National Weather Service: 2.37
Net operation: 2.21
Operating techniques: 2.26ff
Packet Radio: 2.31
Portable antenna mount: 2.24
Radio Amateur Civil Emergency Service
    (RACES): 2.41
Red Cross Safe and Well: 2.28
Resources: 2.42
RMS Express: 2.32
Safety: 2.19
Search and rescue (SAR): 2.36
Served agencies: 2.33
Shelter operations: 2.35
Simulated Emergency Test (SET): 2.23
SKYWARN: 2.37, 2.40
Special event communications: 2.38
Toxic spills: 2.37
Training: 2.21
Winlink 2000: 2.32

Q

Q Signals: 1.19, 4.5
QRP Amateur Radio Club International
    (QRP ARCI): 2.5
QRP DXCC: 3.5
QRZ.com: 2.6
QSL Bureau: 4.24
QSL cards: 1.21, 3.32ff
Quarter Century Wireless Association (QCWA): ... 2.5

R

Radio Amateur Civil Emergency Service
    (RACES): 2.41
RadioReference.com: 2.6
Radioteletype (RTTY): 1.26
    Contesting: 3.53
Remote operating: 3.12, 3.41
Repeater: 1.34
    Amateur television (ATV): 1.68
    Crossband: 1.40
    Linking: 1.39
    Operating techniques: 1.35
    Tones: 1.38
Resources
    Assembling a station: 1.13
    Contesting: 3.61
    DXing: 3.29
    Field Day: 2.17
    HF digital communications: 1.33
    Portable and mobile operation: 1.83
    Public service: 2.42
    Satellites: 1.65
    Slow-scan television (SSTV): 1.75
    SSB and CW operating: 1.22
    VHF/UHF FM and digital: 1.45
    VHF/UHF weak signal: 1.57
Reverse Beacon Network (RBN): 3.18
RST system: 1.18, 4.7

S

Satellites: 1.58ff
    Doppler effect: 1.61
    FM repeater: 1.63
    Linear transponder: 1.64
    Modes: 1.63
    Operating techniques: 1.63ff
    Orbital elements: 1.62
    Orbits: 1.58
    Resources: 1.65
    Tracking: 1.61ff
School Club Roundup: 2.10
School programs: 2.9
Scouting: 2.10
Section Emergency Coordinator (SEC): 2.40
Simulated Emergency Test (SET): 2.23
Six Meter International Radio Klub (SMIRK): 2.5
SKYWARN: 2.37, 2.40
Slow-scan television (SSTV): 1.71ff
    Digital SSTV: 1.73
    Equipment: 1.71
    Resources: 1.75
    Software: 1.73
SO2R (Single Op 2 Radio): 3.55

Social media: 2.5
    Facebook: 2.5
    Instagram: 2.5
    Pinterest: 2.6
    Twitter: 2.5
    Yahoo Groups: 2.6
    YouTube: 2.6
Software
    ADIF (Amateur Data Interchange Format): ... 3.13
    Analog SSTV: 1.73
    Contesting: 3.54
    Digital communications: 1.25
    DX Keeper: 3.12
    Ham Radio Deluxe: 3.12
    JT65: 1.29
    Logger32: 3.12
    Logging: 3.12
    N1MM+: 3.54
    Satellite tracking: 1.61ff
    Win-Test: 3.54
    WriteLog: 3.54
    WSJT: 1.51
Sound card: 1.24
Special events: 1.38, 3.10
    Public service communications: 2.38
Special Service Club: 2.2
Split frequency operation: 3.20
Sporadic E: 1.53
Spotting networks: 3.16, 3.46
SSB and CW operating resources: 1.22
Station setup: 1.9
Straight Key Century Club (SKCC): 2.5
Summits On The Air (SOTA): 1.80, 3.9
System Fusion: 1.42

T

Tablet
    Connections: 1.26
    Digital communications: 1.24
Technical Specialist (TS): 2.4
Triple Play WAS: 3.3
Tropospheric ducting: 1.50
Tucson Amateur Packet Radio (TAPR): 2.5
Twitter: 2.5

U

Universal Coordinated Time (UTC): 1.21
US Amateur Radio Bands: 1.16, 4.1
US Power Squadron ARC: 2.5
USA-CA (County) Award: 3.7

V

VHF/UHF Century Club (VUCC): 3.6
    Application: 4.18
VHF/UHF digital data modes: 1.43ff
    Resources: 1.45
VHF/UHF FM and repeaters: 1.34ff
    Resources: 1.45
VHF/UHF operation
    Activity nights: 1.47
    Aurora: 1.53
    Band plans: 1.46
    Calling frequencies: 1.46
    Contesting: 1.56, 3.40
    DXing: 3.27ff
    Earth-Moon-Earth (EME): 1.54ff
    Grid locators: 1.47
    Ionospheric forward scatter: 1.50
    Meteor scatter: 1.50
    Meteor scatter with WSJT: 1.51
    Meteor showers: 1.52
    Mobile... 1.81
    Portable operation: 1.55
    Propagation: 1.48ff
    Resources: 1.57
    Sporadic E: 1.53
    SSB and CW techniques: 1.50
    SSB, CW and digital modes: 1.46ff
    Tropospheric ducting: 1.50
Volunteer Examination: 2.8

W

Win-Test: 3.54
Winlink 2000: 1.28, 1.44
    Public service: 2.32
WIRES-X: 1.41
Worked All Continents (WAC): 3.4
    Application: 4.15
Worked All States (WAS): 3.3
    Application: 4.20
    Map: 4.13
Worked All Zones (WAZ): 3.6
WriteLog: 3.54
WSJT: 1.51
WSPR: 1.31ff

Y

Yahoo Groups: 2.6
Young Ladies Radio League (YLRL): 2.5
Youth programs: 2.10
YouTube: 2.6

Z

Zulu time: 1.21